DESIGN IN CHAUCER'S *TROILUS*

DESIGN IN CHAUCER'S TROILUS

Sanford B. Meech

SYRACUSE UNIVERSITY PRESS

Library of Congress Catalog Card Number: 58-14391

© 1959, SYRACUSE UNIVERSITY PRESS

This work has been published with
the assistance of a Ford Foundation grant.

MANUFACTURED IN THE UNITED STATES OF AMERICA BY
BOOK CRAFTSMEN ASSOCIATES INC., NEW YORK

Preface

As its title indicates, this book is a study of the artistry of the *Troilus*. Its method is essentially close textual analysis—scrutiny of the poem in relation to its principal source to determine trends in Chaucer's recasting of the story. His borrowings from the *Filostrato* and his departures from it will be noted with equal particularity. The latter will be connected, when possible, with ancillary sources, and his adaptations of these will be examined to the same end as his use of the main one. Broad cultural influences, religious, social, and literary, will also be taken into account, though not pursued as topics of investigation for their own sake. The poem is to be considered for itself, not for its illumination of literary history or the history of ideas, but in all the light that can be brought to bear upon it from these disciplines.

As the title further indicates, the book rests on the assumption that the creative process in the *Troilus* was to some extent a deliberate conscious affair. So resting, it will presume to deduce the author's guiding principles, and, if mainly in their aesthetic aspects, not to the exclusion of any others. Conjecture about an artist's purposes, as I am uneasily aware, has been stigmatized as the intentional fallacy. What he meant in the heat of inspiration, it has been said, is indeterminable even by himself; and, even were it determinable, quite immaterial, for the product must be taken for what it is regardless of the creator's aspiration. I cannot but feel, however, that the intentions of the creator of a masterpiece are worth seeking and that the major ones, at least, can be plausibly inferred from the work itself in its ordered perfection. I cannot but believe, specifically, that Chaucer's in the *Troilus* are well worth seeking and that they can be uncovered, inexplicit though he was about them and made the more elusive of our understanding, as he has been, by the passage of over half a millennium. Any notion that we may gain of them will alert us to particulars which we might miss without it and, at the same time, check facile interpretation of parts which does not square with what appears to be the over-all design. In a work as extensive as the *Troilus,* the deduction of intent from process seems feasible enough. Patterns of thought persist through its generous length and modes of expressing them also. In both, modification of source is highly consistent. Subliminal inspiration must be allowed Chaucer, along with conscious purpose, and the line between these phases of creative power cannot be sharply drawn. Yet the second appears to maintain control and to an approximable degree.

Correlation of the *Troilus* with the *Filostrato* for the unfolding of the story will lead naturally to measuring the worth of the one poem on the scale afforded by the other. Comparison of Chaucer to Boccaccio should yield a fair rating of the former, if allowance is made for differences in intention. A change, however ingenious, is not *ipso facto* an improvement. Sometimes, it may be, the Italian's directness will prove more effective for his generally simpler aims than the subtlety of the Englishman for his complex ones. The latter is not to be accounted superior merely because he has set himself loftier tasks. He must accomplish these as fully as Boccaccio did his tasks if he is to be credited with an advance.

The *Troilus* should conceivably be set against a genre for critical evaluation as well as against this single work of Boccaccio's. If it were, what should the genre be? The poem has been given the titles of romance, novel, and tragedy—each by distinguished critics.[1] The fact is, as most of them recognize, that it resists confinement within any type to which it may be assigned. If it conforms most nearly to the romance, the genre of the *Filostrato,* it approaches the novel more closely than that or any other exemplar of the type in acuteness of characterization and in general breadth of view. To grant that it may be considered a romance and at least an anticipation of the novel does not preclude classification of it as a tragedy. After all, the author chose to call it by that name, and it conforms to the definition of tragedy which he rendered from Boethius' *Consolation* in his translation thereof and to the similar one which he put in the mouth of his Monk. There is the essential fall from high place, though atypically the high place is in the world not of state but of love. Should we defer to Chaucer and judge his work as tragedy in the medieval sense of the term, we have an abstraction to go by which was clear-cut and universally accepted in his time but, alas, only journeyman exemplifications of this—the Monk's collection, for instance, or Boccaccio's Latin compendia behind it. Finding them unworthy as standards of comparison, we should be tempted to resort to classic drama or to the Elizabethan for tragic touchstones. If we pursued the latter alternative, we could show no less easily that the *Troilus,* as tragedy, anticipates Shakespeare than that, as romance, it anticipates the novel. It may seem presumptuous to liken the hero to Hamlet as some have done, but a moment's reflection will convince us that his resemblance to the Dane, his infinite superior as a literary creation, is greater than that to any of the Monk's tragic figures from Lucifer to Bernabò Visconti or to any in the compendia of Boccaccio. Then, too, the admission of the comic in the *Troilus* accords somewhat with Shakespeare's practice in tragedy, while it does not at all with medieval definitions of the genre, however much in conformity it may be with medieval usage in the romance and other types. Possessed of both derivative and anticipative qualities, the poem is *sui generis,* we must conclude, in its combination of all these. We shall be advised, therefore, to evaluate it on its own terms, turning to literary history to sensitize our judgments but not to formalize them.

Being of this opinion, I shall look for such timeless excellences as magnitude, coherence, intensity, and verisimilitude, but shall try to recognize achievement of them through more or less original procedures of our poet, if it so comes, as well as through his employment of time-hallowed conventions. Since, as I have indicated, I rely heavily upon comparison of his work with the *Filostrato* and other specific sources to reveal his methods, whether traditional or revolutionary, I shall make use of all reasonably well-attested identifications of borrowings. I shall draw also upon the scholarship devoted to general literary influences, neglecting, however, one very considerable branch of it, that devoted to the presumed effect upon Chaucer of rhetorical theory. I eschew treatment of this effect, not because I question its presence in the *Troilus,* but because, after diligent attempts, I have found myself utterly unable to separate it from other influences.[2] Biographical and supporting historical research I shall neglect also, and without apology, for it is peripheral to the basically critical interests of this book. I shall do no more than note one argument for the influence of a patroness as an instance of the tenuousness of such speculation and record interpretations of several passages for dating simply as illuminative of the contexts themselves, accepting the conclusions most generally favored for period of composition without reanalysis of the evidence. And I shall not deal with phonology or metrics. Though the magic enhancement which sound gives to sense is the very heart of poetry, I shun consideration of it because of its irreducible uncertainties.[3] Making December, 1956, my *terminus ad quem,* I have forgone citation of Chaucerian research of any kind published after that month.

As for scholarship devoted to Boccaccio other than as a source for Chaucer, I shall draw upon it hardly at all. Since I approach the *Filostrato* and other

works of his contributory to the *Troilus* as materials for Chaucer's transforming art, and not as the transformations, which they laudably are, of antecedent literature and of the Italian's personal experience, I need not be concerned with their particular sources, the general literary background of their
author, his life before the courtship of Maria d'Aquino, nor even, very much,
with this to him most momentous affair.

The print I shall use of the *Troilus* is that given by Professor Robinson
in his first edition of the works of Chaucer. And I shall rely heavily upon the
scholarly apparatus which he has provided in that edition.[4] Of the three
states of the poem which have been distinguished in the manuscripts, his
text represents the *y*, supposed by him to come from a revision by the poet
himself of the *a*. The latter is generally believed to be Chaucer's first completed draft because of its more literal rendering of the *Filostrato* in certain
contexts in which it varies from the other two. Robinson does not accept
readings of the remaining state, the *β*, since he judges them "to be rather
scribal than authoritative."[5] Professor Root's edition, which I shall turn to
for its apparatus but not its text, represents the *β* state. In his belief, it is
that state which incorporates a genuine revision, with the distinctive readings
of *y* being merely scribal.[6] Fortunately, as Robinson observes, "the differences between the *y* text and Mr. Root's *β* version are few and unimportant." Accepting his view—without exhaustive investigation, I must confess—
that the *β* peculiarities are unauthoritative, I shall disregard them. I shall
consider *a* variants, however, to determine Chaucer's revisionary procedures
by comparing them with *y* readings. All among the former which I shall
have occasion to cite are included in Robinson's textual notes as well as in
Root's much fuller collection.

For the *Filostrato* I shall depend upon the text offered by Vincenzo
Pernicone.[7] This editor has classified the numerous manuscripts of the poem
into three groups and constructed his text on the basis of accord between all
three or between two when one diverges. He does not give variants in his
edition. In an article published after it,[8] he conjectures that some variants
are due to revision by Boccaccio, but remarks that these are but substitutions
of one word for another and, rarely, of one construction for another. None
of the few which he cites in the article can be shown to have been in the
manuscript of the poem used by Chaucer.[9] As reviewers of his edition have
noted, his text of the *Filostrato* is superior to that prepared by Moutier because it is based on many more manuscripts. The differences in readings
between the two, however, are, with occasional exceptions, of no significance
for the literary study of the *Troilus*. A few lines of Chaucer's adaptation are
closer to Pernicone's text than to Moutier's; a few, closer to the latter than

to the former. I shall turn to Moutier's text (as reproduced by Griffin and Myrick[10]) only when *Troilus* approaches that more nearly than the other. I shall also be much indebted to the interpage translation which accompanies the reproduced text, although I shall render the *Filostrato* in my own words. The numbering of stanzas is the same in Pernicone's edition as in Moutier's so that my references to the former will conform to those of Chaucer scholars who have worked from the latter or from Griffin and Myrick's reprinting of it. To forestall question, I may remark that the form "Troiolo" which I shall use throughout is the regular full spelling of the hero's name in Pernicone's text—not "Troilo" as in Moutier's edition and the reprint of it.

My indebtednesses of a personal kind are many. Syracuse University granted me a research leave in 1947 to work on this study. The late Professor Karl Young, who made me a Chaucerian, gave encouragement to it in its early stages. Professor Robert A. Pratt communicated many useful pieces of information through correspondence. Colleagues of mine at Syracuse, Howard O. Brogan, Edwin H. Cady, Donald A. Dike, and Mary H. Marshall, read sections of the typescript and offered helpful suggestions about them. My wife prepared the typescript and contributed to its improvement.

Contents

CHAPTER I.   THE ACTION IN ITS COURSE

※ ※ ※ ※

CHAPTER II.   PHYSICAL PARTICULARS AND TIME AND THE SUPERNATURAL

CHAPTER III. FIGURATIVE ASSOCIATIONS IN SEVEN AREAS

✶ ✷✷ ✶

CHAPTER IV. COMPOSITES

The Action in its Course

Introduction: Proportions and Emphases

I N the following sections of the present chapter, Chaucer's reworking of the *Filostrato* will be traced in textual order, with selective illustration of trends as they manifest themselves in fusion and by degrees. Salient trends will be accorded exhaustive and schematic analysis in Chapters II and III: in the former, modifications of the source as to physical particulars about the characters and their world and as to the time factor and the supernatural; in the latter, modifications of it as to patterns of figurative expression. In Chapter IV, syntheses will be attempted of change in the narrator's role, in the roles of the principal actors, and, lastly, in the story as a whole.

The coherence of adaptation, which is to be demonstrated systematically in later chapters, will be suggested as far as possible in this exploratory one. As we move from stage to stage of the narrative, attempt will be made to show that our poet's departures cumulate to produce major changes in proportion and emphasis. These it will be expedient to define here in Section 1 in order that we may have a broad framework in which to place the multifarious details later to be encountered.

Consideration of his changes in the large will bring out the marked increase in scope and complexity which he effected in the story and the maintenance, notwithstanding, of an essential unity. He makes more than Boccaccio of the lives which affect the hero's life and modifies the experience of that central figure in such manner as to give it universal significance. With heroine, confidant, and rival all more fully and delicately realized than in the *Filostrato* and with the social milieu no less elaborated, the *Troilus* is more panoramic of human nature than its original. And, since it raises issues of God's purveyance apropos of the vicissitudes of the hero, it extends our

3

view from purely mundane affairs to the dispensation which encompasses these and all things. Diversification of incidents and multilevelled interpretation of many of them set up complex oppositions, which, dynamically integrated as they are, produce a mounting excitement both intellectual and emotional.

In the *Filostrato,* the hero pre-empts attention. Sympathy is with him almost exclusively; what happens is judged mainly from his point of view. Since that is a narrow one, the concentration upon him is exceedingly restrictive. He sees and is seen as the devotee of love. All else but his passion is of slight concern to him or to Boccaccio as the interpreter of his life. The prince is no epic hero standing for his people but merely the representative of a small and rather precious lot—young men who give their all to love. His misconceptions are not of Oedipean magnitude; the disappointments resulting from them, at best pathetic. Subjugated to Criseida by the godling Amore, he rationalizes the inevitable by persuading himself that he has been delivered into the hands of the best of ladies. Fortune so orders things as to disabuse him. By her very nature she must take away what she has given and does so, for any evidence to the contrary, without orders from any higher power. She banishes Criseida from his embraces and thus insures her defection, for the avid lady will have a bedfellow, be he who he may. The failure of his mistress to return begins such education as Troiolo has; the sight of his gift to her upon Diomede's captured garment completes it. There is no liberating illumination of his soul, either before or after death, and, hence, no catharsis. Speculation is not his forte. The woman responsible for his engrossing passion is drawn with great sardonic effect as the wanton clumsily pretending to modesty. Her emotions, however, are so primitive that they do not admit of the fine dissection to which his are subjected. And she, even less given to thought than he, offers few judgments on events which complement his significantly. Pandaro is a competent intermediary—hardly more, if one excepts a vein of individuating cynicism. Diomede is but the necessary supplanter without even that distinction.

Despite its limitations and because of the disciplined artistry which imposed them, the *Filostrato* is a masterpiece of construction, tightly unified and well proportioned. The credit is mainly Boccaccio's. For, if Benoit de Sainte-Maure invented the story of the fickle Trojan as seems to be the case,[1] it was the Florentine who gave it form and made it one of the immortal legends of our culture.

In Benoit's *Roman de Troie,* a spacious history of the Trojan conflict from the offenses which caused it to the dispersion of the contending hosts, the love affair in question was but a minor sequence and one much interrupted by accounts of warfare. Briseïda, though described early in the romance, did not figure in it until nearly its midpoint, when she was granted to her father Calcas, who had gone over to the Greeks. There we learn that she had been the mistress of Troïlus, previously known to us only for his services to his country. They are shown together on the night before she rode out of Troy and then on that ride. When he parted from her outside the walls, his supplanter immediately began courtship, and from that point at intervals we find a good deal about Diomedès' genuine ardors and the lady's changing dispositions toward him and toward her old lover, a good deal also about the battles between the rivals and their mutual hatred, but nothing of moment about love longings in Troïlus. His sensibilities other than outraged pride do not concern Benoit. The theme of the love sequence is not devotion and consequent misery in the prince but faithlessness in the lady.

Boccaccio freed the sequence from the encroaching background of warfare; extended it backward to the enamorment of the hero, and promoted him from a supporting role to one which commands most of our interest and sympathy. His plot, then, has an ascending action to complement the descending. There is ironic contrast, not only between the man's loyalty and the woman's faithlessness, but also between his views on love in the two phases of the action and between her courses in the one and in the other. And within the first phase, there is an ironic curve, Troiolo being toppled from the real comfort of his boasted freedom from love into real misery and thence raised to a deceptive happiness. To bring hero and heroine together and to provide a listener encouraging of their self-revelations, Boccaccio introduced a confidant, Pandaro, whose name he took from a king inconspicuous in the *Roman* as warrior and unconcerned with love at first or second hand. The heroine he renames Criseida and translates from the single state to that of widow.

In his expansion of the sequence, Boccaccio made skillful use of a number of resources.[2] He borrowed details from the love story of Achillès and Polixenaïn which runs concurrently through the *Roman* with that of Troïlus and Briseïda. He took something from the Latin abridgment of Benoit by Guido de Columnis, the *Historia destructionis Troiae*. And he drew directly from life. As he told his beloved in the prose Proemio to the *Filostrato*, he had chosen the affair of Troiolo for recounting because of its similarity to his own in point of bereavement, and would express his sorrows at present separation from Maria through Troiolo's at loss of Criseida and also his joys before separation through the latter's, though these, he averred, were of a more substantial kind than any he had so far enjoyed. As to what was written of Criseida, he said tactfully, all that was *favorable* was to be credited by Maria to herself. A thrifty artist, he took much from his *Filocolo*, then partially completed. This rambling version of the old tale of Floris and Blancheflor was, like the *Filostrato,* a vehicle for the utterance of his own love. Then too he incorporated material here and there from Dante, Ovid, and poets less enduring than they, as well as, in one notable passage, from the poet philosopher, Boethius.

Chaucer develops Boccaccio's version of the affair with much of the originality displayed by the latter in expanding Benoit's. He omits, modifies, and adds with the independence of a true creator.

His omissions, while numerous and sometimes considerable, are overmatched by what he adds, so that his poem extends to nearly half again as many lines as the *Filostrato.*[3] Had Chaucer and Boccaccio been at substantially the same stage of development when writing of Troilus, the former by allowing himself wider scope would have had some potential advantage in attempting a comprehensive imitation of life. As it was, with our poet the older and more practiced artist at the time of composition,[4] he had a very material one.

Expanding the *Filostrato* unevenly, he changes the proportion between the ascending and descending actions and also heightens the tonal contrast between them. He employs almost exactly twice as many lines as Boccaccio to relate what happened up to the capture of Antenor but not very many more than his author to tell of this and all subsequent events, so that nearly three-fifths of his production is devoted to the ascending phase as against only some two-fifths of the *Filostrato.*[5] He is thus continuing what Boccaccio began, giving preponderance to the part of the story which the latter invented to supplement Benoit. In his leisurely treatment of the upward course of love, Chaucer stylizes passion and refines it and yet turns its conventions to humorous account. While not slighting the hero in this part, he devotes much more attention than Boccaccio to the lady and the confidant—to the latter's stratagems and to the former's outward and inward responses to them. The successive stages of enamorment, courtship, and enjoyment are all made more glowing by Chaucer's pen and more richly variegated. The reversal and decline, on the other hand, he keeps relatively stark and somber, concentrating upon the hero's sorrows and intensifying the bitter irony of his disillusionment. The contrast between the two phases of the action and withal their basic unity are perfectly epitomized in his opening lines:

> The double sorwe of Troilus to tellen,
> That was the kyng Priamus sone of Troye,
> In lovynge, how his aventures fellen
> Fro wo to wele, and after out of joie,
> My purpos is, er that I parte fro ye.

6

With the *Filostrato* all before him as he wrote, Chaucer was wont to draw on later contexts in it for additions to earlier ones, deriving germinal ideas from the descending phase for development in the ascending and from junctures late in each phase for development at points antecedent therein. Surer of what was to come than his predecessor could possibly have been, he was able to prepare more expressly for it and hence to improve continuity in motifs and in character portrayal. His reordering of Boccaccio's presentation and his dovetailing of new materials with the old evidence structural capacities of the highest order.

In developing both phases as given to him in the *Filostrato,* he resorted a great deal to books as scholars have shown—to the faithful rendering of it into French prose by one "Beauvau, seneschal d'Anjou," to sources employed by Boccaccio, and to a variety of other works.[6] He drew also, it may be presumed, upon personal experience, but since he is as reticent about that as his author was communicative, one cannot pinpoint what he derived therefrom. Using the close translation, *Le Roman de Troyle et de Criseida,* along with the original throughout, he profited from its phrasing in hundreds of instances, as Professor Pratt discovered, and in many of these for phrasings pertinent to my study. He exploited the *Roman de Troie* particularly for circumstances of the exchange of prisoners and its aftermath, and supplemented borrowings therefrom with very minor ones from Guido's *Historia.* Portraits of the lady and her two lovers supplied him by Benoit he filled out from portraits of the same by Joseph of Exeter. He altered and extended the consummation sequence of the *Filostrato* by free but indubitable and extensive resort to the sequence in the *Filocolo* in which Florio comes at long last to the couch of Biancofiore, and he derived his valediction to his poem from Boccaccio's to this diffuse prose romance. Still another romance of the Italian's, the stately *Teseida,* yielded short passages which Chaucer incorporated here and there into his fabric—most notably purple descriptions of times of day and year and the account of the flight of Arcita's soul made to serve for the flight of Troilus'—and, besides these, scattered details of Arcita's funerary arrangements incorporated into the Trojan hero's anticipations of death. As for Statius' *Thebaid,* which inspired the *Teseida,* a digest of it supplies the bulk of Cassandre's disquisition to Troilus, and the poem is also a topic of conversation for Criseyde and Pandarus. Petrarch afforded a song for Troilus at the beginning of the action; and Machaut, among other things, a song for Antigone somewhat later in it. Dante's *Comedy* served as a mine for vivid imagery and for notions of the other world infernal and celestial, and, more generally, as a model of the sublime in vernacular poetry. Ovid, Chaucer's lifelong favorite among classical authors as Boccaccio among Italian, made

7

substantial contributions. Directly or indirectly, his *Metamorphoses* supplied a great deal of the mythological element in the *Troilus,* which gives it so convincing a semblance of antiquity and, along with that, so strong an impression of divine power and human weakness and misery, particularly in the amatory sphere. Other works of his proved useful on occasion, as, for example, the *Heroides,* which supplied Oënone's letter for Pandarus to cite. Through intermediaries, if not directly, Horace gave Chaucer several figures and—accidentally—the conception of Lollius as an authority on Troy. Boethius' *Consolation of Philosophy* provided the controlling issues, as well as a number of particular contexts, the most considerable being Troilus' paean to Love apropos of enjoyment of Criseyde and his soliloquy on predestination inspired by prospective loss of her. And, to conclude, the *Roman de la Rose,* the *Epistles* of Seneca, and other works, too numerous even to mention, yielded bits for incorporation at one juncture or another.

In combining what he took from the *Filostrato,* these ancillary sources, and his own imagination, Chaucer organized as large a part of the narrative into distinct episodes as Boccaccio, and he extended more episodes and more sequences of episodes to really substantial proportions than the latter had done. As was the case with the *Filostrato,* scarcely a fifth of the *Troilus* is taken up by the author's digests of intervals and by utterances of his substantially independent of particular events,[7] so that four-fifths remain for units of action so clearly defined as to deserve the names of episode or scene. In the one work as in the other, there are many short scenes and many of moderate length;[8] but only in Chaucer's a number of really long ones—five ranging from three hundred odd to nearly eight hundred lines, as against only one in Boccaccio's of something over three hundred.[9] And for every lengthy chain of episodes in the *Filostrato,* there is a longer one in the *Troilus,* with a tightened chronological linking. A steadier and richer progression is possible in these fairly massive episodes and episode clusters of Chaucer's poem than in their slighter correspondents in the original. The characters of the main actors can be more gradually and delicately unfolded and relationships between them made more intricate.

Turning now from this brief analysis of the poems by their episodic and extraepisodic components to a more extended one by the direct quotation of people of the action and statements of the narrator *in propria persona,* we shall find that Chaucer employs these two elements in the same proportion as Boccaccio, but that he changes the ratios between the line totals of the actors as well as the tenors of their parts and speaks in his own person to very different effect than the Italian writer. In his poem as in the *Filostrato,* the conversations, epistolary correspondence, and self-communings which

8

are directly reported of any and all personages in the fiction take up three-fifths of the total number of lines.[10] There is a higher proportion of this element, of course, in some books of the *Troilus* than in others, but the fluctuation from book to book is roughly parallel to that from corresponding range to range of the source.[11] In each poem virtually all of it comes within episodes.[12] We may consider this first, leaving the lines of the narrators, which in and out of episodes constitute two-fifths of the poems, for analysis further on in the section.

As to apportionment of direct discourse,[13] Boccaccio quoted his alter ego Troiolo as much as all the other characters together, reporting Pandaro and Criseida each in slightly less than half as many lines as the prince and dividing the slight remainder of quotation about evenly between Diomede and a small company of extras. Chaucer tends to equalize distribution by reducing the number of lines assigned to the hero and by increasing the number of those given to his friend and his mistress. The confidant, with more than twice as many lines as in the *Filostrato,* is now the character most extensively reported; the hero, with somewhat fewer than in the original, now less extensively than he but not a great deal less; the heroine with only a moderate increase in lines, still less than her lover, though again not a great deal. Diomede's speaking part is absolutely but not proportionally increased, while those of all bystanders constitute together only a slightly larger fraction of the whole than in the *Filostrato.*

The prince remains the central figure—even during the period of amatory negotiations when he is much offstage—for Criseyde and Pandarus are always considering his merits, and Chaucer has more to say about him than about the lady and much more than about the friend. With ampler room in which to express themselves, however, these fellows of his command more attention and sympathy than in the original, and even the rival presents himself in sharper focus. The lover is ennobled and intellectualized in his responses—improved in all qualities of heart and mind which he possessed in the *Filostrato,* if not given essentially different ones. Yet, despite the improvement, Chaucer recognizes the defects which inhere in these as in all qualities far more acutely than Boccaccio. The confidant is given a new and more distinctive personality in the *Troilus,* as extroverted as his master's is the opposite, but tactful and sympathetic for all the bustle which is his and for all the ego-satisfaction in intrigue and display of worldly wisdom. The heroine is reindividualized, though not, as her relative, more sharply defined. In her discourse, Criseyde captivates us with a sprightliness and gentle charm quite foreign to Criseida and betrays a complex motivation which excites the psychoanalyst latent in us all, as her original's transparent sexuality could not do. Her partial concern for self, however, leads to disillusionment for her lover as surely as the uncalculating appetite of Criseida and with finer and no less bitter ironies. The new Diomede convicts himself of insincerity in love as the old did not and thus comes to stand in more explicit opposition to the hero. Among the minor characters, Cassandre, Deiphebus, and Ector, taken over from the *Filostrato,* speak with higher breeding and affability than in that poem and thus contribute to the courtly atmosphere of the adaptation. And the new speakers, Eleyne and Antigone, chime with them and the four principals in graciousness of address.

To begin a more thorough analysis of the reworking of the discourse of the four main characters by considering that of the hero's, it may be said that his bent to self-communing is accentuated and that his superiority to others in dignity of thought and expression is notably enhanced. Possessed like Troiolo by love and its joys and sorrows, Troilus is even more wont than he to vent his feelings to the air.[14] And in such outlet as also in communication with those about him, he ranges more widely in ideas than his model and in modes of conveying them. Troiolo showed himself concerned only with love and with that passion essentially as it possessed himself. Except in his song to Venere with its Neoplatonic universalization of love, he did not generalize upon his experience with any profundity. And though he protested that his was a sublimated emotion, the figurings of it which stand out in his lines are the elemental images of fire, not the rare figures derived from the conceitful religion of love nor the many but slight ones taken from the equally cerebral feudalization of relations between courtly lovers. As emotionally involved as Troiolo with equally poignant if briefer rhapsodies to prove it, Troilus conceives of his connection with his mistress even more idealistically than the other, and speculates, as Troiolo did not, about the place of man in the dispensation of God. Among his figures, which are more numerous and elaborate than Troiolo's, there are many and striking abstracts —as of amatory worship and particularly of feudal service in love. And, while visual figures are more prominent too in his lines than in the latter's, the imagery of fire, the consuming fire of passion, is materially reduced.

As for the confidant, his part is so fattened that he emerges more completely from type into individuality than in the *Filostrato* and thus contrasts more meaningfully with the hero. His lines, as before, are devoted almost exclusively to conversation.[15] This would be inevitable, it must be admitted, since his commitment is, not as the prince's to meditate upon his own love, but to persuade and arrange for another's. But, as Chaucer shapes him, it is obvious that he is a born talker, verbalizing so much more than in the *Filostrato,* not merely because the suitor is more despairing and the lady more

10

resistant, but because he adores argument and pontification. There are substantial changes in his lines throughout. Increase in them, however, comes almost entirely before the consummation,[16] during the period, that is, when business justifies these oral pleasures. The new resources which he manifests at this time would have been superfluous in the era of Troilus' possession of Criseyde and futile thereafter; and the new exuberance, out of place in tragic circumstances. Pursuing the same goal in the ascending action as Pandaro, Chaucer's intermediary is more sententious with both lover and beloved and more devious in bending the latter to his will. His learning, while extensive, is limited to the earthly sphere, being devoted to the furtherance of love. He lectures Troilus on the theory and practice of courtship and Criseyde on the suitor's knightly accomplishments and on her obligation to show pity—in the most tangible way—to so worthy a man. In his debates with Troilus on destiny, he opposes the worldling's easy assumption that one can weather the alternations of Fortune to the prince's deterministic pessimism, which, though as indemonstrable, is more thoughtfully considered. His pedantry and general busybodyness are not offensive but delightful, relieved as they are by his own humor and put in amusing lights by the responses of friend and niece. He makes even more than Pandaro of the anomaly of his presuming to counsel in love when himself a failure in it. His parading of time-worn instances provokes ironic comment from Troilus, and his patronizing assumption of simplicity in Criseyde is refuted as soon as he acts upon it. Ostensibly their leader, he is incited to activity by calculated resistance from both. Whereas the figurative vehicle of Pandaro's thought differed essentially from Troiolo's only in being less rich, Pandarus' is distinguished from his lord's in a number of positive respects. It is as generally prosaic in association as Troilus' is poetic; very often proverbial, as the latter's seldom is; and with a considerable admixture of similes and illustrations, proverbial and nonproverbial, whereas the prince shows an overwhelming preference for the immediacy of the metaphor.

In recasting the lines of the heroine, Chaucer gives her a mixed style, which approaches now her uncle's and now her lover's; a range of thinking from the one man's pragmatism to the other's metaphysics; and affection as tender as either's, but in conflict, as theirs are not, with fear and a strong instinct for self-preservation. Her self-communings, which were more extensive than Pandaro's, he increases considerably, but her words to auditors even more.[17] If then she is brought closer to the hero in introspective tendencies, she is so also to the confidant in the urge to prevail in argument when circumstances permit.[18] Unlike Criseida, Chaucer's lady has more to say to her first lover than he to her, and, not only maintains sovereignty over him like

11

Criseida, but specifically claims it as the latter did not. And though deluged with words by Pandarus, she counters his disingenuous arguments more skillfully than the earlier heroine the blunt solicitations of Pandaro. She shows herself as practical as her uncle and far more selfish, with concern for security now her flaw instead of rank concupiscence. Yet she is once allowed speculation in divinity as abstruse as Troilus'. Her figurative associations are considerably enriched. Some resemble those of the poetically endowed hero and some those of her homely, proverb-loving relative. She does not have the consistent pungency, however, of the latter. Nor does she often quite match the lofty and beautiful imagination of Troilus; the romantic aura which invests her is the product more of what he and the author say about her than of her own poetic inspiration. It is noteworthy that she is never permitted, as Troilus sometimes is, to image sexual desire as flame or even heat, Criseida's not infrequent figures of this kind being totally suppressed, while Troiolo's more numerous ones are kept in part.

The rival in Chaucer's poem carries the burden of conversation when with the heroine as in Boccaccio's. He shows himself as bold in two quoted interviews with her as in the one in the source, but more tactful and more sophistic. Private reflections attributed to him in the new work manifest a gay unconcern which gives the lie to his protestations, whereas the one bit of self-communing in the old expresses trepidation consonant enough with them.[19] Echoes in his wooing of the phraseology of the first lover thus become unmistakably ironic, as they were not in the *Filostrato*. To the further heightening of irony, the lady, who is made more resistant to the ennobled hero and more assured with him, is represented as meeker with the debased rival and more encouraging of his advances, though credited with remorse for her infidelity and hinted to have postponed physical surrender for a considerable time.

Let us proceed now from the lines of the several characters to the envelope which contains them, statement, that is, by the author speaking *in propria persona*. In each poem, it includes in varying amounts: further reportage of thought, speech, or writing of the characters, but in indirect discourse, paraphrase, or mere summary; transitions from one utterance, or one event, to another; mention or description of details of physical appearance and dress, of stage business and settings, and of times of day and year; and, finally, the expression of attitudes and opinions, either limited to the fiction or extended to life in general. All of these constituents in the *Filostrato* are freely altered in the *Troilus*. And the last two are more than proportionally increased; Chaucer concretizes the action with far greater particularity than Boccaccio and offers much more numerous and extended comments upon it.

In his elaboration of the world of appearances, he perfects the illusion of actuality and brings the visible and tangible to bear upon the invisible and intangible far more powerfully than his original. He establishes the chronology of sequences as if he were a meticulous historian. And he dwells on the planets in their courses, their influences, the seasonal and diurnal appearances effected by their rotation, and the inexorable passage of time for enforcement of moods or concepts. He plots motion as carefully as time, following his actors from place to place in Troy and from room to room indoors, without ever losing them in undefined space as his original sometimes did. Like the discourse invented for his characters, the backgrounds provided for them are a mixture, effective whether entirely conscious or not, of antiquity and contemporary life, with both strains giving verisimilitude if both invested with romantic glamor. His Trojans go, not to churches, but to temples, yet they live in very medieval palaces and display themselves in medieval dress or armor, just as they may refer familiarly to old gods and yet sometimes speak in the idiom of Christianity. All this would have permitted the medieval auditor to eat his cake and have it still—to imagine that he was being given a genuine picture of another age and clime and yet to feel for all its strangeness that in the human essentials it was like his own and hence "real" in current terms. He could sympathize with the persons of the drama as beings oriented at least partially to his modes of thinking and also enjoy a full melancholy realization of their pastness—of their being at one with the snows of yesteryear.

In the process of elevating the heroine, Chaucer bestows upon her a more magnificent establishment than she possessed in the *Filostrato* and brings her into the royal circle at the house of Deiphebus, while suppressing every allusion in that poem to her social unacceptability, both in her own discourse and in that of others. Though made a great lady who can properly claim sovereignty in love, she is so feminized in her person and so gentled in behavior that she appears the quintessence of soft womanhood. No longer does she elbow a jostling crowd or dart angry glances at those who displease her. And instead of casting herself into the embraces of her lover, she yields tremblingly to them.

The masculinity of the hero is similarly emphasized. When in arms, he is more impressive than Mars and, in bed, dominant, as the male is supposed to be, once he is assured of possession. Before that, however, he is put in the quasi-comic situations of addressing his mistress from a pretended sickbed and of being thrown insensible into her bed by Pandarus. Highs and lows in his appearances on stage bring out the ambivalence of love—excellent, it can be inferred, because cherished by so knightly a figure, suspect because stripping him willy-nilly of his dignity and happiness.

The go-between, who is given powers of encouragement commensurate with the lover's need for it and of persuasion commensurate with the lady's shamefastness, manifests his zeal by continual scurrying between them and his easy friendship with both by playful wrestlings. He can match either in weeping, ready with tears as he is for persuasive effect and unable to stem them when genuinely moved.

Diomede, who requires no intermediary, possesses himself symbolically of Criseyde by taking her horse's rein on the ride out of Troy and by winning her glove on his first call at her tent.

As to the role played by the narrator, Chaucer expands it as consistently as he increases the mass of objective correlative. Boccaccio had very little to say directly about his own thoughts and feelings, except in his Proemio—which his adapter does not use. He really had small need to in the poem itself, since, as he had told his beloved, the hero was to be his surrogate, with the latter's responses to love projections of his own. In the body of the *Filostrato*, he commented only rarely upon what was transpiring and then always briefly and obviously. He addressed a general audience only twice and even his particular one, Maria d'Aquino, but three times. The style in which he wrote as narrator is very close to that with which he endowed the hero as far as figurative language is concerned, though negatively distinguished from it, of course, by general avoidance of the personal lyric note.

Chaucer presents himself as an outsider in love and no more than a translator in the literary sphere and yet presumes to pronounce upon love (and all existence for that matter) and to clothe what is palpably his own thought, not his Lollius', in studied rhetoric as well as in the plain language of daily use. Unidentified with any character, he can be both humorously and seriously critical of all his puppets, though displaying warm sympathy for every one but Diomede and an amused interest even in him. As sympathetic an observer of love in the ascending action as Pandarus in that phase, he shares with him a keen awareness of its comic incongruities. The naiveté which, unlike him, he affects permits sly sallies against the passion. Even sometimes in the ascending action and frequently in the descending, he leaves Pandarus' realm of thought and enters the prince's by concerning himself with divine causation. He dwells portentously upon the subordination of man to higher powers. No Dante, however, he treats this in impressionistic fashion rather than schematically. He leaves unresolved the issue of human freedom under an omnipotent deity, assuming the responsibility of his characters over and over again and frequently proclaiming the divine control of events without ever attempting a doctrinal explanation of their compatibility. And though he condemns worldliness in his Epilog with edifying fervor, he has not done so consistently before it nor tried to do so. He has given warnings of disaster, indeed, from the very first, but he has not applied them to the negation of hopes or delights currently unfolding. Instead of maintaining the consistency attainable by him as omniscient author, Chaucer prefers to enact the process of illumination which his audience must experience if it is to appreciate his poem to the full. He convincingly simulates a gradual change in his point of view, moving from preponderantly worldly toward preponderantly extraworldly attitudes, and by so doing he strengthens the contrast between ascending and descending actions which is central to his ironic purpose.

To keep his hearers—and readers—with him in this aesthetic experience, he is careful to maintain a close rapport throughout. He addresses them on any and every occasion with easy if deferential familiarity, confessing shortcomings with ingratiating modesty, deferring to the wisdom allowed to them his betters, and professing the same lively concern for these people of flesh and blood as for the creatures of his imagination. The breadth of understanding, sympathetic and yet objective, which distinguishes him as narrator from all those creatures, is accompanied by a rich variety of style. His writing in his own person surpasses the utterance of every one of his characters in its flexibility, its ready accommodation to all levels of discourse. He equals hero and confidant in their several extremes, while his Criseyde only approaches these. He can be as chatty in his confidential asides as Pandarus and as elevated as Troilus, and, indeed, loftier when he essays the epic manner called for by the pretended antiquity and genuine substance of his tale of love.

In combining the elements with which he works—comment as narrator, objective correlative, and direct discourse of characters in all their ramifications—Chaucer's controlling principle seems to be to oppose circumstances, attitudes, and values in such a way as to produce a dynamically balanced whole. His structural ideal, I believe, for the *Troilus* is artistic unity emergent from lifelike diversity. And, in my opinion, he accomplishes it with eminent success, such flaws as he may have left unremedied being too slight even collectively to compromise the soundness of his ambitious pattern.

In working for significant oppositions, Chaucer is carrying farther what Boccaccio most ably began. He extends the range of contrasts of the *Filostrato*. And he develops them more variously, making some forthrightly ironical in the manner of his author and some but lightly so, and leaving still others as ambiguities to be resolved or not as the reader pleases.

It is to be noted, however, that he is no more inclined than Boccaccio to develop oppositions into strenuous conflicts for the persons of the drama. In his poem, as in the *Filostrato,* paired forces are so unequal that a contest is either impossible or soon decided. What is sought in both is not the suspense of dubious battle but the impression that passions are really ruling and that the powers behind them and behind events are practically, if not theoretically, unopposable. With the characters natured and ideated as they are, struggle is not to be expected of them even if it is to be assumed that they have free will. In both works, Love can overcome the hero instanter and Fortune have her way with him completely, and, in the *Troilus,* the planet goddess Venus readily inclines the heroine to love for all her timidity and prudent shamefastness. In that poem, too, it is indicated that God controls all, though in ways and for ends that pass human understanding. On the human level, Criseida's resistance to the confidant is merely token, and Criseyde's, while more prolonged, still so and therefore to be treated archly. There is no real struggle between friendship and family honor in either Pandaro or Pandarus, though a lively fear of discovery and a sense of shame which will not quite down. And even these do not inhibit either in his brokerage. Rendered obedient by Love, both Troiolo and Troilus yield humbly to the lady's decision to leave Troy despite the gravest doubts of its wisdom. Finally, Chaucer makes it as plain as Boccaccio that Diomede's first visit to her in camp decides the issue of her loyalty. Subsequent tears notwithstanding, Criseyde is as effectively his from that moment as Criseida.

As to contrast in the *Filostrato,* the basic one, as it had to be by the nature of the story, was between hero and heroine, and the principal irony derived from it, of course, the return of faithlessness for fidelity. This contrast centered upon amorous motivation. Troiolo looked for spiritual as well as physical fulfillment. Even when he spoke of bodily delight, he avoided all grossness. Criseida, on the other hand, was preoccupied with the flesh. Revelations of herself bore out her cousin's dictum about the libidinousness of women. Such pretenses to modesty as she attempted were transparent and soon forsaken. She anticipated and exulted in the sexual act with unsublimated frankness. Idealizing love as he did, the prince would sacrifice place and reputation to preserve it, but the lady would not flee with him lest people talk. Impersonally lustful, she found Diomede at once attractive, whereas Troiolo possessed by true devotion remained completely indifferent to other charmers however long she tarried. The irony of these differences between the two was enhanced by anomalies existing within his role and within hers. Troiolo's exalted position in the great world was at variance with his abject one in the kingdom of love; Criseida's profession of modesty and truth, at odds with her performance. Pandaro, as his role demanded, had to press for action when the prince and lady hesitated, appear hopeful when they despaired, but these necessary tendencies of his were not elaborated nor made to contribute vitally to irony. The occasional displays of amatory cynicism which he was permitted were, however, ironic counterpoint to the ill-founded sublimations of his master. Ironic also was the anomaly of his own situation—unsuccessful in love, he presumed to counsel others. Diomede's quick supplantation of the hero was the capping irony, but imperfect in that it did not oppose victor and vanquished as unworthy and worthy of success.

What Boccaccio did so thoroughly in the core relationship, Chaucer extends to all that proceed from it. With him it is nature or artistic second nature to turn the coin—to show reverse as well as obverse. This is his procedure, not only with the individuals of the story and their particular relations, but also with values taken for granted in the *Filostrato*. Keener than Boccaccio in perception of incongruities, he treats them with more tolerant amusement. Sympathy with the hero does not make him savage toward the lady as it did his author. And as he tempers the ironic element, he renders it complex. As Miss Dempster has so well shown, he learned a great deal from the *Filostrato* about irony, and in learning came to improve upon the model.[20] In his version of the tragedy, the heroine appears a victim as well as the prince, and the intermediary is as much her tool as she is his. The mysteries of divine causation which he brings into it Chaucer leaves as such, accepting orthodoxies but not resolving all questions raised by them. On the earthly plane, Troilus and Criseyde are opposed as whole-souled and divided personalities, instead of as amorous idealist and wanton; he and Pandarus, not only as indrawn pessimist and hopeful doer, but also as metaphysical and worldly minds; and he and Diomede, newly, as true and merely pretending lovers. Anomalies are emphasized in the roles of hero, heroine, and confidant. Troilus is both a more impressive public figure and a meeker lover than Troiolo. Criseyde parries the solicitations of the confidant longer and more skillfully than Criseida but is self-deceived in her schemes for besting her father and gives prudential encouragement to Diomede even more openly than Criseida. Pandarus, whose failure in love is stressed beyond Pandaro's, presumes to be more doctrinaire about the passion than his relatively taciturn original. While making the affair in which these three participate more romantically ideal than it was in the *Filostrato*, Chaucer derives a richer humor from it. He cannot but be amused at the extravagances of sentiment which Boccaccio accepted with prevailing seriousness, even though he surpasses his author in realizing

17

for us the nobility of sex love. Recognizing the defects of its virtues even on the plane of earth, he brings us to consider its vanity in the divine scheme of the Universe.

The achievement of oppositions, if a constant purpose of his, as I have asserted, is still but a mediate goal, not the ultimate one. These, it goes without saying, he calculated to produce responses in his audience broader than appreciation of structural excellence. What were the total responses, we must ask ourselves, which he hoped to elicit from the young folk of both sexes, whom he professes to serve as amatory historian but finally warns against all earthly entanglements; from the good ladies, whose displeasure at the mis-exemplifying of their sex he affects to fear; from the moral Gower and the philosophical Strode? Since it transcends technique, the question cannot be resolved by purely objective analysis of the text. And no final answers to it are attainable by other approaches, as the continuing flood of interpretation of the *Troilus* makes all too evident. Answers I shall venture nonetheless, in the hope that they may serve their turn in the present state of our knowledge and critical prepossessions.

I shall begin by asserting that he sought to communicate as fully as possible to all segments of his potential audience. This, though limited to the fortunate in society, still represented a variety of tastes and moral standards. That he wished to keep the favor and interest of all is evident from his assiduous culti-vation of rapport—with the moral and philosophical at the end at least and with the amorously inclined pretty much throughout, with womanfolk ill represented in Criseyde no less than with male gentry vicariously exalted in the worldly perfections of Troilus. It is possible, however, that he was dis-ingenuous in his cultivation of some or all contingents, for he speaks as narrator with obviously calculated art. Granting the possibility, I still believe that he strove for honest contact with every sort of mind and heart. No doubt, he counted on wiser or more enthusiastic response from some quarters than from others, but it does not appear that he disprized any of them. If he over-taxed literal intelligences with his ironies, he did not seek obfuscation. He was not, I think, merely placating the ascetic and orthodox while catering by preference to courtly amorists with praise of love and justification of it on the basis of a heretical determinism. Nor was he bent, vice versa, on making his poem throughout the vehicle of an otherworldly message to the illuminated or illuminable, while leaving it superficially exaltatory enough of passion to hold the interest of romance-hungry ladies and gentlemen. He was not offer-ing one line of thought and feeling for the appreciation mainly of one party and its contrary for that of the other, but the two arrestingly juxtaposed for absorption by all to the top of their several capacities.

18

The opposition of divine infiniteness to human limitations seems to have been intended, as in Greek tragedy, to arouse awe at the first and pity for the second and to educe dramatic irony from strivings of the protagonist and his associates contrary to celestial dispensation. And the protagonist is brought to full recognition of his error though not, indeed, until death has freed him from carnality.

The ultimate moral is distinctively Christian. The poet informs young folk that the proper course for them is to disprize this life and its feigned loves and to fix their hearts upon Him from Whom only comes perfect love.

Heartfelt though this conclusion appears to have been, the *Troilus* is not consecrated exclusively or even in the main to the discouragement of worldly affections. Chaucer does not set the example of the all-absorbing piety which he seemingly regarded as the ultimate wisdom. Immediately before recommending it he announces the *Legend of Good Women* as a project of his— this to be a work which would exalt the female role in love however much it might expose the male. He testifies not infrequently to love's improvement of Troilus and its joyousness for both hero and heroine in so completely unqualified a fashion that he cannot have expected his audience to sense reservations at these moments about the worthwhileness of the passion. Nor, I think, did he expect any substantial portion of it to infer a tidy opposition between what he said of love in happier courses of the action and what in less happy—to discover that the former was deduced with flawless logic from a set of purely worldly postulates and that the latter was deduced, with equal logic and to higher purpose, from the only true postulates, the spiritual. What he hoped to effect, it appears, was something much simpler and less rigid: to prepare for the somber ending by reminders, scattered through the ascending as well as the descending action, of the existence of forces irresistibly productive of change, and yet to make fleeting love attractive for itself in the one phase of the story and for the increase of pathos from its extinction in the other.

He sought to make this love of compelling interest, and friendship also, by portraying the persons involved with fidelity to life and only secondarily to codes of behavior formalized in literature. What he invites thereby is contemplation of the intricacies of human nature, sympathetic contemplation, indeed, but always questioning. He elects to leave relations between his men and women a debatable and hence an immortal issue instead of constricting them within some dated formulas. Had he proposed, less wisely, to give his public a model of courtly love, he would never have chosen a story in which the heroine violates the basic tenet of fidelity, a story which in the *Legend of Good Women* is condemned by no less an authority than the God of Love.

And had he wished to exemplify friendship in classical perfection he would not have made the confidant's position even more dubious than it was by promoting him from cousin to uncle of the heroine. It is true that she is brought closer to courtly standards in the *Troilus* through elevation in rank, strengthening of resistance, and purgation of sensuality. It is true also that the hero, perfect enough by these standards as Boccaccio drew him, emerges an absolute paragon of humility and of all other virtues which were a man's passports to amour courtois. And the confidant not only plies his trade with more finesse than in the original but becomes also an inexhaustible well of amatory doctrine. But the qualities in all three which give them conventional standing must have attracted the medieval reader, along with the modern, as manifestations of personality, of native fineness and gentle breeding, rather than as illustrations of the rules of a polite game. And to these qualities of theirs are added traits, no less fascinating, which are inessential to courtly love, with some positively inimical to it. Even early situations are reworked by Chaucer to bring out equivocal aspects of their individualities, and the debacle is so handled as to emphasize the miscarriage of their expectations founded upon the amatory code. Diomede, exposed more plainly as an adventurer, wins the much refined heroine as easily from the ennobled hero. And she is made to suffer pitifully for her unforeseen weakness along with the deserted prince.

In his treatment then of all relationships in the *Troilus*—between man and man, and man and woman, between mortals and God or his lieutenants—Chaucer endeavors to communicate to us a many-sided conceptualization of experience. He would share, that is, his confirmed habit of thought, an essentially humanistic way of viewing life, which is so balanced and judicious that it can recognize unwisdom in mundane aspirations and partial failure to achieve even these and still accept the hurly-burly of this earth, not only with tolerance and urbane amusement, but with zestful interest and with a sense of its importance. This he transmits to us by example—by his many personalized responses to the action, too calculated not to have been so intended, too coherent in spirit to raise doubt of underlying sincerity despite the shifting point of view.

The above conceptions of Chaucer's purposes, though suggested to me by precedent commentators, do not coincide precisely with the opinions of any one of them and are quite divergent from the views of a good many. So wide is the spread of informed opinion on the *Troilus* that agreement with one camp involves contradiction of another. I can think of but two propositions likely to command universal acceptance—and both, only if vaguely phrased. The first is that the poem is somehow a success. Not denied, to my knowledge, since Legouis, this proposition should go unchallenged inasmuch as it avoids estimate of the completeness of success. The second proposition is that the piece is diversified in style and content. While no one could deny variegation of matter and manner, there has been no little disagreement as to how deep this goes and as to how compatible it is with achievement of a coherent total effect. Critics there have been, at least in earlier days, to whom it seemed a serious weakness in technique.[21] Others, while reconciled to it by and large, have excepted certain passages from approval, passages which, in their views, are inharmoniously adjusted to the whole.[22] Scholars who have concentrated upon phenomena of courtly love in the poem have naturally given only incidental attention to contrary elements, and, if not wishing them away, have tended to skirt the question of their compatibility with the former.[23] Investigators attentive above all to medieval orthodoxies of religion and morality have, as naturally, stressed Chaucer's concern for these, while differing among themselves as to its manifestations.[24]

Among critics following every special interest, there are not a few, happily, who approach the poem as the product of an artist who is an original genius though working with traditional materials, an individual shaped, but not cribbed, cabined and confined, by his milieu. Of their number is Professor Kittredge, the most influential of all Chaucerians, who writes of its creation:

> The magician has marked out his circle, and pronounced his spells, and summoned his spirits. He knows their names, and the formulas that will evoke them, and the task that he shall require them to perform. And lo! they come, and there are strange demons among them, and when the vision is finished and the enchanter lays down his wand, he finds on his desk—a romance to be sure, which his pen has written; a tragedy, in the sense in which he knew the word. . . . Everything is as he had planned it. But when he reads it over, he finds that he has produced a new thing. Nothing like it was ever in the world before.[25]

However various their bents, all who have looked, with Professor Kittredge, for enlargement and even breaking of molds no less intently than for conformities or dutiful adjustments, have found the former in abundance as well as the latter, have sensed tensions between inherited forms and fresh insights, and have come to value these as contributory to the peculiar power of the *Troilus*.[26] And they have seen behind the contrarieties, even those least reconciled, a turn of mind so distinctive and so consistent that it leaves its cachet upon the whole and gives it spiritual unity. This is an inquiring turn, which shuns neither sympathy nor judgment but which, in its very awareness of good and evil with all their shadings, is disinclined to total commitments. Its essence has been defined in more than one way, but perhaps best, by Professor Lowes, as detachment.[27]

It is now high time to support generalization by proof and so to begin the examination, side by side, of Chaucer's and Boccaccio's unfoldings of the story. In order that comparison may be as effortless as possible, the *Troilus* will be divided into blocks of varying but always manageable size, each constituting a distinct stage of the action, and the *Filostrato* into blocks as closely correspondent to these in content as is possible. A section will be devoted to each block in the adaptation along with the corresponding one in the source. Sections 2 and 3 will carry us through Book I of the *Troilus*; 4, through most of Book II; 5, to the end of it and into Book III; 6, to the end of that book; 7, all through Book IV; and 8, 9, 10, and 11, through Book V.

Entrances of Hero and Heroine — and of Narrator

THIS section will follow the more or less parallel courses of the poems only up to the moment when the confidant must come on stage if the action is to progress—that is, through Part I of the *Filostrato* and precisely half through Book I of the *Troilus*. Both authors state their themes, appeal for inspiration, and address themselves to lovers. Then taking up the story *ab initio,* they tell of Calchas' flight to the Greeks and of his daughter's successful appeal to Hector for exemption from paternal guilt; develop the festival of the Palladium as the occasion of the hero's enamorment; and chronicle amorous meditations of his subsequent to that holy exercise.

Chaucer adapts Part I with considerable freedom, though he diverges from it less widely than he will from Parts II and III, which tell how the confidant thrust himself into the affair and brought it to fruition. Expanding I by only a fifth,[1] our poet works changes nonetheless which are determinative of many that are to follow.

Boccaccio began Part I with appeals to his lady for poetic inspiration and to fellow sufferers for prayers to Love for himself, who, like Troiolo, must live removed from sweetest pleasure. After this allusion to his own affair which echoes the longer mention of it in the prose Proemio, he did not refer again to his amatory status in this part and but seldom thereafter.[2] And, as observed in the preceding section, he was chary throughout of personalized comment upon what transpired in the fiction.

Not using the Proemio at all, Chaucer completely transforms the first stanzas of his source.[3] He lets it be known immediately that his interest in love is not that of a participant but of a hopeless ousider. He invokes Thesiphone as a patroness appropriate both for the sad story and for himself

23

its sorrowful teller. He dares not appeal to the God of Love, he confesses, because of his "unliklynesse." He solicits the prayers of lovers for members of their kind in good and bad estate, assuming a priestlike function in the amatory cult which is consonant with his renunciation of love for himself. The role here established resembles Pandarus' instead of the hero's. Out of love, Chaucer would serve lovers in a literary capacity, as Pandarus, unsuccessful in it, would minister more immediately to his friend and to his niece. Yet he cannot be identified with the confidant as Boccaccio with Troiolo, for his sympathies will lie no more with him than with Troilus or with Criseyde and his ways of thinking will not be limited to this worldling's but will encompass and transcend those of all characters.

When Chaucer takes up the story, he proceeds rapidly until he comes to the first extended episode. He adapts Boccaccio's account of Calcas' flight and of Criseida's resort to the protection of Ettore with relatively minor changes, as, for example, particularization of the father's modes of foreknowledge and attribution of the vicissitudes of the War to Fortune, both of which prepare us for the stronger suggestions of destiny that are to come.[4] But he thoroughly reworks the episode of the Palladian festival at which Troiolo was represented to have fallen in love under circumstances reminiscent of Boccaccio's own enamorment on a Holy Saturday in the Neapolitan church of San Lorenzo.[5] In adapting it, Chaucer sharpens the irony of the prince's subjugation by Love and feminizes the appearance and behavior of Cupid's agent, the heroine of the piece. With characteristic exactitude, he narrows its dating from springtime to the month of April.

The hero of the *Filostrato* was declaiming against love and womankind on the basis of personal experience, when by chance his eye lighted upon Criseida. One glance changed his opinion. This reversal yields the immediate irony that he had to eat his words and the delayed one that possession of the new adored would amply confirm their truth. Boccaccio points up the former with a stanza-long exclamation against the blindness of mundane minds. As for the lady, he describes her as a statuesque beauty and relates that, at the moment when Troiolo spied her in the crowd, she was making a place for herself by shoving—a display of spirit which greatly commended her to the prince.

Chaucer gives us quite different first impressions of both hero and heroine. He begins by dropping from the former's speech the complacent reference to amatory experience, thus freeing him from suspicion as a light-of-love. The irony of the situation he emphasizes in both grave and comic vein—to the magnification of the lover and to the rousing of amusement at his expense. To make the point for the proud and worthy in his audience that resistance to passion is futile he dwells upon the lofty rank and character of the victim. Yet for all the princeliness attributed to Troilus, the poet images him as skipping carthorse brought to its senses by the whip and as snail fain to draw in its horns. In presenting the heroine he stresses, not haughtiness, but muliebriety. Boccaccio's description of her as tall and with every member proportional to her height, he adapts as follows:

> She nas nat with the leste of hire stature,
> But alle hire lymes so wel answerynge
> Weren to wommanhod, that creature
> Was nevere lasse mannyssh in semynge.

And, while recording that her behavior was "somdel deignous," he does not permit her to elbow the crowd. Troilus will continue to be represented more heroically and more humorously than Troiolo. The womanliness, here stressed, of Criseyde's person prefigures the soft feminine charm which is to be hers throughout the poem, despite the well developed sense of self-interest and self-preservation which it overlies.

In rendering Boccaccio's account of the lover's psychic ups and downs between first sight of Criseida and first conversation with Pandaro,[6] Chaucer makes, among other changes, the particularly notable addition of a song for the hero.[7] This tour de force, which he derives from Petrarch, is an admirable summary of the anomalies of love—a thematic statement of the ironies of desire. It is a cluster of paired opposites. Woe comes from love, a supposed good. Its every torment seems savory to Troilus; and the more he thirsts, the more he drinks. Unless he consents, how may he have within him so much of this living death, this sweet harm; and, if he consents, what right has he to complain? And so on.

In introducing the lyric, Chaucer makes his first reference to an author whom he will repeatedly pretend to have been his principal source:

> And of his song naught only the sentence,
> As writ *myn auctour called Lollius,*
> But pleinly, save oure tonges difference,
> I dar wel seyn, in al that Troilus
> Seyde in his song, loo! every word right thus
> As I shal seyn; and whoso list it here,
> Loo, next this vers he may it fynden here.[8]

As Professor Kittredge demonstrated in his long study, "Chaucer's Lollius,"[9] the poet strives to give his work the semblance of genuine antiquity by claiming this particular source and by variously reiterating his dependence upon authority as well as by introducing a multitude of "classical touches" —details of Trojan life, that is to say, and bits of mythology. The pretensions

25

as to sources may be taken up all together at this point, with the supporting classical touches left for consideration in Section 6 of the next chapter.

First of all, those to a basic original. In the Prohemium to Book II, which stresses the fidelity to source of that book, the phrase applied in I to Lollius reappears as follows:

> For as *myn auctour* seyde, so sey I,
>
> *Myn auctour* shal I folwen, if I konne.[10]

And it is here specified that the language of this author was "Latyn"[11]—as the reader would have surmised by himself from the form of the name in the earlier passage. Chaucer cites "myn auctour" once more in Book II and five times in Book III.[12] Near the end of the action, he makes a second reference to Lollius by name:

> The whiche cote, as telleth *Lollius,*
> Deiphebe it hadde rent fro Diomede
> The same day.[13]

In all these citations, Chaucer is working for effect, not for discharge of obligation. Like many a medieval—and modern—writer, our poet is ascribing a parentage to his brain child which will sustain the character he wishes this to bear.[14] To create the illusion that his story was a real antique, Chaucer is crediting it to an authority, whom he had reason to suppose a contemporary of Horace. In the *Policraticus* of John of Salisbury, which he knew, lines of Horace are quoted which recommend the "Troiani belli scriptorem" —that is, Homer—to a friend Lollius, but which could easily be mistranscribed to mean that, not Homer, but the friend was the writer who was being praised. Professor Pratt has found such a mistranscription in a twelfth-century manuscript of the *Policraticus;* and, in a fourteenth-century French translation of the work, this misrendering of the quotation from the Roman poet, "Car il dit, que lolli fu principal escrivain de la bataille de troye."[15] No wonder then that Chaucer pretends to be following this literary ghost in his *Troilus* nor that in the *House of Fame* he associates him with Homer, Dares, and Dictys, and with the more recent Guido de Columnis and "Englyssh Gaufride," as upholder of the fame of Troy.[16] Here was an ancient with a reputation. As source for the *Troilus,* he had the additional advantage of being lost to posterity; claims to fidelity to him were unchallengeable.

To enforce the venerability of his romance, Chaucer lets us know in it that he was familiar with other ancient authorities on Troy. In Book I, he directs his audience to Homer and to the allegedly pre-Homeric Dares and Dictys for supplementary information about the war; and, in Book V, to

Dares alone for a full account of the martial exploits of Troilus.[17] On four occasions, he makes vague reference to "olde bokes," and claims of his work at its end:

> Lo here, the forme of olde clerkis speche
> In poetrie, if ye hire bokes seche.[18]

When taken with Trojan local color in the poem and its supernatural machinery and approximations to the epic manner, the claims of ancient derivation compel the imagination of the modern reader as they must have of the medieval. Chaucer continues to achieve what he presumably sought for—not belief, unless among the naive—but willing suspension of disbelief.

The indications of dependence on authority—these just mentioned which stress its antiquity and many others which do not[19]—all serve to develop a second important fiction, that he feels himself unqualified to attempt original treatment of his theme. This contributes to his pose of being an outsider, a stranger to love, who must apologize and defer to his presumably love-seasoned public.[20] In pretended concern for sources as in pretended deprivation of love, he renders himself the opposite of Boccaccio. The latter tells his tale with but two references to an original—both of the vaguest, namely to "la storia."[21]

Entrance of the Confidant

THE visit of the confidant to the enamored hero, which comes in the first quarter of the *Filostrato's* Part II and the latter half of Book I of the *Troilus,* provides for character contrast through dialogue, while bringing matters to a state where courtship can begin. In both versions, the contrast here as later is partly determined by the age-old roles of the speakers. The lover must be timid and pessimistic; otherwise, the confidant would be superfluous. The latter needs to be hopeful and persuasive if he is to impose his will first upon the suitor and then upon the lady. Even in Boccaccio's version, however, the two men are differentiated beyond the minimal requirements of plot, and in Chaucer's far beyond these. While the Italian poet may have derived suggestions for their devoted friendship from many sources,[1] his presentation of it is fresh and vigorous, and the Englishman's is no less so for all his dependence upon the *Filostrato* and despite any use he may have made of ancillary sources.[2]

In the scene in the *Filostrato,* the lover speedily abandoned one position of resistance after another as the confidant assailed them frontally. Troiolo would not burden his friend with the cause of his sorrow but admitted that it was love when pressed in the name of friendship. He doubted that Pandaro, himself unsuccessful in courtship, could help another, and hesitated to identify his adored because she was a relative of the would-be procurer. Countering these objections in turn, Pandaro won her name and proceeded straightway to confirm the lover in his choice. Criseida was worthy of him. She was also accessible; for all her inconvenient virtuousness, she would yield to solicitation, since all women are amorous with no inhibitions but fear of discovery. If secrecy were observed, the affair would turn out happily for

28

all concerned. Troiolo was heartened by this but still dubious of his chances. The lady, he feared, would prove resistant when approached by her cousin, if only to impress him; Pandaro was therefore to ask her for no more than consent to be loved. But upon assurance that he was an old hand at such business, the confidant won carte blanche to proceed with her as he would.

From this exchange of theirs, it appears that the lover was scrupulous in some degree as well as very fearful; the confidant, on the other hand, so cynical about the whole female sex as to be untroubled about seducing any woman, even his own relative, and sure enough of his persuasive powers, despite their failure in his own case, to promise Troiolo unqualified success. There was no hesitancy in him because there was no division of loyalties. He was all the hero's man. Though not unmindful of Criseida's reputation, he was ready to imperil it for the welfare of the lover. Her happiness would come with her suitor's, he trusted, but that was incidental.

Chaucer virtually doubles the length of the scene,[3] here beginning the expansion of the ascending action which, as observed in Section 1, is so disproportionate as to reverse the ratio between it and the descending. The part of the confidant is expanded as it will continue to be until he accomplishes his purpose of bringing the lady to the lover's arms. He delights in talk for talk's sake—in display of wisdom for his own satisfaction as well as for the benefit of his captive auditor. He embroiders arguments even of the most obvious purport, and having won all his objectives with them, turns to lecturing Troilus on amatory principles. Though a born pedagog, he is no dullard. He is more inclined to ironic humor at the prince's expense than was Pandaro, and turns his wit even against himself. His admissions of personal failure in love bring out the disparity between theory and practice much more sharply than the less sprightly ones of his original. Whether gay or grave, he is determined to be a manipulator, using humor as purposively to disarm his adversary as sober appeal and dialectic to beat down resistance. The drives here revealed in him will manifest themselves also in his negotiation with Criseyde along with sustained ingenuity in gratifying them. He is not allowed easy triumphs, however. Troilus in this scene is provided with delaying tactics, as the lady will be in later ones. Made pessimistic about Fortune as well as love, he is genuinely more sceptical of comfort offered than was Troiolo. Nevertheless, he feigns greater reluctance to confide than he feels and, for policy's sake, lets Pandarus go on urging his services after he is of a mind to use them. He has spirit enough, despite his melancholy, to gibe at the sententiousness of his friend, matching the latter's humor at his expense with criticism of that amiable weakness.

The first expansion by Chaucer which we need consider in this episode is of Pandaro's rejoinder[4] to the cavil that he is unpromising as a second in love since he has failed as a principal. In the *Filostrato,* the confidant had supported his claim to utility with analogies of the man unguarded against poison saving another from it and of the dim-of-sight proceeding safely where the clear-sighted cannot. Pandarus takes over the latter well-worn analogy and links half a dozen more to it, betraying thereby the extraordinary fondness for the proverbial which is to be the hallmark of his style. With also characteristic ingenuity he uses his instances, not merely to dismiss his failure as immaterial, but to represent it as a positive advantage; it will point the way to success, he argues, since contraries are mutually illuminating.[5] Neither here nor elsewhere, however, does he cite any mistake or shortcoming of his as lover from which Troilus might profit through avoidance. His failure is left a mystery and, it would appear deliberately so, since an explanation was available; Pandaro, in the speech from which this of Pandarus' is derived, confessed that he had loved unhappily because he had not loved secretly. Made to prefer the lore of others to straight autobiography, Pandarus draws from Oënone's letter to Paris[6] a case which exemplifies his own—that of Phebus, who, though the discoverer of medicine, could not heal himself of the sorrows of love. The citation has a double effect. It further manifests the sententiousness of the speaker, and, with its cozy reference to Paris as Troilus' brother, it strengthens the illusion of historical authenticity created by Chaucer's many citations of his supposedly ancient "auctour." With the same double effect, Pandarus goes on to compare his weeping friend—censoriously—to Nyobe,

> Whos teres yet in marble ben yseene.[7]

Ably and long though his friend has spoken, Troilus continues to be difficult, proceeding much more cautiously than Troiolo to the decisive step of confessing the identity of his beloved.[8] Instead of bursting into tears as Boccaccio's hero, he reclines so inertly that Pandarus fears a lapse into frenzy or even into death. Loudly crying "Awake," he reproaches the prince's inattention, comparing him to the ass insensible to melody. The narrator informs us that Troilus is artful in his silence, maintaining it not only out of caution but also on the principle that one should pretend to eschew what one really wants. When the prince does speak, it is to observe tartly that he is not deaf and to dismiss his counsellor's pretentious wisdom as unavailing:

> suffre me my meschief to bywaille,
> For thi proverbes may me naught availle.
>
> Nor other cure kanstow non for me.
> Ek I nyl nat ben cured; I wol deye.

> What knowe I of the queene Nyobe?
> Lat be thyne olde ensaumples, I the preye.

His protest has as little deterrent effect as he could have wished. Pandarus renews his solicitation and is presently adducing another "olde ensaumple," the plight of Ticius in Hell. Hard pressed for an argument against confession, Troilus produces one which will serve, not merely against this step, but against any action whatsoever. Fortune has shown herself his foe, and she is invincible:

> Ne al the men that riden konne or go
> May of hire crule whiel the harm withstonde;
> For, as hire list, she pleyeth with free and bonde.

Pandarus denies that Fortune has a particular animus against the lover, and, though accepting the figure of the wheel, uses the mutability which it implies as a reason for hope. Likely enough, he says, the unconstant goddess may soon give Troilus cause to sing. His is the short view; his advisee's the long one—heed only for the next upswing as against realization of ceaseless turning and of the inexorable power thus manifested. The opposition in perspective was not even hinted until much later in the *Filostrato,* and then weakly. Advanced to this first conversation in the *Troilus,* it will be continued and broadened in subsequent discussions between the two men. Until the debacle, Pandarus will go on assuming that with ordinary luck and good management one can somehow ride the wheel from day to day, and will concern himself very little about the extent or derivation of Fortune's might. Troilus will continue in awe of the goddess and will recognize an authority above and utterly controlling her—a Supreme Being whose prescience entails necessity. This view will strengthen the pessimism induced by amorous melancholy. At the present juncture, however, he so far yields to Pandarus' hopefulness about the human state as to name his mistress and thus to commit himself to action. The final push to the step is a bit of byplay of the friend's. Shaking the lover playfully, he exclaims, "Thef, thow shalt hyre name telle." He will resort to such jocular familiarity again and again to break tension as he does here.

In the remainder of the episode, Pandarus is as encouraging as Pandaro with no more scruples about seducing his niece than he had about seducing his cousin. And he is wittier, though less gross, and far more doctrinaire.[9] After extending congratulations as did Pandaro upon the choice of beloved, he waxes ironical at the prince's change of attitude toward love and then proceeds to instruct him in matters amatory. He reminds Troilus ironically of his having called Cupid "Seynt Idyot" and Cupid's servants "verray Goddes apes." Despite his jesting tone, he conceives of free love as more than secrecy and appetite, which Pandaro thought its all-sufficient components. According to his exegesis, as according to the narrator's at the beginning of the *Troilus,* the lover's is a ceremonial way of life; indeed, in a fanciful sense, a religious one. The prince must atone for his blasphemies against Cupid by formal repentance of heresy. As to the beloved, Pandarus is as sure of her eventual capitulation as Pandaro, but much more delicate in guaranteeing it. Instead of a bold assertion of female concupiscence, he offers the polite generality:

> Was nevere man or womman yet bigete
> That was unapt to suffren loves hete,
> Celestial, or elles love of kynde.[10]

Like his original, he dismisses the lover's fears as to how the lady will receive a tender through a kinsman and wins complete discretionary powers.

The transition between the intermediary's first conversation with the hero and his first with the heroine is very quickly effected in the *Filostrato,* more slowly with new circumstances in the *Troilus.*[11] Boccaccio, who had begun his Part II with the one, proceeded directly in this same part to the other, bringing the confidant from prince to lady in three lines. Chaucer, who has included the men's conversation in his Book I, tells us of separate activities of theirs at the end of that book, interrupts the action with his Prohemium to Book II, and then has something more to say of Pandarus before reporting the interview with Criseyde.

In the last stanzas of Book I, he records that Pandarus devoted some time to laying plans and that Troilus distinguished himself by valor against the Greeks. Here, then, each of them is perfected in his kind—the one as an intrigant zealously forehanded in his dubious profession, the other as a properly manly aspirant to love. The process is continued for the former after the interrupting Prohemium, as will be seen in the next section.

Preliminary Negotiations

PANDARO conducts extensive negotiations between his friend and his lovely relative before he ventures to demand an assignation from the latter; and the subtler Pandarus, even more protracted ones before he devises a stratagem which eventually yields the opportunity for him to propose a tête-à-tête. To this phase of the story Boccaccio devotes stanzas 34-132 of his Part II; Chaucer, the first 1351 lines of his Book II, that is, one and three-quarters times as many as the other poet.

His Prohemium[1] marks the turn from sorrow toward happiness in the narrative and calls attention to its supposed antiquity and possible strangeness and to his fidelity in rendering it. After a forecast of clearing skies for his poetic bark,[2] he invokes Cleo, the Muse of History,[3] an appropriate patroness, since he is asking, not for original inspiration, but for the humble faculty of converting his "Latyn" original into English rhyme. As a mere translator, reduced to that function by his inexperience in love, he will accept neither praise nor blame. He would have us, his audience, recognize that time brings changes in modes of speaking and thus be tolerant of any deviations that there may be from current practice in this Trojan courtship. The self-exculpation and the defense of old approaches to love are patent artifices. Nowhere is Chaucer freer with his material than in the present book, and, however aberrant the course of love traced in it, the deviations are not peculiar to antiquity. The poet is tickling our curiosity with his apologies for the exotic in his source while continuing the fictions of its genuineness and his naive fidelity to it. He may also be forestalling criticism of the fun to be poked at wooing or of the coming glorification of the flesh —criticism, that is, from opposed camps, the amorists or the ascetics.[4]

Resuming the narrative thread, he invents circumstances which further the irony of the adviser's personal failure and dates them precisely and to fine tonal effect, with recourse for the atmosphere to several sources.[5] On the third of May, evidently an inauspicious time[6] for all the month's delights —particolored flowers all about and Phebus spreading his beams in "the white Bole"—Pandarus experienced a grief in love which troubled his rest the ensuing night. He is roused next morning by the swallow Proigne as she laments her metamorphosis and the cause of it—violation by her husband, Tereus, of her sister. Oblivious of this reminder of passion's potentialities for sorrow, the hapless lover betakes himself to his niece's palace, once he has determined that the moon is in a state favorable to journeying. As usual, he is being careful about the next step or two while relatively feckless about ultimate consequences. And, if Professor Farnham is correct,[7] the precaution which he takes here is popularly, not learnedly, astrological. The misfortunes of Pandarus—and Proigne—are contrapuntal to the joys of the season; while the latter are a bland setting for Criseyde's introduction to love, the former hint at miseries to proceed from it.

Time, as we shall discover, is treated with more nicety and to greater effect throughout the *Troilus* than it was in the *Filostrato*. The May third dating is of particular importance in this dimension. It introduces the long sequence to which this section is devoted and keeps it close to the enamorment of the hero, for Chaucer has put that in April, instead of vaguely in the spring after Boccaccio's fashion, and will indicate later on, as does his authority, that both came within the same year. From Pandarus' reverse in love on the third to his bringing Troilus a letter from Criseyde at the end of the fifth, every action is allotted to a day, and with the exception of the reverse itself, to a specific part of a day. The vernal atmosphere created in the dating is sustained by nature sketches of the afternoon and evening of the fourth day as well as by incidental references to the season. The course of action in the partly corresponding scenes of the *Filostrato* appears blurred by contrast and even spasmodic. They are devoid of seasonal reference; one infers, but only infers, that Pandaro discovered and communicated his friend's love before spring was over. Time of day is never indicated in them, and their continuity is not unbroken.

Having dispatched Pandarus from his own house to Criseyde's on the morning of May fourth, Chaucer returns to his source for the first conversation between the relatives but adapts it very freely, as is most immediately obvious from his doubling of its length.[8] Here he continues the reinterpretation of the heroine which he began in the temple scene and that of the confidant begun in the scene in Troilus' chamber, as well as the dignification of the hero as a virtuous, warlike prince, to which a number of earlier contexts have been devoted. Uncle and niece are made to reveal their subtle natures in a battle of wits, and the former to exalt his master to the utmost in his effort to carry the day.

In the conversation as reported by Boccaccio, there was scant finesse on either side. Pandaro worked out no strategy to win his cousin, but came posthaste to her from Troiolo and stated his case forthrightly. Despite the haughtiness which she had shown in the temple, Criseida failed to offer a dignified resistance here on home territory. She received Pandaro without attendants and took him into an apartment not dignified by the author with a description. Throughout the ensuing conversation, the advantage was with the visitor. She involved herself in contradictions; he, never. Indeed, his frankness made self-contradiction impossible. Criseida affected shock at his proposals but so clumsily that her insincerity was blatant. In writing her speeches, Boccaccio developed antifeminist irony with a heavy hand. She reproved Pandaro for uncousinly solicitation with tears standing in her eyes, but qualified the rebuke by an admission that, if anyone might have her love, it would be Troiolo. Conceding the cogency of the hoary argument that love is to be seized before age ends opportunity, she asked how she might do so and then how Pandaro had discovered the prince's affection for her. After being told of Troiolo's ardors of two days before and then of the present day, she gave her promise to satisfy her cousin's request—the drift of which, she said, was plain to her. That acknowledgment renders her immediately following "let it suffice thee if I see him" quite obviously *pro forma*.

In the *Troilus*, both parties strike one as more finished products of courtly breeding; they are more gracefully affectionate with one another than in the original and much, much more devious. Sharing the good manners and artfulness of the court and also, it may be fancied, some family predispositions, they are individuals nonetheless, differentiated in more complex fashion than in the *Filostrato*, if not more sharply. The confidant is made witty and sententious as in his scene with the prince, and the heroine is represented as like her uncle in both respects. Her maneuvers, indeed, are often counterparts of his. But hers are executed with a feminine lightness of touch very different from his sometimes heavy-handed insistence. Instead of gibing at his proverbial worldly wisdom like the supermundane Troilus, she imitates it, but in moderation with one saw at a time instead of a spate of them. It does not appear that Chaucer refashioned her character after any one model in literature or real life,[9] but rather that he drew upon broad knowledge of womankind to create an essentially new gestalt. The quintessence of femininity, his heroine commands our interest as successfully as she is represented to have controlled her relative and her lover. When with the prince, Criseyde will establish ascendancy over him more explicitly than Criseida, and in this her first conversation with the friend she proves herself a match for him, as her original did not. Indeed the honors of word play pass from the man's side to the woman's, although the ultimate result is more or less the same. It is now he who lapses in consistency. She keeps her defenses logically intact and tolls him into contradictions.

Chaucer brings out the social deftness of his pair by making them perform in company before they engage in private conference. To replace the few lines in which Boccaccio tells of greetings and preliminary chat which passed between the two in convenient privacy, he gives us many stanzas reporting converse between them while others are present.[10] He establishes at once that his heroine is a person of consequence, one whose native intelligence would have been exercised and strengthened by the demands of high place. When Pandarus arrives at her "palays" on the aforesaid fourth of May, he is directed by her "folk" to a paved parlor, where he finds her seated with two ladies and, with them, listening to a maiden who reads of the siege of Thebes. This tableau keys not only the conversation in the presence of these attendants but the entire episode and much that follows it. With considerable establishments of their own and entrees into royal society, the heroine and her kinsman will live elegantly as well as the prince and, like him, with only hard-won opportunities for privacy. Successive details of their privileged existence are realistically convincing of the eminence to which Chaucer would raise them, and the constant surveillance which is the penalty of such eminence for a woman leads to much scheming on the part of the confidant and to quasi-comic situations for all concerned. The poet conforms to the tradition of courtly love in elevating the lady and increasing the difficulties of her pursuit but turns these, when he wishes, to humorous account.

The first exchanges between niece and uncle in this parlor are affective upon two levels—on the surface, conveying their warmth and nimbleness of spirit and, beneath it and without their awareness, recalling the omnipresent threat of destiny. Criseyde welcomes her visitor with the flattering remark that she has dreamed of him thrice that night—a dream more portentous than she can realize. Making conversation of the book, he asks if it is of love, and she picks up the hint of amorous involvement with a laughing reference to his mistress. What she tells him of the volume—a work resembling the *Thebaid* of Statius[11]—is ominously suggestive. She has been hearing of the parricide of Edippus and been interrupted at the point where Amphiorax is plunged into Hell. These predestined tragedies exemplify the hapless state of man as well as contribute to the antique coloration of the poem, just as did the lament of Proigne in the preceding scene. In the dolorous Fifth Book, Cassandre will draw extensively on the Theban saga to interpret Troilus' dream and to show him, as she says, how Fortune overthrew lords of old, Amphiorax among them, and in the Fourth and Fifth respectively, Criseyde and Troilus will allude to the vindictiveness displayed by Juno toward the Theban line. Here Pandarus dismisses the story as speedily as he does all gloomy topics and bids his niece share with him in some observance to the month of May—an invitation which she rejects as not befitting her widowhood.

Sensibly unabashed, he tries other tacks to put her in such mood that she will be receptive when he has privacy to divulge his mission. He rouses her curiosity by declaring that he could delight her with a bit of news and then—as he knew he must—withholding it for the moment. When she chances to ask how Ector fares, he seizes the opportunity to bracket Troilus with that great man. Bringing the latter into the conversation as "The wise, worthi Ector the secounde," he indicates that he means a duplicate, rather than a lesser, paladin by claiming for him every perfection, civil and military, which is acknowledged in this brother and illustrating the military by a vivid account of his prowess on the day before. The extended praise of the suitor is in accord with the requirements of courtly love. A lady capable of true love will bestow it only upon a man whose worth is attested by reputation; Pandarus is assuming that Criseyde is such a one; and the as yet undeclared candidate whom he recommends would qualify by the most exacting standards. Though motivated by friendship, the testimony is evidently meant by Chaucer to be taken at face value, since, as we have seen in Book I, he has gone beyond his source in exalting the prince, not through a character, but speaking to us directly. And he will do so again here in Book II and in those that follow. He is bent upon restoring the martial glory attributed to the prince in the *Roman de Troie,* which was largely neglected by Boccaccio in his borrowing from that poem, and bent also upon complementing this glory with every other distinction to be expected of a romantic hero. The linking with Ector, here established through Pandarus, is taken from the *Roman,* Guido's adaptation of it, or both. As it is the apogee of praise, Chaucer will repeat it often as he proceeds. Having lauded Troilus thus to perfection, the confidant takes his leave but is stayed by Criseyde, as he must have anticipated. Her remark, to hold him, that she has business to discuss, is sufficient hint to her well-trained attendants to stand apart.

With the opportunity to divulge thus created for him, Pandarus still proceeds discreetly, approaching the grand revelation by a long circuit. Despite this further conditioning, his niece affects more shock when it is made than Criseida and, upon recovery, a greater adamancy against commitment, so that he must plead with her at length and earnestly. This private converse of theirs is very freely adapted from the tête-à-tête in the *Filostrato*, drawing upon most of the stanzas in that, indeed, but very seldom rendering them stanza for stanza and interpolating much new material.

The confidant's opening presentation of his case is greatly subtilized.[12] Pandarus affects hesitation and even timidity about disclosure and great sorrow for the prince when he finally comes to it, appealing again to his niece's curiosity in the first instance and newly to her pity in the second. Alluding tantalizingly to his good news once her matters of business have been dealt with, he puts off her appeal for it, with the excuse that he fears to offend her. Urged to plain speaking, he yields, plants a kiss to certify his good intentions, and clears his throat; then launches forth, with the patronizing thought in mind that he must be simple to meet her supposed simplicity—a presumption which he justifies to himself characteristically with a sentence from his traditional store:

> For tendre wittes wenen al be wyle
> Thereas thei kan nought pleynly understonde.

He labors the point, more briefly made by Pandaro, that good fortune should be seized when it presents itself. With the crucial moment approaching, he takes her hand, declares he means well and bids her not be fearful. Urged again by the now trembling and pallid lady, he reveals at last that she is loved by Troilus. He puts the onus of two deaths upon her, declaring in a flood of tears that the prince will die if scorned and that he, the faithful friend, will then cut his own throat with the very knife which he now shows her. This is pushing moral responsibility to the limit, extending the tenet of courtly love that the beloved must yield or be guilty of murder so that it applies to the aide along with the principal. The fine bit of acting with the knife is a parallel, probably half humorously intended by Chaucer, to the business taken over later from the *Filostrato* of the hero's purposing death with his sword beside his swooning mistress. It is followed by bland reassurance; Pandarus would have his niece believe that he expects her only to make Troilus better cheer—not a jot more—and that such favor will not compromise her since friendship between the sexes is never interpreted amiss in Troy.

Now that Pandarus has declared himself, his real difficulties begin. So far he has had pretty constant encouragement from his niece, but from here on he will find her an elusive opponent, alternately docile and indocile as Criseida with Pandaro, but never to be pinned down as the earlier heroine.[13] She begins with a request for advice, thinking discreetly, "I shal felen what he meneth." This evokes a flood of *carpe diem* philosophy from her uncle, much more profuse than Pandaro's essay in this sphere, and completely revealing of his true intention as in the lines:

> Go love, for old, ther wol no wight of the.
> Lat this proverbe a loore unto yow be:
> "To late ywar, quod beaute, whan it paste."

Having brought him into the open, she reproaches him for unnatural solicitation, as Criseida Pandaro, but more tearfully. Pandarus counters by repeating the threat of his lord's death and his own—an effective move, since, as Chaucer now tells us, she is the fearfullest person imaginable. Self-possessed as well as timid she thinks to herself,

> It nedeth me ful sleighly for to pleie;

and, recalling the proverb,

> Of harmes two, the lesse is for to chese,

decides to promise good cheer to Troilus rather than to destroy her relative. She asks Pandarus if he requires only cheer from her, and having received the inevitable answer already proved false, agrees to give this much, but this much only. She listens complacently to his account, even more extended than Pandaro's of the lover's transports on two previous days,[14] until he lets the wish slip out that he may see her wholly his master's. Then,

> "Nay, therof spak I nought, ha, ha!" quod she,
> "As helpe me God, ye shenden every deel!"

His highly equivocal reply that he meant "naught but wel," she gracefully accepts—doubtless in the spirit in which it was offered. They part understanding one another perfectly. Pandarus goes off very content, and Criseyde should have been even happier, for she has had all her own way. Humanly flattered by the admiration of Troilus, she has so proceeded as to be sure of hearing further about it. Cautious, however, to the point of timidity, she has taken no irrevocable step, and, demure as wary, she has preserved decorum to the full. She remains no less sovereign in love than in the conduct of her establishment—to be entreated not bidden, and, if compliant, at her own pace, however imploring her uncle, however desolate her lover.

39

Chaucer and Boccaccio continue with the heroine for a space before following the intermediary into conference with his friend. The latter takes Criseida into her chamber for brief meditation on what she has just heard from Pandaro. Expanding this scene, Chaucer brings Troilus past the lady's window to give her new food for thought and reports her stream of consciousness at greater length than his authority. And he adds to this expanded scene two wholly original shorter ones, in which he provides still further motivation for her enamorment.

In the single episode of the *Filostrato,* Criseida, with nothing to distract her, proceeded briskly to review the pros and cons for accepting the newly offered love. She asked herself why she should not venture, untrammelled as she was and capable of keeping an affair hidden—why she should not enjoy fleeting youth and do as others had done. Her suitor was handsome, accomplished, and royal. The clandestine love which he proffered was more exciting than marriage, in which ease of possession leads to satiety on both sides. Yet, alas, all such love has its inevitable disquietudes. And there would be the particular danger, in an affair with Troiolo, that his superiority in rank might lead him to scorn and at last desert her. If he did not and the affair went on for a long time, it would eventually be discovered and her reputation lost for ever. At this point, Boccaccio stops quoting her, though noting that more oscillations followed.

In his elaboration of the scene,[15] Chaucer exalts the object of the lady's thoughts, refines these, and suggests the control of destiny over what befalls. His product is as glamorous as devotees of the courtly way of life and love could possibly demand and, at key moments, evocative in the seriously-minded of that awareness of universal forces which is requisite to later appreciation of the story as a tragedy.

While Criseyde is tranquillizing herself in the solitude of her closet with the reflection that a woman need not reciprocate a man's love unless she please, she hears shouts heralding the presence of the one who adores her. Troilus is approaching from the Dardanian gate, on his way home from a successful skirmish. This, as Chaucer observes, is the prince's lucky time:

> With that com he and al his folk anoon
> An esy pas rydyng, in routes tweyne,
> Right as his happy day was, sooth to seyne,
> For which, men seyn, may nought destourbed be
> That shal bityden of necessitee.

Mars himself, says the poet, could not be as imposing as this puissant knight in battle-dinted armor, and the crowd acclaims him as, after Ector, their mightiest defender. This triumphal spectacle, compounded from several returns from battle described in the *Roman de Troie*,[16] contributes to the restoration of the martial glory attributed to Troïlus by Benoit. And the effect of it upon Criseyde, which Chaucer seems to have adapted from the account in the *Roman d'Eneas* of the impression made upon Lavine by its hero,[17] helps to explain the lady's gradual yielding of her heart. The tribute of the populace and Troilus' modesty in receiving it so powerfully affect her that she exclaims "Who yaf me drynke" and thinks it pitiful to bring so worthy a man to death.

Having attributed this traditionally proper sentiment to her, the poet hastens to add that it did not lead to precipitate surrender. Anticipating that some envious person might call hers a "sodeyn love," he writes,

> For I sey nought that she so sodeynly
> Yaf hym hire love, but that she gan enclyne
> To like hym first, and I have told yow whi.

To absolve her still more completely of lightness and also to resume the destinal motif, he notes that Venus was in a position favorable to Troilus and had been also at the time of his nativity.[18] In the *Filostrato*, the beneficence of the goddess to Troiolo is recognized only by the hero himself —and, in her planetary aspect, solely in his hymn to her which comes after possession of the beloved. The recognition here in the English poem of her astrological influence will be supported by others all earlier than the one in the Italian; namely, in the Prohemium to Book III (adapted from the first stanzas of Troiolo's hymn), in Troilus' prayer to her and the other planetary deities, which he offers before entering Criseyde's little closet, and in his thanks, first to all seven and then to her "the wel-willy planete" along with Cupid and Hymen rendered after he has made himself at home there. The goddess is thus duly honored for winning for the hero the love to which her son masterfully subjected him.

Having provided visual stimulus to love, Chaucer returns to his source for the heroine's debate with herself. In adapting it, he eliminates sensual implication and avowal of social inferiority and increases concern for worldly advantages. His great lady has the attitudes idealistic and yet practical of her class. Imaged glamorously by him, she can express herself with homely vigor, reverting at times to the proverbial as in her conversation with Pandarus.

In the hopeful phase of her argument, she proceeds very gradually from assuming that she will give her lover no more than kindness to thinking that she may grant him her love, whereas Criseida started with the latter supposition. She begins by saying that, although it might not do to grant him this,

41

It were honour, with pley and with gladnesse,
In honestee with swich a lord to deele,
For myn estat, and also for his heele.

Contrariwise, it would be dangerous to repulse him utterly, since, as the king's son, he might jeopardize her already precarious position. There should be measure in everything, she thinks sententiously, for though drunkenness is proscribed, total abstinence is not required. She dismisses possible gossip as of no concern to her if she doesn't give cause for it, but then reflects that Troilus is the worthiest of any woman's love save Ector and is moved to contemplate giving such cause. Her valuing the suitor for rank as well as virtue is innocent enough by any reasonable standard and thoroughly in accord with the tenets of courtly love. Nevertheless, it reveals a potential which will lead to tragedy. When confronted with a new lover and in even greater need of a protector than here in Troy, she will cast accounts again and decide in his favor, this time purely from self-interest.

In the counter phase of her debate, Criseyde, like her original, recognizes that love is productive of many griefs and includes that of desertion among them, but she does not anticipate that the prince will reject her as being socially beneath him. Like Criseida, she now admits to fear of scandal, pointing up the danger in her own manner with a saw about tongues and bells alike unstoppable. Pithy though Chaucer makes Criseyde in this and other unhopeful observations, he is careful to maintain for her the proper aura of romance; *inter alia,* he carries an elaborate and beautiful figure through this entire phase: as a cloud overspreads the sun and then is put to flight by winds of March, so a cloudy thought dimmed her bright hopes and then, passing out of her soul, left them to shine again. This metaphor of early spring leads into the pleasant actualities of Maytime of the two following episodes.

In these scenes added by Chaucer[19] and ascribed by him to the afternoon and evening of this momentous fourth of May, the background of nature invests Criseyde with its own loveliness and quickens her amorous sensibilities. The numerous females attending her evidence her high station, while one of them in the first scene acts as a moving advocate of love.

In the first and longer one, she descends from the closet of her meditations to her garden, where she makes many a turn under blossomy boughs along with a great company of her women—her three nieces, Flexippe, Tarbe, and Antigone among them. The last of these sings a song, composed, she says, by a Trojan maiden of high estate. It is a profession of service to Love for his gift of a perfect lover and of thanks to Him for the happiness and, more especially, for the improvement derived from the amorous way of life, and also a defense of that way against misguided critics. This lyrical testimony of the highborn maiden and Antigone's assertions of its truth so impress Criseyde that love becomes less frightening to her than before and conversion to it, as Chaucer observes, much easier. Female exaltation of Love in this garden before the affair is well under way balances Troilus' manly exaltation of Him in another garden after it is consummated. The latter replaces Troiolo's hymn to Venere of the same time and place.[20] As Professor Young observed,[21] the hymn in the *Filostrato,* a tribute to the goddess for her general beneficence and her particular favors to the singer probably suggested to Chaucer the insertion of a woman's tribute to Love in a similar setting. This marks the real beginning of Criseyde's passion, as that the complete fulfillment of her possessor's. The man's song, while suggesting the addition of a woman's, could not provide its necessarily feminine content. For this, as Professor Kittredge discovered, Chaucer turned to a lai of Machaut's, the *Paradis d'Amour,* which represents itself to be the utterance of a lady, and took over all of its concepts, though rearranging and rephrasing them.[22]

Dusk brings the next scene. At its coming the heroine retires indoors with her attendants and is brought to rest by them. Yet vernal influence is not shut out. In a cedar beneath Criseyde's window, a nightingale sings its heart out to the bright moon, carrying on in its wordless fashion the tribute paid to Love by Antigone in the garden, and finally lulling her to sleep to close the day for her as its sister Proigne began it for the confidant. No wonder that with such musical suggestion the lady comes to dream of Troilus and to dream of him symbolically as the king of birds—of power to tear her heart from her bosom but of such devotion that he exchanges his for hers.

This climax is true to both Freud and art. The dreamwork achieves wish-fulfillment through combination of experiences of the waking day: the Martian hero of the afternoon is transformed into a creature winged, as is the singer of the evening. Artistically, the eagle which he becomes is a perfect symbol for Troilus—a royal and mighty fowl and, in its whiteness, pure as well as splendid.

The action of the bird in Criseyde's dream will have its antithesis in that of the boar in Troilus' at the far end of the story. This beast, the supplanting Diomede, will slumber through the kisses lavished upon it by the unfaithful lady. Chaucer's opposition of the widely separated dreams is an instance of his control of structure even more striking than his paralleling of Troilus' song by Antigone's—of his planning the whole from the early stages. This which he devises for his heroine implies Troilus' love for her, while that which he will modify from the *Filostrato* for the prince calls Diomede's love into question. In the original of the latter, the dream of the forsaken Troiolo, the boar was anything but sleepy, crashing into view as it loudly did and then ripping out Criseida's heart with its tusks. Irony came only from her willingness to be eviscerated. In fashioning Criseyde's dream, Chaucer has transferred the tearing out of the lady's heart from the boar Diomede to the eagle Troilus and added the meaningful circumstances that the despoiler replaces that organ with its own. According to Mario Praz, who pointed out the common inspiration of the two dreams of the English poem by the one in the Italian, Chaucer may have resorted also to Dante for the first, deriving from him, it seems, the resplendence of the royal bird.[23] As we shall see in later sections, the dream contrast between the suitors so favorable to Troilus[24] combines with many others, to produce a truly thematic opposition.

After the episode of the dream, the poet gives us three, in which Pandarus is respectively with Troilus, with Criseyde, and again with Troilus, these being allocated to the night of May fourth (the night of the dream), to the daylight hours of the fifth, and to its night. These are consolidated from a dateless and otherwise loosely organized series of events in the *Filostrato*.[25] The adaptation, though of about the same length as the original, diverges from it in many large and small respects.

Boccaccio, it is to be remembered, allowed but one scene to Criseida for meditation after her cousin's visit, a daytime one in her chamber in which she pondered her future without witnessing a return from battle of her lover. Concluding this already discussed scene, he returns to Pandaro. The confidant, we learn, had gone straight from Criseida to Troiolo and reported success with her. He then accompanied the prince on an impromptu stroll past her house. This unspectacular appearance of her lover—the first since she had known him to be such—sufficed to captivate the impressionable lady. She desired him above everything else, Boccaccio testifies, and regretted time lost through unawareness of his love.

Ready though she was to enjoy it, Troiolo did not press his advantage and Pandaro did nothing more to help him until urged to do so. The former devoted himself to polite amusements for an unspecified period, engaging Criseida during that time in no more than exchange of glances. Appeal to Pandaro for counsel elicited the suggestion of a letter. The long one which Troiolo immediately composed described his extremity with warmth but perfect delicacy and begged favor for himself, the lady's unworthy servant.

When Pandaro brought her this declaration, she protested that she could not accept it but put it all the same into her bosom. One reading of it after his departure made her resolve to find time and place for an assignation. It was not for her, she thought, to die of desire nor to let another do so; at that instant she would be in her lover's sweet arms pressed face to face.

The apparently lethargic Pandaro, back with her only after repeated urging by his friend, got her promise of an answer and again departed. The letter she produced was as grossly self-contradictory as her yeas and nays to her cousin in their first conversation. She wrote that she could not give what was wanted, but then that Troiolo might have her a thousand times over, and ended with a prayer to God to satisfy his desire and hers. The ill-concealed sensuality of this missive contrasts effectively with the sublimated emotions of Troiolo's. Taken as soon as finished by the intermediary (whose leaving her Boccaccio had apparently forgotten), it was sped by him to Troiolo and hopefully interpreted by the lover, as it well deserved to be.

Chaucer combines into one the episodes in which the confidant reported to the prince on the first talk with the lady and advised him to write her a letter, and he eliminates Pandaro's departures from her presence after delivering that letter and after soliciting a reply to it so that pressure upon her is uninterrupted. He compresses the epistles into brief digests and expands dialogue and stage business, in both ways coming closer to play form. As usual, he gives the heroine a fuller measure of shamefastness and mother wit than Boccaccio chose to do; her lover, more of princely glamour; and the confidant, a greater penchant for scheming and sententiousness.

Troilus, having reached his palace after passing Criseyde's on the way from the Dardanian gate, dispatches one messenger after another in search of Pandarus. The latter arrives in time for supper and stays the night in the prince's chamber. Advising the writing of a letter to his niece, he counsels the prince to ride past her dwelling in appropriate state after it has been delivered and then gives him pedantically detailed instruction in the *ars dictaminis*.[26] The parade, which he is arranging so foresightedly, will take the place of the unpremeditated stroll of Troiolo with his friend. The epistle composed under his direction is merely summarized, but the résumé preserves the humble idealism of the full text in the *Filostrato*.

Chaucer's account of Pandarus' visit to Criseyde on the fifth resembles his of the call on the preceding day in that it brings out the charm and subtlety of both parties and provides an impressive physical setting for their exchanges. Finding his niece apprehensive when he calls upon her betimes this morning, Pandarus breaks tension with a jest at his own unhappiness in love, evidencing tact in this procedure and incidentally reminding us again of the anomaly of his pretensions. For privacy's sake, he takes the lady into her garden and there produces his friend's letter, sparing her modesty by seizing her and thrusting the letter into her bosom. Cued by her smile, he ventures his "beste japes"—such good ones that she thinks she will die of laughter. Criseyde, having led him inside for dinner, retires before it to her chamber with some of her women and there finds opportunity to read the letter. Surprising him abstracted on her return to the hall, she tags him by the hood as playfully as he has wrestled with her in the garden. After they have dined, Pandarus tolls her to a window by the street and, once her folk are away, implores a reply to the letter, which he divines she has read, and so effectively that she retires forthwith to a closet to write. According to Chaucer's very brief digest of her epistle, she committed herself to Troilus only "as his suster, hym to plese." Returning with it to Pandarus by the window, she seats herself beside him and, while held there in conversation, is soon favored with a display of her lover as stirring as his return from battle. Though he now passes by in weeds of peace, he cuts a properly heroic figure—still the man on horseback leading his stalwarts. His humble deportment toward her by no means lessens the effect. Moved as she is, she nevertheless rejects her uncle's suggestion of an interview.

Taking leave of her at eve, Pandarus speeds to the lover, whom he finds in bed—in both literal and figurative darkness. With the light provided by the ever helpful friend, Troilus reads the letter from his beloved and draws hope from it as Troiolo from the franker one of his lusty mistress.

In both *Filostrato* and *Troilus,* receipt of the heroine's communication is the last incident in this phase of preliminary negotiations—the last action in it to be crystallized as a scene. What transpires before the affair moves into its next phase is, in both, summed up very quickly—to wit an increase in the lover's ardors concomitant with that in his hopes and a palliation of these ardors only through the unsatisfactory medium of further correspondence.[27] In both, it is indicated that he continued in this uneasy suspension for some time. Boccaccio notes that Troiolo cried for relief "day and night," that his ardor increased "from day to day" and that he wrote to his lady "many times"; and Chaucer, that Troilus waxed in desire "day and nyght" and wrote "Fro day to day."

Commitment to a Tryst

THE solace of letters is not enough. As true friend, the confidant must seek further comfort for his prince. He must come to some understanding with the lady about her eventual reception of the latter in such place as he can enjoy her. And he must represent that understanding to him as an unshakable guarantee of possession. Having brought the lover to a new plateau of hope, the friend may leave him there for a time before guiding him to the last height, possession itself. This middle stage of the confidant's operations is expeditiously presented in the *Filostrato*, at far greater length and very differently in the *Troilus*.

Boccaccio limited it to two conversations, with an invocation between them and notice of a lapse of time after the second. He devoted the last eleven stanzas of his Part II to a call of Pandaro upon his cousin, which resulted in the making of an assignation by the lady herself. To mark the importance of this step and to signalize the joys of Troiolo which would proceed from it, the author paused to invoke fresh illumination from his guiding star Maria. After this appeal in the first two stanzas of Part III, he returned to Pandaro, now departed from Criseyde; followed him to a temple where Troiolo chanced to be; and there recorded his comment on the situation and the prince's rejoinder. And in a single stanza, the twentieth of this part, he credited Troiolo with exemplary behavior through what was apparently a longish period of waiting.

As for Chaucer, he replaces the scene between Pandaro and Criseida with a long series of ingenious maneuvers and adapts that between Pandaro and Troiolo to link with the new series and to terminate it. His Pandarus contrives an innocent meeting between the lovers at the house of Deiphebus, with

47

the latter an unsuspecting cat's-paw. That the brother should function in this capacity was suggested to our poet by an episode near the close of the *Filostrato* in which he succored the lover, though without being tricked into doing so. Chaucer ends Book II at the climactic moment in the sequence when Criseyde is on the threshold of the chamber at Deiphebus' where Troilus awaits her, and he begins Book III with an invocation of Venus. This, which has the milestone function of Boccaccio's apostrophe of Maria, owes nothing to it but nearly everything to the first stanzas of Troiolo's hymn to the goddess, which comes at the farther end of Part III. In the triangular conversation which follows this Prohemium, Criseyde accepts Troilus as her servant, but it is Pandarus who definitely implies fruition, conjuring the enamored pair to come to his house when he shall invite them. Neither says him nay. Since this conversation brings the affair to about the same point as that between Pandaro and Criseida at the end of Boccaccio's Part II, Chaucer can attach to it a version of the conference between Pandaro and the lover, which his author reported after the exordium of Part III. To achieve continuity he stages the latter in the chamber of his previous scene instead of in its original locale and changes the time from day to night. After parting the two friends on the morrow, he gives a long account of Troilus' improvement by reciprocated love in placé of Boccaccio's one stanza on the subject. All told, he has taken over three times as many lines as his authority to bring the prince from dateless prospects to certainty of early bliss and to the exemplary conduct thereby inspired.[1]

The expansion accomplishes a number of substantial results. First of all, the affair is taken out of the social vacuum in which it seems, somewhat unnaturally, to exist. The heroine and confidant, as well as that public figure the prince, are brought into contact with fellow mortals as they would be inevitably in real life whatever their stations and however extreme their concentration upon love and their desire to shield it from the common gaze.

Then, the contact is such that it emphasizes the aristocratic complexion of the affair. The heroine, who has already been dignified with a great establishment by Chaucer, is now made the intimate of the brother and sister-in-law of her royal lover, and the confidant is put on the same footing. Elevation in society gives her new dignity in the world of love. The hero vows service in the humblest and most reverential terms, and she accepts it with complete assurance as but her due.

Made explicitly sovereign as the rules of courtly love demand, she is further perfected according to its standards by being given adequate motivation for eventual surrender. In the *Filostrato,* she was left suspect of undifferentiating appetite since she came willingly to her lover's embraces without the assay of previous conversation. The interview arranged for her by Pandarus allows a thorough testing, and Troilus passes with distinction.

Yet this interview and the episodes which lead up to it all exploit the comic side of love with as much brilliance as they do the romantically ideal. Concern for secrecy inherent in the system leads to the most unheroical expedients. To come to audience with his beloved, the prince has acquiesced in Pandarus' decision that he feign illness and must therefore make his profession of love, not on his knees, but flat on his back. Even the paladin of the two street scenes cannot maintain full dignity in this posture, the less so because of his trepidation at so crucial a juncture. And the lady is not exempt from humorous inspection self-possessed though she is. For we know that she is the dupe of Troilus' feigning throughout that triumphant hour when she is most sovereignly condescending to him.

The sequence, high comedy that it is, affords Pandarus splendid occasion for the display of those qualities which make him useful to the lover and delightful to us. He is confirmed in the wiles, sententious persuasiveness, and nimble humor with which Chaucer has earlier endowed him, and he is permitted to exercise them with greater boldness than ever and to better effect. He lies to his niece more roundly than before and is not caught out as in his first conversation with her. He lies as egregiously to Deiphebus, despite the ceremonious respect he pays him, and then to all the fine folk assembled by that royal scion. He brings off what he will without a hitch. Under his instruction Troilus is for once successfully disingenuous, and the deceived respond like puppets to the strings. The man's zest for intrigue is wholly engaging, whatever objection there may be to his motives.

Lastly, it is to be observed that the sequence is designed to complement the next and equally ingenious one. Professor Lowes has remarked that "the whole situation in which Pandare 'ladde [Creseyde] by the lappe' to the bed where Troilus lay is with marvelous skill made to foreshadow the great scene where the parts are reversed, and 'Troilus he brought in by the lappe' to Creseyde." [2] The parallels, as will be shown, are numerous and mutually sustaining in point of irony. Anticipation in the one sequence and recall in the other evidence once more the poet's care for structure and his ability to control large masses of detail.

His procedures in the first, which accomplished the results above mentioned, must now be traced with some particularity. To scan them will be to see Chaucer at the peak of his invention. He diverges more widely here from his basic source than ever before or than he will again except in the complementary sequence which follows.

A change of some kind, if not so radical a one as he effects, was mandatory at this point because of earlier changes. Having transformed the intermediary from a blunt to a subtle pleader and the heroine from an inept to a skillful adversary, he cannot accept their primitively simple conversation at the end of Part II. In it Criseida soon allowed that she was all Troiolo's in spirit though insisting still that she would keep her virtue. Pandaro seized upon the admission to bid her fix a time for receiving his friend. Her defenses crumbled at this touch. Avowing that her blood was congealing at the request, she consented to it in principle, and, when assured by a pledge of secrecy, she made the assignation—the place, her own abode, the date that of a festival when some with her would be temporarily away.

Part VII of the *Filostrato* supplied the germinal idea for a replacement of this elemental negotiation, as Dr. Cummings has pointed out.[3] It was there related that Troiolo, sometime after his dream of the boar, became so reduced by grief that he took to his chamber and his bed. His brother Deifobo there surprised him complaining of his mistress and heard enough to piece out the whole affair. Without betraying his discovery to Troiolo, the kind visitor betook himself to other brothers and arranged with them to dispatch their female connections to the sufferer's bedside. Presently the lover's room was filled with women—among them Ecuba, Polissena, Andromaca, Elena, and Cassandra, with each save the last endeavoring to comfort the patient. She alone knew his secret, having overheard Deifobo reveal it to the brethren. Unable to restrain her gossiping propensities, she twitted the prince for involvement with the baseborn Criseida and thus drew from him a spirited and honorably mendacious defense of his mistress as well as a bitter rebuke of herself.

Cassandra, an unpromising tool for the courtship, is left where she is by Chaucer, while the helpful brother is brought forward to speed it as the unwitting cat's-paw of Pandarus. The ascending action is enlivened by the ingeniously adapted material from the descending, and that somber phase will be relieved of trivia inapposite to it—the kindly officiousness of the brother and the eavesdropping and pointless malice of the sister. The lover himself will be represented to summon her to his bedside for a private interpretation of his dream and she to give it in inspired wisdom and with fittingly ominous reminiscence of the fall of princes.

The all-important change made by our poet in the situation which he moves forward is to reduce actual illness to mere feigning. From this every other invention proceeds and from it the general lightening of tone, the transformation of sorrow and bitterness into seriocomic moods. And ironic contrasts result from it backward and forward. Troilus has been in imminent peril of death according to Pandarus, but he must now counterfeit if he is to appear even indisposed. Tricking Criseyde here by resort to bed, he will swoon under her displeasure in the next sequence and be cast helplessly insensible into her sheets. And after he has survived this experience, half comic to us if all serious to him, he will be bedridden, as Troiolo was, by unrelievedly tragic disappointment in his exiled mistress. Foreseeing its potentialities with the eye of genius, Chaucer may well have made the change entirely on his own initiative. The one source suggested so far for his happy thought of illness feigned is questionable as such though interesting as an analogue.[4]

The new sequence begins crisply—with conversations of Pandarus, in quick succession, with Troilus, Deiphebus, Criseyde, and Troilus again.[5] Promising the doleful lover an interview with his mistress and assuring him proverbially that persistence will win, the confidant asks which of his brothers he loves best. When he is told that it is Deiphebus, he sets off without pausing even to reveal the intent of the query. Coming to Deiphebus, he alleges that Criseyde is in danger of oppression and prays him to invite her to an audience on the morrow and to have some of his brethren present, all for the purpose of impressing her adversaries. The chivalrous prince, who has always been "lord and grete frend" to Pandarus, agrees at once to help his "frend" Criseyde, proposes to summon Eleyne to hear her case, and bids the confidant invite Troilus to hear it. The intriguer speeds to his niece and, calling attention to his sweat as evidence of urgency, produces the circumstantial lie that "false Poliphete"[6] is about to renew legal action against her. The lie is convincing because, as Criseyde's reply shows, it is based on past unpleasantness from this quarter. Anticipating from experience that the litigant will have the support of Antenor and Eneas in mulcting her of property, the lady despairs of contesting the suit. Understandably therefore, when the zealous Deiphebus comes in person to extend his invitation while she and her uncle are still discussing the peril, she accepts with alacrity. The discussion of banditry at law suggests Chaucer's own England. But the lady's mention of Antenor and Eneas, those notorious traitors-to-be, gives local color to the anachronism. And her dread of the former is a grace note of irony; for it is his capture by the Greeks which will bring her exchange and thence her ruin.

The fabrication so successful at this juncture will have its parallel in the sequence to come. Pandarus will prepare his niece, then his overnight guest, for the emergence of Troilus from the shadows of her bedroom by telling her that the lover has just entered the house in an anguish of jealousy of one Horaste. Despite profession of complete ignorance of the man, the lady will be as readily deceived by this invention as by that about her familiar adversary.

After Deiphebus has come and gone, Pandarus leaves his niece to return to Troilus. Sketching his machinations, he instructs the lover to go to his brother's house that very night and, when there, to pretend an access of fever, which he is to say will confine him to bed into the morrow.

Troilus carries out his orders to the letter, and is bedded down at the house of his brother, with supererogatory concern on the latter's part for the illness and supererogatory enlistment of the patient's favor for Criseyde.[7] This farcical seclusion of the hero parallels his hiding, from one night to the next of the following sequence, in a stew at the house of Pandarus, though there is the difference that he remains in the first covert to receive his lady and leaves the second to come to her. The one confinement, suggested by Troiolo's illness late in the *Filostrato,* and the other, adapted as we shall see from Florio's daylong seqestration in the *Filocolo,* are developed with the same sympathetic humor. Displaying the noble Troilus in these passes, Chaucer implies Puck's dictum "What fools these mortals be" and in the spirit of that observation.

Once he has the lover abed at the house of Deiphebus, the poet brings us immediately to the morrow and to the party there which the host has arranged—with Eleyne, of course, among those present, Criseyde with her nieces Antigone and Tarbe, and the always indispensable Pandarus.[8] At dinner, the conversation turns to the hero, first to the ailment which confines him in another room and then to his merit, with much amateur medical opinion elicited by the former topic and extravagant hyperbole by the latter. Criseyde sits complacently through it all, rating herself best qualified to cure him and rejoicing in her power of life and death over one so highly praised. Rising from dinner, the company engages in chitchat until Pandarus brings up his niece's alleged difficulty. The account which he gives of it is so disparaging of poor Poliphete that his audience curses the villain no less enthusiastically than it has exalted the prince of the blood.

This interlude provides a social climate appropriate to refined love at the same time that it develops the comedy of situation. Royalty is at its charming best in giving cues, and its dependents are most adept in following them. Deiphebus warmly laments his brother's illness, and all chime in. Eleyne, who holds Criseyde's hand, espouses her cause before it is presented, and all promise their aid as soon as the case has been laid before them. But the cues sincerely given by royalty have been inspired by the wiles of Pandarus.

Suggested by the congregation of ladies in the *Filostrato* at the lorn lover's bedside to cheer him with song and instrumental music, the interlude has its parallel in the next sequence, the supper party at Pandarus' house, which was inspired by the festivities of Biancofiore and her companion maidens in the *Filocolo*. Both social occasions are presented by Chaucer with effective realization of the charms of polished intercourse and with full value derived from situational comedy. Pandarus will rival Deiphebus in hospitality, and yet be as intent while host upon the main business in hand as while a guest of this prince.

The first occasion is terminated by Eleyne's query as to whether Ector or Troilus know of Criseyde's plight. This gives Pandarus the opening to start a procession to the little chamber where his master lies, which reaches its climax at the end of Book II with Criseyde about to enter that sanctum.[9] Going to it first by himself on the pretext of determining whether Troilus will receive visitors, he is so elated as to be bawdy with him:

> God have thi soule, ibrought have I thi beere!

This elicits a smile from the idealistic but evidently broadminded suitor, his first since he beheld hapless lovers in the temple of Pallas, and the last outward sign of mirth in him until he laughs from the vantage of the eighth sphere at the woe made on earth for his death. Pandarus returns to the great chamber with alleged instructions from his lord to bring in Eleyne, Deiphebus, and Criseyde, but takes it upon himself to leave his niece where she is, for the moment, lest the sickroom be overheated by so many bodies. Brought to Troilus, his brother and sister-in-law have to endure a rehearsal of the lawsuit by Pandarus and, to cap this, a new deception by the lover. He asks their advice about documents submitted to him by Ector and thus posts them down a stair into an arbor for nearly an hour of hard reading. With the coast clear, Pandarus returns to the company to fetch Criseyde, advising all that the three great ones await her and earnestly bidding them not be noisy lest they disturb the patient. The book ends with the lady in transit and besought by her uncle to act decisively to save her admirer's life. After all his machinations, Pandarus is no further along than Pandaro was when he began his solicitation.

Still, he is on the high road to success, and the Prohemium to Book III,[10] which interrupts the action, is a due recognition of his triumph. And more important than this, it heralds the period of Troilus' delights, marking its commencement as gloriously as the hero's thanksgivings to Venus and divine partners of hers will highlight its climaxes and as the author's farewell to the goddess, Cupide, and the Muses at the close of the book will signalize its end. In the first thirty-eight lines of the Prohemium, Chaucer celebrates the universal and beneficent influence of Venus, at once goddess and planet; and, in the remaining eleven, he calls upon her to infuse his naked heart with feeling and upon Caliope to lend her voice. Like the first five and a half stanzas of Troiolo's hymn[11] which they render quite faithfully, the first thirty-eight lines dignify earthly love by including it among the manifestations of the great unifying force symbolized by Venus, a force which inspires Jove himself as well as all the levels of creation. In appropriating this utterance of a character for himself, the poet gives it new authority in the eyes of the reader. And by moving it from near the end of the ecstatic period of the affair to the very beginning, he prepares the reader to appreciate the faith held by the lover in the nobility of amorous fulfillment, to accept the fact of his improvement by it in mundane virtues, and even, conceivably, to speculate on the unrealized potential for transcendence of the flesh in a love as aspiring as his. When he presumes to invoke the goddess after the extended tribute to her might and goodness, Chaucer lets it be known, however modestly, that he envisions a momentous raising of his theme. And in the appeal to Caliope for her voice, he signifies his hope of a truly poetic afflatus for his endeavors on this higher plane, here following Dante who bade the Muse inspire his song as he came to celebrate the heavenward yearnings on Purgatory after leaving the despairs of Hell.[12] For Book II, as will be recalled, our poet was content to rely on the pedestrian Cleo, since he pretended to no more than faithful versifying of his source.

When he returns to uncle, niece, and Troilus, now all in the latter's chamber,[13] he satisfies the expectations created in the Prohemium, at least in some measure, by patterning the relationship between the lovers according to feudal ideals, but he by no means abandons the critical spirit of comedy. With all three principals now brought together as they never were in the *Filostrato,* he effects new cross illuminations of character, in which the comic and the romantic are closely blended, just as he will in the next sequence, in which Pandarus is kept with the lovers until the moment of consummation. Alluding to her plight, Criseyde prays Troilus for continuance of his "lordshipe" and quite unhinges the already nervous suitor by this reversal of their relationship in love:

> But, Lord, so he wex sodeynliche red,
> And sire, his lessoun, that he wende konne
> To preyen hire, is thorugh his wit ironne.

The conventionally proper, if still amusing, loss of tongue, does him no harm with his mistress. And his "manly sorwe," which, Chaucer tells us, would have moved a heart of stone, causes the sympathy-questing Pandarus to weep as if he were turning to water. Nudged and exhorted by her uncle for a commitment, Criseyde will have one first from the suitor as to his intentions. To her leading question, he replies that he will do her perpetual service and recognize her authority even to infliction of the death penalty; and she receives him into her service on these terms with the elastic reservation, "Myn honour sauf." After the warning,

> A kynges sone although ye be, ywys,
> Ye shal namore han sovereignete
> Of me in love, than right in that cas is,

she promises him a joy for his every woe and seals the promise with a kiss. From these favors, one less optimistic than Pandarus might hope that "honour" would come to mean reputation for chastity rather than chastity itself. The uncle, without being so crude as to assert the former interpretation, leaves scant doubt that it is his, for he gives assurance of another private meeting with a laugh extremely suggestive in its context:

> "But I conjure the, Criseyde, and oon,
> And two, thow Troilus, whan thow mayst goon,
> That at myn hous ye ben at my warnynge,
> For I ful well shal shape youre comynge;

> "And eseth there youre hertes right ynough;
> And lat se which of yow shal bere the belle,
> To speke of love aright!"—therwith he lough—
> "For ther have ye a leiser for to telle."

An entente having been thus reached, the procession arranged by Pandarus may now reverse itself.[14] Deiphebus and Eleyne return from the arbor to the sickroom; Criseyde makes her adieus to royalty and departs under the escort of Pandarus; the brother and sister-in-law finally take leave of Troilus upon the hint that he would sleep; "and hom wente every wight."

Before consideration of the final episode in the sequence, it may be observed that the uncle's maneuvering of his puppets within Deiphebus' establishment foreshadows the skillful deployments at his own. Here, Troilus is bedded by day as well as by night in a little chamber; there, Criseyde, for the night only and in a little closet. On the hither side of each of these small rooms, there is a large one in which a group is kept for multiple, but luckily oblivious, chaperonage—at Deiphebus' house, his chatting guests, at Pandarus', his niece's sleeping women. On the far side of each there is a retreat which makes possible the deception of the group—the arbor into which Deiphebus and Eleyne retire unbeknownst to his guests, the stew from which Troilus is conducted to the closet, her attendants all unwitting. The use Pandarus makes of contiguous apartments at his own house was suggested by the practices of Biancofiore's attendant Glorizia in the *Filocolo*. Since there was nothing to suggest such deception in the sequence featuring Troiolo's illness in Part VII of the *Filostrato*, it would appear that Chaucer, when transforming this into the intrigue at the abode of Deiphebus, already had in mind what he was to draw from the *Filocolo* for the intrigue at Pandarus'.

As for the closing scene at Deiphebus' house, the nocturnal unburdening of confidant to lover,[15] it brings out, as did its daytime original in the *Filostrato*, the irrevocability of the heroine's commitment and the speaker's fear of discovery now that he is sure of success—fear for her and for himself. But like the original, too, it may leave us wondering whether the go-between is to be thought of as suffering very much from guilt feelings and whether the hero's endorsement of his conduct is meant at all as a directive to us or merely as a dramatic utterance. Chaucer's intention, like Boccaccio's, is seemingly to bring out the warmth of the friend's devotion and of the prince's gratitude rather than to stress a moral conflict in the former or to resolve it in his favor through what the latter has to say. Pandarus is made to dwell longer than Pandaro upon self-justification—upon his comradely benevolence untainted by hope of gain—but longer also upon the expediential matter of secrecy. And the new hero is as challengeably absolute in his position as the old, warranting the confidant's motives with equal vigor and attesting the sincerity of his own approbation with the same offer, made *pro forma* of course, to win a sister or sister-in-law for the go-between. Partly at least to complement his preceding and virtually original scene in which love service is offered in its most ideal extreme, Chaucer has seen fit to keep in this one the extravagant idealization of friendship presented to him in the source. Here as there he would have us admire, I think, the outgoingness of the human spirit and still pass judgment, if we will, on the channelling. The immoderation of the two speakers should evoke a critical response. If it does not by itself, Pandarus' forbodings of discovery and shame, as they are expanded from Pandaro's, can hardly fail to set us thinking, little though they inhibited him.

Links with past and future in Boccaccio's version of the scene are augmented in Chaucer's. Pandaro connected it in time with his discovery of his friend's love by referring to that event as of the current year, "ugnanno"; Troiolo, though alluding to it also, failed to give us any chronological hint. In parallel contexts, Pandarus says he made the discovery "to-yere," that is, in the current one, and Troilus puts it, more definitely and therefore more memorably in "Aperil the laste."[16] Next, Troiolo made an elaborate but linkless asseveration of secrecy; Troilus, a yet more elaborate one, which includes a dramatically ironic foreshadowing of his death just as it will occur:

> And, if I lye, Achilles with his spere
> Myn herte cleve.[17]

Lastly, the whole interchange here between Pandaro and Troiolo with worry and warning on the one side and thanks and reassurance on the other was to be echoed in their conference on the morning after consummation; and the adaptations of these two episodes for Pandarus and Troilus are as closely parallel as the originals.[18] In both *Filostrato* and *Troilus,* each of these emotive if actionless scenes marks the end of a great advance through action and crystallizes the reactions of confidant and hero to it.

In his stanza of transition from the first of these talks to the confidant's resumption of business, the Italian author conveyed the impression that some time intervened, and in his dozen of like function, the English naturally makes it even stronger.[19] Troiolo controlled his amorous impulses, said Boccaccio, though every day seemed a hundred, devoting the nighttime to thoughts of love and the daylight hours to martial exploits. Chaucer credits the hero with the same praiseworthy and, apparently, long persistent behavior. He tells us also that the prince had converse with the lady and rendered such thoughtful and discreet service to her

> That wel she felte he was to hire a wal
> Of stiel, and sheld from every displesaunce.

These circumstances serve the double purpose of the parades by her house and the interview at Deiphebus'—to idealize the hero as lover and to give the heroine romantically acceptable motivation for surrender. And the poet reinforces them as regards the second purpose by noting that there was voluminous correspondence between the lovers.

Union

IN Chaucer's poem as in Boccaccio's, the confidant at last sets the affair moving again—this time, to consummation. In each poem, arrangements for it are made and carried out and the lover routed back to his palace for retrospective conference with his helper in a sequence of a day, a night, and a day. In each, too, a longish span of possession is granted him, to his delight and consequent improvement in all chivalric virtues, and the happiness of this time is exemplified for us in two episodes—his second nocturnal meeting with the heroine and his retiring to a garden with the confidant to celebrate his love in song. Pandarus, however, is represented to have laid plans utterly different from Pandaro's, and Troilus, as a result, to have attained to bliss by another course than that of his original. Even when at last in each other's arms on this first night, Chaucer's lovers manifest joy in fruition and sorrow at dawn's approach only in part as Troiolo and Criseida were moved to do. On their second together, they comport themselves very differently than Boccaccio's pair, and, in the garden scene, Troilus has another song than Troiolo's.

Of the last seventy-odd stanzas of Part III of the *Filostrato,* some forty were devoted to the consummation sequence and the remainder to the happy period thereafter. Only ten of the former were required to bring the hero to the moment when he could claim the ultimate favor of his mistress. The "desired time" having come, presumably but not explicitly the festival indicated by Criseida in an earlier context, Pandaro summoned her for final instructions and then Troiolo, who, with curious insouciance, had gone away on a military mission. The prince made his way to her house that night with the seemingly accidental advantage of overcast weather. Criseida, having

58

heard him enter, sped those with her to rest by pretending sleepiness, descended a staircase to come to him in his lurking place, and after long exchange of caresses took him up the stair to her chamber. About twenty more stanzas concerned what went on there till daybreak, with the lady's warmth of temperament being made evident from the start. And some ten more brought the hero back to his own chamber for joyous meditation, and—after incidental notice of Criseida's like reverie—the confidant also to that chamber for review of the situation. Of the stanzas following the sequence, a few were given to the second conjugation, one to Troiolo's state of happiness, a considerable number to his hymn to Venere, and four to his exemplary behavior as inspired by possession. The last stanza of Part IV forecast the loss of his joy through the inconstancy of Fortuna.

In the free adaptation in Book III of the sequence and what follows, Chaucer expands the former three and a third times, while covering the latter as expeditiously as Boccaccio.[1] And the sequence, though elaborated throughout, is enlarged most greatly at its beginning. Pandaro's arrangements, Troiolo's coming to his mistress' house and ascent with her to a chamber amounted to hardly a quarter of it, whereas what completely replaces all this—Pandarus' machinations prolonged to the verge of consummation at his own house and the compliances with them of hero and heroine—constitutes three-fifths of the longer chain.[2] It is in this replacement that all but the last of the parallels to the preceding sequence are to be found. Chaucer returns to the *Filostrato* for the communications of the lovers when they are alone in bed, drawing on all of the stanzas devoted thereto but adding as much as he takes from them.[3] He refines the transports of the woman, gives the man dominance in the sexual act, and poetizes the thoughts of both. As to the rest of the sequence, the hero's return to his palace for meditation, the heroine's afterthoughts incidentally described, and the confidant's joining his friend for talk, our poet reproduces the first two quite closely, but appends to the second a visit of Pandarus to the lady before she has risen, and moderately expands the third, with due care to maintain its parallelism to the friends' conversation at the house of Deiphebus, which winds up the complementary sequence.[4] And as for the succeeding period of happiness, Chaucer gives an account of the lovers' second night shorter even than the brief one in *Filostrato* and largely independent of it, tells us a little more than Boccaccio about the hero's way of life after this, substitutes a brief paean to Love for his diffuse hymn to Venere, and essentially reproduces the testimony to his improvement by love.[5] Saving the final and transitional stanza of Part III to use in beginning his next book, Chaucer concludes Book III with a stanza of farewell to Venus and the Muses and another of summation.[6]

59

The changes just presented which he makes in the sequence and its aftermath are traceable to several quarters. In Pandarus' devices for tolling Criseyde to surrender of her person, there is much reminiscence, as already suggested, of those which Chaucer invented for him to bring her into private conference with Troilus at the brother's house. And there is extensive adaptation, both in the approach to consummation and in the consummation itself, of circumstances set forth in the *Filocolo* of the experience of Florio, Biancofiore, and her attendant Glorizia in the "Torre dell' Arabo" and some use also of incidents prior to this experience. One occurrence in the approach, the lover's swooning under the displeasure of his mistress, was suggested by Troiolo's faint during the negotiations for Criseida's exchange, which is recorded in Part IV of the *Filostrato*. The new song for the hero is taken from the *Consolation of Philosophy,* as also an excursus of the heroine's upon false felicity.

Since the contribution of the *Filocolo* to the sequence is not yet as generally taken into account as its impress warrants, there will be detailed analysis of it in this section. Its influence upon Chaucer's stanza of instruction to his "litel bok" will be treated briefly in the text of Section 11, while its likely, but not certain, effects upon other contexts are remarked only in notes to other sections.[7] Professor Young first showed it to be a source of the *Troilus,* establishing in an early article its strong impress upon this one sequence.[8] And in Chapter IV of *The Origin and Development of the Story of Troilus and Criseyde,* he reproduced and supplemented the case presented in the article for Chaucer's exploitation here of the *Filocolo* and then presented evidence for his recourse to it earlier and later in his poem. In *The Indebtedness of Chaucer's Works to the Italian Works of Boccaccio,* Chapter I, Professor Cummings took the stand that influence of the romance anywhere in the *Troilus* had not been and could not be established. Though he made a sound point in noting the absence of verbal resemblances in the parallels adduced by Young, his scepticism led him to minimize some parallels unduly and to ignore others worthy at least of consideration. In an article devoted primarily to confirming the use of the *Filocolo* in the *Franklin's Tale,* which also Cummings had denied, Professor Lowes took occasion to criticize the former's methods of disposing of Young's evidence for its use in the *Troilus* and to support this evidence to the extent of adducing a new parallel in the consummation sequence.[9] Others have mentioned the influence on the *Troilus* disputed by Cummings but without marshalling new evidence or analyzing the old. As for myself, I have found nothing decisive to add to Professor Young's arguments for it outside the sequence, and, except for the one for it in the "litel bok" stanza, I feel these to be not absolutely compelling. But

I can supplement his demonstration of it within the sequence and rather materially, adducing verbal resemblances to meet Professor Cummings' objection.

To insure clarity for the parallels old and new which I shall draw between the sequence and parts of the *Filocolo*, I shall begin with a digest of the work, an economically patchy one, in which long stretches not contributing to the *Troilus* will be slighted and episodes providing inspiration to Chaucer will be outlined more or less fully as their fruitfulness to him dictates. Even the patchwork will give some notion of the extravagance of incident in the fiction, in which gods descend to earth, human beings are metamorphosed, and soulless things become sentient. Only perusal of the rambling text itself will bring home the want in it of disciplined artistry. To educe high comedy and exquisite romance, as Chaucer does, from this rococo confection is a feat of no mean order.

Books I, II, and III of the *Filocolo* carry Florio, its protagonist, from birth to that time in his young manhood when he left the homeland to recover Biancofiore, who had been packed off into slavery. He, the son of the King and Queen of Spain, and she, the orphan of a noble Roman couple, were brought up together in the royal palace in Marmorina and fell precociously in love as Venere willed. Learning of Florio's enamorment and disapproving it as socially unsuitable, his parents effected a separation by domiciling him at the court of Duke Feramonte at nearby Montorio. Biancofiore, whom they kept with them, gave her departing lover a ring, the clouding of whose clear vermilion stone would indicate that she was in straits. And soon she was. Florio persisted in amorous melancholy at Feramonte's court despite the consolations offered him by his host and by his tutor, Ascalione. The King and Queen, hoping to cure melancholia by eliminating its cause, contrived an accusation of poisoning against Biancofiore and had her condemned to the flames. So eager was the King to see the sentence carried out that he could not sleep and reproached the night for not passing and the sun for delaying its appearance. He was to be disappointed; next day she was cleared in judicial combat by his own son, prudentially incognito and supernaturally assisted by Venere and Marte. Lodged again in the palace, Biancofiore was to fall into new misfortune. In deference to the urging of the Queen, who naturally welcomed a putative rival to Florio, she gave her veil to one Fileno, when he besought a token to wear in martial games. Learning of the favor from the recipient himself, who naively exulted in it, Florio was presently upbraiding her by letter from Montorio and thirsting for the blood of Fileno. That hapless youth was prompted to flight by a dream and, coming at long last to a secluded countryside, abandoned himself to the most profound despair. The prince fared better, his pangs of jealousy eventually subsiding. Back in Marmorina, however, his mother and father continued intransigent. When Italian merchants chanced to sail into the harbor, the pair summoned them and effected sale of Biancofiore—with her lifelong attendant, Glorizia, as an appurtenance—stipulating that they depart with their prize immediately but not troubling to ask where they planned to take her. King and Queen then gave out that she had died and erected a sepulcher to lend color to the lie. Florio, recalled from exile, attempted suicide at the supposed tomb of his beloved and, in so doing, forced the truth from his mother. With instant resolve to go in quest of Biancofiore, he adopted a pseudonym "Filocolo" under which to travel, enlisted Feramonte, Ascalione and others as companions, and extorted funds from his now softened but still disgruntled father.

Book IV carries Filocolo, king's son now turned private adventurer, through many hazards to union with Biancofiore and eventually to public nuptials. Somewhat more than half of it is devoted to his progress from Marmorina (situated near "colli d'Appennino") to Alexandria, whither he traced her through questioning of informants in place after place. The rest concerns his eventful stay in the latter vicinity.

Of his experiences en route, only two are of present interest. Proceeding by land from Marmorina to Alfea, where the vessel equipped by his father was to await them, Filocolo and his companions came upon a fountain, which turned out to be Fileno metamorphosed—still vocal but reduced by weeping to the liquid state. Ashore again after traversing the sea from Alfea, they participated with gentry of Naples in a round of storytelling—each story to bring up a question of love, and each question to be adjudicated by Fiammetta, the "queen" of the game. The fourth of the many related was the one destined to supply Chaucer with the plot of his *Franklin's Tale*.

In port at last in Alexandria, Filocolo and his shipmates were so fortunate as to be lodged with a host as cooperative as he was well informed. According to the latter, Biancofiore was luxuriously and all too securely confined just outside the city. The Admiral, its potentate, had acquired her from the Italian merchants and was holding her along with other maidens for present delivery to his master, the King of Babylon. Their abode was a place of marvels, with a plaisance on its lofty roof, where the Admiral was wont to test the virginity of his purchases by an infallible tree and stream, and with the choicest of many splendid rooms distinguished by an image of Cupido, whose eyes of carbuncle served very well for illumination. This was Biancofiore's chamber by right of beauty. The stronghold, the "Torre dell' Arabo," was guarded day and night by an Arabian eunuch, the castellan to whom it owed its name, and by many stalwart emasculates under his command. To enter it, the host advised, Filocolo must win the friendship of this officer, Sadoc.

Eager though he was to put this counsel into practice, the hero could think of no promising first step. Passion at last supplied it. As he was viewing the tower one day, he fancied a maiden at a window to be Biancofiore and was thrown into such heedless frenzy that he galloped to the very walls and dismounted to kiss them. Challenged by Sadoc, he had but to exert his charm to mollify him. That day and afterwards he cultivated the eunuch so skillfully that the latter was presently offering to smuggle him to Biancofiore in a basket of flowers. On the night before this dangerous expedient was to be tried, Florio roomed with Sadoc and spent most of it in prayer to all the gods, but especially to his patrons, Venere and Marte.

The next morning he was spirited into the finest of the many floral offerings which stood beside the tower awaiting the Admiral's disposition as festal gifts to this maiden and that. As he cowered in his basket, the latter did what was expected and chose it for his favorite Biancofiore. Toying fondly with the blooms soon to be hers, he exposed the hero's locks but did not see them thanks to the interposition of Venere. The chosen basket was hoisted by a rope to an upper story window, where Glorizia was waiting to receive it —stairs within, as we learn elsewhere, being reserved for the use of the Admiral. The woman cried out as Filocolo too hastily disclosed himself but managed to cover her surprise and, with the goddess lending an invisible hand, to carry him still basketed into the chamber of Biancofiore.

Alone with him there, Glorizia was fertile of stratagems which would prepare her lady for the happy shock of finding him on the premises and which would permit him to administer it after she was asleep in her fourposter. As the first step, the confidante secreted Filocolo in an adjoining room where he could while away the time by peeping into this one. Then she sought out Biancofiore, who was in still another, and began conditioning her for what was to happen that night by fabricating a vision anticipative of it. Cheered thereby, the lady came with fellow maidens to her chamber to spend the day with them in music and dancing—to the insatiable delight of her peeping lover. When night ended the festivities, Glorizia lowered the curtains of the bed and brought Filocolo in to hide behind them. Quizzing the heroine beside it in such fashion as to mitigate surprise, she elicited answers from her which must have pleased him—among them a protestation of innocence anent his jealousy of Fileno. Sleepy at last, the attendant quitted the chamber, leaving Biancofiore to fall asleep and Filocolo, as planned, to reverse that process for her.

Awakening followed in due course, then a ceremony of marriage of the common-law variety, and, finally, consummation. After less intimate attentions to the sleeper, Filocolo took to stroking her naked form to wake her. A leading question from Biancofiore about the ring she had given him long ago led him to declare that he would espouse her with it. And at her prompt suggestion, he did so before the convenient image of Cupido, rising and appropriately vesting himself, as she did, for the purpose. Speeding with what she presumed to be news to Glorizia, Biancofiore brought it to pass that the latter returned to the chamber and celebrated the occasion with instrumental music. When she had left, the lovers consummated their marriage, to the accompaniment of propitious supernatural manifestations.

A terrifying reverse ensued, but as was to be expected from these signs, it led quickly to security and lasting happiness. At the end of the next night, the Admiral surprised the lovers asleep, purposed to skewer them then and there with his sword, changed his mind but not in kindness, and gave orders to have them bound and suspended from the window of Filocolo's undignified entrance. Further orders brought them to the stake for burning, but Venere and Marte effected their rescue. Impressed by the divine favor to his victims, the Admiral approached Filocolo in friendship and, learning— this being a small world—that the youth was his nephew, arranged a public marriage for him and royal entertainment afterward.

Book V winds up the story by returning Filocolo and his bride to Marmorina and edifies it by bringing all parties into the Christian fold. The fountain revisited became Fileno again, a rival no longer but a friend in good standing. In Rome, the orphaned Biancofiore found collateral relatives of satisfying eminence. And there her husband forsook his gods, who, it would seem, had done very well by him, and was baptized under his old name. A zealous convert, Florio persuaded all with him to accept the faith and, when at home once more, was as successful with his parents and his future subjects.

To return now to the sequence in the *Troilus,* we find the confidant, at the start of it, carefully preparing for the crucial night at his house and the lover supplementing his friend's efforts.[10] That no one may wonder at his absence the prince invents an alibi, to wit that he

> moste at swich a temple allone wake,
> Answered of Apollo for to be;
> And first to sen the holy laurer quake,
> Er that Apollo spake out of the tree,
> To telle hym next whan Grekes sholde flee.

This pseudoclassical consultation of the god may have been suggested to Chaucer perhaps by the Admiral's recourse to the tree surmounting the

"Torre dell' Arabo." According to Filocolo's host, the tree, reputedly planted there by Diana and Cerere, would drop a blossom on the head of any damsel placed beneath it by the master if she were a virgin, while a fountain adjoining would become clearer and more beautiful.[11] Whether thence derived or not, the alibi is highly appropriate for Troilus, being consonant with his very real interest in the future and his belief in divine foreknowledge.

Pandarus shows that he too has an eye to the future—though as usual only to the immediate future—by timing his visit to Criseyde[12] by the heavens:

> Right sone upon the chaungynge of the moone,
> Whan lightles is the world a nyght or tweyne,
> And that the wolken shop hym for to reyne,
> He streght o morwe unto his nece wente.[13]

His prevision of darkness and, perhaps also, of guest-detaining weather has no counterpart in the *Filostrato,* though there the night of union chanced to be dark and cloudy. Overriding Criseyde's objection that it is already raining, he soon prevails upon her to sup with him at eve. She asks if Troilus is to be present, remembering, no doubt, the promise made by her uncle of a rendezvous at his house. Swearing that the prince was out of town—a lie derived perhaps from Troiolo's actual absence on a military mission—he renders the oath immediately suspect by a hypothesis:

> Nece, I pose that he were;
> Yow thurste nevere han the more fere;
> For rather than men myghte hym ther aspie,
> Me were levere a thousand fold to dye.

His author, says Chaucer demurely, has not informed him as to what Criseyde thought of this, but only that she consented to be with Pandarus,

> And, as his nece, obeyed as hire oughte.

Her last words give him full powers while neatly absolving herself of responsibility:

> Em, syn I most on yow triste,
> Loke al be wel, and do now as yow liste.

Whether Pandarus' hint that Troilus may be on hand owes anything to Glorizia's covert anticipations of Filocolo's presence,[14] and even this is indemonstrable, Criseyde is unlike Biancofiore in becoming suspicious.

Troilus' secret observation of her arrival for supper,[15] however, unquestionably reflects Filocolo's peeping at his beloved. Apropos of the lady's approach with her retinue, Chaucer exclaims:

> But who was glad now, who, as trowe ye,
> But Troilus, that stood and myght it se
> *Thorughout a litel wyndow in a stewe,*
> Ther he bishet syn mydnyght was in mewe.

As Professor Young pointed out, Troilus' confinement in the stew parallels Filocolo's in a room adjoining Biancofiore's; and the espial, through a little window, of Criseyde coming up the street with her many male and female retainers, the other hero's of Biancofiore entering her chamber with fellow maidens:

> Filocolo, che *per picciolo pertugio* vide nella bella camera
> entrare Biancofiore, di pietá tale nel viso divenne, quale
> colui che morto a' fuochi è portato.[16]

Publishing as he did before several states of the text of the *Troilus* had been differentiated, he lacked one clinching bit of information; namely, that in the earliest or a state *pertugio* was rendered literally. The third line of the passage quoted above from the γ state appears in the a as:

> *Thurgh out an hole* with yn a litil stewe.

The social evening from which Troilus is excluded also derives in part from the *Filocolo,* as Professor Young suggested,[17] but only in part. And it is both like and unlike the party at the house of Deiphebus. It is as lively as that dinner, but its gaiety is interrupted by a moment of the highest seriousness. After supper,

> He song; she pleyde; he tolde tale of Wade,[18]

festivities suggested, it appears, by the music and dancing of Biancofiore and her fellows. But when Criseyde would depart, the author transports us in a flash from the cheerful little scene to the stark immensities of night:

> But O Fortune, executrice of wyrdes,
> O influences of thise hevenes hye!
> Soth is, that under God ye ben oure hierdes,
> Though to us bestes ben the causes wrie.
> This mene I now, for she gan homward hye,
> But execut was al bisyde hire leve
> The goddes wil; for which she moste bleve.
>
> The bente moone with hire hornes pale,
> Saturne, and Jove, in Cancro joyned were,
> That swych a reyn from heven gan avale,
> That every maner womman that was there
> Hadde of that smoky reyn a verray feere.

The phenomenon and the generalization introducing it may seem too weighty for the immediate result but not if we consider that this leads to consequences of tragic magnitude. And the awareness here created of the vanity of human intention will remain with us for the rest of the poem. Its sudden evocation and the startling contrast to the envelope of comedy insure that the awareness will be lasting. The conceptualization of the Universe is majestic and humbling, an ordered monarchy, with Fortune, as Dante conceived her, a minister of God[19] and, as was the received opinion, the planets also his agents, all carrying out His will in ways inscrutable to men. The conjunction which disposes for Criseyde must have been impressive to the audience of Chaucer's day. Saturn and Jupiter were to be conjoined in 1385 for the first time since 769, with extraordinary consequences anticipated and, after the event, presumed. And the moon was to be with them in Cancer after spring had come, with the combination supposedly productive of rain.[20] Carrying the present back to Homeric Troy, the medieval auditor would readily accept the inevitability of the momentous downpour. And he would assume that it came in a Maytime, bringing Criseyde to union, as would be appropriate, in the burgeoning season and, presumably also, just a year after Pandarus first spoke to her of love.[21] The disclosure of cosmic forces ends as abruptly as it began. Pandarus makes a jest, and we are back in the gay intrigue. Eager to get his niece to bed, he is presently suggesting dispositions for the night, Criseyde to lie in a little closet where the storm will be inaudible, her women in part of the large room of the festivities contiguous to it, and he, separated from them by a curtain, in the remaining part.[22] With this arrangement and with Troilus already in the stew beyond the closet, the stage is set for romance—and for farce. Pandarus surpasses himself here in the handling of terrain, and if, as seems likely, his tactics stem from Glorizia's employment of two contiguous chambers, they are still very much his own.

When he has seen everyone to bed, Pandarus betakes himself to the stew, there to encourage his friend to follow him into the closet.[23] But before the timid lover will venture this, he prays to deities of the sky for astral favor and then, very briefly, to the goddesses of fate. Beginning with the likeliest of supporters, he begs Venus to inspire him and also, for the love she bore Adoun, to intercede with her father planet to protect him against the possible maleficence of Mars and Saturne at his birth. He then implores help from Jove himself, for love of Europe; neutrality from ruddy Mars, for love of Cipris; help from Phebus, for Dane's sake, and from Mercurye, for Hierse's; and neutrality, again, from Diane.[24] And he concludes with this appeal to the Parcae:

O fatal sustren, which er any cloth
Me shapen was, my destine me sponne,
So helpeth to this werk that is bygonne.

The prayer is consonant with the astrological assumptions made by the author not many lines before and consonant also with the Prohemium in expressing particular reliance upon Venus, at once goddess and planet. Functional in its enforcement of the theme of destiny, it is appropriate to the speaker, who has been and will continue to be fate-minded. Pandarus' reaction to the prayer is also in character. Fixing on the timidity manifested in it rather than on the foresight, he asks if this "wrecched mouses herte" is afraid of Criseyde's bite. And he conquers hesitancy with action, opening a trapdoor and conveying Troilus through it "by the lappe."

The hero's praying while with Pandarus in the stew is a circumstance so apropos that it could well have occurred to Chaucer without literary suggestion. Yet I would offer the conjecture that he derived it from Filocolo's praying on the night before he was to be hidden in the basket. The lover lay that night with Sadoc and spent most of it in devout supplications:

> Niuno iddio rimane in cielo, a cui le sue voci non
> si muovano. A tutti promette graziosi incensi se a quel
> punto l'aiutano, e Marte e Venere piú che tutti gli
> altri sono pregati: e ultimamente gl'iddii degli ombrosi
> regni di Dite da lui sono tentati divotamente d'umiliare,
> acciò che a' suoi disii non si oppongano.[25]

Though Filocolo did not astrologize, he appealed first to the celestial and then to noncelestial deities as Troilus does and, like him, when in nocturnal seclusion with a confidant.

All is not won when Chaucer's pair have come to Criseyde's place of rest. Troilus must remain silent and, in the darkness, unobserved, while Pandarus fables and argues with his niece.[26] Once the uncle has closed the door to her women's chamber, he can hold forth to the top of his bent, for the storm drowns his voice to those without but offers no impediment within. Startling Criseyde from slumber by his moving about, he attacks her straightway with a fiction quite as alarming as that of the lawsuit. Since she retired, he says, Troilus has come, braving the rain and climbing in "through a goter," all because of hearsay that she loves another; madness and death are in the offing. She is so cast down at being suspect that she not only laments this alleged misfortune but proceeds to generalize that felicity is impossible on the earthly plane. Pandarus assures her that she may right matters if she will, and a debate ensues as to the time of righting, she proposing the morrow and he insisting on the present moment. She seeks a compromise, offering a ring of hers to be taken to Troilus as stopgap consolation, but her uncle will accept no half measures. At last, she yields to him, moved as Chaucer asserts by justifiable benevolence to the lover. Troilus may be fetched, and she will rise from bed in the meantime. Bidding her stay where she is, Pandarus gives the lover his cue to materialize from the darkness:

> and Venus, I the herye;
> For soone hope I we shul ben alle merye.

The conference between the relatives resembles the long one between Glorizia and Biancofiore in the circumstances under which it takes place. In this the confidant addresses the heroine in her bed while the hero listens under cover of darkness; in that, the confidante interrogated the heroine about to retire, with the lover hidden behind the bedcurtains. And, as Professor Young has shown,[27] Pandarus' allegation that his friend is jealous has its parallel in Biancofiore's reference to her lover's jealousy of Fileno and would appear to have been suggested to Chaucer by that allusion and by the chain of episodes in the *Filocolo* of which it would remind him. Glorizia's asking her mistress whether she would welcome any other man, if she could not have Filocolo, evokes the inevitably negative reply and in that reply, casual mention of his misjudgment of her: "avvegna che egli a torto ebbe già opinione ch' io amassi Fileno, il quale me molto amò, ma da me mai non fu amato."[28] With Fileno as long prominent in the story as he was—as rival, fountain, and man again[29]—even this mere fragment of a sentence would have been hint enough to the associative mind of Chaucer to turn Filocolo's long-past suspicion of this unfortunate into the present suspicion of Horaste[30] attributed to Troilus by his friend. Developing the hint from general recollection of Filocolo's period of jealousy and possibly also of particular moments in it,[31] the poet evolves a dynamic situation from the bedtime chat of Glorizia and Biancofiore. Tranquil preparation of an innocent's mind for what she will discover only later becomes strenuous assault on it to force an immediate and recognizably decisive yielding. As Pandarus' big lie[32] seems to come from Filocolo's jealousy, his little one that Troilus effected entrance through a gutter appears to derive from that hero's being smuggled into the tower through a window.[33] A verbal borrowing from that incident, to be noted later on, will establish Chaucer's awareness of it.

The fiction of a rival may or may not have been intended by the poet as a bit of ironic counterpoint to the reality at the end of the story. But the pessimistic response to it which he gives the heroine plainly forecasts his own concluding generalization,

> thynketh al nys but a faire
> This world, that passeth soone as floures faire.

69

Her excursus is a formal dilemma, taken from Boethius,[34] to prove

> Ther is no verray weele in this world heere.

Man must either realize or not realize that all earthly joy is transitory. If he does, anticipation of loss spoils his delight; if he does not, his is the false happiness of ignorance. The timing of this reflection could not be better. Close as it is to the lady's surrender and to great consequent joys, it puts the one in an ironic light and casts doubt productive of tension upon the other. And it is psychologically credible. The shock of being distrusted is enough to produce a strong emotional reaction in the timid Criseyde, and that the reaction should be despair of happiness on earth is in character for one as anxious as she for security and peace. Yet the clothing of her thought is unquestionably drab by modern standards. Versified dialectic, however satisfactory to Chaucer's contemporaries, falls short of our expectations from a charming heroine in crisis.

Pandarus' cuing of the lover to present himself to Criseyde leads to business between the trio[35] as prolonged as the debate which he has just won. With the issue of jealousy now pressed by the lady, it is Troilus' turn to suffer, and the confidant must exert all his ingenuity to hold his gains and to consolidate them. The interplay of the three temperaments, yielding comedy as well as pathos, is a graceful antimasque to the wholly romantic consummation.

At the outset, all seems to be well. If Criseyde is struck dumb by her lover's sudden appearance, her uncle is ready, as ever, to break tension:

> But Pandarus, that so wel koude feele
> In every thyng, to pleye anon bigan,
> And seyde, "Nece, se how this lord kan knele!
> Now, for youre trouthe, se this gentil man!"
> And with that word he for a quysshen ran,
> And seyde, "Kneleth now, while that yow leste,
> There God youre hertes brynge soone at reste!"

Presently, Troilus is promoted from the floor to a seat on the lady's bedside, and the friend, assuming himself to be superfluous, retires to the fireside and a book. This he pretends to scan by a light taken from the fire.

But the optimism of Pandarus is premature. Criseyde reproves her servant at length, if mildly, for the jealousy which she has been told he feels. So keen is her sense of injury, that she questions divine justice, demanding of Jove if he does well to permit the guiltless to suffer. She ends with well-meant comfort, an offer to clear herself in any way satisfactory to Troilus, but lets a few tears escape. For every tear, the lover feels a deathly constriction at his heart. Kneeling in supplication, he topples into a swoon.

Pandarus casts the inert one into bed, strips him to his shirt, and, with his niece, applies first aid:

> Therwith his *pous* and paumes of his hondes
> They gan to frote, and wete his temples tweyne;
> And to deliveren hym fro bittre bondes,
> She ofte hym kiste; and shortly for to seyne,
> Hym to *revoken* she did al hire peyne.

Troilus is resuscitated and told that all is forgiven, and the friend can take his ease again by the fire.

Chaucer draws on several sources in the above complex. He still must have the *Filocolo* generally in mind when he makes Criseyde discourse on jealousy, and perhaps, as Professor Young suggests, he derives particular subtopics of hers from that romance.[36] Her interjected questioning of Jove he owes to Boethius.[37] The swooning of Troilus was suggested to him, as pointed out by Mario Praz, by Troiolo's faint in the presence, not of the heroine, but of Greeks and Trojans assembled to negotiate her exchange.[38] That it was is certain for there are verbal identities between the lines on the former's resuscitation by friend and mistress-to-be and the account of the latter's by father and brothers:

> e le sue forze morte,
> ora i *polsi* fregando ed or la faccia
> bagnandogli sovente, come accorte
> persone, s'ingegnavan *rivocare*.[39]

Moved forward and changed in circumstances, the swoon balances the feigned illness earlier invented for the lover, giving Pandarus opportunity to bundle him into Criseyde's bed, as the other to escort her to Troilus'. And it anticipates the rarified sentiments of consummation while harking back to the comedy at the house of Deiphebus. Fainting at the sight of tears is as conclusive a demonstration of sensibility as could be imagined, one so extravagant, indeed, that it moves the friend to demand "O thef, is this a mannes herte?" and the beloved "Is this a mannes game?" The questions put in their mouths serve to convey the ambivalence of their creator toward romantic sentiment; we may smile, it is hinted, as we sympathize.

Bedded to save his life, Troilus is permitted to remain for love. As Chaucer blandly says, Criseyde can find no reason to bid him rise once she has exacted oaths of her devising. This oath-taking, Professor Young remarks, has its parallel in Biancofiore's proposing a marriage ceremony before the image of Cupido.[40] Though Criseyde recurs after it to the sore point of jealousy, she forgives anew and asks forgiveness for the pain she has caused. Assured by this double condescension, Troilus seizes her in his embrace, and Pandarus exits with a matchless curtain line:

> Swouneth nought now, lest more folk arise!

Now is the time for Venus to fill Chaucer's "naked herte" with "sentement," now the time for Caliope to lend her voice. Here, if ever, he must rise to the heights anticipated in his Prohemium. And rise he does, creating the first great night of love in our literature[41] and one not to be surpassed until by Shakespeare's of an also starcrossed pair. A compound mainly of *Filocolo* and *Filostrato,* it sublimates love more beautifully than either, evoking from bodily delights the transport of spirit proclaimed but not realized in these works.

In presenting the first raptures after the departure of the confidant,[42] Chaucer resorts only to the former of the romances. The rhetorical question with which he introduces the consummation appears to have been taken from this source. Filocolo in his basket awaiting its inspection by the Admiral was timid "come la gru sotto il falcone o la colomba sotto il rapace *sparviero.*"[43] Adapting the second simile for Criseyde,

> What myghte or may the sely larke seye,
> Whan that the *sperhauk* hath it in his foot?

our poet gives her the timidity traditional for her sex upon approach of the male, a shyness not conspicuous in Criseida. And he confirms it by a literal circumstance, her quaking, this suggested possibly by Biancofiore's trembling as she woke to her lover's caresses.[44] With his prayer in the stew now answered, Troilus thanks the planetary deities, "the blisful goddes sevene." And masterful as even a courtly lover might be on such occasion, he demands,

> Now yeldeth yow, for other bote is non!

To assure him of her willingness and at the same time to let it be known that she is no helpless victim of wile or force majeure, she replies,

> Ne hadde I er now, my swete herte deere,
> Ben yold, ywis, I were now nought heere!

Joys ensue the sweeter for past bitterness. Chaucer bestows approval upon the lady's contribution to them with a humor asceptic like Pandarus':

> For love of God, take every womman heede
> To werken thus, if it comth to the neede.

And he figures embracement of each party by the other as the entwining of tree by woodbine. He offers literal description, however, only of the lover's

72

intimacies, sparing, as always, the modesty of the heroine, while yielding the hero the utmost of masculine perogative:

> Hire armes smale, hire streghte bak and softe,
> Hire sydes longe, flesshly, smothe, and white
> He gan to stroke, and good thrift bad ful ofte
> Hire snowisshe throte, *hire brestes rounde and lite*:
> *Thus in this hevene he gan hym to delite,*
> And therwithal *a thousand tyme hire kiste,*
> That what to don, for joie unnethe he wiste.

For this, I feel sure, he went to the *Filocolo*—to the account of what its hero did as he lay beside the still sleeping Biancofiore. In his adaptation, Chaucer has particularized female anatomy and yet eliminated the grossness of the original:

> Egli la scopre e con amoroso occhio le rimira il dilicato petto, e con disiderosa mano tocca *le ritonde menne, baciandole molte fiate*. Egli stende le mani per le segrete parti, le quali mai amore ne' semplici anni gli aveva fatte conoscere, e toccando perviene infino a quel luogo ove ogni dolcezza si rinchiude: e cosí toccando le dilicate parti, *tanto diletto prende, che gli pare trapassare di letizia le regioni degl' iddii.*[45]

Troilus gives pious thanks immediately for "this hevene," rendering them in three stanzas to Love and, in the first of these, also to Venus and Imeneus. This stanza, as Professor Young pointed out,[46] bears the impress of the *Filocolo*. Intending a marriage ceremony, Filocolo called on Imeneo, Giunone, and Venere to be present, and, as a surrogate for these three deities in the ritual, Biancofiore suggested the image of Cupido; the lover called on it to be their Imeneo and their Giunone; and later on, Imeneo, crowned with olive, actually presented himself in their chamber, along with Citerea and Diana.[47] The prominence thus accorded the god of marriage would seem to have prompted mention of him in the thanksgiving of Troilus, neither a husband nor intending ever to become one.[48] The second stanza of the thanksgiving, our eclectic poet drew from the *Paradiso,* converting praise of the Mother of Christ to the Son of Venus.[49] And for the third, according to Professor Young, he may perhaps have returned to Filocolo's address to the image.

From acknowledgments to divinities Troilus goes on to professions to his mistress. He confesses his unworthiness of her, asks guidance, promises good conduct, and calls for the death penalty if ever he should chance to disobey her. This submission is a variant of his more formal one at the house of Deiphebus. And her brief acknowledgment here is likewise a variant of her specific acceptance of fealty in that place. With the obvious reminiscence of their earlier contract, the present one might but need not have been partly inspired by the nuptial vows of Filocolo and Biancofiore.[50]

Chaucer has proceeded thus far with his account of the privacies of the Trojan lovers abed without recourse to Boccaccio's version.[51] At this point, he turns to the latter's and draws at least something from every stanza of it to bring his own up to the time of parting. To maintain the tone which he has set, he modifies and expands it with some freedom,[52] resorting to the *Filocolo* again at two junctures and to the *Divine Comedy* at still others.

In the *Filostrato*, as will be remembered, the prince came by himself to Criseida's house after instruction from Pandaro to do so, secluded himself there until she was free, and then went with her up a staircase to her bed-room—circumstances, as we have seen, all rejected by Chaucer. The consummation scene, which he is to use, began with Troiolo and his hostess stripping for bed. At the lover's request, the lady put off her last garment and, without further prompting, wrapped herself in his arms. Moved at this juncture to apostrophize the night so sweet to them, Boccaccio pronounced it beyond his powers to describe. He attempted some accounting, nonetheless, of the embraces, kisses, and endearments which filled it, interrupting the narrative to exclaim against misers for their rejection of such delight. Cock-crow turned it to sorrow. Troiolo, wondering that he did not expire, declared that he would be patient of necessity if assured of her love. Criseida obliged with protestations of constant ardor, and he took his unhappy leave.

Chaucer passes over the frankly physical in this scene, adds ornament, and enlarges the narrator's emphatic response. Having already brought his heroine through a femininely timid surrender, he is in a position to dispense with Criseida's relatively bold approach to love. Taking over Boccaccio's apostrophe to the night, he personalizes it with the wistful question,

> Why nad I swich oon with my soule ybought,
> Ye, or the leeste joie that was theere?

And he extends the accompanying aporia into an insistently humble profession of dependence upon his "auctour" and of willingness to be corrected by those "that felyng han in loves art."[53] To the night-long demonstrations of love recorded by Boccaccio he adds a circumstance to symbolize union concretely and aristocratically. His lovers exchange their rings, and Criseyde gives Troilus

> a broche, gold and asure,
> In which a ruby set was lik an herte.

The exchange, as Professor Young remarked,[54] comes presumably from the use of Biancofiore's ring in the marriage ceremony.[55] The ruby in the brooch, whether or not suggested by the stone of vermilion hue in that ring, links with Pandarus' early figuring of Criseyde as a ruby to be set in a ring, to wit her suitor, and Troilus' late one of her as a ruby fallen from a ring, to wit her palace.[56] It links also with the ruby in the signet used by the prince to seal his first letter to her.[57] The azure of the brooch, signifying constancy as the red of its stone passion,[58] reminds us that Criseyde offered a "blewe ryng" to her uncle to take to the allegedly jealous Troilus,[59] the same, it may be supposed, that she has now exchanged for a ring of his. Having added the business of tokens, Chaucer adorns Boccaccio's interjection against misers with an arcane, yet lively reference to their archetypes, Mida and Crassus, a reference suggested by the *Purgatorio*.[60] Lastly, he enriches his author's bare mention of cocks as indicative of dawn's approach and the responses to dawn attributed by him to hero and heroine. In the former of these responses there was no apostrophe of anything in nature; in the latter, a very brief one of the day.

The cock, "comune astrologer,"[61] beats its wings and crows, Lucyfer rises in brilliance as the messenger of day, and after her, a group of stars—Fortuna Major.[62] Moved by these unwelcome harbingers, Criseyde demands of night why it does not tarry now as it did for Almena and Jove. Declaring it to have been created by God to afford rest to all, she accuses it of stinting that office and, as punishment, calls for its perpetual constraint:

> ther God, maker of kynde,
> The, for thyn haste and thyn unkynde vice,
> So faste ay to oure hemysperie bynde,
> That nevere more under the ground thow wynde!

Troilus stigmatizes day as a spy with bright eyes at every cranny, bidding it sell its light to the engravers of small seals; and calling the "sonne, Titan" a fool for desertion of his mistress "the dawyng," the prince exclaims,

> What! holde youre bed ther, thow, and ek thi Morwe!
> I bidde God, so yeve yow bothe sorwe!

As pointed out by Professor Lowes,[63] insertion of these twin addresses to night and to day and its luminary appears to have been suggested by the apostrophe of the father of Filocolo to both night and the sun. Though the King expressed reverse wishes—for the former to depart and the latter to come—so that he might hasten the pleasure of seeing Biancofiore burned, he apostrophized them in the same order, employed the word "emisferio" and misbestowed the beloved of Tithonus upon Titan, the Sun:

O notte, come sono lunghe le tue dimoranze: piú che essere non sogliono! O il sole è contra il suo corso ritornato, poi che egli si celò in Capricorno, allora che tu la maggior parte del tempo del nostro emisferio possiedi, o Biancofiore credo

75

che con le sue orazioni prieghi gl'iddii che rallungare ti facciano, quasi indo-
vina al suo futuro danno. Ma folle è quello iddio che per lei di niente
s'inframette, ché a lui non fia mai per lei acceso fuoco sopra ad altare né
visitato tempio. Di se medesima gli può ben promettere sacrificio, perciò che
quando tu ti partirai dal nostro emisferio, io la farò ardere nelle cocenti
fiamme. . . . Et tu, o dolcissimo Apollo, il quale disideroso sí prestamente
suoli tornare nelle braccia della rosseggiante Aurora, che fai? Perché dimori
tanto? Vienne. . . ."[64]

Drawing probably on a dawn piece of Ovid's[65] as well as on his own invention,
Chaucer has created tone poems for hero and heroine which greatly surpass
this their likely but very grim original. After bestowal of the apostrophes
upon the pair, Chaucer is content to return to the *Filostrato* for converse
of theirs with which to end his scene. This he renders with general fidelity
to sense.

He also substantially reproduces the brief account of the hero's return to
his palace and meditation there,[66] and the even slighter one of the heroine's
state of mind after her lover's departure.[67] At that point, however, he inserts
an episode, short too, but of great functional importance.[68] Taking advantage
of his shift of consummation from the lady's house to the go-between's, he
brings Pandarus to her for another bedside conversation. Roguishly solicitous
about disturbance of her slumbers by the rain, her host asks how she fares.
"Nevere the bet for yow . . . ," she replies, "ye caused al this fare," and
thereupon hides her blushes with the sheet. The uncle offers his sword for
his own execution but belies his words by forcing a kiss. Who could hold out
against such an amusing person, whose offense after all was really a favor?
"God foryaf his deth," Chaucer impiously observes, "and she al so Foryaf."
This comic interlude, I would very conjecturally propose, may have been
inspired by the surprisal of Florio and Biancofiore by the Admiral on their
second morning in the tower and his passing intention to dispatch them
with his sword.[69] Derived thus or not, it completes the mildly ironic framing
of the consummation, provoking our smiles at the lady's attractive pose of
innocence, as the bundling of Troilus into bed invites amusement at the
sensibility which confirms his love. And the humor of this interlude affords
a respite between the ardors of the night and the earnestness of the following
scene, the cautionary visit of the go-between to the lover which Chaucer
adapts from the *Filostrato*. Moreover, it stands in opposition to the confidant's
talk with the heroine after the parliament. Parallels between it and this much
later episode, taken over from the *Filostrato,* are effective for both irony and
pathos. On that occasion, as on this, she will shield her face from Pandarus,
but to hide tears instead of blushes. Blaming him again, she will be genuinely
reproachful and with cause enough in her impending banishment from Troy.

The conference between Pandarus and Troilus, reported after the former's chat with his niece, preserves the tenor of the original.[70] Troiolo expressed gratitude to his friend for the night just past, was cautioned to maintain discretion, and promised that he would. So Chaucer's pair—with Pandarus, as usual, made more sententious than Pandaro.

Like Boccaccio, Chaucer proceeds immediately from this final episode of the consummation sequence to the second night of love,[71] agreeing with him that it followed hard upon the first. He moves it, as he has the first, from the lady's house to the confidant's. And he reworks it so thoroughly as to completely change its tone. Boccaccio stressed sensuality—and the woman's more than the man's. During intercourse, his heroine expressed her pleasure in the frankest of hyperboles, and the hero as extravagantly but without her animal gusto. Each kissed the other's mouth, eyes, and bosom. They parted sorrowfully, Boccaccio recorded, but with arrangement for prompt return to their delights so that they might temper their sufferings and enjoy youth while it lasted. Chaucer eliminates the amorous declarations of both parties and replaces what was said of kisses with a magnification of their happiness in purely abstract terms. He gives Troilus a stanza of complaint against the sun as incisively poetic as the longer apostrophe to day and sun on the previous dawning and possibly inspired, as that seems to have been, by the diatribe of the father of Filocolo.[72] And for Boccaccio's hedonistic phrasing of plans for future meetings, he substitutes lines suggestive, not of persistent appetite, but of the reversal presently to ensue:

> They twynne anon, as they were wont to doone,
> And setten tyme of metyng eft yfeere.
> And many a nyght they wroughte in this manere,
> And thus Fortune a tyme ledde in joie
> Criseyde, and ek this kynges sone of Troie.

The stanza of the *Filostrato* which effects transition from this episode to that of Troiolo's song in a garden Chaucer supplements from a much earlier one, to the exaltation of the lover's happiness at the time.[73] Staging the garden scene very much as Boccaccio did,[74] he substitutes for the long hymn to Venere a relatively short one to Love adapted from a metre of the *Consolation of Philosophy*.[75] With the fine opening stanzas of the hymn already borrowed for his Prohemium and the rest inadequate to glorify love at this climax, Chaucer must find a replacement. The metre is a perfect one since it dignifies sexual attraction by identifying it with the cohesive principle of the Universe, as did the stanzas taken over for the Prohemium,[76] and wording that identification with at least equal beauty. The utterances of the concept, first by Chaucer *in propria persona* at the beginning of the book and now

77

near its close by Troilus, serve to bracket the hero's period of joy as a time when love seems all-sufficient—not a competitor with Heaven but Heaven's manifestation on earth.

Chaucer offers testimony, immediately after Troilus' song, to the hero's perfection by love in mundane virtues, as Boccaccio did after Troiolo's,[77] remarking, with this authority, the prince's military prowess, his hawking and hunting, his encouragement of the worthy, and his undeviating politeness. As for prowess he adds, as he has before, that the hero stands next to Ector. The simile of an unhooded falcon applied to Troiolo making himself attractive for Criseida's inspection Chaucer adapts for his heroine doing the like for his hero. This gracile figure he must have felt to be unsuitable for the second warrior of the realm. The transfer is analogous to that of the simile of the sparrowhawk's prey from Filocolo to Criseyde.

Our poet marks the change from weal to woe much more impressively than the Italian. Boccaccio, in the last stanza of his Part III, remarked Fortuna's coming withdrawal of favor from Troiolo and launched into narrative in Part IV without preamble.[78] Chaucer bids farewell to Venus, her son, and the Muses at the end of Book III, with acknowledgment of their inspiration of its prevailingly happy content;[79] and, in the Prohemium to Book IV, exclaims against Fortune for her treacherous nature, foretells what she will do to Troilus, and calls on the Furies and Mars to aid him henceforth. The farewell harks back to the invocation of Venus, "lady bryght," and of Caliope, which concludes the Prohemium to Book III, while affording the strongest of contrasts for the invocation immediately to follow. It reads:

> Thow lady bryght, the doughter to Dyone,
> Thy blynde and wynged sone ek, daun Cupide,
> Yee sustren nyne ek, that by Elicone
> In hil Pernaso listen for t'abide,
> That ye thus fer han deyned me to gyde,
> I kan namore, but syn that ye wol wende,
> Ye heried ben for ay withouten ende!

Here is the fairest of the old mythology, with nothing lost in transmission through *Teseida* and *Paradiso*;[80] in the apostrophe to the Herynes and Mars, as we shall see, its darkest pessimism and fear.

Separation in Prospect

CHAUCER'S Book IV, to be considered entire in this section, covers the same span of action as Part IV of the *Filostrato*. All but the first twenty of its stanzas, as all but the first thirteen of the source, are given to events of a day and a night. And of the twenty, the sixteen after the Prohemium report the same circumstances before this sequence as did the thirteen: the battle momentous for the capture of eminently exchangeable Trojans, the arrangement of a truce, and Calkas' successful plea for the recovery of his daughter by exchange. The sequence includes the same episodes in adaptation as in source: the public negotiation of the exchange, attended by the lover; lamentations separately of hero, heroine, and hero again, with each lamentation interrupted by the confidant; and then—as arranged by him —the last nocturnal meeting of the pair. In adaptation as in its source, these stand in powerful opposition to consummation and the subsequent plateau of happiness, providing anatomization of the sorrows of love as detailed and sharp as any attempted before of its transcendent joys.

In Book IV, Chaucer continues to reshape the *Filostrato* to his own ends, but through additions—and deletions—less radical than he ventured in the ascending action. He enlarges Part IV, but only by a quarter.[1] This moderation, after the lavishness of treatment of Parts II and III, might be thought to reflect a flagging of energy. It seems, however, to be due to a commendable sense of proportion. Boccaccio, for whom separation was the personally significant phase of the story, analyzed the emotions induced by its prospect even more fully than those consequent to love fulfilled. Long protraction of his Part IV would therefore have been supererogatory, not to say tedious. What Chaucer sets himself economically to do is to modify the responses of

79

the characters in conformity with his earlier changes in their portrayal and to strengthen the theme of destiny both through such modification and through comment *in propria persona*. As before, he desensualizes the heroine and remotivates her accordingly. While he can no longer enliven the go-between with humor and artifice, he confirms for him a mastery of dialectic and of the worldly wisdom enshrined in proverbs. And he greatly strengthens the melancholy fatalism in Troilus, whch he has already established as a dominant prepossession. His own pronouncements on destiny reinforce the prince's on the artistic plane, though not necessarily on the philosophic, quickening our apprehension of doom without insistence upon a dogmatic rationale. Contrariwise, they make us doubtful of Criseyde's plans to manipulate her foreknowing parent and hence to reverse fate, and, in so doing, they anticipate the irony of her failure in Book V.

In adapting Part IV, Chaucer resorts, as always, to his "bokes." He continues to depend upon the *Consolation* for ideology and to supplement it at elevated moments with the *Divine Comedy*. And now that he has come to the fateful battle, the point at which Benoit began the love story, he naturally turns to the *Roman de Troie* more often than before[2] though not to the extent that he will in Book V. And he turns also, it seems, to Guido's redaction of this, the *Historia destructionis Troiae*, as perhaps he did on an earlier occasion or two.[3]

His Prohemium[4] at once states the argument of the rest of the poem and sets the mode of treatment—acute realization of ironies tempered by sympathy constant and warm. Fortune, deceiver of fools, who laughs and grimaces at it.[5] Chaucer's heart bleeds at this and his pen "Quaketh for drede." His concern extends to the not guiltless tool of Fortune as well as to the innocent dupe; compelled to follow authorities who assert that Criseyde forsook her lover or was at least "unkynde," he sorrows that they had cause to speak her ill. And with Dantean reminiscence,[6] he invokes the most ominous of divine patrons:

> O ye Herynes, Nyghtes doughtren thre,
> That endeles compleignen evere in pyne,
> Megera, Alete, and ek Thesiphone;
> Thow cruel Mars ek, fader to Quyryne,
> This ilke ferthe book me helpeth fyne,
> So that the losse of lyf and love yfeere
> Of Troilus be fully shewed heere.

This appeal harks back to the invocation, likewise Dantean in phrase, which opened Book I. Here, Chaucer calls on all three daughters of Night to help those thrown from her wheel, is to reject Troilus and elevate Diomede upon him with the sadder phase of the action; there, upon Thesiphone alone, the "cruwel Furie, sorwynge evere yn peyne," for aid in telling how the hero's chances went

> Fro wo to wele, and after out of joie.

The last three lines of the quoted stanza Chaucer should have revised of course. Yet the intention which they suggest of swift and therefore astounding progression to ultimate catastrophe is not fundamentally violated. Though he is to need two books to finish the story instead of the anticipated one, he keeps to the tragic highroad in both and, in the Fifth, even somewhat quickens the pace set by Boccaccio.

His version of events leading to the parliament[7] contains several elaborations of Boccaccio's which are worthy of note. First of all he gives them a seasonal dating. Ector decides upon battle, he tells us

> whan that Phebus shynyng is
> Upon the brest of Hercules lyoun,[8]

that is at some time in later July or earlier August. This, as Professor Tatlock pointed out,[9] seems meant as a *terminus a quo* for later references to time —at the end of this book, Criseyde's fixing the day of her return by the course of the moon and, in the next, Troilus' dwelling on its progress within the designated period. Though Chaucer professes ignorance on the point, the battle presumably followed hard upon the decision to wage it. And it may be assumed that the events between the battle and the parliament came in quick succession. As to the fight itself, the capture of prisoners and the request for a truce, our poet lends realism to the first by specifying weapons; rephrases the second—in partial conformity with Benoit's account[10]—to cut down the number of Trojans taken; and, in his final draft of the third, shifts the ignominy of asking the truce from Priam to the Greeks, again in conformity with Benoit—and with Guido also.[11] Coming to Calcas' longish appeal to the Greeks for a prisoner of theirs to exchange for his daughter, Chaucer reinforces the argument that Troy and its citizens will soon be all theirs by giving the speaker particulars about his divination and about the animosity of Phebus and Neptunus toward the city.[12] The prophet's circumstantial guarantees of doom for the state complement the author's forecast in the Prohemium of the downfall of its second Ector; they magnify the destinal forces arrayed against Troilus by attestation of their power over the entire nation. Finally Chaucer records that the exchange is to be of Antenor—not for the woman alone as in the *Filostrato*—but for her and the captured Greek "kyng Toas." This particular, justifiable perhaps as military realism, may have been inspired either by Benoit or by Guido.[13]

81

The episode of the exchange is reconstituted in the *Troilus*.[14] While the hero's dismay at the proposal of the Greeks is taken over with little change, the summary negotiation is expanded into a full-fledged debate among the Trojans. Boccaccio's word for discussion, "parlamento," probably suggested to Chaucer the parliamentary session which he gives us—as British a phenomenon as the lawsuit earlier purported against Criseyde. King Priam causes "his parlement" to be held; Ector speaks against the exchange as an un-Trojan offense to womankind; the generality censure him for proposing to deprive them of Antenor, greatly needed in their opinion; and the decision is reached "by parlement" and "pronounced by the president" to yield Criseyde for the baron. Ector's opposition accords with his patronage of the lady after her father's flight, which Chaucer took over from the *Filostrato*, and with the assumption, invented by the poet for Deiphebus, that the paladin would be on her side in the lawsuit.[15] Like the kindnesses to her of Deiphebus and Eleyne, these of Ector contribute materially to the feudal ideality of the poem. By reporting the majority opinion that Antenor should be redeemed for defense of the city, Chaucer gives himself opportunity for ironical comment:

> O Juvenal,[16] lord! trewe is thy sentence,
> That litel wyten folk what is to yerne
> That they ne fynde in hire desir offence;
> For cloude of errour lat hem nat discerne
> What best is. And lo, here ensample as yerne:

to wit, that the Trojans would exchange harmless Criseyde for one who "was after traitour to the town"[17]—

> O nyce world, lo, thy discrecioun!

While the comment may reflect particular troubles in England as Professor Brown suggested,[18] it functions as the broadest of generalizations, extending the fallibility evident in hero and heroine to all mankind. It echoes the line,

> O blynde world, O blynde entencioun!

apropos of Troilus' scorning Love at the moment when he was to be transfixed, and also the line,

> Though to us bestes ben the causes wrie,

apropos of Criseyde's intention to leave Pandarus' house immediately before the downpour portentously induced.[19] The parliamentary "ensample"— explicitly of folly—suggests also the prevalence of evil. As Mr. Speirs remarks,[20] Antenor's traitorousness to the city parallels Calkas' to it and the lady's to the hero. Having added debate and *ex cathedra* remark, Chaucer brings the scene to a close. Troiolo's swoon, which ended it in the *Filostrato,* he naturally passes over, since he has used the circumstance in the approach to consummation.[21]

Following Boccaccio, he transports the lover from the parliament to palace chamber for solitary ritualization of anguish.[22] The account which he gives of this diverges from his authority's in significant particulars, though never widely.

After appealing to his lady to pity his own misery, Boccaccio told of Troiolo's manifestations of his—dashing head against wall, beating himself, and pouring forth tears, sighs, and objurgations. He then reported a long plaint, in which the hero successively addressed Fortuna, Amore, his soul, his eyes, Criseida, and the father who would recover her. In the stanzas to the goddess, Troiolo asked why she would deprive him of his beloved rather than of such secondary interests as Priamo or other relatives. Of Love, he asked what was left for him now; of his soul, why it did not flee the body; of his eyes, what they had now to do. Apostrophizing his absent mistress, he predicted death without her comfort and deplored the suddenness of parting —this with the remark, curious from so ardent a lover, that a delay would have accustomed him to the prospect of separation. Calcas he vehemently wished dead.

Our loveless poet omits Boccaccio's stanzas to his mistress, giving us in their place a stanza which likens the hero to a tree winter-bereft. Having sublimated grief momentarily with this Dantean figure,[23] he accepts the frenetic demonstrations of it set down by Boccaccio, reproducing them untempered. And he keeps all of the apostrophes of the plaint. When he comes to that to Criseida, however, he drops the last stanza, which too commonsensically assumes palliation of grief by time, and subsitutes for it a properly romantic one, an apostrophe to lovers with a plea therein for remembrance of the speaker when they shall visit his grave.[24] The concluding diatribe against Calcas the poet reduces, purging it of express wish for the death of the traitor, though he has preserved the even more unpleasant indifference to family, expressed in the address to Fortuna. That he has kept presumably as warrant of the hero's idealization of love, as in a previous scene, his offer to procure a sister or sister-in-law for Pandaro as testimony of his appreciation of friendship.[25]

Chaucer adapts the argument between confidant and prince[26] which follows the latter's grieving by himself in such fashion as to preserve its substance and yet to vivify the dialogue. His changes here are in line with the more considerable ones which he effected in earlier colloquies of the two, reindividualizing each man as these did and subtilizing contrasts between them.

According to Boccaccio, the grief-stricken lover summoned Pandaro to his chamber and inspired tears by tears. The latter confessed astonishment at the reversal but was presently offering consolation as his role demanded. He argued that he, frustrated in love, should be sorrowing, not Troiolo who had long enjoyed it. And he suggested the taking of a new mistress. Many charming ladies were available, he said, and a new affection would drive out the old. Troiolo rejected the counsel, pointing out its inconsistency with the proposer's own behavior in love and calling for death as the one possible surcease. Pandaro then advocated rape. Again the lover took exception; the act would be harmful to the state and probably offensive to Criseida because damaging to her reputation. To ask her of his father, he went on, would be futile, for Priamo would demur, not only at breaking his compact with the Greeks, but also at allowing his son a mésalliance. Pandaro countered the objection to rape with the assurance that Criseida could accustom herself to loss of reputation as well as Elena and urged Troiolo to be daring, upon the ground that Fortuna aids the bold, and with subsequent brief promise of his own support in every peril. The lover held out for his mistress' prior consent, and Pandaro promised him speech with her that evening.

In Chaucer's version, Pandarus comes to his friend without a summons, needing none because he too has been at the parliament. His attending it implies his consequence, just as the familiarity with Deiphebus earlier attributed to him by our poet. Like Pandaro, he weeps and expresses amazement at the reversal, phrasing this anew however, as a comment upon Fortune. Asking,

> Who wolde have wend that in so litel a throwe
> Fortune oure joie wold han overthrowe?

he generalizes,

> Ne trust no wight to fynden in Fortune
> Ay propretee; hire yiftes ben comune.

The surprise thus pathetically and even naively admitted points up the contrast between his previous optimism now refuted and his friend's melancholy fear of the goddess at last borne out. Like Pandaro again, he decries the prince's sorrow at loss of a love thoroughly exploited and urges the consolation of a new mistress. Chaucer even permits him an additional stanza to enforce the attractions of other charmers, this summarizing a passage of Ovid[27] and ending characteristically with a proverb,

> Ech for his vertu holden is for deere,
> Both heroner and faucoun for ryvere.

The poet is careful, however, to absolve him of baseness, indicating that he spoke, not from conviction, but

> for the nones alle,
> To help his frend, lest he for sorwe deyde.

Troilus responds to empty consolation and heretical advice to the same effect as Troiolo but with greater spirit. Apropos of the latter, he exclaims,

> Now foule falle hire for thi wo that care!

As to the former, he likens Pandarus to a posthaste offerer of the cliché,

> Thynk nat on smert, and thow shalt fele none,

and then challenges his argument that it is better to have loved and lost than never to have been loved at all as contradictory of an earlier proposition:

> Whi gabbestow, that seydest thus to me
> That "hym is wors that is fro wele ythrowe,
> Than he hadde erst noon of that wele yknowe?"

This reference to an *obiter dictum* of Pandarus' on the morning after consummation[28] takes the place of Troiolo's own generalization that sorrow inflicted upon the happy by Fortuna surpasses all other. A concession made by Troiolo—that love may decline under various circumstances—Chaucer transfers to the friend, relieving the hero again of tepid rationality as he did by passing over the like concession about grief in the prince's apostrophe to Criseida.

Chaucer renders Pandaro's alternate proposal of rape without notable change but drops from the lover's answering speech the conjecture that his father would be snobbish about Criseida. Having endowed the lady with a palace and retinue, the poet cannot accept this reflection upon her social status.

As for Pandaro's rejoinder to the lover's cavils against violence, Chaucer softens a bit of gratuitous cynicism in it, while invigorating the whole as a clarion call to action. The flippant remark about Criseida's dispensing with her reputation,

> Passisene ella come fa Elena,
> pur ch' ella faccia la tua voglia piena,

he converts into the equivalent but politer,

85

> Thenk ek how Paris hath, that is thi brother,
> A love; and whi shaltow nat have another?

He then inserts a stanza which ends with a caveat more arresting than any remark in the original:

> And if she wilneth fro the for to passe,
> Thanne is she fals; so love hire wel the lasse,

a warning which should raise doubt in us, if not in Troilus, when she wills precisely this in the night to come. Pandaro's saw that Fortuna aids the bold Chaucer takes over as entirely in character for his sententious go-between. And he expands the former's bare promise of support into memorable panache:

> I wol myself ben with the at this dede,
> Theigh ich and al my kyn, upon a stownde,
> Shulle in a strete as dogges liggen dede,
> Thorough-girt with many a wid and blody wownde,
> In every cas I wol a frend be founde.

Manifesting an epic spirit uncalled for by earlier events, the declaration is convincing because true to the speaker in idiom.

Troilus is not overborne by it. Like Troiolo, he insists that he will act only with the lady's approval. And like his model, Pandarus promises opportunity that night to learn her will.

Chaucer makes the transition to the next scene in the same way as Boccaccio and presents it without any noteworthy departure from him.[29] In his poem as in the source, Fame spreads the news of the exchange throughout Troy, and the heroine, duly affected by it, has the aggravation of a visit by female friends. They blunder to perfection, first congratulating her on re-union with her father and then misinterpreting her tears as shed for loss of their society.

He is a little freer with the lady's private indulgence in grief after this ironic interlude.[30] Structure-minded as he is, he maintains its parallelism to the solitary grieving of the hero returned from the parliament. He is at pains, however, to feminize her as he has before and to distinguish her reactions to misfortune more subtly and significantly from the man's than they were in the Filostrato.

Boccaccio told briefly of weeping, beating of breast, and tearing of hair, and then reported complaint of hers at moderate length. Regretting that she had been born, his Criseida purposed death, if not through heartbreak, then by starvation. How could she maintain life in exile, she wondered, since her soul would remain behind with Troiolo. Would he not try to hold her by love or force? Could he bear a sorrow unendurable to her? She wished her traitorous father dead and questioned the justice of Heaven which permitted her to suffer for his guilt.

Chaucer particularizes the sorrower's appearance with romantic effect and retones her plaint to make it consonant with earlier utterances which he has modified or invented for her. Criseyde's hair, he writes, is "sonnyssh," and the fingers with which she rends it are femininely and aristocratically "longe and smale." Her tears issue "as shour in Aperil ful swithe." Still given to the proverbial mode by which he has typed her, she likens her to-be-lovelorn self to a fish out of water and a plant uprooted. Still timid, she attributes her choice of starvation as the means of suicide to fear of sword and dart. She approaches the poetic heights in a stanza substituted for Criseida's fancy that her soul will remain with the beloved in Troy; in this, after bequeathing her spirit to complain eternally with Troilus', she declares:

> For though in erthe ytwynned be we tweyne,
> Yet in the feld of pite, out of peyne,
> That highte Elisos, shal we ben yfeere,
> As Orpheus with Erudice, his fere.

She is not permitted to wish her father dead nor to reproach Heaven for making her pay for his crimes. The mild line,

> O Calkas, fader, thyn be al this synne,

is the only echo of the pair of stanzas in the original expressing these strenuous reactions.

When he goes on to the confidant's visit to the lady, Chaucer devises a speech for Criseyde at the outset, and at the close extends one for Pandarus, but leaves what falls between more or less as it was in the *Filostrato*.[31] The close parallelism of this visit to the confidant's immediately preceding one to the lover is preserved, while linkage is established with the consummation sequence through the heroine's new stanzas. Pandarus' new ones are to be remembered later on, foretelling as they do the ingenuity which she will manifest that night though, ironically, not its misapplication.

In the source, the heroine, surprised abed in tears, hid her face from Pandaro. Exclaiming at the sorrows of the day, he counselled her to refrain from useless and self-destroying grief. Presently he was weeping too. When in possession of himself again, he told of Troiolo's grief and desire to be with her. She declared her sorrow to be more for her lover than for herself and expressed eagerness to receive him; then lapsed into tears. Pandaro bade her compose herself, warning that knowledge of her present state would move Troiolo to suicide. He would oppose the lover's coming to her, he said, if he thought she would continue in it. She should so proceed as to alleviate, not increase, the prince's woe. Unresentful that her cousin was more concerned for his friend's welfare than her own, Criseida promised to discipline her feelings.

Let us now consider Chaucer's opening of the scene. He keeps the detail of the lady's hiding her tear-stained face in her arms. As remarked in Section 6, he has anticipated this in his original little episode after consummation,[32] providing an ironic parallel to it in Criseyde's hiding her blushes from Pandarus then archly triumphant. The speech which he gives her on the present occasion is of three stanzas. The first is a sad echo of her *pro forma* blaming of Pandarus at the other juncture—"ye caused al this fare." Here naming him the "cause causying" of joys now turned to sorrow, she wonders whether she should bid him welcome or no. The second stanza is reminiscent of an utterance given her by Chaucer in the approach to consummation; its opening lines,

> Endeth thanne love in wo? Ye, or men lieth!
> And alle worldly blisse, as thynketh me.
> The ende of blisse ay sorwe it occupieth,

recall her excursus apropos of Troilus' alleged jealousy,[33] in which she reached the conclusion,

> Ther is no verray weele in this world heere.

The third stanza is adapted from the first of Pandaro's opening speech, with his mention of sorrows observed turned to declaration of sorrows felt. It is dramatically more appropriate for her than its original to the maladroit comforter.

As for Chaucer's ending of the scene, he expands Pandaro's final

> Però levati su, rifatti tale
> che tu alleggi e non creschi il suo male

into two stanzas, sententious throughout and in their last three lines unconsciously pathetic:

> Women ben wise in short avysement;
> And lat sen how youre wit shal now availle,
> And what that I may helpe, it shal nat faille.

Criseyde will be fertile of schemes indeed, but of schemes which countenance her going. And with her wit so employed, Pandarus cannot help at all, for her power over the lover is absolute.

In the *Filostrato*, a very short episode follows Pandaro's visit to the lady. Half of its first stanza brings him back to Troiolo—presumably in the latter's palace. The rest of that stanza and the next three contain his encouragement of the prince on the basis of the visit. The fifth and last stanza gives Troiolo's terse reply and notes Pandaro's departure.

According to Professor Root's deductions from the manuscripts,[34] Chaucer elaborated this episode by degrees. He first adapted it rather freely but without any major addition. He then determined to introduce a soliloquy for Troilus between the first two stanzas of this draft, which correspond to the first and second halves of Boccaccio's intial stanza.[35] But before composing the soliloquy, he altered the first of the two stanzas to lead up to it and wrote a new stanza[36] to link it to the second. At last, he dropped eighteen stanzas into the slot thus provided. These give us the prince's views on predestination, as adapted for him from a passage in the *Consolation of Philosophy*.[37] The episode thus completed in the *Troilus* is more than four times the length of its correspondent in the *Filostrato*.[38]

The first lines of its opening stanza, lines unchanged from the first draft, tell us that Pandarus came upon the prince in a temple. This localization, so appropriate for Troilus' metaphysics, was probably suggested to Chaucer by Boccaccio's staging an early conference of the friends in a temple[39]—one which our poet had shifted to the house of Deiphebus. The remaining lines of this stanza as he revised it and the opening lines of the next, the first, that is, of the eighteen-stanza block, prepare for the soliloquy by advising us of the despair which inspired it.

Throughout his monologue, which occupies the rest of the block, Troilus holds to the opinion that everything that befalls must befall. He begins with a forthright statement of this tenet and applies it no less positively to his own case:

> "For al that comth, comth by necessitee:
> Thus to ben lorn, it is my destinee.
>
> "For certeynly, this wot I wel," he seyde,
> "That forsight of divine purveyaunce
> Hath seyn alwey me to forgon Criseyde,
> Syn God seeth every thyng, out of doutaunce,
> And hem disponyth, through his ordinaunce."

Then remembering that the learned have differed on the issue under consideration, he exclaims that he does not know which of them to believe. Yet in the following review of contrary positions, he shows himself to be thoroughly committed to his original statement. He gives favorable attention to the argument that God's foreknowledge of all that is to come is determinative because infallible. He proceeds to the argument which reverses this order of causation—to wit, that the inevitability of what is to come is the basis of foreknowledge—but finds no comfort in it. Whether it be true instead of the other makes no practical difference, he reasons, since it too concedes necessity. Summing up, he ends:

> and thus the bifallyng
> Of thynges that ben wist bifore the tyde,
> They mowe nat ben eschued on no syde.

The stanza following the soliloquy contains a prayer of Troilus to Jove and a statement by the author that Pandarus came in while the former was disputing with himself. The prayer is linked very neatly to the soliloquy by its referral of the truth of "al this thyng" to the god. But the notice of the friend's coming is a clumsy transition to his speech, ignoring as it does the entrance provided for him at the very beginning of the episode. How Chaucer made this slip is hard to explain whether or not one accepts Root's deduction that the stanza was added to the first draft before the soliloquy was composed.

Pandarus' encouragement to the prince, unchanged from that draft, is a little longer than Pandaro's and different in one particular of comfort offered. Claim that the lady's sorrow exceeded the lover's is replaced by assurance that she will find some means to forestall the exchange, an assurance consonant with Pandarus' dictum, uttered to her, on the readiness of the female mind. As in the source, the hero's response to consolation is approving but exceedingly terse.

The soliloquy, the longest single addition to the *Filostrato* in Book IV, is a moot passage. Eminent Chaucerians differ considerably as to Chaucer's intent for it and his success in achieving whatever that intent may have been. Professor Kittredge pronounces generally favorable judgment: "In details, to be sure, the passage is open to criticism, and it is undoubtedly too long; but in substance it is dramatically appropriate, and it is highly significant as a piece of exposition. For Troilus finds no comfort in his meditation."[40] Professor Curry approves the soliloquy without reservation, and expressly for its contributions to the destinal atmosphere of the book and to the hero's standing as a thinker.[41] Chaucer, in inserting it, he assumes, "is primarily the objective artist, deliberately putting back of the story's action *for purely dramatic effect* the conception of Destiny which actually finds expression there." As to the thought processes of the character, he writes, "Troilus's naturally philosophical mind is represented as reasserting itself and as urging him to push to their logical conclusions the Boethian principles which he has espoused all along." Professor Patch argues that the soliloquy is artistically fashioned for the speaker but to expose his weakness of character—not to dignify him philosophically or to key the book. In it, he declares, "the

90

prince exonerated himself of all guilt for his disaster so that he might pity himself the more justly. . . . There is no reason for thrusting this foppery upon Chaucer himself. Furthermore it is quite characteristic of Troilus, who all through the poem at every turn of the plot, blames Fate or Fortuna for whatever occurs." [42] Professor Root similarly praises the author and damns the protagonist, finding the soliloquy an artistic corroboration of earlier indications that Troilus is a sentimentalist, one with whom, "emotion and desire become an end in themselves rather than a spur to action." [43] Professor Tatlock dissents as to its psychological appropriateness, "But though such a man might have so reasoned if he could, it is not in character, and is one of the merely contemporary and artificial passages, similar to the *sentence*-element of the poem." [44] Professor Young observes that one result, whether intended or not, of Chaucer's providing this speculation for Troilus is to perfect him as a literary type: "The erotic code and romantic convention are explicit in requiring the lover's presence in church. . . . Troilus's long meditation and touching prayer in the temple, therefore, give salience to one aspect of his courtliness." [45] And Professor Kirby would have it that the particular tenor of the meditation is reflective of *amour courtois*: "My point is that the whole concept of courtly love was something entirely foreign to the idea of free will." [46]

As for my own views, they are as follows. Chaucer's main purpose in adding the soliloquy was to strengthen the impression of doom in the descending action. If such was the case, he must have meant it to be taken seriously—as at least a fairish intellectual performance, that is, on the part of Troilus, whether weakly self-pitying or not. He knew, of course, that the line of reasoning in it was assailable, no less an authority than Dame Philosophy having controverted the original thereof to her own satisfaction. Yet he would seem to have counted on it to inspire the reader with a sense of tragic inevitability, since comments in his own person in this book and the next are plainly directed to that end, most notably that opening the latter:

> Aprochen gan the fatal destyne
> That Joves hath in disposicioun,
> And to yow, angry Parcas, sustren thre,
> Committeth, to don execucioun;
> For which Criseyde moste out of the town,
> And Troilus shal dwellen forth in pyne
> Til Lachesis his thred no lenger twyne.

This declaration and the soliloquy support one another no less substantially than—in Book III—the poet's attributing the rain to a planetary conjunction and the lover's praying to deities for astrological assistance. Whatever its vulnerability on the philosophical plane, the soliloquy has an appearance of logic which is effective on the literary. Its argument is sequential, if anything, too orderly for a man racked by despair. The lack is, not of semblance of reason, but of transfiguration of reason into poetry—the same lack as in Criseyde's demonstration of the impossibility of true happiness on earth. By the time Chaucer gave Troilus this speech, his fine conception of him as a poetic thinker would appear to have faded a little. After consistent enrichment of the figurative element in his discourse, he here adapted for him a passage of the *Consolation* quite bare of imagery and neglected to improve it with any notable figure. He seems even to have forgotten for an instant that the product was to be a soliloquy, for he lets the speaker address a nonexistent audience—"nowe herkne, for I wol nat tarie." In content, however, if not in style, it will pass muster as a dramatic utterance, being a plausible extension of the hero's tendency to generalize anent his own case and to fall into melancholy fatalism when he does so. Such tendency, if not atypical of his kind, the courtly lovers, is so exceptionally strong in him as to be individualizing.

Troilus' nocturnal visit to his mistress climaxes Book IV of the English poem as Troiolo's, Part IV of the Italian. It comprises the last third of that book as Troiolo's, that third of Part IV.[47] And like the latter, it falls into two unequal sections: the first and smaller centered upon the lady's swoon; the second reporting protracted debate—her arguments for compliance with the exchange, her lover's futile counters to them.

The first section of Boccaccio's account runs as follows. When Troiolo was due, Criseida came to him as was her wont with lighted torch—a stage direction to be expanded, presumably from memory of the consummation night, when, bearing a torch, she descended a stair to reach the dark and remote place where he had secreted himself. Overcome by sorrow on the present occasion, she fainted in his arms. Composing her apparently lifeless body—deposited, one must assume, upon the floor—he drew his sword to send his spirit after hers, but not before a curtain speech. Reproving Giove and Fortuna for this unexpected bereavement, he declared that he was about to fulfill their wishes:

> a quel che voi volete, ecco ch'io vegno.

Since it was their pleasure, he would leave this world to take his chances of reunion with Criseida in the next. With farewells said to beleaguered city and appeal made to the supposedly departed to receive his soul, he would have dispatched himself had she not most opportunely sighed. Restored to full consciousness in his arms and learning why his sword was unsheathed, she declared that, had he used it against himself, she would have plunged it into her own bosom. Without lingering on this grisly thought, she invited him to bed. Much of the night, she estimated, was already spent, for the torch had burned far down. The course to bed is left to our imagination—if we wish, up the staircase as on the night of consummation.

In adapting this action,[48] Chaucer makes simple but necessary changes in staging and retones the nearly farewell speech of the hero. Troilus, he says,

> Ful pryvely hymself, withouten mo,
> Unto hire com, as he was wont to doone.

The last clause is a blind reference, since our poet has shifted the first and second nights of love from the heroine's abode to the confidant's and described no others. Yet it is not implausible. Why should Troilus not have beaten a path—discreetly, of course—to his mistress' own dwelling? And being vague, the statement may pass unchallenged, whereas the explicit one that the heroine came forth with a torch "com' era usata," if taken over from the original, would have set any alert reader to fruitless racking of his memory. Light there must be, however. Chaucer replaces the torch with another illuminant, making his heroine tell time by this after her swoon, as Criseida did, after hers, by the former:

> For, by the morter which that I se brenne,
> Knowe I ful wel that day is nat far henne.

The change from a light borne by the hostess to one not carried by anyone eliminates the question of what happened to the combustible when she fainted, and also leaves it to be inferred that the scene began where it ended— in her bedchamber. As for the prince's words over her insensible form, Chaucer gives them spirit. His hero conceives of intended suicide, not as submission to the wishes of Jove and Fortune, but as an act of defiance:

> Fy on youre myght and werkes so dyverse!
> Thus cowardly ye shul me nevere wynne;
> Ther shal no deth me fro my lady twynne.

Not because it will please them, he says, but because they have slain her, he will follow her soul high and low. And mindful of his repute, he adds:

> Shal nevere lovere seyn that Troilus
> Dar nat, for fere, with his lady dye.

Here is resolution as heroic as is Pandarus' offer of self and kin in the cause of friendship. If inconsistent with the determinism of the speaker, it is emotionally plausible at this crisis and congruent with his intrepidity afield. Devo-

93

tion to the cause of love renders him, like Troiolo, indifferent to all others. He takes unapologetic leave of the city which needs him and of father and brothers and implores Criseyde to receive his spirit. For weal or woe, she recovers in time to save him—as Criseida, her servant. And, if she cries out "for fere" at sight of the drawn sword, as the hardier Criseida did not, she too declares that she would have turned it against herself, had its owner carried out his resolve.

In the second phase of the night, the fateful discussion abed, the heroine is dominant according to both authors. Confident of her supremacy, she begins, as each reports her, by telling, not asking, her lover what should be done, and persists in her decision to comply with the exchange despite his cogent objections and moving pleas. She forces acceptance of the worse as the better reason, in part by sophistries and cajolery, but in the main by sheer determination to prevail. If he seeks comfort from her rationalizations, it is only because he has no alternative. She has willed; as her principled subject, he must concur. Intended to meet his doubts, the rationalizations serve better to justify her in her own eyes—to give her specious assurance that she is planning what will be best for them both and consequently that she is unselfish, as true to love in her way as he in his. Dramatic irony is thus two-edged. At the expense of the hero, who is to lose love because of the compliance which it virtuously inspires. At the expense of the heroine, who will be degraded along the way down which self-deception is to lead her.

Though the irony is basically the same in original and adaptation, it is more tellingly developed in the latter. Expanding the interchange considerably,[49] Chaucer makes the lady more fertile of strategems and more emphatic in her assurances of constancy, so that she will later appear the more egregiously self-misled. And he permits the hero sharper criticism of reliances of hers, so that their tenuousness may be immediately apparent and that his willy-nilly acceptance of them may strike us even more forcibly as an abnegation of judgment. As concerned for empathic response to the ironies as for clear recognition of them, the poet works for a measure of sympathy for the victor in the argument as well as for the vanquished. Exalting the latter somewhat in an already noble role, he marshals for the former such charms and quasi virtues as are at all compatible with her essential frailty.

In the *Filostrato*, the heroine opened the debate with a succinct presentation of her views. After a preamble of two stanzas propitiatory in its assurance of heartfelt grief, she made her first point—that the exchange could not be opposed—in a single stanza; and her second—that it would not bring permanent separation—in but half a dozen more. Having enumerated circumstances boding well for reunion in five of these, she promised in the sixth to do something to insure it, namely to persuade her avaricious father that she could safeguard his possessions in Troy if released by him.

Criseyde's opening speech, more than twice as long as Criseida's, is a masterpiece of persuasion, tactfully unassuming, impressively circumstantial. She begins with a half dozen stanzas of propitiation: what she is to propose, she remarks disarmingly, comes in true female fashion on impulse; it will mean an absence of but a week or two; it is to be kept short; and it is offered merely as a suggestion, for her intent is to do whatever Troilus commands. Coming to the points made by Criseida, she disposes of the first in a stanza, but lets her invention run on about the second in violation of the promise of brevity. She devotes nine stanzas instead of five to hopeful circumstances, and, in one of them, commits herself to return within ten days, as Criseida did not until under pressure of remonstrances from Troiolo. And in place of Criseida's one stanza assuring persuasion of the father to her return, she has seven.

As for these last, in the first four she particularizes the appeal to the selfish interests of the parent suggested in the original. She will bring "moeble" of her own to Calkas and represent it as sent in trust by friends of his, with more to follow if he should permit her to go back as his intermediary. The expense she justifies in a proverbial vein reminiscent of Pandarus' at its homeliest:

> Lo, Troilus, men seyn that hard it is
> The wolf ful, and the wether hool to have.

Further, she will promise Calkas restoration to Priam's favor, through her influence at court, if peace should come. In the remaining three stanzas, she decries divination and proposes to shake his reliance on it so that he will not disprove her arguments by that means. Making light of the science, she counts on the blinding force of avarice:

> For al Appollo, or his clerkes lawes,
> Or calkulyng, avayleth nought thre hawes;
> Desir of gold shal so his soule blende,
> That, as me lyst, I shal wel make an ende.

If he tests her statement by "his sort," she will interrupt him to declare that he has misunderstood the gods, given to ambivalences as they are, and to outright lies; and, specifically, that cowardice led him to such misinterpretation at Delphi—cowardice consonant with the generalization "drede fond first goddes." That Criseyde should work out faith-shaking arguments for later use against her father was probably suggested to Chaucer by the circumstance recorded in both Benoit and Guido that, when scolding Calcas for desertion, Briseïda was critical of Apollo, his informant.[50] Since their function is confessedly expediential, these arguments need not all be taken as convic-

95

tions of hers. One, indeed, the dismissal of gods as mere figments of the mind,[51] is wholly incompatible with her fervent addresses to pagan deities this same night as well as on other occasions. Yet doubt of her father's modes of knowing must be genuine, however wishful; were it not, she could but accept the fall of the city and all its consequences, among them permanence of separation.[52] Her scepticism as to the priest's foreknowledge stands in direct contrast to the reliance on dreams and omens which Troilus is later to exhibit; and the hopefulness which this scepticism allows her does also to the lover's deterministic melancholy, past, present, and future. Both lead to dramatic irony in her future,[53] and the contrasts underscore it. For these effects and others, Chaucer elaborates his original considerably in the transition from her speech to the prince's rejoinder and in the latter itself.

According to Boccaccio, the youth wavered between belief and disbelief in the hopes which Criseida had propounded and, while in the former state of mind, enjoyed love with her and some unquoted verbal dalliance. Doubt still lingering, however, he then warned that delay of her return would make him kill himself; surmised that Calcas would dissuade her from ever coming back; and, as a logical conclusion, implored her to flight—an escape in which both of them would be indifferent to breach of Priamo's commitments and secure against his vengeance in the fealty to themselves of the remote peoples to whom they would resort.

Departures of Chaucer are principally as follows. Before he reproduces the account of the hero's uncertainty and enjoyment of love and conversation, he inserts a stanza attesting, on written authority, the sincerity of the heroine both in her speech just quoted and generally during this period. To complement the last seven stanzas which he gave her, he inserts two in the lover's speech between its threat of suicide and its anticipation of Calcas' dissuading her from return. In these two he permits Troilus to burlesque her style while disputing her thought—to deny as proverbially that she can outwit her father as she has asserted this capacity, to match her wolf and wether apothogem, for example, with

> that on thenketh the beere,
> But al another thenketh his ledere.

Proceeding from this insertion about Calcas to what the hero said of the priest in the original, our poet moderately expands and particularizes Troiolo's forecast of fatherly propaganda. He does the same with the hero's plea for elopement, strengthening this with practical assurances as to wherewithal for life in exile, which are more extended than the cynical write-off of Priamo, which he suppresses. Among these assurances, the remark that Criseyde has treasure to pool with the speaker's is positive, if incidental, testimony to her

status, like her own mention of "moeble" above noted. Having thus rounded
out the counterproposal of the lover, Chaucer makes no less free with the
lady's rebuttal, which immediately followed in the original.

As there reported, this began with an oath of constancy—as brief as it was
trite—by arrows of love in the speaker's bosom. Then came objections to elopement on the grounds successively: of the disloyalty incident to it on Troiolo's
part, of the inevitable damage to his honor, of that to hers, and of satiety eventuating from ease of intercourse in a shared exile. Lastly, there was a bit of
sophistry about besting Fortuna by indifference, videlicet compliance, and,
to make that palatable, an unqualified promise of return on the tenth day.

In Chaucer's revision, the lady's assurance of faith is more elaborately put;
her cavilling at flight, much trimmed down; and her determination of the
time of return, rendered memorable by astronomical periphrasis. If she prove
false, Criseyde is made to implore, may Juno inflict upon her the Stygian
punishment of Athamante, may Attropos sever her vital thread, and may
Symois reverse its course; and, after the first of these invocations, she takes
to witness every deity, minor along with major.[54] At all this, the reader may
well exclaim, like Hamlet at the play, "If she should break it now!" She
goes on to censure the abandonment of city and kin proposed by the lover,
but more briefly than Criseida; repeats, in substance, the latter's caveats about
damage to his and her reputation; but totally ignores the threat of propinquity
to sexual appetite. Compression of the indictment and suppression of the
concern for libido absolve the heroine respectively of harshness and sensuality,
while the former partially protects the hero against loss of our sympathy in
that it de-emphasizes an issue which, from the angle of its presentation, is
much to his discredit. In her conclusion, Criseyde rationalizes the docility she
preaches a little more lengthily than Boccaccio's heroine, and prefixes a poetic
to the baldly arithmetical commitment to return:

> And trusteth this, that certes, herte swete,
> Er Phebus suster, Lucina the sheene,
> The Leoun passe out of this Ariete,
> I wol ben here, withouten any wene.
> I mene, as helpe me Juno, hevenes quene,
> The tenthe day, but if that deth m'assaile,
> I wol yow sen, withouten any faille.

Her mention of lunar progression carries us back to our poet's own dating of
Ector's combat decision by the presence of the Sun in Leo and anticipates his
hero's reckoning of days by the horns of the moon, which he expands for
him from Troiolo's.[55] Such objectification of time serves to maintain our
awareness of it; and that awareness, to insure empathy for the lover's agonies
of waiting.

The heroine's promise of return on the tenth day failed to end debate in the original, and is allowed no better success in the adaptation.

In the former, Troiolo, though professing himself satisfied with this definite assurance, still importuned her to remain in the city. Criseida countered at some length, reproaching him for want of trust and for aggravation of her grief by his own and then appealing to him to be continent during her absence. The appeal—gratuitous to so true a lover as the hero and dramatically ironic from a mistress so soon to be faithless as she—evoked a more serious response than it deserved. In one stanza of this, the prince declared her attraction for him to be unshakable, and, in the remaining three, explained what the attraction was—nothing superficial, not beauty, birth, ornaments, or riches—but loftiness of character as constantly attested by her demeanor. Conduct of hers presently to be chronicled was to put this praise in as ironical a light as her guarantee of return. Here and now, dawn brought the parley to a close and, with it, Part IV of the *Filostrato*.

In the *Troilus,* this wind-up of the debate, while adapted quite unslavishly to end Book IV, is subjected to but one change material enough to be noted here. That comes in Troiolo's final speech. The first stanza of this declaration, the one vowing fidelity, Chaucer keeps *mutatis mutandis* for his hero, but not the other three. In their room, he devises a speech for Criseyde. In the first and wholly new stanza of this, she acknowledges the fidelity pledged in his one by Troilus; in the remaining three, which roughly correspond to the last three of Troiolo's speech, she analyzes the appeal of her lover for her, as Boccaccio's hero had analyzed Criseida's for him. She professes that neither the prince's rank nor prowess compelled her heart but intrinsic excellences of his—moral virtue founded upon truth, gentle heart and manhood, scorn for all waywardness, and, specifically, restraint of sexual appetite. This testimonial by the betrayer herself forestalls her later justification of her breach of faith; it gives us reason to suppose that the accusations of him in the letter which Chaucer will compose for her are red herrings. Since it is an assurance of her love as well as a tribute to the object thereof, it strengthens the irony of desertion to come in the same way as the asseverations by Juno, Attropos, and Symois which she has been made to utter. And the irony here of her misreading of herself is as mordant as that of Troiolo's overestimate of her which it replaces. Lastly, as Professor Young has observed, the reversal of roles of praiser and praised brings both male and female into behavioral conformity with the feminist ideology of courtly love: "Instead of receiving the praises of a social superior, she rises to the dignity of a *domina* controlling her vassal, and conferring upon him a favor."[56]

Parting of the Ways

IN the book which is to complete his poem, Chaucer deals variously with Parts V-IX of the *Filostrato* to achieve effects which it will be the task of the present and following sections to discover. The first 686 lines of this last book comprise an account, longer by a fifth than Part V, to which it corresponds, of the heroine's departure and of the hero's life from that unfortunate event up to the time set for her return—an account to be examined with its original here in Section 8. Lines 687-1099 treat of her defection in camp, at half again the length of the short Part VI—Section 9. Lines 1100-1540 cover the hero's experience from his disappointment on the tenth day through his quarrel with Cassandra, in half the space of Part VII, which is the longest of Boccaccio's concluding five—Section 10. And lines 1541-1869 wind up the action, moralize upon it, and convey the author's valediction to his product in the same number of lines, but by no means in the same way, as the brief Part VIII accomplishes the first two of those tasks and the still briefer Part IX, the last—Section 11. Against the 1869 lines of Book V, there are 2016 all told in the five corresponding parts.[1] The reversal, late in the book, of the hitherto constant expansion of source, creates the impression that the last arc of the descending action plunges the most swiftly, with misfortune following harder than ever upon misfortune. This effect may well have been conscious with Chaucer, in view of his previously evidenced sense of structure.[2]

As for his adaptation of Part V, to which this section is limited, it manifests several trends so distinct as to appear purposive—each as likely to have been intentional as the aforesaid quantitative reversal much later on. Chaucer here continues to strengthen the theme of destiny both in his own pronouncements on divine causation and in lines given to his characters. He heightens consciousness of time in this period of its crucial importance and informs us more exactly than Boccaccio about place. And by various devices, but especially by his favorite one of contrast, he sharpens characterization of the principal actors—the three long on the stage and a new fourth, Diomede, who conducts the heroine to camp and succeeds the hero as cavaliere servente. To oppose this Greek triumphant in love to the Trojan loser, Chaucer departs from the *Filostrato* and from the *Roman de Troie* (and its derivative the *Historia destructionis Troiae*) to deny him a jot of amorous sincerity, and agrees with *Roman* and *Historia* against his main source in giving this rival the effrontery of a declaration on first sight. The heroine he gentles, as he has done consistently, to the enhancement of her charm as before and with revelation for the first time that soft womanliness may lead to dangerous compromise. The hero Chaucer improves as tragic victim, strengthening in him both the poetical imagination to idealize the love for which he will die and the propensity, ominously suggestive to the reader, of forecasting doom from dreams and auguries. And he opposes the confidant to the prince, at greater length than Boccaccio, on the issue of knowledge of the future.

Though he does not supply a Prohemium for this last book as he has for each of its predecessors, Chaucer signalizes its opening with a pair of arresting stanzas, in turn predictive and retrospective. The first ascribes the coming separation of the lovers directly to the Parcae and ultimately to Jove.[3] As remarked in the preceding section, it contributes to the theme of destiny along with the soliloquy created for Troilus. The second stanza records that Phebus has thrice melted the snows and Zepherus brought back green leaves as often since this royal scion was attracted to the charmer now to be taken from him. This notice of time, however it is to be interpreted,[4] implies the care for fact of the historian, and the cyclical phrasing of it borrowed from the *Teseida*[5] impresses upon us life's ceaseless, irreversible progression. Having thus set his tone, our poet turns to the episode which Boccaccio related without preamble at the start of his Part V.

This was the transfer of Criseida, encompassing Priamo's delivery of the lady to Diomede and the latter's of her to Calcas, together with the journey connective of these events. The escort came for her, we learn, on the day following the tryst of Part IV—to what point in Troy, however, we are not told. Wherever it was, Troiolo was there too, venturing nothing, but asking himself reproachfully why he did not, *inter alia*, defy his brothers. When in the saddle to depart, Criseida gave way to indignation. She silently upbraided Giove and Fortuna for cruelty and threatened them with perpetual insult. Her countrymen she flouted ostentatiously, expressing scorn to Diomede, in

100

their presence, at exchange of herself, a woman, and not deigning farewell to any but her own people when time came to put spurs to her horse. Troiolo accompanied her through the defense perimeter with many companions and, for some part of the way, with Antenore. Though disciplining his feelings to extend a welcome to this causer of his woes, the prince betrayed his love for Criseida by emotionality of parting and by concomitant snubbing of Diomede. The Greek was himself smitten with her at the moment of divining the Trojan's love. Brought by him to her father—apparently without court-ship—she received Calcas' tenders of affection in sad silence.

In utilizing the above,[6] our poet adjusts notices of time and place, suppresses irefulness in the heroine, and makes the rival a trifler in love and consequently audacious in its pursuit. Diomede was on hand to receive her, it is specified, "at prime"; and Troilus, it is further specified, had stationed himself to witness the transaction "at the yate ther she sholde out ride." The hero's self-reproaches for inaction Chaucer takes over except that involving the unpleasant notion of combat with his brethren. He relieves the lady of her silent defiance of Giove and Fortuna, her voiced criticism of effecters of the exchange, and her pointed omission of good-byes, and denies her even that poor outlet of driving spurs into her mount. Apropos of the first of these suppressions, it will be remembered from Section 7 that Chaucer turned the lover's plaintive reproach of the same two deities into a challenge of their authority. One may infer that he denies the one what he gives the other on the basis of sex. Criseyde, though made capable of projecting sceptic arguments against her father, is too feminine, as he would conceive her, for the defiant impiousness to be expected of a warrior, even so god-minded a one as the prince. Troilus, it may be noted, is aggrandized at this juncture when his mistress is being softened—given in place of "piú compagni" a following more expressly royal, "an huge route Of knyghtes." With these, he is made to accompany her, not merely "infin di fuori a tutto il vallo," but

Passyng al the valeye fer withoute.

Having placed him just inside the wall for the start of the procession ("at the yate ther she sholde out ride") Chaucer must have him continue with her at least some distance beyond it. He may therefore have deliberately substituted "valeye" for "vallo" (wall) rather than have mistaken the latter for "valle," as has been suggested.[7] Antenor's appearance, not definitely localized in the original, he fixes at this new stopping point. Like Boccaccio, he represents the hero to have mustered up a welcome for the exchangee but, upon parting from the lady, to have found not a word to say to her escort.

For his author's assertions that Diomede took note of this unceremonious and disturbed behavior, inferred love for the woman from it, and was himself secretly taken with her—"nascosamente sé di colei piglia"—our poet gives us the following:

> Of which the sone of Tideus took hede,
> As he that koude more than the crede
> In swich a craft, and by the reyne hire hente.

In the new "As" clause, he implies that Diomede's perceptiveness is highly sophisticated and, in the new predication "by the reyne hire hente," that the rival is to be masterful as well as cunning. This symbolic gesture he seems to have derived from the *Roman de Troie*—from the line introducing Diomedès' guidance of Briseïda after her lover's departure,

> E li fiz Tydeüs l'en meine,

as may be inferred from identity of naming and similarity of action.[8] His rejecting of psychic entanglement for the guide, which is concurrent with his giving him so decisive a move, is not inspired, however, by the *Roman;* lines therein immediately after the one just quoted establish enamorment by prediction of sorrows for the Greek. The departures above noted from the *Filostrato* in Chaucer's report of Diomede's response to the hero's leave-taking prepare for a long addition to that source.

This passage of fourteen stanzas fills the blank between the said response of Diomede and the heroine's reunion with her father—a void left by Boccaccio's transfer to a later point[9] of proposal by the Greek and the lady's equivocal reception of it which Benoit had reported at length as occurring on the journey.[10] Chaucer's insert begins with a silent appraisal of the situation by Diomede, continues through his declaration of love, and ends with Criseyde's answer to that. The first few lines of the appraisal, all of which was invented for the new suitor by Chaucer, show him to be the antithesis of the old:

> Al my labour shal nat ben on ydel,
> If that I may, for somwhat shal I seye.
> For at the werste it may yet shorte oure weye.
> I have herd seyd ek tymes twyes twelve,
> "He is a fool that wole foryete hymselve."

They undercut the profession of love service which is to follow, establishing that it is, not the honest echo which it might appear of the hero's tenders, but an empty travesty. Though a mosaic—with several of its points taken from the long speech Benoit gave to Diomedès en route, with one at least from Boccaccio's adaptation of that speech for his Diomede to utter when in camp,[11] and with still others of Chaucer's own devising—the proffer is a coherent manifestation of character, sophistic throughout, with conventional humility most competently applied to mask assurance. Beginning with an oath of unqualified obedience to her commands, the Diomede of Chaucer prays Criseyde to rely on him as the Greek with whom she is now best acquainted, to think of him as a brother, and—neatly punning—since Greeks and Trojans serve "O god of Love" not to be wroth with him "for the love of God." [12] He assures her that he has never loved before; implies that he has loved her sight unseen; and concludes that, if allowed, he will serve her better than any of his fellow knights, all of whom he flatteringly assumes will be competitors for so fair a lady. Criseyde, though too sorrowful to take in more than an occasional word of all this, is still possessed enough, as our poet summarizes her reply, to thank Diomede for his trouble and, in particular, for his offer of "frendshipe," to accept the latter, and to promise that she "wol do fayn that is hym lief and dere" with trust duly reposed in him. Resembling the extended report of Briseïda's answer in some particulars[13] and equivalent to it in encouragement, the summary of Criseyde's breathes a gentler spirit, with replacement, by euphemistic reference to the proposal, of frank interpretation of it and, by polite assumption that the proposer means well, of questioning of his and all suitors' intentions.

To conclude the ride, Chaucer adopts Boccaccio's stanza on the meeting of daughter and father with particularization of the latter's welcome and amelioration of the former's response. He relates that Calkas bestowed embraces and kisses upon the lady, as Benoit that the pair exchanged them, and that she broke her sad silence to the extent of professing gladness at reunion.[14]

Leaving her in unwelcome paternal care, Chaucer brings us back to the hero en route to his palace and keeps us with him in his whiling away of time as Boccaccio did to the end of his Part V.

The latter began with circumstantial treatment of Troiolo's solitary misery throughout the day of separation and its night and of his communing next day with Pandaro until the decision was made to visit Sarpidone. Secluded in his chamber, the prince wept, cursed gods and men, and tormented himself with recollections of the preceding night, now joyful by contrast. Next morning, he sent for Pandaro, who for some undisclosed reason had been unable to come to him before. He confessed despair to him of ever seeing the lady again and complained of dreams of flight and capture and of falling through space as destructive of his rest. In rejoinder, Pandaro exhorted his friend to be hopeful like other lovers in adversity, to discount dreams as induced by melancholy and auguries along with them, and to seek diversion in this time of truce by going with him to some pleasant spot afar to enjoy the hospitality of one of the allied kings. Consenting to amend, Troiolo proposed Sarpidone as the host to divert them. An afterthought troubled him—that Criseida might return, during his junket—but Pandaro met it by arranging to post an observer who would keep them informed.

Cutting, adding, and shifting, Chaucer accentuates the contrast in orientations of the speakers—founds the prince's melancholy more explicitly than Boccaccio upon predestinarian forebodings and elaborates the counsellor's repudiation of these, takes from the former his one very minor proposal, that as to a host, and gives it to the latter.[15] In his version of the lover's grieving by himself, he gives us the tears, curses, and recollections of the past night reported of Troiolo in his solitude and adds to these material taken from Troiolo's opening speech to the friend. He links the confession of mortal despair which begins this speech to the recollections of the happier night to form one uninterrupted soliloquy for Troilus and renders the despair more attractive than it was by making the speaker express concern for his lady as well as for himself. He then tells in his own person of the dreams of pursuit, capture, and falling which Troiolo mentioned at the end of the speech to Pandaro.

To mark the transition from the prince's lonely vigils to his conference with the friend, Chaucer inserts a picture of the dawn which Boccaccio barely mentioned as the time of summons to the latter—a picture of fading stars and moon and whitening eastern sky which is derived from a stanza of the *Teseida*.[16] He supplies an explanation for the confidant's failure to come on the preceding day, namely attendance on Priam, which is consonant in its suggestion of importance in the state with his being on hand for the parliament, a detail also added to the original. To replace Troiolo's address to Pandaro, which as just noted he has drawn on already, Chaucer gives his hero a speech convincing, because absolutely convinced, of death. It contains instructions to Pandarus to superintend the burning of the speaker's body, his funeral feast, and palestral games; to offer Mars the steed, sword, and helm of the deceased and Pallas, the shield; and to collect his ashes in a golden urn to give to Criseyde—particulars archaeologically realistic as well as tonally effective which the poet culled from the *Teseida*.[17] Following the instructions in the speech and justifying them there is brief mention of dreams present and past and of owl's cry of two nights together as sure indications of death. Troiolo, it will be remembered, alluded only to the former and to these as disturbing of his rest, not explicitly as predictive. At the end comes a prayer to Mercurye to guide the to-be-disembodied soul—a prayer which Chaucer will have fulfilled at the end of the book. With the hero

104

put on record as a believer in dream-interpretation and augury, our poet considerably expands the friend's denunciation of them while keeping his preceding counsel of hopefulness within its original compass. Dreams, Pandarus is made to say, have been attributed to infernal, physiological, psychological, seasonal and lunar influences, as well as to divine inspiration and, being thus multiply explainable, defy interpretation; it is unworthy of mankind, he adds, to fear them or the cries of owl or raven. However attractive his reasoning and however questionable the particular dreams which Troilus had, the reader has been too thoroughly conditioned to forboding by Chaucer to side with his sceptical character.[18] As in the *Filostrato*, the confidant goes on to advise diversion. He suggests it, however, in the town instead of out and does not leave the choice of host to the lover, but, as in the French prose translation, himself proposes Sarpedoun.[19] This king he places "nat hennes but a myle." Troilus assents. Since they have so short a distance to go, Chaucer understandably omits worry on the lover's part about missing his lady if she returns and answer to it on the confidant's.

The social interlude, which he has now to render, was tersely presented in his source. Whether afoot or on horseback we are not told, Troiolo and Pandaro traversed some four miles to Sarpidone's abode. The perfect host, he had hunting to offer, the company of ladies, music, and banqueting. The prince, however, took pleasure only in memories of his lady, and was soon insisting to Pandaro that they depart. Kept there through the fifth day by the latter's persuasions, he then betook himself homeward. The ironic fuility of Troiolo's impatience is brought out en route when, in response to his wondering whether he will find his mistress returned, Pandaro is made to think to himself that, with Calcas of the mind he was, the tenth day, the month, and the year would pass before she would be seen again.

In his own short version of the interlude,[20] Chaucer keeps the focus on the prince's impatience, limiting himself to changes in detail. He particularizes the entertainment to bring out its delightfulness and hence to exalt the fidelity of the lover indifferent to it; he tells of the richness of the bill of fare, specifies both wind and string instrumentation, and puts the ladies to dancing. He laments the fruitlessness of Troilus' hopeful preoccupation with his beloved:

> But weylaway, al this nas but a maze.
> Fortune his howve entended bet to glaze.

In the argument about time of departure, he makes Pandarus hold out for a full week and thus accounts for more of the period up to the tenth day. And he is careful, incidentally, to have him speak of riding home so that the plebeian possibility of walking is eliminated. On the way, Troilus voices hope that Criseyde may have returned and is even so ebullient as to sing. Pandarus is as sceptical in thought as Pandaro but kind enough to say—ambiguously—that she will come as soon as she can.

With the pair home again, Boccoccio and Chaucer concentrate upon the lover's meditations up to the tenth day, quoting the hitherto verbose friend no more and letting him temporarily fade from view.

In the *Filostrato*, the two, having betaken themselves to a chamber, had been there but a little time when Troiolo proposed that they go to see Criseida's house. When before it he exclaimed metaphorically to Pandaro of its change from light to darkness. Then he rode on through Troy, recalling to himself how Criseida had behaved at this spot and that, and begging mercy of Amore after acknowledgment of His victory over him. He also visited the gate of her departure, but not, it appears, on this ride, and there reviewed circumstances of the unhappy event and wondered whether she would ever return. Sometimes he fancied bystanders were aware of his woebegone condition. He whiled away the time with songs about his love, of which a specimen of five stanzas is given—an appeal to Amore for death and for conveyance of the soul thus released to Criseida's bosom. Ever and impatiently counting off the days and nights, he fancied the sun to be off course and its horses slow, but took comfort in the thought that when the moon should be horned as it was at the lady's going she would come back. Observing the Grecian tents from some unspecified point of vantage, he was wont to imagine the breeze therefrom to be sighs of his lady and to conjecture where among them she was situated. In the last stanza of the part, Pandaro, who has not been mentioned since the pause before Criseida's house, is belatedly remembered, it being said here that he had been with the sufferer all the while giving such comfort as he could.

Chaucer improves the lover as poet and, by accounting more exactly for time than Boccaccio and visualizing action more clearly, succeeds also in enhancing the semblance of reality.[21] His Troilus and Pandarus, who have whiled a week away at Sarpedoun's instead of a mere five days, spend not a little while, but all that remains of the day of their return in the former's chamber and all the following night. Their visit to Criseyde's abode thus put off till the next morning evokes, instead of the one diffuse figure of light and darkness from the hero, a chain of sharp images, the longest and most splendid in either poem:

> O thow lanterne of which queynt is the light,
> O paleis, whilom crowne of houses alle,
> Wel oughtestow to falle, and I to dye,
> Syn she is went that wont was us to gye!

> O paleys, whilom crowne of houses alle,
> Enlumyned with sonne of alle blisse!
> O ryng, fro which the ruby is out falle,
> O cause of wo, that cause hast ben of lisse!
> Yet, syn I may no bet, fayn wolde I kisse
> Thy colde dores, dorste I for this route;
> And farwel shryne, of which the seynt is oute!

Here fused are three figurative motifs for Criseyde already established: of light in a world otherwise unillumined for her lover, of the ruby indispensable to its setting, and of a heavenly being in the cult of love—the first motif, pervasive in the *Troilus* as it was in the *Filostrato;* the second, appearing in Pandarus' anticipation of this ruby completing the ring, his master, which is particularized from Pandaro's figure of gem and ring; and the third, of occasional, but more frequent occurrence than in the source. The desire literally to kiss the doors, which was suggested perhaps by the *Filocolo,*[22] intensifies the figuring of the palace as a shrine. It is indicated, as in the *Filostrato,* that the lover continues directly from this holy place to others associated with his mistress, and, as it is not in that work, that his friend rides with him. During this progress, he is made to recall her happy laughter and grace to himself as in the source, but not the occasional loftiness also there remembered—instead her singing "So wommanly." The appeal for quarter to victorious Love is allusively rephrased:

> Now blisful lord, so cruel thow ne be
> Unto the blood of Troie, I preye the,
> As Juno was unto the blood Thebane,
> For which the folk of Thebes caughte hire bane,

with echo, in the allusion, of Criseyde's pairing herself with Juno's Theban victim, Athamante, and anticipation of Cassandre's recounting the falls of Theban princes as analogues of Troilus', which she will have divined.[23] His sentimental reminiscences at the gate are dated after those at the other places associated with the lady as in the French prose translation of the *Filostrato,* not left chronologically indeterminate as in the original.[24]

Abandoning strict time sequence at this point, Chaucer, like his author, remarks that the lover suspected people of curiosity about him. And like Boccaccio he speaks of the prince's devoting his privacy to song, but replaces the unarresting, if artful, plaint to Amore of five stanzas with one of a stanza to Criseyde, in which she is vividly imaged as the star which must show its beams again by the tenth night, if the singer now voyaging in darkness is to escape Caribdis. After this substitution, Chaucer reworks the account of the lover's preoccupation with time, transposing and heightening his thoughts

107

on sun and moon. Boccaccio, not having mentioned the latter orb in Part IV, had here belatedly to remark—in his own person—that Troiolo had seen it horned on leaving Criseida's house before quoting him as in hope of her return when it should present the same appearance with new horns. In his Book IV, our poet indicated a change to be due from old to new horned moon by putting Phebus in Leo for the capture of Antenor and making Criseyde promise not long after that she would return ere Lucina progressed from Aries quite to the end of Leo, and hence has prepared the astronomically minded reader for the stanza he now gives Troilus, in which the prince recalls seeing the old horns after his night with Criseyde and prays Latona to post round her sphere since the lady will come again when the new shall spring.[25] The complaint of solar dallying, which is not chronologically significant, he modifies only to make explicit its implied reference to Pheton's misadventure. He visualizes the lover as pacing the city walls when the breeze reaches him from camp, and turns the brief report of his fancying it the lady's sighs into an elaborate and directly quoted conceit, this ending with the marvellously echoic lines

> for in noon othere place
> Of al this town, save onliche in this space,
> Fele I no wynd that sowneth so lik peyne:
> It seyth, "Allas! whi twynned be we tweyne?"

And in capping this phase of the action, he orients us chronologically once again by specifying that it extended through the ninth night; then remarks the friend's presence throughout as Boccaccio had done.

The Heroine's Moral Eclipse

BOCCACCIO brought rival and heroine back on stage in his Part VI, and Chaucer does so toward the middle of Book V.[1] The Italian briefly exhibited Criseida alone and grieving in the enemy camp; led Diomede to her for a substantial episode on her fourth day there, in which he represented the caller to have doubted of success in wooing but to have assayed to good purpose; and capped the scene with a psychophysical vignette of this new suitor and the observation that the qualities limned in it so affected her that she abandoned her intention to return to Troiolo. Expanding the part by half, Chaucer transforms it in such ways as to convict Diomede of lighthearted adventuring, to accentuate the lady's unsteadfastness but with increase not diminution of pity for her, and to sharpen the irony of her betrayal of the faithful hero alike for him and for herself. As he reports the heroine before Diomede's call, she realizes her error in consenting to the exchange with more ironic self-criticism than in the *Filostrato* and considers escape with more fearful awareness of its perils. He makes Diomede survey his chances before the visit, instead of at its beginning; and with the zest and coolheadedness of a gambler, not the insecurity and desperate resolve of a lover. He introduces portraits of Diomede, Criseyde, and Troilus after the rival's introspection, drawing on Boccaccio's vignette of him in the first portrait and on Benoit and Joseph of Exeter in all three for bodily and spiritual features effective for comparison and contrast of the sitters. The visit, for which these prepare, he moves from the fourth to the tenth day so that the lady may be unworthily engaged through the very span when Troilus is expecting her return in perfect trust. In adapting Boccaccio's presentation of the episode, Chaucer purges the suitor's arguments of all untactfulness, and with the help of Benoit and his redactor Guido, makes the heroine's response even more coyly encouraging. Cogitation of hers upon the visit, which Boccaccio ascribed to no particular hours, he fixes in the night after it with the time-telling moon on its way out of the Lion. And he creates a second visit for Diomede on the morrow, when Troilus is again faithfully waiting at the city gate, and attests the rival's progress in it emphatically though briefly. Criseyde's subsequent course, on which the *Filostrato* is silent, he exemplifies with manifestations of favor to Diomede taken in part from Benoit, but he balances these prejudicial circumstances with pitifully self-accusing lament on her part drawn from that source. To insure sympathy yet further from the reader, he concludes with a warm display of his own.

In the first stanzas of Part VI, Boccaccio testified to the profuseness of Criseida's weeping after arrival in camp; then reported her plaint at sight of Troy afar. Confessing to the mistake made in refusing to elope with Troiolo, she feared it irreparable but purposed to attempt escape with indifference to resultant gossip.

Chaucer gives the heroine a new plaint before he comes to her tears and slightly extends the one inspired by the distant prospect of the city.[2] In the new utterance, Criseyde declares her case hopeless because she cannot wheedle her father and because she will be arrested as a spy or raped if she tries to steal through the lines. The admission of her failure with Calkas completes the irony begun in Book IV with the attribution to her of elaborate schemes against him and to Troilus of spirited warning that they would not avail against this oldster "in sleght as Argus eyed." The conjuring up of dangers of escape evidences the same timidity and the same proneness to yield to it in self-excuse as the argument of a happier day that she must not jeopardize her position at court by rebuffing the influential Troilus. In the lament adapted from Criseida's, there are two significant changes. Confession of error in rejecting elopement is so rephrased in part as to make the ironic point of blindness to the future; lacking one of Prudence's three eyes, Chaucer's heroine admits, she has been sightless in that direction though well apprised of past and present.[3] Assertion of indifference to gossip is prolonged so much as to evidence a still lively dread of it. And a line in the extension,

Felicite clepe I my suffisaunce,

supporting her intent to return at cost of good name, is pathetic in its dependence on that "worldly selynesse" which the speaker herself recognized to be vain when confronted with but petty trouble in the closet at her uncle's.

Boccaccio, having given us his heroine's decision to rejoin Troiolo, proceeded very quickly to Diomede's interposition. In the stanza after her lament, the

110

poet remarked that a new lover was soon to turn her from this intent and then expanded this statement by saying that Diomede made use of every argument to penetrate her heart, and with success. In the next, we read that Diomede came to her ere she had been in camp the fourth day to find her in tears and greatly changed. In a third stanza, the thought is attributed to him that to replace the lover for whom she was evidently mourning he would have to be a very sovereign artist indeed and consequently that the hour was to be lamented in which he went for her to Troy. In a fourth, however, it is said that as a man of great daring and courage he resolved to disclose the rough assaults that Amore made him feel for her and the manner in which he was first enkindled; and that, seating himself, he opened conversation.

Modifying these stanzas and supplementing them, Chaucer continues his reinterpretation of rival and heroine and his glamorization of the hero. As for the first stanza, he changes its opening statement that she would be turned from her intent very soon, "tosto," to one more creditable to her reserve —that she would be "er fully monthes two"; and he replaces the supplementary prediction that Diomede was to use every argument to win her with a lively notice of schemings before action. Diomede, he says,

> Goth now withinne hymself ay arguynge
> With al the sleghte, and al that evere he kan,
> How he may best, with shortest taryinge,
> Into his net Criseydes herte brynge.[4]

The next stanza, which brought Diomede to Criseida, he reserves for use a little further along, and draws on the third and fourth, which presented the rival's thoughts on coming to her, for reflections of his beforehand.[5] While keeping the difficulty of courtship central in the aspirer's mind, he phrases it as a titillation to him not a worry. His Diomede, who has ventured a proposal already on the comfortable grounds that "at the werste it may yet shorte oure weye," is not the man to take possible failure seriously in his planning for another:

> "But for t'asay," he seyde, "it naught ne greveth;
> For he that naught n'asaieth, naught n'acheveth."

Asking himself if he is not a fool to woo a lady sorrowful for another, he answers that one who succeeds under such disadvantages might boast of being a "conquerour," and then concludes, as one ever bold and feckless:

> Al sholde I dye, I wol hire herte seche!
> I shal namore lesen but my speche.

With Diomede thus revealed in his privacy, Chaucer gives us parallel summarizing impressions of him, of the lady whom he is about to visit, and of her first lover.

The vignette of the rival given by Boccaccio after the visit reminded our poet that there were likenesses of Diomedès, Briseïda, and Troïlus in the gallery of many portraits, Greek and Trojan, which Benoit presented early in his *Roman,* and portraits of them also in the gallery, similarly placed, in the late twelfth-century Latin poem, the *Frigii Daretis Ylias* of Joseph of Exeter. Whether he went back of these galleries to their common source, that given in the sixth-century *De excidio Troiae historia,* purportedly by one Dares the Phrygian, is very doubtful; but he seems to have consulted the gallery in the Latin prose redaction of the *Roman,* the *Historia destructionis Troiae* of Guido de Columnis. He drew on both Joseph and Benoit for each of the three portraits, but in each more on the former than on the latter.[6] In the stanza presenting Diomede, he resorted to them for robustious martial qualities in this individual, which Boccaccio but weakly suggested by the adjectives "forte e fier":

> With sterne vois and myghty lymes square,
> Hardy, testif, strong, and chivalrous
> Of dedes, lik his fader Tideus.

The particulars that the rival was "of tonge large" and heir of Calydon and Argos he derived from the *Filostrato*—respectively from the vignette and from Diomede's own boasting to the heroine. In the stanzas given to Criseyde, he combined particulars adapted from Joseph and Benoit, first of her appearance and then of her spirit, with both manifesting ultrafemininity. She was medium of stature, with tresses rippling down her back, perfect in beauty save for joined eyebrows, and with compensation, as Chaucer put it in Dantean figure, in the orbs beneath them—"Paradis stood formed in hire yën." She was sober, simple, charmingly mannered, and always inclined to pity, if "slydynge of corage." In the two bestowed on Troilus, Chaucer adapted such details from Joseph and Benoit as would put the hero at least on a level with the rival in might and prowess and infinitely above him in moral worth. He was tall and perfectly proportioned, hardy as a lion, true as steel, virtued among the best of mankind, and second to none in derring do.

These portraits, conforming to a long tradition and in particular to the extended instances of it in the above-mentioned versions of the Troy story, are perfectly functional, I believe, though there is scholarly opinion to the contrary.[7] They sum up the surface resemblances and the basic disparity in character of victor and loser and the attractions, equally compelling in feminine and masculine kind, of heroine and hero along with their essential difference in point of constancy. And they do so at the proper juncture: at the first point when the rival is sufficiently known to us to make triangular comparison and contrast very telling and just before that episode is to be presented in which the fate of all three is to be settled once for all. It is a time when the charm of the heroine must be accepted by us as great enough to inspire pursuit in the present lover and desire still in the absent, her weakness as sufficient to explain countenance of the former's suit, the practical advantages which he can offer as weighty enough to overbalance for her the moral claims of the Trojan admirer, and these claims so incontrovertible in terms of courtly love as to merit guilty regret from her and pity and ironic reflection from ourselves. Neither supererogatory nor inadequate these portraits recall and enforce previous impressions on the one hand and are certified by them on the other.

With preparations thus made for the crucial scene, Chaucer raises the curtain with a stanza adapted from the one which opened this episode in the *Filostrato*.[8] He changes its time as already remarked, and he supplies specific indication of place. His putting it on the tenth day after Criseyde's exit from Troy reminds us of her promise to Troilus, just before that exit, to return by the tenth, and points up the irony to come of the prince's futile waiting on the appointed day. The original dating of the fourth prepared for this irony, it cannot be denied, but less pointedly, and might serve also to recall, ironically, that Troiolo spent five days with Sarpidone in fond memories of the lady and hoped on his way home to find that she had come back.[9] Replacement of the statement that Diomede came to her on some decent pretext by the specific one that he came to Calkas' tent with commerce pretended with its owner promotes realism in itself.

It also prepares for stage business more realistically detailed than in the *Filostrato*. In his next stanza, Chaucer transforms Boccaccio's remark that Diomede seated himself and led up gradually to his desires.[10] That he may keep Criseyde the poised and well-provided hostess which he represented her to be in her own palace, Chaucer makes her welcome and seat Diomede and then brings in men with spices and wine to sustain them in their conversation. From this starting point, he leads their talk along the path established by Boccaccio, though with some significant departures from it.

Very freely adapted from the converse of Diomedès and Brisïda in the *Roman* as they rode to camp, that of the rival and Criseida in the *Filostrato* four days later is ordered as follows. Topics brought up by Diomede as approaches to a proposal are presented in summary form. Criseida's responses, not even digested, are said to be innocent of his intent and alternately productive in him of "grieve doglia" and "lieta speranza." Assuming in his declaration, which is quoted at length, that her sorrow was for a lover in the city, he argued that she should renounce this man as doomed, like all Trojans, to die at the hands of the Greeks. And as his authority on this point, he cited the foreknowing Calcas, while taking credit to himself for voluntary assistance to the latter in the exchange. He went on to disparage her country-men as barbarous in comparison to the Greeks and to assure her that she could find a worthier lover among his people than among hers. Blushing as he said this and tremulous of voice, he averted his gaze, then offered himself as a candidate on the strength of his royal origin. Criseida thought his boldness great and showed displeasure in her glance. She thanked him nonetheless for his concern for her safety. She presumed to censure his disparagement of the Trojans, denied experience of love save with her late husband, and avowed wonder that a royal personage, as the speaker had insisted he was, could be drawn to a woman of low station like herself. But still, she was not sorry to be loved by him, she confessed, and, further, if the Greeks won as he predicted, she might become more favorably disposed to his suit. Diomede, sure of ultimate grace from these concessions, did not presume to try for more, but departed after a brief reassertion of his fidelity.

Keeping the scene to its original length,[11] Chaucer variously modifies it to emancipate the suitor in heart and yet render him more tactful and more pressing and to keep the heroine from admission of inferiority and display of temper and make her compliant with the stepped-up demands of the former.

As for Diomede on the attack, the poet takes over the summary of his opening moves from the *Filostrato,* but changes the flat assertion that the lady missed their drift to an equivocal "It semed nat she wiste what he mente." And he omits the following statement, indicative of real love in the man, that her responses now pierced his heart with heavy grief, now gave him joyful hope. Intent as he is upon the theme of destiny, Chaucer naturally preserves Diomede's argument from the fated destruction of the city and his support of it by Calcas' authority,[12] while dropping his claim to furtherance of the exchange, a favor which Criseyde obviously was in no mood to ap-preciate. He also suppresses the invidious comparison of her fellow Trojans and the Greeks, though not the assurance, pertinent to his suit, that she will find a worthier lover among the latter than among the former. He permits Diomede the blushing, tremolo, and averted gaze recorded by Boccaccio, trusting presumably that the private cynicisms which he has attributed to the Greek will lead the reader to take some of this as play-acting. And he keeps the following proffer of love, which, though couched in the humble terms of feudal service employed by the Trojan prince, contrasted tellingly with the latter's modesty and good breeding in its boast of royal origin. He adds to this a plea for audience on the morrow and emphasizes that plea in a new transitional stanza to the lady's reply by observing in his own person that she granted it—if with a proviso, the patently futile one that the guest would not speak of "swich matere."

The changes he is to make in this reply accommodate it to those which he has effected in the suitor's discourse and render it both more attractively lady-like and more discreditably yielding. His heroine, like Criseida, expresses appreciation for solicitude—not for Diomede's, however, since his claim to a part in her exchange has been suppressed, but for her father's. And since the suppliant's invidious comparison has also been dropped, she has no occasion to upbraid him for disparagement of her countrymen, though, like Criseida, she speaks in their praise. And like her, she denies experience of extramarital love. Alluding to Diomede's claim to distinguished ancestry, she professes amazement, not that he is demeaning himself to covet her, but that he would "scornen any womman so," to offer love, that is, to any representative of the presumably virtuous sex. Yet she hedges at once and further than her original. If she omits saying that she is not sorry to be loved, she concedes, with her, that reciprocation is a possibility, if the Greeks take the town. She then grants audience on the morrow, as Chaucer has anticipated she would, and confesses preference for Diomede with strong, if coy, implication that it will be fruitful:

> If that I sholde of any Grek han routhe,
> It sholde be youreselven, by my trouthe!

> I say nat therfore that I wol yow love,
> N'y say nat nay; but in conclusioun,
> I mene wel, by God that sit above!

These lines, so compromising of her loyalty, are derived from the *Roman* and the *Historia*—from Briseïda's answer in the former to Diomedès on their ride to camp, which Chaucer merely summarized when dealing with the occasion, and from the abbreviation of that reply in the latter.[13]

After such encouragement, Diomede began to press his suit "al fresshly newe ayeyn." And, according to Chaucer, he possessed himself of the lady's glove on this occasion as, according to Benoit, at the end of the ride. Not until "it was woxen eve" did he leave the tent.[14]

Our poet brings his heroine through the night in two stanzas and disposes of the morning visit which she has granted Diomede in another. In the first of the night stanzas, he tells us that Venus the evening star was following the course of Phebus, who had already left the sky, that Cynthea was urging her chariot out of the Leoun, and that the Zodiac was displaying its "candels," when Criseyde went to rest in her father's bright tent.[15] This corruscating picture is the strongest of reminders that the term of her promise is approach-

115

ing its end. In the following stanza, he states that, abed, she turned over in her
mind

> The wordes of this sodeyn Diomede,
> His grete estat, and perel of the town,
> And that she was allone and hadde nede
> Of frendes help,

and thus fully determined to remain. The prudential motivation here indicated replaces the prepoderantly sexual implied in the last two stanzas of
Boccaccio's Part VI.[16] In these, the Italian described Diomede as tall, fair of
person, young, fresh and very pleasing, strong and haughty, conversationally
disposed, and prone to love; then remarked that these things, "le quai cose,"
pondered by Criseida after his call cooled in her the wish to return and
that new hope partly routed her torment. Chaucer, in his next stanza, the
one in which he invents a morning visit, ascribed the rout of torment to that
call, noting that Diomede stilled her sighs and finally relieved her of most
of her pain.[17] The sketch of the rival, not used here, suggested the insertion of
all three portraits before the visit, as already noted, and contributed the
particular of loquacity to that of the Greek.

Having given Diomede three occasions to press his suit—on the ride to
camp, on the day promised for return, and on the next—instead of the one
allowed him by Boccaccio on her fourth day in camp, Chaucer has been at
greater pains than his author to motivate Criseyde's defection.[18] Before he
brings us back to Troilus for his experiences on and after the promised day,
our poet draws on Benoit for details of the lady's progressive inclination to
Diomede and for her sorrow at thus falsing the Trojan and resolve to compensate by fidelity to the Greek, and then speaks *in propria persona* on her
behalf.

He mentions gifts of hers to Diomede—the bay steed he had won for her
from Troilus, a brooch which had been the latter's present, and a sleeve from
her wardrobe to serve as pennon—and relates that she showed pity and kindness to the present suitor when he was wounded by the old. The first and
third of the gifts and the favor shown to the disabled warrior were recorded
by Benoit, while the second gift was implied in Part VIII of the *Filostrato*
through Troiolo's discovery of his brooch on Diomede's captured garment.[19]
Chaucer's notice of it here, which prepares for its turning up with the
captured vestment much later on, is accompanied by the mild censure "and
that was litel nede." The gratuitous affront, thus underlined, to Troilus' memory is offset somewhat by the compassion reported for Diomede, though that
boded as ill for his predecessor—the many tears for his bleeding wounds and
careful tendance of them. However guilty, she has not lost her womanly

responsiveness to the immediacies of suffering. As to whether she rebestowed her love along with her pity Chaucer will not commit himself but puts the onus of asserting this ultimate disloyalty upon his authorities,

> Men seyn—I not—that she yaf hym hire herte.

Remarking that "the storie telleth us" no woman ever sorrowed more than Criseyde did on forsaking Troilus, he gives her a soliloquy adapted from parts of the long one which Benoit devised for Briseïda immediately after he had reported her moved by the wounds of Diomede.[20] Criseyde foresees that she will be in disfame to the world's end, particularly among women, for her betrayal of one of the gentlest and worthiest of men. Since, however, it is too late to amend in that quarter, she promises herself pathetically to be constant to the new lover,

> To Diomede algate I wol be trewe.

She bids the old godspeed,

> As for the gentileste, trewely,
> That evere I say, to serven feythfully,
> And best kan ay his lady honour kepe,

promises him "frendes love" and her "good word," admits that she is forsaking one who is "gilteles," and ends with a curtain line as poignantly effective as Pandarus' on the night of consummation was comically so:

> But al shal passe; and thus take I my leve.

Having presented her thus appealingly contrite, our poet credits her with some resistance and makes such capital as he can of her compunction.[21] No author specifies the length of time between her meeting and her surrendering to Diomede, he says, and, though the Greek wooed her straightway, he had more to do to win her. He will not chide her further than the record necessitates and would excuse her, if he could, because of her sorrow for untruth.

But excuse her he cannot, for he must follow the record if he is to have a tragedy. However remorseful, she must be left to carry out her guilty decision as the human instrument of Troilus' destined fall. Chaucer must devote the rest of the book to the hero's progressive miseries, of which her sin is the cause. To insure due empathy for the sufferer, he will keep them generally as acute as in the *Filostrato* and consequently as evidential of the magnitude of that sin. At one point, he will supplement the original to her discredit, inventing a letter for her which compounds guilt with disingenuity. In this very belated reply to missives from Troilus, Criseyde presumes to censure him for impatience, excuses her tarrying on the grounds of gossip about their love and of rumor, admitted to be unbelievable, of infidelity on his part, and ends with a promise of return, which cannot but be delusive however consolatory in intent.

Her change in course, begun with complacence to Diomede on their ride and ending in these unpleasant evasions to Troilus, has long been one of the most debated phenomena of Chaucer's poem. At least as productive of the necessary ironies as Criseida's defection in the *Filostrato*, it is not as convincing as hers, perhaps, on the plane of characterization. Boccaccio, having made his heroine from the start a quester for sexual satisfaction, could plausibly bring her from sorrow for one man to interest in another within the span of a single day. Our poet, who has given the lady pretensions at least to sublimated love, is for that reason less plausible, some have said, when he comes to the shift even though he develops it more gradually than the Italian.

Professor Cook argued that Chaucer's characterization of her was consistent, but on the vulnerable premise that it was uniformly pejorative. In his view, the poet adhered faithfully to the traditional representation of the lady as a baggage, presenting her as despicable *ab ovo*—begotten by a traitor, unfilial to him, calculating in her acceptance of Troilus, prone to illicit love, invariably politic, concerned for the appearance only of morality, and, in consequence of all this, naturally unfaithful at last.[22]

Professor Tatlock, holding that the poet considerably elevated the heroine in her time of prosperity, was of the opinion that he handled her sudden fall without primary concern for truth to her individual psyche, though perhaps with a moral implication: "Chaucer's purpose here may well have been to promote not the lifelike but the dramatic. Yet a second purpose is also possible. . . . I am not at all sure that the fundamentally Catholic Chaucer . . . had not come to the feeling that it really was the nature of the first *amour* which led so quickly to the second." The morality, if intended, is implicit. There is no clear foreshadowing of her lapse from grace, according to Tatlock, no gradual development of weakness into treachery. As a man of his times, Chaucer could not be expected to present a personality in evolution, would feel obliged to keep the lady, though much changed by him, to her authentically chronicled downward course: "Further in early literature human character is apt to be conceived and presented as static and not changing; to be given two Criseyde's (as we pretty much are) is unusual, and a whole series of steps would be amazing. . . . But the chief reason is still more medieval. History and story had not yet made their declaration of mutual independence, and this traditional story to all practical intents was history."[23]

Professor Mizener expressed views in part ·resembling Professor Tatlock's

He hypothesized that Chaucer conceived of a character as "a group of un-changing fundamental qualities" and of the relation between the character and events in the narrative as "one of congruence rather than of cause and effect," and, so conceiving, worked for dramatic effect rather than for dis-covery of motivation. To achieve such effect in the betrayal, he fudged characterization a little; his procedure, according to Mizener, "leaves us knowing that Criseyde has betrayed Troilus and yet visualizing her, as we have from the start, as gentle, tender-hearted, loving, and honorable. In other words, Chaucer's arrangement is calculated to leave our sense of Criseyde's character as little affected as possible by our knowledge of her act, it does the best it can to prevent our substituting for the Criseyde we have known all along the character we must invent if we are successfully to imagine Criseyde's yielding to Diomede." [24]

Other scholars have granted that Chaucer elevated the heroine very con-siderably in her better times but held nonetheless that he attributed qualities to her in these times which can well account for her subsequent decline. If they do not stress the same traits as contributory to her fall, they are at one that he calls attention to flaws in her nature plainly and insistently enough to prepare for it. They concur that, when the devoted mistress of Troilus, she is potentially the encourager of Diomede, and, when the latter, still recog-nizably her old self, even if, as one of them would have it, progressively debased by association with Diomede.

Dr. Dodd emphasized self-interest and amorous temperament as the deter-minants of her behavior. Denying that indulgence with Troilus can be in-ferred to have worked a change in her system of values, he asserted that "in giving her love to Diomede, Criseyde did nothing which was not in accord with her nature and character as revealed in the first part of the poem. She shows the same tendency to decide matters in accord with her own inter-ests. . . . There is the same strong appeal to the amorous disposition as in the affair with Troilus. In short, the Criseyde of the latter part is the Criseyde of the earlier; only circumstances are changed." [25]

Professor Kittredge also rejecting the possibility of deterioration through her first affair, would consider her flaw to be, not a scheming bent nor pro-nounced sexuality, but the inability to say no: "As Cressida is at the be-ginning, such is she to the end; amorous, gentle, affectionate, and charming altogether, but fatally impressionable and yielding. Her strength of will is no match for her inconstant heart." [26]

Believing, like Kittredge, that she was uncontaminated by first love, disinterestedly enamored of Troilus, and most impressionable, C. S. Lewis pinpointed her vulnerability as fear: "Fortunately Chaucer has so emphasized

119

the ruling passion of his heroine, that we cannot mistake it. It is Fear. . . .
And from this Fear springs the only positive passion which can be permanent
in such a nature; the pitiable longing, more childlike than womanly, for
protection." As clinging vine she is contaminated by her new oak, according
to Lewis: "Such a woman has no resistant virtues that should delay her
complete degradation when once she is united with a degrading lover. The
same pliancy which ennobled her as the mistress of Troilus, debases her as
the mistress of Diomede. For when she yields, she yields all: she has given
herself to the Greek *tamquam cadaver,* and his vices are henceforth hers." [27]

Professor Kirby, while recognizing that her first lover was a model of
courtly virtues and her second not, saw no change in her: "It must be insisted
that Criseyde is the same person at the end of the poem that she was at
the beginning. . . . She finds herself in a strange place, friendless, indifferent to her father, fearful, amorous, beautiful, intensely interested in men.
She soon realizes the absolute impossibility of return and therefore decides
to make the best of things. What better proof than this is required to demon-
strate that she is an opportunist and that in no pejorative sense?" And he held
her behavior to be in character, not as proceeding from any one trait, but as
the resultant of many: "It is not merely fear nor pity nor affection, not
destiny nor disillusionment nor lonesomeness, not beauty nor common sense
nor passion, that provides the open-sesame to Criseyde, it is rather the combination of all these, and others, which helps us to condemn and condone our
heroine; above all, to understand and appreciate her . . . as Chaucer intended
we should." [28]

My own opinion of Chaucer's treatment of the heroine and what befalls
her is that it is designed to achieve maximum dramatic effect and yet to keep
her the same dividedly motivated person throughout and that it is successful
in both aims. Making his heroine even more compliant when with Diomede
than Boccaccio's sensual Criseida and the rival concomitantly less worthy
of favor than he was in the *Filostrato,* the poet intensifies the irony of dis-
placement of the exemplary hero. And he carries exposure of the Greek so
far that he creates the obverse of this irony, giving her a mere trifler for the
proven servant she has expediently forsaken. He adds a further irony and
makes her cognizant of it, as she perhaps is not of the other: that she who has
consented to the exchange to preserve her reputation is to incur and deserve
eternal obliquy. He achieves all these ironies, it seems to me, without sacrifice
of psychological verisimilitude. I hold with Dodd, Kittredge, Lewis, and
Kirby that his representation of Criseyde as a personality is self-consistent and,
with the last, that it educes plausible behavior from, not one, but a complex
of enduring traits. I would distinguish the being he portrays as an individual

of strong but divided concerns. Troilus can and does give his whole being to love, and Pandarus his to friendship. Criseyde, while capable of genuine attachment, cannot be oblivious to peripheral consequences of it for herself. Though directed more than a little by her heart, she would assure herself always that reason certifies its dictates to be safe and to her advantage. As long as fear or hope of consequences can be squared with generous impulse, all goes well—at least by the standards of courtly love. Timid in actuality and ready for an excuse to be kind, she is not one to controvert Pandarus' assertions that she must yield a bit to save Troilus' life and his own. Inclined to the prince on his merits, she is not less so for the justification, which conveniently occurs to her, that rebuff might incur a dangerous antagonism. When the exchange impends and calls for purchase of love with her good name, she forfeits the chance through well-meant, but not selfless, rationalization. With return to Troy closed by her own fears as well as by parental veto, she accepts the only alternative to loneliness and possible oppression, mindful as usual of herself, if now first to another's harm, and yet pitiful too—as always—with tearful compassion for the wounded Diomede and a considerable if profitless residue for Troilus forsaken. And the residue persists some time apparently, for pity seems to have been a motive for her tardy letter according to Chaucer—"I take it so." If its yield therein is only deceit, the fault may be attributed to circumstances rather than to the baneful influence of Diomede as Lewis speculated. Once committed to writing, she must prevaricate to spare the remnants of Troilus' hope and of her long cherished reputation, though she might indeed have lied with more restraint. The habit of shifting responsibility for what she has willed, so innocently amusing in scenes with her uncle, continues operative but, under changed conditions, to distasteful effect. The letter is certainly the low as well as the last point of her course, but, however low, a credible terminus, as well as a powerful reinforcement of irony at the cost of the already miserable Troilus.[29]

Attrition of the Lover's Hopes

W ITH Criseyde to be heard from no more except by letter, Chaucer brings on Troilus all hopeful of her return on the tenth day. As Boccaccio did in his Part VII, he traces the hero's decline from this fond optimism into a despair so enervating as to confine him to his chamber.

In Part VII, three sequences of events were presented at length and the periods severally following them in short space. Troiolo invented excuse after excuse for his mistress' tardiness on the tenth day while he was awaiting her beyond the city gate, and he returned to it, still trustful, on the eleventh. Thereafter his hopes inevitably faded. Dreaming one day of the tearing out of the mistress' heart by a boar, he interpreted this as a supplantation, attempted suicide, and, when kept from it by Pandaro, wrote a letter, at his friend's suggestion, to test her. Since she did not answer, he became still more grief-stricken and took to bed. A caller, Deifobo, surprised him in amorous lament, and sped to other brethren to tell them of the affair thus uncovered and to be overheard in his turn by Cassandra; dispatched with other ladies by the menfolk to console Troiolo, she presumed instead to chide him for involvement with the lowly Criseida and was paid back with contumely. As days passed after this contretemps, the prince recovered strength, though not good spirits.

In the corresponding range of his Book V, not much more than half as long as Part VII,[1] Chaucer contrives to build up an impression of necessity, while eliminating all circumstances prejudicial to the dignity of the hero and to the tragic elevation now requisite. Compressing the first sequence and its aftermath only moderately, he preserves the irony of the prince's self-deluding hopes on the tenth and eleventh days and the pathos of his subsequent relinquishment of them. In the second, he adapts the dream to new purposes, omits the attempt at suicide and the consequent humiliation for the paladin of physical thwarting by his friend, and compresses the letter without sacrifice of poignancy. He substitutes a single episode for the third sequence, perfectly functional as that was not. Since he has made use of Deifobo in the ascending action, he dispenses with him here. His hero, when bedridden, summons Cassandre to interpret the boar dream, is enlightened as to the past and its implications for him, and disputes the central issue of Criseyde's truth, not the peripheral one of her social acceptability. Cured by rage at his sister, he quits his bed, not days after her going as in the *Filostrato*, but forthwith.

As Boccaccio developed the first of the three stages, he made the ironic most of the conflict between Troiolo's will to believe and the logic of hard fact. In his full account of the tenth day, he complemented the lover's fantasies with scepticism on the part of the friend, and, in the digest of later days, reduced the prince to despair as abject as these rationalizations had been extravagant. Troiolo, having gone to and through the gate at hour unspecified, kept watch with Pandaro till past midday and, after an intermission, watch again till past nightfall. He comforted himself with the notions, successively, that her fond parent was detaining her, that she was waiting for the cover of darkness, that a surge of happiness in his bosom forecast her appearance, and, at last, that her promise had been, not to return on the tenth day, but to do so after ten, that is, on the day still to come. The alleged premonition of her coming moved Pandaro to cynical reflection and inward laughter. Disappointed on the eleventh, which he also spent outside the gate, Troiolo could not but grieve though experiencing revivals of hope for some time thereafter. Then he lapsed into tears, and, suffering jealousy as well as desire, lost appetite, slept poorly, and shunned all company. He became so wan and sad of face and so debilitated as to call down upon himself the unwelcome solicitude of father, brothers, and sisters.

Except for the slight modifications now to be mentioned, Chaucer reproduces this chronicle with substantial fidelity.[2] Time-minded, he brings us back to Troilus still in that "ilke nynthe nyght," in which he left him some four hundred lines before, and specifies that the prince sent for Pandarus betimes —as Phebus was mounting in the east,

> And Nysus doughter song with fressh entente.

Metamorphosed for betrayal of her father, the lark is a proper harbinger of the day of Criseyde's breach of compact, as the swallow, the outraged Proigne, was for that day, long past, in which Pandarus began the fatal intrigue.[3] With concern also for place, Chaucer posts the friends, not outside the wall this morning, but on it as a better point of vantage, and he visualizes Troilus in suspenseful behavior there on both the tenth and the eleventh days:

> And fer his hed over the wal he leyde;
>
> And up and down, by west and ek by este,
> Upon the walles made he many a wente.[4]

He gives Pandarus the practical excuse of dinner for the intermission of watch after midday on the tenth, which the hero offered in the French prose translation of the *Filostrato*.[5] Irony, which Boccaccio kept on the human level, our poet extends to the destinal by observing of the friends after this recess:

> Fortune hem bothe thenketh for to jape![6]

To continue lunar reckoning, an effective time-binder of earlier episodes of his, Chaucer makes Troilus recall Criseyde's promise of return before the moon should pass through the Lion and take comfort that the period thus defined had another day to run. It is comfort as specious, of course, as Troiolo derived from twisting his lady's commitment in terms of days.[7] The poet reproduces all circumstances of the hero's pining but his tears, and objectifies that of weakness of limb by giving him a staff for support.[8]

Dashing of hope by actuality, the ironic essence of this stage of the action, Boccaccio continued into the next. Moved to suicide by the dream, which he thought divinely inspired, his hero took heart again from counsel of Pandaro but only to be confirmed in grief by application of that counsel. The beast which Troiolo visioned charging out of a wood to stand over Criseida and rip out her heart, he correctly identified as Diomede, on the ground that the latter had a boar for his crest in memory of his grandfather's triumph in Calydon. And the lover as rightly assumed from her complacency under violence that her affections went with the heart. Pandaro, to whom he confided this interpretation, prevented ill consequence, wresting a knife from the grief-enfeebled warrior and forcing him to sit down to receive a lecture. In it, he rebuked the attempt at suicide as a breach of friendship; argued that interpretation of the dream, as of all others, was dubious; and counselled that, if Troiolo should find his fears to be true and wish therefore still to die, he should seek his end, not by his own hand, but in honorable battle against the Greeks with the counsellor beside him. Impressed by this seeming common sense, though atremble still with rage and full of tears and sobs, the prince confessed hastiness and asked how he might check the dream. Pan-

124

daro suggested that he test Criseida by letter; failure on her part to respond would signify desertion; an answer, according to its nature, either that or the opposite. She might, he said, have good reason for tarrying.

Troiolo composed a long epistle forthwith. Mention in it of the lapse of forty days since parting determines the time of the episode. Beginning humbly, he wrote that as her servant, he dared not complain whatever the justification to do so. He presumed, nevertheless, to hypothecate a new love as the likeliest explanation of her tardiness. And he gave a circumstantial account of his miseries—the weeping and loss of sleep and appetite consequent to this suspicion, avoidance of social pleasures, and tantalizing preoccupation with the quarter in which she dwelt, the mountains encircling it, and the waters and the sun privileged to repair thither as he was not. Ingratiatory enough to express concern for her possibly matching unhappiness, he besought her return or some assurance of it. He threatened suicide if left hopeless and called attention to his tear blots as evidence of present woe. Well calculated though it was to inspire pity, the letter brought no answer for many days. Troiolo took silence as a confirmation of his dreams, grieved therefore, yet went on hoping.

Chaucer cuts and modifies, with past and future in mind as well as the present.[9] He alters the dream to oppose it to an early one which he has added and trims the dreamer's exegesis to leave room for an interpretation by Cassandre later on. To spare him even momentary loss of face, he eliminates the suicide prevented and censured by the friend. And he edits the letter to perfect the hero in loverly decorum, refining thought and word so that the victim now on the way to immolation and soon to reach it may appear spotless to the courtly eye.

In Chaucer's version of the dream, the boar is not ravishing the lady's heart but drowsing through her caresses. Such easiness, whether it implies satiety or not, is consonant with the nonchalant reflections attributed by our poet to Diomede on the ride to camp and between that occasion and his first call. And it contrasts with the gallant behavior of the eagle of Criseyde's slumbers of a May long past. In the dream before the affair, which Chaucer devised for her under inspiration of the one given Troiolo after it in the *Filostrato*,[10] the bird seized her heart and, more generous than the boar, replaced it with his own. Now that Criseyde has abandoned the treasure freely given by the eagle Troilus, she must wheedle the boar, it appears, for such poor substitute as he may choose to lend. Waking from the dream of her abasement, Troilus avows it to be from the gods as Troiolo had asserted his to be[11] and, like him, draws the inevitable conclusion of betrayal. But he does not follow the latter in identifying the beast as Diomede. If granted this insight, he would have small reason to call on his sister for an exegesis as Chaucer is to make him do.

As for self-destruction, he does no more here than mention it as a possibility. Why was he kept from attempting suicide like Troiolo? Professor Praz argued that Chaucer rejected the incident because it somewhat duplicated the hero's preparation to kill himself when he believed his swooning lady to be dead.[12] It seems unlikely, however, that the poet would object to the parallelism as such, since he created the closely parallel sequences at the houses of Deiphebus and Pandarus and gave the lover's dream a twin in Criseyde's. What he found inappropriate, I suggest, was the humiliation of the prince. He had not scrupled, indeed, to make Troilus a comic pawn of his friend in the sequences just mentioned, a timid and hypersensitive lover who must be coached in everything and even lifted into his lady's bed. But that was in the ascending action. Now near the end, Chaucer, I think, would guard the prince's dignity, insure him the stature which he must have to die a tragic hero. The poet could and did accept the enfeeblement of the lover in this late period but not the shame to which weakness exposed him. He would not let us see the paladin bereft of weapon by the fameless confidant nor compelled to listen to him in impotent and tearful rage. Having dropped the business of suicide, he was obliged to prune the confidant's remarks since most of them concerned it. All that he kept, and that changed in detail, was the argument that the boar dream—as every other—defied positive interpretation.[13] He sacrificed a bit of heroism, the friend's offer to die with his master in battle against the Greeks. But he had provided compensation much earlier by attributing to him an even grander gesture, the offer to risk his kinsmen's lives as well as his own in rescue of Criseyde.[14]

Chaucer's hero, like Boccaccio's, asks his friend how he may resolve suspicion created by the dream, is counselled to sound out his mistress with a letter, and proceeds immediately to write one. As on previous occasions, he is milder than Troiolo and less insistent. Like him, he promises to eschew complaint against her as temerity unbecoming a servant. And though he does not keep the promise, he violates it less flagrantly than his model. He abstains from the hypothesis of a rival, which Troiolo impolitically set down. He conveys as much solicitude in wishes for her well-being as the latter in concern expressed for her possible unhappiness. Trading on her pity as he must under the circumstances, he does so with more restraint, however, than Troiolo. He cites only tears and loss of health in evidence of present woe and the second most briefly. And though he indicates in his plea for a reply favorable or unfavorable that the former will mean his death, he does not threaten suicide. Mention in Troiolo's letter of the lapse of forty days since the heroine's departure is changed in Troilus' to an indication of the passage of two months. This emendation makes the plea for mercy ironically coincident with Criseyde's final abandonment of intent to return:

> But God it wot, er fully monthes two,
> She was ful fer fro that entencioun![15]

More susceptible to pity, it appears, than Criseida, though equally disloyal, Chaucer's heroine answers promptly. Her letter, as Chaucer summarizes it, is the same in essence as the other's tardy response, which Boccaccio digested at a later point.[16] It contains assurances of eventual return as well as of present affection, which our poet characterizes as "but botmeles bihestes." Understandably, it fails to hearten Troilus. Like Troiolo, who had had no reply from Criseida at this juncture, he pines so much that he must take to bed.

The last sequence in Part VII of the *Filostrato* carried the bedridden lover through a call paid by his brother to the squabble with Cassandra, which was badly off key for tragedy and, though productive of irony, productive of it from a side issue. Deifobo came upon him as he was apostrophizing Criseida and surmised the liaison. Too tactful to apprize him of this deduction, he communicated it to other brothers that they might send women of the family to divert the sufferer—and, inadvertently, to Cassandra, who chanced to be within earshot. When in the sickroom with many ladies, she disclosed the affair and branded it a mésalliance. The exposure nettled Troiolo, and the disparagement of his mistress stung him to the quick. He briefly denied that he had compromised her, then upheld at length her worthiness of any great man's heart, arguing that virtue constituted nobility and that hers was so abundant as to make her more royal than his snobbish sister.

There was dramatic irony, of course, in his exaltation of the undeserving. Yet the issue of the lady's faith, which should be the pivot of the irony, was not in debate. Cassandra's sneer at the rascality and inconsequence of the father was not predictive of the daughter's treachery. And Troiolo's censures of gossiping and class consciousness, because valid as generalities, deflected irony in some part from himself to his sister—from the self-deception of protagonist to the pointless discomfiture of a minor figure.

Abashed into silence, she was glad to leave the chamber, and she never returned to it as her companions were to on subsequent days. Troiolo at last grew strong enough to quit it, accustomed as he became to grief and eager again for battle. He had also the meager consolation of a letter belatedly sent him by Criseida, which, as Boccaccio summarized it, was all temporization.

In the *Troilus*, the hero's visitations by Deifobo and Cassandra and her fellows are replaced by private conference of his with the sister, a substitution much shorter than the original.[17] Chaucer's prince, like Troiolo, takes to bed sometime after the boar dream, though, unlike him, he has had a prompt reply to his letter. Preoccupied with the dream, which he takes to be a revelation from Jove, he summons Cassandre to him, relates it, and asks her to interpret it. This recourse cannot be held against him as a violation of the canon of secrecy.[18] True, he is implying interest in Criseyde through his concern for a dream about her, whether he admitted cohabitation or not. But he is not risking the honor of his mistress, for he is consulting the Trojan analogue to a Christian holy woman, a prophetess who goes by and deserves the name of Sibille,[19] not the mean eavesdropper and gossiper of the *Filostrato*.

Cassandre's exegesis proves her a seer and, through its convincing wisdom, does much to strengthen the theme of destiny.[20] She begins by telling her brother that, to come to an understanding of the dream, he must,

> a fewe of olde stories heere,
> To purpos, how that Fortune overthrowe
> Hath lordes olde.

After this ominous hint that the goddess has some misery in store for him, she recounts the slaying of the Calydonian boar by Meleagre and its unhappy consequences and notes the descent of Tideus from the slayer. Thus far— through four stanzas—Chaucer has given her words in direct discourse, re-sorting to Ovid's *Metamorphoses* for the affair in Calydon.[21] In the next four stanzas, derived from summaries of the *Thebaid* of Statius and from that poem itself,[22] she is reported in indirect discourse on the exploits of the leaders in the Theban War and particularly on their deaths—Tideus' in-cluded. Her account of the War, though not contributing to the identifica-tion of the boar, serves to impress upon Troilus—and upon the audience—the grim potential of the forces of destiny. In a final stanza, in direct discourse again, she identifies the animal as Diomede, Tideus' son, and makes the bald assertion that the rival is "inne" and her brother "oute."

Troilus controverts the central point thus raised of the heroine's faithless-ness as hotly as Troiolo the immaterial one of her social unacceptability. Though Cassandre has merely particularized what he has already feared, he attacks her pretensions to divination and declares that she might as well have ventured to accuse the paragon Alceste as to malign Criseyde. The wrong is entirely on his side and the irony, in consequence, all at his expense, as artistically it should be.[23] Cassandre departs without the guilty embarrassment noted of her in the *Filostrato*. Made whole by anger, Troilus straightway leaves his bed, purposing to find evidence for or against his sister's pronounce-ment.

Finale

ALL too soon the hero has proof positive of supplantation by Diomede. He seeks to kill him in battle, but dies—frustrate of this vengeance—by another's hand. To complete the action with these misfortunes and to moralize upon his poem and give it valediction, Chaucer employs the same number of lines, it so happens, as Boccaccio took to do the like.[1] Yet his reportage of events diverges from his author's now and again, and his moral summation and leave-taking of what he has created are radically different from the latter's of his production. Resorting to other masterpieces and boldly combining adapted with invented elements, he gives us a finale consonant with the story as he has reinterpreted it—a loftier ending for a more ambitious whole. His creative imagination has not flagged. *Finis coronat opus.*

It will be convenient to take up the ending in two segments—the first and longer mainly narrative and dependent in large part upon the *Filostrato,* the second much more independent of it and with less of narration than of other elements. In the former, V. 1541-1771, he brings the lover from suspicion to certainty of betrayal and thence into combat with Diomede, as Boccaccio did in the first twenty-six stanzas of his Part VIII. In the latter segment, V. 1772-1869, he fashions a complex mosaic, drawing on the *Filostrato* still but reordering, transmuting, and supplementing it with the greatest freedom. Boccaccio recorded the hero's demise in stanza 27 of Part VIII, declaimed on it in stanza 28, and cautioned young men about mistresses in the remaining stanzas, 29-33, of that part; then wound up his poem in the eight stanzas of Part IX by commissioning it ambassador to his own lady. In the first two stanzas of V. 1772-1869, Chaucer addresses his female constituency, apologizing for himself and then giving counsel which is the obverse of his

129

author's to young men. In the remaining twelve, termed by scholars the Epilog, he apostrophizes his poem with an artist's solicitude; then chronicles the hero's death, traces the ascent of his soul, and declaims on his end; admonishes the young of both sexes to forsake earthly love for heavenly; disprizes pagan worship; humbly commends the poem to Gower and Strode; and concludes with prayer in noblest Christian phrase.

The story line at Chaucer's disposal in the first twenty-six of his author's Part VIII ran as follows. Linking with Part VII by mention of sorrow already felt by the lover, Boccaccio remarked that it was now aggravated by the death of Ettore. He did not elaborate on this event, but went on to say that his hero persisted in love, writing Criseida many letters and even contemplating a visit to camp in pilgrim's disguise. The letters brought response but such as did not allay but increased the writer's suspicions. And chance presently supplied proof that he had interpreted the boar dream aright. In the first episode of the part, brief but crucial, the prince heard that Deifobo was parading with a vestment ravished from Diomede; overtook his brother; and, examining the prize, found upon it a brooch which he had given Criseida on his last night with her. In the immediately succeeding and longer episode, Troiolo lamented with Pandaro, where we are not told but presumably in the privacy of his own dwelling. Having expatiated on the lady's sin, he swore to grieve her by killing Diomede if he might, chid Giove for inaction and implored him to kill her. Then, in reproach to Pandaro for having prevented his suicide and challenged his identification of the boar, he asserted the divine origin of dreams and wished that he had died after dreaming. He promised, however, to wait for death in battle as his friend had suggested, and declared that he would not mind going to the other world if he could send Diomede before him. In a quandary, Pandaro managed only a short and disjointed reply—that he blamed Criseida to the utmost, that he had acted as he had for love of his friend and at the sacrifice of his own honor, and that he prayed the gods to disable her for further sinning. Fortuna still ran her course, Boccaccio ironically observed, despite such lamentations; she loved Diomede and left Troiolo to weep. There were many violent encounters between them of the latter's seeking, but the goddess did not permit either to dispatch the other.

Though preserving the sequence of events, Chaucer works some meaningful changes in their presentation. He makes Ettore's death the occasion for solemn pronouncements on destiny. He emphasizes the heroine's untruth by a letter in illustration and de-emphasizes the suspiciousness of the hero. He tempers the prince's animosity toward her after the confirmation of betrayal.

And he compensates for his failure in vengeance against Diomede by exalting his general prowess.

As for Chaucer's elaboration of matter before the first episode,[2] it begins with enforcement by the poet himself of the lesson in the fall of princes which he has made Cassandre offer to her brother. Fortune now plucked Troy's feathers he observes, describing her in Dantean terms as Jove's agent for change in statehood as in all things.[3] Fate had unalterably determined an end for Ector he goes on to say, and then tells—after Benoit[4]—of its eventuation, namely death by the hand of Achilles, not in fair combat, but with the victim off his guard. The death implicitly foreshadows Troilus',[5] since that is to be at the same hand. And in adapting the mention by Boccaccio of the one brother's sorrow for the other, Chaucer links his hero expressly with Ector by calling him next to the deceased in worthiness. As for the mourner's persistence in love, Chaucer accepts from the *Filostrato* his consideration of pilgrim's disguise[5] and his actual recourse to correspondence. Having epitomized the latter in Boccaccio's fashion, he replaces the terse summary of the lady's response, "parole belle e promesse grandi sanza effetto," with a directly quoted epistle of six stanzas. Except for a flourish adapted from an early missive of Troiolo's and one or two from Criseida's answer to that missive,[6] it is all new with Chaucer. And, as argued in Section 9, he has made it psychologically plausible for his heroine. Circumstances, one gathers from this letter, have brought out the defects of her nature but not changed it substantially. Still concerned for appearances as in her gentle encounters with Pandarus, she is now driven to graceless expedients to keep face. Having accepted Diomede for selfish reasons and at the risk of her good name, she reproaches Troilus for egocentric impatience and, to justify her delay, alleges gossip about their erstwhile love and gossip also about infidelity on his side. Still touched by pity, as the narrator himself suggests, she can yield to it only so far as to keep hope alive with assurances of an impossible return. The letter heightens irony and compassion for both sender and recipient—for Criseyde as reduced to mean shifts by her own weakness, for Troilus as paid off in such base coin. And his reaction, as presented by Chaucer, carries irony still further. Though shaken by it as Troiolo was by Criseida's equivocations, he cannot quite believe her false, as that less trustful lover did his mistress.

Chaucer accomplishes disillusionment in the episode of the brooch, taken over, with some change but not enlargement, from the *Filostrato*.[7] As remarked in Section 9, he has prepared us for the appearance of this keepsake on a garment of Diomede's by mention of it in Book V as one of Criseyde's gifts to that prince. He cites Lollius here for Deiphebus' capture of the garment, as, in Book I, for the text of Troilus' first song.[8] Having eliminated the lover's identification of the dream boar earlier in Book V, he cannot present the discovery, in Boccaccio's vein, as the clincher of this specific inference but treats it as a resolution of uncertainty.

In the succeeding episode, which, unlike Boccaccio but like the French prose translator, he specifically places in the lover's home, he shortens and changes his complaint, in part at least, to the lamenter's advantage, while keeping the confidant's response essentially as it was.[9] After he has faithfully rendered the indictment of the lady with which Troiolo began, Chaucer tones down the unpleasant animus of the following wishes. His hero would make Diomede's "sydes blede"[10] as Troiolo would try the sword against him, but not expressly, as the latter, to bring sorrow to the mistress. Troiolo besought Giove to do away with Criseida after wondering whether His just glance was turned elsewhere and His lightning in repose; Troilus speaks to the same effect but less insistently:

> "O God," quod he, "that oughtest taken heede
> To fortheren trouthe, and wronges to punyce,
> Whi nyltow don a vengeaunce of this vice?"

Like Troiolo, Chaucer's hero, rebukes the confidant for scepticism about dreams and proposes to die in battle but naturally does not refer to the thwarting of suicide, since that incident has been suppressed, nor to the friend's counsel to die in war, if die at all, which was contained in it. And though he might, he does not entertain Troiolo's compensative thought of sending Diomede to the shades before him. Pandarus, so ready of word in happier times, can find no more so say than Pandaro—can offer no solace but only excuse himself, renounce his niece, and wish her dead.

After shaping this episode, Chaucer moderately expands Boccaccio's very brief account of the lover's subsequent frustrations.[11] Taking over the comment of that authority on Fortuna's favor and disfavor respectively to rival and hero, he adds to it a generalization anticipative of the otherworldly conclusion of his own poem:

> Swich is this world, whoso it kan byholde:
> In ech estat is litel hertes reste.
> God leve us for to take it for the beste!

He cites "olde bokes," for the knighthood and might shown by Troilus in many battles[12] before he renders what Boccaccio had to say about the prince's futile encounters with Diomede;[13] then refers us specifically to Dares[14] for worthy deeds of the hero lest there be any doubt of his capacity. This reference terminates the first of the two segments which constitute our poet's finale.

132

We may approach the second by examining, somewhat more particularly than at the outset of the section, the correspondent matter in the *Filostrato*. The stanza after the one given to the encounters with Diomede set forth that few Greeks who opposed Troiolo came out alive but that Achille slew him on a day when he had killed more than a thousand. The next iteratively proclaimed: such end had Troiolo's love for Criseida, such end his sorrow, such end his splendor, and such end his vain hope in her. The next five stanzas, the last of Part VIII, are cautionary to young men. In direct address, the author prayed them, "per Dio," to bridle their steps to evil appetency and to mirror themselves in Troiolo's love, the history of which would keep them from trusting too lightly in women. The young lady, he generalized, eager for lovers and vain of beauty, is amoral and inconstant; many of the sex are additionally objectionable because of pride of birth. Then defining the acceptable feminine type he counselled that all exemplars might be pursued but, still, that choice should not be hasty. He bade the youths pray to Amore that He grant Troiolo peace in His domain and themselves the boon of loving so wisely that they might not incur death. In Part IX, the poet apostrophized his "canzon." He and this product of his own woeful love had brought their bark to port after a dangerous voyage. Now it must seek out his lady to disclose his sorrows and to beseech her either to return or to pronounce his death.

After citing Dares for the achievements of the hero, Chaucer breaks tension with two stanzas, also original, addressed to the ladies.[15] He beseeches them not to be angry with him for Criseyde's shame, implying innocence of it as a mere translator and giving assurance that, if it be their pleasure, he will write of the virtuous Penelope and Alceste. This proposal, he goes on to say, he is making primarily, not for men, but for women, who are betrayed through false folk, and he bids God give the latter sorrow. "Beth war of men," he concludes, "and herkneth what I seye!" A deft reversal, certainly, of Boccaccio's caution against the fair sex, and gallant however tongue-in-cheek.[16] Here Chaucer has resumed his genial intimacy qua narrator; he appears the love poet, once more, who would be en rapport with his audience—deferential to its tastes, sympathetic with its trials, disarmingly ingenuous on the surface if most equivocal beneath. Thus toned, the address is a grateful relief after the grim chronicle of Troilus' misfortunes. On the other side, as a transition to the Epilog if not perhaps even a part of it,[17] the passage is provocative in effect and presumably by intention. It challenges speculation because it is ambivalent—if contrary in one aspect to otherworldly precept soon to follow, as confirmative of it in another. The offer to write of Penelope and Alceste, prospectus, that is, of the *Legend of Good Women*, indicates that the poet will so far jeopardize his present conclusion against sex love as to make love attractive through its product, the constancy of the heroines, but will substantiate the warning, no less inevitably, through the martyrdoms to which that devotion brings them. That is to say, what he has done with the love of Troilus, he will do over again in some fashion with the loves of faithful women. Are we to infer that the case against earthly passion has not been settled for him, despite his unequivocal pronouncement to the young, and may therefore be reopened with some lingering hope of reversal? Or are we to infer that it has been but that the love convicted *sub specie aeternitatis* is still fascinating to him for its evanescent beauty—as well as, presumptively, to his female clientele? The latter view seems indicated. It is the reading called for by his self-dramatization here as elsewhere, the one aesthetically appropriate at this juncture and consonant with the warm yet discriminating humanity of the whole.

With the ladies propitiated, Chaucer turns to his opus now to make its way in the world:

> Go, litel bok, go, litel myn tragedye,
> Ther God thi makere yet, er that he dye,
> So sende myght to make in som comedye!
> But litel book, no makyng thow n'envie,
> But subgit be to alle poesye;
> And kis the steppes, where as thow seest pace
> Virgile, Ovide, Omer, Lucan, and Stace.

Apprehensive of the diversity of English and its spelling, he prays God, in the next stanza, that the poem may not be miswritten or mismetred and that, wherever read or sung, it be comprehended.[18] The anticipation of a comedy, like the forecast of the *Legend,* is a gesture of compensation, an implied evening of the balance; some work with a happy ending[19] is to complement the *Troilus* insofar as it ends unhappily, as that exalting women is to complement it with respect to its disparagement of them. The instructions given it are in the self-depreciatory vein which the narrator has affected from the outset. Terming himself only a "makere," a craftsman, that is, on the lowly plane typical of vernacular writing, he bids his "litel" piece eschew envy of other "makyng" and show reverence to "poesye"—the literature above this plane.[20] In so speaking, he has departed from Boccaccio's concluding apostrophe to the *Filostrato*[21] and turned instead to the valediction to the *Filocolo,* of which the former presumably reminded him, adapting from it expressions of the modesty traditional for authors.[22] As he goes on to voice concern for the transmission of his book, he manifests a pride in workmanship,[23] which qualifies his borrowed humility and is of this world worldly like his mentions of literary projects. Though mundane in spirit, such pride is not a denial

134

of the heavenly counsel to follow but an affirmation of its importance. The creator shows himself intensely serious about his work; we must respond in kind to its following and most exalted stanzas.

In the first of these, adapted from a stanza of the *Filostrato,* Chaucer brings the hero to his death.[24] Boccaccio recorded that few Greeks who braved the Trojan survived and that, one day, after he had dispatched more than a thousand, Achille slew him "miseramente." Our poet, having credited him with the death of thousands and likened him to Ector, concludes exclamatively:

> But weilawey, save only Goddes wille!
> Despitously hym slough the fierse Achille.

The linkage with Ector reinforces that made at the latter's death in glorification of the less famous brother. "Save only Goddes wille," though timeworn, is powerful in context as a formula of acceptance, implying faith as the answer to the mystery of wasted potentials.

In his next three stanzas, Chaucer traces the course of the hero's soul after its release from the body.[25] These come from the three in Boccaccio's *Teseida* on the course of Arcita's. The latter were inspired, in their turn, by the account of Pompey's in Lucan's *Pharsalia* and drew also upon the "Somnium Scipionis," that fragment of Cicero's *De re publica* preserved by Macrobius, and upon Dante's *Paradiso.*[26] Though Chaucer followed the *Teseida* quite closely, he certainly had the "Somnium" in mind and perhaps also the *Pharsalia* and *Paradiso.*[27] Like Arcita's, Troilus' soul rises to "the eighthe spere,"[28] sees the planets, and hears their music; contemplates the little, sea-embraced earth, and despises all that is terrestrial; sees the mourning beside its corpse and laughs at human folly; then goes to the place appointed for it by Mercurye. Modifications of the *Teseida* may be noted at two points. The depreciation of earth seen in perspective by Arcita,

> e ogni cosa da nulla stimare
> a rispetto del ciel,

is expanded, with recall of the "Somnium" and Boethius' *Consolation,* for Troilus, who, we are told:

> fully gan despise
> This wrecched world, and held al vanite
> To respect of the pleyn felicite
> That is in hevene above.[29]

And the terms for human folly, "vanitate" and "tenebrosa cechitate" are replaced by the single but more explicit "blynde lust"—appetency, that is, for temporal satisfactions, including, though not limited to, the delights of carnal love. In these stanzas, which seem to have been added to the first draft,[30] Chaucer affords Troilus the same illumination, after experience, as he provided for himself, the dramatized narrator, in the *Parlement of Foules,* before his vicarious contacts with love in the dream garden. As he claimed in early stanzas of the *Parlement,* he had been reading the "Somnium Scipionis" until bed- and dream-time and had learned from it that the Younger Scipio was visited by the Elder in sleep, shown earth and the heavens "from a sterry place," and advised to contemn this life. The celestial perspective at the end of the one poem of love, as that at the beginning of the other, is supplemental to close-up views of incident, confirming glimpses of misdirection, and, though not destroying impressions of love's beauties, establishing the compatible and necessary truth that they are fleeting.[31] In both cases, the reader is illuminated by the opposition of earth to universe; and, in the *Troilus,* the protagonist also, though in the *Parlement* the poet-dreamer gives no sign of clear understanding. With illumination, Troilus achieves the victory in defeat, the spiritual autonomy, expected of the tragic hero. It must be granted that he has not won it by wrestling with his adversities as the hero should. And consequently the crosses, while to be taken as deserved, cannot be further justified as directly productive of goods of the spirit. Still, there is warrant of a benevolent providence in his posthumous emancipation, and that is reconciling. Wherever "Mercurye sorted hym to dwelle"—and on that point we are not informed[32]—he repairs thither in a state of grace we may be sure. And moved by this transcendence, we are prepared to respond sympathetically to the narrator's counsel of renunciation.[33]

In the stanza after the insertion, Chaucer mourns the hero's demise in Boccaccio's fashion, chanting "Swich fyn" has Troilus for love, "Swich fyn" his "worthynesse," "estat real," "lust," and "noblesse" and then generalizes characteristically,

> Swych fyn hath false worldes brotelnesse![34]

In the next two, he calls upon the young and therefore amorous of both sexes to forsake the vanity of this world "that passeth soone as floures faire" and to give their love to the Creator and Redeemer, concluding

> For he nyl falsen no wight, dar I seye,
> That wol his herte al holly on hym leye.
> And syn he best to love is, and most meke,
> What nedeth feynede loves for to seke?

This appeal maintains the tension of the lover's death, whereas Boccaccio's exhortation to young men which it replaces,[35] is anticlimactically petty, how-

136

ever vital his personal experience may have made him think advice about mistresses to be. And the appeal is not merely an emotionally valid response to present circumstance. It continues and climaxes the opposition, strongly if intermittently developed, between the short and long views of human inclinations. True, the latter is now forthrightly recommended for the first time, but not inconsistently with all previous representations.[36] If this step is a long one, it is not the first in its direction. "Feynede loves" cannot but include the affair just ended, and the rejection of them therefore negates such apparent endorsements of this love as the narrator has permitted himself in the ascending action.[37] Yet the judgment is one which his presentation of events since Criseyde's yielding to the exchange has prepared us to consider. Further, the all-inclusive denigration of the world stresses its impermanence, and this threat to happiness has pervaded the last two books and been recognized on occasion in the earlier ones.

A stanza disprizing paganism[38] appropriately follows the Christian appeal and in its iterative rhetoric matches the "Swich fyn" stanza which precedes. With repeated "Lo here's" Chaucer points up the fruitlessness, demonstrated in the story, of reliance on the old gods and, with a final one, implies condemnation of pagan poetry as reproduced, supposedly, in the *Troilus*,

> Lo here, the forme[39] of olde clerkis speche
> In poetrie, if ye hire bokes seche.

As in the appeal, he is providing a corrective which follows logically from events and is therefore artistically sound, whether conditioned by extra-artistic factors or not.[40] His comment on pagan worship applies particularly, of course, to the hero, as the outstanding pietist, and suggests as a further cause of his misfortunes the inevitable one of his having been born before the Christian dispensation.[41] It is not an indictment of the poem but of the culture represented. A caution against the subject matter, it suggests an approach— a learning from error—which may be profitable. The assertion that the poem embodies "the forme of olde clerkis speche" is therefore not self-incriminating either seriously or ironically.[42] Indeed, as earlier professions of fidelity in translation, it shifts responsibility from the poet to his alleged sources. He has not been an advocate of error, he would have us believe, but a recorder of it and here at last a censorious one.

In the opening lines of the next stanza, he submits the poem for correction to "moral Gower" and "philosophical Strode."[43] It is conventional, of course, to make such an appeal.[44] But to address it to such men as these[45] is to imply confidence as to the essential merit of the work submitted. The request, whether sincere or *pro forma*, assumes that the product is worthy of their attention, is moral and philosophical to some degree though about a "feynede" love in pagan times.

The Epilog concludes with a prayer to Christ for one and all.[46] Exemplifying the resort to Him urged upon the young, it is an appropriate last stroke and, with Dante's verbal genius reinforcing Chaucer's,[47] a very beautiful one.

Scholars agree nowadays that the Epilog is a striking performance in itself and the great majority believe, as I do, that it is congruent with the rest of the poem. Among the minority, Professor Curry calls it "dramatically a sorry performance" and declares that "the poet, without having given the slightest hint of warning, suddenly denies and contradicts everything that has gone before in the poem," though he proceeds to say that "Considered by itself, the Epilog is a poem of great beauty."[48] Also of the minority, Professor Tatlock writes: "His sublimation of earthly to heavenly love and of pagan to Christian faith can leave no one unmoved," but goes on, "The feeling in the Epilog is in no way foreshadowed at the beginning or elsewhere; it does not illumine or modify; it contradicts."[49] The majority assert the compatibility of the Epilog in terms varying with their conceptions of the whole—Professor Malone, perhaps, as broadly as any: "It differs in point of view from the body of the poem, but the difference makes the whole richer and nobler than it could have been otherwise."[50]

Now that we have followed Chaucer in his adaptation of the *Filostrato* from statement of theme to final moralization, we may begin a more thorough analysis of aspects of his workmanship which have been distinguished here or there in this survey. In the next chapter, we shall compare his treatment of physical particulars in nonfigurative contexts with Boccaccio's and, also with that author's, his handling of the interrelated elements of time and the supernatural in such passages. Both poets' metaphors, similes, and the like of matter, time, and the supernatural are to be reserved to Chapter III, where they will be examined in conjunction with other associative figures.

CHAPTER II

Physical Particulars and
Time and the Supernatural

Preview

T HE sections of the chapter are devoted as follows to like elements in source and adaptation. Sections 2-5, to information given about the characters and their man-shaped environment which may affect our sensory imagination: 2, 3, and 4 respectively to material about age, person, or dress, about the wasting effects of passion and consequent possibilities of death, and about expressive behavior apparent to the eye; 5, to material about dwellings or other locales of action and about movement in them. Section 6, in order, to the mixture of the contemporaneous and the antique, to the timing of events, to the treatment of divine causation, and to the use of appearances in nature as reinforcements of idea or mood.

Chaucer, it will be seen, freely modifies and considerably enriches the *Filostrato* in all the areas above delimited. The trends in his procedure which will be brought out in the several sections may be anticipatively summarized as follows.

Referring less often than his author to the youthfulness of the heroine, he adds details about her person with emphasis upon muliebrity. He offers more particulars also about the appearance of the hero with complementary stress upon his manliness; and he notes his youth only in connection with strength and prowess, whereas Boccaccio, in more numerous and varied allusions to it, linked it rather with Adonis-like qualities. Chaucer adds a little to the one portrait of the rival in the source but not enough to make it more soldierly than the new companion portrait of the true lover. Leaving the confidant undescribed as in the source, he promotes him from cousin to uncle of the lady, and thus and in other ways suggests that middle age was at least approaching for him.

141

He gives her a fear of death so acute as to preclude her chancing it as an escape from anguish of mind or body and therein a new motive for temporization. He invents a feigned illness for the hero which stands, in some part, in comic opposition to his genuine attacks of love-sickness, and he transforms his swoon in parliament into one at his friend's house induced by hyper-romantic sensibilities and productive of results contrastingly burlesque. In the descending action, however, in which the lover must have the stature of a tragic victim, Chaucer spares him the indignity of physical subjugation by the fameless confidant. And he builds up his preoccupation with death from the very start, to the increase of our forebodings. Contrastingly, he gives a flippant turn to the rival's one mention of dying as hypothetically in prospect. The go-between he allows to be jocular about the plight of his lord, yet keeps him solicitous as he was in the *Filostrato* and inspires him to capitalize upon it more ingeniously for the persuasion of the beloved.

While leaving demonstrations of sorrow substantially as they were with weeping paramount among them, he significantly modifies behavior indicative of other emotions. As for the heroine's deportment, he purges it of resentment against her nation, forwardness with the first lover, and testiness with the second, and makes it more disingenuous yet more engagingly affectionate toward the seducing relative. He emphasizes the hero's dominance in the act of love to the credit of his masculinity, after he has intensified his conventional diffidence in courtship and attributed to him an equally chivalric modesty in the rejection of popular acclaim. He permits him to display warm affection toward his friend, but not, as Boccaccio made him do, through kissing and close embrace. He introduces symbolic aggressions for Diomede which contrast with the Trojan's meek carriage in wooing. He endows the go-between with a compelling vigor of behavior and an unerring knack for the gesture appropriate at the moment.

He is more exact than Boccaccio as to the locales of action and gives more details about them. Like him, however, he does not map Troy, diagram any of its buildings, nor itemize even a single room, but notes particulars of setting, now here now there, in connection with what is immediately transpiring. His fuller, if still economical, indications of background for individual scenes contribute to their verisimilitude, along with the clearer visualization, above noted, of the conduct of the actors. And these as they accumulate help to suggest that the whole story is a carefully factual piece of history, the more so as, however scattered, they are generally compatible with one another. Many of them—far more than in the source—attest an aristocratic mode of life, for the heroine especially, but also for her uncle, her prince, and his brother Deiphebus. The juxtaposition of apartments in the new locales, the houses

142

of the brother and the confidant, is such as to permit elaborate stratagems, while the lady's establishment is made commodious enough for a wide range of developments. The street, which Chaucer specifies to lead past it from the gate of Dardanus to the lover's palace, serves for his impressive parades in her sight.

Lastly, as to the interrelated elements of time and the supernatural. Chaucer heightens antique color by pretense to a classic source and enrichment of mythological allusion but contemporary color too by increase of Christian touches and the already mentioned particularization of dress, psychophysical response to love, and domestic settings. He revises the chronology of the action and makes it more precise. He achieves a boding sense of destiny far stronger than that conveyed in the original. And he exploits the phenomena of seasons and of night and day more often than Boccaccio and more arrestingly.

Through the changes summarized in the preceding paragraphs, our poet modifies characterization and enlarges the scope and significance of the story, while maintaining due semblance of reality for the medieval and even the modern reader. Dignified by Chaucer with a palace and manners of court and rendered more softly appealing, the heroine seems quite another woman. Made so tender as to faint at her tears, so doughty as to appear a Mars in armor, the hero now more perfectly exemplifies the romantic contrarieties of sensibility and prowess. His friend is individuated through vivacity of movement and gesture, as his rival is confirmed in type by forward behavior. The courtship, highly self-contained in the original, is brought into intimate association with a social environment; persuasion of the lady at her own house, at Deiphebus', and at Pandarus' goes on with bystanders just out of earshot. The protagonist, the mouthpiece in the *Filostrato* for notions of divine causation, is kept as emphatic as in the source upon the absolutism of Love and the mutability of Fortune and directed to the key issue of free will and necessity, though not permitted to resolve it. The narrator assures us *in propria persona* of the control of Fortune, Fates, and planets by a Supreme Being and signalizes His power, mediately exercised, both over the affair and the great war. The author's pronouncements on destinal forces, with those of the hero and occasional ones of the more earthbound heroine and confidant, build up an impression of inexorable fate essential for tragedy, yet do not destroy the also necessary one of individual freedom and responsibility. Most of the religious ideology is indifferently Christian or pagan, and hence neither alien nor anachronistic. Christian phrases, though frequent in the lines of the characters and the narrator, presumably would not register as anachronisms with the fourteenth-century public because of their unobtrusive familiarity, while the also frequent mythological allusions, because exotic, would be convincing of antiquity. The practices in love, and the physical appurtenances of living, medieval insofar as they are distinctive, could be taken as Trojan by a public innocent of archaeology. And many of them are not distinctive—as possible in one age as in another. A fusion of the dateless, the contemporary, and the past, Chaucer's Troy, like Shakespeare's, must have enforced belief when given to the world and can essentially command it still.

In each of the following sections of the chapter, all relevant matter from the *Filostrato* will be presented first; and then all from the *Troilus,* in parallel arrangement and with indication of what is and is not derived from the former. Since the known contributions of secondary sources to Chaucer's reworking of the *Filostrato* have been registered in Chapter I, notice of them will generally be limited to cross-reference to I in the notes. Dissection of the two poems into units as small as the phrase and even the single word will involve profuse citation of both in the notes. For reasons of economy, references to the *Filostrato,* which has been editorially numerated only by stanza, will be by stanza number without indication of the line or lines particularly at issue and hence inexact in all but the occasional cases in which all eight of a stanza are concerned. References to the *Troilus* can and ordinarily will be exact.

Age, Person, and Dress

I N this, as in the next two sections, we shall take up successively what relates to heroine, hero, rival, confidant, and traitorous priest in the Italian poem; then repeat the process with the English.

There are nine contexts in the *Filostrato* which signalize the lady's youth. She was called "giovinetta" by the narrator and Pandaro, "Giovane donna" by Troiolo and Diomede, and "una mia figliuola giovinetta" by Calcas.[1] Persuading her to an affair, the cousin adduced her time of life:

> ed a te, stando in vestimento bruno,
> giovane ancora, d'amar si concede;

and she argued with herself on the same score:

> Io son giovane, bella, vaga e lieta,
> vedova, ricca, nobile ed amata,
> sanza figliuoli ed in vita quiëta,
> perché esser non deggio innamorata?
>
> La giovinezza mia si fugge ogni ora,
> debbol' io perder sí miseramento?
>
> Chi mi vorrá se io c' invecchio mai?[2]

The narrator observed that she and Troiolo planned for ready satisfaction of their desires that they might use "la lieta gioventute" while it lasted.[3] But, at the end, he implied that the youthfulness which qualified her for love had its drawbacks by generalizing upon the fickleness and vainglory of the species "Giovane donna."[4]

As to her person, the most extended account of it is given, appropriately, in the scene in which Troiolo falls in love:

Ella era grande, ed alla sua grandezza
rispondeano li membri tutti quanti,
e 'l viso avea adorno di bellezza
celestiäle, e nelli suoi sembianti
quivi mostrava una donnesca altezza.[5]

There are suggestions here and there of delectable blondness. The narrator spoke of her "biondi crin" and "bianco petto," "fresco volto," "fresche guance e dilicate," and "occhi lucenti"; Troiolo, of her "bianco petto," "bel viso splendido e lucente," "chiaro visaggio," "dilicata faccia," and "fresca cera."[6]

Attestations of her beauty without reference to coloring or other quality are very numerous. Some of these put it beyond compare. Thus the narrator termed her "piú bella ch' altra creatura" and "piú ch' altra donna, bella."[7] Troiolo would have it that she was "avanza Pulissena d' ogni bellezza, e similmente Elena"; twice, that there was never so beautiful a lady as she; twice, that no lady was her equal in beauty or any other respect; that her countenance was unrivalled in beauty; and that her eyes were so too.[8] Pandaro called her face "bellissima."[9] And, eschewing superlatives, the narrator recognized her beauty in nine more contexts,[10] the hero in thirty more,[11] and the confidant in nine.[12] The lady conceded her own attractiveness as quoted above, and Diomede assured her of it in their one conversation.[13] The insistence that she was handsome, with the true lover most iterative, makes us feel physical endowment counted, and heavily—despite his protestation to her on the last of their nights,

Non mi sospinse ad amarti bellezza.[14]

Her attire was somber. She made supplication to Ettore, we are told, "in abito dolente."[15] Distinguished from other worshipers of Pallade by her black weed,

Tra li qua' fu di Calcas la figliuola
Crisëida, quale era in bruna vesta,

she attracted notice from Troiolo in that garb,

l' occhio suo vago giunse penetrando
colá dov' era Criseida piacente,
sotto candido velo in bruna vesta,

and, in it, won his heart,

Piacendo questa sotto il nero manto
oltre ad ogni altra a Troiol.[16]

Thanking Amore afterwards for subjugation to the fair one, the prince declared,

non fu giammai
sotto candido velo in bruna vesta,
sí bella donna, come mi par questa.[17]

Pandaro argued, in lines already quoted, that love was permissible for her clad though she was "in vestimento bruno," and Troiolo challenged the god to kindle flames "sotto la bruna vesta."[18] About to be parted from the hero, she exclaimed,

Or vedova sarò io daddovero,
poi che da te dipartir mi conviene,
cuor del mio corpo, e 'l vestimento nero
ver testimonio fia delle mie pene.[19]

As Griffin points out[20] the black wear was intended throughout as a sign of Criseida's widowhood, but, when combined with the white veil, also as a reminiscence of costume affected by the still husbanded Maria. While the latter intention is irrelevant to the development of the story, the former is pertinent since the widowhood thus emphasized gave the heroine freedom and a sharper appetite for love. Readiness for it was evidenced most dramatically when she cast off her shift at her bedmate's request.[21]

To proceed to Troiolo, it may be first noted that there are somewhat more allusions to his youth than to Criseida's. There is the narrator's remark, already mentioned, that he and she so planned as to make the most of youth.[22] This suggests, though but incidentally, that the commodity was essential to him in love as well as to her. On one occasion she referred to the prince as "giovinetto."[23] The narrator so designated him on five; remarked that he sauntered about the temple of Pallade in the fashion of "giovinetti"; spoke of a group, including Troiolo and Pandaro, as "li giovani Troiani"; and called the lover "il tapinello giovane" at a particularly unhappy crisis.[24] The friend rebuked his contemporary after the parliament with this question,

Or se' tu sí 'nvilito
come tu mostri, giovin valoroso?

and later proposed that, if Troiolo continued bent on death, they should seek it together in warfare "come giovani pregiati" rather than as the prince had attempted through disgraceful suicide[25]—thus twice implying that the hero was of an age to play the man but was not living up to that potentiality. The narrator would have it that Troiolo's youth was his downfall, cautioning "giovinetti" at the end against the passion incident to their years and bidding them mirror themselves in his misfortune.[26] What made Criseida a siren as naturally conditioned him to be a victim.

Account of his person is limited to the generalities that he was strong and good looking. Strength is implied in various allusions to his martial prowess and explicitly mentioned in two of them—the narrator's statements that the flames of love respected neither the "forza corporale" in Troiolo nor the "prodezza" and that, inspired by Amore after fruition, he sallied out "sí forte e sí fiero" that all the Greeks were in terror.[27] Pandaro, however, singled out good looks as the physical attraction in his friend, and Criseida likewise; he recommended the prince to her as possessed of every virtue and as "chiaro nel visaggio"; she assured herself,

> costui è bel, gentil, savio ed accorto,
> che t'ama, e fresco piú che giglio d'orto.[28]

This figure of the lily and others of the floral kind, applied to him as noted in Chapter III. 7, inevitably suggest an Adonis rather than the great warrior he was alleged to be. That she continued to prize his beauty to the night of parting appears from her asseveration at that time,

> se Dio mi guardi la tua faccia bella;

and that he assumed that she had valued it appears from his rhetorical question after the dream as to what similar attraction,

> qual piacer nuovo, qual vaga bellezza,

had drawn her to a rival.[29]

The lover improved nature with art, both while courting,

> e spesso si rinnuova e cangia vesta,

and when in possession,

> si rifaceva grazïoso e bello,
> come falcon ch' uscisse di cappello.[30]

The only articles of ornament or use to be singled out, however, were associated with his misery, not his pride: the tear-bathed "gemma" with which he sealed his first letter to Criseida; the "fermaglio d' oro," successively his, hers, and Diomede's; and the sword and knife grasped with suicidal intent.[31] Never portrayed in armor, he was given a falcon to carry aristocratically on his wrist when escorting his mistress out of Troy and credited with the bold thought of seeking her in pilgrim's disguise though not with execution of it.[32]

Diomede, to judge from the one stanza epitomizing him, might have been a physical replica of Troiolo, if not his psychic double. With the exception

of "grande," adjectives applied to him in its opening lines had been to the
first lover:

> Egli era grande e bel della persona,
> giovane fresco e piacevole assai,
> e forte e fier.[33]

These attributes, with glibness and amorosity, inclined the lady to him, the
stanza informs us. His "ornato vestimento" captured by Deifobo was the
accidental medium of Troiolo's disillusionment, since it bore the "fermaglio"
which the latter had given his mistress.[34]

The confidant, while never visualized, was designated a youth. He was
introduced as a "troian giovinetto" of rank, and, as noted above, casually
included among "giovani Troiani" and made to speak of himself and Troiolo
as "giovani."[35]

Calcas, begging the Greeks to console him as an oldster, a "vecchio cattivo,"
watered with tears, "e la canuta barba e'l duro petto."[36] Though his age
moved them, it naturally did not placate his victims. Criseida made unkindly
reference to him as an old man on two occasions; Troiolo, on many, neither
of them attributing his treason to his years but each one assuming these to
be productive of avarice.[37]

Chaucer, we shall find, modifies Boccaccio's representation in all three
areas of age, person, and dress.

In the first, he de-emphasizes the youthfulness of the parties to the affair.
Lacking the personal reasons of Boccaccio for insistence on the heroine's and
hero's, he chooses for artistic ones to leave them young, but not to stress the
point, and to guard against the supposition that they were less than man and
woman grown.[38] While he accepts references to her youth in argument for
love, he drops all others and, as will be shown in Sections 4 and 5, endows
her with social poise and the adult responsibilities of a great household, this
including three nieces. He passes over all indications in the source that the
hero was young except the final moralization and notes the fact but twice on
his own initiative, both times in connection with bodily might and accomplishment. In adapting the stanza which summed up Diomede, he chooses
not to render "giovane." He also omits the scattered designations of the confidant as young without replacement of any kind, and, though giving him new
bounce, lets it be guessed that he was the lady's senior by making him her
uncle instead of cousin. She and Troilus, Chaucer seemingly would have us
assume, were in their twenties; Pandarus, older by some years but not a great
many.[39] Her father he keeps contrastingly senescent.

As to the persons of the several actors, our poet brings out the charms of
the beloved even more fully than Boccaccio; builds up the physical impressive-

149

ness of the Trojan lover; does no more for the Greek than rework the one description of him given in the *Filostrato;* and like his author, has not a word to say about the semblance of the go-between.[40] The disparity is inherent in the roles. Her beauty must be stressed as the *sine qua non* of the tragedy. Combat potential of the native prince must be too—as a secondary attraction for her and as a merit indispensable to the reader's acceptance of him as true courtly lover and hero. The like in the foreigner, who is but briefly on stage, has to be attested only at that time. What Pandarus may have been in body is immaterial, destined as he was, not to win love for himself, but to procure for his master, to serve a paladin not to be one. Filling in the picture of the lady, gradually and impressionistically built up in the *Filostrato,* and visualizing the hero independently of that source, Chaucer insists on the femininity of her person and the manliness of the suitor's. Concomitantly, as is to be noted in Section 4, he eliminates all behavior of hers which manifested an unwomanly vigor. And, as will appear in the next chapter, he rejects figures applied to her and to the prince which were not compatible respectively with quintessential femaleness and maleness and applies new figures which are.

Lastly, as to costuming, Chaucer takes over most of the scanty particulars in the *Filostrato* about clothing, ornament, or weapons and adds to them always realistically[41] and often with symbolic implication. Keeping the lady in the black indicative of widowhood, he introduces a ring and brooch, both significantly colored, for her to bestow upon the hero and mentions a glove and sleeve as favors of hers to the rival beside the single gift to him which was recorded by Boccaccio. He creates two scenes in which Troilus is displayed on horseback to his mistress, respectively in the accouterments of his military trade and in his "beste gere." He retains the sword, but not the knife, with which the hero proposed suicide; gives the confidant a sword and knife for play-acting.

Let us now examine in detail what he chooses to give us about the heroine's time of life, her semblance, and her dress.

There is argument in his poem as in Boccaccio's that she is of an age for love but none of the casual allusion to her youthfulness recurrent in the source. More delicate than Pandaro, who reasoned that she was a widow and therefore sensual, Pandarus cites her beauty and "youthe" to his friend as incompatible with austerity, then doctrinalizes:

> But trewely, it sate hire wel right nowthe
> A worthi knyght to loven and cherice,
> And but she do, I holde it for a vice.[42]

He prompts her to love by expatiating on the unpleasant prospect of old age, as Pandaro did by reminding her that she was still young.[43] And Criseyde tells herself that she may love because she is independent and "Right yong," where Criseida so concluded from the circumstances that she was young, fair, rich, noble, and a widow.[44] As Dodd points out, such logic on the part of uncle and niece is in accord with the principle of amour courtois that "to be in love is the normal condition for suitable young people."[45] They need not, of course, be in the first flush of youth in order to qualify. If the lady's complacent "Right yong" is not put in question by her own thought later on that love was a delight to her "al come it late," it must be by the narrator's gratuitous admission,

> But trewely, I kan nat telle hire age,[46]

as well as by his invention of three nieces, all old enough to serve her and one, at least, to doctrinalize on love.

As to what is given in the *Troilus* about the person of the heroine, it may first be noted that there are no fewer than eleven contexts which bring out her womanliness, and most of them with particulars. Chaucer is careful to stress that quality in his introductory portrait of her in the temple adapted from Boccaccio's. Changing assertion of her tallness to a denial of low stature, he rejects "donnesca altezza" in favor of sheer muliebrity:

> She nas nat with the leste of hire stature,
> But alle hire lymes so wel answerynge
> Weren to wommanhod, that creature
> Was nevere lasse mannyssh in semynge.[47]

At consummation, he presents her in the nude as Boccaccio did Biancofiore in the climactic scene of the *Filocolo,* dwelling even more than the latter upon softness and delicacy of members:

> Hire armes smale, hire streghte bak and softe,
> Hire sydes longe, flesshly, smothe, and white
> He gan to stroke, and good thrift bad ful ofte
> Hire snowisshe throte, hire brestes rounde and lite.[48]

When she is in despair after the parliament, Chaucer would still have us visualize her as ultrafemale. He expands the line of the *Filostrato,*

> e' biondi crin tirando si rompea,

into the lines,

> Hire ownded heer, that sonnyssh was of hewe,
> She rente, and ek hire fyngeres longe and smale
> She wrong ful ofte;

151

and, with resort to the French prose translation, gives us the following lines instead of the laconic "scapigliata" applied to the heroine in the original,

> The myghty tresses of hire sonnysshe heeris,
> Unbroiden, hangen al aboute hire eeris.[49]

The portrait of her, derived from Joseph of Exeter and Benoit,[50] which he inserts before the scene in camp with Diomede, reinforces his earlier visualizations. Its first lines,

> Criseyde mene was of hire stature,
> Therto of shap, of face, and ek of cheere,
> Ther myghte ben no fairer creature,

are similar in effect to those devoted to her as she stood in Pallas' temple. And the next lines, telling of her hair worn in tresses down her back, suggest as womanly a profusion of this crowning glory as the mentions of it in disarray.[51] Concession of one blemish—joined eyebrows—is a token of the honesty of portraiture which encourages belief in the excellences claimed. Thus insistent upon the femininity of Criseyde, the narrator would have his hero duly appreciative of it. He makes him address her as "wommanliche wif" and "fresshe wommanliche wif," discourse to Pandarus "of hire womanhede, And of hire beaute," lament that grief must be wasting her "fresshe, wommanliche face," image to himself "hire shap, hire wommanhede," and recalls how at a certain house he had heard her singing

> So wommanly, with vois melodious.[52]

Lightness of coloring, indicated or suggested of her a number of times in the *Filostrato*, is much more frequently so in the *Troilus*. The narrator, as already quoted, speaks twice of her sunny hair and once of her snowy throat, with the first mention of the hair an elaboration of Boccaccio's of "biondi crin." He speaks also of "Hire white brest" and "hire brighte face," where the latter remarked her "bianco petto" and "fresche guance e dilicate."[53] And without precedent from him, he refers to "hire eyen cleere" and to "hire brighte hewe" and "Hire hewe, whilom bright," and calls the lady "Criseyde, brighte of hewe," "Criseyde the brighte," and the hero's "lady bryght."[54] Troilus, like Troiolo, mentions her white breast.[55] Independently of him, he refers five times to her "eyen cleere" and once to her "eyen brighte"; calls her his "lady bright" four times, and once "bright Criseyde."[56] And Diomede twice addresses her as his "lady bright."[57] Though "bright" and "cleere" are tired adjectives,[58] they serve at least to maintain the impression created by fresher terms. As will be seen in Section 7 of the next chapter images of light applied

152

to her suggest even more powerfully than the like applied to Criseida that she brightened eye and heart.

Like Criseida, she is declared supreme in beauty by both narrator and hero. Writing in his own person, Chaucer makes the assertions that there was none so fair as she in Troy, that she was first in beauty, and that she was fairer than Eleyne or Polixene—claims correspondent in sense to ones made in the *Filostrato*.[59] At the moment of his swoon, he describes Criseyde as once the fairest to be seen; and, in the portrait inserted before the visit of Diomede, he tells us that none could be fairer than she.[60] Troilus, at consummation, believed her the fairest he had ever seen; and, when offered the consolation for her exchange that there are fairer ladies than she, he bids Pandarus not compare her to "creature yformed here by kynde."[61] When Criseida went no farther than to allow herself to be "bella," Criseyde reflects that she is "oon the faireste" and so considered by men throughout Troy—

> Al wolde I that noon wiste of this thought.[62]

Allusions to her beauty without superlatives are far less numerous than in the source—only ten all told;[63] Chaucer is not one to do things by halves.

In costuming the lady, he naturally does not keep the white veil—a private reminiscence of Maria's wear—but he as naturally accepts the dark attire —a reminiscence of the same, but also the sign of widowhood. Like the French prose translator, he makes it immediately clear that such was the heroine's state, rendering "in abito dolente" descriptive of her in the opening scene with Ettore as follows:

> In widewes habit large of samyt broun.[64]

Coming to the temple scene, he visualizes Criseyde "In widewes habit blak," "in hir blake wede," and "in blak" and accentuates contrast between clothes and wearer with the lovely figure that so bright a star was never seen "under cloude blak."[65] His Pandarus concerns himself with her attire as indicative of a restraint which he would dispel, urging in successive invitations to the dance,

> Do wey youre barbe, and shewe youre face bare;

> And cast youre widewes habit to mischaunce![66]

On the same occasion the confidant quotes Troilus as referring to her as the one "That stood in blak."[67] The fancy of Criseida's that, separated from Troiolo, she would be truly a widow and her black apparel a mark of true sorrow is changed for Criseyde into the conceit, more congruent with the religion of love, that she would lead the life of a recluse,

> And, Troilus, my clothes everychon
> Shal blake ben in tokenyng, herte swete,
> That I am as out of this world agon,
> That wont was yow to setten in quiete.[68]

There is additional color symbolism in the "blewe rying" offered by Criseyde to her host of a night for transmission to her fellow guest—which may be the ring exchanged by her before dawn for one of the latter's—and likewise in the gold and azure brooch with its heart-shaped ruby which she pinned upon his shirt.[69] The blue of the ring and brooch promised constancy, and the red of the stone, passionate love[70]—assurances eventually to be disproved. Her surrender to the rival is emblemed in her gifts to him of her sleeve and Troilus' brooch and steed, and in the glove exacted from her before she made these offerings.[71]

Turning now to the hero as Chaucer presents him, we shall consider his age, person, and dress, not sequentially, but all together, since the poet combines these factors in key passages.

He begins, as Boccaccio did, by commenting that the worthy's great prowess did not avail against the assault of Love.[72] But, unlike him he turns that prowess to advantage in courtship. He inspires Pandarus in the first visit to his niece to equate Troilus with the more famous Ector and to declare that "Hire myght is wyde yknowe."[73] He then brings the hero straight from the front with his veterans that she may inspect him from her window. Mounted, ironically enough, on the bay steed which she was to have from, Diomede as a prize of war and then to restore to its captor,[74] Troilus cut a most gallant figure on this "his happy day":

> So lik a man of armes and a knyght
> He was to seen, fulfilled of heigh prowesse;
> For bothe he hadde a body and a myght
> To don that thing, as wel as hardynesse;
> And ek to seen hym in his gere hym dresse,
> So fressh, so yong, so weldy semed he,
> It was an heven upon hym for to see.

> His helm tohewen was in twenty places
> That by a tyssew heng his bak byhynde;
> His sheeld todasshed was with swerdes and maces,
> In which men myght many an arwe fynde
> That thirled hadde horn and nerf and rynde.[75]

Impressed by "his excellent prowesse," "his shap" and other attractions, she inclined to him from that moment, the poet tells us,

> And after that, his manhod and hys pyne
> Made love withinne hire herte for to myne.[76]

Pandarus saw to it that this should happen. When with his friend on the ensuing night, he proposed, not only, as Pandaro did, that the hero should write a letter immediately, but also that he ride past her house in his "beste gere." [77] Like Boccaccio's prince, Troilus impressed the letter with a seal. This, vaguely designated in the original as "la gemma," is identified, with probably symbolic intent, as "The ruby in his signet." [78] The contrived display before the lady's window was as telling as the return from battle, though without its pomp and circumstance. The narrator exclaims:

> God woot if he sat on his hors aright,
> Or goodly was biseyn, that ilke day!
> God woot wher he was lik a manly knyght!

and assures us that she approved

> His person, his aray, his look, his chere. [79]

Made thus impressive in public appearances that he may attract the fair and be appraised by us as deserving of her love, he is reduced to confusion when he would possess her so that he may be credited with the merit, complementary to valor, of awe for his acknowledged suzerain, and also that the one aspect of his being may be amusingly contrasted with the other. Giving the command, "don this furred cloke upon thy sherte, And folwe me," Pandarus must pull him "by the lappe" from stew to closet; and, when his friend there swoons, he must reverse the process, stripping him to the shirt for resuscitation and exclaiming the while "O thef, is this a mannes herte?" [80] Criseyde chimes in with "Is this a mannes game?" [81] And, when her lover has recovered his senses and pretends a rival, she demands,

> Wol ye the childissh jalous contrefete? [82]

Soon, however, she has yielded to masculine demands, and, as noted above, he and she exchange rings in token of their love. [83]

Fruition improved him as it did Troiolo, both in the social sphere and on the field of battle. So careful of good form as to keep changing his apparel, [84] he was always the first to arm himself for combat and, save Ector, the most fearsome when it was joined—

> And this encrees of hardynesse and myght
> Com him of love, his ladies thank to wynne,
> That altered his spirit so withinne. [85]

In his last hours with the lady, he was faithful as ever, and she duly appreciative of his excellence. Like Troiolo, he would have dispatched himself

155

by the sword when he took her swoon for death, that he might continue her servant in the other world.[86] After recovery, she declared that it was not extrinsic attractions—neither rank nor martial accomplishment—which had won her but intrinsic qualities—virtue grounded on truth, along with gentle heart, "manhod," and control of appetite.[87] In this tribute, denial of concern for station and prowess is a rhetorical overstatement, of course, as is that of care for beauty in Troiolo's protestation to his mistress, from which by reversal of speaker and hearer, it is derived. Obedient to Criseyde's wishes because of that truth which she had praised, he did not defy the exchange but squired her out of the city next morning—like Troiolo—"With hauke on honde."[88]

Since he and Diomede are from this point consistently opposed to one another by Chaucer in nature as in fortune, what relates to them may best be considered together. As for their twin portraits by his hand, that of Diomede attests brawn and mettle, but the longer one of Troilus is yet more exaltatory of both physique and courage, specifying the one to be perfect, the other unsurpassed:

> This Diomede, as bokes us declare,
> Was in his nedes prest and corageous,
> With sterne vois and myghty lymes square,
> Hardy, testif, strong, and chivalrous
> Of dedes, like his fader Tideus.

> And Troilus wel woxen was in highte,
> And complet formed by proporcioun
> So wel that kynde it nought amenden myghte;
> Yong, fressh, strong, and hardy as lyoun;

> . . . .

> And certeynly in storye it is yfounde,
> That Troilus was nevere unto no wight,
> As in his tyme, in no degree secounde
> In durryng don that longeth to a knyght.[89]

Having introduced these virile sketches, Chaucer is inconsistent, it must be said, in keeping for Troilus the rhetorical question attributed to Troiolo as to what new beauty had attracted his mistress.[90] And by taking over for him the conception and renunciation of a visit to camp in pilgrim's disguise,[91] he perhaps hints an indecisiveness in love antithetical to martial resolve, though he gives very plausible reasons for abandonment of the project. He prepares for the appearance of the lover's brooch on the captured garment of the rival, as Boccaccio did not, by anterior mention of it as a gift of the lady's to Diomede, and he identifies the garment more exactly—and more medievally—than his author, rendering "ornato vestimento" as "cote-armure." [92]

156

His parting advice to the young of both sexes conveys the implication of Boccaccio's to young men—that the hero was of an age dangerously susceptible in matters of the heart.[93]

Pandarus, temperamentally the opposite of his friend in many ways, is still a kindred spirit. If never labelled young[94] as Pandaro was and if implied not to be so by uncleship at least, he is, like him, a constant lover and therefore wholly on the prince's side in the affair. In the process of suborning his niece, he goes so far as to threaten suicide with a knife, and, after it has been accomplished, shows but mock compunction, jestingly offering her a sword for his decapitation.[95] An uncle, indeed, but of latitudinarian species, he is one whom she can presume to take playfully by the hood.[96]

As in the *Filostrato,* her father has lost at home the respect due his years, though pitied for them by the Greeks. Calling himself an "olde caytyf," this tearful "olde greye" wins their consent to the exchange.[97] Criseyde does not wish the old man in Hell as the ungentle Criseida was permitted to do, but she schemes even more elaborately than the other to take advantage of his senile avarice to deceive him.[98] And Troilus speaks as unflatteringly of the ancient as Troiolo, though less often.[99]

Now that we have seen how Chaucer adapted his source with respect to age, person, and dress, we may return to the *Filostrato* in the opening pages of the next section to determine what it had to offer about the impress of passion upon the lovely heroine and the several more or less stalwart males.

Ravages of Passion

IN the *Filostrato*, the long and acute sufferings of the Trojan lover stood out against the momentary trepidation of his rival, the vicarious if unremitting concern of his friend, and the soon-dispelled anguish of the lady. Pallor, loss of sleep, appetite, and eventually strength, the prepossession that death was near, and the recurrent wish that it might come abundantly evidenced in the hero that total commitment to love which was the merit of merits in amour courtois, yet established no less plainly that such devotion cost him more than the love chosen was worth. Troiolo's douleurs, accumulating from the moment he saw Criseida, cannot but preponderate in our memories over the ecstasies of a period which was disposed of in a small segment of the whole. She grieved on her own account and on his, but in a briefer span than he and with somewhat less desperation even in that. Her languishings further illustrated the costliness of love so thoroughly brought out in his case, while her recovery from them contrasted ironically with his faithful persistence in self-torment. Diomede was opposed with implicit irony as easy winner to commendably but vainly anguished loser. The confidant, solicitous about the wretchedness of his friend, used it with his cousin as an argument for favors, risking disfame in as firm conviction as Troiolo that love would insure the latter's happiness. Shaken by the reversal, he could not but share the prince's forebodings though he persisted in attempts at consolation.

As the party besought, Criseida had small cause to pine or even to anticipate sorrow until the parliament. And the new hopes which she built on Diomede's call only four days later permanently appeased her torment, we may surmise, since Boccaccio was henceforth silent about it.

158

Before reversal, if shamefast enough to blush occasionally when solicited by Pandaro and to aver that the day on which she first listened to him should have been her last, she made up her mind, very promptly, not to lose color from repression of desire—not to risk her life by it nor her lover's when she had so pleasurable an alternative.[1]

But she was calling in all earnestness upon Death as soon as banishment threatened, wishing that she had been smothered at birth, resolving to drive soul from body by starvation if it did not depart of itself, and fancying that lamentations would break her heart.[2] By the time Pandaro entered her chamber, her face was corpselike, with loveliness gone from it, and around each eye "un purpureo giro."[3] Moved by his account of Troiolo's sorrow, she expected and wished to die sans respite.[4] Her swoon when with the prince was so deathlike as to convince him that she was indeed a corpse.[5] Learning, upon recovery, of his intended suicide, she declared that she would not have survived him had he accomplished it; and, later on, that he was killing her with his doubts about her constancy in exile and that, if it should be he who turned inconstant, she would kill herself.[6] In camp, her cheeks grew "pallide e magre" from nights of weeping, and the loss of beauty became in turn a cause of sorrow.[7] She decided upon scandalous flight in preference to death from grief[8] but was kept from fleeing or dying by the rival. Diomede, who had noted the change in her appearance and interpreted it aright, urged her to cross off every Trojan as doomed, and, accepting him as servant, to recover her beauty for his delight.[9] His words prevailed.

A humble suppliant and by nature faithful, Troiolo was always exposed to the anxieties of love. And his reaction to them was intense. Feeling betrayed itself in his countenance; feeling disrupted rest and diet and led even to temporary invalidism. He often wished to die, and he, Pandaro, and Criseida all found it conceivable that he might succumb. Since prospects of death and actualities of psychophysical response both bulk large in his career, it will be worth-while to consider them separately. We may take up the latter first.

His face, Troiolo complained not long after enamorment, had lost its color; and the narrator tells us that at this early time,

> Aveagli giá amore il sonno tolto,
> e minuito il cibo, ed il pensiero
> multiplicato sí che giá nel volto
> ne dava pallidezza segno vero.[10]

Put to the blush when forced to identify his beloved for Pandaro, he was soon writing her, conceitfully, that he could not wish health to her until he had that commodity himself.[11] And with fruition near, he devoted his nights, if not unhappily, still rigorously to thoughts of love.[12]

The exchange, of course, intensified the psychosomatic manifestations. During the parliament, Troiolo's father and brothers had to labor long and hard to bring him out of a swoon, in which

> 'l viso suo pallido e smorto e tinto
> era tututto, e più morta parea
> che viva cosa.[13]

After he had retreated to his palace, he was told by Pandaro that his eyes seemed already "morti."[14] Next day, afflicted more with rage than sorrow, he shook in every limb when Criseida was surrendered, and colored hotly as he left her with Diomede.[15] And the night following was wretched. Troiolo indulged in lamentation, and, as he told Pandaro afterward, he slept but little and, when asleep, dreamed of flight, peril, and capture, then felt a start as if he were falling.[16] These impressions and his waking fears the friend diagnosed as the effects of "malinconia."[17] The prince changed countenance at sight of his mistress' empty house, and he fell into the delusion that his pallor was exciting comment.[18] He went on counting the hours by night as well as by day until the time appointed for Criseida's return.[19]

Still more miserably wakeful after she had failed to come and forgoing food and drink, he wasted away as never before—

> né l' averia alcun riconosciuto,
> sí pallida e smarrita avea la cera;
> del corpo s'era ogni valor partuto,
> e tanta forza appena ne' membri era
> che 'l sostenesse—

with the unwelcome consequence of family solicitude about this transformation.[20] When he chanced to sleep, he dreamed of the boar.[21] He was so enfeebled that Pandaro could wrest the knife from him which he had seized after the dream and force him to sit down for a lecture.[22] Though trembling with rage at first, he accepted the counsel that he write Criseida and used the occasion to tell her of his loss of sleep and appetite and consequent unrecognizability.[23] He took to his bed because she did not answer; there confessed to Deifobo that he was "alquanto deboletto" though promising recovery to harass the Greeks, and rebuked Cassandra for asserting that his pallor was for Criseida; and—after a slow convalescence—realized the promise to his brother.[24]

With sorrows thus harrowing his body, it follows, poetically, if not medically, that Troiolo should expect death as their final consequence. He would have been less than human had he kept this presumption to himself; and Pandaro, most remiss had he failed to trade on it with Criseida. And, when unhopeful of succor for his miseries of flesh and spirit, the lover could not but wish for death as well as predict it.

He was early soliloquizing that it would be a comfort and that, to please his beloved, he would obey should she cry "Ucciditi."[25] Approached by Pandaro, he implored him not to witness his dying and confessed that, because of love, he had come close to self-destruction a thousand times.[26] He wanted to die of shame, he went on to say, because the mistress he desired was the cousin of his friend.[27] The latter quoted him to Criseida as fearful of death and lamented that she could and might inflict it.[28] Despite concessions from the lady, Troiolo fantasied about expiring to Pandaro and hinted the possibility in his letter to her.[29] This the friend delivered as the plea of an apparently dying man.[30] With succor near, the prince imagined that it might come too late, and the broker warned her that, if she killed this paragon, she would indeed have cause to count her beauty dear.[31] The former, at last in her arms, marvelled that he did not perish as dawn approached, but survived to acknowledge to Pandaro that he owed him his life.[32]

Thinking to expire of grief in the parliament, Troiolo after he had shut himself up in his chamber repeatedly wished that he might, and spun out a conceit that Calcas' life was the occasion of his death.[33] He greeted Pandaro with "i' son morto," declared he would rather die than follow the latter's proposal of a new mistress, called on Death fervently and at length, wished that he might have died at the moment of enamorment, and countered the further suggestion of rape by saying that he would die rather than offend the lady in the slightest.[34] The confidant informed Criseida of the lover's death wish, to her great sorrow, and warned that his friend would kill himself if he should find her cast down.[35] In this instance the cousin may not have been exaggerating, since Troiolo came to the verge of self-destruction when she fell into her deathlike swoon.[36] After her recovery from this, the prince warned that his near suicide was an earnest of what he would do if she failed to return as promised, adding that, should she leave on the morrow, she must think of him as dead.[37] Next day, after wondering whether it was not better to die in rebellion against the exchange than to live on in torment, he again begged her to return lest he expire.[38] Alone, he cursed the day of his birth and, in Pandaro's hearing, wished that he had fallen dead when he let her go, and revealed that he had spent the night apostrophizing Amore and the lady for mercy or death.[39] As the time approached for fulfillment of her promise, he besought the god not to carry vengeance to the point of death and then, contrarily in a song, to deliver his soul from the body.[40]

With his life made odious by her nonreturn, Troiolo drew the inference from the boar dream that it was displeasing to God and tried to kill himself.[41]

Thwarted by Pandaro in this, he twice threatened suicide in the letter which he wrote Criseida at the friend's suggestion.[42] Discovery of the brooch made him call for death; lament his ill-starred birth; and vow to seek an end in battle, concomitantly, of course, with revenge upon Diomede.[43] And perish at the front he did, but unavenged.[44]

The rival, if genuinely subject to love, was not afflicted by it. A bold man, he resolved to present his own case to Criseida were he to die for it.[45] And the effort cost him no more than a fiery blush and a quaver in the voice.[46]

As remarked above, Troiolo acknowledged that he owed his life to his companion.[47] Pandaro took it as a breach of friendship-that the prince, who he had supposed would die at his command, persisted in suicidal efforts against his wishes, and he offered to die with him in battle to turn him from ignominious self-destruction.[48]

And in this death-toned poem of Boccaccio's, even the cowardly traitor must protest his readiness to expire. Were he to be refused his daughter, he told the Greeks, he would as soon die as live.[49]

Chaucer, in expanding the *Filostrato*, considerably increases the total of psychophysical response and expectation of death, and he modifies both with significant result, though without disturbance of the controlling impression that the hero, first in emotional capacity, was therefore first both in desert and in self-deception.[50] Criseyde, paling at every danger and markedly apprehensive of any threat to her life, is in this fearsomeness, as in other respects, a more softly feminine creature than Boccaccio's heroine, and as such more appealing but not more dependable. Troilus is a devotee of love even more quintessential than Troiolo in sensibility and foreboding. *Qua* devotee he is presented to us with as much sympathy throughout as in the original, but with a new and critical humor in the ascending action. Diomede, relieved of apprehension while the Trojan was confirmed in it, becomes his diametrical opposite. The go-between is made more emphatic about his friend's liability to death and his own readiness to die with him—to partially comic effect in solicitation of the lady, at other times to our unreserved conviction of his earnestness.

Acknowledgment by Troilus of his mistress' right to determine whether he should live or die is congruent with the figurative pattern of rule and service which, as shown in Section 3 of the next chapter, is the most meaningful one for their relationship. And literal report of his sufferings and of Criseyde's, and Pandarus' efforts to dispel them is complemented by the metaphorical representations of the lover as patient and of the other two as his physicians, which are collected in Section 5 of that chapter.

To begin with Criseyde, we may scrutinize first her physical responses to emotion and then her inclinations toward death and cancelling apprehensions about it.

In the period of courtship, her shamefastness and timidity are repeatedly evidenced by the former. Pandarus, when he had gone no farther than to hint that something momentous was afoot, found it necessary to exhort her thus:

> Beth naught agast, ne quaketh naught! Wherto?
> Ne chaungeth naught for fere so youre hewe! [51]

She blushed after seeing Troilus in his military glory and almost fell when she reflected on the dangers of an affair with him.[52] She colored at his next ride past her window, and, like Criseida, upon being quizzed about a letter of his.[53] The fiction of a lawsuit made her change "al hire hewe." [54] She turned red when Troilus emerged from the shadows of the closet in her uncle's house and again when Pandarus returned to it in the morning to jest about what had transpired.[55] Having changed color thus often out of modesty or fear, she did so at last because she loved—namely, when the hero had to leave her at the end of their second night.[56]

Banishment in prospect and actuality took its toll. She was pale before her uncle came to console her for the exchange, claimed "siknesse" when he was with her, and presented as ghastly an appearance to his sight as Criseida to her cousin's:

> She was right swich to seen in hire visage
> As is that wight that men on beere bynde.
>
> Aboute hire eyen two a purpre ryng
> Bytrent, in sothfast tokenyng of hire peyne.[57]

Insensible like Criseida in the lover's arms, she gave him equal reason to believe her dead, losing color, becoming cold to the touch, and with eyes "throwen upward to hire hed." [58] Next day, she all but toppled from her horse at sight of Calkas,[59] Troilus, at home, lamented that her fair face would become "pale, and grene" [60] and not mistakenly. Weeping anights made her face pale and her limbs lean, just as it blanched and thinned Criseida's cheeks.[61] As in the source, Diomede presumed to counsel a recall of beauty lost.[62] In her final pronouncement, the disingenuous letter to Troilus which our poet devised, she claimed sickness as an excuse for her delay.[63]

As for dying, he represents her to have been in terror of it from the first and—hyperbolically—to have almost expired of one trepidation and another, making it evident that she would never turn to death as an escape, however strenuous her professions. Timidity insured her from self-destruction no less plainly than shallowness saved Criseida.

Introducing her in sorrow after her father's flight as Boccaccio did his heroine, Chaucer adds the explanation,

> For of hire lif she was ful sore in drede.[64]

In the first conversation with Pandarus, he gives her the incidental remark,

> I am of Grekes so fered that I deye,

and then the funereal responses to her visitor's invitation to love:

> Allas, for wo! Why nere I deed?

and

> For so astoned am I that I deye.[65]

She nearly expired of fright, as the poet himself tells us, at the uncle's counterthreat of dying with his master,[66] but relented to save two lives. On the night of consummation, the alleged jealousy of Troilus made her exclaim "now lyve I to longe!" and protest "if that I be giltif, do me deye!" [67] At parting on their next night of love, she fancied, as he did, to feel "dethis wownde." [68]

Alone after the parliament, she threw herself on her bed,

> In purpos nevere thennes for to rise.[69]

There, like Criseida, she called for death, lamented having been born, and fixed on starvation as a means of suicide, but prefaced this choice with a timid reason all her own,

> I shal doon thus, syn neither swerd ne darte
> Dar I noon handle, for the crueltee.[70]

Her appearance, Chaucer observes, manifested death longings to Pandarus, and, as he also records, she cursed her birth in the latter's hearing.[71] The uncle's account of the hero's woe moved her to predict death for herself, as Pandaro's did Criseida.[72] Like her original, she assured the hero that she would have committed suicide had he killed himself during her swoon.[73] She and Troilus both lamented birth.[74] She would pay with her life, she vowed to him, if she did not wheedle Calkas as promised; and Chaucer assures us that she was sincere in so speaking and "starf for wo neigh, whan she wente." [75] But one of her objections to the proposal of elopement indicates that she was by no means ready to leave this earth:

If this were wist, my lif lay in balaunce.[76]

Following the hyperbolical Criseida, she told her lover that present distrust of her plans was killing her and that any future doubt on her side of his fidelity would do so too.[77] In camp, she wished again that she had never been born, but dreaded escape as rendering her liable to condemnation as a spy.[78]

As has been made evident, Chaucer presents the heroine's attitude toward death and her psychophysical reactions with some originality, reworking the scanty material of the *Filostrato* pertinent thereto and supplementing it considerably. He is no less free in dealing with the hero's, which are so much more fully recorded in the source. Expanding in his case as in hers, he maintains the lover's unhappy precedence in anticipation of death and somatic responsiveness to woe.

As for the responsiveness, which we are now to consider, Chaucer emphasizes that it signified melancholia and threatened madness. And the particulars of it which he invented or adapted from the source are symptomatic of that disorder of mind and body referred to in the *Knight's Tale* as "the loveris maladye Of Hereos." [79] Some of them conformed particularly enough to physiological theory of his day to have made the affliction scientifically acceptable to his contemporaries despite inevitable awareness on their part that it occurred more often and catastrophically in books than in even the courtliest circles.

From enamorment up to reversal, he attributes psychophysical manifestations of emotion to the hero far more extensively than Boccaccio. He thus perfects him by the standards of amour courtois. Yet, as his author did not, he brings out the absurdity latent in the system, opposing this, if genially, to its noble idealism. The sickliness expected in courtship becomes humorous when it is feigned as at the house of Deiphebus; and the expected swooning likewise, though genuine, when it produces such consequences as at the house of Pandarus.

The poet gives his hero, newly introduced to love, a song on the contrarieties of "this wondre maladie"; supplies the information,

That sexti tyme a day he loste his hewe;

then tells us, after Boccaccio, that love deprived him of sleep and appetite and affected his complexion, and, independently of that author, that the victim disguised the fire of love by congruent pretense of a fever.[80]

With Pandarus on stage, Chaucer makes him ask the prince whether it was the Greeks that had caused him to be "leene" and the latter reply that he was not "thus sik" out of fear.[81] When Troilus seemed deaf to exhortation,

165

the counsellor feared that he might lapse into a "frenesie" if not die, but we learn from the omniscient narrator that this silence was calculated—a bait for urging as much as a defense against it.[82] Still, the lover blushed, like Troiolo, at the thought of identifying his mistress and quaked besides.[83] Pandarus, possessed at last of the secret, ticketed the irony of his lord's plight by recalling fleers at the lovesick:

> And some wolde mucche hire mete allone,
> Liggyng abedde, and make hem for to grone;
> And som, thow seydest, hadde a blaunche fevere,
> And preydest God he sholde nevere kevere.
>
> And some of hem tooke on hem, for the cold,
> More than ynough, so seydestow ful ofte.
> And som han feyned ofte tyme, and told
> How that they waken, whan thei slepen softe.[84]

Criseyde heard from her uncle that the suitor was "pale and wan," and had the privilege, after the former's departure, of seeing how modestly Troilus could blush at the plaudits of the multitude on his return from battle.[85]

The two men involved themselves and others in farce when they pretended that he had a touch of fever. In commending the ruse to him, Pandarus argued that it would mask true indisposition, and the prince rejoined in accepting it:

> Iwis, thow needles
> Conseilest me that siklich I me feyne,
> For I am sik in ernest, douteles,
> So that wel neigh I sterve for the peyne.[86]

Hoodwinked by his brother's "sikliche manere," Deiphebus had him tucked in warmly for the night and lamented the indisposition at the dinner party next day.[87] While Eleyne complained too and the group expertized on fever, Criseyde thought complacently that it was she who could best serve as his physician.[88] Pandarus confirmed the others in their solicitude by dispositions allegedly for his friend's comfort, and confirmed the heroine in her self-esteem by the plea,

> Sle naught this man, that hath for yow this peyne![89]

Bringing her to the bedside of the patient, he played out the comedy by exclaiming "God do boot on alle syke," and the latter sustained him with apologies for inability to rise.[90] But, since all depended upon their miming, Troilus was genuinely affected; his heart beat faster, his color came and went, and his voice lapsed into a quaver.[91] Success achieved, Pandarus promised a meeting at his house as soon as the representedly bedridden one could walk; the latter, in assurance of secrecy after possession, declared that he was quaking even then when there was no one to overhear.[92]

Like Troiolo, Chaucer's prince spent the nights remaining before enjoyment in contemplation of love.[93]

Pandarus sought to impose upon his niece with another fiction of illness in the lover when both were at his house—this time a mental one:

> And he is come in swich peyne and distresse
> That, but he be al fully wood by this,
> He sodeynly mot falle into wodnesse,
> But if God helpe; and cause whi this is,
> He seith hym told is of a frend of his,
> How that ye sholde loven oon that hatte Horaste;
> For sorwe of which this nyght shal ben his laste.[94]

Her reproaches to Troilus for the jealousy of which he was innocent did actually bereave him of his senses—as Chaucer informs us with some medical erudition:

> Therwith the sorwe so his herte shette,
> That from his eyen fil ther nought a tere,
> And every spirit his vigour in knette,
> So they astoned or oppressed were.
> The felyng of his sorwe, or of his fere,
> Or of aught elles, fled was out of towne;
> And down he fel al sodeynly a-swowne.[95]

Turning this unexpected result of his fiction to advantage, Pandarus pitched the insensible one into his mistress' bed and, with her aid, restored him to such health that he might leave him to his own devices, quitting the chamber with the triumphant jest,

> Swouneth nought now, lest more folk arise! [96]

The transfer of swooning on the lover's part from parliament to consummation night relieves him of a public indiscretion in the period when he is being dignified for his tragic end and brings out his sensitivity with robust but tolerant humor at a time permissive of comedy.

Delighted on the next night of love as on the first, Troilus felt such woe at its end that he changed color along with his tender mistress.[97] Even at its best, the course of true love was not altogether smooth.

In the descending action, the general pattern of Troilus' physical reactions is close to Troiolo's, though there are differences here and there. His sensi-

167

tivity, presented seriocomically in the ascending, is brought out here with tragic intensity.

Change of countenance signalled his emotions in parliament instead of swooning, and, according to Chaucer, he was "pale and wan" upon arrival in his chamber.[98] There, he

> wex so mat, that joie nor penaunce
> He feleth non, but lith forth in a traunce;

and Pandarus, having seen him, warned Criseyde not to receive him with tears,

> But ye wole have hym wood out of his mynde.[99]

Like Pandaro, the friend challenged the prince for his immoderation:

> Whi list the so thiself fordoon for drede,
> That in thyn hed thyne eyen semen dede?[100]

Next day, the latter could hardly sit his horse for woe, and, like Troiolo, was aquiver on seeing Diomede at hand to receive the lady.[101] He paled at leaving her with the rival, as the other had flushed.[102] Waking that night, he lamented; and, sleeping, dreamed of danger, capture, and falling—both very much as Troiolo had done.[103] The dreams Pandarus, like Pandaro, attributed to "malencolie."[104] At sight of the lady's empty house, Troilus nearly fell from his horse, and, like Troiolo, changed countenance.[105] He fancied that his pallor and thinness excited comment, as the latter that pallor did—a delusion which Chaucer ascribes to "malencolie."[106] And, like Troiolo, he measured the time by night as well as by day until she should return.[107]

More and more suspicious, as the days passed after the tenth,

> He ne et ne drank, for his malencolye,

and

> He so defet was, that no manere man
> Unneth hym myghte knowen ther he wente;
> So was he lene, and therto pale and wan,
> And feble, that he walketh by potente;

questioned by Priam and others, he diagnosed his case equivocally as heart trouble. This pining comes in substance from the *Filostrato,* though with the specification of melancholy added and the realistic particular of the staff.[108] So too, with changes in detail, the ensuing dream of the boar.[109] Chaucer's omission of the struggle for the knife after the dream spares the hero a debasing revelation of feebleness. In his letter to the heroine in camp, Troilus, like Troiolo in his, professed to be changed to the point of unrecognizability, and, with adaptation of a conceit in an earlier letter of Troiolo's played upon the fancy that health could come only from her.[110] Unsatisfactory answer sent him to bed as want of a reply did the other, and there

> He ne eet, ne dronk, ne slep, ne no word seyde.[111]

Anger at Cassandre's interpretation of the dream instantly revived him.[112] But he was still "in his malencolie" when he chanced upon the clincher of it, his brooch upon Diomede's garment.[113]

As with the hero's bodily manifestations of feeling, so with the prospects of death for him, Chaucer elaborates in descending as well as in ascending action but, again, much more in the earlier phase.

In this phase, he increases the lover's own preoccupation with death somewhat; greatly reinforces the confidant's use of his friend's peril as an argument with the lady; and, not only stresses her fear of the danger, but also attributes to her a very human satisfaction in this evidence of her conquest. The forebodings of Troilus are obviously *au grand sérieux*. But we need not take Pandarus' predictions of love death quite at their face value, since he invented the lawsuit against Criseyde and the prince's fever and jealousy. It was easy for her to credit the predictions, since she was constitutionally apprehensive and by no means unaware of her fatal charm. All three accepted the tenets of amour courtois: Troilus, especially in conceding to the mistress the power over him of life and death; the intermediary, especially in urging her consequent responsibility to be merciful; and Criseyde, in being impressed by both the power and the obligation. Of course, she, like Criseida, eventually violated the principle of female responsibility, and Pandarus carried his insistence upon it to disingenuous lengths.

The rays from Criseyde's eyes so affected Troilus at first sight

> That sodeynly hym thoughte he felte dyen,
> Right with hire look, the spirit in his herte—

with the consequence to be expected that the organ would stop beating and his breath fail.[114] In soliloquies thereafter he twice hoped for mercy from her to keep him from death, though once, like Troiolo, longing for that eventuality.[115]

Like Troiolo, he bade the confidant not stay to see him die and revealed that it was love that made him wish his end.[116] He went on to plead "lat me sterve" and to vow belligerently "I wol deye," provoking the rebuke from Pandarus that such despair was folly and would be even after twenty years

169

of unrewarded love service.[117] Brought by the latter to name his lady, "wel neigh with the word for feere he deide." [118] He called on Venus to give help ere he should die, but declared to his friend that he would rather expire than so far presume as to compromise his lady.[119]

In the speech in which he disclosed to her the prince's affection,[120] Pandarus insisted that this great man was in mortal peril and she responsible. Presenting the issue as an open one,

> The noble Troilus, so loveth the,
> That, but ye helpe, it wol his bane be.
> Lo, here is al! What sholde I moore seye?
> Do what yow lest, to make hym lyve or deye,

he presumed nonetheless to decide it for her. He vowed to die, if his friend met death, represented him to be wishful of it, then hypothesized:

> If it be so that ye so cruel be,
> That of his deth yow liste nought to recche,
> That is so trewe and worthi, as ye se,
> Namoore than of a japer or a wrecche,—
> If ye be swich, youre beaute may nat strecche
> To make amendes of so cruel a dede.
> Avysement is good byfore the nede.

And, after specious assurance that she need be no more than friendly to save a life, he concluded:

> So lat youre daunger sucred ben a lite,
> That of his deth ye be naught for to wite.

Chidden for this speech, he charged her flatly with murder of her lover and himself.[121] Criseyde promised pity but would yield no more, she said, even if both threatened deaths should result.[122] Persistent, the uncle let her know that Troilus had expected death when in the palace garden and been hardly restrained from it in his chamber; then begged once more for the prince's life and his own.[123]

Criseyde recalled all this when seeing the mighty warrior pass by her window:

> Lo, this is he
> Which that myn uncle swerith he moot be deed,
> But I on hym have mercy and pitee;

and, as Chaucer interprets, she was moved by his dependence more than by any other consideration:

> But moost hir favour was, for his distresse
> Was al for hire, and thoughte it was a routhe
> To sleen swich oon, if that he mente trouthe.[124]

170

Merciful as the medieval code of love required, she was partly so, it seems hinted, out of an innocent—and timeless—vanity.

Troilus, fearing to write her lest he might unwittingly offend, warned Pandarus:

> Than were I ded, ther myght it nothyng weyve.[125]

Yet he ventured composition. Upon delivery of the product to the lady, Pandarus claimed that his friend would not live long without an answer —this a modification of Pandaro's forecast at the same juncture.[126] Pressing again for a reply, he begged her, "doth hym nat to deye,"[127] and won his point. After Troilus had ridden by as prearranged, the uncle asked if it befitted a woman to destroy so fine a specimen, to which loaded question she could respond only in the negative.[128]

In the sequence of feigned sickness, there was naturally much about dying. Pandarus, inferring that his friend would rather die than betray his love, suggested the ruse as a safe cover for wooing.[129] Chaucer interprets Criseyde's reaction to praise of her lover at the dinner party in the same way as to the spectacle of him in armed triumph. Her heart laughed, he says,

> For who is that ne wolde hire glorifie,
> To mowen swich a knyght don lyve or dye?[130]

As already noted, Pandarus implored her not to slay this man who was in pain for her.[131] Presenting her to the bedded Troilus, he said:

> Lo, here is she that is youre deth to wite.[132]

The prince, having made his declaration, vowed to kill himself, soon and without regret, if it displeased her.[133] Pandarus gave her the alternative of ending woe or slaying them both right there; begged her to have pity for the lover and not put him to death; and declared that, were he a god, he would make her pay with her life for reluctance to accept Troilus as a servant, knowing him as she did to desire nothing but her honor and to be at point of death.[134] Assured by Pandarus that the lady was really soon to be his, the prince was eased of the woe "that made his herte swelte," but yet recalled that he had been near death only the last April.[135]

The consummation sequence was also productive of funereal remark. Pandarus, as already quoted, told his niece flatly the night would be his friend's last because of jealousy.[136] To her suggestion of an audience on the morrow, he replied,

> Ye ben to wys to doon so gret folie,
> To putte his lif al nyght in jupertie;

171

and, to her offer of the blue ring to be transmitted to the lover,

> that ryng moste han a stoon
> That myghte dede men alyve maken;
> And swich a ryng trowe I that ye have non.[137]

This personage, he said, was no trivial lover, to be put off with mere words, but one,

> so gentil and so tendre of herte,
> That with his deth he wol his sorwes wreke.[138]

At Criseyde's tears for his alleged jealousy, Troilus felt "The crampe of deth" about his heart and cursed the time that he was born; then, believing "he nas but deed," collapsed to the floor.[139] Frightened after recovery by her harking back to the jealousy, "hym thoughte his herte deyde."[140] In possession, he thanked Love for helping him in a quarter where he had been likely to perish, but acknowledged to the lady a suzerain's right to make him live or die.[141] Like Troiolo, but more insistently, he expressed the notion at dawn that parting threatened his life.[142] And when back in his own chamber with the confidant, he granted, like Troiolo, that he would have been dead without his aid. [143]

At the next dawn with Criseyde, he shared her fancied sensation of "dethis wownde." [144]

In the descending action, Chaucer moderately reinforces the insistence upon the hero's dying so very strong in the source. He passes over very few of the passages relating to it, and none of significance except the attempted suicide, and more often expands than condenses in adaptation. Here and there he gives new reminders of the specter—in several cases, very memorable ones.

Near death in the parliament, Troilus preferred it to separation.[145] Retreating to his chamber, he invoked death, cursed the day he came into the world, reproached Fortune for not having slain him rather than deprived him of the lady, anticipated an end as miserable as Edippe's, called on his soul to leave the body and follow Criseyde and on her to receive it, apostrophized lovers who would visit his tomb, and named Calkas as his bane.[146] He was "Neigh ded for smert" when Pandarus came to him; and the latter proposed a new mistress, Chaucer tells us, not from conviction, but

> To help his frend, lest he for sorwe deyde.[147]

Troilus, as close to dying as before, replied that he would rather do so than be unfaithful, exclaimed "thow sleest me with thi speche," and called for his quietus in a long apostrophe to Death.[148] Pandarus then made his second proposal, abduction—venturing it, as his thought is represented, "rather than my felawe deye." [149] Still recalcitrant, Troilus exclaimed "whi nyl myn herte breste?" [150] The confidant, repeating the proposal, urged action even if it brought death in civil conflict, but the lover, though tempted, said that he would rather die than seize the lady without her consent.[151] As indicated in the notes, most of the above allusions to death have correspondents of some sort in the *Filostrato*. Of those, which do not, the one most memorable is the prince's fine, if sentimental, apostrophe:

> O ye loveris, that heigh upon the whiel
> Ben set of Fortune, in good aventure,
> God leve that ye fynde ay love of stiel,
> And longe mote youre lif in joie endure!
> But whan ye comen by my sepulture,
> Remembreth that youre felawe resteth there;
> For I loved ek, though ich unworthi were.

Pandarus, on going to the lady, told her that the lover and he had been almost sorrow-slain, as Pandaro that the former had wished death; and, like Pandaro, warned that the prince would destroy himself if she received him in her present sorrow.[152]

Chaucer tells us that Troilus was in full purpose to die when he soliloquized on predestination in the temple and makes him conclude with a prayer to Jove to effect his death or relieve his and his mistress' sorrow.[153]

During his last night with the heroine, Troilus was as near death from his own hand as Troiolo and talked about dying very much in the latter's fashion. He would have made an end with his sword had Criseyde remained unconscious.[154] Abed, he, as she, lamented birth.[155] If she failed to come back to him, he said, he would commit suicide; would die, if Calkas kept her.[156] Should she submit to the exchange as she purposed, he was "but ded." [157]

Next day he asked himself whether it were not better to die in opposing it than to live on in torment and besought the departing lady to keep her promise and thus not cause his death; then, returning to his chamber, anathematized his birth and wished that he had perished at her going—all this in Troiolo's vein.[158] Receiving Pandarus on the next, he predicted that he would not live till morning; bade him attend to his funeral rites, offer Mars his steed, sword, and helm and Pallas his shield, and give Criseyde his ashes in an urn of gold; explained that he was sure of death because of his "maladie," his dreams past and present, and the two-nights shrieking of the owl; and besought Mercurye to guide his disembodied soul.[159] This pas-

173

sage, added by Chaucer, illustrates the speaker's death fixation in a most memorable fashion while contributing also to the antique semblance of the poem. Later in the ten-day period, Chaucer gives the prince a song imaging his future as a voyage to death in place of the one in the source appealing to Amore for release of soul from body.[160]

Like Boccaccio's hero, Troilus thought death the only solution when the lady failed to return and was confirmed in this belief by the boar dream,[161] though, unlike him, he did not attempt suicide after it. And, if in his letter to her he did not threaten to do away with himself as his original, he made it clear that her disfavor would mean his end—as, for example, in the gracious valediction:

> And fareth wel, goodly, faire, fresshe may,
> As ye that lif or deth may me comande![162]

From discovery of the brooch, he was as bent upon death—and revenge —as Troiolo. When with Pandarus, he invoked it, wondered that she could have been so cruel as to slay him, lamented his birth, and vowed to seek his death in arms.[163] In pursuit of it, he wrought havoc among the Greeks, but as Fortune willed, neither killed nor was killed by Diomede in their many desperate encounters, dying at last—futilely—at the hands of Achilles.[164]

As for the rival, Chaucer effectively nullifies the single hint of his liability to death, adding to his resolve to attempt the lady even if he should die for it the cynical *non sequitur*,

> I shal namore lesen but my speche.[165]

Thus on record, the adventurer cannot be thought greatly discomposed when, as in the *Filostrato*, he turned red and quavered in the course of his wooing.[166]

Pandarus, who, except for paling on one occasion and claiming that he might swoon on another, appears as physically unaffected by his master's griefs as was Pandaro, is made, however, much more assertive of willingness to die for the hero. And if his threats of suicide to Criseyde may be taken *cum grano salis*, the offer to Troilus of his and his kinsmen's support in abduction breathes the most desperate resolve. More insistent than Pandaro, as we have seen, upon the parlous state of his friend, he is permitted to justify himself more explicitly by the obligation to save the prince's life. And thus self-exculpated for pandering and all the deceits which it involved, he shows as little compunction about the lady as the confidant in the *Filostrato*. His own unhappiness in love, like Pandaro's, is obscured by preoccupation with the hero's. Though there is more frequent and more ironically effective reference to it than there was to his original's, it is a side issue with him as with us. He is wrapt up in friendship as the prince in love.

Taking upon himself the responsibility for Troilus' fate with positive enthusiasm, he was confirmed in it expressly by his grateful lord:

> My lif, my deth, hol in thyn hond I leye.[167]

In his first talk with Criseyde, as already noted, the uncle threatened her, conditionally, with his as well as the lover's death:

> But if ye late hym deyen, I wol sterve—
> Have here my trouthe, nece, I nyl nat lyen—
> Al sholde I with this knyf my throte kerve,
>
> . . . .
> . . . . If that ye don us bothe dyen,
> Thus gilteles, than have ye fisshed fayre;

and then, after she proved difficult, absolutely:

> I se ful wel that ye sette lite of us,
> Or of oure deth! allas, I woful wrecche!
> Might he yet lyve, of me is nought to recche.
>
> . . . .
> But sith I se my lord mot nedes dye,
> And I with hym, here I me shryve, and seye
> That wikkedly ye don us bothe deye.
>
> But sith it liketh yow that I be ded,
> By Neptunus, that god is of the see,
> Fro this forth shal I nevere eten bred
> Til I myn owen herte blood may see;
> For certeyn I wol deye as soone as he.[168]

Such was "the sorwful ernest of the knyght," that the always timid Criseyde could vision a corpse encumbering her premises,

> And if this man sle here hymself, allas!
> In my presence, it wol be no solas.
> What men wolde of hit deme I kan nat seye,

and she determined so to proceed as to safeguard her honor but also his life.[169] Pandarus, having favored her with a specimen of the lover's woeful discourse, pled that to quote all of it would cause him to swoon; then made the best possible apology for himself and a final appeal for them both:

> But for to save his lif, and elles nought,
> And to noon harm of yow, thus am I dryven;
> And for the love of God, that us hath wrought,
> Swich cheer hym dooth, that he and I may lyven! [170]

"Wel neigh ded for routhe" at the lover's impatient woe,[171] he proposed the stratagem of feigned illness to remedy it. And when he had brought Criseyde to the bedside of the feigner, he implored,

175

> For love of God, make of this thing an ende,
> Or sle us both at ones, er ye wende.[172]

After she had left the chamber, he there protested to Troilus that he had engaged in procuring, not from hope of material reward, but out of concern for him, and the latter most thankfully agreed. This exchange of theirs is derived from one between Boccaccio's confidant and hero, but, as Dr. Slaughter has pointed out, with significant reinforcement of the former's apology and the latter's assuring reply; the go-between is made to say to the lover that he acted only to alleviate the distress,

> For which wel neigh thow deidest, as me thoughte,

and the beneficiary to encourage this other to continue in his course,

> sith thow has idon me this servyse,
> My lif to save.[173]

Troilus acknowledged, after consummation, that he owed his life to the intermediary, but almost word for word as Troiolo then put it.[174]
With the lover after the parliament, Pandarus was "ful ded and pale of hewe." [175] His first proposal, so callous toward his niece, that Troilus should replace her, Chaucer explains away, as already noted, as a hasty expedient to keep the prince from death; and his second of abduction was ventured for the same end.[176] In urging it, the counsellor promised:

> I wol ben ded, or she shal bleven oure;

and then, more explicitly:

> I wol myself ben with the at this dede,
> Theigh ich and al my kyn, upon a stownde,
> Shulle in a strete as dogges liggen dede,
> Thorugh-girt with many a wid and blody wownde,
> In every cas I wol a frend be founde.[177]

Though he was to live on, no line could have been a truer epitaph than the last of this passage. He was to tell Criseyde presently that he and Troilus had almost expired of woe, and, after the boar dream, to lament, because of the dreamer's misery, that he, the spectator, had ever been born.[178]

Committed as he was to friendship and self-exculpated in that commitment, he professed, on several occasions, to prefer death to her dishonor or his own,[179] yet went on risking both; suggested that she inflict capital punishment for what he had done but suggested this humorously.[180]

He lost color and a night's repose for his own love before he solicited

176

Criseyde on Troilus' behalf; once spoke in jest to her of fasting for it; and twice, in earnest, to the prince of dying on that account.[181] Understandably sympathetic with the latter's woes because of personal experience, he is in the ironic position of attempting for another what he could not achieve for himself.

To conclude this section with traitorous father, it need only be remarked that, as in the *Filostrato,* he professed a readiness to die if his child were not restored to him.[182] Returning to the source in the first pages of the next section, we shall consider behavior of Criseida, Troiolo, Diomede, Pandaro, and the father which visually signals their states of mind and heart.

Expressive Actions

THE *Filostrato* had a good deal to offer our poet in the way of visualized behavior for hero and heroine, if very little in this kind for rival and confidant. What it pictured of the Trojan pair was generally bravura, manifesting the violent passions which, as noted in the preceding section, affected their appearance and rendered them death-conscious. Undemonstrativeness in the Greek followed from his exemption from suffering. Pandaro, who had reason enough for displays of feeling, was permitted but few, it may be assumed, because his was only a supporting role.

The lady's deportment, as Boccaccio presented it, suggested lively emotion but neither much sweetness nor the assured dignity of rank. She manifested resentment against her countrymen, desire and grief to an extreme in her affair with Troiolo, a momentary pique with Diomede, something, but not much, of the tranquil affection of a kinswoman for Pandaro. And she fell short of patrician charm with all of them.

As to her public behavior. She knelt in prudent and lachrymose supplication to Ettore.[1] But as she stood crowded by the temple door, she made room for herself while drawing the mantle from her face and in such manner as to impress Troiolo with her spirit:

> Piacque quell' atto a Troiolo e 'l tornare
> ch' ella fe' 'n sé alquanto sdegnosetto,
> quasi dicesse:—E' non ci si può stare.—[2]

Mounted for the distasteful trip to camp, she clapped spurs to her horse after she had let the Trojans know how little she thought of them and pointedly refrained from a farewell glance at anyone.[3]

In commerce with Troiolo, she was encouraging from the first and soon ardent. She returned gaze for gaze as he strolled past her window on the very day she had learned of his regard.[4] When she heard him enter her house for their first night, she signalled her awareness with a cough, and, joining him as soon as possible, she shared a thousand embraces and even more kisses.[5] Professing embarrassment, when abed, about removal of her last garment, she cast it off nonetheless and wrapped herself in his arms to experience with him love's "ultimo valore."[6] Locked in embrace all night, they gazed constantly upon one another.[7] She kissed his eyes in return for the like attention to hers.[8] Their talk of past sorrow was interrupted by more osculation, but neither words nor action by sleep, and

> saziarsi l'un dell' altro non potieno,
> quantunque molto fosse il fare e 'l dire
> ciò ch' a quell' atto appartener credieno.[9]

Desire of embracing fired them again at dawn, and Criseida asked and received a last embrace before kissing him goodbye.[10] With Troiolo back in her arms for a second night, she opined that she was the most delighted of females and that anyone would die out of hand in order to win

> un poco sol di cosí gran piacere.[11]

They exchanged kisses on mouth, eyes, and breast.[12]

Tearful immediately before and after leaving Troy,[13] Criseida strenuously postured grief at the prospect though still capable of sharing love with Troiolo. After her gossips had left her, she threw herself on her bed and there beat her breast and tore her hair.[14] She hid her face in her arms at Pandaro's coming and again after she had conversed with him.[15] When the lover came, she exchanged kisses in their welcoming embrace; then raised her eyes to his and lapsed into the deathlike swoon.[16] She could propose bed, however, after recovery of her senses.[17] Close, if teary, embraces ensued.[18] Clasping as straitly at dawn, they parted after a full thousand kisses.[19] Next day they gazed into one another's eyes and clasped hands before the final separation.[20] After it, Troiolo in thinking of her recalled joyous laughter.[21] The reminiscence is the only notice of such merriment in her in the entire poem; the most that was previously recorded was arch smiling at the cousin.

Before she answered Diomede's tender which she was speedily to fancy, the lady reproved his boldness with a hostile glance,

> a traverso mirandol dispettosa.[22]

As for deportment with Pandaro, she rose to greet him when he appeared for his first visit, but, though hostess, did not lead but was led by him to a place where they might talk.[23] She asked him smilingly why he gazed at her with such intentness, barely held back the tears after his disclosure that Troiolo was her lover.[24] When the envoy came again, they saluted one another from afar, then clasped hands.[25] Coy at first about the letter which he had brought, she soon smiled and put it in her bosom.[26]

Troiolo's actions, while often parallel to hers, do differentiate him from her to some extent. He could be dissemblingly gracious in public. He assumed the initiative in love-making, though no more ardent in it than his partner; and, of course, had far greater occasion than she to manifest love sorrow. And, owing so much to the intermediary, he showed affection toward him more warmly.

As for his behavior in public view. At the feast of Pallade, he sauntered about the temple, laughingly pointing out now this fond lover now that.[27] His was the pride that goes before a fall, for, at sight of Criseida, he was held in gaze as the others by their ladies.[28] On the ride with her out of Troy, he had the grace to make Antenore precede him,[29] though not to exchange courtesies with Diomede.

In private, he yielded occasionally to tears up to possession and, as noted above, shared physical transports with her during that happiest time. He wept before Pandaro came to his chamber for the first time and in the course of that visit.[30] The friend apprised Criseida of the lover's sadness on this occasion and also on an earlier, when he had seen him bow his head near tears.[31] In his stroll by her window, the prince scrutinized her for possible effects of Pandaro's solicitation.[32] Having mentioned weeping in his first letter to her, he moistened the gem with which he sealed it on his teary cheeks.[33] In the first night of love, he was the mentor, though of a cooperative pupil; he gave the first embrace, prescribed nudity, led her to kiss his eyes by kissing hers, proceeded from eyes to face and bosom, and—near tears— gave more than kiss for kiss, it seems, at parting.[34] In the second, he and she were equal in act and she alone vocal about sensual delight.

From the "parlamento," of course, he became more copious in weeping[35] and more violent in other displays of emotion. Resuscitated by his father and brothers on that occasion, he started to his feet and made for his palace without a glance at anyone.[36] He gave way to self-torment when locked in his chamber—prostrating himself, knocking his head against the wall, and beating his face with his hands, and breast and arms with his fists.[37] This fury at an end, he took to his bed for mournful soliloquy.[38] Coming to Criseida by Pandaro's arrangement, he was naturally beside himself when she swooned in the welcoming embrace; he rained kisses upon her face, tested all her members for sign of life, and, judging her dead, composed them in seemly

180

fashion and drew his sword to end himself, but had instead to speed her opportune recovery by taking her into his arms.[39] As remarked in the discussion of Criseida's behavior, they managed to enjoy love that night and, next day, gazed into one another's eyes at parting. On the night of that day, Troiolo twisted and turned abed, embracing his pillow in default of the lady.[40] And after the boar dream, he was to run for a knife hanging in his chamber.[41]

Friendship also moved him to lively displays of feeling. Ashamed to reveal that he desired the cousin of his intimate, he fell back on the bed and hid his face when pressed to confession by Pandaro in their first session.[42] And he lowered his gaze after protesting that he expected nothing unseemly from her.[43] With assurance of seduction from the lax relative,

> Troiolo destro si gittò in terra
> del letto, lui abbracciando e basciando;

and, with good report from him of progress toward it, the lover was to embrace him a thousand times and kiss him as often.[44] Promising discretion before his first night with her, the prince looked his friend assuringly in the face.[45] And in thankfulness for it afterward, he threw himself on Pandaro's neck, kissed his forehead, and repeated the kiss; later, took him by the hand into a garden whither he repaired to sing of love.[46] After the reversal, he again threw himself upon the friend's neck, but weeping; and again took him by the hand, but to go on sorrowful pilgrimage to Criseida's empty house.[47] For once hostile, he struggled with him desperately for the knife.

Diomede, assured enough to seat himself in Criseida's presence, did recognize the presumption of his address by lowering his gaze midway.[48]

Pandaro was allowed few signs of attitude despite his importance. Leading Criseida by the hand into her own "loggia" for their first conversation, he laughed and chatted before fixing his gaze portentously upon her, and he was moved to smile by her curiosity about Troiolo.[49] They took one another by the hand upon his return, and he smiled when quizzing her about the letter which he had brought from the lover.[50] Her wretchedness after the parliament moved him to tears.[51] Weeping with Troiolo on that day and afterward, he had had occasion to laugh at his timidity in their first conference and was to have occasion in next to their last to use force against him.[52]

Last and least as usual, Calcas had tears at his command to sway the Greeks.[53]

Now that we are to proceed from *Filostrato* to *Troilus*, some generalizations may be offered as to trends of adaptation. Chaucer pictures the action of the four principals more fully than Boccaccio, as he does the persons of three of them, and again to the enhancement of realism. Modifying the patterns of their behavior as he expands, he creates fresh impressions of their natures and of the relations prevailing between them. The heroine, whose physical womanliness he stresses, is gentled in her deportment toward the public and toward her lovers while made more socially assured with these individuals and even playful with her relative. The first lover, given the semblance as well as the reputation of a warrior prince, is credited with new demonstrations of the humility appropriate to his knightliness and yet allowed the masterfulness of his sex at the proper moment. The second, visualized as a burly male, has a taking hand to match his predatory spirit. And the confidant is mass translated into energy—denied portraiture as in the source but vividly realized, as not there, through behavior expressive of his attitudes toward kinswoman and friend. Perfected with them in charm of manner, he is a sovereign manipulator and entertainer.

As for Criseyde and, first of all, her demeanor in public. She knelt weeping before Ector like Boccaccio's heroine.[54] In the temple scene, though defensive like her, she was less aggressively so. Stationing herself near the door and behind others—as Chaucer explains—from fear of shame, she showed spirit delightful to the prince but by a glance that said "What! may I nat stonden here?" not, as Criseida, by a sweep of the arm for standing room.[55] She made so favorable an impression on Deiphebus and Eleyne in the new sequence involving them that they extolled "hire manere." [56] Sighing instead of scolding, when the time came to ride out of Troy, she neither put spurs to her horse as Criseida did nor disdainfully averted her gaze from the spectators.[57]

She is given opportunity for display of tenderness to the lover before consummation as Criseida was not, but is made more shamefast than her original up to surrender and, after, less ardent in response to the lover's caresses. As Troilus rode by from battle, she recalled what her uncle had just told her about him,

> And with that thought, for pure ashamed, she
> Gan in hire hed to pulle, and that as faste,
> Whil he and alle the peple forby paste;

seated threafter in cogitation, she "heng hire hed ful lowe." [58] Pandarus, with her when the prince rode past again, had to beg "O fle naught in." [59] But when he had brought her to the lover's bedside at Deiphebus' house, she was composed and kind. To keep the alleged sick man healthfully recumbent, she

> Gan bothe hire hondes softe upon hym leye;

cast her eyes upon him "Ful esily and ful debonairly" before accepting his service on her own terms; and, after acceptance, took him in arms and kissed him.[60] Her proffer to the confidant in the latter's house,

> Have heere, and bereth hym this blewe ryng,[61]

indicates as much good will as temporizing prudency. The token being rejected, she consented to receive Troilus as soon as she could get out of bed, but was urged "liggeth stille, and taketh hym right here." [62] If as a matter of discipline she kept the lover kneeling for some time after his appearance at this cue, she kissed him at last and bade him seat himself.[63] A woman wronged by his alleged jealousy, she must chide him for it and then torment him into insensibility by shedding "a fewe brighte teris newe" and hiding her head in the sheet.[64] A loving one, she whispered in the ear of the swooner that she was not angry, collaborated with Pandarus in first aid, supplemented that with kisses, and, after resuscitation, laid her arm forgivingly over the prince and bestowed more kisses.[65] Alone with Troilus, however, she trembled when he took possession.[66] All that Chaucer tells us about her subsequent behavior that night as distinct from the lover's is that she kissed him, pinned her brooch upon his shirt,

> And hym in armes tok, and ofte keste;[67]

and all that he tells about it as shared with Troilus is that she and the prince wound one another in arms, experienced "the grete worthynesse" of love, wondered in each other's arms whether they were there or dreaming, exchanged rings, interrupted talk with kissing, and neglected sleep.[68] Some adapted from the *Filostrato* and some original, these particulars are invariably so phrased as to avoid any suggestion of lustfulness in the heroine. And in our poet's reworking of the second night of love, Criseida's exclamation about sexual delight is omitted along with all details of physical endearment on her part—as on Troiolo's.

He takes over nearly all details of her sorrowing after the reversal, however, changes them little, and adds nothing very material. Like Criseida, his heroine was copious of tears until visited by Diomede,[69] and, like her, extravagant in other maifestations of grief while still in Troy. Falling on her bed after the gossips' departure, she tore her hair, wrung her fingers, and beat her breast.[70] In her uncle's presence, she twice buried her face in her arms.[71] She laid her face upon Troilus' bosom, as she lost her senses in the embrace of welcome.[72] Gazing upon him and taking him in her arms after recovery, she proposed that they hie to bed.[73] There they embraced and kissed, if sadly.[74] After she was in camp, Troilus spoke in reminiscence of her joyous laughter as Troiolo of his lady's.[75] Diomede inferred that she had a lover at home since he had never seen her "laughe or maken joie." [76]

A more practiced hostess than Criseida, she did not wait for the visiting Diomede to seat himself but

> Welcomed hym, and down hym by hire sette;

and she had servants at her disposal who brought spices and wine.[77] Not taking exception to his address as the other did, she lowered her gaze after reply instead of eyeing him askance before.[78] And, tender as well as polite, she was moved by the hurt which he later sustained from Troilus:

> tho wepte she many a teere,
> Whan that she saugh his wyde wowndes blede.[79]

Her deportment as niece is far more extensively and charmingly reported than her original's as cousin. It evidences more warmth, humor, and social deftness than the other's and, of course, a greater concern for appearances. When the confidant appeared for his first visit, she rose, like Criseida, for salutation, but took his hand to seat this guest instead of leaving it to him to choose a place for conference.[80] A jest of hers about Pandarus' mistress made them both laugh.[81] At his hints of vital news, she cast down her eyes; and, at his amoral presentation of it, she burst into tears—not restraining them like Criseida.[82] But when he pretended to be off in dudgeon, she held him "by the lappe." [83] On his next call, a quip from him about his lovelorn state made her laugh so heartily that "it thoughte hire herte breste." [84] Proceeding to a secluded spot compliantly arm in arm with the jester, she would not take the letter he presented, as Criseida did its counterpart, yet smiled after he had thrust it into her bosom.[85] Witticisms of his then ensuing so amused her

> That she for laughter wende for to dye.[86]

Elsewhere on the premises, she repaid his playful violence in kind:

> Er he was war, she took hym by the hood,
> And seyde, "Ye were caught er that ye wiste." [87]

At Deiphebus' house, "Al innocent of Pandarus entente," she went arm in arm with him to her lover's chamber.[88] Invited by her uncle to his own house for supper, she laughingly—and ineffectually—pled rain as an excuse.[89] Next morning there she had reason enough to hide her face from him in the bedclothes.[90]

184

While Chaucer thus variously invests the heroine with more womanly charm than she mustered in the *Filostrato,* he takes care to make her royal lover the finer gentleman. And since he would be reticent about sexual ardor on her part, he chooses to present the intimacies of the climactic night as originating almost in toto with the man. He keeps the prince as demonstratively melancholy for love as he was in the *Filostrato* and—that irony may be served—as scornful of hapless lovers before enamorment.

In the temple scene, his Troilus behaved toward them with the ironic merriment of Boccaccio's prince; then cast up the brow as if to say how wise am I and thus further to provoke the God of Love.[91] Wounded, like Troiolo, by this deity, he too delighted in gazing upon the fair one.[92] When in the new episode of his triumphal return from battle the populace applauded him, he proved as modest as he had been overweening with the lovers—so much so, Chaucer informs us,

> That to byholde it was a noble game,
> How sobrelich he caste down his yën.[93]

And he so far masked his sorrow as to kiss the returning Antenor whereas Troiolo merely drew him into the cavalcade.[94]

Like the earlier hero, he progressed from weeping to joyful caresses in the ascending action, though, thanks to Pandarus, by a very different path. Drowned in tears before the first conversation with that worthy, he was twice reproved in it for them.[95] As in the *Filostrato,* the friend told the lady that the prince had bowed his head sorrowfully on an earlier occasion and the narrator informs us that he wet his signet with his tears.[96] Riding past Criseyde's house as Pandarus directed, the lover humbly, even fearfully saluted her.[97] In bed at Deiphebus', he apologized for inability to kneel to her, might have risen had she not restrained him, and made his declaration

> With look down cast and humble iyolden chere.[98]

And in the closet in Pandarus' house, he knelt by her bed until, at long last, she gave him the word to sit down; hung his head at her reproachful sorrow and sank to his knees again before loss of consciousness.[99] Turning dominant upon recovery,

> He hire in armes faste to hym hente,

stroked her naked body to the accompaniment of a thousand kisses, puncuated thanksgiving with more osculation, gazed protractedly upon her face, bestowed kisses upon her eyes, and strained her to him again and again[100]—all this beside actions of his lumped with hers which have been cited above.[101]

After the parliament, Troilus, like Troiolo, was often in tears[102] and now and again impelled to other displays of woe. Like him, he hastened to chamber from that assembly to vent his feelings masochistically before subsiding upon his bed.[103] Joining the heroine when night came, he reacted to her swoon with the tenderness and desperation of Troiolo;[104] and, with Troiolo's mixture of sorrow and delight, he enjoyed her love for the last time.[105] Like his original again, he cast his eye appealingly upon the lady as they parted next day outside the city and tossed sleeplessly in the ensuing night, regretting that he had only a pillow to embrace.[106]

In adapting the prince's behavior toward his friend, Chaucer keeps it indicative of trust and dependence but notably minimizes one aspect prominent in the source—that of physical contact. Whereas Troiolo responded to Pandaro's initial encouragements by embracing and kissing him, apparently face to face, Troilus acknowledged Pandarus' by embracement only, and expressly in a kneeling posture; and while the earlier hero hugged and kissed the intimate a thousand times for good progress claimed with the beloved, the latter reverently "held up bothe his hondes" to him at the same juncture.[107] In new scenes, on Criseyde's street and at his brother's house respectively, Troilus "bekked on Pandare" by way of friendly salutation and took a broad jest from him with a smile[108]—the only smile on his part to be mentioned after enamorment. In an episode transferred to that house from a temple, Chaucer's prince confirmed promise of discretion, as Boccaccio's had done, by steadfast gaze.[109] But, when in his own palace with Pandarus after consummation, he knelt to thank him instead of falling on his neck and kissing his forehead as the other was reported to have done with Pandaro.[110] And though, like Troiolo, he led the companion by the hand into a garden when he resorted to it to sing of love,[111] he did not hang upon the latter's neck when grief-stricken by the parliament as his original was allowed to do. He cast his eye appealingly upon the friend, Chaucer tells us, after he had viewed the empty palace of his mistress.[112] This distraught glance is the last visualized indication of attitude toward the helper, since the struggle for the knife is to be eliminated.

Our poet's relieving the hero of Italianate clasping and kissing of the friend is the more notable in that it runs counter to his accentuation of physical endearments lavished by the former upon the mistress. Whatever his motives may have been in playing down such effusiveness toward the fellow male, one result is to forestall conjecture of even latent homosexuality. And, making him kneel instead to his benefactor, he brings out his idealistic humility in friendship, as he brings it out in love by putting him in that posture before the mistress. The conduct of the henchman toward the lover, as we shall see presently, he styles to indicate a close but normal relationship.

Before taking up the actions of Pandarus, we have three small particulars to note about Chaucer's Diomede. He presumed, as Boccaccio's did not, to take the rein of the lady's horse for the trip to camp and to exact a glove from her on his first visit, though, like his original, he showed diffidence on the latter occasion by a sideward glance.[113]

As for the intermediary, our poet increases visualization of his behavior in the ascending action proportionally even more than that of heroine or hero in the same span, though not in the descending where liveliness would have been out of place. Multiplying this character's gestures toward both the others, he is careful to balance warmth with humor as well as to temper familiarity with some deference. The comic spirit evidenced in Pandarus keeps his avuncular affection from seeming mawkish, his friendship from being suspect of abnormality, his vicarious delight in love from coming unpleasantly close to voyeurism—in each case despite the heightening of emphasis upon the particular emotion. And, if a concomitant of easy morals, the spirit is dis-arming even with those readers least inclined to absolve him for seduction. The intimacy which permits humor does not negate rank. Pandarus, himself a lord, can fetch and carry for the prince but not be served by him; play the masterful uncle with Criseyde in private and yet treat her ceremoniously at his supper party. Amusingly protean in his deportment, he remains a self-consistent personality throughout, as will appear from the following surveys of his behavior with Criseyde and of that with Troilus.

His first call upon the lady establishes the technique for solicitation of alternating gaiety and gravity—pressure and relaxation of pressure. At the start. he joined with her in laughing at his own involvement in love.[114] In gingerly approach to the disclosure of Troilus', he kissed her; gave a little cough; then gazed at her intently, as Pandaro did on this occasion; and finally requested that she give him her hand.[115] Tears poured from his eyes, when, rebuffed for the news, he spoke of suicide and enforced the threat with a gesture—

Al sholde I with this knyf my throte kerve.[116]

He bowed his head after further pleading and started up as if to leave her when that was ill-received.[117] Stayed by her, he smiled, like Pandaro, at request for information about the suitor.[118]

When he called again, he proposed that they repair to her garden, and, as already noted, they went to it "arm in arm yfeere."[119] Once there he stared

187

at her in amazement at refusal of the letter which he had brought, and, not waiting for her to take it as Pandaro did with Criseida, he

> hente hire faste,
> And in hire bosom the lettre down he thraste.[120]

This presumption he salved with "his beste japes." Pressing for a letter in reply after they had gone indoors, he "held his hondes up, and sat on knowe," in mock serious appeal for "the labour it to sowe and plite." [121]

As earnest of his concern for the lawsuit which he was to invent, he opened a later visit with this evidential claim to haste:

> O verray God, so have I ronne!
> Lo, nece myn, se ye nought how I swete? [122]

Convinced, she went to the house of Deiphebus next day to gain support against the alleged litigant, and there, as remarked above, proceeded from the great chamber to Troilus' small one "arm in arm" with her uncle.[123] Leading her "by the lappe" to the prince's bedside, Pandarus seemingly almost wept for illness feigned.[124] And, at his friend's appeal for mercy, he

> wep as he to water wolde,
> And poked evere his nece new and newe.[125]

Rendering thanks to Cupid and Venus for concessions from his niece, he went down on his knees and raised face and hands to heaven.[126] He permitted himself a significant laugh[127] in promising a meeting at his own house, at which the lovers should have time enough, as he put it, to converse.

Inviting her at a later date to sup with him, "he swor hire in hire ere" that, if she did not accept, he would never come to her again.[128] He took her in his arms when she appeared for the engagement and laughed when rain prevented her departure.[129] At bedtime, he turned ceremonious:

> Tho Pandarus, hire em, right as hym oughte,
> With wommen swiche as were hire most aboute,
> Ful glad unto hire beddes syde hire broughte,
> And took his leve, and gan ful lowe loute.[130]

Returning clandestinely with Troilus to where she lay, he murmured in her ear that she should keep quiet.[131] And coming back alone in the morning, he pried under the sheet which she had drawn over her face, made his playful offer of a sword for his own decapitation, and

> With that his arm al sodeynly he thriste
> Under hire nekke, and at the laste hire kyste.[132]

Against all these details of behavior toward the lady in the ascending action, there is but one in the descending—and that one borrowed from Pandaro—weeping for her misery directly after the parliament.[133]

As would be expected, Pandarus' deportment toward the friend confirms intimacy even more strongly than that toward the niece. The go-between was obligated to more constant attendance upon the suitor than upon the sought, preoccupied with his welfare to the neglect of hers, and more inclined to robustious humor in the man-to-man relationship than in the avuncular. The humor Chaucer blends with the preoccupation throughout the ascending action.

So in early scenes in the lover's establishment. When Troilus, abed in his chamber, seemed at last ready to identify the beloved,

> "A ha!" quod Pandare, "here bygynneth game."
>
> And with that word he gan hym for to shake,
> And seyde, "Thef, thow shalt hyre name telle." [134]

And the lover's assurance of modesty of desire, which followed the naming, made Pandarus laugh as Troiolo's similar one made Pandaro.[135] According to the report which the uncle gave Criseyde of time spent in "the paleis gardyn," [136] he was so manly as to participate in exercise with Troilus and so solicitous as to play the lurking spy. They diverted themselves there with jumping and dart-throwing after they had canvassed strategy against the Greeks. Pandarus strolled apart when the friend said he would doze, but, noting groans, returned to "stalke hym softely byhynde." Hearing out a lament to Love, he stole away and again came back, this time with comic—and disingenuous—reproof for sleepiness. After the session with Criseyde in which he had told of this incident, Pandarus—repeatedly summoned by the anxious prince—"com lepyng in atones," jested about the summoner's impatience, and, when chambered with him for the night, affected teasingly to withhold details of the visit to the niece:

> Ly stylle, and lat me slepe,
> And don thyn hood; thy nedes spedde be! [137]

Returning with a letter from her after Troilus had gone to bed again on the next night, the ever-serviceable one provided illumination for its perusal:

> Have here a light, and loke on al this blake.[138]

At Deiphebus' house, he leapt into the chamber where Troilus was feigning illness and made bawdy pronouncement "in his ere." [139] Yet he had tears on

189

tap to impress the lady, when, as already noted, he brought her to the suitor.[140] Alone with him there after dark, he perched on the bedside to implore discretion in all earnestness.[141]

At his own house, he made speed to bundle friend with niece. Having sat through the former's prayer in the stew, he thrust the "furred cloke" upon him which he had providently brought and drew him "by the lappe" forthwith into her closet.[142] With the one pawn on his knees before the other and she speechless in confusion, Pandarus "that so wel koude feele In every thyng," ran for a cushion and offered it playfully to the suppliant—"Kneleth now, while that yow leste."[143] She took this hint and bade the lover seat himself, but it was the confidant who specified the place, namely within the bed curtains, where, as he said, each might hear the other better.[144] The point settled,

> he drow hym to the feere,
> And took a light, and fond his contenaunce,
> As for to looke upon an old romaunce.[145]

Reactivated by the prince's swoon, he cast him on the bed, stripped him to his shirt, and, with Criseyde, applied remedy so successfully that withdrawal to the fireside was again in order and, before long, an exit.[146]

The comic triumph had its dangers, as he well knew. Visiting Troilus in his palace on the morrow, he greeted him soberly and sat down on his bed there to implore caution.[147]

Adversity subdued him. Tearful as he softly entered the lover's chamber after the parliament, he stood in gaze with folded arms; then, like Pandaro, was moved to profuse weeping by his friend's example.[148] And he stared at the ground when rebuked for the suggestion of a new mistress.[149] Returning the next day, he greeted Troilus soberly and sat down on his bed [150] to give him such comfort as he could. Though he spent the night with him after the interlude at Sarpedoun's,[151] he had, so far as we are told, no counsel to offer.

As for the lady's father, Chaucer keeps the circumstance that he wept on her account before the Greeks, and specifies, as Boccaccio did not, that he took her in his arms when she arrived and kissed her "twenty tyme." [152]

Visualizing the behavior of the five characters more extensively than Boccaccio, Chaucer gives fuller information about locales and correlates action with setting more precisely. As will appear in the next section, his representations as to place are so much more explicit than his author's that they strengthen verisimilitude throughout and so divergent from the other's in some parts of the story that they change the course and tone of events. The stage data in the *Filostrato*, being very meager, left the field open for improvisation.

Place

B OCCACCIO treats place to significant effect but with the utmost economy. He concentrates action in a very few locales and leaves these spatially uncon-nected; is always terse about settings and highly selective in correlation of movement with background. That such is the case will appear from the following schematic review of what he does with temples, mansions, the city's defense perimeter, and the land beyond it.

Temples are the only public edifices he mentions. After he has concluded his first and unlocalized episode of Criseida's audience with Ettore, he prepares for the enamorment scene by informing us that the Trojans had kept up "li divin sacrificii" and, above all, their devotions to Pallade and that the city fathers, when spring came, arranged for the accustomed honors "al Palladio fatale." [1] He then brings us to the site of these honors, a large and noble temple—not to tell us anything about the pagan rites—but to picture Criseida by the door and to follow Troiolo about, with reminiscence apparently of a very recent Easter Sunday in San Lorenzo of Naples.[2] Later in the story, he tells us that Pandaro came upon his friend "in un tempio pensando" and took occasion to implore secrecy in the love soon to be enjoyed.[3] The "parlamento," we may infer, was held inside the city and in some public building,[4] but it is not assigned to one.

Three dwellings figure in the action: those of hero and heroine, between which most of it is divided, and that of Sarpidone, the locale of a minor interlude. What is stated or implied about them is realistic in terms of Boccaccio's own period but never archaeologically.

Troiolo's establishment is always called a palace[5] and thus, but only thus,

191

indicated to be magnificent. References to companions or friends of the prince without indication that any of them were domiciled with him and to servants without specification of their number[6] afford no clue as to the size of the building. And the one accommodation to be singled out is the "camera" —presumably, if not demonstrably, always the same bedroom.[7] Though his entertainment of "compagni" after the Palladian festival and at least one conversation with Pandaro must have taken place elsewhere in the palace,[8] we are not told in what part. In scenes in the chamber, there is careful account of Troiolo's going to bed and rising from it, if not of his every movement,[9] but hardly any of Pandaro's disposition of himself.[10] The hero's persistent recourse to the chamber, and to its inner sanctum the bed, is the objective correlative of his withdrawal into a private world organized on the convictions that love was the sole good and oblivion the only alternative to its enjoyment. In one sequence, the apartment might suggest the womb to disciples of Freud, so great is the emphasis placed upon its being closed and dark. Attendants who were in it after the parliament quitted the chamber, "ma pria le finestre serraro"; left thus alone "nella camera sua serrata e scura," the prince indulged his feelings, then went to the door "che serrata avea" and opened it that he might dispatch a valet to Pandaro; and the summoned one was presently in the room "oscura e cheta." [11]

The lover, so devoted to his chamber, sought an outdoor hideaway at but two periods: at the one, as reported by Pandaro, in "selve ombrose," at the other, as directly stated by the narrator, in "un giardin." [12] Neither spot is located in relation to the palace or otherwise.

As for the lady's abode, Boccaccio's failure ever to call it a palace suggests that it was inferior to Troiolo's, but his several designations of it as "casa" and his one as "magione" all occur in contexts which imply some pretentiousness. We learn from these passages that it housed a considerable group, boasted a second story, and had windows on the street side as well as a door.[13] She must have been well up the social ladder—though far below the prince as we are often reminded.

The "camera" is the featured room in her dwelling,[14] though not as constantly the stage for action in it as Troiolo's in his. It is her retreat before and after the first night of love, and their rendezvous on this and all subsequent nights. Alone in it at three junctures before consummation, she is never clearly postured; in the later scenes there, however, she is dispatched to bed, and, except in one, with Troiolo on hand to lie there.[15] In that one—immediately after the parliament—Pandaro, who came to assuage her grief, is left unpostured while doing so.

Action in the house not assigned to the chamber and, in part, expressly outside it is presented to us as follows.

When Pandaro came to her for the first time, he and she proceeded from some point not specified to an apartment vaguely denominated "una loggia" [16] —there to converse, we learn, but not whether seated or standing. A little later in the day we find her ogling Troiolo from a window,[17] but where the window we cannot tell. Upon the cousin's return, she quitted companions of hers who were seated at a spot unnamed [18] and went to meet him at some other and, apparently while standing there, to receive from him the prince's letter of declaration. The two following appearances of his—to urge an answer and to collect it—are reported without indication of place or posture; the next—to win an assignation—is fixed in the "loggia" of his first visit.[19]

Criseida was upstairs with housemates of hers, but not demonstrably in her chamber, when she heard Troiolo enter below to keep the appointment.[20] Hidden, as instructed, " 'n certo loco remoto ed oscuro," he assured Criseida, when she descended to him with apologies for the confinement of his royal splendor, that this "particella" was dearer to him than his palace.[21] After they had embraced there and kissed a thousand times—one wonders what happened to the torch she bore—he went with her up the stair[22] to those delights which he had purchased with token sacrifice of rank in the dark corner.

Preliminaries to chambered joy were the same on their second night as on the first.[23] And on the undescribed nights between the second and the last they were still so, as we gather from the lines introducing that terminal occasion.

Boccaccio, having chronicled the lover's eagerness for it, informs us:

> Crisëida, quando ora e tempo fue,
> com' era usata, con un torchio acceso
> sen venne a lui.[24]

Fainting this time when taken into Troiolo's arms, she was disposed by him as a corpse, but recovered to find herself again in arms and to infer suicidal intent from the sword which he had drawn and expiration of a great part of the night from "il torchio consumato." [25] One is left to wonder what Troiolo did with the sword while snatching up Criseida, and—as on the first night —what befell the torch.

Some hours before these transports, she had received female visitors, "le quali esser solean sue compagnesse"—certainly outside the chamber, though where outside not determinable.[26] Their unwelcome call is the only social occasion for her to be developed in the entire poem. Despite the implication

193

of more such contacts in the phrase just quoted and in reminiscence of Troiolo about her later on,[27] we are left to feel that she, like the prince, was set apart by love.

Sarpidone's dwelling is implied to be splendid by designation of the owner as "baron possente" and inclusion in the list of entertainments which he offered to his guests of hunting, the attention of many ladies, music, and superlative feasts.[28] Troiolo's distaste for all this accords with theoretical renunciation in his happy time of every interest but love; contrasts diamatically with his practice in that era—hawking and hunting, patronage of deserving youths, and ingratiation of everyone.[29]

Progress from building to building is treated even more sketchily than action within. Streets, which must have connected them, are left to be assumed. Distance is indicated only between Troiolo's abode and Sarpidone's, and the specification of "quattromila passi"[30] in this instance raises a question, left unresolved, as to whether the latter was within the city limits or not. Riding is specified on but two occasions, Criseida's departure to camp and Troiolo's subsequent pilgrimage to her house and other places associated with her.[31] Nocturnal trips from the palace to her house would naturally be made on foot to avoid attention and daylight ones might be as well, but it is curious that Boccaccio does not mount the prince and his also aristocratic confidant for the jaunt, expressly longish, to Sarpidone's.

The fortifications, once mentioned early in the story,[32] are important to it only from the time of Criseida's departure. Witnessing Priamo's surrender of her to Diomede somewhere in town, Troiolo accompanied her—with others —"infin di fuori a tutto il vallo"; then rode back to Troy and his palace.[33] That the route led through a gate appears only later, when we read of Troiolo awaiting the tenth day,

> El se ne gía talvolta in sulla porta
> per la quale era la sua donna uscita.[34]

Where he stood when he viewed the camp during this interval is not revealed.[35] On the tenth day, he waited outside the gate with Pandaro until noon, anxiously scrutinizing all who approached, and waited again outside it from some time in the afternoon until starshine, mistaking a cart in the twilight for his lady, and making the sentries keep it open for two hours after they had clamored that all must come in—citizens and strangers, villeins and their beasts.[36] The unusual wealth of detail for this day helps us to share Troiolo's suspensefulness. He kept as long vigil there, it is tersely indicated, on the eleventh as on the tenth.[37]

No man's land objectifies the lovers' separation, but is unimportant as a

194

stage for events. As might be expected, it is not clearly mapped. The battle which brought Antenore's capture was waged, we are told, "ne' campi piani."[38] And we learn from the record of the first days of separation, that the hero could gaze at "li Greci attendati davanti a Troia," and the heroine, at the walls, palaces, towers and fortresses of the city.[39] Somewhere near the shoreside camp, however, there were "monti," for in his letter to her the prince expressed envy of them, as well as of the sun and "l'onde discendenti al mare," on the ground that they enjoyed sight of her which was denied to him.[40]

Lastly, as for the camp itself, though tents are mentioned collectively,[41] no settings are provided for any of the action there—Calcas' appeal to the Greeks, his reception of his daughter, her self-torment up to the fourth day, or her talk with Diomede on that day. Nearness to the sea appears from several contexts—most memorably from the hero's letter to her, in which sympathy is expressed anent tempests from that quarter.[42]

In the *Troilus,* hints about locale are quite numerous, as may be seen from the pertinent entries in Professor Magoun's article, "Chaucer's Ancient and Biblical World."[43] According to Dr. Mayo, however, they are generally so slight as to be of only minor functional importance.[44] This I deny. It can and will be shown that they constitute a substantial advance over the less numerous and even terser particulars of the *Filostrato*. Taken together, they lend more verisimilitude than Boccaccio's, because more often exact as to settings and dispositions in them. A few are antiquarian or meant at least to be so: namings of a Trojan gate and river and of legend-rich places outside Troy,[45] and imaginings of devotion in the local temples. Many more—largely those about domestic arrangements—are of Chaucer's own period, as scholars have pointed out.[46] Realistic in effect because familiar, they serve also to aristocratize the milieu. Various new details about the heroine's establishment warrant its medieval splendor, while one or two about the hero's are similar in implication. And houses, bestowed on Deiphebus and the confidant that the latter may execute stratagems in them, are such as to impress us likewise with the consequence of the owners. Dignified by state at home and honorable reception abroad, the lady can presume to claim sovereignty in love and have it acknowledged most humbly, as will appear in Section 3 of the next chapter.

We may begin with the following steps taken by Chaucer: retouching the episode of the Palladian festival, transferring the friend's preconsummation appeal for secrecy from a temple to a house, inventing as alibi for the prince a vigil in a temple, putting him in one at a time when in the original he apparently stayed in his own room, and, contrariwise, thoroughly Anglifying the "parlamento." He clarifies the notice of pagan piety with which Boccaccio introduced the enamorment scene by rendering "divin sacrificii" as honor paid to "goddes" and by glossing the Palladium—anachronistically—as "a relik."[47] In the scene itself, he is as uninformative as his author about the temple and the rites, but explains the heroine's stand by the door as motivated by shame—presumably for her father.[48] Moving the confidant's appeal to the prince for discretion from a temple to the latter's chamber in Deiphebus' house, Chaucer supplies new pagan color by making the lover offer to swear secrecy "in all the temples of this town Upon the goddes alle."[49] The alibi with which he provides Troilus for the consummation night—vigil in "a temple" to learn of the future from Apollo speaking out of a holy laurel tree[50]—is, if pseudo—, still effectively classical. And he appropriately sends him to "a temple" for the soliloquy on predestination at an hour when the unsoliloquizing Troiolo seems to have been in his chamber.[51] The parliament, though unlocalized as in the source, is made procedurally so English as to bring to the mind's eye some Trojan equivalent of Westminster Hall.[52]

Next to be considered is Chaucer's treatment of domestic establishments: his adaptation of the source with respect to the hero's, the heroine's, and Sarpedoun's, his introduction of the houses of Deiphebus and Pandarus.

In dealing with the hero's, he follows Boccaccio rather closely, yet strengthens the impression of princely grandeur in several ways and increases verisimilitude by fuller correlation of act with setting. Like his author, he always calls it a palace.[53] If, like him, he fails to enumerate a resident staff or even to specify one, he substitutes a "knyght" for the "valletto" on duty in it after the parliament, and denominates those accompanying the prince abroad, not his companions, but *his* knights or *his* folk, that is to say, expressly his dependents and, in the former case, dependents of rank.[54] The first episode in the palace, the master's entertainment of a group, he leaves unplaced as Boccaccio did.[55] All others assignable to its interior he locates in chamber either expressly or by implication.[56] He traces the lover's movements to and from the bed as circumstantially as his author[57] and, as the latter did not, visualizes the confidant also in relation to that one piece of furniture.[58] Toning down the prince's embracements of his friend, as noted in Section 4, so that there can be no suspicion of homosexual tendencies, he accentuates the intimacy by representing the latter to have spent at least two nights with the former in the palace chamber as well as another in the one put at his disposal by Deiphebus.[59] The lover's seclusion in chamber, with and without the bosom friend, objectifies his divorce from the world as persistently as in the *Filostrato*. And his closing every door and window after his return to it from the parliament, the attendant knight's having to open the door to admit Pandarus, and the latter's entering to find it in darkness are as meaningful particulars as those in the corresponding sequence in the original.[60] While Chaucer tells us nothing new about the interior of the hero's dwelling, he does supply it with a pleasance—to match the garden and the arbor which he attributes respectively to the heroine's and Deiphebus'. In adapting for Pandarus Pandaro's report to the lady of his discovery of the love which the prince felt for her, he not only visualizes the action more sharply but transfers it from a wood unlocalized to "the paleis gardyn, by a welle" [61]—within the garden, that is to say, of the suitor's palace. Boccaccio's statement *in propria persona* that the lover resorted after consummation to a garden our poet leaves as vague as he found it,[62] but now naturally to be interpreted as signifying Troilus' because of the relocation of the discovery episode.

As for the heroine's establishment, Chaucer exerts himself to make it impressive of her consequence. If, like Boccaccio, he uses the neutral term "hous" to refer to her dwelling, he also employs the honorific one of "paleys." [63] He indicates, as his author did not specifically, that people residing with her were numerous, male as well as female, and all of dependent status, and he brings out these facts through memorably circumstantial action.[64] He lets it be known, if casually, that she had much movable property and treasure.[65] He visualizes the undescribed "loggia" of the original as a paved parlor, gives the lady a closet to retire to as well as a chamber, and a hall besides for dining, and appends a large well-kept garden, while implying, with Boccaccio, an upper story and a broadish façade.[66]

With sets thus specified, he can trace movement about the premises more exactly than Boccaccio. That he does so will appear from the following review of stage business which he invents for adapted scenes here as well as for completely new ones.

In those within the ascending action, business devised for uncle and niece contributes to the comedy of manners, blending his deviousness and her romantic charm. In the first sequence in her house, Chaucer brings Pandarus to the paved parlor, where she and other ladies were listening to a maiden read of Thebes, makes the hostess rise to take him graciously by the hand and seat him "on bench," and notes withdrawal of bystanders to give the two the privacy they evidently desired; records that she witnessed Troilus' parade from her closet and that, before and after that event, she was seated there in contemplation; follows her down a stair to the garden and, with her women, along its paths; and then brings her indoors to be put to bed by them in her chamber.[67] In his second sequence, he records that Pandarus went with her from chamber to garden to deliver the prince's letter;[68] then develops a complex of activity centering in the hall, to which he speeds the pair from the garden. Criseyde left her uncle in hall to go with women of hers to chamber and, having read the letter there, returned to dine with him; led by him after dinner to a window, presumably in the hall, she left him again to compose the answer which he urged upon his knees, retiring this time alone to her closet; then rejoined him at the window, and, sitting by him "on a stoon Of jaspre, upon a quysshyn gold-ybete," gave him her epistle and presently saw Troilus pass by for the second time.[69] It was to insure her witnessing this parade, which he had prearranged with the lover, that the confidant held her by the window. In the one scene at her house during his machinations to bring her to Deiphebus' and in the one in which he invited her to his own, no setting is provided, but it is recorded in the one that he sat beside her and in the other that he whispered in her ear.[70] With her acceptance of the uncle's summons to dinner, action is diverted from her home until the day of the parliament.

The ladies who called on her that day, Chaucer specifies, she received in hall; then brings her, as his author did, to chamber and bed for lamentation before and after the confidant's arrival.[71] Keeping the friend's assumption in this retreat that the prince would join her there at night,[72] he presently fulfills it but with necessary modification of the source and some improvement.[73] Boccaccio, harking back to his accounts of the consummation in her house and the following assignation, stated that on this night, she advanced as usual, with lighted torch, to greet Troiolo; Chaucer, who has transferred the earlier meetings to the house of Pandarus, covers the shift as best he can by writing vaguely that the lover "Unto hire com, as he was wont to doone." Thus putting the case, he implies that the meeting was, not outside, but in the chamber, so that he does not have to bring the pair to it after the hostess has recovered from her swoon. Relieving the lady of a torch in hand before the swoon and making her mention after it, not this illuminant, but "the morter which that I se brenne," he eliminates the puzzle of what befell the light while she was insensible; and he resolves the question as to what the prince did with his weapon when he had to comfort her, telling us that he "leet his swerd down glide." [74] Their behavior abed he is content to leave more or less as it was.

Let us turn now to the action which he develops at the home of Deiphebus. As noted in Section 5 of the preceding chapter, the inspiration for the sequence culminating in this new locale came from a very different and much later one of the *Filostrato*, the visits paid the bedridden lover in his own chamber by Deifobo and by ladies of the royal family. In Chaucer's sequence, the heroine appears as the darling, not only of the hero, but also of his exalted circle;[75] he as the properly humble, if feigning, lover; and Pandarus, who manages everything, as intrigant nonpareil.

Deiphebus' abode, to which they severally repaired, though called only a "hous,"[76] is worthy of the princely host and so arranged as to facilitate comic machinations and romantic consequences. The focus of action, as in the palaces of hero and heroine, is a bedroom—this a small one in which Troilus remained pretendedly feverous from the night before his brother's dinner party through the night after.[77] It was somehow connected with "the grete chaumbre" on one side and, by a stair, to "an herber greene" below it on another.[78] Pandarus, having quitted his host and fellow guests after dinner, for a word with Troilus, came back to the large chamber with the suggestion that Deiphebus and Eleyne accompany him to the little one—and they only for the moment, lest the room become overheated—but that Criseyde join them presently. Unbeknownst to those left behind, brother and sister-in-law proceeded from sickroom to arbor—to read material commended to their attention by Troilus who had chanced on it "at his beddes hed."[79] Pandarus then went back for his niece, and, conducting her to the bedside, "gan in at the curtyn pike."[80] She manifested such tenderness to the incumbent by act[81] and word that Pandarus fell on his knees in thanksgiving.[82] And he ventured to forecast a rendezvous in his own house, thus advancing as far as Pandaro did at Criseida's in winning a promise from her to receive the suitor there.[83] Escorting his niece out of the chamber before Deiphebus and Eleyne returned, Pandarus came back to spend the night on "a paillet" beside his master, rising from it, however, to sit for a time on the "beddes syde,"[84] there to talk about the future, as Pandaro canvassed it with Troiolo in an unidentified temple.[85] Transfer of the discussion to the bedroom makes for continuity in the sequence and brings out the intimacy of the friends. They spent several other nights together, it will be recalled, in Troilus' chamber at home.

We may now direct our attention to Pandarus' own establishment. It was here, presumably, that he spent the night before his first visit to Criseyde, tossing abed because he had experienced "a teene In love."[86] And, more important, it was expressly in his "hous"[87] that he achieved the union of friend and niece, as he had implied at Deiphebus' that he would. Machinations to this end which Chaucer devises for him parallel those to effect the tête-à-tête at the brother's. Arrangement of a supper party matches suggestion eventuating in the dinner party; strategic utilization of three contiguous apartments,[88] the like of two and an arbor; advantage quickly taken of the lover's honest swoon, steady build-up of his pretended sickness. The counterpoint is too insistent and too comically effective to have been accidental. Chaucer may have had the later sequence already crystallized in his mind when he created the earlier, and certainly harked back to that one while he was at work on this. In this, as remarked in Chapter I, Section 6, he supplemented his own invention by recourse to both *Filostrato* and *Filocolo*. Troilus' swoon is Troiolo's moved back from the parliament and duly adapted; his and Criseyde's commerce abed after he has completely recovered derives in part from Troiolo's and Criseida's on their first night in her chamber, while many details here and there in the sequence come from the climactic one of the prose romance, in which Florio possessed himself of Biancofiore with the aid of Glorizia. The end product of Chaucer's joiner work is an intrigue complex to an extreme.

He makes it clear and believable by tracing action meticulously from point to point. Troilus, concealed since midnight in "a stewe" at his friend's, spied Criseyde coming to the house with her retinue on the next evening.[89] Fed well by her uncle and delightfully entertained, she yielded to his importunity to stay the night. She was to rest, he told her, out of earshot of the storm "in my litel closet yonder," while he took station "in that outer hous" as warden of her women and they reposed "in this myddel chaumbre that ye se." The chamber obviously is that in which the party had been going on; the outer house, most likely, a part of it to be shut off by a curtain; and the closet, an inner room as indicated by its quietness.[90] The curtain—"travers"—was drawn; everyone who had no further business in the chamber departed; and Pandarus, having conducted the lady bedward with her women, bowed himself out with the assurance that they would be on call "Here at this closet dore withoute."[91] When heroine, attendants, and all others were abed, Pandarus, solicitous of the hero, "gan the stuwe doore al softe unpynne," sat down inside for a brief conference, then "gan undon a trappe," to lead him through it into the closet.[92] After he had closed the door between closet and the room where her women slept, the uncle proceeded to work on the recumbent Criseyde with the fabrication about her lover's jealousy, including in his big lie the little one that Troilus

> Is thorugh a goter, by a pryve wente,
> Into my chaumbre come in al this reyn.[93]

When the prince came forward, Pandarus brought him by degrees to favor, making a jocose offer of a pillow to kneel upon, proposing that he be seated on the bed, withdrawing to the fireplace for pretended reading by a candle lit from it, starting up to cast him when aswoon into bed, returning with the candle to the fireplace and presently taking his leave after all was well.[94] Troilus did not quit the bed till dawn and then most reluctantly; Criseyde kept to it until her host returned in the morning and mollified her with avuncular jest and embrace.[95]

200

The second night of love Chaucer moves from the lady's house to the confidant's,[96] as he has the first, briefly indicating that dispositions in the several apartments here were repeated. He seems also to imply that the lovers came here for later nights.[97]

The last dwelling to be considered is Sarpedoun's. As in the *Filostrato,* its magnificence is only implied—by the rank of the owner and his lavish hospitality.[98] Chaucer promotes him from "baron possente" to "kyng." And though he omits hunting from the list of entertainments, he gives new particulars about the others—banquet, music, and female society. Troilus' indifference to all this, like Troiolo's, contrasts with socially exemplary deportment in the period of happiness.[99]

Unlike Boccaccio, our poet supplies clues as to the relation of dwellings to one another and the rest of town. Along with his various indications of layout in the establishments of Criseyde, Deiphebus, and Pandarus and his addition of a garden to the prince's, these clues are persuasive of reality, enabling us to follow movement from place to place as the former to trace it within confines. The hero, of course, is the character to be featured in transit, Chaucer presenting him more frequently and impressively than Boccaccio as the man-on-horseback.

It is in the new episode of Troilus' return from battle that the most important clue is given. As Criseyde was sitting in her closet, "Ascry aros at scarmuch al withoute"; men cried in the street that the hero had routed the Greeks; and her people shouted,

> A, go we se! cast up the yates wyde!
> For thorwgh this strete he moot to paleys ride;
>
> For other wey is fro the yate noon
> Of Dardanus, there opyn is the cheyne.[100]

Passing by, as thus anticipated, en route to his palace, he cut a most gallant figure—the honorably battered leader of two troops of cavalry.

He followed the same route when, at Pandarus' suggestion, he essayed a second parade. And the latter did his part by keeping her close to one of her front windows,

> Lo, Troilus, right at the stretes ende,
> Com rydyng with his tenthe som yfere,
> Al softely, and thiderward gan bende
> Ther as they sete, as was his way to wende
> To paleis-ward.[101]

Question and answer by the window—

"Nece, who hath araied thus
The yonder hous, that stant aforyeyn us?"
"Which hous?" quod she—

establishes that the street was well built up here, though assurance given by
the uncle elsewhere on the premises that he would not harm her "for the
citee which that stondeth yondre" seems to imply that the area was at some
remove from the center of things.[102]

In the period of intercourse, Criseyde was often at a window to salute her
lover "whan that he com ridyng into town"[103]—necessarily along the self-
same street. And he must have traversed it on a ride—with Pandarus—from
his palace to view her then empty one.[104] He would have used it, presumably,
to reach her palace on the night after the parliament and on any previous
nights that he may have ventured thither; and Pandarus would have too on
his errands between the palaces.

The houses of the uncle and of Deiphebus, it seems hinted, were not far
from Criseyde's; and the abode of Sarpedoun, which Boccaccio put at "quat-
tromilla passi" from the lover's, is relocated as "but a myle" away and thus
as easily within the city limits.[105] The hero and confidant traversed the mile,
our poet makes specific, on horseback.[106]

Chaucer names a city gate—as has been noted—in his original episode of
the hero's triumph and locates it, within earshot of Criseyde's palace, at the
foot of her street. Neither naming nor exactly locating the gate of her
departure, he recasts Boccaccio's accounts of that event and of the lover's subsequent visits to the portal in such fashion as to permit the inference that it
was the Dardanian of the new and earlier episode and—whether we draw this
inference or not—to enable us to visualize movement in its vicinity with
satisfying clarity. Troilus, he informs us, waited for his mistress "at the yate
ther she sholde out ride"; thence, accompanied by many knights, rode with
her "Passyng al the valeye fer withoute"; and, with farewell said at that limit,
turned back to the city and his palace.[107] Back at the gate after visiting
Sarpedoun, the prince reminisced of conducting her from it "to the yonder
hille."[108] And he was wont to mount "the walles" for the view they offered
of the camp.[109] On the tenth day, he stationed himself on the walls with
Pandarus till "noon," and, after a recess for dinner, saw to it that the porters
should keep the gate open; as dusk thickened, craned over the wall with such
delusive expectancy that he, like Troiolo, mistook an approaching cart for the
lady; but had to ride homeward disappointed when "The warden of the yates"
at last called in those outside.[110] Returning to this gate next day, he made
many a fruitless turn upon the walls.[111]

Cavalry engagements imply the existence of some fairly level ground between town and camp,[112] though, as just noted, a valley and hill are distinguished on Criseyde's route from the one to the other. Fortunately for pathos, no inequality was great enough to obscure the view; she, like Criseida, could torment herself with sight of the walls and buildings of Troy;[113] and, as noted, Troilus, like Troiolo, with sight of the camp. Chaucer, with his accustomed particularity, makes his heroine define the interval as traversable on horseback in "half a morwe." [114]

As was not the case in the *Filostrato,* one enemy tent—Calkas'—is distinguished from the many.[115] Brought to it from Troy by Diomede, Criseyde received him hospitably therein on the tenth day, and, that night, weighed her chances as she lay abed in the "faire brighte tente."[116] The sea, by which the camp must have stood, is mentioned indeed, but not in connection with it.[117]

To give his hero—and his audience—the perspective of eternity, Chaucer raises him posthumously to "the holughnesse of the eighthe spere" and turns his gaze upon

> This litel spot of erthe, that with the se
> Embraced is.

By this celestial ascent, derived in the main from the *Teseida,*[118] the poet converts him very expeditiously from short- to long-term evaluations.

Time and the supernatural, interrelated in this passage as often throughout his poem and Boccaccio's, will occupy us in the last section of the chapter.

Time and the Supernatural

FOUR aspects of the *Filostrato* and then of the *Troilus* are to be considered in this section. The period flavor, whether medieval or ancient, of allusions to the supernatural, of the physical particulars discussed in earlier sections, and of notices of source. The linking of events in time. The ideology of causation in allusions to the supernatural, and in assumptions of planetary influence with or without supernatural overtones. And the reinforcement of concepts or feelings by impressions of cyclic phenomena in nature concurrent with them.

The material in the *Filostrato* relevant to these aspects is of but moderate amount. Having chosen the Trojan love story expressly because of its parallelism to his own,[1] Boccaccio did not labor its pastness. Within the span of his action, he worked out an extensive time nexus beginning with the parliament and short chains of episodes before and after it, but left many stretches chronologically indeterminate. Concentrating upon the aggressions of Amore and Fortuna, he failed to provide a comprehensive and majestic scheme of divine causation. The atmosphere of season, day or night, he exploited only sparingly.

As to period flavor, he did little to remind his audience that the legendary era to which he had transported them was culturally remote from their own and nothing to suggest that such remoteness need be taken into account in interpreting the story. He rarely cited authority for his version of it, and then without pretense that the original was ancient.[2] He presented a hero medieval, not classical, in his affections—a hero so consumed by love for a woman that, as recorded in Sections 3 and 4, he paid for it at times in health, and over and over again with fear or hope of dying; for it, often gave

204

way to tears, and, after the parliament, to masochistic excesses. Born too soon to have the benefit of archaeological investigations, Boccaccio could not even conceive of period sets and costuming and hence—as noted in Sections 2 and 5—was blithely anachronistic about *realien*. Myth, upon which he was to become a distinguished authority, he did use for period effect but only to a limited degree.

Working up the polytheistic atmosphere indispensable for his ancient story, he did not attempt to be exotic nor trouble to be always completely pagan. He made a great deal of those stand-bys of medieval literature, Amore and Fortuna; once exalted the stand-by Venere at length while allowing her brief notice at other times; gave incidental recognition to Marte and Ercole, Apollo, the Muses, and Pallade, familiar deities all; and paid their superior, Giove, the due of repeated mention. The last, if kept recognizably his Olympian self, is equated in function at least once with the Almighty of Christians. And that Almighty is brought to mind more or less strongly in frequent citations of "Iddio" or "Dio," that is, of God par excellence.

There are sixty occurrences of these variant terms but no more than ten of "Giove." As to the latter, Boccaccio spoke *in propria persona* of Jove as wont to be invoked by other poets.[3] His hero, when fancy free, gave thanks for this condition to "Giove, dio vero, da cui viene ogni grazia"; in song to Giove's daughter Venere, credited him, under her influence, with animation of all things and succor of humanity, while not forgetting the god's erstwhile pursuit of women and presumptuously declaring that she had exalted his mortal self above the divine lover; came to accuse Giove and Fortuna of the supposed death of Criseida, and, apropos of her actual treachery, demanded of "sommo Giove" whether his just eyes were now indifferent to misdeeds, whether his fervent lightnings were in repose.[4] The lady reviled the great Olympian and Fortuna for her exile; and Pandaro speculated unhappily about Giove's inclinations in the matter.[5] As for the sixty occurrences of the terms "Iddio" or "Dio"—in wishes piously phrased for mundane advantage, in thanks for worldly favors already received, in asseverations, in exhortations, and in *obiter dicta*—a few bring out specific attributes of the Deity, the rest, of course, imply His power, and all, needless to say, give speech, not an antiquarian, but a contemporary flavor. All but two[6] are in the lines of characters. There are many in Troiolo's—from which his asseveration "per quello Iddio . . . che 'l cielo e 'l mondo ugualmente governa" and his blessing of "Iddio che tanto cara donna diede al mondo" may be singled out as paralleling his acknowledgments in the hymn to Venere of Giove's creation of life and provision for mankind.[7] In Criseida's, there are many too, though none which signalizes particular aspects of divinity.[8] Among the many in Pandaro's lines, the assumption that he was displeasing to "Dio" and Fortuna may be noted as a parallel to the hero's and the heroine's coupling of Giove and that goddess; and the following as explicit tributes to the power and wisdom of God: his remark, "Sará che Dio vorrá, ultimamente," his appeal to "Dio che può ciò che gli pare," his remark "solo Iddio sa il ver di quel che fia," and his asseveration by "Dio, che tutto quanto vede." [9] Like Troiolo, he conceived of the Supreme Being as Creator, thus referring to Him without name in the clause, "poi che colui che 'l mondo circoscrisse fece il primo uom." [10] As for the other characters, one is reported to have thanked God and one quoted as taking His name in asseveration and ejaculation. [11]

Fortuna, not subordinated to the Almighty in the contexts in which they are together cited, stands throughout the poem for unpredictable and therefore seemingly arbitrary change. Though mentioned far less often than He, this dangerous free agent is more compelling of attention, as will be shown later in the section.

Venere receives a longer tribute than any other deity—the aforementioned hymn of Troiolo. In this, wherein repeatedly identified as both goddess and planet, she is credited with benefic influence, extending from Giove downward through man to the lowest order of creation, and thanked for direction of it upon the singer. [12] Outside the song, however, she is mentioned only three times, on each occasion by the hero and very briefly, and on but one with explicit acknowledgment of might. [13]

There is frequent reference in the narrator's lines and the hero's and occasional in Criseida's and Pandaro's to Amore. [14] He is never called a god, though twice implied to be divine by designation as the son of Venere. [15] Capable, like Fortuna, of procuring woe as well as weal and therefore terrible, he more nearly resembles that being as characters and narrator all unphilosophically conceived of her than his own mother as sublimated by the hero. Like the one and unlike the other, he seems to work independently of the Supreme Being. [16] As will be shown in Section 3 and 8 of the next chapter, his influence is consistently represented through the traditional metaphors of armed assault and inflaming. The hero, who felt it most, addressed him often as "signore," [17] a term which neither he nor any other speaker ever applied to the Almighty—Jove or God.

As for other deities, Apollo, connected with literary endeavor by the narrator, was represented by him to have been Calcas' informant and erroneously supposed by Troiolo to have been Cassandra's. [18] And the prince implied the god's association with the sun. [19] The Muses the narrator celebrated, with Apollo and Giove, as inspirers of song. [20] Winged Fama he pictured as spreading the news of the exchange.[21] He chose the festival of Pallade as the occasion, apparently fortuitous, of the enamorment and made his hero refer to her as a patroness of learning.[22] Both spoke of Marte as patron of war, and the character of him also as a servant of Venere.[23] The latter adduced Ercole too as subject to love.[24] And he further showed himself a polytheist by occasional generic reference to divinities, with support in this vein from other actors.[25]

There are a few metaphors of supernal kind to be remarked here, which will be more carefully considered in the second section of Chapter III. All these—except the representation of Maria as a combined Jove, Apollo, and Muse and several of Criseida as a goddess unidentified—are Christian, womanly beauty being figured as angelic or paradisiacal, amorous enjoyment as Paradise, the want of it as Hell, and pangs of love as martyrdoms.

As has been observed, the mythological coloring of the *Filostrato* is somewhat weak—routine save for the hymn to Venere, adulterated by touches indifferently pagan or Christian or positively the latter, and scanty in total for so long a work. Advertising pastness, it does not disguise the fourteenth-century spirit which prevails. Troiolo came to his sad end because he lived by the amatory mores of that century, not because he subscribed to a creed outworn.

In the dating of events, the second aspect of the work which we have to consider, there is the same economy as in the suggestion of period. Boccaccio achieves verisimilitude by exactness here and there—particularly in the fateful ten-day span—but does not attempt an inclusive timetable. He leaves the duration of the action a matter of pure conjecture, not specifying how hard the enamorment followed upon Calcas' escape, whether the burgeoning season of Deifobo's call was the next after that of the enamorment or not the next, nor at what remove from the call the death of the hero ensued.

In the ascending phase of his story, he provides the following, often vague, information about time and no more. The war had been going on for some time before the priest's flight and his daughter's consequent appeal to Ettore, and many combats took place between these linked events and the vernal festival of the Palladium.[26] Immediately after the ceremony—a morning affair —Troiolo betook himself to his palace and there retired to chamber.[27] Pandaro had his first conference with him in that apartment several days later; proceeded directly from it to Criseida's abode, where he mentioned a sojourn, two days earlier, with the hero in shady woods as well as the conference just ended; and, returning to Troiolo, companioned him in a stroll past her house.[28] Sometime afterward, he prompted the suitor to declare himself in writing and, still later, the beloved to respond in kind.[29] After further lapse of time, he obtained a promise from Criseida to receive the lover "alla futura festa" when some of those with her would be away.[30] He briefed her for consummation, at the date, one may guess, which she had thus set, and summoned Troiolo, who chanced to be distant on warlike mission, to brief him also.[31] The lover spent the fleeting hours of darkness at her house and, back in his own palace, received Pandaro in the morning.[32] A second night of love was soon in order;[33] and others, projected on that night, were enjoyed, it appears, over a considerable period.[34]

In the descending action, it is not stated but may be presumed that the capture of Antenore led quickly to Calcas' proposal of his exchange for the heroine, and that request quickly to the "parlamento," with which the ten-day sequence begins.[35] This, the one long time-unit in the poem, occupies nearly as much space as the entire ascending action and takes up most of that allotted to the descending.[36] The relatively close attention paid in it to chronology serves the ends of both pathos and irony. Pandaro, we learn, went from hero to heroine and back again on the day of the parliament, and the lover spent the ensuing night in her chamber.[37] There, after lengthy debate, she promised to return "al decimo giorno."[38] Troiolo asked how he could hold out so long; she, contrariwise, professed astonishment that a man strong in arms should quail at temporary separation[39]—a suggestive difference in point of view. Leaving his mistress at cockcrow, Troiolo was on hand, in some part of the day thus heralded, to escort her out of town, and he spent the rest of it and all the following night in the solitude of his chamber.[40] Pandaro, there in the morning, proposed visiting a magnate as pastime to the tenth day; and the lover, praying for its speedy advent, chose Sarpidone for their host.[41] To the latter they went straightaway, but, before they had spent three days with him, Troiolo was proposing an exit; Pandaro, demanding ironically if the tenth had arrived and insisting that they remain two days longer, kept his friend there through the fifth.[42] On the homeward journey, the prince's speculation that his lady might already have returned moved the friend to the aside that the tenth day, the month, and the year would pass without sight of her.[43] Hardly were they back in the former's chamber before they quitted it again for a tour of the city.[44] Eagerly impatient to this point, Troiolo so continued in the days remaining to the tenth as appears from the chronologically imprecise account of them.[45] The hope which he permitted himself was already out of date. Though Criseida had grieved acutely for the separation, she was soon to forget him altogether, and was well on the way to doing so after hearing Diomede on the fourth.[46] At the gate on the appointed day, Troiolo kept up his hopes with successive excuses for her—the last, after nightfall, that she had said she would remain with her father, not until that day, but through ten.[47] Thus wishfully misremembering, he came back on the morrow to be again disappointed.[48]

His subsequent wretchedness, though treated in moderate compass, is made to seem interminably drawn out. Hope and health waning, he fell asleep one day to dream of the boar and Criseida; and—to test her constancy, as Pandaro advised—promptly wrote a letter, in which he referred, among other matters, to the passage of some forty days since her departure and to the coming of springtime.[49] He awaited a reply for many days, but getting none, was reduced to bed, where he was visited in quick succession by Deifobo— who also mentioned the spring season—and by ladies of the royal circle.[50] Confined long enough to be frequently revisited by the latter, he presently gained strength from animus against the Greeks and false encouragement at last received from Criseida and took part in many battles.[51] While in protracted sorrow for the death of Ettore, he dispatched many more letters to her and sent Pandaro to camp during truces; thought many times of going there in disguise; received from that quarter an abundance of empty promises.[52] After spying his brooch on the garment captured from Diomede, he took part in every battle and destroyed multitudes, but, though exchanging blows many times with the rival, did not kill him and met death at another hand.[53]

Turning from the chronology of the poem to the next aspect to be examined, the matter of divine causation, we may review the already-discussed representations as to the Supreme Being, Venere, and Amore, and then take up the role of Fortuna. After that, we must give some attention to dreams concerning the affair and to the fate of the city peripheral to it.

Under the name of "Giove," the All High is exalted in general terms in the hymn to Venere and thanked or blamed for specific outcomes in several contexts; under those of "Iddio" or "Dio," paid high but incidental tribute in many others. Shadowy withal as far as direct influence is concerned and accorded no authority over the potent Amore and Fortuna, He is unimpressive as a causative force. In the hymn, Troiolo asserted Venere's sway over the cosmos, attributed the emotion which delightfully possessed him to her influence, and implored the planet goddess, as a boon within her scope, to keep Criseida his for a long time.[54] Since the prayer was not granted, the assertion of sway—the only explicit statement in the romance of a constant ordering of the world—has no pertinency to the subsequent course of events. Amore, pictured by the narrator as the deity who accomplished the subjugation of Troiolo and acknowledged throughout by the victim as his master, is, indeed, a potent figure. Yet he is not a majestic one, a petty tyrant as he appears to be, without restraining commission from the All High.

As to Fortuna, the protagonist shared the suspicions entertained of her by friend and mistress and corroborated by the narrator, holding her as they did to be a capricious opponent who was free to act as she pleased. And he was more consistently defeatist about her than either of the cousins. The go-between was committed by his role to the assumption that the principals could shape the future at least in some degree. Thus, in the first visit to Criseida, he argued that she had a splendid opportunity to capitalize on her attractions, though he chose to magnify it by contrarily hopeless estimate of his own plight in love,

> Lascia me pianger che 'n malora nacqui,
> ch'a Dio, al mondo ed a fortuna spiacqui.[55]

Hesitant, if attracted, she begged him not to tamper with the dispensation which Fortuna had in store for her, and, after he had gone, reflected as follows on hazarding her good name:

> Assai è vano
> fidarsi alla fortuna, e ben vedere
> quanto uopo fa, non può consiglio umano.[56]

When she had so far suppressed fear as to grant an assignation, Pandaro manifested it to the extent of imploring Troiolo to proceed cautiously lest "ria fortuna" destroy his anticipated happiness.[57] The latter, who as remarked above was to thank Venere for love, presumed to chide the other being when dawn brought the first night of it to an end.[58] And the narrator held her responsible for what befell Troiolo after his thanksgiving:

> Ma poco tempo durò cotal bene,
> mercé della fortuna invidïosa,
> che 'n questo mondo nulla fermo tene:
> ella gli volse la faccia crucciosa
> per nuovo caso, sí com' egli avviene,
> e sottosopra volgendo ogni cosa,
> Crisëida gli tolse e' dolci frutti,
> e' lieti amor rivolse in tristi lutti.[59]

The three affected by the "nuovo caso" responded diversely. The lover complained against Fortuna when alone and with Pandaro after the parliament, and against both her and Giove as he contemplated suicide beside his swooning lady.[60] The friend, counselling initiative, averred that Fortuna was one to help the bold but reject the timid.[61] And the mistress, though supposing that she had been born in evil hour and was now tormented by Fortuna, assured Troiolo that they could get round this enemy by insouciant compliance.[62] Quitting the town, she promised Giove and Fortuna incessant vituperation as long as she was away.[63] After he saw the telltale brooch, the prince complained of birth in evil hour,[64] as she had been moved to do by the prospect of exchange and Pandaro by frustration in love. Insistent to the end on the irony of mutability, the narrator observed that Fortuna ran her course, giving joy to the new lover and sorrow to the old though sweet vengeance to neither; then intoned of the former's death that such was the end of his love and grief, such the end of his magnificence.[65]

Though ending with the fall of the prince, the *Filostrato* is not a tragedy even by the norms that Boccaccio was later to establish in his *De casibus virorum illustrium*. And it is not one, of course, by the old Athenian standards for conceptualization of destiny, as well as in other respects not at issue here. The action is supernaturally determined, indeed, but not by one sublime combination of forces. The Supreme Being and His inspirer Venere are remote; Amore and Fortuna, all too near, are true only to their by no means exalted natures. Astrological influence is linked with divine only in the hymn and is elsewhere but casually implied. And what is said of Troiolo's dreams and of the forecasts for his nation does little to strengthen the destinal atmosphere.

The dreams are not such as to convince us that his future was strictly predetermined. Those of the night after Criseida's departure may be taken as of warning kind despite the friend's sceptical comment, but the perils in them are only vaguely anticipative of what was to come.[66] The dream of the boar forty days later was, as Troiolo correctly interpreted it, revelatory of a seduction entirely or substantially accomplished, and his confirmation of the interpretation after Pandaro's questioning of it proved merely that the gods had kept him up to date.[67]

Doom for the city is brought to our attention only as Calcas predicted it, and his foreknowledge, though important to the story, is not a featured element. He went over to the Greeks because he had learned from Apollo of their eventual victory and argued for exchange of Antenore on the ground that victory was near.[68] To persuade Criseida to relinquish the Trojan lover, Diomede cited her father's prophecy and won admission from her that it might be realized.[69]

As to the last aspect of the poem to be dealt with in this section, we shall find that physical concomitants of time above or on the earth are seldom noted and always very simply. Troiolo, in his song to Venere, dwelt on her luminosity *qua* planet, and also celebrated the springtime consequences of her influence though without visualizing them.[70] The spring of the enamorment was imaged by the narrator as reclothing the meadows with grasses and flowers and making the fauna spruce and lustful; that after the separation, by Troiolo and Deifobo respectively, as manifesting itself in painted flowers and new grass which turned the meadows a thousand colors, and as doing so in meadows freshly green.[71] These conventional strokes were all that implied the harmony of the one spring and the pathetic contrast of the other with current moods of the hero. As little sufficed to associate nights and dawns with what transpired in them. Calcas ventured on treasonable flight, as he later told the Greeks,

> che 'l chiaro giorno fu tornato bruno.[72]

The night in which Troiolo first stole to the lady's house was—to his satisfaction—dark and cloudy; and that of his next approach, without a star.[73] Cockcrow signalled unwelcome dawn, when they were first enchambered and when last.[74] The lover was to recall that on quitting her house this last time he had seen the old moon horned and to assure himself that he would have her back when the new should be so.[75] Early at the gate in this belief on the tenth day, he was still vainly hopeful when the sun's light died and an occasional star appeared, and he persisted there until the sky had become all starry.[76] Nighttime, once longed for, now came too soon.

In all four aspects under consideration, Chaucer's poem is much richer than the *Filostrato*. As to the first, he has reinforced the semblance of antiquity with obvious care, yet has taken over some modern touches and added many, furthering the illusion of truth to life, paradoxically, from as free a mixture of past and present as Boccaccio's. The actualities of both times, he elevates of course, in philosophic vein or in romantic. The complexity of the fusion of eras has been brought out by scholars in our age, who have made fruitful studies of his work from diverse points of view.[77] As to the second aspect, Chaucer is far more precise about chronology than his author—to the advantage of verisimilitude throughout, often to the strengthening of continuity, and here and there, variously, to the development of the meaningfulness of event. There has been illuminating investigation of this aspect also.[78] As to the third, he takes over most of Boccaccio's interpretation of circumstances in terms of forces more powerful than man but so modifies and adds to the borrowing that he leads the reader to new and loftier conclusions. Bringing to his attention, as the former insistently did, the apparent arbitrariness of Fortune and the seemingly unbridled masterfulness of Love, Chaucer proceeds to impress upon him that these entities are not self-directed and anarchical but instruments, along with others, of a grand design. The Supreme Being, he asserts, commissions Fortune, the planets, and the Fatal Sisters; and he implies, through Troilus, that God has power over Love the boisterous male, while himself attesting the effective relationship between the Almighty and gentle Venus, which Troiolo acclaimed in the source. These acknowledgments of the omnipotence of God along with recognition, in a soliloquy added for Troilus, of His prescience and the consequent alternatives of conditional or absolute necessity, elaboration of the issues of the foreknowledge of Calcas and of the predictive value of dreams, magnification of the role of Fortune, and heavy reinforcement of astrological influence are cumulatively more than sufficient to give the English poem a lowering aura of destiny inexorably in process. Thus invested, the work comes closer than the *Filostrato* to tragedy as cultivated by the great Athenians, though, as I have remarked in the Preface, it defies assignment to any one genre past, contemporary, or after its time. Scholars have been somewhat at odds about the destinal component with respect both to Chaucer's intentions and achievement.[79] In my view, he seems to have developed it with concern for metaphysical illumination as well as for artistic effect but to have put the latter first; has made the element unquestionably one of the great strengths of his poem and accomplished this because he put art first. He dramatizes, not systematizes, ideas of causation, evolving them from his own progressive response as narrator to what is going on and from that of his characters and pitting hero against go-between and lady in *ad hoc* dispute. Had he been scholastically precise, he would have exegetized the contradictions which resulted from such procedure. Leaving them unresolved, he preserves the impact of emotional conjecture; and, like many a purveyor of tragedy before and after him, convinces without argument that the outcome was awesomely inevitable and yet that the actors were somehow free enough to merit interest—praise and blame. As to the final aspect, Chaucer improves upon the *Filostrato* very conspicuously in the use of natural phenomena to objectify divine causation and to complement the moods inspired by the vicissitudes of love. He supplies more numerous and far more striking impressions of appearances in nature than that poem had to offer. The ornate splendor which he achieves in many of them is a dignification of style consonant with his philosophical enrichment of matter. Both, as scholarly investigation has shown, are in accord with the precept of Dante and Boccaccio and their practice.[80]

In our survey of the first aspect, Chaucer's blending of past and present, we may quickly review his already discussed objectification of love, visualizing of the Trojan scene, and pretense to ancient sources, and then consider at great length his conflation of Christianity and paganism.

213

As will be recalled from the third and fourth sections of the chapter, he accepted Boccaccio's presentation of the hero as one so possessed by love of a woman as to be sometimes debilitated and much occupied with death and to be very tearful and on one occasion physically violent against himself. Reinforcing these—and other concomitants—of amorous devotion, he improved the prince as courtly lover, made him an even better exemplar of that medieval species than he was in the original. The apology in the Prohemium to Book II for the suitor's possible deviations from current practice, while a deliberate hint of Trojaninity, is not supported by the record of his behavior.

As will be remembered from the second and fifth sections, Chaucer was considerably more explicit than Boccaccio about costume and setting. His particularization of the former was never antiquarian; and of the latter, very seldom so, being limited to a detail or two about the environs of the city, the naming of one of its gates, and the spuriously classical invention of an oracular laurel. Living before the days of classical archaeology, he, like Boccaccio, could visualize the past only imaginatively and therefore as very much like the present. The jewelry which he mentions, the articles of clothing, the arms and armor might all have been worn by his aristocratic contemporaries; and the abodes of Troilus, Criseyde, Deiphebus, and Pandarus, insofar as he describes them, are no less up-to-date. Fourteenth-century readers would savor the familiar as realistic in comfortable disregard for anachronism. And present ones, though they may question combat on horseback, gloves and sleeves for Criseyde, a coat-armor for Diomede, or something else, should accept most particulars readily enough. After all, they would have some difficulty in proving that this or that recognizably medieval detail was not—by accident—a fairish approximation to pre-Homeric fact.

Allusions to sources in the *Troilus* have been brought together in the second section of Chapter I. Those to be recalled here are: the frequent citations of "myn auctour," that is, of Horace's friend Lollius miscredited with composition about Troy; a reference to Homer, Dares, and Dictys; another to Dares; four more to "olde bokes"; and this final comprehensive statement,

> Lo here, the forme of olde clerkis speche
> In poetrie, if ye hire bokes seche.

Other indications on Chaucer's part that he was following authority, like the very few given by Boccaccio, do not make the point that it was old. All subserve his pose of humble dependence; and those listed, of course, the further pretense that he was giving the world a faithful replica of ancient literature. The second, we may assume, is, as the first, a purely artistic device not a Chattertonian hoax. Insistence on a classical main source for his poem and on also venerable ancillary ones is supported by due provision of mythological color. Though shading, as we shall discover, into Christian tones, the color is applied with obvious concern for period effect and achieves this end without prejudice to others as important.

In his handling of the supernatural, Chaucer gives strong advertisement to paganism and hence antiquity but introduces much that is indifferently pagan or Christian and not a little that in concept or phrase is definitely the latter. He cultivates the illusion of an alien religious climate with far greater assiduity than Boccaccio, alluding to many more of the old divinities—to recondite as well as familiar bits of myth. Yet he rationalizes all the planetary deities by astrology, as his author did Venere and her father; invests her son with a cult apish of the Christian; and makes Fortune acceptable from the monotheistic point of view by explicit subordination to God or His sometime equivalent, the chief of the heathen pantheon. Like Boccaccio, he not only astrologizes that chief but presents him ambivalently as Olympian and as *the* Deity. And while he finds occasion to use the term "Jove" with whatever meaning more than twice as often as his author, he employs the everyday one of "God" to designate the Supreme Being many times more than the other poet and, by and large, with clearer Christian echo.

In the *Troilus,* there are over twenty occurrences of the name "Jove," as against ten of "Giove" in the *Filostrato,* and also three of the name "Jupiter"; and, as against sixty of the variants "Iddio," "Dio" in the source, about two hundred and ninety of the term "God" for the Supreme Being in the English poem, and also some thirty of the word "Lord" with the same sense, as well as some twenty of the phrase "parde." As will appear from the following survey, exclusively pagan touches in contexts about Jove or Jupiter—pursuit of women, resort to thunder, patronage of nativities—are balanced by touches as much pagan as Christian—power of creation, control of Fortune, enthronement. And in passages about God, we shall find the latter concepts attached to Him along with that of omniscience and the peculiarly Christian one of salvation. The familiar "God," "Lord," and "parde" which occur often enough in the lines of the narrator and notably oftener in the lines of the characters do not overshadow the less numerous but more attention-provoking "Jove" and "Jupiter" so essential to the pagan atmosphere. Rather they combine with the latter to suggest that the Trojans were constantly mindful of one great deity, however many more they might acknowledge and whatever unworthy superstitions they might entertain about Him, and that the narrator, dramatized as a culler of heathen books, remained cognizant of the One. The suggestion must have given medieval readers some feeling of spiritual community with the Trojans and the historian, without prejudice to the illusion

215

that the latter had carried them backward in time. Such feeling for those acquainted with polite society and literature would not be vitiated by the frequent tacit assumption on the part of all speakers that God, whom they duly magnified, might be invoked or cited in concerns altogether mundane. And stock pietistic phrases, "God woot," "for love of God," and others, helped no doubt to make speech sound lifelike to every subject of Richard II—compellingly real because of their currency in his day.

Mentions of Jove or Jupiter occur as follows. In the Prohemium to Book III, the narrator celebrated the vivifying effects and amorous metamorphoses of Jove for which his planet daughter was responsible, much as Troiolo had done in the first stanzas of the hymn to Venere.[81] In Book V, he wrote that Jove committed to the "angry Parcas, sustren thre" the destiny which he had in disposition for the Trojan pair; later, generalized, apropos of Fortune's reduction of their city, that she wrought change "Thorugh purveyaunce and disposicioun" of this high god; but lumped him with the pantheon in a concluding dismissal of the lot.[82] Troilus, in prayer to planetary deities before consummation, appealed to Venus to enlist the astrological influence of her father and to Jove, directly, to be helpful for the love of Europe, by him ravished in taurine form.[83] Alone after the parliament, he wished that Jove had put Calkas in his clutches and besought the enthroned deity for remedy or death; and, when with the beloved, chid Jove and Fortune even more defiantly than Troiolo for her seeming demise, but took heart from her recovery to pray Jupiter that they might soon be together again.[84] As we learn from the narrator, the lover fell to cursing Jove—and other deities—for her departure, yet, when oppressed by the boar dream, credited the god with having sent it "of his purveyaunce."[85] Changing front again, he prayed Jove to give Cassandre sorrow for her unwelcome confirmation of this inference.[86] During her first night with Troilus, Criseyde called on Jove to extirpate the lover's jealousy and demanded of this "auctour of nature" if it was to his credit that the innocent should suffer, as she was doing because suspected; at cockcrow, challenged night for not tarrying as long as when Almena lay by Jove.[87] As the narrator informs us, she besought Jupiter to give mischance to the negotiators of her exchange.[88] She exclaimed "O Jove" when about to swoon on the hero's breast; and, when in discourse with him, asseverated, "Or ellis se ich nevere Joves face."[89] Having heard Diomede's baleful predictions about her city, she besought Jove, "for his grace" to deliver it soon.[90] Pandarus, when newly apprised that she was his friend's choice, bade him fare aright "for Joves name in hevene."[91] At one juncture, he swore to her—inter alia—by "Jupiter, that maketh the thondre rynge" and, at another, "by natal Joves feste."[92] And he declared that Troilus could not know of her wishes

216

unless Jove had whispered them in his ear.[93] Lastly, Eleyne called on Jove for the discomfiture of Criseyde's enemy, of whom she had heard from the wily uncle.[94]

Occurrences of "God," "Lord," and "parde" have now to be surveyed, and, first, those in the lines of the narrator.

In his account of the planetary conjunction, he sublimated God as the authority above Fortune and "influences of thise hevenes hye"; in the overtly Christian Epilog, bade young folk turn from earthly affection to their Creator and Redeemer and gave the example for worship of Him as the triadic One; but, in the Prohemium to Book III, had written casuistically,

> God loveth, and to love wol nought werne.[95]

At the beginning, he had called on lovers to supplicate God for their fellows and for himself as amatory writer, in parody of the "bidding prayer" of Christian liturgy.[96] And, in the course of the story, he appealed to God a dozen times for intercession in matters of the heart.[97] Brought to contemn the world by Troilus' woes, he made the more becoming appeal,

> God leve us for to take it for the beste;

yet continued so mundane as to pray the Deity that another work, a comedy, should come from his pen and that the present one should be properly transmitted and understood.[98] Conjecturing divine influence as well as wishing it, he thanked God for the happy outcome at Pandarus' house, remarked that Criseyde recovered from her swoon and that Troilus rode on from her empty palace "as God wolde," and qualified his lament for the hero's death with a "save only Goddes wille." [99] He resorted to the formula "God (it) woot" a dozen times and implied omniscience twice more by remarking that only God and Pandarus knew what was up and that only God and Troilus knew whether the latter had become woeful.[100] Exclaiming, "O myghty God" on one occasion, he employed the asseveration "and God toforn" on another, and a little later, the explicitly Christian "also God me save."[101] He resorted twice to the exhortatory "For love of God." [102] He found occasion for "parde" in a hypothetical question about Criseyde's behavior.[103] And the exclamation "Lord," signifying the One, appears very frequently in his lines.[104]

In Troilus', not half as numerous as the narrator's, "Lord" appears nearly as many times; "parde," more times; and "God," more. In the long soliloquy created for him after the first draft of the poem, the hero debated the compatibility of God's prescience and man's free will, favoring the negative side though with admission of uncertainty.[105] When secure of his mistress, he

217

had looked to Him to make Love do his duty, singing in his paean to the inferior being:

> So wolde God, that auctour is of kynde,
> That with his bond Love of his vertu liste
> To cerclen hertes alle, and faste bynde,
> That from his bond no wight the wey out wiste.[106]

And abed with her, he had prayed God to quench the light of day and to discipline the overhasty Sun and his love the Morrow.[107] First and last, he expressed some twenty wishes to God variously concerning himself, the mistress, friend, rival, or others involved in love.[108] Lovers, who had heard him scorn them were thanking God, he fancied, for his inclusion in their number.[109] And he predicted eventual help from God against the Greeks.[110] Thinking of Him again as the author of nature, the prince declared that he would not reveal his secret happiness "For al the good that God made under sonne" and flattered Criseyde with the dictum "God hath wrought me for I shall yow serve." [111] He employed the locution "God (it) woot" many times and once an equivalent.[112] Among a dozen miscellaneous asseverations of Troilus by God, one signalized His omniscience again; another—adapted from Troiolo—His universal sway; and two—"God so wys me save" and "God so my soule save"—His redemptive power.[113] The exhortatory "For (the) love of God" appears frequently in his discourse and "For Goddes love" once.[114] Frequently too "parde," with its variants "pardieux" and "depardieux." [115] And so the exclamation, "Lord" signifying the Almighty, besides two prayers addressed to Him under this appellation.[116] The first of the prayers incorporates the by now familiar concept of His enthronement.

Criseyde, with fewer lines than Troilus, employed the words "God," "parde," and "Lord" about as many times as he. In her apostrophe to night paralleling his to day and the solar Titan, she conceived of the dark time as shaped by God for respite and, since it had proved too hasty for this function, wished that it might be bound forever to their hemisphere by the "maker of kynde." [117] Frequently, though not as often as the prince, she directed wishes to God apropos of herself or fellow Trojans.[118] She sometimes anticipated His guidance in this world without praying for it.[119] And she thanked Him at several junctures for mundane favors already received.[120] Now and again she supported an assertion with "God woot" or an equivalent thereof.[121] Like Troilus, she employed many other asseveratory phrases involving God and was, indeed, more addicted to such than he. Several of hers, as of his, recall the doctrine of salvation; and one, "by that God that bought us bothe two," more arrestingly than any of his.[122] She appealed to her hearers "for (the) love of God"—or "for Goddes love"—quite as frequently as the prince;

and, once, "For his love, which that us bothe made." [123] Like Troilus a Gallic swearer, she employed "parde" and its variants "par dieux" and "depardieux." [124] She once took vow "by that ilke Lord that made me," and was moved occasionally to the ejaculation "Lord." [125]

Pandarus, with more lines than heroine or hero, named "God" a few more times than either, but less frequently in impressive fashion, while making occasional use, as they did, of the synonym "Lord" and the oath "parde." His quite numerous wishes to God for himself and others range in mood from the serious to the jocose. [126] Several phrases of his imply that future weal depended on God and several more that present weal was due to Him. [127] A curiously anachronistic attestation of divine power is his "Ensample" of heretics, who, converted through God's grace, hold Him most in awe. [128] Another tribute to it, echoing Troilus' "Almyghty Jove in trone," is his ejaculation "O myghty God . . . in trone." [129] As for divine omniscience, there are many "God woot's" in his lines to suggest it, if uncompellingly; and a variant—adapted from Pandaro—to signalize it with greater force. [130] Another formula of asseveration, the salvationist "And God so wys be my savacioun," appears twice in his discourse. [131] And there are others, some often repeated but none particularly striking. [132] As prone to asseverative statement as niece and friend, he lacked their poetic touch. He made one exhortation "for the love of God, that us hath wrought" and—like them—many "for (the) love of God" or "for Goddes love." [133] "Parde" he used a good deal. [134] At one point, he swore "by that Lord that formede est and west" and, at several, ejaculated "Lord." [135]

As for the supporting cast, Deiphebus, Eleyne, and Calkas, each named God once; and the Greek Diomede, several times. [136]

The Christian tone which recurs with varying strength in mentions of the Supreme Being is present also in diverse metaphors later to be noted and in the following nonmetaphorical utterances: Troilus' ejaculatory "How devel maistow brynge me to blisse?" and Pandarus' "the devel have his bones!" "Fy on the devel!" and "the devel spede hym that it recche"; the narrator's already mentioned glossing of the Palladium as "a relik"; and Criseyde's observations:

> It sate me wel bet ay in a cave
> To bidde and rede on holy seyntes lyves,

and

> Shal I nat love, in cas if that me leste?
> What, par dieux! I am naught religious. [137]

219

Fortune, subordinated by the narrator as already remarked to "Jove" and "God," is frequently cited in the *Troilus* without acknowledgment of this relationship. All that he and his characters have to say about her will be considered later in the Section.

So, too, mentions of the Parcae: the narrator's already noted reference to them as subordinate to Jove, an allusion to the trio and one to Atropos by the hero; and one to that sister by the heroine.

Venus was presumed benevolent by the narrator, hero, heroine, and confidant, as she had been by Troiolo, who alone mentioned her in the source. Speaking of her as planet, Chaucer remarked that she was in favorable position at the time of the hero's return from battle and in not unfavorable at his birth, by way of partial explanation of the impression the prince made upon Criseyde in that triumphal return.[138] In lines of the Prohemium to Book III which he took from Troiolo's hymn, the poet, addressing her as luminant of the third sphere and as the Sun's "lief" and daughter of Jove, proclaimed her wholesome influence to extend from her father and Mars down through all creation; and, in lines appended to these, besought inspiration from her as "lady bryght" and then—to make sure that his work would do honor to Venus—also from the Muse Caliope.[139] His alluding to lovers as servants of the former and to himself as their "clerc" hints a formal devotion to her analogous to that earlier and more clearly indicated for her son. At the end of the book, he addressed this "lady bryght, the doughter to Dyone," along with her blind and winged offspring, "daun Cupide," and all nine Muses, wishing them eternal laud—now that they were to leave him —for guidance so far.[140] Troilus had invoked Venus in his initial conference with Pandarus and exalted her in his second without mythic or astrological embellishment.[141] Appealing to all planetary divinities except Saturne when about to venture into Criseyde's room at the friend's house, he began with Venus. Her he begged to inspire him and—for love of boar-slain Adoun—to seek remedy from her father if Mars or Saturne, the malefic orbs, had been potently situated at his birth or she impotently.[142] As the narrator informs us, the prince gave thanks to "the blisful goddes sevene" upon taking Criseyde into his arms.[143] And after enjoying her, he included Venus and Imeneus in a tribute primarily to Love:

> Thi moder ek, Citherea the swete,
> After thiself next heried be she,
> Venus mene I, the wel-willy planete!
> And next that, Imeneus, I the grete.[144]

Years later, he was to curse Cupide and Cipride—along with Jove, Apollo, Ceres, Bacus—in a revulsion of feeling caused by his lady's departure.[145] On

220

the night before her going, she had expressed thankfulness to Cipride and also prayed to her under name of Venus.[146] Pandarus made asseveration by Mynerve, Jupiter, and Venus and by the last alone; assured Cupide and Venus on his knees that they might felicitate themselves for his friend's acceptance into his niece's service, which he termed a "merveille," and praised the latter deity for another encouraging circumstance.[147]

The son celebrated with Venus in contexts noted above,[148] is kept more prominent than she and, as in the *Filostrato,* differentiated from her by recognition of his masculine aggressiveness. Yet there are material changes which, on the whole, bring him closer to his mother, de-emphasis of wounding and inflaming on the negative side, sublimation on the positive. Usually called "Love" as always "Amore" in the source and once allowed the synonymous appelation of "Charite," he is named "Cupide" in passages already cited and others, and, in specific attestation of divinity, referred to sometimes as a "god" and sometimes particularly as "God of Love." [149] As will be brought out in detail in the next chapter, he is accorded figurative treatment substantially different from that in the original. In its second section, it will be shown that a cult is developed for him after the pattern of the Christian, according to precedent well established in courtly love literature but not followed in the Italian poem. Narrator and confidant take on priestly functions. Troilus appears in the guise of reclaimed heretic, and Criseyde is misjudged a saint. In the third section, we shall find that violent subjection of human beings by Love which was featured in the source is on the whole de-emphasized, whereas the orderly feudal relationship between conquered and conqueror is given more stress. Troilus, for example, is made to address the deity as "lord" a little more frequently than Troiolo as "signore," and the new character Antigone to iterate that term in her few lines.[150] The de-emphasis of armed assault—Section 3—is accompanied naturally enough by some reduction in the item of amorous flames, for which the god's arrows were traditionally held responsible—Section 8. Most of the impressions of Love, figurative and nonfigurative, are conveyed in a few blocks of stanzas: the narrator's Prohemium to Book I and part of his account of the enamorment, several apostrophes of the hero to the god, counsel given him by the friend in their first interview and his response, and the song with which Antigone favored her aunt. In the Prohemium, Chaucer implied his priestlike office; and in the temple scene, educed the ostensibly serious doctrine of submission to the deity—along with some ironic humor—from transfixion of the prince.[151] Alone after the experience, Troilus like Troiolo humbled himself to the god but in more expressly feudal terms.[152] His friend prescribed repentance to Love for past insults and, having obtained it, gave him consolation of no

221

less priestly tone.[153] In the already mentioned thanksgiving to Love, Venus, and Imeneus on the night of consummation, Troilus exalted the first above the others, addressing him as "thow holy bond of thynges" and asserting in Christian phrase that all were lost "But if thi grace passed oure desertes."[154] And in the song adapted from a metre of the *Consolation* which replaces Troiolo's to Venere, he paid Love the noblest tribute in the poem, developing at length the concept of the just quoted phrase "thow holy bond of thynges."[155] Reduced to the despondency of preconsummation days by the lady's exit, he addressed the god, like Troiolo, as a vengeful conqueror.[156] Against all this and more on the part of the honest lover, there is only the word play on "god of Love" and "love of God" and a hasty profession of obedience to the "god" on the part of Diomede. And there is nothing of moment on Criseyde's. Exaltation of love from the female point of view is left to the niece Antigone. She obliged with a song composed by a highborn maiden in thanksgiving to that "lord" for provision of an ideal lover.[157]

Apollo is represented, as in the source, to have determined the affair indirectly; presumed by the hero to be capable of astrological influence; and also called to mind in many astronomical, but not astrological, contexts by myth-colored reference to the sun[158] and in two passages in which a human being is likened to him.[159] The god's warning of the fall of the city, which, as in the *Filostrato,* prompted Calkas to flee and later to bring his daughter to him, is strengthened by other indications of that event. And it is asserted that the deity was procuring the catastrophe as well as foretelling it. In his expansion of Boccaccio's notice of the warning, Chaucer eruditely stated that it came from the diviner's "god, that highte thus, Daun Phebus or Appollo Delphicus," and added punningly that Calkas corroborated it by "calkulynge."[160] When exchange was at issue, the priest, not content as in the original to give the Greeks an unsupported promise of success, told them that he had learned from Apollo, as well as through astrology, casting of lots, and divination by birds, that Troy would soon be in ashes and explained that Phebus and Neptunus willed this cataclysm because "kyng Lameadoun" had failed to reward them for walling the town.[161] Aware of her father's gloomy conviction, Criseyde assured Troilus on their last night together that she would deal with it so effectively as to win the old man's consent to her return.[162] Against such temptation as she would offer of financial advantage from this return, said she,

> al Appollo, or his clerkes lawes
> Or calkulyng, avayleth nought thre hawes.

Should he test her veracity in temptation by casting of lots, she would distract him in the process and question his interpretation of "the goddes" on the ground of their ambivalence. And, venturing that they were figments of human terror, she would brand his response to oracular revelation at Delphi as cowardice. The scepticism of this argument is evidently *ad hoc*, since it occurs in no other allusions of the heroine to the supernatural. As she was to find ere long, it did not sway her father. And the reader, cognizant as everyone must be of the outcome of the War, at once recognizes it to be pathetically futile. Her lover, god-minded even in deceit, pretended as alibi for his first sojourn with her, a vigil by a laurel through which Apollo spoke; and, in his prayer on that joyous night to the planetary deities, appealed in all earnestness to Phebus for love of Dane, who became the laurel.[163] Including the god in comprehensive cursing after her departure, Troilus did not deny his power.[164] The narrator did, of course, by denigration of worship paid him and other deities, but too late to nullify our conception of his influence.[165]

Let us now revert to the hero's astrological prayer as a starting point for consideration of Mars, Saturne, Mercurie, and Diane. The first two, as already noted, are referred to as malefic in its opening appeal to Venus; and Mars is apostrophized, for her love, not to be so on the present occasion.[166] The chaste moon goddess is besought only not to be wroth; but Mercurie, like Venus, Jove, and Phebus, to be helpful for the sake of a beloved—in his case, Hierse.[167] Outside the prayer, there is one mention of the planet Saturne without mythological color and one of the god as father of Juno in an unsceptically fervent asseveration of Criseyde's by that goddess within the hour of her scheming to undermine the piety of Calkas.[168] Mars, though disprized by the narrator in the end along with Apollo and Jove,[169] is accorded awesome mention in his lines, the hero's, and the confidant's. Having celebrated the appeasement of "fierse Mars" in the Prohemium to Book III as Troiolo in his hymn, Chaucer called on this "cruel" deity, "fader to Quyryne," in that to Book IV, together with the Herynes, to help him bring the story to its sad conclusion.[170] He identified Mars as "god . . . of bataille" in a simile applied to Troilus and spoke, like Boccaccio, of the prince's devoting his days to this patron of war.[171] The lover, anticipating death, instructed Pandarus to offer his steed, sword, and helm to Mars, and his shield to Pallas.[172] The confidant invoked the "cruel" and "dispitouse" god along with the Furies for death if he meant harm to Criseyde, made asseveration to her "By Mars, the god that helmed is of steel," and adjured his friend "for the love of Marte."[173] The lady appealed to Troilus "for the love of Cinthia the sheene," and Cassandre informed him of Diane's avenging herself through the Calydonian boar, while the former, Troilus, and the narrator made reference to the moon under the names respectively of Lucina, Latona, and Cynthea.[174] The lover, after giving Pandarus the just mentioned instructions about disposal of his effects, besought Mercurye to guide his soul after death; and the narrator, in his otherwise Christian Epilog, represented the prayer to have been granted.[175]

Beside the seven planetary divinities and Love, Fortune, and the Parcae, supernatural beings of antiquity alluded to more than once in the *Troilus* are Pallas, Juno, and Neptunus, the Muses and the Furies. The narrator, as in the *Filostrato*, made mention of the Palladium.[176] The hero referred incidentally to the wrath of Pallas against Aglawros and, as already noted, willed his shield to the goddess.[177] Criseyde prayed to her under the name of Pallas and again under the name of Minerva, and made two asseverations by her under the former.[178] Pandarus made asseveration "by the goddesse Mynerve."[179] As for Juno, Troilus alluded to her wrath against the Thebans; the heroine made two asseverations by her on the night of parting, the first with allusion to her punishment of Athamante and the already mentioned notice of her fathering by Saturne, the second with the designation, traditional for the Virgin, of "hevenes quene"; and the uncle, on that night, looked to her for aid.[180] He swore "By Neptunus, that god is of the see," and Calkas as previously remarked, associated Neptunus with Apollo in enmity against Troy.[181] The narrator appealed to Cleo to be his "Muse" for allegedly literal translatorship in Book II; and, as already stated, invoked Caliope after Venus at the beginning of the climactic third book, and at the end of it apostrophized the

> sustren nyne ek, that by Elicone
> In hil Parnaso listen for t' abide,

along with the love goddess and her son in thanksgiving for guidance to that point.[182] In the Prohemium to Book I, he appealed for help in writing his tearful verses to Thesiphone, the "goddesse of torment," the "cruwel Furie, sorwynge evere yn peyne"; and in that to Book IV, along with Mars as already noted, to the

> Herynes, Nyghtes doughtren thre,
> That endeles compleignen evere in pyne,
> Megera, Alete, and ek Thesiphone.[183]

And Pandarus, as previously recorded, called on that god and "The Furies thre of helle," while Cassandre had something to say about them to her brother.[184]

With review completed of supernatural beings prominent in varying degree in the *Troilus*, a bare list may be given of miscellaneous pagan touches. This will include all references to human beings, other than characters of the story, in some way affected by the old deities, whether left human by them, metamorphosed, or raised to godhead; every allusion to a deity mentioned but once; and every unspecific one to "goddes." Some material in it will receive fuller treatment later in this section or in the second section of Chapter III. Even as digested here, the numerous items bear impressive witness to Chaucer's zeal for antique coloration. In the narrator's lines, a single reference is made to each of the following: Proigne, changed into the swallow, and Tereus her brother-in-law; Janus, "god of entree"; gold-loving Mida; Dyone, Nyght, Quyryne, who, as already recorded are named respectively as mother of Venus, mother of the Herynes, and son of Mars; lion-killing Hercules; Fame, bearer of tidings; Mirra, botanically transformed; Mynos, the judge of souls; the wind Zepherus; Ceres and Bacus; Ixion, "in helle"; "Nysus doughter," impliedly a bird; and the faithful Penelope and Alceste.[185] In the lines of the hero, a single one to each of the following: Nyobe, whom Pandarus had previously mentioned; Adoun, Europe, Dane, Hierse, and Aglawros, as already noted, respectively beloved of Venus, Jove, Phebus, and Mercurie and hated by Pallas; Imeneus, associated with Cupide and Venus, and the "Morwe," with the solar Titan, as already noted; blind Edippe; Proserpyne of the underworld; many-eyed Argus; Escaphilo, metamorphosed as the owl; "folk of Thebes" afflicted by Juno; Caribdis, monster of the Sicilian strait; Pheton, "The sonnes sone"; and Alceste, who died for her husband.[186] Criseyde is made to speak of the murder of Layus by his son Edippus, and of Amphiorax's swallowing up by the earth as recorded in the romance of Thebes which was read aloud by her maiden; to allude, as previously observed, to Almena's possession by Jove; to imagine herself ending in Elysium with Orpheus and Erudice or, maddened like Athamante, in Styx; and to swear fidelity "on every god celestial" and "on ech goddesse,"

> On every nymphe and deite infernal,
> On satiry and fawny more and lesse,
> That halve goddes ben of wildernesse.[187]

Pandarus is made to refer to Oënone's letter to Paris for Phebus' enamorment with "the doughter of the kynge Amete," to speak of the tearful Nyobe and of vulture-eaten Ticius; to utter an asseveration involving Cerberus; and, as reported in indirect discourse, to swear "by stokkes and by stones" and by the gods resident in heaven that rather than offend he would be with "Pluto kyng" as deep in hell as Tantalus.[188] Diomede claimed that the Greeks would become fearsome even to the Manes, "which that goddes ben of peyne,"

225

and made allusion, though without supernatural details, to the fateful Theban War.[189] Cassandre alluded to a number of such circumstances in that struggle after speaking of the divinely sent Calydonian boar.[190] And Calkas, as already noted, brought up Lameadoun's breach of contract with divine wall builders.[191] Finally there is occasional mention of "goddes" without identification by name or species in the lines of narrator, hero, and heroine; and one in Pandarus'.[192]

From our long analysis of the supernatural for period flavor, we may proceed to consideration—fortunately somewhat briefer—of the chronology of the *Troilus*, the second of its aspects to be taken up in the section. In the ascending action, to which he devotes twice as many lines as Boccaccio,[193] Chaucer lets it be surmised that the winning of the lady took about a year, concentrates events in a few days within that span, and provides clear transitions from one time of day to the next in the sequences which he evolves. In his moderately expanded version of that large fraction of the descending from Ector's resolve to do battle through the hero's vigils at the gate,[194] he indicates that three years had elapsed since the enamorment, links Ector's decision and subsequent occurrences astronomically, and postpones Diomede's call on the lady to make it synchronous with Troilus' hopeful waiting at said gate. And in his abbreviation of the small remainder of the descending action,[195] he makes several not insignificant adjustments in the time pattern. His procedures strengthen verisimilitude and continuity, of course; and, as will appear, put some matters in a new or stronger light.

At the outset, he reminded his audience that the siege lasted "neigh ten yer"[196] but did not assign Calkas' flight and his daughter's resort to Ector to any one of the ten. Indicating with Boccaccio that some time elapsed between these circumstances and the Palladian festival, he narrowed the latter's dating of the ceremony from springtime to April.[197] Like Troiolo, Chaucer's hero went straightway to his chamber from it; like him was visited there by the confidant some days later but still—as we eventually learn—in April.[198] Pandarus, instead of going directly from lover to beloved as Pandaro appears to have done, took time to work out an approach.[199] Such care forecast the wiliness which he was to display as intrigant and hinted a flattering estimation of his niece's powers of resistance.

Having suffered a reverse in his own love "on Mayes day the thrydde" and spent a restless night therefore, Pandarus rose in the morning to betake himself to Criseyde's palace.[200] His mentions while there of his talk in chamber with the prince and of an antecedent sojourn with him in the garden, adapted from Pandaro's of the former and of a sojourn in shady woods, differ from the originals as to time. Chaucer's worthy assigned the episodes—not, as

Boccaccio's, to the current day and the day before it—but to "this other day" and "This other day, naught gon ful longe while."[201] The redating here, made by our poet because of his separation of the visit to the lady from that to the hero, evidences his care for consistency even in minutiae of time. After the uncle's departure at an hour unspecified, Criseyde sought her closet, then her garden, where she remained until dusk; and, going in again, retired for the night.[202] Pandarus, summoned by his friend, supped with him and, with him, took to bed,[203] not to rest, however, but to lay plans for the next day. He returned to his niece's palace, "by-tyme A-morwe," with the letter exacted from the prince; there dined; stationed himself and her, "after noon," by a window from which Troilus could be seen; and took his leave only "whan that it was eve."[204] He brought her answering missive to the suitor abed in darkness.[205] Between this tightly constructed sequence of three days and the next, that involving Deiphebus, of two, there is an interval of considerable but undefined length.[206]

The gathering at Deiphebus' house was promoted by the go-between, before and after dinner time on the day before it took place.[207] Troilus, according to instructions, went to his brother's house at night to be tucked in for a pretended bout of fever.[208] "An houre after the prime"—as "meeltide" was approaching—Eleyne came to the establishment, Criseyde too, and others.[209] Well fed by the host, the group was skillfully manipulated by Pandarus after dinner.[210] Deiphebus and Eleyne, who were sped through Troilus' bedroom to "an herber greene," remained there "the mountance of an houre,"[211] during which time the recumbent lover forwarded himself with Criseyde, his friend assisting. The uncle escorted her out when the pair in the arbor reappeared, and Troilus congeed his brother and sister-in-law.[212] Pandarus returned to the chamber to stay all night with his lord.[213] A remark of the latter to the former at this juncture gives the month of their first conference and establishes that the present sequence came less than a year after it:

> Frend, in Aperil the laste,—
> As wel thow woost, if it remembre the,—
> How neigh the deth for wo thow fownde me,
> And how thow dedest al thi bisynesse
> To knowe of me the cause of my destresse.[214]

Pandarus' vague promise, made while Criseyde was still in the room, that a rendezvous at his own house would follow when the lover should be up and about,[215] implies that there was to be little delay. It appears, however, that some time elapsed before the tryst was effected.[216]

227

Pandarus initiated the climactic two-day sequence by paying a morning visit to his niece,

> Right sone upon the chaungynge of the moone,
> Whan lightles is the world a nyght or tweyne,
> And that the wolken shop hym for to reyne,

and persuading her to sup with him at eve despite the unpromising weather.[217] At eve she came, as joyously observed by Troilus from the stew where, "syn mydnyght," he had been concealed.[218] Purposing to return home after supper and entertainment, she was deterred by the onset of rain due to the conjunction thus described:

> The bente moone with hire hornes pale,
> Saturne, and Jove, in Cancro joyned were.[219]

With the new moon in Cancer, May is indicated or possibly early June; a year must therefore have passed since the enamorment but, unless Pandarus dallied unprecedently after his triumph at Deiphebus', only one.[220] According to the astrology of Chaucer's time, the conjunction could be held responsible for precipitation.[221] That he had in mind the occurrence of this rare phenomenon in the spring of 1385 is a matter irrelevant to the present study.[222] The storm was so loud as to give the host an excuse to lodge Criseyde in the closet, where it could not be heard, and to deafen her attendants in the next room to sounds in this one.[223] Conducted to her bed after the "voide" had been drunk,[224] the lady was soon waked by her uncle to give audience to the prince and, ere long, taken into the latter's embrace. Blameworthy by Christian standards, she was not by those of courtly love, having honored the prescription of slowness to yield as the poet was careful to establish through his astronomical dating. Cockcrow presaged the dawn; and, the weather evidently having cleared, so did the ascension of Venus and the star group Fortuna Major.[225] Willy-nilly, Troilus repaired to his palace, while Criseyde remained abed; Pandarus came to the latter in the morning, and, sent for by the former, remained with him till night.[226]

The period from consummation to reversal Chaucer treats even more expeditiously than his author though he seems to indicate later on that it was slightly over two years long. Like Boccaccio, he records that a second nocturnal meeting was effected soon after the first.[227] As his author did not, he specifies that there were many subsequent ones.[228] Particularizing an observation of Criseida's, he makes his heroine remind the hero on this last night together that they had often kept apart a fortnight for discretion's sake.[229] His hero, like Troiolo, went repeatedly to a garden for devotional song, distinguished himself when battle was waged and, in times of truce, rode out to hawk and hunt, while so deporting himself in society as to be an ornament to it.[230] All this helps, if vaguely, to account for the passage of time, while the hero's extra-amatory pursuits attest his worthiness to be a lover and his and his mistress' abjuring of contact for periods of a fortnight indicates due care for scandal and freedom from lustful appetite.

As has been seen, Chaucer assigns episodes up to the reversal almost entirely to ten days: one in April, another in that month, three consecutive ones early in the next, two consecutive in a month unspecified, and three consecutive in a May presumably one year after the spring of the enamorment. Episodes thus assigned, with the transitions which link them in chronological sequences, constitute 85 per cent of the line total of Books I-III.[231] There are at most three episodes not thus assigned, all so short as to add up to but a small fraction of the remaining 15 per cent, namely: Criseyde's audience with Ector, sometime before the April festival; the lovers' second night together, shortly after their first; and, if what is represented to have taken place "ful ofte" can be called an episode, Troilus' resort to garden to sing of love.[232] The concentration of action in a few days of one spring, in three of the next, and in two somewhere between them would make it easy to turn these books into play form. In the descending action, to which we are to proceed, Book IV and most of Book V would be as readily convertible.

Chaucer begins his account of events before the parliament with an astronomical indication of date. He tells us it befell,

> whan that Phebus shynyng is
> Upon the brest of Hercules lyoun,
> That Ector, with ful many a bold baroun,
> Caste on a day with Grekes for to fighte,

sometime, that is, in later July or early August.[233] He expressly disclaims knowledge of the length of time between this resolve and the day-long battle which ensued.[234] And, though he stresses Calkas' eager haste,[235] he does not account precisely for the intervals between the battle and the father's petition to the Greeks and between that successful appeal and the parliament. However, as Professor Tatlock has pointed out, later astronomical passages establish that resolve to fight, waging of battle, fatherly appeal, and arrangement for negotiation cannot have occupied more than a very few days.[236] What we are left to infer from the *Filostrato* is thus made definite in the *Troilus;* action which led to the sequence beginning with the parliament was dramatically swift. And the astronomical passages in the sequence with the one just quoted, vivid as they are, keep us well reminded of the inexorable progress of time. The summer of parting Chaucer is to fix in relation to the April of enamorment by notice that three springs had come since Troilus fell in love.[237]

In his moderate expansion of the sequence, which in the *Filostrato* is well patterned chronologically, our poet schedules a few events more precisely than the Italian, reschedules a few, and replaces others; and, by one device and another, enhances the already poignant significance of the time factor. Changes bearing on it we shall find in all three phases of the sequence: that of happenings in and near Troy through the ninth day, that of the lady's behavior in camp, and that of the hero's fruitless waiting at the gate.

As to the first. Chaucer accounts for time on the day of the parliament and the ensuing night no less exactly than Boccaccio.[238] The term anticipated of separation he brings more strongly to our attention than the latter. He makes Criseyde limit it to ten days at an earlier point in the conversation of that night than Criseida; at the point when the latter promised to return on the tenth, not only keeps that bare statement for his heroine, but complements it with an astronomically phrased equivalent, namely to return before the moon should pass beyond Leo; and inspires her at dawn to pray for reunion "or nyghtes ten." [239] Like his authority, he represents the woman to have been significantly readier to undergo a brief parting than the man. In transition, to the next day, he interjects that the sun had thrice melted the snows and Zepherus brought back green leaves as often,

> Syn that the sone of Ecuba the queene
> Bigan to love hire first for whom his sorwe
> Was al, that she departe sholde a-morwe—

a statement which, with the dating of the resolve for battle in July or August, seems to me clearly to indicate a period of three years and several months.[240] He provides a *terminus a quo* for the events of the day by specifying that Diomede appeared "at prime."[241] And, with authority from Benoit, he makes this escort profess love on the ride to camp and thus reveal himself to be an insouciantly sudden claimant.[242] Like Boccaccio, he follows the hero to chamber after his parting from the lady outside the town and chronicles his solitary woes up to dawn, while taking care to insert a reference to the ten-day term in his nocturnal lament.[243] By picturization of daybreak he accents the circumstance taken from the *Filostrato* that the prince summoned his friend at that hour, and he realistically explains that the latter had been kept from offering comfort before by enforced attendance on Priam.[244] Representing in conformity with the source that they proceeded to Sarpedoun to while away the time, he keeps them a full week with this host instead of five days.[245] And, having brought hero and confidant back to the former's palace at the week's end, he keeps them there overnight before he dispatches them on pilgrimage to love-hallowed spots, whereas Boccaccio indicated that

230

they undertook the expedition on the day of their return—the fifth by his calculation.[246] Circumstances recorded by that author after the pilgrimage without clear statement of time, ours presents no more exactly, but he does let us know just how far he has gone with the hero before reverting to the heroine:

> This longe tyme he dryveth forth right thus,
> Til fully passed was the nynthe nyght.[247]

Chaucer leaves no doubt that Criseyde had temporized fatally by the end of the tenth day but makes it also clear that she did not proceed with wanton haste to satisfaction of the new lover. He thus preserves more sympathy for her than Boccaccio for Criseida without impairing the validity of the hero's periodic despair in the days after the tenth. And, as remarked in Chapter I,[248] he makes her failure of Troilus credible by suggestion that it resulted from the timidity with which he has characterized her in the ascending action. No sooner does he turn to the exiled lady than he puts in her mouth an anticipation of dire consequences of attempt to cross the lines, thus preparing us to doubt the intention to make such attempt which he is to adapt for her presently from Criseida's.[249] His statement,

> But God it wot, er fully monthes two,
> She was ful fer fro that entencioun,

may be taken to imply a slower waning of good purpose than Boccaccio's that soon—"tosto"—a new lover turned her from it.[250] Postponement of Diomede's call from the fourth to the tenth day[251] allows her a longer period of unshaken faith and yet strengthens the irony of betrayal by synchronizing her coquetry, not with the hero's briefly described ardors at the house of Sarpedoun, but with his hopeful waiting at the gate, recounted in full and prepared for ever since the night of her promise to return. Inspiring the suitor to ask permission to repeat his call on the morrow and the lady to grant it and specifying that the former remained till eve came "And al was wel," Chaucer conveys an even stronger impression than Boccaccio of the aggressiveness of the one and the yielding temperament of the other.[252] He emphasizes her violation of the promise to rejoin Troilus ere the moon should traverse Leo by picturing the night sky above her tent with that orb about to leave the sign.[253] In her nocturnal reflections, his heroine gave weight to Diomede's value as a protector, not as Criseida did in hers of unspecified date to his capacities for love.[254] On the morrow, Chaucer tells us, the Greek kept his appointment and argued so well

> That alle hire sikes soore adown he leyde.[255]

231

Thus matching the hero's return to the gate on that day which he is to take over from the *Filostrato*, he continues to prepare for an irony of synchronous opposites. Before he accomplishes it by return to Troy, he inserts a number of stanzas about the lady's subsequent relations with Diomede. In one of them he makes the negative assertion that no author states how long it was before she forsook the Trojan for the Greek and the positive,

> For though that he bigan to wowe hire soone,
> Er he hire wan, yet was ther more to doone.[256]

In the last phase of the sequence, Chaucer is as attentive to time as in the others. Returning like Boccaccio to the hero on the tenth day, he is careful to remind us that he has brought him through "that ilke nynthe nyght" and to establish that the lover summoned his friend early next morning to proceed to the gate.[257] He accounts for their doings through the day and into the night with all the precision of Boccaccio and all his suggestion of tense anxiety.[258] And as that poet afforded ironical reminder of Criseida's promise in terms of days through misconception of it on Troiolo's part, so Chaucer through his hero's misconception of Criseyde's as phrased in terms of lunar progression.[259] Disappointment at the gate on the next day he chronicles succinctly in the manner of his author.[260]

Compressing the rest of the descending action in free adaptation of the latter, Chaucer occupies himself very seldom with dates but then to good purpose. He represents his hero, like Troiolo, to have declined in health as in hope with the passage of days, to have dreamed of a boar, and, after immediate discussion of the dream with the confidant, to have undertaken a letter forthwith to the tardy heroine.[261] He makes free, however, with indications of time in the missive, changing the length remarked of the lady's absence from forty days to two months and dropping, along with other matter, the allusion to springtime.[262] The change to two months puts the appeal for return ironically in that period when, according to Chaucer's earlier statement, she was to be far from such intention; and the omission of reference to spring avoids conflict with his summer dating of Ector's still quite recent resolve to do battle.[263] He devises a single conference of the hero with Cassandre some days after the writing of the letter in place of the chain of visits to him recorded in the *Filostrato*: Deifobo's, fixed in springtime like Troiolo's letter written some days before it; that of female relatives, including Cassandra, immediately after the brother's; and subsequent ones of the ladies, from which the troublesome sister was excluded.[264] Our poet indicates some lapse of time between the conference and the lover's discovery of the brooch and ensuing lamentation with his friend, as Boccaccio between the visits and these woes; and, like him, a considerable interval again between the latter and the hero's death.[265] At the end, he affords Troilus the corrective of a view of the world after death and thus, in a sense, out of time.[266]

Of the lines in Books IV and V, Chaucer has given 55 per cent to the first three days of the long sequence and another 11 per cent to days also singled out for episodes later in it, but only 10 per cent to the three separated ones so distinguished thereafter.[267] Despite the heavy concentration upon a few within the sequence, the preponderance of lines devoted to focal days is not quite as great in these two Books as in the three of the ascending action, in which as will be remembered it amounts to 85 per cent. Structural resemblance to a play fades in the latter part of Book V.

The next aspect of the poem to engage us is its ideology of extrahuman causation, a topic which has been dealt with by many scholars.[268] When we were analyzing its period flavor, we took account of all references to the Supreme Being—Jove, Jupiter, God—and of all to lesser deities, with the exception of those to Fortune and the Parcae. Here it will suffice to restudy only the most meaningful of the passages thus considered from another point of view and to examine hitherto unnoted mentions of Fortune and the fatal sisters as well as a few contexts without supernatural tinge. The relevant lines may be taken up speaker by speaker, and by speaker in textual order. This approach will reveal more clearly than any other that the ideology is dramatized, not systematized, varying from person to person and shifting under pressure of circumstance even in the individual—as widely in the narrator as in any of the characters. Necessity is implied here, moral responsibility there as art dictates, without obtrusive conflict between these theoretically reconcilable assumptions, but also without any formal accommodation of them. The lively pronouncements of the speakers, though not patterned into a neat scheme of causation orthodox or unorthodox combine to evoke that awe for forces greater than man and that respectful sympathy for his strivings however misguided which are the classic attributes of tragedy.

The narrator, as was not the case in the *Filostrato,* presumes to comment freely on all issues, the causal included. At times, his frame of reference is the universe through the years; at others, the little world of the affair at a particular moment. Consequently observations of his *in propria persona* may transcend those of characters or may not. On the whole, they contribute more powerfully to the destinal atmosphere than those even of Troilus, the foreboding member of the cast. With his privilege of omniscience, the narrator can herald the national disaster, which the prince did not so much as conjecture, and the loss of love, which this victim could speak of—until the very end—only as a possibility. Fortune, portentous in herself, he makes more so on two occasions by derivation of her power from the Supreme Being. On others, however, he, like Troilus, finds fault with her as if she did as she pleased. And he is ambivalent about Love also.

In Book I, utterances of the narrator which we must consider occur in his accounts of Calkas' desertion, of martial vicissitudes, and of the enamorment of the hero. The foreknowledge which inspired the treason he warrants as unqualifiedly as Boccaccio and with greater circumstance, attributing it to astrology and sortilege as well as to consultation of Apollo and denominating that god more imposingly than his authority.[269] Though he emphasizes necessity with respect to the town, he does not for the prophet, and, indeed, suggests that his flight was a free act by stigmatizing it as "this false and wikked dede."[270] The difference in interpretation is artistically expedient. If the great city was subject to fate, it follows that even so exalted an individual as Troilus might be too. The priest, on the other hand, must seem morally responsible to qualify as villain, and a villain he must be to insure maximum pity for the daughter left behind. The Greeks were no more their own masters than the Trojans it appears, for Chaucer goes on to observe that Fortune was spinning the one as the other up and down.[271] The God of Love, he would have us believe, was as absolute in his province as Fortune in the War. He makes sport of Troilus' disprizing the archer and advises all worthy folk against resistance to Love, who could compel submission and would reward it with moral benefits as well as with the obvious pleasures.[272] Dramatically appropriate here, the advice is to be contradicted by the Epilog, equally appropriate after the death of the prince; for, in that, young folk will be presumed able to forgo the kind of affection represented by Cupide and begged to turn from it. With contradiction so long postponed, the dictum about Love contributes not ineffectively to the impression of destiny though of lighter tone than the narrator's later pronouncement on the Supreme Being and his agents.

In Book II, he assigns the reverse in love which he invents for Pandarus to the somehow unpropitious day of May 3,[273] and offers deterministic comment on the triumph invented for the hero and on the lady's reaction to it. After mention of shouts heralding Troilus' approach, he says:

> With that com he and al his folk anoon
> An esy pas rydyng in routes tweyne,
> Right as his happy day was, sooth to seyne,
> For which, men seyn, may nought destourbed be,
> That shal bityden of necessitee.[274]

It is to be noted that he avoids commitment to the generalization by attributing it to others. He ventures astrological explanation, however, upon his own authority, of the effect of the spectacle on Criseyde, asserting that Troilus sped the sooner because Venus was then in favorable position and had been at his nativity.[275]

In the Prohemium to Book III, the narrator—as Troiolo in the corresponding stanzas of his song—acclaims the beneficent influence of the planet goddess upon nature and mankind, her inspiration of Jove to life-giving effects, and her appeasement of Mars.[276] By inclusion of sexual love in the universal order which she symbolizes, he tacitly glorifies the passion which in the Epilog he is explicitly to condemn—here prompting us to be sympathetic to the hero's transient success as there to pass judgment on his life in its entirety. Having brought Criseyde to her uncle's house and told of her entertainment up to the point when she proposed departure, he writes apropos of the conjunction about to cause rain:

> But O Fortune, executrice of wyrdes,
> O influences of thise hevenes hye!
> Soth is, that under God ye ben oure hierdes,
> Though to us bestes ben the causes wrie.
> This mene I now, for she gan homward hye,
> But execut was al bisyde hire leve
> The goddes wil; for which she moste bleve.[277]

The apostrophe, like the Prohemium, hypothecates a purposive ordering of the universe, though in different terms and with new and ominous admission of its mystery. The rest of the stanza establishes that her staying was absolutely determined, but eschews the question as to whether her subsequent behavior was or was not. The narrator observes of the second night of love that it came soon "for that Fortune it wolde"; and of subsequent ones,

> thus Fortune a tyme ledde in ioie
> Criseyde, and ek this kynges sone of Troie.[278]

In the Prohemium to Book IV, he blames the goddess for the coming reversal as did Boccaccio and signalizes her mutability even more piquantly than the latter.[279] Though he addressed her in the preceding book as an agent of God, he has nothing to say here about her obedience to the higher power. Notice of it might have weakened the impression of malicious cruelty which he elects to convey at this juncture.

He reverts in the first stanza of Book V to the concept of pyramidal authority, telling us that Jove committed to the Parcae for execution His destiny for Criseyde and Troilus. Later on he comments that Fortune intended to glaze the prince's hood and still later that she purposed to jape both him and Pandarus[280]—in each instance without suggestion of control from above. This, however, he presently recognizes, observing apropos of Fortune's denudation of Troy that she was commissioned by Jove to effect change.[281] As the end approaches, he twice remarks her frustration of the hero's wishes, both times after the *Filostrato*.[282] For all that he says about supernatural determination, he could not exculpate Criseyde, for to have done so would have been to jeopardize sympathy for Troilus. He would have us assume that she was responsible for her conduct, as is indicated by his mournful wish that he might defend it.[283] Unimpeachably Christian and otherworldly when all is over, he disprizes the old gods, whom he has been countenancing, and prescribes resort to the One, not for mundane advantage, but for salvation.

Troilus, though second to the narrator in illumination, was duly cognizant of controlling forces. He acknowledged Love's power over himself, like Troiolo, from the enamorment—as will be shown in Section 3 of the next chapter. And he once credited the deity with integration of the universe, as Boccaccio's protagonist once did Venere. In the latter's vein, he held fortune to be a capricious tormentor of mankind and his personal enemy. Associating all planets with deities as Troiolo the orb of the third sphere with Venere, he believed them potent in his concerns. More recondite than his original he wondered whether God's prescience left him any free will. Preoccupied with the supernatural he was indeed. To call him pious, however, would be to strain the term a little. Beings to whom he bowed in petition or thanksgiving he challenged when balked. He did not possess the resignation to say humbly to any "Thy will be done" unless the will seemed likely to coincide with his own.

In the first two books, a declaration about Fortune is the one statement of his which requires notice. Having confessed love to Pandarus but not yet accepted help, he opined that she was his foe and that no one might withstand her injuries.[284] This judgment on the goddess, much earlier in the story than the first of Troiolo's, elicits a defense of her from the friend on the same popular level; and accusation and reply prepare us for subsequent, more profound speculations about fate.

In the cheerful third book, he counted unreservedly upon divine good will. He implored five of the seven planetary deities by their past loves to help him with his; a sixth, the chaste moon goddess, not to take it amiss; and the "fatal sustren" who had shaped his destiny, to help also.[285] He thanked all seven for possession of his mistress and then Venus along with her son and Imeneus.[286] And the son, Love, he magnified later on, as the cohesive force in nature, society, and individual relationships.[287]

Under sentence of separation throughout the fourth book, he dwelt on supernatural defeat of his wishes. He upbraided Fortuna, like Troiolo, for taking the lady from him, and he implied his own depression on her wheel by reference to the elevation of others.[288] In the soliloquy given to him by Chaucer in revision,[289] he declared at the start:

> That forsight of divine purveyaunce
> Hath seyn alwey me to forgon Criseyde,
> Syn God seeth every thyng, out of doutaunce,
> And hem disponyth, thorugh his ordinaunce,
> In hire merites sothly for to be,
> As they shul comen by predestyne.

And though he professed uncertainty as to whether necessity were absolute or conditional, he felt sure that the one alternative was no more hopeful than the other, concluding:

> thus the bifallyng
> Of thynges that ben wist bifore the tyde,
> They mowe nat ben eschued on no syde.

In his prayer to Jove which follows the soliloquy, he asked not for patience to bear separation, ordained presumably according to the "merites" of the case, but for rescue from it or death. Intent on suicide when he thought his lady dead, he reproached Jove and Fortune in a spirit more defiant than Troiolo's.[290] Atropos he called on to prepare his bier.[291]

Deprived of the society of the beloved in Book V, he cursed the gods like Troiolo; yet, like him, gave them credit for the instructive dream of the boar.[292] As in the *Filostrato,* of course, this dream did not evidence foreordination, since it came after the mistress had falsed him in intent and perhaps also in act. Finally, he was as sure as Troiolo, after sight of the brooch, that he had been born "In corsed tyme."[293] Needless to say, he held Criseyde accountable for his misery despite his hypothetical determinism.

Criseyde, while made more thoughtful than her original, is not given a preoccupation with causality even approaching the hero's. She generalized, indeed, that worldly joy must be transitory[294] but clung to hope that in her own case the forces of change might be withstood. So cast down at first by the exchange as to suppose that she had been born "in corsed constellacioun,"[295] she rallied to comfort Troilus with assurances of victory over circumstance. She would overcome her father's veto of return, she promised, by shaking his faith in divination with agnostic argument.[296] This sceptical gambit, since it was to be purely expediential, is not at odds with her frequent pietisms.[297] Her reliance on it, however, betrays a woeful underestimation of her parent's foreknowledge and hence of supernatural obstacle to her desires. She presumed, like Criseida, to counsel the hero to master Fortune

237

by indifference, and she assured him that neither time nor the changeable deity could mar her loyalty.[298] With that soon gone, she did not blame any being but herself.[299]

Like Criseyde, her uncle took free will consistently for granted. No metaphysician as was Troilus, he did not ask whether it was compatible with God's prescience. And though a practicing astrologer,[300] he never dwelt on the influence of the planets. Fortune he conceded to bring change as Pandaro had done, but, like him, assumed her to be manageable by the bold.[301] Sceptical of divine revelation as of divine control, he questioned the lover's belief that dreams were identifiably the former even more vigorously than Pandaro.[302]

Calkas represented to the Greeks that he had Apollo's word for the imminent destruction of the city as well as his own findings from astrology, sortilege and augury and added that this god and Neptunus were eager for it.[303] In the *Filostrato,* as will be recalled, the priest, supplied no documentation for his promise of victory. As in the source, Diomede cited the father's foreknowledge to persuade his daughter to relinquish commitments at home.[304]

Lastly, Cassandre told her brother that, to come to an understanding of the boar dream,

> Thow most a fewe of olde stories heere,
> To purpos, how that Fortune overthrowe
> Hath lordes olde.[305]

Discovering from them that Diomede was his supplanter, Troilus, it seems to be implied, would also learn that to fall was the lot of the high and mighty.

Her chronicle of old woes from the gods, Calkas' prediction of the like to come, and the many recognitions by Troilus and the narrator of divine influence give the poem a strongly destinal tone. And the hopes of mistress and confidant to have their way, Fortune notwithstanding, do not impair it since these were unrealized. As we have seen, however, there is no denial of individual responsibility.

It remains to survey Chaucer's exploitation of appearances in nature, the fourth of the aspects of his workmanship to which this section is devoted. Much of this has been touched on in our study of the aspect of chronology but only in a casual way. He is more generous than Boccaccio, we shall find, with particulars about earth and sky, as we have already observed he is with details about the persons of the Trojans, their habiliments, and their abodes. He seeks to visualize time through its phenomena in nature, variously suggesting its speed or tediousness, its conditioning of human event, or its harmony with the latter.

When he is presenting love's nascence, he keeps us well reminded that the season is the fresh one traditionally associated therewith. Boccaccio's dating of the hero's enamorment as of the time which revests the meadows and excites beasts to display their loves he utilizes with modifications, specifying that time to be April, dropping the hint of animal copulation, and noting the hues and odor of the flowers.[306] And he gives us an account of Criseyde's initiation which is redolent of spring. He begins with ornate placement of her uncle's antecedent discomfiture:

> In May, that moder is of monthes glade,
> That fresshe floures, blew and white and rede,
> Ben quike agayn, that wynter dede made,
> And ful of bawme is fletyng every mede;
> Whan Phebus doth his bryghte bemes sprede,
> Right in the white Bole, it so bitidde,
> As I shal synge, on Mayes day the thrydde.[307]

He rouses Pandarus next morning with plaint of the "forshapen" Proigne,[308] an ill omen one may fancy for the affair about to be promoted. Bringing him to Criseyde he makes him propose that they "don to May som observaunce."[309] After the uncle's departure and after Troilus' triumphal appearance, she proceeded to her garden, "shadewed wel with blosmy bowes grene,"[310] and there heard Antigone on the delights of love. With the coming of dusk—finely described by Chaucer if with a touch of parody—she retired indoors and, when it pleased her, sought her couch.

> A nyghtyngale, upon a cedir grene,
> Under the chambre wal ther as she ley,
> Ful loude song ayein the moone shene,
> Peraunter, in his briddes wise, a lay
> Of love, that made hire herte fressh and gay.[311]

In the sequence which he devises at the house of Deiphebus Chaucer interjects the paean to Venus borrowed from Troiolo with its notice of her "bemes clere" and attestation of her influence upon nature as well as man.[312]

In that of consummation, he provides the evening tempest[313] and elaborates upon the approach of dawn. Through the storm raised by God's ministers the planets, he objectifies divine control and furthers the machinations of the resourceful Pandarus. He marks the end of night with pictures of the wing-drumming cock and of Lucyfer and Fortuna Major rising in the east.[314] Its lamentable shortness he emphasizes through aubades given to Criseyde and Troilus, upbraidings respectively of night and of day and the sun.[315] The hero, it may be added, Chaucer inspires to complain of the solar orb when with the heroine for a second time.[316]

Taking from him the song to Venere, he gives him one to the corresponding male figure. In this, Love is addressed *inter alia* as he who causes the elements to hold a perpetual compact, Phebus to bring forth the rosy day and the moon to have lordship of the nights and as he who keeps the avid sea from overwhelming the earth.[317]

When he comes to the reversal, Chaucer makes full use of the world of nature as a magnificent timepiece. In Book IV, he gives the astronomical dating of Ector's resolve for battle which puts it in the summer and emphasizes the heroine's promise to return by the tenth day by adding to it the astronomically equivalent assurance of return before the moon should pass through Leo.[318] In Book V, he relates the summer to the season of the enamorment with the notice that, since that mission, Phebus the golden-haired had thrice melted the snows and Zepherus as often brought back "the tendre leves grene";[319] and he keeps us intensely aware of time throughout the crucial ten days. In free adaptation of the *Filostrato,* he records the hero's longing for the moon to become new horned and his impatience with the sun, as well as his fancy that the wind from camp was the sighing of the awaited mistress.[320] Having chronicled her reception of Diomede on the day set for her return, he visually reminds us of her broken promise:

> The brighte Venus folwede and ay taughte
> The wey ther brode Phebus down alighte;
> And Cynthea hire char-hors overraughte
> To whirle out of the Leoun, if she myghte;
> And Signifer his candels sheweth brighte,
> Whan that Criseyde unto hire bedde wente
> Inwith hire fadres faire brighte tente.[321]

Troilus, he goes on to relate, had sought the gate that day as soon as Phebus had begun to warm the waves of the eastern sea "And Nysus doughter song with fressh entente."[322] The bird, metamorphosed for betrayal of her parent, would seem as ominous of woe as the transformed Proigne who awakened Pandarus. Our poet winds up the vigil with a formal reminder of the wayward lady's astronomically phrased compact—an expression of hope on Troilus' part that he had misinterpreted it.[323]

Brought by Chaucer after death to the eighth sphere,

> he saugh, with ful avysement,
> The erratik sterres, herkenyng armonye
> With sownes ful of hevenyssh melodie,

and, instructed by the manifestation of eternal order, came to despise our mutable earth.[324]

Tendencies of Chaucer's observed in this chapter will appear *mutatis mutandis* in the next on his figurative modes of communication. His poem is richer than Boccaccio's in similitudes of the body, man-made things, and the natural scene, as it is in literal details of physical appearance and reaction, of costume and housing and of season, night, and day. Elaboration in it of the feudal metaphor of the sovereignty of the beloved over the lover complements the dignification of the heroine with a palace and large domestic staff. And parallel to greater concern in it for divine causation is the more extensive and ingenious employment of supernatural figures.

CHAPTER III

Figurative Associations in Seven Areas

Preview

║ N this chapter, expanded from a paper of mine,[1] we are to survey imaginative associations in *Filostrato* and *Troilus*. The formal categories into which I would divide them may be exemplified from the latter poem as follows. The metaphor, a phrasing of a concept in terms for another from a different field of experience:

> For love bigan his fetheres so to lyme;

and the metonymy, a phrasing of a concept in terms for an allied idea, e.g. of the cause as if it were the effect:

> Welcome, my knyght, my pees, my suffisaunce,[2]

The simile, a likening, somehow made explicit, of a concept to one in a different field:

> And thow fordon, as snow in fire is soone,
>
> A thousand sikes, hotter than the gleede,
>
> Al myghte a geant passen hym of myght;

and what Chaucer would call the "ensample" and I the illustration or analogy, a more or less tacit likening sententious in effect. For instance, the plainly implied but not explicit likenings of variety in love making, change in mood, and futile hindsight respectively to variety in workmanship, seasonal change, and tardy medication:

245

Ek som men grave in tree, some in ston wal,

And after wynter foloweth grene May,

But al to late comth the letuarie,
Whan men the cors unto the grave carie.[3]

The first two types equate something, on the verbal level, with something else; the last two bring out a resemblance between one thing and another without such identification. In each work, there are many debatable instances of metaphor—perhaps suggestive at the time of composition, perhaps not. All but the very weakest will be mentioned. Instances of metonymy, simile, and illustration, seldom debatable, will all be noted. In the *Filostrato,* there are four illustrations and over thirty similes, some hundreds of metaphors, if weak ones be counted, and a fair sprinkling of metonymies. In the adaptation, more than fifty illustrations and more than seventy similes, roughly twice as many metaphors as in the source but very few instances of metonymy.

The associations in each work, distinguished above by form, may all be assigned to one or another of seven content patterns and will be so grouped for consideration in the seven following sections. The patterns in the order in which they will be taken up are these. The first includes associations with supernatural beings pagan or Christian and with Christian doctrine and practice. The second comprises those with conquest and relationship between ruler and ruled. The third takes in associations with a variety of human activities—arts, letters, sciences, crafts, and games. The fourth consists of those with the body, its states, sensations, or activities, and its preservation through medical care. The fifth is of those with the brute creation, both in its happy freedom and as it is pursued or controlled by man. The sixth is the pattern of insentient nature. It extends from figures of the single leaf or flower to panoramic ones of ship-tossing seas or of the circling heavens. The seventh pattern is that of fire and of the heat which it engenders and—antipodally —of cooling and positive cold.

In each of the seven sections devoted to a pattern, treatment of the figures in each work which belong to it will be by order of referent, with any applied to referents other than persons of the action coming first and then, sequentially, those applied to the heroine and hero, the rival and the confidant. The few devoted to minor characters will be taken up at any convenient points. With this arrangement, the illumination of referents will be the aspect of the figurative process to stand out. However the complementary aspect, the differentiation of the styles of the several speakers and, by that

246

means, of their characters, will not be neglected, since nearly every association cited will be credited to the individual who made it.

To prepare for the detailed analysis in the seven sections of Chaucer's
reworking of the figurative element, an impressionistic digest of his procedures
may be offered here—first in general and then with respect successively to
the stylistic differentiation of speakers and to the illumination of referents.

Although he expands some parts of the original story more than others,
he treats all with lively associative imagination. The concentration of figurative material in each of his five books is higher than in the corresponding
portion of the *Filostrato,* and the distribution between the five is as even as
between the corresponding ranges in that source. The assumption sometimes
made that the relatively slight expansion in Book IV and most of Book V
and the actual compression at the end of the latter indicate fatigue or tedium
is contradicted by the abundance of figures in each. It is noteworthy, however, that Troilus' soliloquy on predestination in Book IV, supposedly added
in revision, is barer of them than any other long passage. Though congruent
with the lover's other reflections about destiny, the speech does not manifest
the imaginative apprehension of ideas which is characteristic of him.
Chaucer's conception of the hero as poet may have faded a little by the time
he came to revise.

His employment of associations in the seven areas which I have distinguished is proportionally different from Boccaccio's in two significant respects.
Of the total number of illustrations, similes, metonymies, and indubitable
and dubitable metaphors in the *Filostrato,* a quarter may be assigned to the
pattern of conquest and feudal relationship, a quarter to that of the body, a
sixth to that of fire and cold, a tenth to that of insentient nature, and something
under a tenth to each of the three others. Of the total in the *Troilus,* which
is twice as large as in the source, a somewhat bigger fraction may be assigned
to the martial and feudal pattern than that just cited for the original, a much
smaller one to the pattern of fire and cold, and roughly the same fractions to
all the others.

Of his associations in any of the seven areas, only a small proportion is
taken from the *Filostrato*—a quarter in the thermal, a little more than a
tenth in the mythico-religious, and under a tenth in all the others—although,
as might be expected, a higher proportion of the elaborate than of the un-
elaborate ones. Thus independent, Chaucer effects marked changes in all
seven besides increasing the quantitative prominence of one and decreasing
that of another. In the first, the mythico-religious, he evolves a ritualized cult
of love. In the second, the pattern of conquest and dominion, he develops a
more explicitly feudal relationship than Boccaccio between lover and Cupide

247

as well as between lover and lady. In the third, that of arts and so on, he creates several nexuses of conceptions, although no pervasive system, and applies them like the systems in the first two, to contrast the roles in love of the parties to it. In the fourth, the pattern of the body, he adds to Boccaccio's dominant conceptions of love's sweetness and bitterness and of one lover's being the animating force of the other a more elaborate scheme, that of figurative sickness in which the suitor is the patient and the lady and confidant are his physicians. In the fifth, of the brute creation, our poet gives us many homely figures of animals as well as a considerable number of the conventionally romantic sort favored by his author and, through such diversity of association, not only reinforces contrasts between persons, but also stresses disparities within the individual. In the sixth, that of insentient nature, he maintains the concept of luminance as the prevalent one for the impression made by woman upon man and strengthens those of darkness and storm for his state without her. In the last pattern, the only one which he contracts, Chaucer figures amatory sorrow by flames as powerfully as his authority but not sexual desire, reducing the heat imagery for male appetency somewhat and almost wholly suppressing it for the female.

Discrimination of the modes of figurative utterance of the several speakers, it can be shown, he carries much farther than Boccaccio.

In the *Filostrato,* the confidant and heroine are distinguished from the hero by paucity of associations, and he from the narrator speaking *in propria persona* by richness. Of its 5704 lines, 2259 are the narrator's; 1706, Troiolo's; 789, Pandaro's; 747, Criseida's; 98, Diomede's; and 105, minor characters'. With something less than half as many lines apiece as the hero, confidant and heroine each has less than a third as many figures to deliver. And with considerably fewer lines than the narrator, he has somewhat more figures altogether than the latter, and nearly as many very long ones.[4]

As for the incidence of figures of the several content patterns in the lines of the several speakers, there is one very material disproportion to be noted. Almost half of those of the pattern of subjugation and feudal relationship occur in utterances of Troiolo, including the three longest.[5]

As to the distribution of the poem's thirty-five similes and four illustrations, which occur in one or another of the content areas of association, twenty-three of the former come in lines of Boccaccio written *in propria persona,* nine of them and one illustration in the hero's, two each in the confidant's, and one each in the heroine's.[6] Eight of the narrator's and one of the hero's similes and the heroine's one illustration are long.[7] In view of the hero's riches of metaphor and not infrequent employment of metonymy, it is noteworthy that he is so poor in simile and illustration. That he so largely eschews the latter forms in favor of the others may be imagined to reflect the fervor of his passions. Bringing out some likeness between unfused concepts, they are more analytical and, other things being equal, less intense than metaphors or metonymies which equate one concept with another.

Of the forty-six instances of proverbial matter in the *Filostrato* noted by Professor Whiting—proverbs, sententious remarks; and proverbial phrases —slightly more than half are associative figures: fifteen of the just mentioned thirty-five similes, all four illustrations, and seven metaphors. The distribution of these twenty-six among the several speakers is roughly proportional to their line totals[8] and hence not individuating. Only one is tonally extraordinary, the narrator's course similitude of scratching heels for itch of head.[9]

None of the speakers is given to rhetorical conceits. Hardly any of their figures, in my opinion, could qualify as such, perhaps only the narrator's declaration that Maria was his Jove, Apollo, and Muse, and the hero's that Criseida had thrown the water of the smith on his fire.[10]

In sum, Diomede, Pandaro, Criseida, Troiolo, and the narrator are stylistically at one in avoidance of the ingenious and the homely. The rival, on the sole occasion when he is permitted to speak, employs as many figures as his predecessor within utterances of comparable length and none which the latter might not have used. Friend and lady resort to figurative communication less often than the hero proportionally to line totals, thus differing from him in a purely negative way. He is distinguishable from the narrator, whose alter ego he is, both positively and negatively, though only to a limited extent, with somewhat more figures in total, and many more in one pattern, and with notably fewer similes.

In the English poem, the figurative style of each of the five main speakers has its own peculiar quality or combination of qualities.

That of the poet speaking in his own person is richly varied. His publicly displayed personality includes traits of his reflective hero and his pragmatic go-between. Concomitantly, his style embraces all their modes of associative statement. It is not a mean between theirs but matches each at its most typical—Troilus' in moments of poetic inspiration, Pandarus' when most vigorous in homely vein. The narrator freely uses associations of all patterns and alternates between originality and the proverbially familiar, the earthy and the grand, the simple and the conceitful. Similes and illustrations are not infrequent in his lines.

Troilus is the quintessential poet which a romantic lover should be. Like Troiolo's, his lines are more concentratedly figurative than other characters' or the narrator's. For his intensity of thought and feeling as for his original's, the metaphor is the natural instrument of expression. Like him he employs few similes or illustrations. He too prefers figures of rule and service above all others. The proverbial and the homely he largely eschews, although capable of forceful use of both. Lastly and most important, he is gifted with a magical beauty of phrasing which no other participant comes near equalling. At his best, he achieves high emotion with perfect economy of means. The figurative concept may be ingenious in such case, but the wording of it is of the most refined simplicity. And the plain words combine melodiously—

> O soule, lurkynge in this wo, unneste,
> Fle forth out of myn herte, and lat it breste.

> And God, to whom myn herte I sacrifice,
> So sende us hastely the tenthe day!

> The day in which me clothen shal my grave.[11]

Pandarus is made Troilus' opposite in figures. He is more given to similes and illustrations than his friend. The illustration—the instance, example, or analogy—is the form par excellence for instruction and hence natural to his role and temperament. Delighting in sententiousness for its own sake, he will add illustration to illustration. Or he may labor the obvious in a single one—as in the following stanzas intended to assure the lover that Criseyde will eventually yield and that she will be the better mistress for her obduracy:

> Thenk here-ayeins: whan that the stordy ook,
> On which men hakketh ofte, for the nones,
> Receyved hath the happy fallyng strook,
> The greete sweigh doth it come al at ones,
> As don thise rokkes or thise milnestones;
> For swifter cours comth thyng that is of wighte,
> Whan it descendeth, than don thynges lighte.

> And reed that boweth down for every blast,
> Ful lightly, cesse wynd, it wol aryse;
> But so nyl nought an ook, whan it is cast;
> It nedeth me nought the longe to forbise.[12]

The concluding "occupatio" points up the long-windedness of the speaker in the same way as Polonius'

> since brevity is the soul of wit
> And tediousness the limbs and outward flourishes,
> I will be brief.

For, though Chaucer preserves the Trojan from the tediousness of the Dane, he would have us know that the confidant is fond of lecturing. Like the wisdom of Polonius, the former's is mainly of the tried and true variety. The proverbial is a hallmark of his style; he resorts to it much more than prince or lady. Most of his illustrations are proverbial like the one just quoted. So too are most of his similes and some of his metaphors, not to mention remarks of his which are nonassociative. The proverbial is regularly sententious in the illustrative form and not infrequently so in the others. Professor Whiting supposes that Chaucer intended the proverbial flair to be a sign of sophistication in Pandarus. But when it is sententious, it would appear rather to indicate a blend, as in Polonius and many now living, of real enough sophistication and a naive desire to be sophisticated. The proverbial with him is often homely, and as such often lively and vigorous, as in the asseveration,

> So thryve I, this nyght shal I make it weel,
> Or casten al the gruwel in the fire.[13]

His fondness for traditional phrasings is due to no lack of wit of his own. He is often ingenious, as in this irreverent fancy,

> Somtyme a man mot telle his owen peyne.
> Bileve it, and she shal han on the routhe:
> Thow shalt be saved by thi feyth, in trouthe;

and occasionally capable of a truly metaphysical conceit as in the line,

> Algate a foot is hameled of thi sorwe.[14]

But he never rises to the beauty and passion of Troilus, nor does he attempt to do so.

His niece's figurative style is a mean between his and Troilus', less proverbial than the one's, more so in proportion to line totals than the other's; less often homely than the uncle's, seldom elevated as her lover's, and without marked preference for any pattern or inclination to simile or illustration. As the distinctively mannered styles of Troilus and Pandarus are reflective of their several natures, so her middle way with associations is a mirror of her very complex character. A divided personality, she can see life from the points of view of both men, but does not respond to it with the imaginative vigor of either. While the figures applied to her by the narrator and Troilus regularly exalt her beauty and charm, those through which she expresses herself sometimes give evidence of commonsensical prudence at odds with her romantic love.

As for the rival, the few figures in his cynical private reflections are very much down to earth; the more numerous ones in his protestations to Criseyde, as sublimated as Troilus' tend to be on all occasions. The private ones show the others to be insincere and make them a parody, unconscious on his part, of the style of the true lover.

The generalizations just offered about the five speakers in the *Troilus* may be illuminated somewhat by the following quantitative analyses paralleling those given for the *Filostrato*.

The narrator and main characters all have more figures than in the source, both absolutely and in proportion to line totals. With the whole expanded from 5704 to 8239 lines, the narrator has 3418 lines instead of 2289; the hero, 1462½ intead of 1706; the confidant, 1804½ intead of 789; the heroine, 1154 instead of 747; the rival, 153 instead of 105; and minor characters, 247 instead of 105.[15] The narrator and Diomede, whose lines are increased proportionally to the whole, have about the same shares respectively of the new total of figures as they had of the old. Because of the great expansion of the direct discourse of confidant and heroine and the moderate contraction of the hero's, the former naturally have larger shares of the new total than they did of the old, and the latter has a smaller. He still has more figures than either of them; and, although fewer than the narrator, still more in proportion to line totals. As for long ones, he has considerably fewer than the latter but more than friend or mistress.[16]

With less than a fifth of the lines of the poem, the hero makes a third of the associations in the pattern of conquest and feudal relationship—as many as the narrator with two-fifths and far more, of course, than any other character. And he is responsible for more than half of the long ones in this area.[17]

There are seventy-four similes and fifty-two illustrations in the work. The narrator has fifty-two of the former and fourteen of the latter; Troilus, seven and five; Pandarus, twelve and twenty-four; Criseyde, three and seven; and Antigone, two illustrations.[18] Thirteen of the narrator's similes and three of his illustrations are long; two and one only of the hero's; five and six of the confidant's; three of the heroine's illustrations, and both of Antigone's.[19]

As for proverbial associative figures, there are some one hundred and twenty-seven among the over two hundred instances of proverbiality of all kinds cited by Whiting: thirty-four of the similes and thirty-seven of the illustrations just cited and fifty-six metaphors. The narrator has twenty-four of these similes, ten of these illustrations, and sixteen of the metaphors; Troilus, five, four, and seven respectively; Pandarus, three, sixteen, and nineteen; Criseyde, two, seven, and eleven; Diomede, one of the metaphors, and Antigone, two.[20]

Along with the quantitative distinction between speakers in the use of proverbial associations there is a qualitative. The narrator, who employs the most, has a good many which are folkishly rude; the confidant, who employs somewhat fewer, even more which are such; the heroine, with considerably fewer, still a fair number of this kind; but the hero with slightly fewer, only an occasional one which may be considered homespun. In the lines of the narrator we find the following homely proverbial figures: metaphors of singing a fool a mass, glazing a man's hood, piping in an ivy leaf, smiting while the iron is hot, plucking a peacock, drawing in one's horns, and fishing for an excuse; and similes of a carthorse reduced to obedience, and of clawing heels for ache of head.[21] In Troilus' discourse the only figures comparable to these are the analogy for himself of a man hanging by the neck and the cluster of analogies for Calkas and Criseyde beginning with that of bearward and bear.[22] The cluster, as remarked below, may be imitative of her style. Pandarus offers the following: metaphors of making a man a hood above a caul, fishing ill-advisedly, being a mouse's heart, casting all the gruel in the fire, toasting by it, and coming to fetch fire and running home again; similes of an old hat, an ass insensible to music, and a feeble gnat; and illustrations of a whetstone, a man deemed hot because he sweats, and hounds to be left sleeping.[23] Criseyde has a store of homely proverbial figures, smaller than her uncle's but larger than the prince's: a metaphor of telling what she thinks while it is hot; and illustrations of drunkenness being forbidden but not drinking, of a fish out of water, and of the incompatible full wolf and whole wether.[24]

Professor Whiting hypothesizes that Chaucer meant to stamp Pandarus and Criseyde as more sophisticated than Troilus by alloting more proverbs to them than to him.[25] That they have a kind of sophistication not conspicuous in the prince may be granted. Yet he is permitted to be tellingly critical of this wisdom and hence made to appear anything but naive. Having kept warily and teasingly silent, as the narrator informs us, through much sententious exhortation from Pandarus to confide, he replies to the latter's loud "Awake":

> Frend, though that I stylle lye,
> I am nat deef. Now pees, and crye namore,
> For I have herd thi wordes and thi lore;
> But suffre me my meschief to bywaille,
> For thi proverbes may me naught availle.
>
> Nor other cure kanstow non for me.
> Ek I nyl nat ben cured; I wol deye.
> What knowe I of the queene Nyobe?
> Lat be thyne olde ensaumples, I the preye.[26]

Offered proverbial consolation by the friend after the parliament, he remarks:

> Thow farest ek by me, thow Pandarus,
> As he that, whan a wight is wo bygon,
> He cometh to hym a paas, and seith right thus,
> "Thynk nat on smert, and thow shalt fele non." [27]

Criseyde's proverbial reasoning apropos of her plan to cajole her father with goods of her own,

> Lo, Troilus, men seyn that hard it is
> The wolf ful, and the wether hool to have,

he answers proverbially—with analogies for Calkas of the bearward, of the wise who may be outrun but not outwitted, and of the cripple who cannot be deceived by shamming.[28] As Professor Whiting observes, "We are uncommonly close to a desperate parody of Cressida's conversational style"[29] and, as I might add, if not a consciously ironic one, one ironically justified by the outcome.

Lastly as to rhetorical ingenuity, the prince quite holds his own. The following figures in the lines of the narrator may be deemed conceitful: the metaphor of desire breeding in the lover no other fawns but arguments to one conclusion, the simile of alchemical distillation for his weeping, and perhaps the metaphor of Troilus and Troy town sliding knotless through Criseyde's heart.[30] The ingenuity of the lover is evidenced by the following: the declaration to his lady that though mercy be written in her eyes the text is very hard to find, the command to day to go sell its light to engravers of small seals, the question to Love how he may permit repeal after he has taken prince and mistress into his grace and sealed both their hearts, the command to his own soul to unnest and fly forth, and his anticipation of unsheathing the soul from his breast.[31] Pandarus, lively though he is, has only about as many conceits as Troilus: the assurance to the latter that one foot is "hameled" of his sorrow, the command to him to stay close in his hunting station while his helper drives the deer to his bow, the fancy that Troilus is buried in his bed and the indecent one that Criseyde is to be his bier, the implication that her compliance is a miracle worked by Cupid and Venus, and the promise to the lover that the day is set "the chartres up to make."[32] The lady evolves no conceit of truly metaphysical kind nor does Diomede.[33] That Troilus equals his friend and surpasses his mistress and rival in associative ingenuity strengthens the evidence just given of his maker's intention to give him an intelligence at least as active as theirs.

Having surveyed the figures in the poems as delivered by the several speakers, we have now to do so as they are applied to referents. Separation of these aspects is, of course, purely a matter of convenience. They are fused whenever an individual is talking about himself and interrelated even when he is not.

As for figurative representations concerning the narrator, the very few in the source link him with a mistress, while the few in the adaptation bring out his relationship to a public. In supernatural metaphor, Boccaccio's Maria was his Giove, Apollo, and Muse. And in that of insentient nature, she was a light to him as Criseida to Troiolo, and he, like his hero, was committed by love to dangerous seas. Chaucer, allegedly far from Love's help in darkness, can serve the accepted servants of the god in a literary capacity. So functioning, he may prove impercipient of amatory nuances, he admits, as a blind man is of colors. Clerk of those who serve Venus, he beseeches her to flood his naked heart with sentiment.

Divine power, variously attested in both poems as we have seen in the last section of the preceding chapter, is expressed through figure to a limited extent in the *Filostrato* and to a wider in the *Troilus*.

In the source, the influence of Venere is figuratively acknowledged in one passage; that of Amore, over and over again with vivid particulars; that of Fortuna, on occasion though without such touches. In Troiolo's song, Venere is called the lady of every gentle heart and said to impose laws upon the universe. Amore is frequently represented as the conqueror of Troiolo by force of arms and his absolute lord in consequence, and also as joint kindler with Criseida of his flames. The lover professes humble service to the god as to the mistress. Amore is called her lord but once and never allowed service from her, but he is imagined to have inflamed her just as he did her suitor. The god's influence upon Diomede is figured in the same way as that upon the hero and apparently without even covert irony; the narrator speaks of the Greek as attacked and enkindled, and the character himself professes service to the deity. Fortuna is considered almost entirely in relation to Troiolo. Though her operations against him are not, like Love's, vividly presented as warfare, the prince does speak of her as an enemy and an irresistible one.

In the *Troilus*, the scanty figuring of Venere is carried little farther; the extensive figuring of Amore is changed in significant respects; that of Fortuna is somewhat enlarged and in one respect significantly; and metaphorical representation is extended from these deities to others. The narrator, in his Prohemium to Book III, rates Venus law-giver to the universe as Troiolo in his song. Pandarus seems to imply that she worked a miracle with her son and thus to associate her with him in the so-called religion of love. In Troilus' song to Love which replaces Troiolo's to Venere, the god is said to knit the "lawe of compaignie" for human beings, to have governance of earth and sea, and to enforce his behests in the high heavens. Here he is raised for the nonce to his mother's exalted plane. In a number of contexts he is accorded a cult, the fanciful religion of love modelled after the Christian. The narrator and Pandarus are the exegetists of this faith of Cupide; Troilus, its devotee. The god's lordship and the hero's service to him, taken over from the *Filostrato* and enlarged upon as feudal concepts, stand out most prominently in their relationship. That of armed conquest, taken over with these but not elaborated, becomes proportionally less impressive, while the associated one of Love's part in inflaming the prince is suppressed. The occasional figurative suggestions in the source of his influence upon the heroine and upon the rival are eliminated. Fortune is held by Troilus to be his enemy as she was by Troiolo. Her changeableness, stressed in the *Filostrato* but not through figures, is repeatedly imaged in her traditional wheel. There is figurative acknowledgment also of her dependence on the All High, of which there is no hint in the source. She and the influences of the high heavens are His herdsmen, and with His commission she proceeds to strip Troy of its bright feathers. The Parcae, who are mentioned as responsible for the thread of life, have commissioned from Him too. He is called "lord" very, very often and several times referred to as enthroned monarch.

The relationship between hero and heroine is metaphorically presented in the *Troilus* on the whole much as it was in the *Filostrato* but with some noteworthy modifications. It is kept central, of course, with many more figures being applied to it than to any other. And the hero retains his primacy, with many more used of him than of his lady. In the one poem as in the other, the figuring of the man and woman conforms to the usual conception of the roles of the sexes in romantic love. Her attractions are stressed more than his; his feelings, than hers. The power conferred on her by beauty is repeatedly attested and the devotion inspired in him by it. In both, her inconstancy is set against his truth in many figures and with strongly ironic effect. But Chaucer in his figurative associations distinguishes hero and heroine even more sharply than his author and on different bases. He makes Criseyde appear more gently feminine than Criseida and Troilus more of a man than his original both in body and in warlike exploit. At the same time, he accentuates the mistress' authority and the humbleness of the lover. Finally, he develops subtler oppositions than Boccaccio between aspects of her nature and behavior, and stronger ones between aspects of her lover's. Presenting the pair from several points of view, he makes their love an affair of manifold nuances.

In the *Filostrato*, the heroine appears a truly celestial being, but her word proves not sacred. Like Amore, she effects Troiolo's subjugation by missile weapons. She is repeatedly acknowledged to be his lady but without enumeration of her powers in feudal terms. Conscious as she is of her social inferiority, she herself never claims to be lady over him nor to have the authority of a suzerain. Yet, according to Pandaro, she is as bold in undertaking as any king. She is Troiolo's heart and soul, his very life. Declared sweet by him, she finds love sweet and loss of it bitter. Her eyes, he says, hold him forever in the amorous net. She is his light—specifically his star. And she is flowerlike in beauty. Intense flames of desire consume her, but, since she is never said to be enkindled by Troiolo, the impression given is that hers is the impersonal blaze of lust. There is but a single image of heat for her grief at parting, and that a weak one. Once parted, she cools very rapidly in her desire to return. A fiery being and a handsome one, she inflames her lover instantly and forever.

As for Troiolo, enjoyment of the lady seems Paradise to him; want of it is truly an Inferno. He is her faithful servant and one who prizes service in love above all else. Complete though his devotion undoubtedly is, there is no suggestion of manly protectiveness in it. When possessed of her affections, he is called her heart, soul, life, as she is called his. Sweet to her as she to him, he too finds love sweet and deprivation bitter. He is once likened along with her to a singing bird; and once again, when making himself fine for his mistress, to a falcon released from its hood. His captivation by love is imaged as netting and snaring, and his frustration, not his prowess, by the raging of bull and of lion. He is cheered and guided by the light of his mistress, miserable when he no longer sees it. Though certified a mighty warrior, he is repeatedly imaged through flowers and much more memorably than his fair lady. Having referred in the temple to love's fire as a thing of the past for him, he is rekindled at first sight of her. More numerous, though not more intense figures of burning are applied to his desires than to Criseida's. None suggest unsublimated carnality in him, as several do in her. Grief at loss of love inflames him more than his lady, and, whereas she cools, he does not.

In the *Troilus,* the heroine, though gentled, claims absolute power over her lover, and the hero yields himself more humbly than Troiolo for all his greater manliness. His perfect devotion is as misplaced as the latter's, for Criseyde's self-interest is no less incompatible with true love than the questing appetite of Boccaccio's lusty female. So great is her charm, as our poet represents it figuratively and otherwise, that the reader finds the prince's admiration a most natural thing, and in the early stages at least must share it with him. Yet Chaucer does not mislead us. Even in these stages, he brings out the extravagance of the lover's emotions and the admixture of calculation in the beloved's, preparing in light and sometimes comic vein for the graver ironies which are to follow.

His heroine is as celestial in aspect as Boccaccio's, and, as the latter's, her word is supposed holy and proved otherwise. Her conquest of the lover is stressed no more than Criseida's, but her sovereignty over him given far greater prominence. As in the role of Cupide, the new preponderance in hers of the notion of ordered rule over that of lawless aggression helps to create the impression that love is a formal system. Freed of Criseida's sense of social inferiority, Chaucer's heroine asserts her rights as lady in specifically feudal terms. Troilus acknowledges these rights of his own volition more fully and often than Troiolo, and narrator and confidant are as conscious of her sovereignty in love as he. Like Criseida, she is her suitor's heart, soul, and life, and very sweet in his opinion. Though she drinks with him of love's potation, she does not confess thirst for it as he does. Less is said of its bitterness for her than for him, and still less of its sweetness. She feels amorous smart but, again, not as often as her lover. She is frequently represented as his physician but never as receiving or even in need of amorous medicine from him. As in the *Filostrato,* she is jointly imaged with him as singing bird, and the pretty but unheroic figure of a preening falcon, applied in that poem to Troiolo, is transferred to her in the English. Further, she is newly figured in the consummation scene as lark in the claws of a sparrow-hawk and as nightingale momentarily silenced by seeming danger. But in this scene, in which Troilus the sparrowhawk possesses himself of her body, he calls her eyes nets, and in a later one it is remarked that his heart was forever enmeshed in Criseyde's net. Unfortunately, she will not captivate her father, as she has Troilus; Calkas will prevail over her, the lover correctly anticipates, as the bearward over his charge. She is figured, like Criseida, as her servant's light, and far more beautifully. The floral imagery applied to her is, however, no more striking than the occasional figures of this kind used of her original. New figuring of her emotions as spring sunshine and cloud contrasts them with Troilus' imaged as stormy, nocturnal, and winterish. She is never represented as ablaze with stark desire. Not until the affair is threatened is she said to be on fire, and then with love and sorrow mixed. Since she has never been ablaze with sexual passion, her change of heart cannot be imaged as cooling. Suggestions that she has kindled Troilus are of the vaguest. A cautious woman, she disapproves of the heat of impulse displayed by her lover in urging an elopement; in a mixed figure, she bids him slay it with reason.

To Troilus as to Troiolo, possession is heaven; lack of it, hell. The infernal aspect of his experiences is raised to greater prominence than the heavenly by likenings of him to various sufferers in the nether regions. Pandarus' fancy that his friend is a reclaimed heretic enforces the irony of his enamorment though in lightsome mood. Troilus professes service more explicitly than Troiolo and displays greater humility throughout. Inhibited by the same respect for her honor as Troiolo's, he cannot protect her by deeds of valor.

But his service seems the manlier for his being called, not merely her servant, but her knight and also her sword, shield, wall, and the steadfast ground of her happiness. Fighting for his countrymen as he cannot for his mistress, he proves their shield. He is as sweet in her estimation as she in his. But he is a patient instead of a physician. And his figurative sickness is such that it appears to him a living death. More ignominiously subdued by love than Troiolo, he is nevertheless more glorious. Plucked peacock, carthouse chastized, and abashed snail in Pallas' temple, he is a hawk in the physical act of consummation as well as the splendid eagle of Criseyde's dream. Though the death throes of a bull figure impotent rage in him as in Troiolo, two lion images represent his prowess in the field, not futile anger as the one used of Boccaccio's hero. He is as dependent upon the heroine's light as his original and finds the world even blacker without it. To the advantage of his masculinity, pretty floral imagery is much less frequently applied to him than to Troiolo. Less often represented as on fire with passion than his prototype, his love appears less openly physical. And it appears to have been his first love, for the reference in the latter's discourse to earlier fire does not appear in his. His passion now contrasts with the heroine's in point of intensity as it did not before, since the considerable imagery of this kind applied to her sexual desires in the *Filostrato* is virtually eliminated in the *Troilus*. His sorrows, as they are imaged by fire, also appear greater than hers.

The supplantation of hero by rival creates the principal irony in both works. The essential part of this irony is, of course, that the lady forsakes a lover who is a model of his kind. Chaucer enhances it by making the new lover positively unworthy, whereas in the original he differed from Troiolo only in having greater self-assurance.

Boccaccio speaks of Diomede's being taken with Criseida at the first encounter. When the Greek visited her in camp and found her mournful, he feared that one would indeed have to be a sovereign artist to displace her first lover and that therefore he had done ill for himself in going to Troy to fetch her. Nevertheless, says the author, he boldly resolved to inform her of Love's harsh assaults and of how he was first enkindled. He did so, and went on to offer service as Troiolo had and with apparently equal sincerity. His person and address cooled her in the hot desire which she had of returning.

The statements that the rival was taken, assaulted, and enkindled do not appear in the *Troilus,* and there are no new indications, figurative or otherwise, that he was truly in love. For the modest reflection that one would need to be a sovereign artist to win the lady, there is substituted the egocentric one that a man might say he were a conqueror if he had success with so sorrowful a woman. Troilus, contrariwise, had repeatedly acknowledged conquest by this lady as well as by the God of Love even when she was not on hand to be impressed. His protestations of service made in her presence must therefore have been sincere, as his rival's similar ones very evidently are not. Eager for her love though he was, he never schemed cold-bloodedly to win her. His only fishing was for excuses for a jealousy of which he was innocent. Diomede, on the other hand, spent much thought on how he might bring Criseyde's heart into his net and laid out hook and line to fish for her. He was one who knew more than the creed, says Chaucer. Heartfree, he came to her tent as fresh as branch in May.

Finally, as for the confidant in his relations with hero and heroine and with his own mistress, he is very scantily figured in the Italian poem, considerably more often in the English though still not with great frequency. The scarcity of associations for him does not mean, of course, that he is inconspicuous in either work. His personality is impressed upon us in both, but by what he does and what he says about others, rather than by what he says about himself or by comments made about him by narrator and fellow characters. The moderate increase in figures for him in the *Troilus* serves principally to emphasize his own ill success in love and his aspirations as counsellor and hence the anomaly of his position.

In the *Filostrato,* Pandaro defends his ability to counsel though loveless by joined analogies of the man safeguarding another against poison when he cannot protect himself and of the one-eyed walking where the full-sighted cannot. And to reassure Troiolo that he can get Criseida for him, he says that he has the amorous flames in his hands and boasts that he has accomplished greater feats—presumably of the seducing kind.

At the moment when Boccaccio's confidant offers his two analogies, Pandarus gives a long series—of a blind man walking where a clear visioned could not, of a whetstone making sharp carving tools, of the taster of bitterness being the only judge of sweetness, of white seeming whiter when set by black, and of Phebus who could not cure himself of love though the founder of medical science. Unhappy as he is in love, he has no cause, he says, to soar like a hawk. Yet, he preaches of love, even when that passion felt in his own heart has turned him green. He is Troilus' physician, in the narrator's view as well as his own, at times when Criseyde cannot be in attendance. He plans his first approach to her as carefully, we are told, as an architect the building of a house, and later has the timber ready for the framework of a plot. And he promises to drive the deer Criseyde to his master's hunting station. She would have it that he is a fox. Yet he does not claim to have kindling flames, as did Pandaro with the implication of previous triumphs as procurer. And Chaucer's statement that Pandarus knew all the old dance suggests such triumphs only weakly if at all. Though ebullient, he is tactful and sympathetic. He is repeatedly said to be as still as stone; and on several occasions at least, it appears that he is so, not merely to preserve secrecy, but out of concern for the sorrow of others.

Now that we have viewed the figurative element of each work as a whole, we may give detailed attention to the seven content groups which comprise it in each, taking them up one after another in the seven sections to come. In the section which immediately follows, we are to consider the mythic and Christian associations. In it and its successors as in the sections of the last chapter, we shall deal first with the relevant material in the source and then with that in the adaptation.

Religion and Mythology

FIGURES of the supernatural kind in the *Filostrato* are typical of Boccaccio's associative procedures. They are limited to a few conventional themes; they are regularly terse, often, indeed, consisting of a single word; and they are uniform in tone, presenting the attractions and miseries of love with equal seriousness. Although singly not often striking either in idea or in expression, they combine to give strong affirmation of Criseida's desirability and of the intensity of Troiolo's passions. She is a heavenly creature in seeming, the possession of whom is Paradise, the absence, an Inferno. His sufferings, and hers as well, are martyrdoms. Such touches notwithstanding, there is no effective suggestion of a cult of love analogous to Christian worship.

Beginning with what is said of Criseida in otherworldly echo, we may consider, in sequence, its application to her feelings, to the impression which she makes on the beholder and particularly on Troiolo, and to the judgments passed upon her by him and by the public. Thence we may proceed to the figures applied to Troiolo, all of which have to do with his emotions.

The narrator uses the noun forms "martiro" or "martiri" four times for sorrow on her part and three for hers and Troiolo's jointly; Diomede, the form "martíre" once for grief inferred in the lady.[1] Such religious implication as there may be in the term is never developed beyond it.

To Troiolo she is a goddess, as Maria is to his creator; her beauty is angelic; her face, her lover's Paradise. Boccaccio, who tells Maria that she is his "Giove," "Apollo," and "musa,"[2] gives Troiolo as flattering notions of Criseida. The prince wonders whether Amore has dedicated him to the service of a lady or a "goddess" and addresses her, after he has had ample opportunity to resolve this point, as more loved and honored by him than any other "goddess"; and it is remarked by Boccaccio that, in his mind's eye, the lover was forever seeing his departed mistress as his "god."[3] The poet declares that she was so beautiful and so "angelic" to see that she did not appear a mortal thing, once calls her countenance "angelic," and has Diomede do so twice.[4] He pays similar compliment, it may be noted, to Polissena, whom he certifies an "angel" in semblance, and to Maria, whose face also he calls "angelic."[5] In like hyperbolic style he speaks of Criseida's countenance as adorned with "celestial" beauty and as "made in Paradise."[6] And, finally, Troiolo, in his last letter, calls her the "divine" light of his eyes.[7]

Her character is not as heavenly as her appearance leads the hero to believe. Pandaro, though anticipating no difficulty in making her Troiolo's mistress, would remind him that her reputation is "holy" among the people, but his friend is to have good cause to complain that her faith is not as "holy" as he has trusted it to be.[8]

Up to his final disillusionment, Troiolo considers possession of Criseida to be Heaven. Immediately before and after consummation, he thanks Pandaro for having brought him from "Inferno" into "Paradise" and, in his letter addressed to her in the Greek camp, he writes that all his "Paradise" is in her face.[9]

His suffering is frequently represented as martyrization. Beside the three contexts in which his and Criseida's shared unhappiness is so designated, there are thirteen in which his woe is, without notice of hers. In one of these, he declares that the fire which she has kindled in him "is martyrizing" his spirit.[10] In the rest, one or another of the noun forms, "martir," "martiro," "martire," or "martiri," is applied to torment of his—by himself, by Pandaro, or by the narrator.[11] The martyrhood of Troiolo is to his credit in the frame of courtly love and, to some degree, in any idealized amatory ideology, just as dying for the faith is in the Christian frame. But since it brings only temporary reward and much subsequent grief, it raises the question of the worthwhileness of love. Whether to be in love was good or not, Troiolo, in his own view, could not avoid it. In his hymn to Venere, he cites the demigod Ercole as a saving precedent for his own defenselessness against the passion.[12]

The figurization above recorded was suggestive to Chaucer but not sufficiently rich and varied for his purposes. He adapts, rejects, and supplements with great freedom, making associations in the pattern which are more diversified and ingenious than Boccaccio's, notably more incisive, and, in at least several cases, of more compelling beauty and power. He associates hero and heroine together with one mythological unfortunate and the former alone with several more; stresses the infernal character of the prince's experience and once recognizes that of the lady's. As insistent as Boccaccio upon her celestial seeming, he glorifies Troilus' soldierly qualities by comparison of him to Mars, his amatory by linkage with Cupide. And he attests the rival's cunning in a single metaphor while bringing out Pandarus' didacticism in figurative language used by and of him.

Chaucer's most pervasive increment is the working out of an amatory religion, like the Catholic in that it has dogma, forms of observance, and ecclesiastical orders. His exploitation of this fancy, traditional in the literature of courtly love, was duly recognized many years ago by Dr. Dodd.[13] And Dr. Slaughter has recently concentrated upon the application to earthly love in the *Troilus* of the doctrine of grace and related Christian concepts to show that this phase of the development is consequential.[14] To reanalyze the ideology so fully treated by the latter scholar would be superfluous. Christian touches peripheral to it which concern the God of Love or Venus may, however, be noted at this point—first those illuminating the role of the narrator and then those illuminating the hero's.

In the opening stanzas of Book I, the poet casts himself as an apprehensive but fascinated exegetist of the amatory cult.[15] The first clause in his statement,

> For I, that God of Loves servantz serve,
> Ne dar to Love, for myn unliklynesse,
> Preyen for speed, al sholde I therfore sterve,
> So fer am I from his help in derknesse,

implies an office like the Pope's, the "servus servorum Dei"; and the whole expresses the humble spirit of the title, though carrying it to such extreme as to preclude equation of the speaker with the successors of Peter. Even more suggestive of clerical function than this denigratory statement is the parody, which follows, of a bidding prayer, the liturgical form in which the priest instructs his flock to pray for designated groups and individuals. In it, the narrator asks lovers to call on God to speed him in exemplifying the pain and woe of Love's folk in Troilus', to bring the amorously despairing and maligned soon out of this world, and to grant the fortunate due perseverance and the ability so as to please their ladies "That it to Love be worship and plesaunce." He winds up the directive with the following lines,

> For so hope I my sowle best avaunce,
> To prey for hem that Loves servauntz be,
> And write hire wo, and lyve in charite.

His own prayers, one may infer, will be for the continuance in amorousness of the happy as well as for the release from it of the unhappy, since he has recommended supplication of both kinds to others. Though confessedly rejected by Love and making more of the disappointments of his servants

264

than of their successes, he means to be taken here as a spiritual guide in the devotion to which they are committed, not as a guide away from it as in the Epilog. There is irony, doubtless, in the pose, but no forthright condemnation of worldliness. Priestlike status, implied so strongly for him at this juncture, is suggested, conceivably, in the Prohemium to the third book. Appealing to Venus for literary assistance, Chaucer identifies himself as the "clerc" of her servants. While the word in context need mean no more than writer, it readily evokes memories of its original sense of clergyman.

Troilus, once a scoffer at Love, becomes a devotee of the faith of which the narrator is the loveless theoretician and thus evidences the might of the god asserted by the latter. Generalizing from the prince's experience in the temple that the best of people are overcome by passion, Chaucer declares with echo of the Gloria Patri:

> This was, and is, and yet men shal it see;

and he presently exclaims:

> Blissed be Love, that kan thus folk converte! [16]

The hero, in effort to hide his subjugation, speaks jestingly of love as a demanding "lay," of its adherents as an "ordre," and of their amatory pursuits as "observaunces." [17] Joyous to learn of the enamorment, Pandarus expresses surprise at "thus fayr a grace" for one who called Love "Seynt Idyot, lord of thise foles alle." [18] He bids Troilus make formal repentance to the god and is obeyed.[19] He opines that Love has "converted" the hero from his wickedness so that the latter shall become the best pillar "Of al his lay," and supports this view with a stanza-long example to the effect that "converted" heretics hold God most in awe and are strongest of faith.[20] With Criseyde some days later, he represents to her that he overheard the prince saying a "mea culpa" to Love in the palace garden before he came upon him in chamber.[21] Encouraging the lover to solicit her when they shall all be at Deiphebus' house, he plays ingeniously on Christian doctrine:

> Somtyme a man mot telle his owen peyne.
> Bileve it, and she shal han on the routhe:
> Thow shalt be saved by thi feyth, in trouthe.[22]

When Criseyde gives her promise there of comfort to his friend, the confidant exclaims that Cupid may glory in it and Venus make melody; then imagines a miracle:

> Withouten hond, me semeth that in towne,
> For this merveille, ich here ech belle sowne.[23]

265

After consummation, Troilus pays a tribute to Love reminiscent of Dante's to the Virgin and assures the god, late in the action, that he will live and die in his "byleve." [24]

Beside the above instances of suggestion of a Christian-toned cult of sex which involve deification, there are others in which neither Love nor his mother is mentioned. These it will be convenient to treat with the rest of the supernatural figures. All will be dealt with in order of application—to lovers in general, to Criseyde, to Troilus, to Pandarus, and to Diomede.

In several passages about lovers as a class, their bliss is likened to Heaven. And in one of these there is an accompanying equation: true lovers are to lechers as saints are to fiends. Apropos of the hero's coming at last to the satisfaction of his desires, Chaucer makes the general observation that pains "bryngen folk to hevene." [25] Commenting on Troilus' reaction to this event, Pandarus observes that a man who has once been "in hevene blisse" feels otherwise than when he first merely heard about it. [26] Antigone reinforces her point that the sensual are ignorant of bliss with an analogy thus vigorously put:

> Men mosten axe at seyntes if it is
> Aught fair in hevene (why? for they kan telle),
> And axen fendes is it foul in helle. [27]

Chaucer associates the heroine's responses with a variety of things supernal, in contrast to Boccaccio who availed himself only of the concept of martyrdom. In the new and cheerful episode of her visitation by Pandarus on the morning after her surrender, our poet likens to God's forgiveness of His death on the cross hers of the alleged entrapping by Pandarus. [28] Through the humorously outrageous disproportion between the two forgivings, Chaucer heightens the irony implicit in the latter—pardoning of the uncle for what the niece more or less expected and, despite timidity, certainly desired. But about her grief over the exchange, he is entirely serious, leaving no doubt that she was capable of true feeling. He says that, after the parliament, she thought that she had fallen from "heven" into "helle," and also that her appearance at this juncture gave sign of "martire Of deth," here following Boccaccio who says that it evidenced "aspri martiri." [29] She herself speaks of her coming life of separation from Troilus as the state of a female religious—an "ordre," the "observance" of which is to be sorrow, complaint, and abstinence. [30] Chaucer remarks that her tears and Troilus' at prospect of their parting, were more bitter than those of Mirra distilled "thorugh the bark and rynde," bitterer, that is, than the gum of the tree into which this other victim of passion had been transformed. [31] This is, indeed, a wide range of linkings—to God, martyr, nun, and mythological female.

In beauty, Criseyde seems more than human, and Troilus so esteems her. After first seeing her, he, like Troiolo, is uncertain whether it is a "goddesse or womman" whom Love has made him serve.[32] When speaking in his own person, Chaucer testifies to her charms in equally extravagant terms. Boccaccio's declaration that she was "so angelic to see that she did not appear a mortal thing" he expands in this fashion:

> So aungelik was hir natif beaute,
> That lik a thing inmortal semed she,
> As doth an hevenyssh perfit creature,
> That down were sent in scornynge of nature;

and, when his author spoke of her face as "made in Paradise," he describes it as "lik of Paradys the ymage."[33] Finally, on the alleged authority of writers who had seen her, he says that "Paradis stood formed in hire yën."[34] In Troilus' address to her empty house there is the exalted line,

> And farwel shryne, of which the seynt is oute.[35]

The saint's infidelity is an obvious irony, which Chaucer does not neglect. Like Pandaro, his Pandarus warrants her reputation to be sanctified, the one calling it "halwed" as the other, "santa."[36] But her fidelity to a lover does not match her apparently deserved reputation for propriety before she accepted him. Troilus has reason to complain that he believed her every word to be "gospel," as Troiolo that he thought it holy—"santa."[37] Nevertheless, after this complaint, he bitterly reproaches Cassandre for impugning Criseyde's faith and declares that she would have done no worse to slander Alceste, the very paragon of womanly fidelity.[38] The comparison does honor to his loyalty but also illustrates his loverly persistence in self-deception.

Troilus' joys in love are figured as heavenly and his sorrows as infernal. The latter type of association is heavily preponderant. In the *Filostrato,* it will be remembered, there are only two metaphors of Inferno, both of them acknowledgments by Troiolo of Pandaro's having translated him from that region into Paradise. The second of these reappears in the *Troilus,* with classical embellishment, as the hero's thanks to Pandarus for having brought his soul to rest in "hevene" from "Flegetoun, the fery flood of helle."[39] There are a few original figures of Heaven without a balancing Hell in the English poem, as against one in the *Filostrato* in a passage which Chaucer does not translate. Pandarus assures the prince of coming to "hevene blisse"; and Chaucer, in his own person, calls the consummation "this hevene" and "this hevene blisse."[40] But allusions to the pains of Hell without promise of compensating heavenly joys are much more numerous. Pandarus likens Troilus' early woe to the torment of "Ticius in helle," which he glosses as tearing by vultures; the narrator asserts that Troilus trembled as though he were being led into "helle" when he first named his lady to Pandarus, that the lover's pains at separation passed "every torment down in helle," and that, after Criseyde's going, he tossed and turned in his bed like "Ixion in helle"; and Troilus writes to Criseyde that his ease has turned to "helle" and that her absence is to him "an helle." [41] Similar in effect to the comparisons of Troilus to Ticius and Ixion are others of him to mortals, who, though not placed in Hell, suffered as they did from the displeasure of divinities. There is the already mentioned likening of his tears and Criseyde's to those of Mirra. Then, too, Pandarus reproaches Troilus for weeping like Nyobe, whose tears turned to marble; and the prince anticipates ending his life in darkness, like Edippe, and appeals to Juno not to be as cruel to the blood of Troy as she had been to the blood of Thebes. [42] In a metaphor of voyaging, he imagines that Caribdis will devour his "ship" and him with it. [43]

As Boccaccio does not, Chaucer draws on the supernatural to illuminate Troilus' actions and capacities for action as well as his feelings and the manifestations thereof. In some instances, he magnifies him as a warrior to make him the more perfect lover, while, in others, he exalts him for virtues not at all military. In describing his return from battle, Chaucer asserts:

> But swich a knyghtly sighte, trewely,
> As was on hym, was nought, withouten faille,
> To loke on Mars, that god is of bataille. [44]

It was "an heven," he tells us, to see him thus soldier-like; and "an hevene" likewise to hear him sing of love, just as it was to hear the tender Antigone. [45] The poet's remark that "a geant" might surpass him in strength, although concessive, serves as well as the comparison to Mars to suggest Troilus' potency among men. [46] Other figures concern his activities as they affect Criseyde. Pandarus argues that she should not fear scandal through frequentation by the lover, since he who comes to the "temple" is not suspected of eating the "ymages." [47] Chaucer tells us that the prince was too sincere "to synge a fool a masse," that is, to flatter, and observes that his lady appreciated this quality. [48] Images in the tragic part of the action are as grave as these two are light. Troilus rejects his friend's council to take another mistress, saying that it would befit him only if he were a "fend." [49] Pandarus, then suggesting like Pandaro that the old one be ravished away, exclaims,

> But manly sette the world on six and sevene;
> And if thow deye a martyr, go to hevene!

This the only fancy of martyrdom for the lover in the English poem is adapted not from the *Filostrato* but the French prose translation of it—doubtless to heighten the speaker's desperate resolve evident in the original.[50] Troilus' earnestness, recognized in the homely observation of the narrator's that he would not sing a fool a mass, is beautifully illustrated by his own phrasing of desire for her return:

> And God, to whom myn herte I sacrifice,
> So sende us hastely the tenthe day![51]

Like the image of the shrine without a saint, the idea of sacrificing the heart is a perfect union of feeling and symbol. Among the several distinctions which Chaucer accords Troilus, that of poetic power is perhaps the most striking. Poet, soldier, and true lover as he is, it is only just that Criseyde, in an otherwise ungracious letter, should address him as "Cupides sone."[52]

Pandarus is plainly differentiated from Troilus in character as well as in role. To the projection of this highly individual being, occasional passages of mythological or religious coloring make some contribution. The first of these emphasizes at length the irony of a failure in love setting himself up as a counsellor to another lover. As might be expected, Chaucer, who stresses a comparable anomaly in his own case, directs more attention than Boccaccio to the love-starved condition of the go-between. His Pandarus devotes two stanzas to a comparison of himself, for Troilus' benefit, to the god Phebus, who, although capable of curing others with his medical skill, was unable to ameliorate his own suffering when enamored of the daughter of Amete.[53] To make the comparison topical—close to the royal family—the letter of Oënone to Troilus' brother Paris is cited as the source. Chaucer once says that the confidant "preaches," and the character twice uses this word with reference to his own conversation.[54] In all three instances the term may be intended to suggest that he deports himself as if he were a priest of love. The first serves the ends of irony, Chaucer remarking that love often turned Pandarus green, however well he might "preche" of loving. The word is not applied to the discourse of any other character, except once to the wily Calkas'. Troilus, who declares him to be "in sleght as Argus eyed," fears that he will persuade Criseyde to marry, since he is one who can well "preche."[55] In the same scene in which Pandarus speaks of himself to Criseyde as preaching, he declares that he is "shriving" his heart to her.[56] This is assuming a virtue—frankness—when he has it not. Neither the open Troilus nor, for that matter, any other character claims to shrive himself or is said to do so. By inclination, Pandarus is something of a *deus ex machina*. When Criseyde is slow to take Troilus into her favor, her uncle playfully admonishes her:

> Were I a god, ye sholden sterve as yerne.[57]

269

The single religious figure applied to Diomede is explicit about his knowledge of the art of love and suggestive of his cunning. He took heed, says Chaucer, of Troilus' emotion at the parting,

> As he that koude more than the crede
> In swich a craft.[58]

This is typical of the poet's care to make Diomede the antithesis of the hero, the artful as against the feeling lover. By itself it would convey little, but it prepares us for other contexts of similar implication and is illuminated by them.

In the next section, we are to be concerned with figures drawn from societal relationships and from their forcible establishment. More prevalent in source and adaptation than the associations to which the present section has been given, these contribute much in both poems to the definition of man's part and woman's in affairs of the heart and of commerce between humanity and its gods, especially the God of Love.

Subjugation and Feudal Relationship

THE figures employed in the *Filostrato* of strife and of rule and service are cumulatively potent because numerous and because concentrated to a great extent upon Troiolo's status in love, upon his pre-emption, that is, by Amore and the latter's instrument Criseida. The deity, it is impressed on us, made himself the prince's lord by force of arms, and we learn also that the heroine became his lady in the same way. The hero was, and frequently professed to be, their servant. While she too is represented to be subject to the god, his authority over her is not emphasized, but hers over the man. Diomede, in his one utterance, spoke of service to her though not to Amore; and the narrator, at the beginning and end of the poem, implies the same to his beloved. Figuring, martial or feudal, of the influence of divinities other than the love god is very scanty.

Such as there is may be noted before we take up that of his influence, of which there is so much. In the song to Venere, Troiolo calls her the benign "lady" of every gentle heart, declares that she imposes "laws" upon the universe, and hopes that she will "govern" his ardor.[1] He twice speaks of Fortuna as "hostile," and Criseida once; and the lady bids him proceed by insouciance to "conquer" this being, who, she says, never "subjected" anyone of bold spirit.[2] On one occasion he swears by that God that "governs" heaven and earth.[3]

The hero, so sure of himself in the temple of Pallade, is there brought low by the missiles of Amore and has sad cause to remember this overthrow on many later occasions. Boccaccio stresses the irony of the reversal. He speaks of the scoffing Troiolo as one whom Love would "transfix" more than any other before he left the temple, and remarks that he who was so wise in

271

reproving Love's "servants," did not see that the god dwelt with his "darts" in the rays of Criseida's beautiful eyes.[4] Apostrophizing Love after this encounter, Troiolo twice calls him "lord"; thanks him for enforced "service" to the lady; and beseeches the god, whom he fancies to dwell in her eyes, to obtain from them the healing of his soul wounded by the "sharp arrows" of the divinity, if to him the petitioner's "service" is at all pleasing.[5] The arrows, he says, Love impelled when he showed him Criseida's lovely face. According to Pandaro's report to Criseida, the lover in another address to Amore spoke of him as present in his own bosom and as there seeing the soul again prostrate but this time "conquered" by the divine effulgence which held it "bound."[6] In this acknowledgment of subjugation and need for help, he calls Amore his "lord" no fewer than five times and once speaks of lovers as the god's "subjects." Much later, Criseida assumes that it is Love with his "fervent darts" who is moving Troiolo to propose flight with her.[7] After her departure, the prince visits the places associated with their love and speaks once more of his conquest by Amore. But on this solemn occasion he eschews the pretty conventions of the god's residence in Criseida's eyes or his own bosom and describes Love's achievement in the grand manner as if it were a military campaign duly signalized by a triumph:

> Lunga hai fatta di me, Amor, la storia,
> s'io non mi voglio a me gir nascondendo,
> e 'l ver ben mi ridice la memoria:
> dove ch'io vada o stea, s'io bene intendo,
> ben mille segni della tua vittoria
> discerno, c'hai avuta trïonfante
> di me, che schernii giá ciascuno amante.
>
> Ben hai la tua ingiuria vendicata,
> signor possente e molto da temere.[8]

Because of his loss, Troiolo here conceives of Amore not merely as stern but also as vengeful. Nevertheless, he prays to him as before. Adducing his soul's devotion to "serving" Love, he begs him to constrain Criseida to come back.[9]

The ideas of Love's taking arms against Troiolo and having lordship over him appear more fleetingly in a number of other passages. Early in the action Troiolo admits to Pandaro that it is useless to "defend" oneself against Love.[10] Late in it, he asks the god why he had not "struck" him with mortal effect at the first encounter, adding that his "amorous wounds" remind him of his absent lady.[11] Boccaccio twice speaks in his own person of the hero's "wounds," and Pandaro asks his friend whether he supposes himself to have been the only one ever to feel "the amorous stroke."[12] Troiolo calls Love "sire" in one passage not already mentioned and "lord" in two others.[13] Boccaccio speaks of the sweet "kingdom of Love" of which the hero has been made worthy and again of the prince as the "faithful servitor" of the god.[14] The idea of forcible subjugation by passion so prominent in the development of Troiolo's relations with Amore is reinforced by many contexts in which he is represented as attacked or conquered by his own emotions, although not specifically by love personified.[15]

Neither Pandaro nor Diomede claims to serve Amore. The former, however, once refers to him as to a superior, saying that if Love puts him "in his peace," he will obtain a letter from Criseida.[16] And Diomede is said by Boccaccio to have felt the rough "assaults of the god.[17]

Criseida also experiences his might. Troiolo, after being overcome by Love, asks that she too may be; and the prayer is answered. According to Pandaro's report to the lady, the prince urged Amore to enter her bosom, arguing that the deity could win no greater "glory" than by this action.[18] The narrator speaks of her, soon after, as "transfixed" and later observes that she felt the spirit in her heart to be so.[19] Troiolo infers from her first letter that Amore was constraining her, although she was being discreet in it—in his words, "hiding herself behind the shield."[20] On the night before the parting, she swears constancy by those "amorous arrows" which entered her bosom on Troiolo's account, and the narrator tells us that, when still mindful of the first suitor, she answered Diomede as it pleased "her lord Love." [21]

The woman's power over the man is as much emphasized as that of the god. Criseida, like Amore, transfixes the hero with immediate and permanent result. From that moment he deems himself her servant and is quite content with this reversal of their positions in Trojan society because of his mistaken belief that she is innately noble. And Diomede proffers service as unqualifiedly as he, if with immodest haste and boasting. She exercises sovereignty in her first affair, though she does not claim it in this or the second nor call either prince her servant. Conscious, as will be remarked in the next chapter, of her social inferiority to both, she understandably ventures no assertion of dominance. Maria d'Aquino, the model in some part for Criseida, stands with the author as she with the protagonist.

In one of his first stanzas, Boccaccio assures this lady that he has been and ever will be "faithful and subject" to her.[22] Apostrophizing the poem itself in his last ones, he reasons that it has been drawn from his soul

> da virtú nascosa,
> spirata e mossa dal sommo valore
> di nostra donna nel trafitto core,

and bids it go to this sovereign of his thoughts,

273

alla donna gentil della mia mente.[23]

Troiolo, who has made occasion of the Palladian festival to ridicule any gallant betraying devotion to a lady as one so burdened by "his liberty" as to put it "between her hands," departs from the temple no longer "free."[24] He speaks of himself twice afterwards as "wounded" by Criseida, and Pandaro similarly of him twice.[25] And at consummation, the prince declares that her eyes have fixed "the fiery darts of love" in his heart.[26]

She correctly assumes that she will keep her "liberty" in becoming his mistress as she could not if she took a second husband.[27] She is never to speak of serving him, of course; and she calls him "lord" but twice, and in only one of these instances with possible implication that he is her superior in the love relationship.[28] Of the moderately numerous designations of her as "donna," on the other hand, at least fifteen have the meaning of "lady love," that is of "liege" in this relationship—a dozen in Troiolo's lines and three in the narrator's.[29] Though the only "crown" she claims is the soon-relinquished one of her chastity, she is royal by nature if we may believe her cousin, who declares that she would undertake any high enterprise as readily as a "king."[30] In any event, she enjoys the authority of one with the son of Priamo.

Even sanctioned power, as hers is by the tradition of courtly love, is liable to blame if it be abused. Her forsaking of Troiolo is a crime analogous to the betrayal of vassal by lord—a violation of *noblesse oblige*. In his last-quoted letter to her, he writes that if she causes him to take his own life, the shame will be hers for having brought her "subject" all blameless to so dark a death.[31] Her leaving of Troiolo for Diomede is a "betrayal," a "tradimento," as the narrator sees it, and the prince would have Giove do away with her as one who harbors "tradimenti" in her bosom.[32] She deserves to be called of villein kind, as she is in Boccaccio's final mention of her,

cotal fine ebbe la speranza vana
di Troiolo in Crisëida villana.[33]

Troiolo's devotion is represented in several passages as service to Criseida and he, somewhat more often, as her servant. Boccaccio mentions that the prince hoped not to be refused "as servant" and again that he feared she would not receive him in that capacity.[34] As has been noted, the prince thanks Amore for having given him to "serve" so fair a being.[35] In his first epistle to the lady, he speaks of his soul as the "handmaiden" of her worth and asks grace by virtue of desire "of serving well," though admitting that the favor is not merited by his "service."[36] While hymning Venere, he gives thanks to her son for having made him the "true servant" of his newly enjoyed mistress.[37] In his last letter to Criseida, he argues that, if the "servant" is ever justified in complaining of "his superior," he perhaps would be and then refers to himself as a "subject" of hers.[38] His service has been more of heart than hand, although he has striven to recommend himself to Criseida by exercise of arms against the Greeks. Because of his concern and hers for her reputation, he has not resorted to force to thwart the exchange. The clandestinity of their affair, which inhibits action on his part, is in her eyes, however, no demerit but a positive advantage. Opposing his proposal of flight to other lands where they may live openly together, she observes that their love pleases him because to have it he must act "by stealth" and that, if it is to last, it "must, as always, be stolen."[39]

His service, which he counts a privilege above all others,[40] brings him more pain than comfort. Its debits are several times metaphorically expressed in economic, if not particularly feudal, terms. In the period of courtship, he speaks of his life as "beggared of solace," and the narrator tells us that at that time he had sighs in "great wealth," while calling him "beggared of repose" near the end of the story.[41] He informs us that the prince "sold" sighs and complaints at a dear rate to the compatriots of Diomede and that he and his rival often met, "selling" their love to one another dearly.[42]

The new love, so hastily offered Criseida and so readily granted, is a mean cause for a sorrow of such nobility as Troiolo's and, in proportion to its unworthiness, an ironic one. Smitten with her, indeed, as Boccaccio certifies,[43] Diomede manifests a boldness and pride out of keeping with amour courtois. He plucks up courage to approach her within four days, and, to persuade her to forsake the lover he suspects she has left behind, declares that the Trojans are held "in prison" by the Greeks[44] and that the imprisoned are barbarous in comparison to their jailers. Asserting that she may easily find a worthy lover among this fine folk, he recommends himself on the grounds of birth and station. He concludes with the humble yet complacent petition that she take him "as a servitor" if he seems to be of such quality as befits her "ladyship."[45]

Pandaro, though a lover too, never speaks of himself as the would-be servant of the one whom he has wooed in vain nor of her as his lady.

In Chaucer's poem, associations with rule and service are more numerous and elaborate and more variously suggestive than in Boccaccio's; but those with subjection by force, no more frequent or vivid and of no wider application. In consequence, the impression of order on all levels of being is relatively stronger in adaptation than in source; and the impression of stark violence, relatively weaker.

As in the *Filostrato*, associations of the second type are employed almost

275

exclusively to convey the effects of love. And they are restricted even more narrowly to its impact upon the hero. Troilus, like Troiolo, is imagined to have been wounded and thus brought to surrender by love god and lady, but neither she nor Diomede is said to have been assaulted by the god as both were in the source. There is mention, indeed, of amorous wound for Pandarus, but only once.

Associations of the other type Chaucer exploits to the full and in considerable independence of Boccaccio. He works out the authority of the heroine as lady love in specific feudal detail, and manages at the same time to dignify the hero as her vassal. Giving the rival professions of service to the God of Love as well as to her, he opposes both to similar utterances of the protagonist by making them seem empty. As for the god, the poet magnifies his authority in general and over the hero in particular, rejects Boccaccio's one suggestion of it over the heroine, but gives the new character Antigone a song in which female dependence upon the deity is joyously proclaimed. Venus he refers to in his own person as lady and lawgiver as Troiolo did. And he keeps us steadily reminded of the lordship of the Almighty.

Let us consider in order the quite incidental suggestions in his poem of dominion of Pallas, Mars, Pluto, Juno, and a Muse, the more vital ones of the Supreme Being's, a hint or two of the enmity of Fortune, the several tributes to Venus, and the many allusions to her son as conqueror or lordly recipient of human service. We may then proceed to the very numerous passages indicative of feudal relationship between man and woman in love.

Criseyde addresses Pallas as "lady myn," and the narrator employs the term "servyse" for worship in her temple.[46] As he puts it, his warlike hero was, by day "in Martes heigh servyse." [47] To the poet, Cleo is "lady myn"; to Pandarus, the god of the underworld is "Pluto kyng"; to Criseyde, Juno is "hevenes quene." [48] And the lady reproaches Troilus for not taking "the goddes ordinaunce" for the best.[49]

As stated in the preceding chapter, there are thirty-three recourses to the term "Lord" for the Supreme Being.[50] Of these, the narrator's prayer to "the Lord" as He "That regnest ay in thre, and two, and oon" and Troilus' apostrophe, "O Lord, that set art in thi trone," are highly suggestive of kinglike station.[51] Matching the latter are another apostrophe of the hero's, "Almyghty Jove in trone," and Pandarus' ejaculation, "O myghty God . . . in trone." [52] Like Troiolo, Chaucer's hero swears by that God, "That, as hym list, may al this world governe." [53] Assuming this omnipotence, Criseyde would have God "bynde" night fast to the hemisphere.[54] The true All High[55] is the ultimate resort. "God shilde us fro meschaunce," Pandarus early ejaculates, his niece later on, and the narrator later still.[56] Anachronistically, the lady professes her good intentions to Troilus "by that God that bought us bothe two."[57] Chaucer, in the Epilog, urges young folk to forsake this transitory world as but a "faire," and bids them love Him who died upon the Cross "oure soules for to beye," averring

> For he nyl falsen no wight, dar I seye,
> That wol his herte al holly on hym leye.[58]

Fortune, whom the narrator philosophically dignifies at storm time as "executrice of wyrdes," he rails against later on without thought of her authorization from above, calling her "traitour comune" because she seems truest when she is about to beguile.[59] Troilus, newly enamored, believes her to be his "fo."[60] After the parliament, Criseyde opines that he is "lord" of Fortune who disprizes her and that she "daunteth" only wretches, thus agreeing substantively with Criseida.[61]

The narrator, who has observed that Venus was "not al a foo" to Troilus at his nativity,[62] pays her more positive honor in Book III. In its Prohemium, he speaks, like Troiolo, of the "lawe" by her imposed upon the universe and makes reference to "servyse" paid the "lady bryght."[63] And "lady bryght" he calls her at the book's end.[64]

The male deity of love is allowed the universal sway of the female in two contexts and, as in the *Filostrato,* often conceded power over the human heart.

In his first stanzas, already dealt with in the preceding section, Chaucer speaks of lovers as the "servantz" and "folk" of the God of Love and, modestly, of himself as one who "serves" them.[65] These terms, though societal in origin, evoke memories of Christian ideology rather than of order and degree in secular life.

Representing, as Boccaccio did, that Love wounded the hero in the temple, he colors the irony of the event with humor yet offers generalization ostensibly serious in tone. At Troilus' disrespect, he tells us,

> the God of Love gan loken rowe
> Right for despit, and shop for to ben wroken.
> He kidde anon his bowe nas naught broken;
> For sodeynly he hitte hym atte fulle;
> And yet as proud a pekok kan he pulle.[66]

Thus pictured, the bowman is not a majestic nor even a dignified being. And his victim is reduced to comic size by the figure of the peacock and that of the whip-humbled carthorse which follows it. No sooner has Chaucer ventured these base similitudes, however, than he reminds us that Troilus is a prince and speaks of his experience in conventional feudal language. On the higher level, he maintains the antithesis between erstwhile pride and

277

present abjectness introduced on the lower but puts a hopeful construction upon the change. This fierce proud knight, this worthy king's son, has suddenly become "moost subgit unto love." [67]

> Forthy ensample taketh of this man,
> Ye wise, proude, and worthi folkes alle,
> To scornen Love, which that so soone kan
> The fredom of youre hertes to hym thralle;
> For evere it was, and evere it shal byfalle,
> That Love is he that alle thing may bynde,
> For may no man fordon the lawe of kynde. [68]

Subjection, the poet argues, is pleasurable and improving as well as inevitable, and he therefore entreats,

> Refuseth nat to Love for to ben bonde. [69]

At the end of the scene, he alludes to the god's residence "Withinne the subtile stremes" of Criseyde's eyes. [70]

Though repentant for derision of "Loves folk," Troilus still pretends to smile at "servantz" of the deity after he has repaired from temple to palace. [71] In company there, he declares that harm may befall the best of lovers as often as advantage and exclaims,

> Youre hire is quyt ayeyn, ye, God woot how! [72]

Thus ironic for self-concealment, he is fated—ironically—to exemplify the dictum.

Addressing Love in private, he, like Troiolo, calls him "lord," imagines him to stand in the heroine's eyes, and beseeches favor if his "service" be pleasing, but makes no reference to wounds as the earlier hero did. [73] When with the confidant, he admits—again like Troiolo—that resistance to Love is futile. [74] The friend, recalling that Troilus has called the deity "lord of thise foles alle" and spoken ill of his "servantz," bids him address Love humbly as "lord," and the prince complies. [75] From this moment, the hero will be the one most to grieve Love's "foos," according to his counsellor's prediction. [76] As quoted to Criseyde by the go-between, Troilus in earlier supplication to Love, addressed him as "lord," confessed that he had been "rebell" of intent, and begged him to be his "sheld." [77]

At consummation, he terms Love the "holy bond of thynges" and looks to him to succor those "That serven best." [78] And he expatiates on his universal binding power in the garden song derived from a meter of the *Consolation*. [79] In the first stanza he phrases it entirely in terms of human sovereignty:

> Love, that of erthe and se hath governaunce,
> Love, that his hestes hath in hevenes hye,
> Love, that with an holsom alliaunce
> Halt peples joyned, as hym lest hem gye,
> Love, that knetteth lawe of compaignie,
> And couples doth in vertu for to dwelle,
> Bynd this acord, that I have told and telle.

In the next, the singer declares that Love keeps the elements in a perpetual "bond" so that the sun brings forth the day and the moon has "lordshipe" over the nights, and in the next that he constrains the mighty sea. The sublime being of these stanzas is hardly recognizable as the god who petulantly avenged himself on Troilus at the festival. That he is appears, however, from the less exalted final stanza. There hope is voiced that he may please to circle and "bynde" all hearts and to twist the cold ones. After he has given Troilus this hymn, Chaucer records that the prince held every wight lost who was not in "Loves heigh servise." [80]

After the parliament, Troilus ventures mild complaint to the god. Still calling him "lord" as Troiolo did, he asks in legal phrase,

> Syn ye Criseyde and me han fully brought
> Into your grace, and bothe oure hertes seled,
> How may ye suffre, allas! it be repeled? [81]

By way of comfort, the lady argues that he "That serveth Love" must sometimes bear a pain if he would come to joy.[82] Unconvinced by the sophistry, Troilus addresses another complaint to Love after her going. Like its original in the *Filostrato*, it is military in concept:

> O blisful lord Cupide,
> Whan I the proces have in my memorie,
> How thow me hast wereyed on every syde,
> Men myght a book make of it, lik a storie.
> What nede is the to seke on me victorie,
> Syn I am thyn, and holly at thi wille?
> What joie hastow thyn owen folk to spille?
>
> Wel hastow, lord, ywroke on me thyn ire,
> Thow myghty god, and dredefull for to greve![83]

Elsewhere, it may be noted, sorrow and death are conceived of as warring on the prince.[84]

Pandarus, who would succor his friend, is himself wounded, but the supplanting Diomede appears unscathed though professedly subject to the archer god. We learn that the former,

> for al his wise speche,
> Felt ek his part of loves shotes keene.[85]

279

The latter, when accompanying the heroine to camp, argues punningly:

> For though ye Troians with us Grekes wrothe
> Han many a day ben, alway yet, parde,
> O god of Love in soth we serven bothe.
> And, for the love of God, my lady fre,
> Whomso ye hate, as beth nat wroth with me.[86]

He goes on to declare:

> Ek I am nat of power for to stryve
> Ayeyns the god of Love, but hym obeye
> I wole alwey; and mercy I yow preye;[87]

and concludes with an offer of service to the lady. Inventing this hasty solicitation for Diomede, Chaucer would have us believe it insincere. For when he comes to the stanza of the *Filostrato* in which Boccaccio spoke of "rough assaults" which Amore made the Greek feel, he so transforms it as to establish that the new suitor had felt none.[88]

Criseyde, though represented to have been emotionally beset,[89] is never figured as a target of the god. The inference drawn in the *Filostrato* from a letter of the heroine's that Amore was constraining her but that she was warding herself "sotto lo scudo" is reduced in the *Troilus* to the supposition that there was cause for hope, "Al covered she the wordes under sheld."[90] And the few other hints of Amore's use of force against her are eliminated as is the one reference to him as her "signore." In "servyse Of love" indeed, as she confesses,[91] Chaucer's fair one is not expressly in that of love deified.

Unacknowledged by Criseyde, Love receives high tribute from that "goodlieste mayde Of gret estate in al the town of Troye" who is credited with the stanzas sung for the heroine by a niece.[92] Saluting him thus,

> O Love, to whom I have and shal
> Ben humble subgit, trewe in myn entente,
> As I best kan, to yow, lord, yeve ich al,
> For everemo, myn hertes lust to rente,

the maid rendered thanks for her enamorment. It had brought happiness, she acknowledged—and moral benefit as well,

> This is the righte lif that I am inne,
> To flemen alle manere vice and synne.

Anyone who would call loving a vice or "thraldom" betrays envy, in her opinion, or sheer ignorance,

> for swich manere folk, I gesse,
> Defamen Love, as nothing of him knowe.
> Thei speken, but thei benten nevere his bowe!"

Peril in love exists, she implied, only for the unfit:

> And forthi, who that hath an hed of verre,
> Fro cast of stones war hym in the werre!

And she declared specifically that none existed for her. Exalting the divinity —thrice addressed as "lord"—from the feminine point of view and the passion which he inspires, the song complements the arguments for loving which Criseyde has just heard from her uncle.

We have now to turn from the relationship between the God of Love and the amorous to that between the heroine and hero. We shall see that Chaucer has emphasized the feudal nature of the latter. Contributory to the aristocratization of the story, this development also strengthens irony to the extent that it points up the worth and dutifulness of the forsaken lover. On the lady's side, it magnifies her authority without prejudice to the general softening of her character to which our poet is obviously committed.

There is but little suggestion that the gentle Criseyde achieved sway by force—several notices of her wounding the hero analogous to the several of Criseida's doing so; a fancy that she has bound him, and paradoxical designation of her as his adversary. The narrator relates that Troilus left the festival,

> Right with hire look thorugh-shoten and thorugh-darted;

and the prince confides to Love that she has "wounded" him sorely with her gaze and, to Pandarus, that her "darte" will never be loosed from his soul.[93] Addressing her eyes at consummation, he fondly wonders how they could "withouten bond me bynde." [94] And he twice designates her by the oxymoron, "swete fo." [95]

Timid as Criseida was not, she fears that the conquest she has made may lead to her own bondage. Pandarus sought to preclude such fear by assurance in their first talk that he was not asking her to "bynde" herself to his friend by any promise.[96] After the uncle's departure, she inclines at first to proceed with Troilus—yet not too far:

> Ne als I nyl hym nevere so cherice
> That he may make avaunt, by juste cause;
> He shal me nevere bynde in swich a clause.[97]

She reasons, like Criseida, that a lover is to be preferred to a husband with his constraining rights.[98] Then the thought strikes her that even extramarital love is a threat to independence:

> Allas! syn I am free,
> Shold I now love, and put in jupartie
> My sikernesse, and thrallen libertee? [99]

281

And the doubt is as unsettling as Criseida's worry that she might be cast off by Troiolo because his social inferior. Essaying a missive upon the insistence of Pandarus, his niece

> gan hire herte unfettre
> Out of desdaynes prison but a lite,

and wrote that she would not make herself "bonde In love" though fain to be sisterly toward her correspondent.[100] His at last after more evasions, she comes to feel that she will remain so forever, believing, as the narrator testifies, on the day of the fateful parliament

> That al this world ne myghte hire love unbynde.[101]

Though to be separated from Troilus on earth, she will not be, she fancies, in the afterlife:

> Myn herte and ek the woful goost therinne
> Byquethe I, with youre spirit to compleyne
> Eternaly, for they shal nevere twynne.[102]

She is so assured of prerogatives in society and in love as to feel at ease about his rank and is feminine enough to welcome his protectiveness and manly ardor. Correctly formal at the start of their tête-à-tête at Deiphebus', she calls him "Sire"; thanks him, presumably for his interest in her legal troubles; and beseeches continuance of his "lordshipe." [103] She throws Troilus into confusion with this deference, but listens to his proffer of abject duty without the slightest embarrassment and accepts it only upon conditions —among them, this:

> "But natheles, this warne I yow," quod she,
> "A kynges sone although ye be, ywys,
> Ye shal namore han sovereignete
> Of me in love, than right in that cas is." [104]

She comes to thank God for him, as the narrator explains,

> For whi she fond hym so discret in al,
> So secret, and of swich obëisaunce,
> That wel she felte he was to hire a wal
> Of stiel, and sheld from every displesaunce;
> That to ben in his goode governaunce,
> So wis he was, she was namore afered,—
> I mene, as fer as oughte ben requered.[105]

That is to say, she would infer such masculine competency from his attentions as to relax and even to luxuriate in it. And if she later unmans him with chiding so that he swoons, this exercise of sovereignty is but a prelude to surrender—

> Men seyn alday, and reden ek in stories,
> That after sharpe shoures ben victories.[106]

She capitulates to her resuscitated vassal in a most womanly flutter, though mindful to establish that she is situated as she is of her own free will. To his triumphant

> O swete, as evere mot I gon,
> Now be ye kaught, now is ther but we tweyne!
> Now yeldeth yow, for other bote is non!

she answers:

> Ne hadde I er now, my swete herte deere,
> Ben yold, ywis, I were now nought heere![107]

Compliant by volition, she remains the arbiter of the affair in her own eyes and, despite his ultimatum, in Troilus'.

She is his superior throughout, as we are variously reminded, but most often by designation as his "lady," his mistress, that is, in the nonpejorative sense. The word is applied to her seventy-four times with this connotation —thirty-two times in lines of the narrator, thirty-three in Troilus', seven in Pandarus', and once each in a letter of hers and in Cassandre's disquisition[108] —whereas the word "donna" is so appled to Criseida, as will be recalled, only fifteen times—three by the narrator and twelve by Troiolo.[109] Though sovereign as a queen, Criseyde is never figured as such. The uncle's appeal to her for mercy "in the vertu of corones tweyne," whatever it may imply,[110] does not suggest royal status in love.

Her rights as the prince's lady are carefully defined in their first conference—their hour together at Deiphebus' abode. When she asks him to state his intentions, he replies that he would have her favor him sometimes with friendly looks,

> And thanne agreen that I may ben he,
> Withouten braunche of vice on any wise,
> In trouthe alwey to don yow my servise,
>
> As to my lady right and chief resort,
> With al my wit and al my diligence;
> And I to han, right as yow list, comfort,
> Under yowre yerde, egal to myn offence,
> As deth, if that I breke youre defence;
> And that ye deigne me so muche honoure,
> Me to comanden aught in any houre;

> And I to ben youre verray, humble, trewe,
> Secret, and in my paynes pacient,
> And evere mo desiren fresshly newe
> To serve, and ben ay ylike diligent,
> And with good herte al holly youre talent
> Receyven wel, how sore that me smerte.[111]

In her acceptance, she stipulates, after the already quoted limitation of his prerogative:

> N'y nyl forbere, if that ye don amys,
> To wratthe yow; and whil that ye me serve,
> Chericen yow right after ye disserve.[112]

The *quid pro quo* of such dominion, though admitted by neither party to the agreement, is, of course, an ultimate sexual reward. The witness Pandarus assures his friend, as soon as they are in private, "That al shal ben right as thiselven liste" and implies that consummation is not far off:

> Thow woost ek what thi lady graunted the,
> And day is set, the chartres up to make.[113]

The concession of Criseyde's right to inflict the death penalty which the prince made at Deiphebus' he repeats at two later junctures. After possessing her, he declares that God has willed her to be his directress—to make him live or die as she pleases—and bids her slay him if ever he should violate any prohibition of hers.[114] And in his letter to her in camp, he undertakes to die if she signifies that guilt on his part has merited death and bids her farewell as she who may command him life or death.[115] These humilities are very different from the self-righteous declaration in Troiolo's corresponding letter that she would be shamed if she caused her blameless subject to take his own life. Nowhere in the *Filostrato* is there any suggestion that Criseida's ladyship entitled her to inflict the death penalty or any other.

Were Criseyde as honorable as her uncle claimed—

> In honour, to as fer as she may strecche,
> A kynges herte semeth by hyrs a wrecche—

she would have just claim to authority, though, in his view, she did play "the tirant neigh to longe." [116] And even after she has forfeited desert, love and pity inspire gentle handling. Troilus, who suspects from his dream that she has "bytrayed" him,[117] does not presume to employ the word in the subsequent letter. And whereas Boccaccio spoke in his own person of the guilty lady as "Criseïda villana" and of her act as "il tradimento," [118] Chaucer uses no such opprobius term for the deed and plays wistfully with the unlikelihood that those who wrote of her were villainous, not she:

284

> Allas! that they sholde evere cause fynde
> To speke hire harm, and if they on hire lye,
> Iwis, hemself sholde han the vilanye.[119]

Yet she has not escaped full retribution, for, as he later still tenderly observes:

> Hire name allas! is punysshed so wide,
> That for hire gilt it oughte ynough suffise.[120]

The service of Troilus is as much emphasized as the dominion of the lady to whom he renders it. Chaucer reminds us of the hero's dependent status much more often than Boccaccio, expresses it in more explicitly feudal terms, and thus brings out the spirit of devotion with greater force. By his choice of figures, our poet suggests a manliness and dignity in Troilus' stewardship which we are not made to feel in Troiolo's, though in plain fact the one is the same as the other. The furtiveness of the affair he presents as a necessity only, not a virtue.[121] The irony of meager reward for faithful duty and high expectations, which he found already well developed in his source, he considerably strengthens.

Troilus is three times called the "servant" of Criseyde—twice by himself and once by the narrator;[122] four times, her "man"—thrice by himself and once by the narrator;[123] and eleven times her "knyght"—twice by himself, three times by the narrator, once by Pandarus, and five times by Criseyde.[124] The noun "servyse" is applied to his relationship to her nine times—twice each by himself, the lady, and Pandarus, and three times by the narrator;[125] and forms of the verb "serve" are so used fourteen times—ten times by himself, twice by the narrator, and once each by Pandarus and Criseyde.[126] As against these forty-one applications of the five words in the English poem, there are only nine comparable ones of a half dozen in the Italian. Troiolo conceived of himself in single instances as Criseida's "servo," "servidore," and "suggetto" and, in one, of his soul as her "ancella," while using the infinitive "servir(e)" three times for his attendance; and the narrator spoke of him as her would-be "servente" and "servidore." [127]

The passages in which Troilus is labelled Criseyde's "man" may be singled out as illustrative of his devotion. Apostrophizing the God of Love some time after enamorment, he assures him that "as hire man I wol ay lyve and sterve" and that

> myn estat roial I here resigne
> Into hire hond, and with ful humble chere
> Bicome hir man, as to my lady dere.[128]

The narrator tells us that all the prince's thought at this early time was "to ben hire man, while he may dure." [129] And on the day of the parliament, the lover declares to Pandarus that "as hire man I wol ay lyve and sterve." [130] Still of such mind after Criseyde's going, he denominates her the lady

> To whom for evermo myn herte I dowe. [131]

Since his fidelity is matched by obedience and discretion, [132] he richly merits the tribute which she pays him in the soliloquy lamenting her own disloyalty:

> Yet prey I God, so yeve yow right good day,
> As for the gentileste, trewely,
> That evere I say, to serven feythfully,
> And best kan ay his lady honour kepe. [133]

He is made to appear a mighty retainer as well as a true one. Of the terms for him as her adherent—"servant," "man," and "knyght"—the last and most honorific is significantly preponderant in the poem and the only one to appear in her lines. [134] The narrator tells us, as already quoted, that she felt Troilus to be "a wal Of stiel" and potent "sheld." [135] In her last letter, she salutes him *inter alia* as "swerd of knyghthod." [136] And Pandarus, when with her first, reported of the prince's conduct of the day before against the Greeks,

> He was hir deth, and sheld and lif for us. [137]

Figured thus, Troilus seems the peer of the puissant and noble Ector, whom the narrator calls "the townes wal and Grekes yerde" and who braves his townsmen in parliament to "shilde" Criseyde. [138] And so he is in his grander moments, though the butt of Pandarus' wit—and Chaucer's—for swooning elevation to Criseyde's bed.

Deserving of love, the prince endures many rigors to win it. The price of so esteemed a commodity is justifiably high; as his friend Pandarus implies and as he is willing to believe. There is, however, the complementary axiom, also stated by Pandarus, that devotion should be rewarded, and, though it is in the hero's case, the measure is short. Criseyde withdraws her favor while he would still serve her, and, as the ultimate irony, enfeoffs Diomede for lip service only. She proves as capricious as Fortune, whose unwitting tool she is, and thus confirms Troilus' early pronouncement on lovers in general:

> Youre hire is quyt ayeyn, ye, God woot how!
> Nought wel for wel, but scorn for good servyse. [139]

The prince hesitated to confide in Pandarus, the narrator informs us, on the proverbial ground that one often shapes a "yerde" with which one comes to be beaten, [140] but, doing so nonetheless, is committed irrevocably to the rigors of courtship. To give him heart, the friend exalts unremitting service, going so far as to hold it its own reward. He asks should a man despair who

has "love ful deere ybought" through twenty kissless years, and provides the
answer:

> Nay, nay, but evere in oon be fressh and grene
> To serve and love his deere hertes queene,
> And thynk it is a guerdon, hire to serve,
> A thousand fold moore than he kan deserve.[141]

Proceeding to Criseyde some days afterward, he naturally urges reciprocity:

> certain best is
> That ye hym love ayeyn for his lovynge,
> As love for love is skilful guerdonynge.[142]

The hero, prizing such favor as Pandarus claims to have won from her,[143]
comments ruefully nonetheless that he "That hangeth by the nekke" remains
in great disease.[144] Revisited by her uncle, the lady makes concessions yet
declares it to be her intent to love Troilus "unwist,"

> And guerdon hym with nothing but with sighte.[145]

The lover, if freed at Deiphebus' of "al the richesse" of his sighs, still could
not rest anights for wishing "of that hym missed han ben sesed." [146] At
Pandarus' house, offer by the beloved of conference on the morrow, moves
her uncle to exclaim "allas, that were a fair." [147] It would be the thing, he says,
to "feffe" a fool tardily with empty words,[148] but not Troilus. Granted audience straightway, the prince finds her tears harder to bear than "strokes of
a yerde," [149] though he survives them to experience such gladness as is felt
by one rescued from apparently certain death.[150] In reproach of defeatism after
the parliament, his friend observes that a man need not offer the neck till "it
shal of," [151] but events transpire to justify all apprehension. Troilus is reduced
to begging the long absent Criseyde, "In guerdoun" of his having served her,
to do no more than clarify the situation by letter.[152] And he presently finds
cause to soliloquize on her violation of their feudal bond:

> "Was ther non other broche yow liste lete
> To feffe with youre newe love," quod he,
> "But thilke broch that I, with teris wete,
> Yow yaf, as for a remembraunce of me?" [153]

He has only the useless satisfaction of vengeance on the Greek host, who, as
Chaucer twice tells us, paid dearly for his wrath.[154]

To strengthen irony, Chaucer represents the new suitor to have been
emotionally undeserving of acceptance. He eliminates the notice in Boccaccio's
account of the ride to camp that Diomede was taken with the heroine and

makes him venture a declaration, en route, upon the heartfree premise that at worst it will make the way seem shorter.[155] Thus minded, the Greek cannot feel the deference which he professes to his charge:

> So fro this forth, I pray yow, day and nyght,
> Comaundeth me, how soore that me smerte,
> To don al that may like unto youre herte.[156]

And if he seems trepidant in begging his "lady" not to be angry, not to be his "fo," not to wonder at hastiness, he presumes to recommend himself as the best candidate among many worthy knights from whom she may now choose:

> But myghte me so faire a grace falle,
> That ye me for youre servant wolde calle,
> So lowely ne so trewely yow serve
> Nil non of hem, as I shal, til I sterve.[157]

In the *Filostrato,* the rival, postponing suit until the fourth day after the ride, then came to her painfully dubious of success. Fearful that he was not so sovereign an artist as to displace her Trojan lover, he even regretted at the outset that he had been exposed to her charms. In the *Troilus,* he can wait until the tenth day to pay a visit since he has taken full advantage of the transit, and he arrives at the conclusion meanwhile that competition adds zest to what is in effect a harmless game:

> "But whoso myghte wynnen swich a flour
> From hym for whom she morneth nyght and day,
> He myghte seyn he were a conquerour."
> And right anon, as he that bold was ay,
> Thoughte in his herte, "Happe how happe may,
> Al sholde I dye, I wol hire herte seche!
> I shal namore lesen but my speche." [158]

Having given us this meditation of Diomede, Chaucer can be sure that his wooing of the heroine on the tenth day, though close to that reported in the *Filostrato* on the fourth, will carry stronger suggestions of vanity and new suggestions of insincerity. If less disparaging of the Trojans "In prisoun" than Boccaccio permitted him to be, the rival appears no less confident of the superiority as lovers of their jailers.[159] He offers himself no less quickly in such capacity,

> And if ye vouchesauf, my lady bright,
> I wol ben he to serven yow myselve,

and with as much parade of rank.[160] As he did not in the *Filostrato,* he begs audience for the morrow, on the ground of his devotion:

288

> syn that I am youre man,—
> And ben the first of whom I seche grace,—
> To serve yow as hertely as I kan,
> And evere shal, whil I to lyve have space.[161]

And Criseyde grants it, conceding that he could "serve" his "lady" well,[162] though not promising to be that woman.

To wind up the section, we may note the very few applications of concepts of the pattern under study to relations between Pandarus and his beloved, his friend, or his niece. Criseyde denominates the beloved his "maistresse," and he refers to bootless "servyse" in that quarter.[163] Hyperbolically grateful, Troilus promises to "serve" him forever as his "sclave" and declares that, could he "selle" his life a thousand times in a day in "servise" of the go-between, the payment would be all too slight.[164] Pandarus laments that, as seducer, he may think himself a "traitour" to his niece.[165]

Acquired Skills and their Products

FIGURATIVE associations with warfare in *Filostrato* and *Troilus* have been included in the preceding section, and those with medicine, pursuit or control of animals, and seafaring will be, respectively, in Sections 5, 6, and 7. All in the poem with other acquired skills of man and with any instruments or products thereof are to be treated here.

In the *Filostrato*, the total is small, even if expressions which are but dubiously evocative be counted. There are single figures of a master artist, of a ring and its gem, of a pearl, of water of the smith, of clarionlike sound, of looking in a mirror, of the dance, of chess playing, of weaving, of veiling, of girding, of circumscribing, and of teaching; two each of a key, of locking up, and of revesting; and frequent notices of visual memory in terms more or less suggestive of artistic representation. Some of these last are weak in evocation as are the two instances of the locking concept and the one of the instructional.

Pandaro refers to the Creator as the being who "circumscribed" the world; and the narrator, in two mentions of springtime, imagines that it "revests" the countryside.[1]

All the other associations under review are applied to human referents: one each to the narrator, his male audience, and Diomede; a pair to the confidant; and the rest either to heroine or hero. Among the several impressions conveyed, the strongest are of the lady's charms and of Troiolo's preoccupation with them.

As for Criseida, there are, to begin with, several figures in Pandaro's dialogue which concern her union with her first lover and several more in her own dialogue and in lines of the narrator which attest her sorrow at parting from the hero. If she be as wise as fair, the cousin tells her, that is to say if she accepts the lover whom he is recommending, then "is the gem well placed in the ring."[2] Let her essay a letter to Troiolo, he urges, for Amore knows well how "to teach."[3] Wishing her to receive the hero without delay, he says, "Let us complete this web."[4] She promises the go-between later on that, for Troiolo's sake, she will keep her sorrow "locked" in her heart.[5] The narrator speaks of her eyes closed in swooning as "veiled" and of her reminiscence of acts shared with Troiolo as "drawing" or "picturing."[6] According to one reading of the text, he calls intercourse on the last night "the amorous dance."[7]

The lady's beauty and consequent power are diversely imaged. As just noted, Pandaro conceives of her as the proper gem for the ring Troiolo. The narrator once remarks that she appeared like an "orient pearl" and, again that Amore had placed in her hands "the key" of the hero's wretched life.[8] Troiolo successively declares that she has thrown "the water of the smith" upon his flame so that it burns yet more brightly, that he sees the love goddess' virtue "depicted" in her face, that she holds in her hands the "key" of his life and death, and that there were no Trojan knights whom she "would not mate in the middle of the chessboard" in both courtesy and magnificence.[9]

The prince, the most single-minded of lovers, is retentive of Criseida's semblance. Love takes his station, he fancies, in that place within him where he bears "depicted" the "image" which most pleases him; her fair "image," he writes, brings to his heart a thought which banishes all others; and he would wish to have the lady herself always in his bosom as he has there her "image."[10] He keeps Criseida in his heart, he says, in her modest attire as a sure "token" of his pleasures.[11] Her countenance and discourse he "figured" constantly in heart and mind after her departure, as the narrator tells us.[12] In his last letter Troiolo writes that, although against his wish, he still holds her fair face "effigied" in his bosom, here echoing the enamored author's declaration to Maria that she is "effigied" in his sad breast.[13]

With such devotion, sorrow is naturally his lot. Grief, he soliloquizes, "locks" him fast.[14] Boccaccio says that his hero's face was "painted" with sorrow's hue, and the prince himself that he is "marked" in his face with death's color.[15]

There is but a single figure for his virtue as doer not sufferer. While chiding her prince for his proposal of flight, Criseida pays an oblique compliment to his reputation; let him not think of fleeing, she bids, if his fame which "sounds so clear" means anything to him.[16] Well-reputed though he was and true, one would hardly wish to imitate him. Boccaccio would have amorously inclined youths "mirror" themselves, not in Troiolo's virtues, but in his sad love and be appropriately cautious.[17]

Pandaro applies two figures to himself, and Diomede, one to himself. The former, as already remarked, proposes to join with Criseida in bringing the "web" of the affair to completion, and he assures Troiolo that he is "girded up" to help him in all possible ways.[18] Diomede reflects that, to supplant the lover for whom she mourns, he would have to be indeed a "master artist." [19] As will be recalled from the preceding section, this metaphor is replaced in the *Troilus* by that of a conqueror.

In the English poem, associations to be considered are far more numerous and diverse than in the Italian—and on the average as precise, the residue of debatably vague ones in it being proportionately no larger than in the *Filostrato*. As we shall see, the enrichment by Chaucer of the figurative constituent drawn from activities and paraphernalia of civilized living equals his already discussed elaboration of literal statement about the housing, costume, and diversions of the Trojans and evidences as strong a bent for realistic detail.

He applies most of the associations in question to heroine or protagonist but, though none to Diomede, a fair number to Pandarus, and not a few to referents outside the human sphere. In so doing, he stresses the attractions of the lady, as Boccaccio did, and the hero's concentration upon her, but also signalizes the latter's dependability, the infinite resource of the go-between, and the precariousness of existence for all and sundry.

The first of his figures to be scrutinized here are those expressive of fate or chance. Four of Fortune's wheel suggest her power and caprice, and another of her glazing a hood, her delusive intent; and three of spinning by the Fates attest their awesome function, while one of a brittle suspending wire and two of dice bring out the uncertainty of life on earth without hint of a steadfast providence above. The narrator observes at the start, that Fortune wheeled Greeks and Trojans about according to her course; on the occasion of the exchange, that she laughs when someone is thrown from her wheel and that she set Diomede high upon it; and, apropos of hope on Troilus' part, that this was but a "maze" and that

> Fortune his howve entended bet to glaze! [20]

The hero tells Pandarus, at the beginning of the affair, that no one may withstand the harm of her cruel wheel and, after the parliament, apostrophizes lovers high upon it to visit the sepulcher of his death-destined self.[21] Replying to what his friend said to him about the goddess, the confidant grants the ceaseless turning of her wheel but uses this as an argument for better luck to come.[22] According to the narrator, separation of the lovers, which Jove had commissioned the Parcae to bring about, will keep Troilus in pain

> Til Lachesis his thred no lenger twyne;

the prince assumes their control in praying to them before consummation:

> O fatal sustren, which, er any cloth
> Me shapen was, my destine me sponne,
> So helpeth to this werk that is bygonne;

and Criseyde, when still true, would have Attropos break her "thred of lif," if she were to turn false.[23] The usually hopeful Pandarus offers a gloomy argument in urging discretion upon Troilus:

> For worldly joie halt nought but by a wir
> That preveth wel it brest al day so ofte.[24]

The lover was glad or miserable, says the narrator, as the "dees torned on chaunces," and Pandarus seeks to console him with the observation that pleasures come and go in love just as chances befall "in the dees."[25]

Control by the Supreme Being is assumed, however, throughout the poem, as shown in the preceding section. At the end, Chaucer appeals for protection to the Lord,

> That regnest ay in thre, and two, and oon,
> Uncircumscript, and al maist circumscrive.[26]

And he affords his hero posthumous experience of the harmony of God's creation:

> And ther he saugh, with ful avysement,
> The erratik sterres, herkenyng armonye
> With sownes ful of hevenyssh melodie.[27]

As for other metaphorical representations of nature, our poet remarks, in adaptation of Boccaccio, that the meed is "clothed" with new green in April and that holts and hays in May "Revesten hem in grene."[28] Following Alain de Lille, he calls the crowing cock "comune astrologer."[29] And he permits the heroine to reproach night for withdrawing its "derke wede," under which God would have men abide in rest.[30]

She reveals her timidity in various figures. While debating with herself as to whether to accept Troilus as a lover, she expresses her concern for reputation proverbially:

> And who may stoppen every wikked tonge,
> Or sown of belles whil that thei ben ronge?

and after she has decided in Diomede's favor, she does so again:

> Thorughout the world my belle shal be ronge![31]

293

Faced with the necessity of deciding whether or not to receive Troilus at her uncle's house, she phrases her perplexity in Euclidean terms:

> I am, til God me bettre mynde sende,
> At dulcarnoun, right at my wittes ende,

the key word of which lines the always didactic Pandarus misglosses as "flemyng of wrecches," a translation of the name of another proposition than that designated by "dulcarnoun." [32] Were Troilus' scheme of flight known to the Trojans, she tells her lover, "my lif lay in balaunce, And youre honour." [33] When she yields to her uncle's first importunities, she takes account of his plight, again in terms of scales dubiously poised:

> A! Lord! what me is tid a sory chaunce!
> For myn estat lith now in jupartie,
> And ek myn emes lyf is in balaunce. [34]

Yet, as when vetoing Troilus' proposal, she puts her own welfare first. Her fear of loss of freedom is expressed in a conventional but briskly phrased metaphor from the game of chess. The issue is the, for her, purely hypothetical one of matrimony:

> Shal noon housbonde seyn to me "chek mat!" [35]

Pandarus' task it is to counter her trepidation and to rouse her to love. Like Pandaro, he urges the heroine to become the stone in her proper ring, the hero. As the former does not, he promises her a metaphorical cloak and uses another clothing figure to lecture her on female duplicity. With characteristic exactness, Chaucer makes the undefined "gemma" of Pandaro's ring figure a particular one for Pandarus':

> And, be ye wis, as ye be fair to see,
> Wel in the ryng than is the ruby set. [36]

Discreet visitation by Troilus will not be suspected, the uncle early assures her, because of the prevalence in town of love of friends; this sociability she may use as her cover:

> And wry yow in that mantel evere moo. [37]

Leading up to his fiction of scandal involving her and one Horaste, he observes that all women deem it shameful to make a lover "an howve above a calle," a metaphor, which he thus defines:

> I meene, as love another in this while. [38]

294

Figures of physical impression and penetration applied to Criseyde's psychic experience suggest that hers were emotions truly felt. They occur both in the narrative and in remarks of Pandarus. The first is a metaphor of war already noted in the preceding section. Tracing the growth of love in her for Troilus, Chaucer says:

> And after that, his manhod and his pyne
> Made love withinne hire herte for to myne.[39]

Every word of Antigone's in praise of amatory service, as the poet observes, the aunt "gan to prenten in hire herte faste." [40] Pandarus supports his assertion to Criseyde that her lover should be glad that she was hardly won with the following proverb,

> For-whi men seith, "impressiounes lighte
> Ful lightly ben ay redy to the flighte." [41]

But he hastens to make it clear that enough is enough, observing that she has played the tyrant almost too long as well as shown her heart to be properly resistant:

> And hard was it youre herte for to grave.[42]

He assures Troilus that an interview with her will produce good results:

> For in good herte it mot som routhe impresse,
> To here and see the giltlees in distresse.[43]

Beside these images of graving or impressing, there is a late one of picturization to attest her sincerity though this without metaphorical suggestion of depth. Adapting Boccaccio's statement that the heroine spent her first days among the Greeks in recollection of what she and the hero had done, Chaucer writes,

> And in hireself she wente ay purtrayinge
> Of Troilus the grete worthynesse.[44]

The event proves that the impressions made on her mind were not so deep as to be ineradicable. An image, the reverse in effect of those which we have been considering, marks her change of affections. The narrator, forecasting this change, observes:

> For bothe Troilus and Troie town
> Shal knotteles thorughout hire herte slide.[45]

The verb in these lines is repeated in the famous characterization of her as

295

Tendre-herted, slydynge of corage.[46]

Her delight in love shared with Troilus is signalized in three very diverse images. His consideration for her makes her believe that love

Of alle joie hadde opned hire the yate.[47]

In their first night together, they did all their might

For to recoveren blisse and ben at eise,
And passed wo with joie contrepeise,

and on their last, after much sorrow, they turned finally to the "amourouse daunce." [48]

Criseyde's beauty is specifically exalted in two figures and her more general charm in several more. Whether or not there is an allusion to Queen Anne in the following lines of the narrator (a matter which is no concern of ours) and whether or not the poet was thinking of a finely illuminated capital letter, they leave no doubt as to the superlativeness of the lady's aspect:

Right as oure firste lettre is now an A,
In beaute first so stood she, makeles.[49]

The simile complements the testimonies to the angelic or celestial quality of her appearance which have been noted in Section 2. So also Pandarus' exclamation about her countenance, "On swich a mirour goode grace!" [50] His already quoted figure of the ruby in the ring is a blanket tribute, implying her physical charms no doubt but not limited to them. In a neat bookish one, Troilus at once acknowledges her seeming mildness and gently chides her for past difficulties:

Though ther be mercy writen in youre cheere,
God woot, the text ful hard is, soth, to fynde! [51]

In his address to her empty palace,[52] the richest cluster of varied images in the entire poem, he beautifully expresses his idealization of Criseyde. Of the six visual metaphors contained in it, four may be quoted here, although I have already cited the last one as an example of religious metaphor:

O thow lanterne of which queynt is the light,

O paleis, whilom crowne of houses alle,

O ryng, fro which the ruby is out falle,

And farwel shryne, of which the seynt is oute!

The third, it will be noted, is meant to recall to the reader Pandarus' ring figure (which Troilus did not hear), with the palace substituted for the prince as the containing circlet.[53] It is as formally paired with the other as Troilus' dream of the boar with Criseyde's of the eagle. Like Boccaccio's heroine, this bright lady holds the key to her lover's affections; our poet writes:

> For she, that of his herte berth the keye,
> Was absent, lo, this was his fantasie,
> That no wight sholde maken melodie.[54]

According to the narrator, the first view of Criseyde so affected Troilus

> That in his hertes botme gan to stiken
> Of hir his fixe and depe impressioun,

and the first enjoyment of her person so much that he would recall her every word and look,

> And fermely impressen in his mynde
> The leeste point that to him was plesaunce.[55]

And as dawn is ending that enjoyment, the prince declares:

> Ye ben so depe in-with myn herte grave,
> That, though I wolde it torne out of my thought,
> As wisly verray God my soule save,
> To dyen in the peyne, I koude nought.[56]

Chaucer reports of him early in the action,

> Thus gan he make a mirour of his mynde,
> In which he saugh al holly hire figure;

and, late in it, speaks of him—this time after Boccaccio—as

> Refiguryng hire shap, hire wommanhede,
> Withinne his herte, and every word or dede
> That passed was.[57]

Actual or conjectured results of love for the prince are variously phrased. Sorrow, he fears, will "myne" so long in him as to cause death.[58] As already noted, Criseyde and he on their last night together are said to begin the "daunce" of intercourse. Far from anticipating this at the beginning of the affair, he supposed himself to be in the "daunce" of those whom Love does not favor.[59] With his success with Criseyde still uncertain, he puts up a brave front, the poet tells us,

> As though he sholde have led the new daunce,

when in truth he was ravaged by sorrow.[60] He would not have the affair trumpeted abroad, any more than Criseyde welcomes the bells of scandal. Love "to wide yblowe," he thinks, may yield bitter fruit; his sorrow, if "iblowe on brede," will be laughed at; and his affair and Criseyde's, if "iblowe" through his meddling, will make her his enemy.[61] His "song" when Criseyde swoons is but "weylaway." [62] For all her encouragements from the camp, says Chaucer, poor Troilus may "Pipe in an ivy lef." [63] As the lover tells her in a letter, he is "chiste of every care." [64] Misinterpreting the sadness of the prince before the latter's confession of love, Pandarus would have it that the Greeks have laid Trojan jollity "on presse." [65]

Two vivid figures are applied by the narrator to physical manifestations of sorrow in Troilus and one by the character himself to his anticipated death. Having returned alone to his chamber from the parliament, he appeared

> Ful lik a ded ymage, pale and wan,

and, when Pandarus came to him,

> This Troylus in teris gan distille,
> As licour out of a lambic ful faste.[66]

It is in Criseyde's power, the lover writes, to determine

> The day in which me clothen shal my grave.[67]

The great virtue of Troilus in love, as the lady and others see it, is his dependability, his solidity of character. As noted in the preceding section, he seemed to Criseyde "a wal Of stiel, and sheld from every displesaunce" as well as the very "swerd of knyghthod"; to Pandarus, "sheld and lif" for the Trojans; and, to the narrator, "Trewe as stiel in ech condicioun." She calls the prince "My ground of ese" and tells him that what won her heart in him was "moral vertu, grounded upon trouthe." [68] As his lady, in the narrator's words, she "cler stood on a ground of sikernesse." [69] And in Pandarus', he would become the "beste post" of the religion of Love.[70]

As sincere and open a lover as ever lived, Troilus still must resort to certain hallowed techniques and even artifices to forward his courtship. For love is a "craft" or "art," as the narrator himself calls it.[71] He refers to the hero's practice in terms of craftsmanship and learning, while Pandarus gives him a considerable lecture on letter writing—the *ars dictaminis*. According to the poet, Troilus "borneth" his cheer and speech to conceal from others his newborn love, and borrows a "title" of other sickness to hide his real one.[72] Asking tolerance of the prince's courtship if it be different from the current mode, Chaucer observes,

> Ek som men grave in tree, some in ston wal.[73]

The prince, while waiting for Criseyde in his chamber at Deiphebus' house, took pains to get a speech by memory:

> Lay al this mene while Troilus,
> Recordyng his lesson in this manere:
> "Mafay," thoughte he, "thus wol I seye, and thus;"

but her first words thoroughly discomposed him,

> And sire, his lessoun, that he wende konne
> To preyen hire, is thorugh his wit ironne.[74]

The suggestion here of the flustered schoolboy is patent but genial. Pandarus' earlier advice on writing is schoolmasterish, although not condescending; "thou art wis ynough," he assures his friend politely. It recommends the light touch, but is itself pretentious, offering lengthy analogies to the sister arts of music and painting, both of them drawn perhaps from Horace's *Ars poetica*.[75] One should not repeat even a good thing, he says,

> For though the beste harpour upon lyve
> Wolde on the beste sowned joly harpe
> That evere was, with alle his fyngres fyve,
> Touche ay o streng, or ay o werbul harpe,
> Were his nayles poynted nevere so sharpe,
> It sholde maken every wight to dulle,
> To here his glee, and of his strokes fulle.

Nor should one use discordant terms,

> For if a peyntour wolde peynte a pyk
> With asses feet, and hede it as an ape,
> It cordeth naught, so nere it but a jape.

Such advice was surely unnecessary for the modest and tactful lover, as Pandarus, his friend, must have realized. It sheds little light, then, upon the recipient but much upon the giver, for whom advising was meat and drink.

Not a few figures in the areas with which we are here concerned are applied to the counsellor himself. Of these, the most elaborate are architectural. As Troilus, for the solidity of his virtues and affections, is the foundation—the "ground"—of Criseyde's happiness, so Pandarus, because of his ingenuity, can be the erector of their house of love. Chaucer borrows a simile from the *Nova poetria* of Geoffrey of Vinsauf to suggest the care with which Pandarus plotted his first moves:

> For everi wight that hath an hous to founde
> Ne renneth naught the werk for to bygynne

With rakel hond, but he wol bide a stounde,
And sende his hertes line out fro withinne
Aldirfirst his purpos for to wynne.[76]

Speaking of the preparations which the confidant made for the lovers'
meeting at his own house, Chaucer indicates that they have advanced beyond
the planning stage:

This tymbur is al redy up to frame;
Us lakketh nought but that we witen wolde
A certeyn houre, in which she comen sholde.[77]

The architect is also smith, painter, and dancing master (though no
dancer); a whetstone in function as well as a school of warning example; and
like a bell in confident prevarication. Justifying his counselling in a field in
which he has had no luck himself, he tells Troilus:

A wheston is no kervyng instrument,
But yet it maketh sharppe kervynge tolis.
And there thow woost that I have aught myswent,
Eschuw thow that, for swich thing to the scole is.[78]

A question of Criseyde's and his reply make this same point of his unsuccess
in lighter vein:

"How ferforth be ye put in loves daunce?"

"By God," quod he, "I hoppe alwey byhynde!"[79]

Contented with his progress as a go-between, whatever his misadventures as
a lover, he "felte his herte daunce,"[80] his own unsuccess notwithstanding.
Chaucer speaks of him as one who knew "The olde daunce" in every detail.[81]
Affecting straightforwardness when first with Criseyde, Pandarus asks
rhetorically,

What sholde I peynte or drawen it on lengthe
To yow, that ben my frend so feythfully?

but, as the lady views his disclosure, it is a "paynted proces" all the same.[82]
Sensing that the "iren" is hot after she has seen Troilus ride past, the uncle
begins to "smyte" with new solicitations.[83] Developing the fiction of a lawsuit
against her to enlist the sympathies of the group at Deiphebus' house,

He rong hem out a proces lik a belle,

and to rehearse the case again, for Deiphebus and Eleyne only, he "gan newe
his tong affile."[84] Like Criseyde, the prince considers an argument of
Pandarus to be sophistry. Advised by him to replace the lady with a new
mistress, Troilus exclaims that ill should befall any woman who cares for
Pandarus if he can "playen raket, to and fro," as he would have others do.[85]

Corporeal Existence

W E are now to scan the two poems for figurative statement drawn from the life of the flesh—birth, sustenance, illness and cure, blindness, sensation, more or less automatic behavior, dreaming and waking, and ultimate prospect of the grave. All locutions thus derived which are at all evocative or may have been to fourteenth-century readers will be treated here except for metaphors of sensing heat and cold. These are reserved for Section 8.

The material to be examined in the *Filostrato* consists of some miscellaneous associations made but once or twice and several types which are recurrent. Of the latter, the most pervasive is with the sensation of sweetness, while that with bitterness is fairly common.[1] Then there are the fancies, collectively also numerous, that one person is the heart, soul, life, weal, or pleasure of another, in which of course, physical suggestion merges with psychic. The aforesaid concept of sweetness is attached to many of them.

Application is concentrated, as usual, upon the heroine and hero, with more emphasis in her case upon charm than feeling and in his, vice versa. A few figures, however, bear on Pandaro and a few on Boccaccio and his lady.

The one which is applied with any pretense to philosophical generalization is a metaphor of blindness. Apropos of Troiolo's unexpected subjugation by Amore, the narrator exclaims:

> O ciechitá delle mondane menti,
> come ne seguon sovente gli effetti
> tutti contrarii a' nostri intendimenti! [2]

Speaking as lover, Boccaccio employs several figures of sweetness and bitterness and single ones of birth and weeping as well as some metonymies. Maria is all his "weal" and "comfort," his sole "hope," and the "sweetest

301

pleasure" ever desired.[3] She is the cause, nevertheless, of such "bitter" woe in him as the hero's, because, she like Criseida, has departed.[4] His verse is "lachrymose."[5] "Sweet" verses are occasioned by happy times; the long speaking of his piteous song is due in some measure to his "bitter" woes, though the principal reason for its extension "is born" of the hope that she will remember him.[6] Its mission is to declare to her the woes, sighs, and "bitter" plaints in which he remains.[7]

The god Amore is to him a source of sweetness and to Troiolo also. The poet would celebrate the weal of Love's "sweet" kingdom and bids young men pray that the divinity may "sweetly" grant them the grace of loving wisely.[8] The hero twice terms him "sweet."[9]

Criseida's emotional experiences are represented as both sweet and bitter, as the former up to the parting and as the latter after it. In several contexts, the sweetness is represented as experienced by her alone; in others as shared with Troiolo. Before the consummation, he would have Love give her "sweet" sighs, and she reflects, proverbwise, that the "water" of a clandestine affair is a "sweeter" thing than the too abundant "wine" of marriage.[10] Of their first meeting Boccaccio remarks that they embraced with "sweet" joy, that the "sweet" night brought them indescribable delight, and that they kissed one another "sweetly."[11] Outside Troy's walls, Criseida remembers the "sweets" that she had within them.[12] Troiolo, in a letter, begs her to return by that "sweetness" which inflamed their hearts equally and by the "sweet" kisses and "sweet" converse which held them strained together.[13] In later communications, according to Boccaccio, the prince reminded her of the "sweet" time past.[14] The turn from sweet to bitter comes for her with the news of her exchange. She retires to her chamber overcome by "bitter" sorrow.[15] Pandaro, who comes to her from Troiolo, remarks that, wherever he goes, he encounters "bitter" languishing.[16] These qualities of the past and present are opposed in Boccaccio's account of the lovers' last embracings, strait as before, but now more "bitter" with tears than they had been pleasing with "sweetness."[17] Criseida spent her first nights of separation in "bitter" tears, making a "bitter" fountain of her eyes.[18] Diomede urges relinquishment of the "bitter," because fallacious, hope that the Trojans might be saved when he comes to her within four days of the "bitter" parting.[19] In his letter, Troiolo reminds her of unfulfilled commitments made in his and her last "bitter" complaining.[20] He, the inspirer of her joys and sorrows, is nothing but sweet in her opinion, but of this presently.

Outside the sweetness-bitterness pattern, there are only two or three body images of note which represent the lady's emotions. There is the already mentioned proverbial comparison of the delight of water obtained by stealth to that of wine had in abundance. One figure of manipulation seems to have some life in it, that of Criseida's "revolving" every word of Pandaro's in her heart.[21] Another of bodily discomfort is lively enough, no other figure in the poem approaching it for proverbial homeliness. Her female friends, when consoling her amiss, were doing nothing but scratching her in the heels when it was her head that itched:

> né erano altro che grattarla
> nelle calcagne, ove il capo prudea.[22]

A medical metaphor, the only clear instance of its kind in the *Filostrato,* is applied to the sexual satisfaction of women. Generalizing on the widow Criseida's aptness for love, Pandaro observes that every woman is amorous by inclination and that, if to such misery of longing a completely satisfying medicine may be given, foolish is he who does not despoil her:

> e s' a tal doglia
> onestamente medicina piena
> si può donar, folle è chi non la spoglia.[23]

Criseida, who tastes the bittersweet of love, is all in all to Troiolo, literally his friend, metaphorically the heart of his body and his soul, and metonymically his life and well-being and the emotions in him which she has inspired. However designated, she is often called sweet—never bitter. He terms her, after separation, his "sweet" friend.[24] At the consummation, each calls the other "heart of the body," and Troiolo names her "heart of my body" on three later occasions.[25] He denominates her his "soul" six times, twice with the modifier "sweet."[26] He speaks of her as his "sweet life" in one context; as his "weal" in eight—in five of these with a modifying "sweet"; as his "hope" in three—in one with "sweet"; as his "comfort" in two—in one with "sweet"; as his "sweet love" and his "sweet desire," each in two; and as his "disport" in one.[27]

From this quintessence of sweetness, sweet delight for the hero is anticipated, experienced, or recollected throughout the poem. Before soliciting Criseida, Pandaro speaks of the "sweet" conclusion which his efforts will bring.[28] Troiolo, as quoted by his friend, expressed hope for "sweet" peace from his lady, and, in his first letter to her, bids for "sweet" peace and "sweet" joy.[29] Delighted by her "sweet" regard—as the narrator informs us—in casual meetings, the lover is to enjoy her with more "sweetness" than he can derive from mere assurance of consummation, according to the go-between.[30] The sweetness of that event for both parties is dwelt on by the narrator as already noted.[31] The poet speaks of Troiolo's matutinal reminiscence of the "sweet"

303

converse of the first night and terms his return for a second an entrance to "sweets." [32] On the latter occasion, the hero confesses to his lady that he cannot express the "sweetness" with which she has filled his bosom. [33] In his "sweetly" sung hymn to Venere, he mentions "sweet" sighs as among her gifts to him. [34] Fortuna, as the narrator observes, turns the "sweet" fruits of love into sad mourning—to the amazement of Pandaro, who did not believe, as he says, that a time so "sweet" would so soon be ended. [35] The lover concedes that, if Criseida's going had been delayed, long accustomance to the prospect might have made it "sweet." [36] But the hypothesis is contrary to fact, and, despite this startlingly commonsensical recognition of time's healing potential, Troiolo does not become reconciled to her loss but battens upon memories and delusive hope. He recalls how "sweetly" Criseida's glances brought love into his heart, and tells her, on their last night, that she can make his life miserable or "sweet." [37] Without her, he anticipates, death will be as "sweet" to him as life to one to whom life is joyful. [38] Deprivation of the sweetness of her gaze makes life burdensome to him in the ten days after her going, though a hope, delusively "sweet," gives him comfort as the tenth ends without her return. [39] In his letter written after the boar dream, he appeals to her by the "sweetness" which once kindled their hearts as well as by their "sweet" kisses, and in further correspondence, according to the narrator, reminds her of the "sweet" time past. [40]

Before possession as well as after it, the bitter accompanies the sweet in Troiolo's experience. In his first conversation with Pandaro, he heaves a "bitter" sigh, and the go-between in his first with Criseida speaks prospectively of "bitter" death for his friend, while the narrator records that her response to the hero's letters was now pleasant, now "bitter." [41] With consummation imminent, the lover harks back to the "bitter" time and acknowledges Pandaro's service in redeeming him from "bitter" plaints and from perturbation destructive of every "sweet" memory. [42] The confidant terms the exchange a "bitter" circumstance, and Troiolo fears that, with Criseida absent, he cannot avoid grievous and "bitter" languishment. [43] Quitting the gate after fruitless vigil on the eleventh was overly "bitter" to the prince, Boccaccio tells us. [44] The boar dream Troiolo calls "bitter," as also his "sorrow" after discovery of the brooch; and his plaints between dream and discovery are so termed by the narrator. [45]

Expressions reminiscent of corporeal existence beside the iterated metaphors of sweetness and bitterness are scatteringly employed for Troiolo's psychic processes. Though diverse in concept, all bring out the intensity of his experience. He tells his mistress that a flame "is born" from her attractions, and the narrator speaks of the woe felt by the lover at sight of her empty palace as passion newly "born."[46] The poet records that Troiolo envisioned the absent lady with the "eyes of the mind."[47] He twice images the not deeply meditative prince as "revolving" matters in his thought.[48] Of the several contexts, in which words with root meanings of heaviness are applied to the lover's woes, two are rather strongly suggestive of it. He falls half dead, as the narrator says, under the "load" of misery created by the parliament; Pandaro advises that, "however heavy this weight may be," he should take active steps to help himself.[49] Criseida advises that the right procedure with Fortuna is to "turn the back" to her.[50] The prince, as the author chronicles, felt grief so "sharply" before swooning in the parliament that he thought he would die, and pains so overly "sharp" after her going that they brought him to his bed.[51]

Up to the separation, he was all in all to Criseida and, as such, sweet. She speaks of him as her "sweet" lord once; and she, Pandaro, and the narrator, once each, as her "sweet" lover.[52] She calls him "heart of my body" twice; and her "soul," twice.[53] She names him also her "life" and "sweet life," her "weal" and her "sweet weal," her "sweet repose," her "heart's delight," her "love," twice her "sweet love," and twice her "sweet desire"; and the narrator terms him her "sweet well-being" and her "delight."[54] She anticipates being in Troiolo's "sweet" arms and laments removal from his "sweet" countenance.[55] The Greeks, contrariwise, had reason to fear him like "death."[56]

Pandaro's part in the affair is figured only infrequently, and yet once, it must be allowed, by a very lively pair of proverbial analogies. To him, the prince is a "sweet" and dear brother and a "sweet" friend.[57] For him, the confidant addresses Criseida with "sweet" words to put her at ease to hear the suit; for him, as he admits, he has "thrown honor to the ground."[58] And on his own account and the lover's he gives way to "bitter" plaint after she has proved false.[59] At the beginning, he justifies his anomalous pretensions as loveless love-counsellor by the linked analogies of the man who does not know how to guard himself from poison but keeps another safe by good counsel and of the half-blind man who is seen to walk where the full-sighted does not proceed well::

> ma spesse volte avenne
> che quei che sé non sa guardar dal tosco,
> altrui per buon consiglio salvo tene,
> e giá veduto s'è andare il losco
> dove l'alluminato non va bene.[60]

Chaucer insists, like Boccaccio, that heroine and hero each found the other sweet and love-centered experience both sweet and bitter, iterates the concept occasionally employed in the *Filostrato* that each seemed the other's

305

heart, and develops a new figurative theme of sickness and cure. Suppresssing Pandaro's cynical endorsement of male remedy for female desire, the one metaphor in the source drawn from the notion that love could be literally an illness, he often figures his hero's longing and its alleviation by niece and uncle in medical terms and, sometimes, malaise of hers as well. These fanciful inventions, impressive in themselves, are supported by the notices of actual debility of prince and lady, which, as recorded in the preceding chapter, our poet adapted from the original. Still other associations of his with bodily concerns, though not pervasive, are variously arresting as will appear. Whereas none of Boccaccio's figurative statements just reviewed was elaborate or sharply particularized, not a few of Chaucer's now to be considered are thus memorable. And a fair number of his are kinetic in suggestion as against only some half dozen of his author's. They manifest the lively apprehension of event in process, which as shown in the aforesaid chapter, pervades his treatment of stage business and of movement from one locale to the next.

Of his associations at issue, most apply to the relationship between Criseyde and Troilus of course, but a considerable number to relationships between him or her and other persons in the story, a few to the narrator's role, a few to the general human lot, and a small residue to inanimate nature.

Taking up the last three categories first, we may begin with the figures devoted to the condition of man on earth. All are depreciatory. Chaucer adapts Boccaccio's generalization on the enamorment as follows:

> O blynde world, O blynde entencioun!
> How often falleth al the effect contraire
> Of surquidrie and foul presumpcioun.[61]

Apropos of the reversal, he observes that Fortune

> kan to fooles so hire song entune,
> That she hem hent and blent, traitour comune!
> And whan a wight is from hire whiel ythrowe,
> Than laugheth she, and maketh hym the mowe.[62]

And he tells us that Troilus, after release from the flesh,

> dampned al oure werk that foloweth so
> The blynde lust, the which that may nat laste.[63]

His heroine, doubtful of love in prospect, observes of it,

> Ful sharp bygynnyng breketh ofte at ende,

and,

> Ther is no wight that woot, I trowe so,
> Wher it bycometh; lo, no wight on it sporneth.[64]

Confronted with Troilus' alleged jealousy, she declares that worldly felicity,

> Imedled is with many a bitternesse.[65]

And her uncle is to concede "fortunes sharpe adversitee." [66]

Metaphors of the body applied to natural phenomena, though vivid, are too sporadic to develop any theme. The sun Chaucer terms "the hevenes yë," and his hero fancies that every aperture has one of its "bryghte yën." [67] The prince images Mars in a "blody cope." [68] March, the narrator remarks, often changes its "face." [69] In Troilus' hymn to Love, the sea is said to be "gredy" to flow; and in the Epilog, our little earth, to be "Embraced" by it.[70] The hero and Calkas respectively mention "asshen pale and dede" and "asshen dede." [71]

Such bodily figures as Chaucer uses for his own efforts support the humble pose of ignorance of love and dependence on authority. In context, the line of his first stanza,

> Thise woful vers, that wepen as I write

reflects the solicitude of an outsider, not identification with the Trojan lover as Boccaccio's corresponding phrase " 'l mio verso lagrimoso." [72] And, as outsider, the poet would exculpate himself in the Prohemium to Book II:

> Disblameth me, if any word be lame,
> For as myn auctour seyde, so sey I.
> Ek though I speeke of love unfelyngly,
> No wondre is, for it nothyng of newe is;
> A blynd man kan nat juggen wel in hewis.[73]

He must follow that author's account of the consummation, he remarks, to whomever it "sucre be or soot." [74] In the envoy to his little book, he bids it be subject to all poesy and to "kis" the steps which great poets tread.[75]

Let us now go on to figurative concepts employed in representation of Criseyde. Those applied to her emotions and thought processes will first engage us and then those applied to her influence, actual or potential, upon the hero.

Bitterness follows sweetness in her course with this sweet lover and in more than equal measure. The narrator calls the period of their full understanding before consummation "this tyme swete," and observes of their delight in the event,

> And now swetnesse semeth more swete,
> That bitternesse assaied was byforn.[76]

Yet daylight soon comes to part them, and, as he records, they were to curse it "bitterly." [77] He asserts that her weeping on the day after the parliament evidenced "bittre" pain and hyperbolizes as follows about hers and the lover's on the succeeding night,

> The woful teeris that they leten falle
> As bittre weren, out of teris kynde,
> For peyne, as is ligne aloes or galle.[78]

She complained to the go-between of "cruel bitternesse" which pervaded her at thought of the exchange.[79] And, when newly transported to the camp,

> "Allas!" quod she, "the plesance and the joie,
> The which that now al torned into galle is,
> Have ich had ofte withinne tho yonder walles!"[80]

Diomede, as in the *Filostrato*, is made to despise her hope for Troy and Trojans and to call it therefore "bittre."[81]

Another figure of tasting and three of drinking bear on the lady's courses. Underestimating her intelligence, Pandarus fears that, if he subtilizes his presentation of amorous opportunity,

> She shal no savour have therin but lite.[82]

After the uncle has left her to herself, she argues that she may venture part way with Troilus, reflecting proverbially,

> For though a man forbede dronkenesse,
> He naught forbet that every creature
> Be drynkeles for alwey, as I gesse;

but then falls into doubt, imagining that women's lot in love is tears and that

> Our wrecche is this, oure owen wo to drynke.[83]

And Chaucer applies a medical similitude of imbibing to her experience and the prince's throughout courtship. Before we take up this and other figures of cure for her, however, we should survey a few which are miscellaneous in concept.

As the narrator puts it, she and Troilus "flete" in bliss during their first night, but, after exchange, she

> Shal no lenger in hire blisse bathe.[84]

He credits her with "dedly sharp distresse" at the prospect of separation and asks rhetorically,

> What wonder is, though that hire sore smerte?[85]

In reproof of the lover for cavilling about the prospect, she says,

> For if ye wiste how soore it doth me smerte,
> Ye wolde cesse of this.[86]

Criseyde tells Pandarus that her wit is "al to leene" to interpret a covert assurance of his.[87] With more reason for self-criticism, she exclaims when wishing that she had not submitted to exile,

> Prudence, allas, oon of thyne eyen thre
> Me lakked alwey, er that I come here![88]

It appears, however, that her intelligence could be as probing as a pair of nimble hands. Confronted by her uncle with the prospect of love, she thinks to herself, "I shal felen what he meneth, ywis."[89] His every word, the narrator tells us, she "gan up and down to wynde" after retiring to her chamber, as Boccaccio that his heroine turned over Pandaro's in her heart.[90] She went on, he says, "to caste and rollen up and down" the several attractions of Troilus—such extrinsic ones as his rank and fame as well as his personal merits and his gratifying dependence on her favor.[91] Continuing in meditation,

> what to doone best were, and what eschue,
> That plited she ful ofte in many fold.[92]

The narrator remarks that, when first together, she and her uncle

> gonnen wade
> In many an unkouth glad and dep matere.[93]

And Pandarus employs another image of footing it to sway her against rejection of his friend,

> Wo worth that wight that tret ech undir foote![94]

"Hire herte lough," the poet informs us, when she heard Troilus praised at the dinner party; but, alone with him for the last time, she was to declare,

> The pure spirit wepeth in myn herte.[95]

To mark a shift in her initial reflections on love, Chaucer writes,

> Than slepeth hope, and after drede awaketh.[96]

Bringing her to literal slumber, he observes "the dede slep hire hente."[97]

Four figures of remedy for disease illuminate emotional states of hers at widely separated points in the action. Apologizing for her fear reaction to Pandarus' offer of a suitor, she quotes the proverb,

> But cesse cause, ay cesseth maladie.[98]

In the consummation scene, Chaucer devotes a stanza to an analogy which applies to her and to Troilus jointly:

> O, sooth is seyd, that heled for to be
> As of a fevre, or other gret siknesse,
> Men moste drynke, as men may ofte se,
> Ful bittre drynke; and for to han gladnesse,
> Men drynken ofte peyne and gret distresse;
> I mene it here, as for this aventure,
> That thorugh a peyne hath founden al his cure.[99]

Of the women who offered her unwanted consolation, our poet observes:

> But swich an ese therwith they hire wroughte,
> Right as a man is esed for to feele,
> For ache of hed, to clawen hym on his heele!

herein reproducing Boccaccio's remark about them, with substitution of headache for an even less dignified, though certainly more congruent, itching.[100] Repentant for having left Troy, Criseyde again proverbializes:

> But al to late comth the letuarie,
> Whan men the cors unto the grave carie.[101]

It is to be noted that only the second of these passages even implies that malaise afflicting her is sexual appetancy. And even in the second, the cure is not expressly attributed to her lover, though he, of course, provides it.

Having covered the figurative representation of Criseyde's experiences, we may proceed to that of her influence upon Troilus.

He calls her his "herte" twenty-one times and, in twelve of these instances, his "swete herte" or "herte swete," while the narrator once refers to her as the prince's "herte swete."[102] In his first letter, according to the poet's digest of it, Troilus addressed her as his "hertes lif," "lust," and blisse"; and he later names her "my blisse and my solas."[103] He apostrophizes her five times simply as "swete" and twice speaks of her as his "swete fo" and once each as "so swete a wight" and "swete may," and the narrator once terms her the "lady swete" of his hero.[104] That she may become such, Pandarus exhorts,

> So lat youre daunger sucred ben a lite.[105]

She is conceived of as the hero's physician and as one or another medium of cure for him which a healer might employ. Having mentioned the lover's early yearnings for her favor, the narrator sums up,

> Lo, here his lif, and from the deth his cure![106]

In anticipation of her possible refusal of favor, Pandarus ejaculates,

> Wo worth the faire gemme vertulees!
> Wo worth that herbe also that dooth no boote! [107]

And he assures her that Troilus duly swore him to secrecy before revealing "who myghte ben his leche." [108] Accepting the uncle's high estimate of this suitor, she is pleased to think "his lif al lith now in my cure." [109] Troilus, in his first missive, calls her his "sorwes leche" as well as his "hertes lif." [110] Finding the prince abed when he brings him her answer to it, Pandarus declares conceitfully:

> thow shalt arise and see
> A charme that was sent right now to the,
> The which kan helen the of thyn accesse,
> If thow do forthwith al thi bisynesse. [111]

At Deiphebus' house, when everyone else turns physician to prescribe for the alleged sick man, Criseyde smugly reflects, "Best koud I yet ben his leche." [112] With exchange threatened, Pandarus admonishes her not to increase his friend's sorrow with weeping but to seek to assuage it. Reinforcing this appeal metaphorically, he urges,

> Beth rather to hym cause of flat than egge,

be to him, that is, as a magic weapon capable of healing the wounds it has inflicted; and then generalizes,

> Bet is a tyme of cure ay than of pleynte. [113]

Criseyde obediently replies:

> If to this sore there may be fonden salve,
> It shal nat lakke, certeyn, on my halve. [114]

Afflictions, in her phrase, are to be slain. Apropos of his purported jealousy, she tells Troilus that it is her intent "Fully to slen" the anguish in their hearts. [115] When alone after the parliament, she despairs of his future,

> Who shal that sorwe slen that ye ben inne?

but, when with him, asserts that it will be possible to "slen this hevynesse." [116]

Pandarus, on the other hand, once fancies her a bier for his friend. Leaping into the prince's chamber at Deiphebus' he jests,

> God have thi soule, ibrought have I thi beere! [117]

Figures applied to Troilus as her mate will next concern us. Like the figures used of Criseyde as his, they may be divided into two categories—

311

interpretative respectively of amorous experience and amorous influence. To the first belong the concepts of sweetness and bitterness of events for him, his drinking woe and having it fed, his smarting with sharp sorrow and bathing in bliss, his mental vision or lack of it and his manipulation of ideas, his tears of the heart, the sleeping and waking of his passions, their birth and death, and, finally and most important, his sickness of the heart. To the second, only the repeated designation of him as her heart or sweetheart and several others of like import used but once or twice.

There are notable differences between the application of bodily figures to him and that to her. Both are said to drink of love's potation, but only he to thirst for it; amorous smart is emphasized more for him than for her; existence is in some sense a living death for him as it is not for her; she is often represented as his leech or medium of cure, he never as hers.

Beside Chaucer's already mentioned remarkings of a sweet interim for hero and heroine, the sweetness of consummation made more sweet to them by earlier bitterness, their bitter cursing of daylight, and their tears more bitter than aloes or gall,[118] there are several notices in his poem of sweetness or bitterness for Troilus alone. The prince would be secret, the narrator tells us, because he remembers that love advertised

> Yelt bittre fruyt, though swete seed be sowe.[119]

In the song derived for him from Petrarch, Troilus terms love "swete harm so queynte."[120] Pandarus, like Pandaro, hopes that his efforts will achieve "swetnesse" for his friend.[121] With the latter at Deiphebus', Criseyde promises,

> I shal trewely, with al my myght,
> Youre bittre tornen al into swetnesse.[122]

The juncture at which Troilus was alerted for a second night with her the poet terms "the blisful tyme swete."[123] Pandarus counsels his lord to abridge the "bittre peynes smerte" of separation by taking another mistress.[124] In course of rejecting the advice, Troilus, like Troiolo, asserts that death would now be "swete."[125]

Apropos of the hero and heroine's release from sorrow, Chaucer observes, as already noted, that men must drink bitter draughts to be healed of sickness. In his song from Petrarch, the newly enamored prince confesses an anomalous thirst for love without assuming that it might be medicinable:

> If it be wikke, a wonder thynketh me,
> When every torment and adversite
> That cometh of hym, may to me savory thinke,
> For ay thurst I, the more that ich it drynke.[126]

Criseyde implies that his alleged jealousy is the excusable kind that "goodly drynketh up al his distresse." [127] A model of constancy, he tells her in his last letter to be quoted:

> So thursteth ay myn herte to byholde
> Youre beute, that my lif unnethe I holde. [128]

Sighs and plaints at the prospect of her departure combined "to feede" the lover's woe, as the narrator puts it. [129] Contrariwise, as he remarks ironically of Troilus and Pandarus in vigil at the gate,

> longe may they seche
> Er that they fynde that they after gape. [130]

According to Chaucer as already quoted, his hero and heroine "flete" in bliss during the first night, and he also says that the former "felte his herte in joie flete" at prospect of a second. [131]

There are a dozen applications in his poem of the concepts of smarting or sharpness to Troilus' feelings as against the three which have been recorded for Criseyde's. On the night of union, Pandarus tells her that the prince will not speak of jealousy, "how sore that hym smerte," and she asks Troilus to be forgiven "that I have don yow smerte." [132] Faced with separation, the hero is "Neigh ded for smert"; is advised by Pandarus, as already noted, to abridge his "bittre peynes smerte"; replies ironically that his consoler is like one who proverbs,

> Thynk nat on smert, and thow shalt fele non;

and later beseeches Criseyde to rue on his "aspre peynes smerte." [133] After her going, he is "In sorwe," as Chaucer tells us, "aboven all sorwes smerte"; remarks to Pandarus that it is no wonder that one laments who feels "harm and smert in every veyne"; and writes Criseyde that she alone could save him from harm of "alle peynes smerte." [134] Before enjoying his lady, he feels "sharp" desire according to the narrator, and, after losing her, "sharpe" throws and a "sharp" new pain, according to the poet's statement and his own. [135]

At the Palladian festival, he is made to tell lovers—as Troiolo was not —that they are "nyce and blynde." [136] In consequence, generalization by Chaucer on his immediate enamorment,

> O blynde world, O blynde entencoun!

is more patly ironic than Boccaccio's on his hero's. [137] Resorting to similar metaphor near the end, our poet observes of Troilus, in futile vigil by the gate, "his hope alwey hym blente." [138]

313

Unlike Criseyde, who had two at least of the three eyes of Prudence, her lover saw with the one of the affections. As Chaucer testifies,

> By nyght or day, for wisdom or folye,
> His herte, which that is his brestes ye,
> Was ay on hire.[139]

In adaptation of a metaphor applied to Troiolo, the poet states that Troilus

> gan up and down to wynde
> Hire wordes alle, and every countenaunce.[140]

And he says that his hero, on taking to the pen,

> rolleth in his herte to and fro,
> How he may best discryven hire his wo.[141]

Neither of these figures implies calculating shrewdness as do the four of manipulation devoted to thought processes of the lady.

Prideful in the temple, as the narrator images him,

> This Troilus is clomben on the staire,
> And litel weneth that he moot descenden.[142]

Pandarus, wishing to help him after the descent, argues *inter alia*,

> Ek the ne aughte nat ben yvel appayed,
> Though I desyre with the for to bere
> Thyn hevy charge; it shal the lasse dere.[143]

And he cites authority as follows:

> The wise seith, "Wo hym that is allone,
> For, and he falle, he hath non helpe to ryse." [144]

In courtship, the suitor "held after his gistes ay his pas" as Chaucer phrases it, that is, accommodated his gait to the stages of his amorous itinerary.[145] To pray him as Deiphebus did to favor Criseyde was as superfluous

> As for to bidde a wood man for to renne.[146]

After such arduous metaphorical progression, Troilus was deserted by his senses at the very goal. As he knelt contritely by the bedside of his tearful mistress,

> The felyng of his sorwe, or of his fere,
> Or of aught elles, fled was out of towne.[147]

Years later, because of her failure to return on the appointed day,

> His hope al clene out of his herte fledde.[148]

As the dawn came to end their first assignation, it seemed to him,

> for piëtous distresse,
> The blody teris from his herte melte.[149]

There are single metaphors of waking and dreaming for responses of his and several each of quickening and dying. The narrator relates that, as Troilus sat awake, his spirit "mette" it saw Criseyde as she had been in the temple, and that Pandarus sought to "awaken" his friend's temper with jesting words.[150] He tells us that, on due occasions, the hero's desire and affection, his thought, and his whole being began to "quyken."[151] He writes of him also that

> lust to brede
> Gan more than erst, and yet took he non hede.[152]

When new to love, the prince termed it "quike deth."[153] Thanks to this anomalous passion, his erstwhile japes and ruthlessness became "Dede."[154] Pandarus, calling after he had retired, asked jocosely,

> Who is in his bed so soone
> Iburied thus?"[155]

And, as already noted, he was later to announce to his friend that he had brought him his bier—another jest with portentous overtones.[156] At one time, woe of Troilus "made his herte swelte" we are informed; and, at another, that "hym thoughte his herte deyde."[157] When he urged elopement, his cautious mistress responded, "sle with resoun al this hete."[158] Frankly the slave of feeling as she a pretender to rationality, he was ere long to write her of cold care "That sleth my wit."[159]

The many contexts already cited in which she is represented as a cure or curer for Troilus[160] all suggest that his status is figuratively the inactive one of patient, and so too the equally numerous contexts, presently to be taken up, in which the friend is accorded curative potential. So also, the previously mentioned analogy of restoration to health through bitter drink which the narrator draws to the experience of both hero and heroine.[161] And so, perhaps, the question the prince asks himself when he might still frustrate the exchange:

> Whi nyl I helpen to myn owen cure?[162]

As for his influence upon the lady, it is implied by a conventional denomination used over and over again and by some other appelatives employed but rarely. Criseyde names him her "herte" in thirty-one instances, and, in

315

six of them, her "swete herte" or "herte swete"; the narrator, once her "herte" and once her "swete herte."[163] On single occasions, she apostrophizes Troilus as "myn owen hertes list" and as

> Myn hertes lif, my trist, and my plesaunce.[164]

At one point, she calls him "my pees, my suffisaunce"; at another,

> Myn owene hertes sothfast suffisaunce.[165]

And three times, she employs "swete" by itself to address him.[166]

The few figures to be considered for the relationship between Criseyde and Diomede will remind us ironically of some of the many applied to that between her and Troilus. On the way to camp, the hasty rival prays,

> Comaundeth me, how soore that me smerte,
> To don al that may like unto youre herte.[167]

And soliciting her there, he ventures the endearment, "herte myn."[168] Criseyde, who years before included "estat" among the numerous merits of Troilus "to caste and rollen up and down Withinne hire thought," now concentrates upon the practical advantages of the new suitor,

> Retornyng in hire soule ay up and down
> The wordes of this sodeyn Diomede,
> His grete estat, and perel of the town,
> And that she was allone and hadde nede
> Of frendes help,

with the result that intent to remain "bygan to brede."[169] Yielding to it, she presently has occasion to minister to the new suitor, but for literal wounds inflicted by Troilus, not figurative ones made by the God of Love.[170]

There are a good many figures of the body, mainly in Pandarus' own dialogue, to illuminate his connection with the prince, as well as three or four which have some bearing on commerce with his niece.

The former all evidence his sympathy for Troilus; and nearly all, the wish to help him. Several refer to his own ill success in love, never as a matter of primary interest, but always as an issue tangential to his pretensions as love-counsellor. The dominant metaphorical concept is that of curing; others support it in lively but sporadic fashion.

These uniterated concepts may be considered before the medical one. To support the argument that he may help another though not himself Pandarus observes, somewhat like Pandaro:

> I have myself ek seyn a blynd man goo
> Ther as he fel that couthe loken wide;

and then, independently of his original,

> For how myghte evere swetnesse han ben knowe
> To him that nevere tasted bitternesse? [171]

He tells his niece he found it so hard to keep Troilus from death

> That yet fele I myn herte for hym wepe. [172]

Brought near death himself by pity for the wishful prince, he took thought, as the narrator informs us, "Som of his wo to slen." [173] Troilus' new woe after the parliament "slough" the friend's heart, the latter is said to have imagined. [174]

Suggestion of healing activity for Pandarus occurs repeatedly in the first scene between him and his lord and once in that after the reversal. In the former, the confidant applies to himself a mythological analogy derived from Oënone's letter to Paris:

> "Phebus, that first fond art of medicyne,"
> Quod she, "and couthe in every wightes care
> Remedye and reed, by herbes he knew fyne,
> Yet to hymself his konnyng was ful bare;
> For love hadde hym so bounden in a snare,
> Al for the doughter of the kynge Amete,
> That al his craft ne koude his sorwes bete."
>
> Right so fare I, unhappily for me.
> I love oon best, and that me smerteth sore;
> And yet, peraunter, kan I reden the,
> And nat myself; repreve me na more. [175]

He then exhorts Troilus not to be like the fools, persistent in sorrow, that "listen naught to seche hem other cure." [176] Dispraising proverbs and examples offered, the prince says roundly,

> Nor other cure kanstow non for me.
> Ek I nyl nat ben cured; I wol deye. [177]

Pandarus rejoins "put nat impossible thus thi cure," terming "unskilful" the belief,

> That of thi wo is no curacioun. [178]

To persuade the reluctant one to disclose his lady's identity, he argues,

> For whoso list have helyng of his leche,
> To hym byhoveth first unwre his wownde. [179]

Chaucer, having brought the scene to a close with the pair in accord, takes momentary leave of the hero as follows:

> Now lat us stynte of Troilus a stounde,
> That fareth lik a man that hurt is soore,
> And is somdeel of akyngge of his wownde
> Ylissed wel, but heeled no deel moore:
> And, as an esy pacyent, the loore
> Abit of hym that gooth aboute his cure.[180]

In their colloquy after the parliament, Pandarus is thus rebuked by the lover for advising him to take another mistress,

> This lechecraft, or heeled thus to be,
> Were wel sittyng, if that I were a fend.[181]

Apropos of the friend's begging his niece to speak with Troilus, Chaucer writes,

> But theron was to heven and to doone.[182]

He tells us that, when inviting her to dinner, Pandarus swore that she should not elude him

> Ne lenger don hym after hire to cape;

and, as already noted, that confidant and lover when at the gate have long to seek ere finding "that they after gape." [183] These several figures do no more than emphasize the man's obvious persistence.

Several applied to Calkas illustrate paternal solicitude on his part and contempt, fear, and doubt of him on the parts respectively of Criseyde, Troilus, and Diomede. It was "to hele hym of his sorwes soore" that the Greeks yielded Antenor as the narrator informs us.[184] Criseyde promises to make him dream that his soul is in heaven since cupidity will so "blende" it as to make him credulous.[185] Troilus challenges this assurance with the following pronouncements, among others:

> Men may the wise atrenne, and naught atrede.

> It is ful hard to halten unespied
> Byfore a crepel, for he kan the craft;

and tells her flatly that she will not "blende" the oldster.[186] Warning her of the fall of Troy, Diomede concedes that his authority for it may be deceptive, that Calkas may be misleading the Greeks with "ambages"—

> Swiche as men clepen a word with two visages.[187]

As for the potentially suspicious, they must all be made blind. According to the narrator, Pandarus reported to the hero "how that he Deiphebus gan to blende." [188] En route to the sickroom in this lord's house, he urges his niece to make the most of opportunity, "While folk is blent." [189] Troilus, having done so when she joined him, begins to groan,

> His brother and his suster for to blende. [190]

The time presently approaches for consummation, and

> Now al is wel, for al the world is blynd. [191]

After the parliament, the friend would have Troilus hide his grief from Priam and the court,

> Thow most with wisdom hym and othere blende. [192]

And the prince—"his meyne for to blende"—devises a pretext for a jaunt before venturing to the palace Criseyde has abandoned. [193]

With so cautious a lover and uncle, she was needlessly apprehensive about gossips that "dremen" amiss. [194] Abandoning the former for Diomede, she accurately foretold the consequence,

> O, rolled shal I ben on many a tonge! [195]

In this section, Chaucer's exploitation of concepts of sickness and cure has been shown to be by all odds his most significant departure from Boccaccio in the figurative pattern under study. In the next, we shall see that he variously enriches that drawn by his author from the animal world, diversifying it in content, tone, and implication.

The Brute Creation

THE figurative elements of the *Troilus* and its source here to be treated will include associations with man's fellow creatures severally or collectively and as pursued or subjected by him or as doing what they would.

In the *Filostrato,* the total is small, and the bulk of it devoted to the protagonist. He is imaged as bull, lion, falcon, and—with Criseida—as songbird. He repeatedly fancies himself to have been netted, and once specifies that she was responsible. He proceeds from biting criticism of others to gnawing himself in thought. She is similarly masochistic but not for long. Spurred by desire, he must curb this and apply the bit to his amorous mind. Diomede, the boar of his dream, is never associated with the animal world in metaphor or simile, nor is Pandaro. Curbing, however, is prescribed for Cassandra and for young men, while fear is thought to bridle womankind. The ignorant twitter; the censorious may bay. Love, as the heroine once objectifies it, has retentive "claws"; and Fame, as visualized by the narrator, speeds on "wings."[1]

We may quickly dispose of the figures which bear at all upon Criseida. They are rarer by far than in any other pattern. The generalization that nothing but fear of shame "bridles" a woman is offered by Pandaro apropos of his as yet unattempted cousin.[2] At consummation, the narrator images her with Troiolo as a bird delighting in its song:

> e sí come augel di foglia in foglia
> nel nuovo tempo prende dilettanza
> del canto suo, cosí facean costoro,
> di molte cose parlando fra loro.[3]

She received Calcas' welcome taciturnly, he informs us, "gnawing" herself the while in sorrow.[4] And the hero acknowledges the potency of her eyes in one of his metaphors of being netted.

320

We may consider these first among the figures bearing on his experience. In a complaint about the deity who surprised him at the festival, Troiolo recognizes that he is "taken in the snare" against which he has declaimed and fears censure for being "netted" by love in time of war.[5] He will be caught in the "nets" of death, he tells Pandaro, unless succored by him or by the lady.[6] Apostrophizing her eyes at consummation, he declares that they hold and will always hold him in the "amorous net"; and, the next day, he informs the confidant that he has never been so completely in the "nets" of love as at the moment.[7] Beauty, though wont "to net" others, did not move him to love Criseida, he later assures her, but high breeding and demeanor.[8]

The narrator represents Troiolo's early criticism of lovers to have been biting, and the prince imagines that they so regarded it.[9] At exchange time, he is gnawed with his own preoccupations, as he tells Criseida and as the poet reports.[10]

The more hopeful he became during courtship, the more he felt desire "spur" him according to the narrator.[11] That emotion—in complementary metaphor—must be bridled. Pandaro at the outset exhorts him to be patient, "curbing" warm desire.[12] With the lady won, he insists again upon restraint,

> più che mai ti rammento
> che ponghi freno alla mente amorosa,

this time for the sake of her reputation.[13] Troiolo continues as discreet to the end as his friend could wish. Nothing, however, "curbs" the tears he sheds in secret, as we learn from a missive of his to the exiled Criseida.[14] Because of the disastrous consequences of passion for his hero, the author exhorts youth to curb their steps toward it:

> per Dio vi priego che voi raffreniate
> i pronti passi all' appetito rio.[15]

The already quoted image of a songbird flitting among leaves prettifies the lover on the same level as the beloved. That of a falcon, applied to Troiolo alone, associates him with the predator only in the unheroic respect of spruceness:

> ed a' suoi tempi Criseida vedendo,
> si refaceva grazïoso e bello,
> come falcon ch' uscisse di cappello.

It weakens the impression created by the notice immediately before it of his manly bent for hawking and hunting.[16]

Similes of a boar and a lion bring out the violence respectively of his

321

grief and longing for revenge, but not the potency claimed for him in fight, while another of a savage beast emphasizes a change for the worse in his appearance, a change which is accompanied by debilitation. The narrator reports that Troiolo, when alone in his chamber after the parliament, gave vent to sorrow in such manner,

> ch' uom non parea, ma arriabiata fera;

and then particularizes the comparison as follows:

> Né altrimenti il toro va saltando
> or qua or lá, da poi c' ha ricevuto
> il mortal colpo, e misero mugghiando
> conoscer fa qual duolo ha conceputo,
> che Troiolo facesse.[17]

Because Criseida did not return as promised, he lost appetite, could not sleep, shunned company,

> Ed era tal nel viso divenuto
> che piuttosto che uom pareva fera,

while declining so low that he could hardly walk.[18] Her failure to reply promptly to his letter so affected him that he had to take to bed. Visiting him in it, Deifobo sought to raise his spirits by talk of warfare soon to be resumed and was eminently successful:

> Quale il lïon famelico, cercando
> per preda, faticato si riposa,
> subito su si leva, i crin vibrando,
> se cervo o toro sente, od altra cosa
> che gli appetisca, sol quella bramando;
> tal Troiol udendo la guerra dubbiosa
> ricomminiciarsi, subito vigore
> gli corse dentro allo 'nfiammato core.[19]

Thus moved, the sick man vowed that he would soon recover and, because of his hatred of the Greeks, fight harder than ever against them. He kept the promise, of course. Yet, though fulfilling it to their bane, he is never imaged as lionish in combat.

Cassandra he reprimanded for her officious disclosure made while he was still abed. Observing that it would be wiser for her to be silent than to speak "unhaltered," he demanded that she "curb" her ready tongue.[20] He held that she was biting every one.[21] And he chid her for "bestiality" and "brutish-ness."[22]

Lastly, it may be recorded that unwelcome discourse of anonymi is associated with noise of bird or dog. That of the women who visited Criseida after the parliament the narrator calls vain "chirping."[23] When still eager to return to Troy, she was ready she thought defiantly to let anyone "bark" about her who would.[24]

The instances of figurative linkage with animals in the *Troilus* not only outnumber those in the *Filostrato* but are more diverse than they and more often vividly particular. Though most lie within the same areas of association as the few in the source, only half a dozen are derived from it. These all concern hero or heroine. A great many new figures relate to him, but many also to her, a number to the confidant, a pair to the rival, one to her father, three to potential gossips, and several to deities as participants in human affairs. Of the new which bear on Criseyde, some emphasize tender and yielding femininity in the spirit of romance, while others give a homely, every-day turn to her thinking and its consequences. Those bearing on Troilus present him also in contrasting lights. Several bring out his manliness as heroic complement to her femininity; many, his utter subjection to love—poetically in some cases, prosaically and even comically in others. The two in a stanza about Diomede point up his heartfree craftiness, the antithesis of the hero's truth. That applied to Calkas—and his daughter—opposes his will to her intent in ironic fashion. Two illuminative of the confidant point up his own amatory failure; others, his zeal and ingenuity on behalf of the resource-less prince. Thus, contrasts between the major roles and within them are accentuated. And in figurative reference to divinities, which we shall take up first, their efficacy is sometimes opposed to human weakness.

Aprostrophizing Fortune and the influences of the spheres anent the momentous rain, Chaucer declares:

> Soth is, that under God ye ben oure hierdes,
> Though to us bestes ben the causes wrie.[25]

While bringing the story to a close, he reports that she

> Gan pulle awey the fetheres brighte of Troie
> Fro day to day, til they ben bare of joie,

as one commissioned by Jove to transfer power from nation to nation.[26] He writes as follows of the wounding of Troilus by the God of Love:

> For sodeynly he hitte hym atte fulle;
> And yet as proud a pekok kan he pulle.[27]

Troilus, in the song derived for him from Boethius, gives loftier testimony than this to the power of the deity:

> And if that Love aught lete his bridel go,
> Al that now loveth asondre sholde lepe,
> And lost were al that Love halt now to-hepe.[28]

At the end, however, the narrator would have us believe the old gods thin deer, dismissing as profitless the worship

> Of Jove, Appollo, of Mars, of swich rascaille.[29]

And in the long analogy of Phebus which the confidant draws to himself we find the metaphorical assertion that love held this one "bounden in a snare." [30]

Criseyde is figured as prey and taker of prey, and with contrasting implications in each of these aspects. She is represented to be yielding though timid, astute yet less so than she sometimes imagines.

She may be consumed by the years or stung by pity, but is exempt from bite of desire which Troilus feels. At the outset, her uncle admonishes,

> And therfore, er that age the devoure,
> Go love, for old, ther wol no wight of the.[31]

The prince tells her on the last night that he fears supplantation,

> but if routhe
> Remorde yow, or vertu of youre trouthe.[32]

Oftenest associated with the winged order of creation, she is then more the heroine of romance than when linked with any other. At consummation, she is equated with those favorites of love poets, the dawn and night songsters, and in such wise as to imply the softest femininity.

> What myghte or may the sely larke seye,
> Whan that the sperhauk hath it in his foot?

asks Chaucer as his hero takes possession.[33] Her recovery of speech after this loving violence, he celebrates as follows:

> And as the newe abaysed nyghtyngale,
> That stynteth first whan she bygynneth to synge,
> Whan that she hereth any herde tale,
> Or in the hegges any wyght stirynge,
> And after siker doth hire vois out rynge,
> Right so Criseyde, whan hire drede stente,
> Opned hire herte, and tolde hym hire entente.[34]

In adapting Boccaccio's summary of the liaison, he transfers its dainty simile of a falcon from lover to beloved:

> And whan that he com ridyng into town,
> Ful ofte his lady from hire wyndow down,
> As fressh as faukoun comen out of muwe,
> Ful redy was hym goodly to saluwe.[35]

Borrowing for Pandarus the suggestion made by Pandaro that the hero should seek a replacement for the lady about to be exchanged, he reinforces it with an analogy,

> Ech for his vertu holden is for deere,
> Both heroner and faucoun for ryvere,[36]

which, though implying attractions in her, argues as potent ones in other women. The prospect of separation moves Criseyde to fear that her soul may soon wing from her. She would have Troilus come, she tells her uncle,

> er deth, that thus me threteth,
> Dryve out that goost which in myn herte beteth.[37]

.The narrator reverses this fancy when in telling of her swoon he attributes recovery to the hero's ministration,

> For which hire goost, that flikered ay on lofte,
> Into hire woful herte ayeyn it wente.[38]

Possessed of soul again and hopeful, she assures Troilus that, though banished, she will not be so "hid in mewe" that he will have no word of her.[39] Their joy in subsequent talk Chaucer expresses by a similitude taken from the *Filostrato,*

> And as the briddes, whanne the sonne is shene,
> Delited hem, and made hire hertes clere.[40]
> Right so the wordes that they spake yfeere
> Delited hem, and made hire hertes clere.[40]

The figure is eminently appropriate for the heroine whom he has gentled, if not altogether so for his masculinized hero.

New ones of bear, deer, and tame grazing animal are interpretative of other situations of hers in less poetic vein. With a noble lover in prospect as she has just learned from Pandarus, the lady felicitates herself that she is without a husband:

> I am myn owene womman, wel at ese,
> I thank it God, as after myn estat,
> Right youg, and stonde unteyd in lusty leese.[41]

The uncle, having laid an ambush for her at the house of Deiphebus, speaks thus assuredly of it to his friend:

> Lo, hold the at thi triste cloos, and I
> Shal wel the deer unto thi bowe dryve.[42]

Criseyde proverbs like a merchant to justify giving Calkas some of her own wealth under the pretense that it is that of friends sent to him in trust and that more will be forthcoming if he lets her go back to Troy:

> Lo, Troilus, men seyn that hard it is
> The wolf ful, and the wether hool to have;
> This is to seyn, that men ful ofte, iwys,
> Mote spenden part the remenant for to save.[43]

The needless explanation appended to the metaphor is reminiscent of her uncle's pedantries. In controverting the scheme to trick her father, the hero resorts to as homely a proverbialism,

> For thus men seyth, "that on thenketh the beere,
> But al another thenketh his ledere."[44]

Like the figure of Bayard subdued by the carter, which our poet applies in an early scene to Troilus, this one exposes presumption with deglamorizing irony.

Before the lover joins her after the parliament, his mistress has vented her grief in another homely, though poignant, utterance,

> How sholde a fissh withouten water dure?
> What is Criseyde worth, from Troilus?[45]

Thinking of her contrarily as angler in their first talk, Pandarus ventured this caution against obduracy, on his friend's behalf and his own,

> If that ye don us bothe dyen,
> Thus gilteles, than have ye fisshed fayre.[46]

As will presently be noted, she is said to have taken the hero with and without net. She assures him that she can enthrall Calkas without one.[47] Finding the priest set against her return to Troy, she laments that she could never see as she ought until "in the snare."[48]

Troilus is presented to us through animal imagery with even stronger suggestion of contrarieties than his mistress. Associated with diverse species —formidable beast and fowl, the joyous songbird, and some hapless, unromantic creatures—he appears, by turns, virile, precious, and pathetically or absurdly wretched, though always deserving of love once he has become enamored. We learn that he is snared and limed and netted. Desire bites him; his heart is gnawed and gnaws. A peacock at the festival, he is there ignominiously plucked by Love. Yet he comes to seize Criseyde as a hawk the lark, thus substantiating her dream of him as that grander predator, the eagle. He shares delight with her in talk, as one birdling with another in song, and prettily anticipates being made happier by her return than any

326

fowl by that of May. In starker mood, he imagines his soul to be on the wing to death. As prancing carthorse is subdued by a touch of the whip, so he by initial experience of love. Thenceforth, he must bridle himself and does so admirably. Reserve on his part moves Pandarus to conjecture him as insensitive to entreaty as an ass to music. Desire breeds fawns within him. He might have been pulled down by sorrow had not his friend maimed one of its feet, but is so stationed by the confidant that he has an easy shot at the deer his mistress. When she is to be taken from him, he rages as violently—and as resourcelessly—as a dying bull. When in battle, he proves an enterprising lion. He so terrifies the Greeks that they take flight in bee-like swarm. At successive crises in his love life, he is associated with snail, mouse, and gnat. At one, he is an angler perforce, fishing for an excuse for jealousy which Pandarus invented.

Images of liming, snaring, and netting for the enamorment of Troilus are collectively as numerous as those of snaring and netting for Troiolo's and, in several instances, more detailed. After leaving the temple of the Palladium, he sought to be alone, it is explained,

> For love bigan his fetheres so to lyme;

and, when by himself, he ejaculates,

> O fool, now artow in the snare,
> That whilom japedest at loves peyne.
> Nor artow hent, now gnaw thin owen cheyne! [49]

Pandarus wishes well to his niece who has "swich oon ykaught withouten net." [50] The captive apostrophizes her eyes on the first night as,

> Ye humble nettes of my lady deere,

a bolder fancy than Troiolo's on this night that Criseida's held him "nell' amorosa rete." [51] And Chaucer says of his hero at a later time:

> The goodlihede or beaute which that kynde
> In any other lady hadde yset
> Kan nought the montance of a knotte unbynde,
> Aboute his herte, of al Criseydes net.
> He was so narwe ymasked and yknet,
> That it undon on any manere syde,
> That nyl naught ben, for aught that may bitide. [52]

At the end of the aforesaid night, Troilus laments inevitable parting,

> Syn that desir right now so biteth me,
> That I am ded anon, but I retourne. [53]

327

Next day, he finds a saving anomaly in his condition:

And ay the more that desir me biteth
To love hire best, the more it me deliteth.[54]

He is so afflicted by the exchange, however, that Pandarus must exhort:

Lat nat this wrecched wo thyn herte gnawe.[55]

Adapting a remark of Boccaccio's about his hero, Chaucer states that Troilus was convulsed at sight of the rival—"so gan his herte gnawe." [56]

Associations of Troilus with bird life, now to be or previously quoted, all imply true devotion, but in aspects from the sublime to the comic and with prospects occasionally bright if more often the reverse. Love has so limed his feathers that he cannot be the peacock at home that he was in the temple. He sagely purposes "to hiden his desir in muwe" except as he may confess it to advantage.[57] Disclosure of it to Pandarus inspires the friend's mission to Criseyde, and his advocacy and succeeding developments evoke her dream of a white eagle which changes heart for heart. As has been observed in the fourth section of Chapter I, this dream, suggested to Chaucer by the hero's boar dream after separation, stands in opposition to the latter as he recasts it with the quadruped sleeping through caresses of the exiled lady. The one promises a mate both glorious and devoted; the other reveals the mate's successor to be as indifferent as it is gross. The masterfulness, which Criseyde anticipates in her dream, is confirmed by Chaucer's equating of the hero embracing her with a sparrowhawk taloning a lark, though put in question in the same episode by Troilus' fancy that her eyes are nets, albeit humble ones, and, afterwards, by our poet's statement that the lover's heart has been and always will be inextricably in her net. The likening of the couple to tuneful birds, which Chaucer accepted from the *Filostrato*, preserves an impression of the male partner softer than that given by the new couplings of him with hawk and eagle. Transfer to the heroine of the falcon simile, so prettily applied by Boccaccio to the hero on display, eliminates one hint of youthful softness in the man. Another is reduced, I think, by the substitution of a bird for a flower simile employed by the hero in the original. There, he soliloquized that never was rose so fair in the sweet spingtime as he was disposed to become upon his lady's return; in Chaucer's poem, he is made to say:

For was ther nevere fowel so fayn of May
As I shal ben, whan that she comth in Troie.[58]

As Criseyde does hers, Troilus imagines his soul to be winged for flight

328

after the parliament, but phrases the notion more vividly and tellingly than she:

> O wery goost, that errest to and fro,
> Why nyltow fleen out of the wofulleste
> Body that evere myghte on grounde go?
> O soule, lurkynge in this wo, unneste,
> Fle forth out of myn herte, and lat it breste,
> And folowe alwey Criseyde, thi lady dere.
> Thi righte place is now no lenger here.[59]

The peacock figure, which epitomizes the irony of his humbling in the temple, is reinforced by a long equine analogy following hard upon it:

> As proude Bayard gynneth for to skippe
> Out of the weye, so pryketh hym his corn,
> Til he a lasshe have of the longe whippe;
> Than thynketh he, "Though I praunce al byforn
> First in the trays, ful fat and newe shorn,
> Yet am I but an hors, and horses lawe
> I moot endure, and with my feres drawe";
>
> So ferde it by this fierse and proude knyght.[60]

Reduced to conformity by Love as Bayard by the carter, Troilus is expected to curb himself and scrupulously fulfills this obligation. In the first conference with him, Pandarus admonishes,

> Now loke that atempre be thi bridel;

and, in the one after fruition, he implores, with precedent from Pandaro,

> Bridle alwey wel thi speche and thi desir.[61]

We have the narrator's word for it that in the courting period Troilus did not permit himself any rash act or "unbridled cheere." [62] At the very end of the union, Criseyde includes restraint of will among the merits which won and are to hold her love—

> And that youre resoun bridlede youre delit.[63]

Pandarus, though insistent as we have seen on discretion in the lover, was piqued when he first encountered it. Failing to win response to appeals for the beloved's name, he demanded of Troilus if he were somnolent—or

> lik an asse to the harpe,
> That hereth sown whan men the strynges plye,
> But in his mynde of that no melodie
> May sinken hym to gladen, for that he
> So dul ys of his bestialite? [64]

The friend was wide of the mark here, as we must assume from the narrator's *obiter dictum* apropos of the vexatious silence,

> Ek som tyme it is a craft to seme fle
> Fro thyng whych in effect men hunte faste[65]

These lines imply that Troilus was coying as Criseyde would do presently, managing the peremptory manager with something of her finesse.

In his psychic existence, he is fancied a parturient and a fleeing deer; but, in action, a huntsmen likely to bring one down. The narrator conveys his early preoccupation with Criseyde as follows:

> N' yn him desir noon other fownes breede,
> But argumentes to this conclusioun,
> That she of him wolde han compassioun,
> And he to ben hire man, while he may dure.[66]

Sorrow on her account Pandarus would have its victim imagine a canine pursuer, henceforth maimed because he has successfully pled for him to the lady,

> Algate a foot is hameled of thi sorwe! [67]

And, as already quoted, he promises to bring the deer—Criseyde—within bowshot when the suitor shall be in his "triste" at the house of Deiphebus. With feigned sickness and real humility as his arrows, Troilus is successful in the hunting station of a bed.

The simile of a bull which Boccaccio used for his hero grief-stricken by the parliament, Chaucer applies to his in the same torment:

> Right as the wylde bole bygynneth sprynge,
> Now her, now ther, idarted to the herte,
> And of his deth roreth in compleynynge,
> Right so gan he aboute the chaumbre sterte.[68]

Comparison to the lord of the herd makes us think that Troilus still has the physical might requisite for an epic hero, but, since it is to the beast defeated, it reminds us that he is without hope and will seek none. At the great crisis, as at others in his amour, he despairs unheroically of all enterprise before any is tried.

Yet Chaucer states that "he pleyde the leoun" militarily after his first talk with Pandarus and terms him "hardy as lyoun" when drawing his portrait late in the descending action.[69] These clichés attest his prowess more unequivocally than Boccaccio's leonine simile did Troiolo's, applied as that elaborate figure was to the prince, not as fleshed in combat, but only as desiring to be.

The image employed by Pandarus for an early triumph of his master is as glorifying as the two phrases just quoted:

> For nevere yet so thikke a swarm of been
> Ne fleigh, as Grekes fro hym gonne fleen.[70]

Antithetical to this in effect are his associations of the hero *qua* lover with feeble insect and weakest rodent and the narrator's of him as such with the timid snail. It is observed by the narrator that, as soon as Troilus felt the passion against which he had been ranting,

> He was tho glad his hornes in to shrinke.[71]

Impatient to proceed to the closet of his guest the heroine, Pandarus ventures comic reproof to his friend, who has taken time to invoke the planetary deities:

> Thow wrecched mouses herte,
> Artow agast so that she wol the bite?[72]

Years later, he urges him to defy the exchange with no more regard for his scruples of the moment than for his careful piety when consummation was in prospect:

> And rather be in blame a lite ifounde
> Than sterve here as a gnat, withouten wounde.[73]

Wakened in the closet, his niece was to call the jealousy he invented for Troilus a "wikked serpent" and a "wikked wyvere"[74] and to demand an explanation of it from the victim. The latter did his poor best,

> As he that nedes most a cause fisshe.[75]

Diomede stands opposed to his predecessor in the one stanza in which he is characterized through animal association. He is not a reluctant, but a purposive, angler; the user, not the victim, of a net:

> This Diomede, of whom yow telle I gan,
> Goth now withinne hymself ay arguynge
> With al the sleghte, and al that evere he kan,
> How he may best, with shortest taryinge,
> Into his net Criseydes herte brynge.
> To this entent he koude nevere fyne;
> To fisshen hire, he leyde out hook and lyne.[76]

As for Pandarus, a few animal metaphors remind us directly or indirectly of service to the hero, while two others hint ironic contrast between this and his own pursuit of love. His already quoted figures of hameling Troilus'

331

sorrow and driving Criseyde to the prince's bow support claims of past accomplishment at her house and of future at Deiphebus'. The effectiveness of his preparations for the rendezvous at his own wins the tribute of a metaphor from the narrator,

> Dredeles, it cler was in the wynd
> From every pie and every lette-game.[77]

For nocturnal machinations there, he deserves the epithet of "Fox" accorded him by Criseyde in the morning,[78] though he has had the advantage of her willingness to be beguiled. And he convinces us that, with opportunity, he would be as heroic in friendship as he has been crafty when he urges Troilus to thwart her exchange and promises to second the attempt,

> Theigh ich and al my kyn, upon a stownde,
> Shulle in a strete as dogges liggen dede.[79]

The lover takes exception to the proposal as he did to the alternative suggestion before it that he console himself with a new mistress. Having observed of the earlier one that it was incompatible with his friend's persistence in an unrequited love, he asked ironically,

> O, where hastow ben hid so longe in muwe,
> That kanst so wel and formaly arguwe? [80]

In their very first conference, Pandarus had referred to this love, admitting failure therein while asserting utility to the prince in his:

> I have no cause, I woot wel, for to sore
> As doth an hauk that listeth for to pleye;
> But to thin help yet somwhat kan I seye.[81]

An essential function of his—with which we may end the section—was to cope with those ignoble but troublesome species, the gossips. As already noted, he took precautions against every magpie and every other "lette-game" before inviting Criseyde to his house. Having agreed to come, she pled with him, as the narrator tells us, to beware of "goosish poeples speche." [82] He, in turn, would not have her call an attendant, as she thought of doing when he entered her closet, on the proverbial ground,

> It is nought good a slepyng hound to wake.[83]

Taking our leave of associations with quadrupeds, birds, snakes, and insects, we can proceed to the many in the *Filostrato* and *Troilus* with insentient nature—with the living botanical creation and its lifeless complements on earth and in the heavens, with the phenomena of sunshine, starshine, or whatever luminance, and of any darkness or foul weather.

332

Insentient Nature

FIGURES of heat or cold, unless they are drawn from the out-of-doors, will be left for the next section. All other associations in the poems with phenomena not in the human or animal spheres or not peculiar to them are to be treated here, and all with plants or inorganic constituents of nature.

In the *Filostrato*, such metaphors and similes oppose heroine and hero as attractive sought and anguished seeker, but not as soft female and hardy male; do as much, though less often, for the narrator's lady and himself; twice advertise the fickleness of womankind; and are used in several contexts to express divine influence or potential. These applications may be viewed in reverse order.

Troiolo, as Pandaro reports him, confessed his soul vanquished by the "flashing radiance" of Amore.[1] About to write his first letter, he prayed the god to make the effort "fruitful."[2] He declared in his song to Venere that beneficent influence "rains" from her sphere and that she is the cause of the "fruit" of friendships and, in it, blessed God for having put enough "light" in his discernment to fix on Criseida.[3] The narrator, having attributed the exchange to Fortuna, calls it "the lofty thunderbolt," when he reaches Troiolo's swoon in the parliament.[4]

Parallel figures support the expressions of antifeminist doctrine which bracket the story. Just before his enamorment, Troiolo declared that the female heart turns a thousand times a day "as the leaf turns in the wind," and the author, in his caveat at the end against the young woman as a species, calls her "turning always as a leaf in the wind."[5]

At the beginning, middle, and end of his poem, Boccaccio addresses Maria as his guiding light—in the first and last cases, specifically as the star by

333

which he steers his course. In his opening appeal for her guidance, he declares her to be "the clear and beautiful light" by which he lives in the "tenebrous" world and also "the lodestar" which he follows to come to "harbor," and then, shifting his nautical imagery, he calls her "anchor of safety."[6] Undertaking Part III, he addresses her as the "bright light" whose "ray" has thus far guided him, and pronounces it fitting that her "light," redoubled, should now guide him.[7] In his short Part IX, which is a valedictory to the poem, he conceives of his work and himself as shipmates directed by their common "star." They have come to the port which they have been seeking among reefs and on the high seas, ever following through breeze and storm the light of that star which improves his every thought. Anchors are to be cast and such thanks as are due from the grateful pilgrim are to be rendered to their guide, and garlands and other honors to be placed on the ship of their loves.[8]

Criseida, whom Troiolo hoped "the nettle of love" might prick as it did him,[9] is associated with the rose both in her normal loveliness and when blushing, with stone and ice for exemption from feeling, with a fountain for her tears, and—oftenest—with light for charm or resultant sway. The narrator informs us that she surpassed other women in beauty "as much as the rose the violet"; that, hearing of her admirer from Pandaro, she colored and looked like a "morning rose"; and that, after separation from the prince, she was apostrophized by him a thousand times and more as "thorn rose."[10] Alluding to her beauty by paraleipsis, Troiolo told Cassandra that he would not speak of it though universally judged supreme, "because the fallen flower is soon brown."[11] When freshly smitten, he had lamented Criseida's ignorance of his plight as follows:

> Ma quella per cui piangi nulla sente
> se non come una pietra, e cosí stassi
> fredda com' al sereno intero ghiaccio,
> ed io qual neve al foco mi disfaccio.[12]

Subsequently melted, she "made a bitter fountain of her eyes" during the first days in camp.[13] "As the air is colored by the morning," so she became upon Pandaro's first demands.[14] At several junctures, Troiolo called her clear, sweet, and divine "light," and he imagined her house to have been "luminous" while she was in it but as "dark" afterwards.[15] The confidant imaged her and Troiolo in recommended union as "the star joined with the sun," yet fancied that she, the dimmer luminary, was inflaming his friend with the "splendor" of her countenance.[16] At consummation, Troiolo assured the lady that "the star" of her "splendid and lucent face" had been always before him; on their last night, addressed her as a "bright star" by which he proceeded to "harbor"; and apostrophized her absent as "fair light" and "morning star."[17] He had believed her words, he said after the boar dream, to be a truth more certain and open than "the light of the sun."[18]

While few of the nature images applied to Criseida, as we have seen, express response to love, nearly all bearing on Troiolo perform that function. Of the half dozen floral similes for him, but one conveys his drawing power—the lady's estimate that he was "fresher than garden lily."[19] The others concern recovery from, or lapse into, depression. Should she favor his as yet undisclosed passion, he would become, he anticipated, "like a flower in a meadow quick in springtime."[20] According to the narrator, he responded to one assurance of success from Pandaro as flowerets to the morning sun:

> Quali i fioretti dal notturno gelo
> chinati e chiusi, poi che 'l sol gl' imbianca,
> tutti s' apron diritti in loro stelo;

and to another as the whole country side—flowering plants included—to the springtime:

> E sí come la nuova primavera,
> di fronde e di fioretti gli arbuscelli,
> ignudi stati in la stagion severa,
> di subito riveste e fagli belli,
> e prati e colli e ciascuna rivera
> riveste d' erbe e di bei fior novelli.[21]

Overcome by the result of the parliament, he is compared to the lily withering after dislodgment by the plow:

> Qual poscia ch' è dall' aratro intaccato
> ne' campi il giglio, per soverchio sole
> casca ed appassa, e 'l bel color cangiato
> pallido fassi.[22]

"Never was rose as fair in sweet springtime," he told Pandaro after her going, as he was disposed to become upon her return.[23] These similes, more elaborate as well as more numerous than the floral images for Criseida, make him appear at least as exquisite as she—too prettily adolescent to be full man, that martial one he is reputed.

As already quoted, he likened his unapproached beloved to ice safely frozen, but himself to snow wasting in fire. His eyes streaming for her imminent loss seemed "two fountains," Boccaccio tells us, "which poured out water in abundance"; and the weeper spoke of them after her departure as turned to "rivers."[24]

His friend, as noted above, saw him as "the sun" and Criseida as "the star"; she spoke of his "royal splendor"; and the narrator of "the lucid splendor" which he held in store for the royal throne.[25] He, however, depended on her light for guidance, as we have observed. Before she had been solicited, he wished that he might come to the "port" of death and feared, after she had been, that he might die ere he reached the "port" of love.[26] Utterly lost without Criseida, he deluded himself with hope of her return from exile, moving Pandarus to the ironical reflection that he was expecting a wind from Etna,

> Di Mongibello
> aspetta il vento questo tapinello,[27]

a quarter from which in Naples—if not in Troy—it never blew.

No significant image in the pattern under study is applied to the confidant,[28] and not one to Diomede.

Chaucer adapts a few of the figures we have been considering, replaces several with quite different ones, passes over the others without replacement, and introduces many of his own. He applies a meaningful simile to the rival; and another—four times repeated—and several metaphors to Pandarus. Resorting to more varied images than Boccaccio for the protagonist, he keeps the stress upon his emotionalism but reduces the implication of a delicacy almost feminine by dispensing with flower similes which convey this in the source. Conversely, in elaboration of the figurative presentment of the heroine, he brings out more womanliness of feeling than his author while preserving the latter's emphasis upon her charm for man. He presents himself, like Boccaccio, as in darkness and on stormy seas, but as poet only not as poet and lover. Nature metaphors unarrestingly applied in the *Filostrato* to divine things he does not borrow, and introduces but one —Criseyde's fancy that tears must "reyne" from heaven for her woe.[29] He uses a good many figures, on the other hand, to enforce abstractions about love or life in general, whereas Boccaccio thus applied but two, the similes of leaf in the wind for woman's inconstancy.

These clinchers of truth or alleged truth are all pertinent to immediate circumstance, however freely they may extrapolate from it; and all, in character for the several speakers. The confidant's are directed more to mind, by and large, than to feeling; and the narrator's and the lady's, not less to the former than to the latter. Occurring, if unevenly, in each book of the *Troilus*, they sustain a complement of thought to the emotional story more extensive and diverse than it was given in the *Filostrato*. They suggest that the experience of Trojan individuals is common, making us reflect that we

336

too undergo seasons and weathers of emotion, live much in the dark, and may wither or be uprooted if an affection to which we bend is disappointed.

In Book I, Chaucer, having conjured the wise, proud, and worthy to learn form his hero's overthrow not to scorn Love, reasons with them that

> The yerde is bet that bowen wole and wynde
> Than that that brest.[30]

The victim, he relates, kept in mind that love, publicized,

> Yelt bittre fruyt, though swete seed be sowe.[31]

Pandarus adduces the fact that "whit" is set off by "blak"[32] to support his claim that he understands love's joy from acquaintance with its sorrow and hence is qualified to counsel Troilus. Exercising this function, he declares to the mournful neophyte that a suitor should "evere in oon be fressh and grene,"[33] even if courtship should go unrewarded for twenty years. He exhorts him to hope that she who causes his woe may become his comfort and supports the counsel with analogy upon analogy:

> For thilke grownd that bereth the wedes wikke
> Bereth ek thise holsom herbes, as ful ofte
> Next the foule netle, rough and thikke,
> The rose waxeth swoote and smothe and softe;
> And next the valeye is the hil o-lofte;
> . And next the derke nyght the glade morwe;
> And also joie is next the fyn of sorwe.[34]

And he employs another to warn him against philandering:

> Ek wostow how it fareth of som servise,
> As plaunte a tree or herbe, in sondry wyse,
> And on the morwe pulle it up as blyve!
> No wonder is, though it may nevere thryve.[35]

To prepare us for the men's course with the lady in Book II, Chaucer observes in its Prohemium:

> For every wight which that to Rome went
> Halt nat o path, or alwey o manere.[36]

Criseyde, whose uncertainty about the newly offered amour he likens to the variable weather of March, herself generalizes:

> For love is yet the mooste stormy lyf,
> Right of hymself, that evere was bigonne;
> For evere som mystrust or nice strif
> Ther is in love, som cloude is over that sonne.[37]

337

Pandarus, hypothecating a question in the lover's mind as to how it profits him for her to bend as long as she stays rooted, has an axiom ready in like figurative idiom:

> Thenk here-ayeins: whan that the stordy ook,
> On which men hakketh ofte, for the nones,
> Receyved hath the happy fallyng strook,
> The greete sweigh doth it come al at ones,
> As don thise rokkes or thise milnestones;
> For swifter cours comth thyng that is of wighte,
> Whan it descendeth, than don thynges lighte.
>
> And reed that boweth down for every blast,
> Ful lightly, cesse wynd, it wol aryse;
> But so nyl nought an ook, whan it is cast.[38]

Delay is unwise he argues to his niece, for in it

> The folk devyne at waggyng of a stree.[39]

Distressed in Book III by the uncle's fiction that Troilus suspects her, Criseyde laments mankind's unhappy dilemma of either realizing that joy is transitory or weltering in the "derknesse" of ignorance.[40] Chaucer, however, anticipates that God will remedy the distress caused by the lie and justifies his forecast proverbially:

> For I have seyn, of a ful misty morwe
> Folowen ful ofte a myrie someris day;
> And after wynter foloweth grene May.
> Men sen alday, and reden ek in stories,
> That after sharpe shoures ben victories.[41]

In Book IV, he finds Roman wisdom confirmed by the folly in the Trojans of demanding the redemption of Antenor soon to betray them:

> O Juvenal, lord! trewe is thy sentence,
> That litel wyten folk what is to yerne
> That they ne fynde in hire desir offence;
> For cloude of errour lat hem nat discerne
> What best is.[42]

To be bereft of a lady through his countrymen's misjudgment, Troilus is advised by his friend to seek another, on the ground that a new interest expels the old as surely "as day comth after nyght."[43] The heroine, at this crisis, soliloquizes to contrary effect:

> How sholde a plaunte or lyves creature
> Lyve withouten his kynde noriture?
> For which ful ofte a by-word here I seye,
> That "rooteles moot grene soone deye."[44]

Chaucer, moralizing in the Epilog against temporal preoccupations, bids the young disprize

This world, that passeth soone as floures faire.[45]

From this last instance of imagery enforcing generalization, we have now to turn to the many of its application to individuals—to the narrator, Criseyde, Troilus, confidant, and rival.

Pretending to no star such as Maria to guide him, our author confesses at the outset that he is far from Love's help "in derknesse." [46] And in the Prohemium of Book II, he images his psyche as afloat on waves stirred up by love, indeed, but by Troilus' not his own:

> Owt of thise blake wawes for to saylle,
> O wynd, o wynd, the weder gynneth clere;
> For in this see the boot hath swych travaylle,
> Of my connyng, that unneth I it steere.
> This see clepe I the tempestous matere
> Of disespeir that Troilus was inne;
> But now of hope the kalendes bygynne.[47]

As in the *Filostrato,* the dominant image of the heroine is that of light, with significations of beauty and influence. When it is specifically starlight, it may be coupled with that of dependent navigator for the hero as in the source. Figures of clouding, clearing, and shower are introduced to express emotional responsiveness on her part, while that of ice for noninvolvement is taken over in adapted form. She is held the fount of her lover's joy and sorrow; and, as in the *Filostrato,* her eyes are hyperbolized into gushing springs. Botanical imagery, more frequent and diverse than that applied to her there, is as suggestive of compelling pulchritude and more so of sensitivity.

As for the botanical. The narrator tells us that Criseyde became "al rosy hewed" when her uncle adverted to Troilus' first letter and that she "wex as red as rose" when she saw the writer beneath her window.[48] Diomede refers to her as "swich a flour," and Troilus addresses her in his last missive as "Right fresshe flour." [49] Elsewhere, the Trojan calls her the "crop and roote" of beauty and the "welle and roote" of his weal or woe, and the author refers to her as the "crop and more" of all the desire or joys of his hero.[50] He expresses the wish apropos of her seeing the prince ride by for the second time,

> To God hope I, she hath now kaught a thorn,
> She shal nat pulle it out this nexte wyke.
> God sende mo swich thornes on to pike! [51]

Pandarus later indicates that the hope is as yet not fully realized by his already mentioned conjecture of this question in her suitor's mind:

> So reulith hire hir hertes gost withinne,
> That though she bende, yeet she stant on roote;
> What in effect is this unto my boote? [52]

He dismisses his niece's offer, made in his own house, of a ring to give Troilus with an impatient "ye, haselwodes shaken!" [53] Chaucer records that, when taken in arms there by the suitor,

> Right as an aspes leef she gan to quake,

and yet that she soon reciprocated his embraces:

> And as aboute a tree, with many a twiste,
> Bytrent and writh the swote wodebynde,
> Gan ech of hem in armes other wynde. [54]

Asked by Troilus to flee with him, she demands consideration for her repute, which "floureth yet." [55] Chaucer says of her equivocation with Diomede ten days afterward that she spoke as one who had so fixed her heart on his predecessor "that ther may it non arace" [56]—a puzzling statement since it neither squares with her words nor seems ironical.

Apropos of her ignorance of his newborn love, Troilus is made to say,

> But also cold in love towardes the
> Thi lady is, as frost in wynter moone,
> And thow fordon, as snow in fire is soone—

this in adaptation of Troiolo, with the simile of ice for the heroine changed to one of frost, and that for her of an unfeeling stone omitted. [57] Meditating on love disclosed, she sat in her closet, Chaucer tells us, "as stylle as any ston." [58]

Troilus is minded to call her the "welle" of his woe and, again, of his weal and woe, [59] and, as noted above, the "welle and roote" of these opposites. According to our poet, the "welle" of her tears and of the lover's began to "ebben" in their last assignation [60] after most plentiful discharge.

Her momentary shift from hope to fear of friendship with the hero Chaucer marks by a new and lovely stanza:

> But right as when the sonne shyneth brighte
> In March, that chaungeth ofte tyme his face,
> And that a cloude is put with wynd to flighte,
> Which oversprat the sonne as for a space,
> A cloudy thought gan thorough hire soule pace,
> That overspradde hire brighte thoughtes alle,
> So that for feere almost she gan to falle. [61]

He then gives us this "cloudy thought," which includes the already cited generalization that love is "the mooste stormy lyf," wherein "som cloude is over that sonne," and marks the end of the stream of consciousness with another figure of the weather,

> And after that, hire thought gan for to clere.[62]

Reverting at exchange time to this vernal concept of the heroine, he writes that her tears

> Down fille, as shour in Aperil ful swithe.[63]

The words which she and Troilus exchanged then, however,

> Delited hem, and made hire hertes cleere.[64]

Several metaphors of light bear expressly upon the lady's blondness, whereas none in the source more than implies this literally much stressed attribute. Chaucer speaks of her "snowisshe throte," of her hair "that sonnyssh was of hewe," and of the great tresses of her "sonnysshe heeris." [65] For Boccaccio's figure of her supremacy over other ladies in beauty as of rose over violet, our poet substitutes the primacy of the letter A and reinforces this alphabetic figure with the wonderfully because simply effective stellar image,

> Nas nevere yet seyn thyng to ben preysed derre,
> Nor under cloude blak so bright a sterre.[66]

The latter establishes at the very beginning a striking contrast between her fairness and her widow's blacks, a contrast which Boccaccio does not exploit figuratively. And it prepares for the thematic opposition between the light to his spirit, that, for better or worse, she was, and the darkness which the world seemed to him to be without her.

The night after she had left Troy, he wondered who was then viewing his "righte lode-sterre," and in the letter written after some two months he calls her both his "righte lode-sterre" and his "hertes day." [67] The song which he is given to while away the fateful ten days is all one metaphor of dependence upon her beams:

> O sterre, of which I lost have al the light,
> With herte soor wel oughte I to biwaille,
> That evere derk in torment, nyght by nyght,
> Toward my deth with wynd in steere I saille;
> For which the tenthe nyght, if that I faille
> The gydyng of thi bemes bright an houre,
> My ship and me Caribdis wol devoure.[68]

And the expansion for him of Troiolo's apostrophe to her deserted house is powerful in tribute to her luminous aura:

> O thow lanterne of which queynt is the light,
> O, paleys, whilom day, that now art nyght,
>
> O paleis, whilom crowne of houses alle,
> Enlumyned with sonne of alle blisse.[69]

As for the nature figures applied to Troilus, several concern his standing as man and prince and express it a little more precisely than the image of Troiolo as the sun and the two mentions of his splendor did the latter's. Most for him, however, as most for Boccaccio's hero, project dependence upon the heroine or some consequent emotion. The intensity and anguish of love, striking enough in Troiolo's case, are made rather more so in that of Troilus. His inner life, as it is figured, contrasts sharply with Criseyde's, as hers is. She, the aspen leaf momentarily fluttered by the embrace of her lover; he, the tree made bare by wintry blast of harsh adversity. Her emotional uncertainties, like the mild changes of spring weather; his compulsive progress in love, like a mariner's course, storm beset and in a darkness only uncertainly relieved by the light of a single star.

Conceptualization of the hero as flower is all but eliminated. The simile of morning revival of "fioretti" used for joy of his at good news is indeed taken over and without much change:

> But right as floures, thorugh the cold of nyght
> Iclosed, stoupen on hire stalke lowe,
> Redressen hem ayein the sonne bright,
> And spreden on hire kynde cours by rowe.[70]

That of the vernal quickening of the whole countryside used for such joy is taken over too, yet without the "fioretti" and "bei fior novelli" mentioned in it:

> But right so as thise holtes and thise hayis,
> That han in wynter dede ben and dreye,
> Revesten hem in grene, when that May is,
> Whan every lusty liketh best to pleye.[71]

Of his own anticipations in the *Filostrato* that he might become like a flower in spring and like a rose in it, the first is left out and the second replaced by the hope that he may become like a bird in that season.[72] Criseida's pronouncement that he was fresh as garden lily is dropped; and, with the omission of the swoon in parliament, the simile of the withering of lily applied to it by the narrator is naturally dropped too. Thus five of the six

342

instances of association of the hero with flowers are eliminated; and none is added.

Botanical figures for him which Chaucer does add are free of the implication of adolescence given by Boccaccio's. They point up the joy of love, the sorrow in it and the delusive folly, in styles from the prosy level of the proverbial phrase to the exalted one of Dantean rhetoric. Troilus' desire, says Chaucer, was increased by a letter Criseyde sent him "as an ook comth of a litel spir." [73] He likens their first embracements, as we have seen, to the entwining of tree by woodbine, while the contretemps preceding these made her pray Jove to "arace" jealousy from the lover's heart and Pandarus to beg:

> Yee, nece, wol ye pullen out the thorn
> That stiketh in his herte. [74]

Instead of Boccaccio's lily figure for the hero's weakness in the parliament, Chaucer elects to give us a stark one taken from the *Inferno* for prostration manfully postponed to solitude:

> And as in wynter leves ben biraft,
> Ech after other, til the tree be bare,
> So that ther nys but bark and braunche ilaft,
> Lith Troilus, byraft of ech welfare,
> Ibounden in the blake bark of care. [75]

Pandarus thinks, "Ye, haselwode!" when his friend hoped to find Criseyde back in Troy before the appointed tenth day; and, when the lover on that day still expects her, the go-between observes *sotto voce:*

> From haselwode, there joly Robyn pleyde,
> Shal come al that that thou abidest heere.
> Ye, fare wel al the snow of ferne yere! [76]

And the narrator confirms these ironic asides, when he writes after chronicling her defection:

> But Troilus, thow maist now, est or west,
> Pipe in an ivy lef, if that the lest! [77]

Emotion precludes help for the bereft one, as he himself implies after the parliament. Pandarus, he says, must turn him to a "ston" before his sorrow can be allayed. [78]

He is one who melts and freezes in grief and whose eyes are abundant fountains. Like Troiolo, as we have seen, he complained, as undeclared suitor, that he was wasting "as snow in fire is soone" while his lady must remain obliviously chilly. About to lose her, he burst into tears when joined by Pandarus—in Chaucer's phrase,

Gan as the snow ayeyn the sonne melt.[79]

He had been weeping copiously before the friend arrived as our poet impresses upon us with this extravagancy from Boccaccio,

> His eyen two, for piete of herte,
> Out stremeden as swifte welles tweye.[80]

And, according to Chaucer, he "byreyned" her bosom with salt drops when he thought her dead.[81] Inexhaustibly lachrymose, he can write her, months later, of tears which "reyne" from him and declare,

> Myn eyen two, in veyn with which I se,
> Of sorwful teris salte arn woxen welles.[82]

Passing her house in the meantime, his heart turned cold "As frost." [83]

Despite the emotional abandon thus imaged—and signalized further by his threat to kill himself, were Criseyde truant, "also soth as sonne uprist o-morwe" [84]—he is attested properly secretive about his love. Chaucer says of him in the courtship period:

> From every wight as fer as is the cloude
> He was, so wel dissimulen he koude.[85]

According to the poet, he was—next to Ector—"of worthynesse welle," and Criseyde addresses him in her letter as "sours of gentilesse." [86] Deiphebus and others lauded him, the narrator says, as people are wont to exalt a man whom they are praising

> A thousand fold yet heigher than the sonne.[87]

And Criseyde speaks of his honor, "which that now shyneth so clere," at the time when he would compromise it by flight.[88]

He is much beset by the elements, it is fancied, and usually by them on the sea. In his first song, the one borrowed for him from Petrarch to voice the contrarieties of love, he laments:

> Thus possed to and fro,
> Al stereles withinne a boot am I
> Amydde the see, bitwixen wyndes two,
> That in contrarie stonden evere mo.[89]

A little later, he wishes, like Troiolo, for death's haven:

> God wold I were aryved in the port
> Of deth, to which my sorwe wol me lede;

and, presently thereafter, he confides to Pandarus that Love is so oppressive

That streight unto the deth myn herte sailleth.[90]

The confidant gives the assurance, "to good port hastow rowed,"[91] but communicates his own optimism thereby rather than any purposive activity in Troilus. As quoted above, the narrator in the Prohemium to Book II imagines himself to be sailing "Owt of thise blake wawes," and glosses the "see" on which they roll as the "tempestous" subject of the lover's despair. Late in the book, he tells us that Pandarus found his lord abed between hope and "derk disesperaunce."[92] Troilus, in his last song, that of one stanza previously quoted, envisions himself, bereft of the light of his star, to be sailing "evere derk in torment, nyght by nyght" toward his death.

Contrariwise, the rival, from the one figure applied to him, seems to flourish without encouragement:

> This Diomede, as fressh as braunche in May,
> Com to the tente, ther as Calkas lay.[93]

Pandarus, of craft, humor, and sympathy compact, is welcomed by Criseyde to her house with a gay

> What manere wyndes gydeth yow now here?

and reproached by her—not too harshly—at his own for effective contrivance despite his "wordes white."[94] Her sorrow for the exchange so moves him that he cannot keep

> The teeris from his eighen for to reyne.[95]

The narrator tells us that the confidant proceeded to Troilus "as stille as any ston" after delicate negotiation with Criseyde; that he seated himself "stille as stoon" beside the hero hidden in the little stew; that he approached Troilus' bed on the day of the parliament "as stille as ston"; and that, shamed by his niece's defection and sorry for his friend's sorrow, he stood in the lover's presence "As stille as ston."[96] For all his bounce and garrulousness, we are thus assured, he could be quiet when he should—for the sake of concealment as in the first passage, through realization of the importance of a step about to be taken as in the second, and out of tact and right sentiment as in the other two.

In the next section, we are to observe how this considerate stone, his friend, his niece, and the rival are figured in terms of heat and cold after we have seen how their originals were in the *Filostrato*.

Fire and Heat and Cold

THIS last pattern is perhaps the most affective of the seven distinguished in the *Filostrato*, though it has a smaller total of figures than either the pattern of dominion and service or that of bodily existence. In it, metaphorical kindling and maintenance of fire preponderate over metaphorical assuaging or extinction of it; intense heat, over all lower temperatures. Troiolo, ignited by his lady and the love god, finds no surcease in possession or in lasting divorce but is consumed by an ever stronger flame. She too burns, if only for a time; even Diomede is set on fire; and the lovelorn Pandaro claims to have flames in hand with which to kindle passion. Love, we gather, is a strenuous excitement, for man or woman, and, even when welcomed, never much below the threshold of pain.

It is, however, not the same for heroine and hero. Troiolo, in whom love has waxed hotter with enjoyment, proposes flight as an alternative to the exchange and, after the latter is effected, complains of intensification of the amorous fire. Criseida argues that an elopement would quench their torch through propinquity, and cools all too soon when apart from him. She is inflamed by sorrow only at the peripeteia; he before, as well as after it. The reader is made to feel that she is blameworthy for lack of torment, not he for excess of it. Possession by emotional fires, though obviously his misfortune, does not appear a flaw, either tragic or comic, but rather the laudable evidence of true love.

As for Diomede and Pandaro, the two figures of the pattern which are applied to the rival do not distinguish him from Troiolo, but the several employed by the confidant manifest a cynicism of which the enamored prince is innocent.

346

Life expectancy Criseida terms "the path . . . given by celestial fire." [1]
This periphrasis, though it occurs in *carpe diem* argument, brings the
concept of fire to its ultimate extension, dignifying the element as the source
of being.

On the pagan level of divinity, fire is exalted as an attribute of both the
warlike Amore and his gentle mother. As noted in Section 3, he is represented
to have wounded Troiolo, and Criseida as well. She once credits the love god
with "fiery darts." [2] And the prince acknowledges conquest by his "lightning." [3] Without specification of instrument, the hero informs Pandaro that
Amore "kindles" his heart and later blesses him for having done this. [4] According to the confidant, he dared the god to kindle his flames under
Criseida's mantle:

> Dubiti tu sotto la bruna vesta
> d'accender le tue fiamme, signor mio? [5]

In the hymn to Venere, Troiolo asserts that she makes everyone courteous
who is touched by her fire,

> che del tuo foco alquanto è infiammato,

and he prays that she will prolong, hide, and govern his "ardor" and that
of his mistress. [6] He looks, then, to the goddess to control such heat as she
creates, a kindly office which he does not expect from her violent son.

Troiolo's hope for the inflaming of Criseida which appears in his challenge to the son is soon and fully realized. And her course bears out the
dicta of Pandaro that every woman is amorously inclined and feels little
burning anguish when possessed. [7] Although she does not complain of the
heat of love as often as Troiolo, her thoughts about it are, if anything, more
frankly sensual. Assured by his first letter, she reasons that she should
quench her nascent fire through surrender:

> A spegner questo foco
> conviene a me trovare e tempo e loco.

> Ché s' io il lascio in troppo grande arsura
> multiplicare, el potrebbe avvenire
> che nella scolorita mia figura
> si vederebbe il nascoso disire. [8]

In her reply to the letter, she informs Troiolo that he can have her a
thousand times over, if "cruel fire" does not "burn" her[9]—presumably the
fire of her passion. According to Boccaccio's report, the union which she
desired proved to be an experience of delight no less fiery for her than for
the lover. Before mounting to the bedchamber, he tells us, they embraced
with "ardent" joy and kissed as those "who burned with equal fire." [10]

Couched, they embraced one another with "fervor"; often interrupted their subsequent discourse with "fervent" kissing; and at cockcrow, when desire of embracing "was refired," were reluctant to part because more than ever "inflamed" by love.[11] Troiolo, while still abed, expressed hope for another rendezvous to temper their mutual "fire."[12] During their last one, Criseida speaks of the torch which kindles them, but as to be extinguished if they were to elope and live always together:

> ma se tu m' averai liberamente,
> tosto si spegnerá l' ardente face
> che or t' accende, e me similemente.[13]

After she has thus adduced the old pessimistic tenet that ease of access destroys love, she begs him not to increase with his grief the sorrow which "too fiery" affection has put in her mind.[14] Months later, he is to appeal for her return to Troy by that sweetness which "kindled" their hearts in equal measure.[15]

Beside these images of heat for Criseida's amorous desire, there are two for the suspiration which love causes her. The confidant tells Troiolo that her sighs for threatened separation are so "burning" that they exceed the lover's, and, after she has gone, the prince remembers a sigh of hers "of unusual fire."[16]

Of the four of cold which apply to the lady, two figure her resistance to passion without in the least confirming it; the others represent her infidelity, which needs no confirmation. As remarked in the preceding section, Troiolo once supposed her to be "cold as ice beneath a clear sky,"[17] and, at the time, reasonably enough since she did not yet know of his affection. When informed of it, she avers to Pandaro in one stanza that her blood "turns to ice,"[18] but in the very next that she is disposed to be compliant. As just noted, she would quench her flames, not by chaste restraint, but by surrender and fears indulgence only insofar as it may quench the delightful torch by excess of pleasure. According to the narrator, the attractions of Diomede soon made her cool about returning:

> Queste la fêr raffredar nel pensiero
> caldo ch' avea pur di voler reddire.[19]

Whether she burned for the second lover as for the first, Boccaccio does not reveal. But since she yielded herself, it was not mere "lukewarmness," as Pandaro would have the lover believe, that was keeping her in the Greek camp.[20]

Congruent with the notion that Criseida is herself aflame is the even more frequently recurring one that she sets Troiolo on fire. In one instance, the idea that she inflames is explicitly associated with the equally conventional one that she wounds with missiles, Troiolo declaring on the night of union that her eyes have put "fiery darts of love" in his heart, darts with which he is all ablaze.[21] The other images of her kindling of the lover may be considered in textual order and, along with them, the complementary figures of alleviation sought from her. The latter are all contradicted by experience, for enjoyment of her favors does not mitigate his burning as he anticipated but steadily increases it.

The narrator holds that Troiolo was on fire after the festival and that he quickened the blaze by attempted assuagement of it through contemplation of the lady. Having observed that "the ardent amorous flames" did not spare the prince's greatness, he ironizes the ventured remedy as follows:

> ma quale
> in disposta materia secca o mezza
> s'accende il foco, tal nel novo amante
> messe le parti acceser tutte quante.
>
> Tanto di giorno in giorno col pensiero,
> e col piacer di quello or preparava
> piú l' esca secca dentro al core altiero,
> e da' belli occhi trarre immaginava
> acqua soave al suo ardor severo;
> per che astutamente gli cercava
> sovente di veder, né s' avvedea
> che piú da quegli il foco s' accendea.[22]

In a four-stanza lament, Troiolo dwells on the heat contracted from her. He begins with the observations that now she has taken possession of his life, he expects to die of the "fervent" desire wherein he blazes and burns; that sight of her, which should suffice his "inflamed" desires, does not at all, and that his "ardors" are so ungoverned that one would not believe how much his increasing "flame" torments him.[23] Proceeding to address Criseida in absentia, he declares that she is the only one who can allay his fire, yet terms her the flamelet of his heart:

> tu sei quella
> che sola puoi il mio foco attutare,
> o dolce luce e del mio cor fiammella.[24]

He concludes by asking Pandaro if the latter, who sees him "burn in such a fire," can be indifferent to his plight.[25] The friend responds with the proposal of a letter of declaration, and the prince acceding writes, in part, that a "fire" is born of thoughts of her which constantly torments him—an "ardor" with which he feels himself to be consumed little by little.[26]

Analyzing his feelings after consummation for Pandaro's benefit, the hero observes that the fire which he has caught from the eyes and face of his mistress now burns him much more than formerly,

> e vie piú che l' antico
> ora mi coce il foco, che tratto aggio
> degli occhi di Criseida e del visaggio,

and then goes on to say, not only that he burns more than ever, but also that the "fire" which he presently experiences is of a new quality.[27] With his mistress for the second night, he declares that he cannot express the sweetness and "fiery" delight which she has put in his bosom; that he does not believe as formerly that Jove can alleviate his "fire" even after many conjugations; and that she has thrown upon it "the water of the smith" so that it "burns" more than ever.[28] In his hymn to Venere, he pronounces benediction upon a number of things, among them the "fervent" sighs which he has already heaved on Criseida's account and the "fiery" desires drawn from her supremely beautiful aspect, as well as upon God who produced her and gave him such discrimination as to become enkindled for this marvel of creation.[29]

Troiolo's most vivid statement of her incendiary power comes in his rejection of Pandaro's advice to take a new mistress. Sparks passing from her eyes through his, he declares, lit that fire in his heart productive of every virtue and never to be extinguished:

> Da' suoi begli occhi mosser le faville
> che del foco amoroso m' infiammaro;
> queste pe' miei passando a mille a mille,
> soavemente amor seco menaro
> dentro dal cor, nel quale esso sortille
> come gli piacque, e quivi incominciaro
> primiere, il foco, il cui sommo fervore
> cagione è stato d' ogni mio valore.
>
> Il qual perch' io volessi, che non voglio,
> spegner non potrei mai.[30]

Shortly after her departure, the lover recalls how she once "enkindled" his heart with a sigh "of unusual fire" and later writes her that merely hearing about the place where she now lives or seeing someone who comes from there "rekindles the fire" in that organ.[31]

The heat of Troiolo's passion, for which Criseida is expressly held responsible in the above contexts and Amore or Venere in several discussed earlier, is attested in others without such specification: in a few already noted in which his fervor and hers are brought out together, and in a good

350

many now to be scanned in which his alone receives attention. Against all these, there are only two which associate his experience with gentle warmth: the similes of revival of flowerets in the morning sun and of the whole countryside in springtime—applied, as has been observed in Section 7, to responses of his to propitious news.[32]

In the ascending action, he who has spoken slightingly of the "fire" of love, no sooner discovers Criseida than he wishes that she might learn of his "hot" desire.[33] Since he is too fearful to reveal it to her, he imagines himself to be wasting like "snow in fire"[34] while she remains, through ignorance, perforce as cold as ice. When Pandaro finally learns the secret, he expresses astonishment that Troiolo has been able to keep such a "fire" so long hidden from him, and promises eventual remedy, cautioning the prince, however, to control his "hot" desire in the meantime.[35] Thus encouraged, the lover "is kindled" still more.[36] Pandaro fulfills his promise so well that Criseida determines to give satisfaction to the "hot" desire of her admirer,[37] but, since she does not immediately carry out her decision, the latter has to go on suffering for a time. Perceiving "the flames kindled" in the hero's bosom by this delay, Pandaro continues to be insistent with her.[38] Upon consummation, Troiolo feels that "love is roasting him more than ever," according to the narrator, and "becomes still more enkindled" by reminiscence of this delight.[39]

In the descending action, prospect of Criseida's exchange makes him wish that he had passed away on the day he was first enkindled.[40] To counter this melancholy, Pandaro declares that, were he as enkindled as the prince, he would take action, and that love is not wont to be scrupulous about means when the enamored mind is burning.[41] Troiolo answers that he would not risk harm to his mistress, even were his flames a thousand times more enkindled.[42] On the night after her departure, he complains to himself that "the amorous flame" is increasing and, on the next day, to Pandaro that "the amorous fire" so envelops him that he cannot rest.[43] When on the way home from Sarpidone's establishment he naively hopes that Criseida may have returned during the period spent there, his friend reflects ironically that the "fiery" wish of the lover will have time enough "to cool."[44] According to the narrator, Troiolo, disappointed in this and later anticipations, comes to give tearful vent to his "fiery" desires, his lamentations being the greater because his torments are now more "burning."[45] In his last-quoted letter, he says that it is his purpose to expose to her his thought, more "fiery" than ever with love, and all his "hot" longing.[46]

The images so far considered for Troiolo's emotional life stress his appetency, though often enough with recognition of accompanying sorrow.[47]

There are some others which emphasize passions caused by amorousness rather than amorousness itself—grief for separation and anger roused by disappointment and jealousy. Boccaccio describes him after the parliament as "enkindled in the sorrowful fire" and his sighs as "more ardent than fire." [48] Troiolo at that time bids death not delay, saying that the mortal stroke will be a cooling relief because the fire has already inflamed every vein:

> deh, non tardar, ché questo foco m' have
> incesa giá sí ciascheduna vena,
> che refrigero il tuo colpo mi fia. [49]

"Enkindled" with lofty disdain, he presumes to reproach Giove and Fortuna for his imminent loss. [50] He gives no respite to his "inflamed" sighs when in talk with Pandaro soon after he has sustained it. [51] Because of his depression when she fails to return, he flees all social pleasure like the "fire." [52] Planning suicide after his dream of the boar, he tells the confidant that he feels a strong "fire newly enkindled" in his mind, and he trembles with this "kindled" rage even after his friend has brought him to a more hopeful frame of mind. [53] Deifobo's mention of war against the hated Greeks makes vigor course again in the "inflamed" heart of Troiolo, and he shortly recovers his strength because of his "ardent" will to show his might against them. [54]

A single and not very evocative figure represents the lover's outward appearance. When he confesses his love to Pandaro, he is said to be "enkindled" with blushes. [55]

The images of cold or cooling for his affections have been cited with figures of heat—to which they are linked without exception. As we have seen, none suggests that the fire of love ever waned in Troiolo. His anticipations of quenching of desire through amorous satisfaction are disappointed. Death, he comes to realize, is the only agent which can cool his fire. Pandaro's ironical reflection that Troiolo's fiery inclination will have ample opportunity to grow cold ere Criseida's return is essentially a prediction of her behavior, although the imagery in it applies to the lover. The nature images of revival after night and winter suggest cold but mildly and that the coldness of wanhope, not of love.

As for Diomede, the two images of the pattern which are applied to him, though inconspicuous, suffice to hint genuine passion. Having stated that the Greek was taken with Criseida at first sight, [56] Boccaccio says that he presently resolved to tell her how he "was first enkindled." [57] And he informs us that the audacious one turned "red as fire" in the course of his declaration. [58]

There is only one image concerning Pandaro. Applied by himself, it

352

defines his function in all frankness. "Let me proceed," he says encouragingly to Troiolo, "because I have the amorous flames in my hands and speeches designed accordingly":

> Lascia far me, ché le fiamme amorose
> ho per le mani e sí fatti sermoni.[59]

And he goes on to claim that he has accomplished greater feats—presumably of seduction—than the one he is now undertaking.

A metaphor in defiance of gossip completes the list. Making a decision, soon abandoned, to steal back to Troy, Criseida says, "Let the smoke go where it pleases":

> e vada dove gire
> ne vuole il fumo.[60]

This is exceptional as a fire metaphor in that it appeals to the visual imagination rather than to memories of heat. The only others to do so are the images for Troiolo's blushing and for Diomede's.

Chaucer freely modifies the last pattern as he does the preceding six, but compresses it in the process instead of enlarging it as all the others. He resorts to fewer images of heat than his author and does not develop as many at length. Though most of his stress desire, proportionally more of them put sorrow before appetite than do those of Boccaccio. Even ones emphasizing sexual passion do not make it seem quite as intense as their like in the *Filostrato*. Pure flame is differentiated from lustful heat as it is not in that poem, and the idea that fiery devotion may be a hazardous virtue is more often and more explicitly suggested. And, whereas in the original there are very few images of cold, there are a good many in the *Troilus,* all of which serve to enforce the trepidation and misery coexistent with hopeful eagerness in love. These trends in adaptation of the pattern affect our concepts of each of the four parties to the affair, while they make it appear, as a whole, less elementally direct and violent.

The heroine is transformed; the hero, changed somewhat. She does not burn with sensuality, and such temperate affections as she has are inhibited to no small extent by fear, caution, and cool rationality. Her effect upon his emotions is but rarely imaged as a kindling of them; being no longer a hot wanton, she can less properly be thought of as incendiary in her charms. His passion remains flamelike, but is less often so termed than in the *Filostrato*. The disparity between their loves is not the same as it was there, though quite as marked and quite as tragically ironic. In the source, her amorous passion, if as intense as his, was not correspondingly sublimated and

353

therefore not as enduring. In the *Troilus,* hers is the feeble love of a divided personality; his, the strong one of a soul in which emotion is unchallenged by dictates of common sense.

The rival is less estimable than before; the confidant, more attractive. Never said to be enkindled for the lady, Diomede appears a false pretender to love. The go-between is less grossly cynical in such metaphor as he employs.

Replacement of an early generalization of the latter's by one not as carnal foreshadows the refining of passion throughout. In the *Filostrato,* he told the lover that every woman is amorous by inclination and, when overcome, not burningly anguished; at the same point in the *Troilus,* he gives his friend as hopeful assurance, but more delicately:

> For this have I herd seyd of wyse lered,
> Was nevere man or woman yet bigete
> That was unapt to suffren loves hete,
> Celestial, or elles love of kynde.[61]

Through this bracketing of earthly with heavenly love he tacitly sublimates the former.

Its acceptability to the All High, not vouched for here, is implied by the narrator when he wishes well to heroine and hero momentarily at odds:

> But now help God to quenchen al this sorwe.[62]

The utterance, however, is empathic, not doctrinal.

As for Cupide and Venus, there is no mention of his kindling potential, and but one of hers. In a stanza of Chaucer's Prohemium to Book III as in the corresponding stanza of Troiolo's song, the goddess is presumed to set her elect "a-fyre." [63] In Troilus' hymn substituted for Troiolo's, the god is asked to master the tepid, but not by flame:

> And hertes colde, hem wolde I that he twiste.[64]

The rejection of all acknowledgments in the source of Love's incendiary might is harmonious with the subordination of the concept of him as missile-thrower to that of feudal lord. Both serve to de-emphasize lawless aggression.

In the *Troilus* a distinction is explicitly made between lust and love which is never stated in the *Filostrato,* although it is latent in the contrasting implications of Criseida's remarks and Troiolo's about their consuming fires. Antigone, when lecturing Criseyde, presumes to say:

> But wene ye that every wrecche woot
> The parfite blisse of love? Why, nay, iwys!
> They wenen al be love, if oon be hoot.[65]

354

The heroine is made another woman by Chaucer's reworking of the imagery which Boccaccio applied to her emotions and to her influence upon the hero. Criseyde never burns with unmixed desire, much less with concupiscence. Sorrow, on the other hand, does inflame her, and more hotly, it appears, than it did Criseida. The cold of fear tends to inhibit such passion as she has, whereas it was satiety that threatened Criseida's and the attractions of another man which effectively cooled her loyalty. Unlike the other, Criseyde disparages the heat of impulse both in herself and in the prince. In short, a rather selfish concern for safety and reputation replaces the egocentricity of sensualism. No longer gross, the heroine now has more of the defects as well as more of the charming qualities of the conventionally restrained and "proper" female of romantic tradition. Having minimized the heat of the lady's own passions, Chaucer very naturally de-emphasizes the idea that she kindles the hero and the complementary one that only she may quench his fire. To have kept them would have suggested a bold sexual attraction in her person quite at variance with the total impression of her soft femininity.

Chaucer is extraordinarily careful never to permit us to think of his heroine as hotly in love. He avoids saying that she burns until he comes to the exchange and then, of course, with sorrowful rather than amorous passion. The most that he ventures up to this point are two tame figures of heat, neither of them suggestive of desire and each paired with a figure of cold. Writing of her alternations between hope and fear of what an affair will bring, he observes:

> Now was hire herte warm, now was it cold,

and

> Than slepeth hope, and after drede awaketh;
> Now hoot, now cold.[66]

If she is inflamed in her happy nights of love with Troilus, the poet does not say so. The analogies of a merry summer's day following a misty morrow and of Maytime succeeding winter,[67] drawn to her passing with him from joy to sorrow, are far from implying heat in either of them. After the tragic reversal, Chaucer can speak of consuming fires in his heroine because love in her is now chastened with grief. Of her feelings when alone after the parliament he writes,

> And thus she brenneth both in love and drede,

and of her mixed emotions when she is offered consolation by female acquaintance,

355

> Such vanyte ne kan don hire non ese,
> As she that al this mene while brende
> Of other passioun than that they wende.⁶⁸

He again images her as inflamed with sorrow when she is alone in the Greek camp:

> And thus she sette hire woful herte afire
> Thorugh remembraunce of that she gan desire.⁶⁹

The one metaphor of heat which she applies to herself occurs in a confession of unreflective hastiness made on her last night with Troilus:

> I am a womman, as ful wel ye woot,
> And as I am avysed sodeynly,
> So wol I telle yow, whil it is hoot.⁷⁰

This self-depreciation is an artful apology for what she is about to do; namely, to presume to take the initiative in planning for the future. By disprizing herself, she forestalls hurt to masculine pride. The fault confessed is one of which she is eminently free, and, if we did not know this already, her ensuing schemes for tricking her father would clearly show it. The humorous tone of the lines quoted makes it plain enough that she distrusts the emotional unreason which she figures as heat. As will later be argued, her commands to Troilus on this night to moderate his hotheadedness are manifestations of the same distrust.

Fear as well as rationality keeps her passion in check. Three new figures of cold which Chaucer applies to her all bring out this timidity—the two already cited of her alternations between hot and cold at the prospect of a liaison; and the statement that she

> Gan sodeynly aboute hire herte colde,

when only obliquely accused of showing favor to Horaste.⁷¹ A fourth, Troilus' early antithesis,

> But also cold in love towardes the
> Thi lady is, as frost in wynter moone,
> And thow fordon, as snow in fire is soone,

serves, however, only to bring out the irony of his being in love with one who does not know of his passion, as did Troiolo's antithesis of ice and snow, from which it is taken.⁷²

The fancies so prominent in the *Filostrato* that the heroine kindled and might quench the fires of love in the hero are reduced to insignificance in the *Troilus*. Only three contexts develop either notion: an original line of Chaucer's, which employs that of kindling; a modification of an elaborate passage of Boccaccio's, with notions of both kindling and quenching preserved, yet with the lady's agency made less specific; and another original passage in which she is expected to quench, but not desire so much as sorrow.

Though Troilus believed himself to be proof against love, says Chaucer,

> Yet with a look his herte wax a-fere.[73]

Here, obviously, the irony is the essential thing rather than sensory definition of Criseyde's effect upon the male.

A little later on, the poet sees fit to adapt a passage in which Boccaccio images the lover's passion as burning, hoped-for alleviation of the fire as quenching by the beloved, and actual increase of it as further kindling by her.[74] The first stanza of the adaptation, as its correspondent in the *Filostrato*, conveys only the idea that the lover burns:

> In hym ne deyned spare blood roial
> The fyr of love, the wherfro God me blesse,
> . . . .
> And brende hym so in soundry wise ay newe,
> That sexti tyme a day he loste his hewe.

Even here there is some change. Left out is the concrete detail that Troiolo caught fire like dry fuel; added are a delicate suggestion of likeness to mystical experience in the phrase "fyr of love" and an implied reservation following it about the desirability of the amorous condition. In his next stanzas, Chaucer tells us plainly that Troilus hoped to put out his flames by resort to Criseyde and achieved the opposite, but he does not realize her for us as quencher or kindler:

> Forthi ful ofte, his hote fir to cesse,
> To sen hire goodly lok he gan to presse;
> For therby to ben esed wel he wende,
> And ay the ner he was, the more he brende.

> For ay the ner the fir, the hotter is,—
> This, trowe I, knoweth al this compaignye.

The homely generalization at the end gives a half-humorous turn to the irony. Boccaccio was all seriousness in the lines parallel to these. And he imaged Criseida vividly as both quenching and kindling agent; as he puts it, Troiolo hoped to draw water from her eyes which would be soothing to his ardor, but, unbeknownst to him, fire was kindled all the more by them.

The new context in which Criseyde is represented as a potential quencher

357

of grief occurs in the dialogue of Pandarus. Having declared that the prince was miserably concerned about Horaste, the confidant says to his niece that he hopes that matters may yet be well, if only she will cooperate,

> For ye may quenche al this, if that yow leste.[75]

As he continues his appeal for her help, he carries on the imagery of extinguishment, but with a general application:

> Nece, alle thyng hath tyme, I dar avowe,
> For whan a chaumbre afire is, or an halle,
> Wel more nede is, it sodeynly rescowe
> Than to dispute and axe amonges alle
> How this candele in the strawe is falle.[76]

This is an argument against any and all delay. Such suggestion as there may be that Troilus' sorrow is fire is distinctly secondary and so also, in consequence, any suggestion that Criseyde's assistance will be a quenching of that emotion.

As Chaucer gives us a new heroine, so also he considerably modifies the interpretation of the hero's experiences through changes in the imagery of heat and cold. He does not, however, create a radically different personality for the lover, though a more refined and complex one. Significantly, he employs far fewer images of heat for the amorous desires of the prince than Boccaccio, while using about as many for the grief and frustration caused by these inclinations. As already observed, he neglects intimations that the heroine was the agent of combustion, and, along with them, such passages as represent her love and his together as fiery. And, as we shall see presently, he passes over some of the contexts in which Troiolo's love was imaged by itself as heat, and without express notice of kindler or quencher. Nevertheless, the figures for that love which Chaucer adapts from the source and the several which he invents are together sufficiently numerous to create a strong impression of fervor in the prince and hence to contrast him with the heroine whose fires have been regularly dampened. Alive to the consequences of such ardency, he exploits the two figures ironical of it in the source, while rejecting a number of those which are not. Depreciations of heat which he puts in the lady's mouth are tenable indictments of the lover for emotionalism as well as manifestations of her selfish rationality and thus support the opposition of character. Images of cold, applied to Troilus more frequently than to Troiolo, all signalize unhappy preoccupation with love. Three of the four applied to Criseyde, as we have seen, bring out concern for security and repute as jeopardized by loving.

Of the figures of heat or cold for his inner life, those which center in desire may now be reviewed and, after them, such as highlight peripheral emotions.

A few in the first and larger category have been treated already. As noted in Section 7, images from the *Filostrato* of flowers reviving with the day and of the countryside with springtime apply to him at two promising moments; and the linked new ones of sunshine after mist and of May after winter, to him and Criseyde jointly at a third transition.[77] However striking, these suggest only the mildest warmth. A fifth, remarked in Section 5, implies burning out in semijocular mood. It is Pandarus' conceit that his friend's love-longing is an "accesse."[78]

The others in the category bear stronger witness to the intensity of Troilus' desire, as will appear from the following survey in textual order.

Like Troiolo, Chaucer's prince is progressively more inflamed from enamorment to consummation. He echoes the former in saying that he is wasting "as snow in fire."[79] In his first song, the one taken from Petrarch, he asks wonderingly about the coexistence of opposites in love:

> And if that at myn owen lust I brenne,
> From whennes cometh my waillynge and my pleynte?

and again,

> Allas! what is this wondre maladie?
> For hete of cold, for cold of hete, I dye.[80]

He is credited by the narrator with pretending other sickness lest men think

> That the hote fir of love hym brende.[81]

As Troiolo complained that Amore inflamed his heart, so Troilus remarks at the same point that desire assails him "brennyngly"; and at a juncture where Boccaccio said that the hero was kindled still more, Chaucer writes that "hotter weex his love."[82] Pandaro reported to Criseida that the lover spoke of his soul as conquered by Love's lightning; Pandarus that Troilus conceived thus picturesquely of his fire:

> This is the werste, I dar me nat bywreyen;
> And wel the hotter ben the gledes rede,
> That men hem wrien with asshen pale and dede.[83]

According to the brief testimony of the narrator in the *Filostrato*, the hero's ardor went on growing after correspondence had been initiated. Our poet elaborates the statement as follows by drawing on a generalization earlier in the source that love often waxes with hope as fire from added fuel:

359

> But as we may alday oureselven see,
> Thorugh more wode or col, the more fir,
> Right so encrees of hope, of what it be,
> Therwith ful ofte encresseth ek desir;
> Or as an ook comth of a litel spir,
> So thorugh this lettre, which that she hym sente,
> Encressen gan desir, of which he brente.[84]

And he has this to say about the lover's assiduity:

> Fro day to day he leet it nought refreyde,
> That by Pandare he wroot somwhat or seyde.[85]

Somewhat later, he conceives of hope, not as fuel for a raging fire, but as a thawing warmth in the lover's heart. Writing of Troilus' response to encouragement from his friend, he says,

> His olde wo, that made his herte swelte,
> Gan tho for joie wasten and tomelte.[86]

He assures us that the suitor kept his pangs hidden, "though as the fir he brende," herein influenced by the French prose translation of Boccaccio's poem.[87]

Having brought Troilus back to his palace from consummation, the narrator remarks that he now prized her more than ever "for whom desir hym brende" and also that "Desir al newe hym brende," in the latter statement following Boccaccio, who said that Troiolo was kindled the more with recollections of the night.[88] When Pandarus comes to his friend in the morning, he employs the homely image of toasting by the fire to define the latter's present happy situation:

> Be naught to rakel, theigh thow sitte warme.[89]

Troilus is as homely in expressing the enhancement of his passion,

> I hadde it nevere half so hote as now,

not conceiting, as Troiolo did, that the fire proceeded from the lady's eyes and countenance.[90]

Reversal of fortune moves Pandarus to take an expediential line but fails to shake the lover's idealism. When with Troilus after the parliament, the monitor advises relinquishment of a love now threatened by separation, using, among others, this argument,

> Swich fir, by proces, shal of kynde colde.[91]

Reproved for his counsel, he urges ravishment and says that if he had it "so hoote" as Troilus, he would resort to action, much as Pandaro declared that

360

he would do so, were he as enkindled as Troiolo.[92] And as the former ironically reflected after the visit that Troiolo's fiery wish for the mistress' return would have more than time enough to cool, so Pandarus thinks at the same juncture:

> God woot, refreyden may this hote fare,
> Er Calkas sende Troilus Criseyde! [93]

According to Chaucer, the lover's heart was alternately "hoot and cold" during this period and especially on the ninth night after her departure[94] but the chill was produced, of course, by doubt as to her return, not by the sensible process of forgetting which Pandarus had recommended.

With our survey now completed of the many figures which stress Troilus' desire above concomitant emotions, we may proceed to a dozen concerned primarily with his sorrow, a pair critical of his impatience, and one which attests his rage.

When about to leave his newly won mistress at dawn, he is said to feel

> The blody teris from his herte melte.[95]

Home from the parliament, he is likened to a tree leaf-stripped in winter, as has been observed in Section 7.[96] He gave vent there, as did Troiolo, to

> A thousand sikes, hotter than the gleede;

and, bursting into tears when Pandarus joined him, he

> Gan as the snow ayeyn the sonne melte.[97]

Like Troiolo, he thought of death as a cooling relief for the distress inspired by the parliament:

> O deth, syn with this sorwe I am a-fyre,
> Thow other do me anoon in teeris drenche,
> Or with thi colde strok myn hete quenche.[98]

These last lines are sharper and more ingenious than their originals; the fire is stated, not merely implied, to come from sorrow, and the stroke not only is cold but also quenches. According to the narrator as quoted in Section 7, he imagined his heart grew cold as frost when he viewed Criseyde's empty palace; and it "gan to colde" again, we are told, at sight of her brooch on Diomede's captured garment.[99] The alliterative phrase "cares colde" is applied to his sorrows twice by himself and four times by the narrator; and the variant "colde care," once by himself.[100]

Though his anguish on the last night with Criseyde was "queynt" with hope she gave him of her return,[101] he challenged her schemes for this and urged flight then and there. In condemning the proposal as bad for his reputation and hers, she twice disparages impetuosity through metaphor:

> Beth naught to hastif in this hoote fare;
> For hastif man ne wanteth nevere care;
>
> And forthi sle with resoun al this hete.[102]

The contrast is extreme between this lady who advises abolishment of heat by reason and her subject, who, as quoted in the preceding paragraph, saw alleviation for it only through dying.

The anger raised in him by discovery of her keepsake on the coat-armor of Diomede is vented against the rival:

> And, God it woot, with many a cruel hete
> Gan Troilus upon his helm to bete.[103]

The Greek seems exempt from love's fevers and chills. Chaucer eliminates the two images of fire which in the original severally vivify Diomede's inward response to Criseida on first sight and his blushing while in talk with her later. Rejection of the second of the two is immaterial since the literal circumstance of blushing is kept, but that of the first, with its implication of genuine enamorment, materially strengthens the opposition between the precipitate new claimant and the steadfast old one.

As for the intermediary, our poet suppresses the boast made by him in the source that he was a flame bearer and had accomplished greater tasks than the prospective seduction,[104] and resorts to some new figures which present him in more reputable light. Though said to have encyclopedic knowledge of "The olde daunce" as noted in Section 4,[105] Pandarus does not appear to be the bawd of at least semiprofessional status which Pandaro implied that he was. Telling us that his worthy was diligent "to quike alwey the fir" in Crisyde's bosom,[106] Chaucer does not go on to say that he had set it in others. The asseveration which he gives Pandarus to utter when about to bed friend with niece,

> So thryve I, this nyght shal I make it weel,
> Or casten al the gruwel in the fire,[107]

is so plain and hearty that we wink at its intent. So far as homely words can disguise laxity in morals, these do it very well. Solicitude for Troilus, the main justification for corruption of the lady, is twice figuratively attested by the narrator. He tells us that in the first talk with his lord, Pandarus nearly "malt" for woe and pity, and that, in the one after the parliament, his heart began to "colden" at sight of the grieving prince.[108]

To conclude this section—and the chapter—we may note three images of miscellaneous application, all of which depend upon visual aspects of fire. Chaucer speaks of "smoky reyn," and says that,

> The noyse of peple up stirte thanne at ones,
> As breme as blase of straw iset on-fire;

and Pandarus generalizes,

> For also seur as reed is every fir,
> As gret a craft is kepe wel as wynne.[109]

Beside these three, Pandarus' already mentioned analogy of conflagration of a building and Troilus' of red coals being made hotter by banking with pale ashes are strongly visual figures. Appeal to the sense of sight is thus a little more frequent in Chaucer's fire imagery than in Boccaccio's.

CHAPTER IV

Composites

Preview

IN the earlier chapters, I have re-examined many aspects of Chaucer's transformation of the *Filostrato,* but with grateful regard for the scholarship devoted to it throughout our century. In this last chapter I shall conflate the data from the others with more, and shall turn again to precedent criticism of the *Troilus* for light on details of adaptation, trends therein, and the combinative effect of trends.

Section 2 of the chapter will contrast the extensive personalization of attitude of the narrator in the *Troilus* toward his audience, and toward the characters and forces operative upon them, with the very scanty personalization in the source. The purposes of the contrasting are to show that Chaucer strove for empathy by advertising it in his own bosom and by associating listener or reader intimately with himself in responses to events; that he tempered it on the earthly level by his irony of manner, his pretended naïveté about courtship and fruition; and that he raised empathy—and dramatic irony—above that plane by attesting a divine order which precluded continuance of the affair as it will sever all mundane attachments sooner or later.

Section 3 will set the presentation of the four main characters in the *Troilus* against that of the corresponding persons in the *Filostrato.* Dealing with Boccaccio's heroine, hero, rival, and confidant in turn, it will assemble literal statements about each and by each which bear expressly upon character, status, or repute and, as pendants to these, will offer digests of material about the person collected in Chapters II and III. Proceeding to Chaucer's Criseyde, Troilus, Diomede, and Pandarus, it will do the same for each of

367

them, but preface the data for each from the poem itself with a sampling of the scholarship on him or her. Our poet's handling of the rival, so briefly on stage, has evoked little remark and no significant dispute. One may confidently assert that he meant to turn Diomede, *qua* suitor, from a partial to a complete antithesis of the hero and that he achieved this ironic effect with admirable economy of means. His reshapings of the heroine, hero, and confidant from start to finish have preoccupied the critics inevitably and raised among them very material differences of opinion—differences as to the balance between his sympathy for and reservations about all three characters, his motivation of Criseyde, the consistency of this whatever it is, and the extent to which he tried to make the romantic lover a convincingly real person and succeeded in the attempt. Kept from positiveness by the differences between estimable scholars and by my own reluctance to read into the text anything that is not strongly implied in it, I shall venture only middle-of-the-road propositions such as the following. That Chaucer deliberately made Criseyde, Troilus, and Pandarus very attractive; that, on the other hand, he stressed the disappointment of the lover and hence the vanity of his expectations, while bringing out as much, if less insistently, about the heroine and, less insistently still, about the go-between; and that he developed the opposition between potential virtues and their wastage as an artist, alive to religious and moral values, but not inclined to diagrammatic formulations in these—or any—terms. That he substituted believably complex for believably elemental motivation of the lady up to her exile and, having done so, brought off her defection with fair plausibility, as much as could be achieved without slowing the tragedy and diverting attention from the victim. That, keeping the latter always to the fore, he gave him a metaphysical turn as complement to his loverly introspectiveness and carried his despairing passivity into necessitarianism; asserted his public worth more strongly and objectified the claim, *inter alia,* with views of him on parade in armor and in civilian garb. And that, by intellectualizing and masculinizing him thus, he credibly broadened his dimensions, yet did not round him into a being as lifelike as either of his inferiors, the changeful lady or the earthy friend.

The last section will argue on the basis of the precedent two that the *Troilus* better illustrates courtly love and romantic love in general than the *Filostrato* and that, unlike the source, it serves more broadly as an instance of devotion to any and every fleeting "good." Then drawing on Sections 5 and 6 of Chapter II, it will argue that Chaucer by more careful attention to place and time than Boccaccio paid these factors improves linkage of episodes, increases verisimilitude, and more strongly highlights mood and idea. It will next concern itself with our poet's employment of ironic parallelism and show that in using this device he made the most of his author's example and went beyond him. And it will end by asserting the unity of his complex design.

Postures of the Narrator

$\mathbb{B}$ OCCACCIO, a professed seeker of love, called attention to himself as narrator far less than our poet, allegedly an outsider. He would have had trouble in establishing a personality as such very different from Troiolo's, his fictional representative. To inveigh more than the latter against the defection of Criseida, who was Maria d'Aquino's, would have been self-defeating, if, as he claimed, he hoped to ingratiate himself with that lady. And it might have been too patent an irony to exult with the hero in the heroine's seeming virtues since these turned out to be nonexistent. In any event, it would have been tedious to echo Troiolo's shifting sentiments, all most amply expressed. To interpret them with much of the wisdom of the ages was out of the question for a poet as young and perhaps as ardent as the character. Boccaccio, naturally, did not confide about resort to books for a tale meant to apply to his own case. He generalized but rarely on love or anything else. He did not address himself at length to Maria in the romance itself, as distinguished from its prose introduction, and he had as little to say to other potential readers. He expressed hope for God's intervention but once and made only one appeal in His name. And to convey his amazement at the magnitude of joys or sorrows he relied in the main on the easy stock device of proclaiming them beyond description.

The phrases, "if the story says true" and "if the story does not err," which occur early and midway in his poem, are the most explicit suggestions in it of a source.[1] Speculation as to whether the heroine was or pretended to be ignorant of being loved, which also implies one, is the archest of his remarks about her, and that mild enough:

> E qual si fosse non è assai certo:
> o che Criseida non se n'accorgesse
> per l'operar di lui ch' era coverto,
> o che de ciò conoscer s' infignesse.[2]

He has little to offer by way of doctrine other than the following comments: on the blindness of mortal minds, apropos of the enamorment unforeseen by Troiolo; on increase of love by hope, apropos of the encouraged suitor's passion; on the beneficent might of Amore and the instability of Fortuna, apropos, respectively, of the lover's improvement by and loss of love; on the dissolution of all things by death, in anticipation of his quietus; and, at the end of the story, on the sad end of his private life and public glory, on the fickleness and self-esteem of young beauties and the snobbery of many among them with ancestors to boast of, and on the engaging characteristics of a mistress worth having.[3]

He appealed to his lady for inspiration when beginning Parts I and III alleging on the former occasion that she was Jove, Apollo, and Muse to him, his sole hope and mistress of his bosom.[4] Coming to the reversal in Part IV, he told her that he did not need her afflatus then, since he could draw on his own sad experience for composition, but prayed her to return, ere he died of sorrow.[5] In Part IX, he made supplication to her through his completed work personified, bidding it recommend him to the lady when it should be in her hands, recount his woes, and pray her either to return or to command his soul to leave him.[6]

He subjoined to his first address to her an appeal to lovers to pray to Amore for him as one who, like Troiolo, was separated from a beloved.[7] Having brought hero and heroine to union, he counselled anyone who had ever been so favored by the god to recall his own delight to comprehend theirs.[8] At that time, he wished to have misers ask themselves whether money ever gave such pleasure as love could in an instant and, assuming that they would say "yes," pronounced an imprecation upon them,

> Iddio gli faccia tristi,
> ed agli amanti doni i loro acquisti.[9]

Finally, he exhorted young men—"per Dio"—to take caution from the hero's unhappy example and, after commenting upon womankind as cited above, bade them pray to Amore to give Troiolo peace after death and to grant them love which would not be fatal.[10]

He repeatedly made profession that emotions of hero or heroine transcended the power of language to describe them—making it twice in the intimacy of the first person. Who could tell all the joy, he asked rhetorically,

371

aroused in Troiolo's spirit by prospect of consummation.[11] He said that it would be a lengthy business to relate the jubilation of the lovers in chamber for that event and impossible to tell their delight, and averred of the night they spent there:

> Se la scïenza mi fosse donata
> che ebber li poeti tutti quanti,
> per me non potrebbe esser disegnata.[12]

He declared that Troiolo wept so sorely after the parliament that no man could well recount it and that Criseida did the same so sorely that it could not be told.[13] Asking who could give in full her subsequent words of lament, he answered for himself,

> Certo non io, ch' al fatto il dir vien meno,
> tant' era la sua noia cruda e rea;

then went on to report that her agitation upon receiving Pandaro was such that it could not be told.[14] Her plaining in the camp, he said, could not be fully told and would have been contagious had anyone heard it.[15]

These tributes to the hero's and heroine's sensibility, two of which have the warmth of the first person; the addresses to lovers and to Maria and the digression about misers, also with that warmth; and the comments, without it, on love and other matters do make us aware of the narrator as a responsive being, but neither pervasively nor in such wise as to set him above Troiolo in breadth of sympathy or in percipience. He is content, ordinarily, to let the events speak for themselves—as they are well calculated to do.

In the *Troilus,* we are made constantly aware of the existence of the narrator, of his interest in characters, audience, and himself, of his alleged perplexity about some matters, his calm wisdom about others. He is given a liveliness of response equal to that of any character, a range wider than that of any, and a balancing objectivity all his own. His naïveté, an evident irony of manner, points up the lighter aspects of dramatic irony, as his unambiguous concern about God's will brings out graver ones. Generous use of the first person for himself, frequent of the second for a general or particular audience, and occasional of the first again for audience and self are reminders of his identity, closeness to us his hearers, and sense of community with us.

The prominence of the teller in this and other narratives of Chaucer has drawn the attention of scholars. They have considered the part he is made to play in them for its effect, literary antecedents, and possible reflection of extraliterary circumstances. H. Lüdeke, dealing with the first two aspects, made a pioneering investigation, which remains the most thorough. In his monograph, he generalized as follows:

Soweit in der Dramatisierung der Funktion des Erzählers ist keiner von Chaucer's Zeitgenossen gegangen. Die literarische Konvention hatte aus der Kunst des fahrenden Sängers nur wenig variierte formelhafte Wendungen übernommen. Chaucer hat diesen Bestand ungemein erweitert und dem Erzähler auf diese Weise eine Körperlichkeit und Lebendigkeit gegeben, die er sonst nirgends besass. . . . Chaucer hat Sänger und Buch verbunden, indem er den Vortragenden mit der Dichtung zusammen schuf, zu der Erzählung auch den Erzähler hinzudichtete. Der Erzähler ist in der Ökonomie seiner Epik ein wichtiger und unentbehrlicher Faktor geworden. Er ist in weit höherem Grade als bei anderen Dichtern der Mittler zwischen Dichter und Hörer, denn er ist als eine wirklich vortragende Gestalt konzipiert.[16]

Ruth Crosby has touched on the conventional side of the narrator in Chaucer's poems, which Lüdeke treated along with the original, in her study of parallels between them and popular romances meant to be recited.[17] Bertrand H. Bronson has contributed an appreciation of the poet's technique as adapted to oral delivery, with emphasis upon his habitual self-dramatization.[18] In studies devoted to particular works of Chaucer, he and others have discussed the role in these of the narrator.[19] David Worcester has given a section of his book on satire to a persistent feature of the role, the irony of manner.[20] As for possible conditioning of the narrator's part by actualities in the life of Chaucer, Margaret Galway has argued that devotion to the mother of Richard II—Joan the thrice-wed Fair Maid of Kent—was responsible for the postures he affected toward love, but has not won general assent to this hypothesis.[21] Professor Tatlock has offered one, more plausible to me and others: "Chaucer's dwelling on his own inexperience in love . . . is meant merely to head off chaff against his own unromantic personality and physical build while reading aloud among his own social superiors."[22] Father Denomy opines that, beside such motive in the *Troilus* for what he takes to be the poet's dissociation of himself from love specifically courtly, there was a wish to avoid blame for immorality and heresy or to salve his own conscience.[23] Though one must concede that Chaucer manifested scruples in the poem about courtly love, one may question whether denial of exploits in this field could have been very effective as a quieter of remorse for celebrating it or as a shield against moral and religious censure.

The ambivalent attitude exhibited toward love by the narrator in the *Troilus* and preceding and following works was the manifestation, we may assume, of a temperamental objectivity in Chaucer; and the concern again and again shown by the narrator with destiny, and particularly with the issue of necessity and free will, the reflection of a deep-seated intellectual interest. And we may hazard that the geniality and unassumingness displayed were traits actually possessed by the man of whom his disciple Lydgate wrote:

373

Hym liste not pinche nor gruche at euery blot
Nor meue hym silf to perturbe his reste
I haue herde telle but seide alweie the best
Suffring goodly of his gentilnes
Ful many thing enbracid with rudnes.[24]

Yet modesty was a gesture traditional for an author;[25] and warmth, a quality accentuable in anyone. We cannot be sure how much in the persona of the narrator was Chaucer's nature unalloyed; how much, nature heightened by art; how much, pure art.

Interesting as speculation on the point might be, I shall eschew it along with even more dubious conjecture about the influence of Chaucer's private or public life upon his projection of himself in the *Troilus* as narrator. And I shall forgo discrimination of conventional from more or less original elements in that role, limiting myself to analysis of aesthetic purpose and effect.

The narrator serves, I feel, as a unifying presence despite the variousness of attitude and mood allowed him and the concomitant diversity of style. The pattern of response which he exemplifies for us is steadily humane. Shifts in emphasis are gradual and effected without disruption of our first impressions of him, if not without some ideological contradiction. Made to react dramatically, he appears sober and amused by turns at nearly every stage of the action, but becomes prevailingly graver as the catastrophe approaches and more aware of universal implications of the story. He voices interest in everything momentous that transpires and joins us to him in immediate response and progressive illumination by an intimacy as warm as it can be tactfully deferential. We see more in the characters for viewing them with him and come to full realization of the import of events by penetrating his bland simplicities as by weighing his unequivocal pronouncements. Far from diverting attention from the Trojans, he quickens and sharpens it. Lightness of touch preserves him from sentimentality; and power of imagination, from dry sententiousness.

Chaucer composes with the prospect of reciting the story steadily in mind. To tell of Troilus, he begins,

My purpos is, er that I part fro ye,

thereupon requesting,

Now herkneth with a good entencioun.[26]

He addresses himself subsequently in Book I to "al this compaignye," and, in Book II, to any lover who may be "in this place" and to lovers "that ben

374

here." [27] In Book III, he excuses himself to any man who may expect a detailed account of the courtship by saying that it would be lengthy "for to here," and observes, in Book V, that he is abbreviating, "lest that ye my tale breke." [28] Turning to women at the end, he urges, "herkneth what I seye." [29] A dozen times in the story, he carries us forward or backward in it by saying that we are to hear or have heard something from him. [30]

With the poet at the lectern, the narrator's role must have been supremely effective; and not much less, perhaps when, as he anticipated, his poem was recited by another—

> And red wherso thow be, or elles songe; [31]

less now, of course, when there is no one to take his place at the lectern, but still highly effective. The individual who silently absorbs the *Troilus* cannot but feel a partnership with the writer as there self-projected. And Chaucer must have hoped he would:

> Thow, redere, maist thiself ful wel devyne
> That swich a wo my wit kan nat diffyne. [32]

In our consideration of the role, we may take up sequentially: posturing as to sources, doctrinalization about love and the universe, prayer for self, hearers, and the characters, assertion of the affectiveness of what transpires or its indescribability, management of transitions, and claim of abbreviation.

The pretense to use of Lollius or other old writers as an antiquifying device has been previously treated in full. [33] Here we are to consider the ingratiatory, empathic, and covertly ironic effects of alleged dependence on authority.

As for ingratiation, the narrator is apologetically modest about his translatorship. Having pretended in Book I that he has rendered the *Canticus Troili* as exactly as possible from "myn auctour called Lollius," he confesses ignorance-enforced reliance upon that authority as excuse for whatever may prove amiss in Book II:

> Forwhi to every lovere I me excuse,
> That of no sentement I this endite,
> But out of Latyn in my tonge it write.
>
> Wherfore I nyl have neither thank ne blame
> Of al this werk, but prey yow mekely,
> Disblameth me, if any word be lame,
> For as myn auctour seyde, so sey I. [34]

He is even humbler in Book III, where he implies some deviation from the ancient:

> But soth is, though I kan nat tellen al,
> As kan myn auctour, of his excellence,
> Yet have I seyd, and God toforn, and shal
> In every thyng, al holy his sentence;
> And if that ich, at Loves reverence,
> Have any word in eched for the beste,
> Doth therwithal right as youreselven leste.

And putting himself under the correction of those with sensibility in love's art, he begs them to add or excise here at their discretion,[35] and thus to join him in the interpretative process.

Such diffidence about creativity, associated as it is with the fiction of Lollius, is obviously a pose on Chaucer's part, and one contradicted obliquely by concern expressed for preservation of the finished work and by submission of it to the eminent Gower and Strode. Effective on the surface as flattering abasement to the public, it contributes below surface to the ironization of the narrator; gives him the opportunities of a naive recorder, one who, like Gulliver, can be a revealing innocent. No person of the story rivals him in this capacity, neither the unequivocally humble Troilus nor his patently assured friend, mistress, or rival.[36]

Admissions of uncertainty because of lack of information may not only display a historian's scrupulosity, as the one about the inscriptions on some rings;[37] but may also put matters in a comic light by this seemingly grave respect for fact. So, the following cautious stanza about Troilus as suitor yet unrewarded:

> Nyl I naught swere, although he lay ful softe,
> That in his thought he nas somwhat disesed,
> Ne that he torned on his pilwes ofte,
> And wold of that hym missed han ben sesed.
> But in swich cas man is nought alwey plesed,
> For aught I woot, namore than was he;
> That kan I deme of possibilitee.[38]

And so three passages about Criseyde, which elicit amused contemplation of her thinking as gently as the above stanza does of Troilus' emotions. The first, expanded from the *Filostrato*, concerns her thoughts before the hero had declared himself; the wholly original second and third have to do with them when Pandarus invited her to supper and when Troilus was kneeling by her bed:

> But how it was, certeyn, kan I nat seye,
> If that his lady understood nat this,
> Or feynede hire she nyste, oon of the tweye;
> But wel I rede that, by no manere weye,

Ne semed it as that she of hym roughte,
Or of his peyne, or whatsoevere he thoughte;

Nought list myn auctour fully to declare
What that she thoughte whan he seyde so,
That Troilus was out of towne yfare,
As if he seyde therof soth or no;
But that, withowten await, with hym to go,
She graunted hym, sith he hire that bisoughte,
And, as his nece, obeyed as hire oughte;

Kan I naught seyn, for she bad hym nought rise,
If sorwe it putte out of hire remembraunce,
Or elles that she took it in the wise
Of dewete, as for his observaunce.[39]

This subtle irony of alternative explanations by the narrator has its closest
parallel in the less subtle of Pandarus' "innocent" single ones at a time past
innocence—bidding his niece let Troilus sit upon her bed for audibility,
implying that he would spare the eyes of the bedded lover by taking the
candle to the fireplace, and so on.[40] Kept to the oblique approach, the narrator is not allowed the primitive irony—the verbal—of saying the exact
opposite of what one means, whereas Pandarus resorts to it some six times,
Troilus, half as often, and Criseyde, once.[41]

Allusions of his to source material or lack of it still to be considered manifest warm sympathy for the heroine in the descending action, and serve
occasionally to enforce approval of heroine and hero in the ascending. The
misrepresentation,

But wheither that she children hadde or noon,
I rede it naught, therefore I late it goon,[42]

leaves her more generally acceptable as a woman, I would assume, than Boccaccio's assertion of her sterility, however welcome that condition in a mistress
might have been to him. The claim that there was correspondence between
the lady and her Trojan suitor,

That wolde, as seyth myn autour, wel contene
Neigh half this book, of which hym liste nought write,[43]

is a tribute, convincingly fabricated, to their mutual devotion in time of
courtship. And the phrase "but if that bokes erre," as its equivalent in the
Filostrato,[44] gives the weight of authority to assertion of the prince's improvement by love enjoyed. From the reversal, the narrator maintains affection for
Criseyde by showing it himself, but without obscuring her guilt, on which
the tragedy depends. Having announced in the Prohemium to Book IV that
he must report her fault from those who have written of it, he exclaims,

> Allas! that they sholde evere cause fynde
> To speke hire harm, and if they on hire lye,
> Iwis, hemself sholde han the vilanye.[45]

He vouches, on authority, for the sincerity of her schemes for return:

> And treweliche, as writen wel I fynde,
> That al this thyng was seyd of good entente;
> And that hire herte trewe was and kynde
> Towardes hym, and spak right as she mente, . .
> And that she starf for wo neigh, whan she wente,
> And was in purpos evere to be trewe;
> Thus writen they that of hire werkes knewe:

and for the sincerity of her grief at parting:

> And trewely, as men in bokes rede,
> Men wiste nevere womman han the care,
> Ne was so loth out of a town to fare.[46]

Though he cites the "storie" for three gifts made by her to Diomede and censures one of the three with a mild "that was litel nede," he will not commit himself to her reputed yielding of affection to the supplanter; will, on the other hand, attest her penitence:

> And for to helen hym of his sorwes smerte,
> Men seyn—I not—that she yaf hym hire herte.

> But trewely, the storie telleth us,
> Ther made nevere woman moore wo
> Than she, whan that she falsed Troilus.[47]

He would obscure the possibility that she may have compounded her sin by easy yielding:

> But trewely, how longe it was bytwene
> That she forsok hym for this Diomede,
> Ther is non auctour telleth it, I wene.
> Take every man now to his bokes heede;
> He shal no terme fynden, out of drede.[48]

And, with delicate balance between mercy and justice, he professes that he would exculpate her, but implies that fact prevents:

> Ne me ne list this sely womman chyde
> Forther than the storye wol devyse.
> Hire name, allas! is punysshed so wide,
> That for hire gilt it oughte ynough suffise.
> And if I myghte excuse hire any wise,
> For she so sory was for hire untrouthe,
> Iwis, I wolde excuse hire yet for routhe.[49]

He would not have ladies angry with him on her account, he tells them, since

> Ye may hire giltes in other bokes se,

and shows his good intentions toward the sex by expression of preference for Penelope and Alceste to Criseyde as subjects for his pen.[50]

Timidly dependent upon sources for interpretation of heroine and hero as the narrator seems to be, he generalizes confidently enough about the passion which he knows only at second hand, about the forces behind it, and about the organization of the universe. He makes much of extrahuman influence upon the events chronicled and often prays that it will be beneficent to himself, his audience, or the characters. He inspires lively response to divine as to human phenomena by manifesting it himself. Like the persons of the story, he doctrinalizes and prays in both pagan and Christian idiom, as has been fully recorded in the last section of Chapter II.[51] Lip service to the old deities, however out of character for him the English translator, is impressionistically as convincing of the antiquity of the masterpiece as that in character for the Trojans and Diomede. Transcendence of polytheism, achievable by him as it is not completely by any of them, leads to a scheme of unified causation, as meaningful on faith as it is awesomely mysterious to reason. His progress from seeming, if ambivalent, acceptance of the cult of love to unqualified denunciation of all its works raises questions so challenging that debate on them still continues. And the debate is proof of the vitality of the *Troilus*.

Cast in its opening stanzas, as has been remarked in the second section of Chapter III, as the exegetist, the quasi-priest, of the religion of love, the narrator functions off and on in that capacity throughout the ascending action. He calls attention, however, as strongly to the miseries of passion as to its joys and hints a smile sometimes at its extravagances. He solicits prayers at the beginning from joyful lovers but on the strength of their remembrance of former heaviness—prayers for the happiness of some of their fellows, for a speedy release for others from the burden of existence as the only practicable favor. Moved by Troilus' overthrow to admonish the high and mighty not to resist Love,[52] he supports the counsel with a warning as well as a promise: to surrender is to be delighted and improved; to resist is futile. In Book II, he shows a theorist's concern for amatory protocol, excusing Troilus and Pandarus for possibly outmoded behavior and defending Criseyde against the charge of facile enamorment.[53] He adapts in it Boccaccio's truism that desire often increases with hope.[54] Celebrating Venus in the Prohemium of Book III as Troiolo in the first stanzas of a paean to her,[55] he gives the weight of his authority to the exaltation of sex love as an aspect of a beneficent universal force. He returns to earth with the consummation. Apropos of Criseyde's exaction of pledges from her lover, he observes:

> Yet lasse thyng than othes may suffise
> In many a cas; for every wyght, I gesse,
> That loveth wel, meneth but gentilesse.[56]

On Troilus' recovery from grief, he generalizes:

> Thus sondry peynes bryngen folk to hevene.[57]

He gives vivacious approval to her surrender:

> Now is this bet than bothe two be lorn.
> For love of God, take every womman heede
> To werken thus, if it comth to the neede.[58]

He exclaims ecstatically, and yet ominously, of their night together:

> Why nad I swich oon with my soule ybought,
> Ye, or the leeste joie that was theere?[59]

Following the narrator of the *Filostrato,* he attributes the hero's general improvement after possession to the God of Love.[60]

Very different from the above are observations of his about the Almighty working through Fortune, the Parcae, and the planets, which have been collected in Chapter II, Section 6.[61] Directly or mediately the Supreme Being will realize His grand design, he indicates, however mortals in their blindness may strive to accomplish hopes contrary to it. Attachment to anything mundane cannot but end in loss or disillusionment. "Thus goth the world," he observes of Criseyde's change of heart and Troilus' resultant misery; and again of both, a little later:

> Swich is this world, whoso it kan byholde:
> In ech estat is litel hertes reste.[62]

And he appends to the *sic transit* for the prince, which he takes from the *Filostrato,* the melancholy generalization,

> Swych fyn hath false worldes brotelnesse.[63]

From these depreciations of our earth, the narrator's renunciatory advice to the young proceeds as a natural and unforced conclusion. The coexistence in his lines of long and short views of life, both feelingly expressed, creates a tension, which might have been dispelled readily enough to the satisfaction of metaphysicians, but which is left in full force to the lively excitement of all readers.

380

Praying fervently for temporal or eternal favors for himself and his audience, the narrator dramatizes exigencies of flesh and spirit. In despair of inspiration from the God of Love, he resorts to Thesiphone at his beginning:

> To the clepe I, thow goddesse of torment,
> Thow cruwel Furie, sorwynge evere yn peyne,
> Help me, that am the sorwful instrument,
> That helpeth loveres, as I kan, to pleyne;

and indicates that he will add his prayers to those to God which he has solicited for lovers.[64] Awed by love's fire in Troilus, he ejaculates "the wherfro God me blesse."[65] He appeals to Cleo for help with the auspicious second book, and to Venus and Caliope for assistance with the happy third.[66] He is so benevolent as to wish others the joy in prospect for the hero:

> To which gladnesse, who nede hath, God hym brynge![67]

And when the joy is achieved, he prays:

> With worse hap God lat us nevere mete![68]

Attacking miserly disprizers of love, he implores a more ingenious retribution from God than Boccaccio—ass's ears to wear and molten gold to drink.[69] He invokes the complaining Herynes and cruel Mars to help him with the descending action.[70] Apropos of Troilus' jealousy and of its reinforcement by Criseyde's disappointing letter, he ejaculates "God us blesse" and

> God shilde us fro meschaunce,
> And every wight that meneth trouthe avaunce![71]

Of men who betray women, he cries "God yeve hem sorwe, amen!" and thereupon whimsically adjures the ladies:

> Beth war of men, and herkneth what I seye![72]

He prays God that a comedy may proceed from his pen and that the finished tragedy may not be textually corrupted.[73] Rising to highest solemnity at the end, he prays Him to defend us against visible and invisible foes and to make us worthy of His mercy for the Virgin's sake.[74]

He gives pious expression to his concern for the characters as to that for himself and his auditors. Of Troilus' enamorment, he exclaims:

> Blissed be Love, that kan thus folke converte![75]

He invokes the appropriate deity for Pandarus' expedition to his niece's palace:

> Now Janus, god of entree, thow hym gyde![76]

381

Sight of the prince on horseback, he wishes, may have had the proper effect upon the lady:

> To God hope I, she hath now kaught a thorn,
> She shal nat pulle it out this nexte wyke.
> God sende mo swich thornes on to pike! [77]

For the lover awaiting a first interview with her, he prays:

> God leve hym werken as he kan devyse! [78]

He would have an end of their unhappiness before consummation,

> But now help God to quenchen al this sorwe!
> So hope I that he shal, for he best may;

and is grateful when this comes to pass,

> but al swich hevynesse,
> I thank it God, was torned to gladnesse. [79]

Along with such recourse to the divine implying the momentousness of circumstances, there is some explicit statement of their affectiveness. Of Troilus, the narrator says:

> So fressh, so yong, so weldy semed he,
> It was an heven upon hym for to see;

> It was an hevene his wordes for to here;

> Therwith his manly sorwe to biholde,
> It myghte han mad an herte of stoon to rewe;

of the heroine:

> Tornede hire tho Criseyde, a wo makynge
> So gret that it a deth was for to see;

> Aboute hire eyen two a purpre ryng
> Bytrent, in sothfast tokenyng of hire peyne,
> That to biholde it was a dedly thyng;

> In al this world ther nys so cruel herte
> That hire hadde herd compleynen in hire sorwe,
> That nolde han wepen for hire peynes smerte;

of both of them:

> That in this world ther nys so hard an herte,
> That nolde han rewed on hire peynes smerte;

and of Ector deceased:

382

> For which me thynketh every manere wight
> That haunteth armes oughte to biwaille
> The deth of hym that was so noble a knyght.[80]

None of these observations, except the last on Criseyde, is matched in the *Filostrato*.

The narrator also represents, sometimes after the *Filostrato* and sometimes independently, that emotions of heroine and hero were so extreme as to be indescribable. In echo of the source, he asks who might tell half of a joy the prince felt; and, professing inability to relate the delights of consummation, leaves them to the imagination of those who have experienced the like.[81] Without echo, he declares of the transport of the second night that it is beyond every intelligence to describe and that it may not be set down in ink.[82] He rephrases Boccaccio's question as to who could reproduce Criseyde's lament for coming separation and infuses the answer with humility:

> How myghte it evere yred ben or ysonge,
> The pleynte that she made in hire destresse?
> I not; but, as for me, my litel tonge,
> If I discryven wolde hire hevynesse,
> It sholde make hire sorwe seme lesse
> Than that it was, and childisshly deface
> Hire heigh compleynte, and therfore ich it pace.[83]

No mind, he volunteers, could imagine nor any tongue tell the lover's pangs when dawn terminated the last rendezvous with her; and, asking who could describe the prince's woe after her departure, he answers neither could he nor any man.[84]

Affecting closeness to those of whom he tells, he once joins Pandarus and Troilus with himself in a collective first person and once uses the second for the lover. Of machinations of theirs, he says:

> Us lakketh nought but that we witen wolde
> A certeyn houre, in which she comen sholde;

and of the prince's being deserted:

> But Troilus, thow maist now, est or west,
> Pipe in an ivy lef, if that the lest![85]

His use of the intimate first and second persons for communication with his audience has been exemplified already in contextually significant passages and may now be further in transitions and abbreviations.

As was the wont of oral purveyors of literature, the narrator keeps reminding the audience of what has transpired and apprising them of new directions to be taken. In no fewer than thirty of his backward or forward references, he speaks as "I" or to his hearers as "you," or does both at once.[86] In a half dozen of his bridgings, he employs an even warmer "we" or "us":

> Now lat us stynte of Troilus a throwe,
> That rideth forth, and lat us torne faste
> Unto Criseyde, that heng hire hed ful lowe;
>
> Now lat hire slepe, and we oure tales holde
> Of Troilus, that is to paleis riden
> Fro the scarmuch of the which I tolde;
>
> Now lat hem rede, and torne we anon
> To Pandarus, that gan ful faste prye
> That al was wel;
>
> Now lat hire wende unto hire owen place,
> And torne we to Troilus ayein,
> That gan ful lightly of the lettre pace;
>
> Now torne we ayeyn to Troilus,
> That resteles ful longe abedde lay;
>
> And after this the storie telleth us.[87]

Despite the actual enlargement of the story, the narrator pretends steadily to abbreviation.[88] He asks as one who seems to see no reason for embellishment:

> What sholde I lenger sermon of it holde?

> What sholde I make of this a long sermoun?

> What shold I lenger in this tale tarien?

> what sholde I more telle?

> What sholde I telle his wordes that he seyde?[89]

Cogency is evidently his ideal; and a motive for it, consideration for his hearer's time and patience:

> But how this town com to destruccion
> Ne falleth naught to purpos me to telle;
> For it were here a long digression
> Fro my matere, and yow to long to dwelle;
>
> But fle we now prolixitee best is,
> For love of God, and lat us faste go
> Right to th' effect, withouten tales mo;
>
> But al passe I, leste ye to longe dwelle;
> For for o fyn is al that evere I telle.[90]

Humor lurks behind simplicity when he renounces the extraneous at consummation and at Pandarus' visit next morning to his niece:

> Resoun wol nought that I speke of slep,
> For it acordeth nought to my matere;

> I passe al that which chargeth nought to seye.
> What! God foryaf his deth, and she al so
> Foryaf, and with here uncle gan to pleye.[91]

From these last minor illustrations of the enrichment of the narrator's role, we may turn back to the *Filostrato* to survey the presentation in it of the four main characters before considering their treatment by our poet.

Gestalten of Heroine, Hero, Rival, and Confidant

I N the *Filostrato*, the hero, with as many lines as all other characters together and much said about him, commands the lion's share of our attention. Criseida, with much said about her and a good deal to say herself, has a considerable one; Pandaro, with as much to say as she and much to do but with scant remark about him, a small one; and Diomede, quoted on only one occasion and meagerly discussed, a smaller.[1] Troiolo pre-empts interest as the character whose feelings are constantly exposed to us and may be esteemed as well as pitied for his vain loyalty. Confidant and rival, though individualized to some extent, attract notice less for themselves than for their influence upon him. The former's devotion to him, taken for granted, remains incidental, and the latter's to Criseida seems not so far beneath the hero's as to evoke indignation or wry amusement. She may well elicit both these responses but consequently wins little of the pity and none of the esteem which we must accord the deserted lover.

Now proceeding with her more or less as afterward with hero, rival, and confidant, I shall cite literal statements of the narrator and fellow Trojans about her nature, status, or repute along with literal pronouncements of hers which bear immediately upon these matters; and shall review particulars collected in Chapter II as to her person, psychosomatic response actual or anticipated, expressive behavior, and mode of life, indications noted in that chapter of her attitude toward the supernatural, and figurative associations concerning her which have been treated in Chapter III.

As all this should show, she is brought vividly to life as an elemental being. Today at least more believable as spirited wanton than the hero as languishing paladin, she is given motives too simple to be psychologically

386

intriguing. She is allowed all feminine perquisites recognized in the system of courtly love but is left incapable of the idealism in it which gives Troiolo such nobility as he has. Subject with him to dramatic irony, she is not protected from our scorn, as he is to the very considerable extent that he inspires empathy. Her attractions for Troiolo and power over him are extravagantly attested, however; and her delight in their affair and shock at separation, as convincingly, if less insistently, established. Her reputation, it appears, had been untarnished up to their liaison and was kept so until their parting. Her social standing, on the other hand, was dubious. A woman of means but the daughter of a mere priest and a hated one to boot, she was uncomfortably far below her two princely lovers. The lofty spirit claimed for her seems defensive touchiness rather than the charming assurance of one to the manner born. And the high principles also claimed are denied by her own conduct.

The narrator, having only obliquely suggested that she would be faithless, introduces her as, in his view:

> accorta, onesta, savia e costumata
> quant' altra che in Troia fosse nata.[2]

Bringing her back from audience with Ettore to her house, he reports:

> Quivi si stette con quella famiglia
> ch' al suo onor convenia di tenere,
> mentre fu 'n Troia, onesta a maraviglia
> in abito ed in vita,

and therefore loved and honored by everyone who knew her.[3] He characterizes her while standing in the temple as

> negli atti altiera, piacente ed accorta,

and says that she showed there "una donnesca altezza."[4] He offers no further encomia of even this superficial kind, though, as noted in the preceding section, he warrants transient honesty of feeling by pronouncing her transports of love and sorrow for loss of it to be indescribable. He criticizes her abandonment of Troiolo only by indirection—by generalizing on the fickleness of the sex; and he passes no judgment on the lack which he records in her of filial sentiment.[5]

Her cousin—a partial witness—assured the newly enamored Troiolo that Amore had done well by him since she was worth his love and, indeed, a *ne plus ultra*:

> perch' ella il val veracemente, s' io
> m' intendo di costumi, o di grandezza
> d'animo, o di valore o di bellezza.

387

Nulla donna fu mai piú valorosa,
nulla ne fu piú lieta e piú parlante,
nulla piú da gradir né piú graziosa,
nulla di maggiore animo tra quante
ne furon mai;

and went on to say that, though "piú che altra donna onesta," she had the
desires of a widow and would therefore be amenable.[6] With the first night
in prospect, he reminded Troiolo that her reputation was hallowed among
the people.[7] But upon learning of her defection, he told the lover that he
joined with him in blaming her and had no excuse to offer.[8]

Troiolo paid her three high tributes—when he had seen her but briefly,
when she was soon to play him false, and when he came rightly to suspect
that he had lost her. Thus timed, they serve not to define her for us, but to
build up dramatic irony—the second more than the first, and the third than
the second. In his initial letter, he mentioned as attractions for him beside
beauty, her "costumi ornati" and

l' onestá cara e 'l donnesco valore,
li modi e gli atti piú ch' altro lodati.[9]

Parting from her on the last night, he opposed to her abundant "bellezza,"
"gentilezza," "ornamento," and "ricchezza" as qualities not responsible for his
love, even finer ones which were:

Ma gli atti tuoi altieri e signorili,
il valore e 'l parlar cavalleresco,
i tuoi costumi piú ch' altra gentili,
ed il vezzoso tuo sdegno donnesco,
per lo quale apparien d' esserti vili
ogni appetito ed oprar popolesco,
qual tu mi sei, o donna mia possente,
con amor mi ti miser nella mente.[10]

Though he had earlier recognized Criseida's social inferiority[11] and was
presently invalided by doubts of her faith, he defended her heatedly against
the snobbish aspersions of his sister. Equating "gentilezza" with "virtute,"
he declared that the lady was all virtuous—was "onesta" in unsurpassed degree
and "sobria e modesta," "tacita" as befits a woman, manifesting "discrezione"
in act and word, surpassing every Trojan knight "di cortesia e di magnifi-
cenza"—and hence fitter for royal crown that Cassandra.[12] Ere long, he was
to call for divine vengeance upon the object of this praise.[13]

She gave Pandaro to understand that she had never had an amorous
adventure,[14] but quickly showed interest in the one he offered. When alone,
she asked herself why she should not enter upon it:

> Io son giovane, bella, vaga e lieta,
> vedova, ricca, nobile ed amata,
> sanza figliuoli ed in vita quïeta,
> perché esser non deggio innamorata?[15]

Pondering the issue, she judged it no sin to do as other ladies were doing, but feared that she might be discarded by a lover so much above her as Troiolo and recognized that her fame would be lost forever if she were compromised with him.[16] She reproached Pandaro for having brought her to hazard reputation; would preserve it at the cost of acquiescing in the exchange.[17] For having effected this, she wished her father dead.[18] Alleging to Diomede as she had to the confidant that her husband had been her only love, she coquettishly declared herself socially unworthy of this suitor's interest as, long before, she had feared she might be of Troiolo's.[19]

These pronouncements of Criseida and statements of the hero, confidant, and narrator about her leave no doubt of her care for the proprieties or of her rise to social acceptance by princes but give assurance of no trait conceivably admirable except loftiness of temper, and that, however esteemed by Troiolo, not attractive, I would venture, to the average male. Other elements in the presentation of the lady, now to be recalled from Chapters II and III, are more suggestive of appeal yet do not disguise irremediable superficiality and crassness.

She was young, it is emphasized, and supremely beautiful. She had the grace to blush under solicitation and the sensibility to weep, swoon, talk of death, and actually to waste away a little because of separation. In the act of love, she was as overtly sensual as Troiolo. She betrayed pique at both the Palladian festival and her exit from the city and, momentarily, when Diomede spoke too presumptuously. As hostess to her urgent cousin, she manifested the affection of a relative but scantly and finesse in coquetry not at all. No retinue is ever brought into view to dignify her.

Unthoughtful and unresigned, she bade Troiolo ignore Fortuna, whom she herself dreaded, and threatened that goddess and Giove with incessant vituperation for removing her from him. Ennobling recognition and acceptance of a divine purpose were quite beyond her.

She is celebrated in figurative language by Troiolo and other speakers as one compelling of love. That she felt the passion is expressed in figure by herself and others, but not as often or impressively as that she inspired it. Being a woman, she is represented, inevitably, more as the sought than the seeker and, being a woman of elemental type, is not raised to the prince's level of devotion. The glory of love exists in his capacity for idealization rather than in her real beauty or imagined virtues. Celestial in aspect, she is conceived to have subjugated him with missile weapons and to have held him in willing service, though she, the lower born, never made specific claim to power. Like an eastern pearl and held a gem worthy of the ring Troiolo, she had been given the key to his life by Amore. She was sweet, he averred, and his very heart, soul, and life. A rose in beauty, she was the light of his spirit. She had inflamed him forever. She too was inflamed, but rather, it appears, by his availability as a male than by individual excellences in him real or fancied. And her impersonal flame was easy to cool. Esteeming the water of a clandestine affair above the abundant wine of marriage, she proved as ready to take it from one spring as another. The bitterness which Troiolo experienced more constantly from love than sweetness, she tasted for only a few days. His martyrdom was lasting; hers, not.

As for Troiolo, the errors acknowledged in him are heavily overbalanced by homage accorded. Purged of pride by enamorment, he improved with love, it is claimed, throughout the ascending action. If too despondent and passive at crises, he was so, obviously, from the best of a lover's motives—reverence for his mistress and concern for her pleasure and welfare. He would abandon family and nation to flee with her—sacrifice a traditionally binding loyalty, indeed, but for one in his eyes higher. He risked his life against the Greeks solely on her account, yet as effectively for the safety of all as if on theirs. Deprived even of revenge after wasting himself upon a fickle lady, he died, as he had lived, on the whole in vain, yet not altogether for he had kept his faith, been nobly if mistakenly true. By the standards of courtly love—against which no protest is entered—he was essentially perfect.

The narrator, as observed in the preceding section, indentifies himself with Troiolo in point of suffering and speaks feelingly of both his sorrows and joys and of his demise; is moved by his humbling in the temple to exclaim at the blindness of mortal minds and bids young men take caution from his mischoice, yet solicits their prayers to Amore for him in the afterlife. He relates that, after subjection by the god, the prince, though not diverted from amorous thoughts by warfare, worked miracles in arms to be the more pleasing through glory and became "sí feroce e forte" that the Greeks feared him as the death.[20] Encouragement from Criseida, he records, produced further glamorous effects:

> Troiolo canta e fa mirabil festa,
> armeggia e dona e spende lietamente,
> e spesso si rinnuova e cangia vesta.[21]

He notes that, while awaiting possession, the lover gave his days to Marte as his nights to thoughts of love.[22] He devotes four stanzas to the exemplary behavior inspired in him by possession—his frightening the Greeks with a valor raised by Amore, his hawking, his hunting of dangerous beasts, his talk of love and manners, his encouragement of the valiant, his agreeable condescension, as the god willed, to all.[23]

Pandaro recommended the prince to Criseida even more strongly than he had her to him but under the same suspicion, of course, of partiality. Asserting that the Creator had not put a more perfect soul than this man's in anyone, he particularized:

> Egli è d'animo altiero e di legnaggio,
> onesto molto, e cupido d'onore,
> di senno natural piú ch' altro saggio,
> né di scïenza n' è alcun maggiore;
> prode ed ardito e chiaro nel visaggio.[24]

And he assured her later in this their first conversation of the hero's discretion and loyalty.[25] If, as particularly in the declining action,[26] he reproached the prince for despair, it was in disregard of good reasons for passivity or melancholy of which he was well aware.

The heroine agreeably concurred with her cousin's introductory encomia of Troiolo; and, when alone, reflected that the suitor was "gentil, savio ed accorto," and

> Di real sangue e di sommo valore.[27]

Countering his proposal of flight, she reprehended his indifference to the welfare of kin and city and to his reputation and hers, and demanded unfairly,

> Chi crederia che uomo in arme forte,
> un aspettar dieci dí non comporte?[28]

It was no ten-day separation that Troiolo feared but a permanent one, as actually eventuated.

Smitten by the prospect, he showed himself desperate for love and yet not without a conscience. He soliloquized immediately after the parliament, not only that he would have Calcas dead, but also that he could have better borne the loss of his own father, Ettore, Polissena, Paris, or Elena than that of Criseida.[29] Nevertheless, he objected to his friend's proposal of abduction both as contrary to the public weal and as destructive of Criseida's repute and hence perhaps unacceptable to her.[30] And, though asking himself when he saw her turned over to the enemy why he should not precipitate a riot, he did not do so, the narrator tells us, because he feared that she might be slain in the melee.[31]

The material pertinent to him collected in Chapters II and III thoroughly establishes his devotion and suggests an incipient turn for metaphysics, but does little to strengthen the claims cited above that he was a mighty warrior and social ornament.

There are even more allusions to his youthfulness than to Criseida's. In context these give the impression of an Adonis rather than a Mars. No picture of him is supplied, however, either to support that impression or to dissipate it. Unlike the heroine, he is represented to have suffered acutely before and after the ten-day crisis as well as in it. He was prone to lose sleep and appetite and to show it in his appearance; swooned in parliament and had to take to his bed afterward; was ready to kill himself during her swoon, would have later had not the friend prevented, and constantly showed a preoccupation with death. He gave free outlet to his sorrows when alone and when with Pandaro or Criseida; tried to hide them from others as a lover should but betrayed them, nonetheless, to both Diomede and Deifobo. He played the man vigorously enough at consummation; and, with an effusiveness acceptable I presume in Boccaccio's time and place, embraced and kissed Pandaro at high points in the action. Humbled at the festival, he exerted himself henceforth, as his lady did not, to be gracious in public. Still he took no part, as far as is written, in affairs of state. He is accorded a palace, yet this undescribed; servants in unspecified number; and companions, beside Pandaro, of unspecified rank.

He was, though by no means devoted to reflection, more preoccupied with extrahuman influence than was any other speaker. He professed humble subjection to Amore over and over again, if sometimes complainingly. In the hymn to Venere, he conceived of her as a power, not only favorable to his kind of love, but giving life and integration to the entire universe. Dreams he took to be divinely sent for our enlightenment. On the other hand, he blamed Fortuna for ending the first night and—without suggestion that she was dependent on the Almighty—both her and Giove for cutting short the affair.

A poetic spirit, he spoke movingly of himself in figure; the narrator, of him to comparable effect; Pandaro and Criseida to much less. In total, there is scanty figurative association for his attractions, a great deal for his responses. As for the former, he is held to be the ring in which the female gem should be set, the sun to her star, resplendent in station, fresh as garden lily, and —repeatedly—sweet to her and as such her heart, soul, or life. As for the latter, his sorrows were called martyrdoms; enjoyment of the lady, Paradise, but lack of it, Inferno. He was the humble servant of Criseida, but not cast to be or even to seem to be her manly protector. He found love sweet as she did, and more lastingly bitter. In good times, he was spruce as unhooded falcon, joyous as songbird; in bad, roused as bull and lion but to no profit. He revived or wilted like a flower according to circumstances. Bereft of Criseida, he languished in darkness. Flames, which she and Amore lit in him were both intense and inextinguishable.

His supplanter, we are led to believe, was also honestly in love but bold beyond decorum. According to the narrator, Diomede was taken with the lady while inferring the hero's attachment from the latter's behavior, and resolved soon thereafter, as one of great daring and great heart, to divulge his own enamorment.[32] This he did, with unseemly vaunting of royal ancestry and royal prospects, and so glibly as to justify the characterization of him in Boccaccio's subsequent portrait, "parlante quant' altro Greco mai."[33]

As noted in preceding chapters, though represented in that portrait as robust in person and spirit, he had turned red as fire, quavered, and lowered his gaze in the course of solicitation and ended with an appeal for acceptance as her servant; had previously lamented that to win Criseida he must needs be too sovereign an artist, though resolving to tell her of his apparently genuine enkindlement. Appearing in Troiolo's dream as a boar tearing out her heart, the rival is implied to be a lover no less eager than masterful. Not raised to his predecessor's level of excellence as determined by the standards of courtly love, he is not abased to Criseida's; is brought nearer to the former's than to the latter's.

Pandaro conformed acceptably to these standards, we are led to feel, both as a principal in love and as a second. Though he had violated the commandment of secrecy in his own amour, he kept the still greater one of fidelity. Up to the parliament, he exhorted Troiolo to observe the former and counted on him to honor the latter; at that juncture, indeed, recommended neglect of both, yet out of engaging sympathy. There is dramatic irony, of course, in this reversal of himself, but nothing in it to suggest that his commitment to brokerage had been a moral error, a sin from which ill consequences must inevitably proceed. Despite the complication of blood bond with the lady, he neither seriously despised himself at any time nor was ever severely chidden for wooing her for his friend. Never to be criticized by the narrator, he is prepossessingly introduced by him as

> un troian giovinetto
> d' alto legnaggio e molto coraggioso.[34]

Challenged for failure in love when he offered to help Troiolo, he admitted it, but not as a bar to good counselship; alleged breach of secrecy to be the cause, and professed undiminishable suffering.[35] He presumed to instruct his prince, with emphasis upon discretion, and won from him high praise and

full authority.[36] Criseida chid him for urging Troiolo upon her but confessed attraction to the latter immediately thereafter; in a missive to the
prince, complained of his friend's indifference to her honor and reputation
yet wrote on with evident readiness to be seduced.[37] Pandaro, though he had
justified his recommendation as brilliantly to her advantage,[38] felt a twinge
upon winning an assignation for the suitor. To him, he lamented,

> Io son per te divenuto mezzano,
> per te gittato ho 'n terra il mio onore,
> per te ho io corrotto il petto sano
> di mia sorella;

pled in extenuation that he had not done so for gain but only out of friendship; and begged secrecy, not discontinuance of pursuit.[39] The hero promised
silence, lauded the service done him as free from pecuniary motive, and
offered to repay it by seducing Polissena or Elena for so true a friend; having
heard all this,

> Rimase Pandaro di Troiol contento.[40]

When on the morning after consummation the prince declared hyperbolically that he owed his life to Pandaro, the latter replied that he was glad to
have been of assistance while pleading again for concealment.[41] The parliament drove him to further extremes of friendship. Alluding to his own failure
to win a mistress, he urged Troiolo to abandon one duly enjoyed; and then,
in contravention of previous insistence that her repute be safeguarded, proposed defiance of the exchange.[42] The lover dismissed the first idea out of
hand, remarking its inconsistency with his friend's devotion to an unrespon-
sive lady and indicated that he would not entertain the second without the
heroine's approval.[43] Though savage against Criseida when convinced of
her defection by the lover, Pandaro presumed still to justify himself, declaring pathetically to his ruined comrade:

> ciò ch' io fei giá il fei per tuo amore,
> lasciendo addietro ciascun mio onore.
>
> E s' io ti piacqui, assai m' è grazïoso.[44]

Particulars about him to be recalled from earlier chapters are few and in
sum not richly individuating. We are told that he was young, but not how
limbed or featured, nor, outside the amorous sphere, how occupied. He is
represented to have been on such easy terms with his cousin in the ascending action as to take her by the hand and smile and gaze at her, to have had
tears both for her and for Troiolo on the day of the parliament, and later to

394

have been moved to offer to seek death with him in warfare. A comforter by function and thus perforce an optimist in seeming, he exhorted Troiolo to be dauntless with Fortuna and made light of the prince's dreams. He likened himself in the capacity of loveless love counsellor to a warner against poison and a one-eyed leader of the full-sighted and boasted of having amorous flames at his command.

In the *Troilus,* the confidant is given more than twice as many lines as in the *Filostrato* to deliver[45] and brought thereby from partial to memorably full individuation. The rival, permitted to solicit the heroine on the way to camp as well as after arrival and reported more fully in stream of consciousness, is identified unequivocally as an adventurer. The hero, with somewhat fewer but more thoughtful and richly figurative lines than in the *Filostrato* and with more said in his praise, is elevated though not transformed. And with a larger speaking part and wider contacts, the heroine becomes a new woman.

Diversely changed, all four command attention as personalities and invite question about values. Professor Lowes has put the case very strongly, observing "In the first place, the paramount interest of the *Troilus,* as in absolutely none of Chaucer's other work except the greatest of the *Canterbury Tales,* is in men and women"; and then going on to say: "But even more, perhaps, than in the paramount place it gives, not to types, but to living people, the *Troilus* claims kin with the greater *Canterbury Tales* in a certain paradoxical attitude toward the very life in which it manifests so keen an interest." [46]

Scholarship on the poem has naturally been devoted in large part to its richly humanized characters; and, because of the "paradoxical attitude" taken toward them, has as naturally been diverse in emphasis and on some points even contradictory. To refer to everything that has been written about the four principals is out of the question. But critical opinion about each from 1913 to the present should be sampled before I attempt my own summation of Chaucer's development of that individual from the corresponding figure in the source.

As for the heroine, we may take for granted the recognition by most critics of Chaucer's advertisement of liking for her and of his failure to absolve her for change of heart.[47] And we may pass over, as already registered in the ninth section of Chapter I,[48] the majority opinion that the change is motivated sufficiently even for the twentieth-century reader and the minority that it is not. What remains in the scholarship for notice here is mainly the varying approach to her liaison with Troilus.

The comments adduced will be cited as a rule in order of publication.

395

Scrutinizing the *Troilus* for conformity to courtly love, Dodd held that its heroine is presented with unqualified approval as long as she remains faithful to the hero, though with disclosure in that period of a then justifiable susceptibility of heart and concern for her own welfare which will bring her to shame under adverse circumstances.[49] Kittredge, offering much the same opinion, made the point also that she is developed into a more complex being than Criseida and, as an illustration of this, cited her mistaken scepticism about the beliefs held by her father.[50] In two articles, Young showed that there is some diminishment of courtly love ideology in Chaucer's transformation of Boccaccio's heroine but more vital enhancement. In the one, he noted our poet's suppression of the lady's insistence upon furtiveness as a stimulus to love, but his concomitant minimization of sensuality in her.[51] In the other, his elimination by elevating her socially of occasion for the doctrine that rank is immaterial in love, but fortification by the same means of her sovereignty over the princely hero.[52] Curry interpreted her yielding to Troilus to be fated and, hence, it would seem, something for which she could not be held fully responsible. He summed up as follows: "Nature-as-destiny had decreed their passion and destinal forces residing in the erratic stars have determined in large measure the conditions, times, and places which figure in their joyous coming together."[53] Lewis rated this yielding as "By Christian standards forgivable: by the rules of courtly love, needing no forgiveness," and attributed what he called her "subsequent treachery" to a "ruling passion"—fear—which he said is steadily emphasized by Chaucer.[54] Mizener denied that there is implication of any tragic flaw in her, arguing that motive hunting is not one of the poet's primary concerns.[55] Patch asserted that Chaucer would have the lady held morally accountable destiny notwithstanding, and, because accountable, blameworthy for free love with Troilus as well as with the rival.[56] Kirby, giving little attention to moral issues, assembled much evidence to show that Criseyde is fashioned "as a more typical courtly love mistress than Criseida" and so complexly presented as to be "the greatest of courtly love heroines."[57] Tatlock termed her "the earliest full-figure Portrait of a Lady in English literature," but argued that Chaucer does not develop the affair with Troilus distinctively in terms of courtly love and may, perhaps, have thought it a corrupting experience explicatory of her sin with Diomede; he was careful to say, however, that the poet undertakes "not to explain how an attractive woman became faithless, . . . but how infinitely appealing a woman notoriously to become faithless could be."[58] Speirs, approaching the poem "as built upon contrasts between three 'characters'—Troilus, Criseyde, and Pandarus," opined that she has enough in common with her uncle "to make her . . . independent to a considerable degree of the courtly convention," as her lover is not.[59] Robertson condemned her as "self-seeking and vain, an easy victim to the temptations which misled her great mother Eve."[60] More gracious than he, Constance Saintonge dwelt on the lady's charms: a desire to please, inculcated in medieval women of her class, which is ultimately disastrous in her case yet always appealing; and a poise which gives her reserve and hence fascinating mystery.[61] And Lumiansky has pointed out that she is kept from being as acrimonious against the traitorous father as Criseida.[62]

My own views of Chaucer's treatment of the character, which I shall endeavor to substantiate by analyis of it parallel to the analysis I have made of Boccaccio's, may be briefly stated in this paragraph. As will appear from the digest, they have been shaped to a very large extent by earlier criticism. In my opinion, he materially enhances the semblance of courtly love in her relationship with the hero by strengthening her sovereignty, refining desire and elaborating diffidence, motivating her surrender in part by esteem for Troilus' virtue and glory, preserving in full force her concern about scandal, and realizing for her the exquisite deportment more strongly claimed than manifested in the *Filostrato*. He transcends formula, of course, in developing her personality in this relationship: broadens worry about reputation into pervasive fear and adds to that a longing for security and some calculation of advantage, suffuses good breeding with much individual charm, and so emphasizes femininity of person as to make even this generic endowment distinctive. He blandly exposes the disingenuity of resistance to Pandarus and the ego satisfaction in power over her duly esteemed prince while he is exploiting all the charming possibilities in her adherence to the amatory code, and thus gives his audience cons and pros for judgment on her in happy times but does not direct the verdict. Bringing out the influence of destiny upon her in the first affair, he never appeals for exemption from judgment on that score. In the descending action, he makes her seem plainly culpable. He attributes her infidelity to traits which he has previously established and does not exonerate her despite his recognition of the strain put upon them by the divinely inspired exchange. He presents the yielding to Diomede as an offense against her own code of love rather than as one against Christian morality and writes nothing, I believe, which implies that he thought it a consequence of having violated that morality with Troilus. More occupied with the effect of her inconstancy upon the hero than with the weakness itself, he does not urge condemnation by her own or higher standards, seeks instead to elicit as much pity for her as may be entertained without losing sight of the harm done the lover. Yet at the end, he would have us take her lapse as demonstrative of the instability of earthbound affections and renounce them in Christian spirit, love of courtly mode, of course, included. And he suggests the irony of events for her as well as for the hero though not as compellingly.

Qua narrator, the poet is generous with compliment and sympathy for the lady while covert in implication of foible and affectedly reluctant to blame her for the cardinal sin of infidelity. As remarked in Section 2, he hints that she may have been more aware of developments in the first affair than she seemed, but genially endorses her surrender to Troilus by advising every woman to copy it, magnifies her desolation at parting from him, brings in remorse for falsity and wishes that he could excuse her on this ground. Though he expressly anticipates her defection in his opening statement of theme, he speaks as highly as Boccaccio of her way of life on the occasion of her return from audience with Ector:

> And in hire hous she abood with swich meyne
> As til hire honour nede was to holde;
> And whil she was dwellynge in that cite,
> Kepte hir estat, and both of yonge and olde
> Ful wel biloved, and wel men of hir tolde.[63]

He expands and modifies his author's statement that she manifested "una donnesca altezza" at the festival:

> And ek the pure wise of hire mevynge
> Shewed wel that men myght in hire gesse
> Honour, estat, and wommanly noblesse.[64]

In her first scene with the confidant, he characterizes her independently as "the ferfulleste wight That myghte be." [65] He forestalls charge of precipitancy by limitation of the effect upon her of the new episode of Troilus' return from victory:

> For I sey nought that she so sodeynly
> Yaf hym hire love, but that she gan enclyne
> To like hym first.[66]

He takes over but one of Boccaccio's three notices *in propria persona* of hostility to her traitorous parent and that the weakest.[67] And in the portrait inserted before her encouraging reception of Diomede, he credits her with many excellences before noting one serious vulnerability:

> She sobre was, ek symple, and wys withal,
> The best ynorisshed ek that myghte be,
> And goodly of hire speche in general,
> Charitable, estatlich, lusty, and fre;
> Ne nevere mo ne lakked hire pite;
> Tendre-herted, slydynge of corage.[68]

The confidant in Chaucer's poem begins by praising and ends by denouncing the lady as in the *Filostrato* but to somewhat different effect. In congratulating the hero for having fallen in love with her, Pandarus echoes Pandaro's testimony as to gentle excellences but not as to greatness of spirit:

> For of good name and wisdom and manere
> She hath ynough, and ek of gentilesse.
> If she be fayr, thow woost thyself, I gesse.
>
> Ne I nevere saugh a more bountevous
> Of hire estat, n' a gladder, ne of speche
> A frendlyer, n' a more gracious
> For to do wel, ne lasse hadde nede to seche
> What for to don.[69]

He gives the lover assurance that she will be responsive but without resort to Pandaro's argument that as a widow she must be sex-hungry.[70] When consummation is at hand, he would, like his original, have the prince remember that her name is sacred among the people.[71] When exchange looms, he sounds a new note of warning:

> And if she wilneth fro the for to passe,
> Thanne is she fals; so love hire wel the lasse.[72]

And incensed at realization of this judgment, he expresses himself more violently than Pandaro against the fair inconstant:

> I hate, ywys, Criseyde;
> And, God woot, I wol hate hire everemore![73]

Troilus, made less insistent upon divine retribution than Troiolo when she proves false,[74] is never permitted to be specific as the latter mistakenly was about traits in her character worthy of love and esteem. Troiolo's first flattering letter to the heroine is uncircumstantially digested in the English poem, his testimonial at the end of their last night changed to one on her part, and his defense of her against Cassandra eliminated along with that sister's aspersions. Self-probing though Troilus is, he does not presume to grade his mistress, to give her marks for breeding and innate virtue as the kindly but somewhat patronizing Eleyne and Deiphebus are once said to have done.[75]

Criseyde, who confides to Pandarus,

> I am of Grekes so fered that I dye,[76]

displays greater timidity at the news of a lover than her original as well as more shamefastness. Yet taking stock of her untrammelled state after the go-between's departure, she asks herself, much like Criseida,

> Shal I nat love, in cas if that me leste?[77]

She then echoes the earlier heroine on danger to repute[78] but not on the hazard of being socially inferior to the prince. Pandarus' machinations and the storm notwithstanding, she admits full responsibility in effect for surrender of her person:

> Ne hadde I er now, my swete herte deere,
> Ben yold, ywis, I were now nought heere! [79]

Gentler than Criseida, she does not wish her father dead for having arranged the exchange. Like her, she would acquiesce in it to perserve a still un-blemished reputation.[80] When solicited by Diomede, she resorts to Criseida's pretense of lovelessness during widowhood[81] but not to her affectation of un-worthiness of the new suitor in point of rank. Ironically, she is to earn a notoriety far worse by accepting him than would have been hers had she elected flight with Troilus. That consequence troubles her more, we may infer, than the pain resultant to the true lover. For though there is com-punctious recall of his merits in her lament,[82] this seems incidental to the theme prevailing from the first two lines,

> Allas! for now is clene ago
> My name of trouthe in love, for everemo!

Sharing the narrator's tender pity for such remorse, we may nevertheless detect in it the concern for self which appeared starkly in her early valuation of an affair with her king's son as practically advantageous and, no less plainly but more charmingly, in her recurrent ultrawomanly fears.

Impressions given of her person, psychosomatic responses, and carriage and of her domestic establishment, which as shown in Chapter II are all fuller than the like supplied about Criseida, combine to strengthen her ap-peal and to make us lenient toward shortcomings. Assertion of total womanli-ness of form and cataloging of abundant golden hair, snowy throat, breasts round but delicate, slender arms, and touch-inviting sides objectify the femi-ninity of constitution which is the essence of her charm if also, seemingly, of her weakness. Complacent about her power of life and death over Troilus, she cannot anticipate dying with equaniminity except briefly after the parliament and then, if to be sought, by starvation not by cruel sword or dart. She is gently playful with the uncle as Criseida did not attempt to be with the cousin, submits tremblingly to the lover's first embraces if soon as responsive as her original, and shows none of the other's hauteur to Diomede, the crowd in the temple, or the assemblage witnessing the exchange. She is in tears earlier than Criseida and later, while matching her as to swoon and changes in countenance. She is endowed with a palace and garden and many attendants to serve her therein or abroad and dignified with the graceful assurance which should result from such gifts of fortune. At home as at the houses of Deiphebus and Pandarus, she appears before us as the great lady, matured by position even if of an age, as is insisted, appropriate for love.

She shows a capacity for religio-philosophical thinking riper than Criseida's, as has been noted in the last section of Chapter II, though no more effective against disaster. She argues before consummation that worldly happiness must be specious, if one does not know it is transitory, and vitiated if one does, asserts after the parliament that it must end in woe, yet at neither time desists from pursuing it. Too soft for defiance, she does not threaten Fortune and Jove for banishment as Criseida presumed to do, yet, like her, sought to sway the hero by counsel of indifference to the goddess. She has learned enough about agnostic argument to plan to shake her father's confidence as to supernatural revelation, discovers that she cannot unsettle his faith in what he believes and we know to be true. She comes to see the insufficiency of her scheming but is not granted the liberation from all follies achieved for Troilus in the eighth sphere.

As Chapter III has shown, she expresses herself more tellingly in figure than Criseida, sometimes with her uncle's homely vigor sometimes with her lover's poeticality, yet does not consistently equal either of them or the protean narrator. Associations made by others contribute more to her aura as to Criseida's than do those which are self-applied. Departures from the figuration of her predecessor's responses to love make hers seem more conventionally acceptable and appealing, but emphasis remains stronger upon power to evoke passion than upon capacity to feel it.

In figure, the power is glorified as a totality. Of possible constituents, only the obvious one of beauty is often singled out for metaphorical celebration and that, indeed, not many times. Thus, the lady's influence is heavily impressed upon us, but her right to it not certified in terms of character. Deemed celestial in appearance as Criseida was, she is canonized—without due process—by the hero:

> And farwel shryne, of which the seynt is oute.

She asserts the feudal rights accorded a mistress in the system of courtly love, which Criseida enjoyed but did not claim. Troilus acknowledges them

401

more circumstantially and humbly than Troiolo, only to discover that she has enfeoffed Diomede with a keepsake brooch. She is imaged as a ruby, the earlier heroine less specifically as a gem; fancied like her to hold the key to the prince's heart. Like her called his heart and proclaimed sweet, she is represented also as a restorative for him and a physician. It is as much insisted that she is his light, and specifically his star, as that Criseida was; not as much that she is the kindler or might be the quencher of his amorous fire.

In figure, her response to love is differentiated significantly from his. She is never presented as inflamed, like Criseida, with desire alone, though several times as thus affected by grief and longing commingled. Thus desensualized, as is to her honor according to the tradition of courtly love, she appears less capable of ennoblement by passion than Troilus who is shown to be consumed by it. She finds love sweet, of course, as he does, shares delight with him in converse as bird with bird in song after she has recovered from a trepidation like the entaloned lark's or startled nightingale's. But the affair does not mean so much to her that she repeatedly suffers the infernal, bitter, or smarting anguish so often said to be his lot. The prospect of venturesome love may induce an alternation of mood like that of spring weather, but prospect of loss of love does not have the effect upon her as upon him of a wintry blast. In the crisis as before, she keeps her head, seeks to enlist reason in the service of emotion and upbraids Troilus for failure to do the same. Ironically, she fails to achieve the perpetuity of love they both desired and to which his incautious passion might have brought them. He predicts that Calkas will have his way with her as the bearward with the bear, and, finding this so, she confesses that she has always lacked the necessary third eye of Prudence.

The single-minded Troilus has inspired as much comment in our century as the ambivalent Criseyde. His inferiority to her and to her uncle as a timeless characterization and his dominance, nonetheless, of the story have been repeatedly asserted or implied and never controverted.[83] Aspects, however, of his development from Troiolo have been varyingly emphasized and their implications diversely argued, as the sampling of scholarship given in the next paragraph will show. There will be no repetition from Chapter I, Section 7, of pronouncements there cited on the key soliloquy on predestination.[84] We need only recall that one authority denied it to be in character for Troilus, that others, assuming it to be, differed as to whether it was to his intellectual credit or not, and that two associated it with the pattern of courtly love.

In Dodd's view, the prince is shaped to that pattern from the outset, and shaped for our unqualified approbation. "It seems clear, then," he summed up, "that Chaucer conceived the character of Troilus, not as a vacillating, visionary, unpractical weakling; but as a man of strength, with the courage of his convictions." [85] Kittredge agreed that the poet exalts his hero as a model of courtly love, but insisted that the sympathy thus shown for him is blended with a humorous if cosmic irony.[86] Engrossed with our author's intimations about destiny, Curry put a more solemn construction upon the treatment of the lover: "The tragedy of Chaucer's *Troilus* may be defined, therefore, as the representation in a dramatic story of an essentially noble protagonist of heroic proportions who is brought into conflict with circumstances and with the destinal powers—character, Nature, and the stars—and who, because his passions overshadow and becloud his reason and judgment, is brought into subjection to adverse destiny and finally to his destruction." [87] Lewis, tracing the development of the victim not from philosophical but from amatory tradition, would deny him tragic stature. After saying that "As an embodiment of the medieval ideal of lover and warrior, he stands second only to Malory's Lancelot," this critic declared, "Of such a character, so easily made happy and so easily broken, there can be no tragedy in the Greek or in the modern sense. The end of *Troilus* is the great example in our literature of pathos pure and unrelieved. All is to be endured and nothing is to be done." [88] Patch questioned that Chaucer labors unreservedly for pathos; ventured that he may have thought the lover's resourcelessness anomalous for so young and strapping a man and perhaps even explanatory of the lady's willingness to quit him.[89] Kirby, though granting that Troilus appears no more self-reliant in courtship than his original, pointed out that his valiance as warrior and his nobility as lover are brought out much more strongly than Troiolo's and observed of these developments: "The poet was fully cognizant of the courtly conception of love as a great spiritual, ennobling, and regenerative force, and it is this understanding of the courtly love code which seems to me to explain the great transformation of Troilus." [90] In him, Tatlock suggested, Chaucer is conceiving "a traditional ideal which he and others liked to see movingly embodied" rather than a lifelike personality, and asserted "Never again has he anyone so like a 'courtly lover' as hero." [91] And Speirs equated the character with "the swooning, complaining lover of the *trouvère*-Petrarchan convention." [92] Occupied like Curry with religio-moral aspects of Chaucer's presentation of the hero, Stroud interpreted them less somberly, hypothesizing: "Let us suppose that he viewed Troilus *also* as a 'Boethius' who is driven by the alternations of Fortune rather than led by Philosophy up to the levels of metaphysical comprehension traversed in the *Consolation*." [93] Robertson offered a contrastingly bleak exegesis of these aspects: "The three stages of tragic development—subjection to Fortune, enjoyment of Fortune's favor, and denial of providence—correspond to the three stages in the tropological fall of Adam the temptation of the senses, the corruption of the lower reason in pleasurable thought, and the final corruption of the higher reason." [94]

With the precedent of the scholars I have cited, I shall be forthright in stating my own position. That Chaucer brings the course of his hero into correspondence with the tropological fall of Adam I do not believe. That he views him as a Boethius of sorts appears to me a tenable conjecture but, since he makes so much less of growth in perception than of lifelong appetency, not one to be heavily stressed in exegesis. I heartily agree with the experts on courtly love that he perfects him above Troiolo in its terms and feel that in so doing he means to build sympathy for him and even admiration. He would elicit smiles, of course, at particular extremes which he ascribes to him in courtship as well as solemn reappraisal of his whole career when it has ended but never, in my opinion, implies his hesitancies in love to have been unmanly and as such to have palled on the lady. Lewis notwithstanding, the poet raises his lamenting hero to a plane of tragedy, though not to the highest. It is to be conceded that he does not develop in him a personality as richly complex as in Criseyde or Pandarus, yet to be recognized that he makes him more than a type pure and simple of the courtly lover, giving him as he does a wry irony on occasion and a persistent if unfruitful curiosity about supernatural dispensation. He endows him with an intelligence deeper than Criseyde's and the friend's as well as with virtues she lacks and a basic dignity to which Pandarus can lay small claim. He assumes freedom of the will for the prince as he does for them, thus rendering him also praise- or blameworthy and therefore of moral interest. Since he calls attention to destinal forces operative in the story mainly as they affect the protagonist, he promotes identification with him in every thoughtful hearer rather than with either of the two more rounded characters.

Dramatization of the narrator's attitude toward Troilus, pronouncements by whatever speaker definitive of his character, status, or repute, particulars given about his physical existence, concepts of the supernatural attributed to him, and his representation in figure collectively encourage criticism of him beyond the negligible extent to which the like in the source did of its hero; encourage appreciation of him, on the other hand, in even fuller measure than the like did of Troiolo. In the ascending action, he is represented as so enmeshed in love as to prepare us for his eventual destruction, but with so much advertised to his credit by mundane standards and so little against it by worldly or otherworldly ones that he then appears a specimen rather of human potentiality than of human error. In the descending, he is

shown, like Troiolo, to have suffered more acutely than before and now in
vain for the particular commitment of his heart, but is granted, as the earlier
protagonist was not, the boon at last of true appraisal of all worldly devotion.
Illuminated thus after death and held up to us as a warning example, not
against hasty choice of a mistress, but against universal human error, he is
raised from the level of romance to that of tragedy.

In the English poem the narrator dwells somewhat more than in the
Italian upon the improvement of the hero's prowess and deportment by love
and thus bears stronger witness to the nobility of his passion though he does
not conceal its exclusion of other loyalties or the diminution by adversity of
its beneficent effects; shows as warm a concern for his vicissitudes, as has
been noted in the preceding section, despite slyly humorous presentation
of some of them and final deprecation of them all. Attesting the prince's
valor after enamorment much as in the *Filostrato,* he signalizes it again after
the auspicious first session with Pandarus, and at this time pays tribute also to
his social conduct:

> And in the town his manere tho forth ay
> Soo goodly was, and gat hym so in grace,
> That ecch hym loved that loked on his face.

> For he bicom the friendlieste wight,
> The gentilest, and ek the mooste fre,
> The thriftiest and oon the beste knyght,
> That in his tyme was or myghte be.
> Dede were his japes and his cruelte,
> His heighe port and his manere estraunge,
> And ecch of tho gan for a vertu chaunge.[95]

As in the source, he refers occasionally to military or extramilitary distinctions
of the lover as the affair progresses and catalogs them fully at the end of the
ascending action.[96] In that summation, he associates the prince—as was never
done in the *Filostrato*—with his more famous brother, declaring him

> Save Ector most ydred of any wight.

Lastly, remarking no defect in his hero as he does in Criseyde and in
Diomede when he essays formal portraiture in Book V, he presents him
there as a man of outstanding excellence and unsurpassed doughtiness:

> Oon of the beste entecched creature
> That is, or shal, whil that the world may dure.

> And certeynly in storye it is yfounde,
> That Troilus was nevere unto no wight,
> As in his tyme, in no degree secounde
> In durryng don that longeth to a knyght.[97]

405

Pandarus, though taking more frequent exception than Pandaro to his lord's quickness to despond,[98] extols his manly virtues in the lady's presence with stronger particularity. Before he has revealed Troilus' love he speaks to her of him as

> The wise, worthi Ector the secounde,
> In whom that alle vertu list habounde,
> As alle trouth and alle gentilesse,
> Wisdom, honour, fredom, and worthinesse;

rates the younger brother as equal to the supremely esteemed elder; celebrates his routing the Greeks on the previous day; and winds up,

> Therto he is the frendlieste man
> Of gret estat, that evere I saugh my lyve,
> And wher hym lest, best felawshipe kan
> To swich as hym thynketh able for to thryve.[99]

Coming at last to the point that this treasure is hers, he declares:

> Now, nece myn, the kynges deere sone,
> The goode, wise, worthi, fresshe, and free,
> Which alwey for to don wel is his wone,
> The noble Troilus, so loveth the,
> That, but ye helpe, it wol his bane be.[100]

On a later occasion, he reminds her that she is plighted to "the worthieste knyght, Oon of this world."[101]

Criseyde acknowledges the knight's excellence oftener than Criseida and, like her, fails to mark any flaw in it sufficient to palliate defection; exhibits a pride in her lofty conquest as self-centered as the other's passing awe. She approves her uncle's equations of Troilus with Ector.[102] Impressed by them and by sight of the hero martially arrayed, she reflects in private:

> It were honour, with pley and with gladnesse,
> In honestee with swich a lord to deele,
> For myn estat, and also for his heele,

as, contrariwise, it would be a hazard to repulse him; tells herself that she can count on his discretion; and exults:

> I thenke ek how he able is for to have
> Of al this noble town the thriftieste,
> To ben his love, so she hire honour save.
> For out and out he is the worthieste,
> Save only Ector, which that is the beste.[103]

Yet his swooning on their first night moves her to ask, "Is this a mannes

406

game?"[104] On their last, she is permitted, like Criseida, to challenge his proposal of flight as inimical to public weal and to his and her reputations, but with emphasis much reduced upon the former and more damaging issue.[105] Instead of listening at this time as Criseida did to explanation by the prince of his love, she is made to give him reasons for hers:

> For trusteth wel, that youre estat roial,
> Ne veyn delit, nor only worthinesse
> Of yow in werre or torney marcial,
> Ne pompe, array, nobleye, or ek richesse
> Ne made me to rewe on youre destresse
> But moral vertu, grounded upon trouthe,
> That was the cause I first hadde on yow routhe!
>
> Eke gentil herte and manhod that ye hadde,
> And that ye hadde, as me thoughte, in despit
> Every thyng that souned into badde,
> As rudenesse and poeplissh appetit,
> And that youre resoun bridlede youre delit;
> This made, aboven every creature,
> That I was youre, and shal while I may dure.[106]

The reversal of parts serves to warrant his deserts, while yielding the irony that the heroine is confident of her fidelity in lieu of the irony that he relied on it and lodging the privilege of bestowing approbation, as is seemly, in her his domina. In the lament which Chaucer gives her after she has accepted Diomede, the lines,

> For I have falsed oon the gentileste
> That evere was, and oon the worthieste!

and

> Yet prey I God, so yeve yow right good day
> As for the gentileste, trewely,
> That evere I say, to serven feythfully,
> And best kan ay his lady honour kepe,

confirm her earlier testimony and nullify the charges hinted and then withdrawn in the missive to Troilus which the poet composes for her and implies to be not much if any later than the complaint.[107]

The people share her opinion and her uncle's that Troilus rivals Ector, hailing him as "next his brother, holder up of Troye"; and the courtly group assembled at the house where he is feigning illness vie in his praises, to her silent satisfaction.[108]

He seldom offends against the canons of gentility and—after death—perceives and accepts a higher standard. Like Troiolo, indeed, he not only voices animosity against Calkas after the parliament but indicates that he would have preferred the elimination of his own kin to loss of Criseyde.[109] Like him, however, he expresses concern for the state and for her reputation when opposing the confidant's suggestion that he thwart the exchange and restrains his own impulse, next day, to provoke a brawl because he fears that she might be killed.[110] He achieves purgation in the after life if not in this, wins tranquility on the way to his eternal abode wherever that is to be:

> And in hymself he lough right at the wo
> Of hem that wepten for his deth so faste;
> And dampned al oure werk that foloweth so
> The blynde lust, the which that may nat laste,
> And sholden al oure herte on heven caste.
> And forth he wente, shortly for to telle,
> Ther as Mercurye sorted hym to dwelle.[111]

We appreciate this bestowal of wisdom upon one so long concerned as Troilus about the ordering of the universe. And we may wish him well with Mercurye. Committed to this guide posthumously as he has been made to depend in his lifetime upon other pagan deities, he is presented to us, it seems to me, to be evaluated philosophically—like the self-dramatized Boethius—rather than by the tenets of our religion. The appeal by them to "yonge, fresshe folkes" to renounce "worldly vanyte" need not imply that for his failure to do so he is to be viewed as in Christian terms a sinner. He is an ancient, it is stressed, however often he may be permitted to speak of God like a fourteenth-century man and however completely he seems made to think and act like one in his pursuit of love. According to common belief, indeed, he as anyone living before the Redemption might have achieved understanding of God's will through grace and hence could be held accountable for its observance. But nothing in the *Troilus*—not even the attack on paganism in the Epilog—serves to channel interpretation along this course. Treated in the poem as an individual fatally in error, but so treated, not with doctrinal zeal, I believe, but with the dispassionateness of philosophy, he is allowed a speculative mind, an aspiration for the ideal, and a knightly prowess which may understandably hold our regard though we perceive their limitations more and more clearly. Even when we finally view them in minifying cosmic perspective, do we not all cherish the largely prepossessing image of the whole man created by such explicit statements as have been cited above and by the wealth of supporting implication elsewhere collected and now to be reviewed? And would Chaucer, who respects his hero enough to afford him eventual enlightenment, wish us to do otherwise?

Impressions given of Troilus' person, of the effects upon it felt or anticipated of love, and of his lordly state make him a very acceptably romantic figure, though as such not exempt from the tacit criticism of humor. He is visualized in a scene in the ascending action as war leader on horseback, specified to be tall and perfectly proportioned in the formal portrait in the descending, and called young only in these two contexts, in which youthfulness is associated with virile force, so that the allegations of his prowess are more credible than those of Troiolo's, who was never portrayed and often termed young. The intensity of his passion, as of his original's, is evidenced by the gift of tears, psychosomatic misery, and an obsessive mindfulness of death. In the ascending action, he is involved in the new—and comic—situations of a feigned illness and genuine bedside swoon; but, in the graver descending, is relieved of the indiscretion of a collapse in parliament and the indignities of an attempt at suicide thwarted by his fameless retainer and of a public altercation during illness with a waspish sister. Not permitted to be as physically demonstrative to the friend as Troiolo, he is accorded a more conspicuously dominant role in intercourse with the mistress. He is provided, not with companions as Boccaccio termed his hero's anonymous associates, but with knights, with folk—that is, expressly with dependents; is regularly horsed for peaceful as well as for military expeditions; and in these respects and others is shown to enjoy full dignity of caste.

He is imbued with a concern for supernatural influence wider in intellectual range than that distinguishing Troiolo from his fellow ancients if no more productive of spiritual reorientation in this life. Like Boccaccio's single-minded hero, he takes stock of the powers above him as they may help or hinder his own intent, not as they might correct it. More fervent than Troiolo in prayer and thanksgiving for divine assistance, he is made fervent also in complaint that it has been withheld or withdrawn. He respectfully acknowledges the might of all seven planetary deities at consummation; subsequently attributes universal and beneficent power to the god of love, as his predecessor to the goddess; and, when moved by the parliament to question free will, assumes the foreknowledge of the Almighty without impious complaint. Yet he indicts the Almighty's servant, Fortune, as unphilosophically as Troiolo and earlier than he; upbraids her and upbraids Jove in more defiant spirit than Troiolo when the lady swoons; like him, presumes to curse gods and goddesses collectively after her departure.

Capacities of the lover to affect and to be affected are both more abundantly figured in the *Troilus* than in the *Filostrato,* but with emphasis as there upon the latter potential. As in the source, his own employment of figures is distinguished by general richness, a predilection for the pattern of subjugation and feudal relationship, and marked avoidance of simile and illustration in favor of the metaphor with its immediacy.

409

On the one hand, some new associations for him in his own lines and in those of the narrator and fellow Trojans enforce the secondary concept that he is appealingly impressive as man and prince. He is, we read, like Mars in aspect, surpassable in might only by a giant. He is the sword of knighthood, a shield for his comrades in arms, and both shield and wall for Criseyde. He calls himself and is called her knight and her man as well as her servant. He plays the lion against the Greeks. He is the glorious eagle of her dream, a sparrowhawk in the act of love as she the lark. He is the well of worthiness. Small wonder that, as in the source, he proves sweet to her.

On the other hand, many associations, new or adapted from the *Filostrato,* support the primary concept that he is emotionally beset. And, though most of them enforce sympathy for his plight, a few invite quizzical estimate of it. Formerly a heretic in the religion of love, he must do penance. As in the *Filostrato,* possession of the lady is his Heaven, the opposite his Hell, with the latter concept stressed more than in the source. Subjected as in the original by her and by the God of Love, his obligations to them are defined with more precision than they were there. He is a patient, for whose cure both Criseyde and Pandarus are responsible; experiences smart; and, as in the *Filostrato,* finds love now sweet, now bitter. Justly likened at the Palladian festival to a plucked peacock, a carthorse reduced to obedience, and an affrighted snail, he is later captiously accused of mouselike timidity and the fragility of a gnat. Fancied by Pandarus to be a huntsman of the deer his lady, he imagines himself, as in the *Filostrato,* to have been netted by her. As in the source, he is likened in joy to a songbird and in grief to a dying bull. Floral imagery for him in the original, inapposite for a man, is virtually eliminated. The concept of him as imperilled voyager is, however, kept in full force. That of his love as a consuming fire is less emphasized than in the original, but not rejected as the like for hers. In the pattern of inflaming and hoped-for cooling as in the others, he and she are consistently differentiated and, on the whole, to his advantage in terms of courtly love; he is the more enveloped in love's honest blaze.

Diomede is rendered the hero's opposite in love as shown by Kirby, the one scholar who has analyzed the process in much detail. This writer ends his survey of Chaucer's transformation of the rival with the following sentences: "In the story as told in the *Filostrato* he had at least some claim to consideration as a lover but in the *Troilus* he has none whatsoever. The conclusion is inevitable that just as in the case of Troilus, whom Chaucer sought to make the typical lover through the enhancement of his courtly love qualities, in the case of Diomede he strove for the opposite effect and presented him as an example of what a courtly lover should not be. This careful balancing of Diomede against Troilus I consider one of the finest additions to the English poem." [112]

Chaucer effaces Boccaccio's assertion that the rival was taken with the lady while detecting the hero's interest in her; advances wooing by the new suitor from her sojourn in camp to her ride thither and gives him the most light-hearted of reasons for such precipitancy:

> Al my labour shal nat ben on ydel,
> If that I may, for somwhat shal I seye.
> For at the werste it may yet shorte our weye. [113]

Deferring solicitation in camp from the fourth to the tenth day, he establishes that Diomede spent the interval in plotting and, though recognizing difficulties, maintained an insouciant resolve:

> "But for t' asay," he seyde, "it naught ne greveth;
> For he that naught n' asaieth, naught n' acheveth."
>
> And right anon, as he that bold was ay,
> Thoughte in his herte, "Happe how happe may,
> Al sholde I dye, I wol hire herte seche!
> I shal namore lesen but my speche." [114]

And in the portrait of Diomede which he gives us, along with those of Criseyde and Troilus, before bringing the rival to her, he signalizes glibness of tongue as Boccaccio did in the portrait of the character which he offered by itself after he had reported the visit to the lady.[115] In the new version of the call, the suitor protests love even more circumstantially than in the old but with hypocrisy now evident to us because of Chaucer's previous exposures. A little more tactful with the lady, he is still egregiously boastful of his ancestry and consequent prospects.[116]

As observed in an earlier chapter, our poet gives a stronger impression of Diomede's physical and temperamental masculinity in his portrait of the Greek than Boccaccio in his; and ascribes to the rival the significantly confident acts of taking the rein of the lady's horse to bring her to camp and of there possessing himself of her glove, which with other circumstances render suspect the timidities of blushing, quavering, and lowering of gaze taken over for him from the *Filostrato*. Yet there is less emphasis upon combat effectiveness in the portrait of the supplanter adapted from that source than in Chaucer's parallel new one of the first lover. Giving the second the dishonorable advantage of effrontery in love, he does not allow him superiority in warfare, the ultimate test of manliness.

As also earlier observed, he modifies the tenor of imaginative associations as they apply to Diomede's relations with the lady. He makes him profess

411

feudal subordination to her more insistently than in the *Filostrato* and, as he did not there, to the God of Love as well. He undercuts such protestations by allowing the rival to conceive of himself, not as an artist deficient in winning ways, but vaingloriously as a putative conqueror, by representing his purpose to have been to bring Criseyde's heart into his net and his course to fish for her with hook and line, and by terming him "as fressh as braunche in May" at the time of his crucial visit to her tent. And, having symbolized Troilus in the new dream of the lady as a pure white eagle which changes heart for heart, he pictures the boar, representative of Diomede, in the hero's dream as slumbering through her kisses instead of ravishing her heart as in Boccaccio's version.

The trend of Chaucer's procedure with Diomede is obviously to establish that he is devoid of all attributes of the courtly lover except that of soldiership, in which the protagonist at least equals him; and the effect is to heighten the irony both of the lady's turning to him from a servant perfectly deserving and of that worthy's consequent deprivation. Never explicitly judged himself, the adventurer demonstrates by his easy triumph the baselessness of the idealist's expectations from love and hence promotes our acceptance of the disprizing of them in the Epilog.

Like the rival, the confidant is differentiated more sharply from the protagonist in Chaucer's poem than in Boccaccio's. Kept as faithful in love as in the source and as reservationless in friendship, he is given a penchant for intrigue and instruction, a capacity to view himself—as others—humorously, and a lively but unelevated intelligence and mode of expression which combine to make him the most individual of procurers and to oppose him temperamentally to the hero with whom, as to love, he is ideologically in accord.

With this manifold endowment, the character poses questions of interpretation which have been of great concern to scholars in our time. The issue of how to relate him to the tradition of courtly love has been considered extensively and, less often but fully enough, the associated one of how to regard him in terms of friendship, while the problem involved in both these issues of determining the extent and nature of the comic in his make-up has received much attention. Dodd pointed out that, though he is permitted some levity about courtly love, he is made to commend its doctrines enthusiastically to friend and niece and to observe them in his own affair. This interpreter, when summing up, wrote in part: "And further we have seen, I think, that even the satire of Pandarus himself, who has been supposed to express the poet's irony, is no more characteristic than is his sentimentality; and that the inconsistency of the two elements in him helps to make him not only a delightfully humorous figure, but also, like Troilus and Criseyde, an eminently human one."[117] According to Professor Kittredge, he cannot be a sentimentalist because a humorist and man of action; is "a rare but perfectly human compound of enthusiasm and critical acumen"; though thus attractive, lacks sanction under the erotic code for his role of go-between and, in playing it, carries the ideal of friendship to an unjustifiable extreme.[118] In one article, Professor Young cited the *De Amore* of Andreas Capellanus to establish that, despite Kittredge, an intermediary is "a legalized agent in the system of courtly love" and hence that qualms of Pandarus arise, not from any deviation from it, but from the conflict, peculiar to his situation, between claims of friendship and those of family honor.[119] And, in another, he remarked that the confidant's humor is not destructive of courtly idealism and has some precedent in French romances.[120] Lewis distinguished a number of aspects in the characterization of Pandarus—the practical efficiency bestowed upon him, the serious commitment to love, the ironic contrast between failure in practice and readiness to advise, the humor unconscious on his part of garrulity and busybodyness, the skillful raillery, and the lurking uneasiness about his role—and, having done so, concluded, "analysis, with its multiple distinctions, will never exhaust what imagination has brought forth with the unity of nature herself."[121] The extremism in friendship, according to Laurens J. Mills, may be presented to us as of debatable morality, but not obtrusively as such.[122] Patch stressed the declension of Pandarus from effectiveness in guidance to futility, calling this change a tragedy for him and implying it to be illustrative of the conclusion of the vanity of worldliness to which the whole story leads.[123] Except for allowing him such atypical scruples as he had in the *Filostrato*, Chaucer, in Professor Kirby's opinion, makes the confidant a perfect specimen of his kind in courtly love and thus calls for a response from us as favorable to him as that of Troilus upon promise of consummation.[124] Passing over the traditional in the characterization, Tatlock applied himself to its individuating complexity, noting among other traits which he thought evident or inferrible in Pandarus: a bustling vitality, a relish for the proverbial such as Thackeray ascribes to the mentality of domestic servants, and, along with warmhearted concern for friend and niece, a pleasure in sentimentality and voluptuousness at second hand, a snobbish attraction to the great, and a power-hungry delight in intrigue.[125] Speirs thought him put below Troilus in dignity, above in practical wisdom.[126] Robertson saw in him "a masterpiece of medieval irony"—a superficially "attractive little man," by turns sentimentalist and cynic, of limited understanding, and largely devoid of principle.[127] Slaughter, contrarily, sought to establish the thesis that: "Chaucer intended Pandarus's role as intermediary,

413

uncle, and friend to be ideal, and wholly commendable; Pandarus acts always within the limits set by the classical ideal of friendship as Chaucer received that ideal from Jean de Meun." [128]

In my view, Chaucer turns the go-between into an even more patent exemplar of courtly love and of friendship than he was in the *Filostrato;* builds up the lighter irony of his presuming to win for another what he cannot for himself, but not the graver of the eventual negation of that effort; leaves his service to the lover as morally challengeable on the one hand as before, on the other, as little provocative of harsh estimate of him or of the serious reflection about events inspired by the hero's conduct. More pathetic than Pandaro when frustration is inevitable because previously more exuberant in resource, Pandarus is brought no closer to the level of tragedy. For though he has been made more evidently a man of consequence than his original, he has been made also in part a jester and an object of jest, and, thus presented, could hardly be and is not ennobled with the pro- tagonist in the capacity of victim of self and destiny. Neither more nor less uneasy than Pandaro about the subornation of a kinswoman, he justifies himself and is justified somewhat more fully in terms of courtly love and friendship but, of course, is not exempted thereby from adverse moral judg- ment by readers who do not share his attitudes. Since he purposes, and repeatedly purposes, to deceive her and appears to be indulging a sizable ego in machination, he lies open to new peripheral charges as well as to the main one. Yet censure on all counts is mollified by an affection more engag- ingly evidenced in him than in Pandaro toward friend and relative and by a temperament developed for him so conspicuously hearty and robust as to forestall conjecture of sycophancy or decadence. It is hard to think of Pan- darus as a toady or voyeur; easy to forgive him for sleights always amusing, and usually palpable to Criseyde, and for an *amour-propre* both risible and inoffensive; possible to sympathize with his guiding principles though not to accept them. And it is natural to be less concerned moralistically about them than about the also specious ones of Troilus, the protagonist and more exalted spirit.

The narrator, hero, heroine, and Pandarus himself all emphasize his unhappiness in love; the niece mildly blames and the prince unequivocally commends the brokerage to which his friend is irrevocably if sometimes uncomfortably committed; the narrator passes no definitive judgment upon it favorable or unfavorable but does signalize the broker's assiduity, tact, and good intent. Not establishing the confidant's social dignity in the first scene with the hero, as did the narrator of the *Filostrato* by introducing him as a person of lofty lineage, he does so later by referring to him as "the knyght" and to him and Troilus jointly as "thise ilke lordes two" and by specifying his presence at the parliament and his attendance upon the king.[129] Pandarus, when twitted in that first scene with unskillfulness in his own affair, argues more elaboraely than Pandaro that he can be skillful in another's but does not, like him, attribute his personal failure to breach of secrecy.[130] Proceeding to instruct the enamored hero at greater length than his original, he lays as much emphasis upon discretion, wins from him as hearty commendation and as unreserved authority.[131] He earns a tribute from the narrator for taking time to plan his campaign against the lady—as Pandaro did not—before initiation of it.[132] Credited by that authority with a true lover's sleeplessness on the night before he visits her, he is greeted by her in the morning with a jocular allusion to his mistress.[133] Before his great disclosure, he swears to Criseyde that she is the woman he loves best "Withouten paramours" and is answered that he is the man to whom she is most beholden.[134] In making it, he disingenuously protests that, as her uncle, he would sooner see all three of them hanged than play the bawd for his friend and that he is asking no more than that she make the latter better cheer.[135] Undeceived, she chides him for procuring as Criseida did her forthright visitor;[136] like the earlier heroine, debates the offered adventure as one leading potentially to complete surrender, and shows immediate interest in it if less frankly. Pandarus, encouraged to pay her a second call, breaks tension *inter alia* with humorous reference to his ill success in love, eliciting reply in kind from her and hearty laughter.[137] As certain of her surrender after his machinations with Deiphebus as Pandaro was of Criseida's when he had won an assignation from that lady, Chaucer's go-between expresses concern to the hero about services rendered as fully as Boccaccio's and pleads at greater length for secrecy, concluding, as the other did not, with a pathetic allusion to his own failure in love.[138] Troilus, like Troiolo, responds with promise of discretion, assurance that he recognizes the services to have been free of pecuniary motive, and offers to repay them in kind by seduction of any of his female relatives; and as effectively lays the friend's scruples thereby.[139] The narrator attests the general diligence of the intermediary thereafter and his care in planning for the rendezvous at his own house, and apropos of his behavior on that occasion characterizes him as intuitively diplomatic:

> But Pandarus, that so wel koude feele
> In every thyng, to pleye anon bigan.[140]

Troilus, if unhappy about the immediate effect of the friend's attribution of jealousy to him, is as grateful next morning as Troiolo, who had no such ruse to complain of.[141] Answering the lover's thanks for the outcome, Pandarus,

415

like Pandaro, expresses delight in it but pleads even more insistently than the other for continued secrecy.[142] He is rebuked that same morning by his niece for the duplicity of the night but is quickly forgiven.[143] After the parliament, he suggests as did Pandaro, first, abandonment and, then, forcible retention of the lady, the former with as melancholy a reference to his own failure to win love as his original's, the latter with disregard for her reputation less cynically expressed and with willingness for combat more heroically.[144] Troilus rejects the first proposal no less categorically than Troiolo and with even more ironical allusion to the counsellor's amorous fidelity as irreconcilable with it, and is as little disposed to follow the second without the mistress' consent.[145] The narrator, as was not the case in the *Filostrato*, attempts to palliate the first, remarking that it was offered because of desperate concern for the prince.[146] When the lady's infidelity has been established by the hero, Pandarus speaks against her even more violently than Pandaro, attempts as pathetically—and egocentrically—to maintain his credit for friendship:

> And that thow me bisoughtest don of yoore,
> Havyng unto myn honour ne my reste
> Right no reward, I dide al that the leste.
>
> If I dide aught that myghte liken the,
> It is me lief.[147]

Impressions of his gestalt conveyed by the material just cited relating expressly to the spirit are reinforced and sharpened by clues to his time of life, physical being, and concern about the possibility of death for his friend or himself, which as shown in the first five sections of Chapter II are richer on the whole than those given but meagerly to Pandaro's. As uncle to the heroine, he has stronger obligation to guide her aright than his original, her cousin, and more guilt if he does not. So too if considerably older than she, as he might be since he was her uncle and never termed young as Pandaro was on several occasions. It appears, however, that he is not her senior or the hero's by many years, for, though he assumes old age's prerogative of doctrinalization, he affects camaraderie with both parties and is treated by them as a coeval, a mentor in love, indeed, but also a fellow, and, if to be twitted about his futile suitorship, without the slightest implication that it is autumnal. Suffering from his own passion but capable of levity about it, he can imagine that Troilus may expire from his and be so sympathetic as to contemplate death in that event, yet exaggerate the double possibility to sway Criseyde, stage a fever for the hero to the same end, and after his friend's recovery from swoon wax arch about that genuine debility. Though his person as was Pandaro's is left entirely to our imagination, he is physically individuated for us nonetheless—by a liveliness of movement and gesture, which, like his copious energy of speech, reveal him as one vivacious in both jest and earnest. He runs on hopeful mission, makes leaping entrance with good news. At one time or another in his niece's presence, he embraces her, whispers in her ear, thrusts a letter into her bosom, kneels in petition, brings her ceremonially to bed and playfully wrestles with her upon it, affects readiness to kill himself with a knife and to let her kill him with a sword, laughs, weeps, and clears his throat. Laughing and weeping with his friend, he is his partner in vigorous exercise in the garden; within doors, shakes him, provides him with a light, a cloak, a cushion, strips off his shirt, and tosses him into the lady's bed. A guest in the establishments of two princes of the blood, he has one of his own capacious enough for party giving and intrigue and hence evidential of rank.

As remarked in the last section of Chapter II, he is brought into debate with the hero earlier than Pandaro about Fortune and at greater length about dreams and, on these bases, thus more prominently into opposition with him. Arguing, like Pandaro, and more forcefully, that the goddess need not always frustrate her minions and that dreams are to be disregarded as not identifiably prophetic, he is as thoroughly refuted by events and his melancholy friend proved as justifiably apprehensive as Troiolo.

As seen in Chapter III, he is distinguished from all other speakers, as Pandaro was not, by a strong taste for the illustration, the most sententious form of figurative association, and for the homely proverbial in such association irrespective of form. And as there observed, his service to the hero and his own ironically contrasting failure in love are both signalized in figure more often and more ingeniously than Pandaro's. He is represented or represents himself to be: a preacher of the amatory faith, a physician who cannot cure himself, an architect of plot, an individual who knows all the old dance yet treads the measure haltingly, one though blind able to proceed where the clear-sighted fall, a connoisseur of sweetness for having tasted bitterness, a driver of the doe into ambush and a fox but not an exultant soarer like the hawk, a whetstone for one more fortunate than he, and when occasion demands, a stone in stillness.

To sum up Chaucer's presentation of the four principals, it may be said that he characterizes each one more fully than Boccaccio and makes their interrelationship more suggestive; stresses anomalies within the individual and elaborates contrasts between one person and another; broadens our interest in them singly and collectively, without dissipation of the emotional impact of their affair. His Troilus—the central figure though less pre-emptive of attention than Troiolo—surpasses the latter as amatory idealist, impressive warrior, and questing metaphysician; excites warmer sympathy and more thoughtful evaluation in both the ascending and descending phases of the story; and achieves at last a universal, a tragic dignity after he has been exposed at times to the needful criticism of laughter. Criseyde, made less sensual but more timid and therefore more calculating than Criseida, is opposed to the idealistic hero, as a lady not too wanton but too prudent to reciprocate his eternal devotion. Ultrafeminine and pathetically divided between love and other concerns as Boccaccio's heroine was not, she wins more compassion from us than that lusty damsel, but not at the expense of pity due the servant. And, because seemingly worthier of trust than her original as certainly more attractive, she is a more telling instance of the speciousness of worldly goods when she proves equally inconstant. Her uncle, a more genial relative than Criseida's cousin, is quite as latitudinarian a one, a charming humorist indeed, but a deceiver and a relisher of the power obtainable through intrigue and argument. A richly developed character like the niece, he is a more effective foil for the lover than Pandaro, being distinguished from his advisee not merely by the initiative and optimism which the role of go-between necessitates but also by a quizzical, pragmatic temper and a correspondingly prosaic style. Though dedicated to love, he does not cut a romantic figure in pursuit of it for himself or his friend; and, however emotionally involved in the latter's decline, does not attain his tragic stature. Exemplifying the capacities and limitations of workaday folk, he heightens by contrast our sense both of the defenselessness and of the magnanimity of Troilus. The rival is presented as the diametrical opposite of the protagonist in love. Not only hastier than in the *Filostrato* but devoid of the sincerity therein implied, he is as desertless as the other is deserving. He caps the irony of the story, winning without a moment's pain the lady who thought herself unalterably true and grieves that she is not, nullifying thus easily the labors of the ingenious and well-intentioned confidant, and besting the noble hero who dared not speak for himself because he feared he was unworthy, let his mistress depart so that she might preserve her good name, and now hopes with all his heart that she will return.

Chaucer, as has been seen here and elsewhere, keeps the hero to the forefront and primarily to the forefront as a courtly lover, but brings out his strength and weaknesses more sharply than Boccaccio by a fuller development of the heroine, go-between, and rival as variously contrasting characters and broadens the significance of his life by making it an instance not merely of misdirected sexual affection but of contravention of the total scheme of existence as superhumanly ordained. In the concluding section, our poet's organization of his materials into a complex whole and Boccaccio's of his into a simpler one will be briefly viewed, with attention focused upon linkages and oppositions.

Conclusion: The Totality

THE story of the Trojan hero, his mistress, his friend, and the Grecian rival is in Chaucer's telling, as in Boccaccio's, an ambivalent instance of courtly and hence of all romantic love and, in our poet's, further of every mundane commitment. The Italian achieved an effective simple unity by concentrating upon erotic sentiment in the stylized mode introduced by the troubadours and a tension equally simple and powerful by opposing to the weal of amour courtois its also inherent woe and to the adoration of the female which it prescribed the unworshipfulness of a reputed paragon of the sex. Chaucer subtilizes his author's opposition of expectancies and actualities in the clandestine affair and, giving it a more thoughtfully developed cosmic background as well as a fuller and thus more realistic earthly one, extends antithesis from a province of experience into life's total domain, makes the particular a type of the universal. Broadening the narrative and also diversifying its tone with new humor and higher seriousness, he maintains coherence by skillful linkage in time and space and by inducement of uniformly humane response through pervasive dramatization of his own.

The configuration in his poem of amatory doctrine, cultish phrasing thereof and behavior induced by it is even more distinctive of courtly love than that in Boccaccio's, as we may learn from modern analysts of the system,[1] and is better calculated to invest passion with seductive charm. Yet the hero, brought to perfection as chivalrous servant, is involved in quasi-comic situations during courtship and, after death, made to laugh at the values by which he lived, while allowed to suffer as acutely throughout ascending and descending actions as in the source. His domina, partially improved for traditional suzerainty, still betrays him, and for a rival whom Chaucer has

420

thoroughly debased. Like hero and heroine, the intermediary is rendered more attractive to us, but he is not thereby exempted from our judgment for his procuring of a relative or for the unhappy consequences of that act of friendship. And the narrator in the *Troilus*, allegedly deprived of love, signalizes its potential for secular improvement and delight at least as warmly as the amorously engaged one of the *Filostrato*, but its liability to mundane woe also as poignantly as the other and—as he did not—its absurdity when carried to extremes of sentiment and its incompatibility with the universal order. Noting how much is implied against sexual adventure in our poet's handling of the theme, I cannot accept without material reservation such a pronouncement as Lewis', "Thus *Troilus* is what Chaucer meant it to be—a great poem in praise of love." [2] Vice versa, observing how much is conceded to such adventure, I would question the tone at least of such an antipodal statement as Father Denomy's, "Chaucer not only rejects, disapproves of and condemns, he repudiates Courtly Love as vain, ephemeral, and fallacious, the blind effect of passion, and that not only in the Palinode but within the very fabric of the story itself." [3] The poet of course brings out the illusoriness of Frauendienst more and more strongly as he proceeds but not, I venture, with the austerity suggested by the above wording of his intent. Along the way, he keeps us aware of its evanescent appeals and manifests to the very end a sympathetic if critical interest in it.

Broadly as well as tolerantly moralistic, he would have us view the action in relation to divine ordering of the universe. He stresses the influence of Fortune and the planets and indicates that it was exerted according to the will of the Almighty. Scholars have differed somewhat as to the strength and import of destinal suggestion in his poem. [4] To me, this element seems to pervade the *Troilus* and to bring home the futility and blindness, not merely of the three love-questing ancients, but of humanity in general, reliant as it tends to be upon one specious good or another of the transitory world. And without excluding free will and the responsibility of the principals for their own miseries because of abuse of freedom, this element gives the story, I feel, a sense of inevitability which contributes materially to its elevation and power.

Developing wider implications from the affair than Boccaccio, Chaucer also enriches the former's setting of it in the confines of Troy as has been observed in the second section of Chapter II. The ardent Florentine, preoccupied with the business of love, keeps the heroine much to her dwelling and the hero much to his or hers and, concentrating upon the psychic aspects of that business, tells us little about their respective chambers and even less about other parts of their homes or about Sarpidone's establishment,

421

temples, fortifications, and the camp, and neither relates action in episodes closely to *mises en scène* nor traces movement carefully from stage to stage. A convincing interpreter of the life of the heart, he does not associate it as intimately with social existence as it would be in his own world or in ours and fails to project it into sharp visual reality within the bedrooms or outside these sanctuaries. Chaucer permits Troilus to retreat to his chamber and bed as often as Troiolo and sequesters him also at the houses of Deiphebus and Pandarus but accords him a mass reception on triumphal entry into the city. He involves the heroine in a dinner and supper party at the just mentioned houses and confers attendants upon her for these occasions and for her time spent at home. He supplies a closet for privities in her establishment as well as a chamber, indicates other apartments in it, and appends a fine garden. And he visualizes action clearly in relation to settings within doors, on the walls of Troy, and in Calkas' tent, and accounts precisely for comings and goings. He thus creates a fuller semblance of physical actuality than his author and achieves it without great loss of psychic intensity. For, though he introduces new locales, he keeps the story centered in that haven of feeling, the prince's chamber, where with the world locked out the exigencies of the heart seem all important. And to whatever spot he moves, he never allows us to be long forgetful of them.

Attentive to time as well as space, he exploits this factor likewise more effectively than Boccaccio, as has been shown in the last section of the second chapter. The Florentine, accoutering and housing the Trojans as if they were his contemporaries, did make them pagan on the surface but not with such care even on this level as to produce the illusion of antiquity. No more meticulous about the dating of events, he keeps us poignantly aware of time in the suspenseful ten-day period, yet fails to define the length of ascending or descending action and does not construct extended sequences before this period nor after it. He draws but little on seasonal or diurnal aspects of nature to heighten mood. And he turns as infrequently to the panorama of the heavens to objectify divine causation. Chaucer, making more of time, enforces idea and mood thereby and increases verisimilitude. By pretense to a classical source and by systematic infusion of the old mythology, he emphasizes the temporal remoteness of the story to the enhancement of its exotic appeal, though he leaves it assimilably fourteenth-century in *realien* and in basic ideology. Without constructing a precise schedule for the whole, he implies historicity by frequent specifications of time, builds sequences in the ascending action to the material benefit of continuity, preserves the long one which Boccaccio initiated with the parliament, and dates it relatively to the beginning of the prince's love. He derives atmospheric background for experiences of his characters from the spring, from dawn, full daylight, .evening, and the night. And in coursings of the planets, he pictures destiny impressively.

Occurrences separated in time or space he ties together by likeness which calls attention to unlikeness, herein following the lead of Boccaccio to achieve a coherent and progressive irony.

In this process which underscores anomalies of experience or response in the persons of the story, the youthful creator of the *Filostrato* had much to teach Chaucer, mature though our poet was when he undertook to adapt it. Boccaccio, disengaging from Benoit's romance of the Trojan War the strand of Diomede's supplantation to give it an elaborate reworking, and prepending to this a shorter though considerable account of Troiolo's enamorment, courtship, and enjoyment of his lady, took care to develop oppositions of incident within both new and borrowed phases of the action and also between them.

At the Palladian festival, Troiolo as quoted in derision of lovers when about to be made one by Criseida, asserted that woman turns like a leaf in the wind. With the simile confirmed to the hero's astonishment by what she eventually does, the narrator applies it again to the young of the sex in his concluding moralization.

Calls of Pandaro alternately upon hero and heroine during the period of solicitation bring out in strong contrast the sincere and elevated reaction of the one to love and the disingenuous, patently carnal of the other. So too the letters of the period which are quoted, the suitor's first one and the lady's reply.

The exultant hymn to Venere given the lover during possession is balanced by the song which expresses his anxiety in the first ten days of her absence. Summation by the narrator of the improvement worked in Troiolo by love which caps the account of his happiness with her is followed immediately by prediction of evil to come from Fortuna.

In the descending action, hope is set against despair, with the latter regularly verified by event. Complimented for virtue by the hero on their last night after she has given him firm assurance of return, she will offer encouragement to his successor within four days and break her promise for the tenth. Troiolo, shaken by various dreams on the night after her going and, later on, by that of the boar, takes comfort from his friend, only to be beset again by the fears which they inspired. Possessed by these fears, he defends his mistress nonetheless against the aspersions of the eavesdropper Cassandra; turns to vilification of the absent one when they are substantiated by discovery of the brooch.

Chaucer, who so unequally expands the ascending and descending actions as to reverse the proportion between them, reinforces oppositions by what he does with both, though, as might be expected, in greater measure by his very inventive treatment of the former. Having a version of the whole before him must have been a considerable advantage, as Hubertis M. Cummings pointed out many years ago.[5] He could sharpen contrasts evolved by Boccaccio between happenings not far apart in time and do more than his author to associate immediate developments with those to be treated much later. Capitalizing on these possibilities with his accustomed freedom, he achieves a symmetry, a balance, in episode and detail rightly lauded by Professor Patch as of signal effect for dramatic irony.[6]

Through figurative media, he stresses human impercipience, from which such irony arises. He makes the hero call lovers blind before his unforeseen enamorment, which prompted Boccaccio as narrator to comment on the blindness of earthly minds; then can and does render that generalization to heightened ironic effect. He employs an analogy of "a blynd man" for himself as love-ignorant amatory poet and—adapting the *Filostrato*—gives Pandarus one to apply to himself as lovelorn go-between. He gives more than one assurance that the affair was so managed as to keep even intimates of the principals well hoodwinked. He remarks anent the rainstorm produced by a rare conjunction that such high causation is hidden from us; is moved by the folly of the Trojans in parliament to speak of the cloud of error encompassing humanity; conceives of Fortune as blinding those who trust her and of hope as doing the same to the forsaken Troilus; reports that the latter posthumously condemned human striving as pursuant of "The blynde lust"; and quotes Criseyde as hoping to blind her father's soul with avarice and as confessing, when unable to trick him, that she lacked Prudence's eye for the future.

Chaucer sets song against song as divergent interpretations of the life of the heart. To the hero greatly perplexed before his friend intervened, he gives one about love's contrarieties, while to a new character, Antigone, another so unequivocally eulogistic of the passion as to sway the heroine toward amorous adventure. He supplies Troilus when in possession with a song as optimistic from the masculine point of view as Antigone's from the feminine and, after possession is terminated, with one more than matching in anxiousness his first about contrarieties—both of these as replacements for lyrics of Troiolo respectively similar in tone.

Concatenations as ironic as that of the songs pervade the *Troilus*. Some will be worth recalling as illustrative of the artistry of our poet.

Several are initiated in the long sequence beginning on a May the third. Pandarus, he relates, is awakened for his fateful first visit to his niece by the metamorphosed Proigne lamenting the wickedness of Tereus. The heroine is lulled to sleep after the uncle's call by Proigne's sister bird, the nightingale, and dreams of a white eagle exchanging its heart for hers—a symbol for Troilus antipodal to the boar for Diomede, which in Chaucer's version of the hero's dream years later will slumber through her caresses. On the morning when Troilus will summon Pandarus to await the faithless lady at the gate, the metamorphosed betrayer of a father—Nysus—will be singing aloft. The uncle, opening conversation with Criseyde in the May-time by question about the book to which he found her listening, is informed that it is of Thebes and in particular that it recounted the death of Layus at the hand of Edippus and the descent of Amphiorax to Hell. The awesome saga thus introduced in thoughtless chat is to be grimly associated with the hero of the Trojan legend. The prince, overwhelmed by negotiation of the exchange, will vow to end his life "as Edippe, in derknesse"; in the crucial ten-day interval, will pray Cupide not to be as cruel to the blood of Troy as Juno was to "the blood Thebane"; and, summoning Cassandre to interpret his dream of the boar, will be told by her of the overthrow by Fortune of Theban lords—Amphiorax among them—with the implication that he may see his fate in theirs.

Other suggestive linkings are to be found in the sequences which Chaucer develops principally at the houses of Deiphebus and Pandarus—linkings between them, and in them to later ranges of the action. Criseyde is tolled to each house under false pretenses—to the one for a dinner, to the other for a supper party. In the former, Troilus has a private conference with her from a bed where he lies in feigned illness; in the latter, he comes to her bedside and is brought to genuine swoon by her reproaches for his alleged jealousy. Like Troiolo, he will be ready to kill himself when he thinks her dead on the last night, but is kept from telltale faint in parliament as well as from ignominiously futile struggle with the confidant for a suicidal weapon. The fiction of legal chicanery of Antenor against Criseyde employed by Pandarus in the first of the twin sequences is a foreshadowing in lightsome vein of the narrator's portentous observation, re the exchange of that warrior, about his impending betrayal of the city. And the fiction, used by the uncle in the second, of her having given his friend cause for jealousy of Horaste is one of the fact that she will misbehave with Diomede. She is moved by the allegation that her lover is jealous to conclude that true bliss is impossible on earth, as she will be by the negotiation of the exchange, and as the narrator will be by backward view of the whole story. When Pandarus approaches her bed after dawn has banished Troilus from it, she covers her face to hide blushes and reproaches the visitor coyly for her involvement, as she will hide tears from him when he finds her abed after the parliament and speak of joys he effected as turned to woe.

In the descending action, Chaucer modifies ironies provided by Boccaccio and considerably fortifies them. He sets against the heroine's defection soon to come even more solemn promises of return than those written for her by his author and, instead of the tribute paid to her by the lover, an admission of his worthiness of her everlasting love. Troilus, like Troiolo, finds that the comfort for his dreams offered him by the friend is specious. Momentarily convinced of death after the restless night following Criseyde's departure, he prays for guidance of his soul by Mercurye, of which, despite subsequent hopefulness, he is ere long in need. Portraits of hero and heroine ranged by Chaucer beside that of Diomede adapted from the *Filostrato* contrast spotless excellences of Troilus with the blemished of the other two. Supplying an answer to the hero's epistle to her in camp which he adapts from the *Filostrato,* our poet opposes the disingenuity of her use of the pen to the sincerity of her correspondent's, as Boccaccio had done with the pair of letters he quoted in the ascending action. And he represents Troilus to have controverted the indictment of his lady by a true seeress as determinedly as Troiolo the attack on her by a spurious one and then, like the earlier protagonist, to have been forced to denunciation of the mistress by incontrovertible evidence of her faithlessness.

Impressionistic review of Chaucer's procedures of adaptation having now been completed with illustration of his development of ironic tie-ups, a bold summary is in order. He brings all four principals into more explicit lip service to the code of courtly love than Boccaccio and contrasts them as to realization of word in deed more precisely in terms of that system. At the same time, he makes the affair a more dateless exemplar of romantic love common to all ages by feminization of the heroine, sublimation of the hero, enlivening of the rival as that lover's antitype, and humanization of the go-between both as friend and relative. And manifesting in their relationships the control which God is believed to exercise directly or mediately over all of us, he universalizes the pursuit of love in ancient Troy as an instance of the vanity of human wishes. Attentive beyond Boccaccio to place and time, he appears thereby the truer historian, integrates his more elaborate version of the story by closer linkage of events both temporally and spatially, achieves more of three-dimensional realism by sharper visualization of setting and action against it, and now glamorizes now minifies the behavior of the characters through glimpses of nature's pageant. Such supplementation of the original in literal particulars is matched by enrichment of it in figurative associations. Congruent, they refine contrast and broaden its significance,

426

multiply tensions accordingly but organize them into a unity no less powerful than Boccaccio's for being more complex. This unity achieved with much
art rests upon unity of spirit.

An understanding, sympathetic yet dispassionate, pervades the *Troilus*, an
understanding which encompasses diverse manifestations of human nature,
finds all of interest, discriminates smilingly or gravely but never with severity,
and can therefore communicate to us a view of the whole in which tolerance
and critical perception are harmoniously blended. Until the Epilog, the
oppositions which Chaucer effects are oblique rather than polar whether
between virtues and defects in individuals, between persons, or between the
endeavors of these mortals and what is celestially decreed for them. We can
be amused by his Diomede and charmed by Criseyde while recognizing the
heartlessness of the one and the halfheartedness of the other; grant Troilus'
worldly merits, yet smile at the absurdities in which the plots of his friend
involve him; appreciate the latter's motives in procuring for the prince
without being put off by his joviality from condemning them; and savor the
delight which he won for his master with the help of a storm, though we
must anticipate that destiny so impressively evidenced in this phenomenon
will overwhelm them both. And even the polar opposition in the Epilog of
heavenly to mundane affection cannot obliterate our memories of the fine if
soon withered fruits which the latter yielded to the hero. Our zest unspoiled
by the finale, we begin the poem again and again, which as its author prayed
with some worldliness has been spared the ravages of time.

Notes

PREFACE

1. Professor Young's "Chaucer's *Troilus and Criseyde* as Romance," *PMLA.*, LIII (1938), 38-63, is the definitive presentation of the case for considering the poem a romance. He shows that Chaucer brought the story closer to the genre than it was in the *Filostrato* by changing some of the urban reality of the source into romantic glamor and by increasing and refining the element of courtly love and that he did *not* divorce it from the genre by elaborating psychological analysis or by making the confidant an earthy and comic figure. Granting the insights gained from earlier consideration of the *Troilus* as novel, he asserts that fuller ones are to be derived from approach to it as romance. An article which he praises with characteristic generosity, C. S. Lewis' "What Chaucer Really Did to *Il Filostrato*," *Essays and Studies*, XVII (1932), 56-75, maintains a less specific, but compatible, thesis that Chaucer's transformation of his source was "first and foremost a process of *medievalization*." In the *Allegory of Love* (Oxford: Clarendon Press, 1936), pp. 176-97, Lewis, however, attributes this process, not to the influence of romantic narrative, but to that of the allegory of the *Roman de la Rose*.

Distinguished medievalists have presumed to call the *Troilus* a novel though with recognition, of course, of its ties with older forms. For example, W. P. Ker, in *Epic and Romance*, 2d ed. (London: Macmillan, 1908), p. 367, refers to it as "the poem in which medieval romance passes out of itself into the form of the modern novel"; Professor Lowes, in "The Prologue to the *Legend of Good Women* Considered in its Chronological Relations," *PMLA.*, XX (1905), 821, as "a full-fledged modern 'problem novel' "; and Professor Kittredge, *Chaucer and his Poetry* (Cambridge: Harvard Univ. Press, ᶜ1915), pp. 109, 112, as "the first novel, in the modern sense, that ever was written in the world" and as "an elaborate phychological novel." John Speirs considers Chaucer in the *Troilus* to be "poet, dramatist, novelist in one" but finds that the work in its leisureliness "more resembles a great Tolstoyan novel than a Shakespearian play," *Chaucer the Maker* (London: Faber and Faber, 1951), pp. 49-50. The novelist, Frederic Prokosch declares it to be the "loveliest as well as the first of our English novels" and supports his judgment with a brilliant appreciation of the work, "Geoffrey Chaucer" in *The English Novelists A Survey of the Novel by Twenty Contemporary Novelists*, ed. Derek Verschoyle (New York: Harcourt Brace, ᶜ1936), pp. 3-16, with quotation from p. 3.

In *The Medieval Heritage of Elizabethan Tragedy* (Berkeley: Univ. of California Press, 1936), pp. 137-60, Willard Farnham singles out aspects of Chaucer's adaptation of the *Filostrato* designed "to make it into a tragedy according to his understanding of the term," p. 138. As this scholar temperately puts the case, "The originality of the *Troilus* is multifarious, and the work can be appreciated critically from many widely different angles of observation. But viewed as a tragedy in the tradition set by Boccaccio's *De Casibus* its originality chiefly consists in its discovery that a story of serious misfortune gains enormously in force of tragic impact when it is plotted at greater length than that of any story in the *De Casibus* or the *Monkes Tale* and with more leisurely attention to the details of setting, dialogue, and action," p. 137. D. W. Robertson, Jr., in his study, "Chaucerian Tragedy," *ELH.*, XIX (1952), deduces Chaucer's conception of tragedy from statements in the *Monk's Prologue* and *Tale*, pp. 1-11; and presents the *Troilus* as following, "in its general outlines," the theory which he attributes to the author, pp. 11-37. Summarizing his—to me—overly positive analysis of the work, he asserts, "There is thus a remarkable logic in the events of Chaucer's tragedy, an intellectual coherence that is rooted firmly in Christian doctrine and Boethian philosophy. The tragedy of Troilus is, in an extreme form, the tragedy of every mortal sinner," p. 36. Walter Clyde Curry, essaying classification of the poem in his "Destiny in Chaucer's *Troilus*," *PMLA.*, XLV (1930), 162-65, opines: "This dramatic narrative, founded ultimately upon a mediaeval philosophy, occupies a sort of middle ground artistically between the ancient Greek tragedy and the modern tragedy of Shakespeare," p. 164. In the Introduction to his edition of the *Troilus*, pp. xlix-1, Professor Root concedes that "it is a tragedy in the medieval sense of the term," but goes on to say: "And yet the story does not make on us a really tragic effect. It is rather a tragic story handled in the spirit of high comedy." ◆That spirit is emphasized in Mark Van Doren's appreciation of the poem in his book, *The Noble Voice* (New York: Holt, c1946), pp. 257-82. Gordon H. Gerould opines in his *Chaucerian Essays* (Princeton: Princeton Univ. Press, 1952), p. 84, that the *Troilus* may be considered a tragedy, "even though very many of its scenes are conceived and executed in the spirit of comedy."

2. The abundant scholarship devoted to Chaucer's rhetoric has established that there is a great deal in rhetorical treatises available to him which may well have shaped his art in the *Troilus* as well as elsewhere. But there is always the competing influence of the rhetorical practice of his sources to be reckoned with, even in passages of his not taken from any one of them. This difficulty is pointed up by Robert A. Pratt. Alluding to the article of Daniel C. Boughner, "Elements of Epic Grandeur in the *Troilus*," *ELH.*, VI (1939), 200-10, which plausibly argues that our poet was influenced by the principles of high style enunciated in Dante's *De vulgari eloquentia* and Boccaccio's *De genealogia deorum*, Professor Pratt suggests that the example of the *Teseida* "may have had more to do with Chaucer's decision to rework the story of *Il Filostrato* in a heightened manner" than these precepts (or, incidentally, than the example of the *Divine Comedy* also noted by Boughner), "Chaucer's Use of the *Teseida*," *PMLA.*, LXII (1947), 611-12.

3. Despite the extensive and competent investigations which have been made of Chaucer's metrics and of the qualities and quantities of his vowels and consonants, no one can be sure that he is reading the lines as the poet would have uttered them. And even if one were positive of this, he could not deny that his responses to sound patterns must be highly subjective. See, however, Dorothy Everett, "Chaucer's 'Good Ear," *RES.*, XXIII (1947), 201-8.

4. Boston: Houghton Mifflin, c1933. In the second edition of Robinson's works of Geoffrey Chaucer (c1957), the text of the *Troilus* and the Textual Notes to it are taken virtually without change from the first; the Explanatory Notes, occasionally expanded in cognizance of recent scholarship. Since I have gone directly to as much of this scholarship as concerns me, I need not refer to his citations of the same. My references by page to his scholarly apparatus as printed in the first edition will only slightly inconvenience users of the repaginated second.

5. For Robinson's constitution of the text of the *Troilus*, see his first edition of the Works, pp. xxxvi and 1023-24.

6. For Root's findings and conclusions about the manuscripts, see his edition, *The Book of Troilus and Criseyde* (Princeton: Princeton Univ. Press, 1926), pp. li-lxxxix, and also his *Textual Tradition of Chaucer's Troilus*, Chaucer Soc., Ser. I, XCIX (1916 for 1912), *passim*, esp. pp. 248-72.

7. *Il Filostrato e il Ninfale Fiesolano*, Scrittori d'Italia, No. CLXV (Bari: Gius. Laterza & Figli, 1937). See pp. 353-67 for Pernicone's listing of manuscripts and statement of principles of textual construction.

8. "I manoscritti del 'Filostrato' di G. Boccaccio," *Studi di filologia italiana*, V (1939), 41-82. See p. 81 for Pernicone's characterization of Boccaccio's revision.

9. The information given in the article, while insufficient to classify the manuscript used by Chaucer, does suggest that he did *not* use manuscripts of certain types. Group β has the form Griseida instead of Criseida. Subtype p of β has an order of lines in one stanza different from that followed by Chaucer in his adaptation. Subtype b¹ of group γ lacks one stanza rendered by him and subtype b² omits another. This negative evidence is useless for the present study. As Pernicone remarks in the notes to his edition, p. 373, an English scholar, William A. Walker, hoped to study the manuscripts of the *Filostrato* to determine the affiliation of the one employed by our poet. But, through correspondence with Mr. Walker (whose address was kindly supplied to me by Professor Pratt), I have learned that he has given up the project.

Pernicone has not carried out his own intention, stated in his article, p. 81, of publishing an edition of the *Filostrato* with textual notes.

10. *The Filostrato of Giovanni Boccaccio A Translation with Parallel Text by Nathaniel Edward Griffin and Arthur Beckwith Myrick* (Philadelphia: Univ. of Pennsylvania Press, 1929). The only notable change made by them in Moutier's text in vol. XIII of his *Opere volgari di Giovanni Boccaccio* (Florence: il Mugheri, 1827-34) is the substitution of the form "Criseida" for that of "Griseida."

CHAPTER I *The Action in Its Course*

Section 1 *Introduction: Proportions and Emphases*

1. It has been argued that a fuller version, than that now extant, of Benoit's principal source may have given him the love story. Until one is unearthed or more evidence is presented for any such having ever existed, the credit for inventing the story may be left to the French poet. According to Constans, the definitive editor of his work, *Le Roman de Troie, SATF.*, 1904-12, VI. 182-91, he composed it in the period 1155-60. The last fifth of his work (11. 24425-30316) is based upon the fourth-century *Ephemeris belli Troiani*, a Latin work purportedly translated, at one remove, from the autograph war report of a Dictys the Cretan who served with the Greek host), with only secondary dependence upon the sixth-century *De excidio Troiae historia* (purportedly translated directly from the autograph report of one Dares the Phrygian, a supporter of the Trojans). The preceding four-fifths, however, is based upon the latter. And it is in this range that the love triangle is developed. In the text of Dares, as it has come down to us, Troilus and Diomedes are prominent as warriors on their respective sides and Calchas as a turncoat soothsayer, but Briseida has no part in the action. There is nothing relating to her, except a brief psychophysical description—this in a gallery of portraits of Greeks and Trojans which is presented before the account of the siege is even begun (Chs. xii-xiii). She is left free for attachment to Troilus or any other hero, since no mention is made of her experiences with Achilles or Agamemnon. With no indication of parentage except her name—a patronymic unrecognizable as such by one innocent of Greek—she is left free also for fathering by Calchas or any other man of years. There is not even a hint, however, of any new liaison or blood relationship; Troilus and Diomedes encounter one another, indeed, but only as national enemies, and Calchas pursues his traitorous course untrammeled by parenthood. All that Dares gave Benoit, then, was an opening for the exercise of creative imagination.

2. As stated in my Preface, analysis of Boccaccio's sources is not germane to my purposes. They are extensively treated in Karl Young's *The Origin and Development of the Story of Troilus and Criseyde*, Chaucer Society, Second Series, XL (1908 for 1904), Chs. I and II and Appendix A, and in Griffin's Introduction to his and Myrick's edition of the *Filostrato*, pp. 24-70. On Boccaccio's changing the name Briseida to Criseida, see Ernest H. Wilkins, "Criseida," *MLN.*, XXIV (1909), 65-67. On his possible indebtedness for Troiolo's courtship to Benoit's account of Diomedes', see R. M. Lumiansky, "Aspects of the Relationship of Boccaccio's *Il Filostrato* with Benoit's *Roman de Troie* and Chaucer's *Wife of Bath's Tale*," *Italica*, XXXI (1954), 1-4. See also Lumiansky, "The Story of Troilus and Briseida according to Benoit and Guido," *Spec.* XXIX (1954)), 727-33.

3. The increase is 144 per cent, from 5704 lines to 8239.

4. The *Filostrato* was completed in its author's twenties; the *Troilus*, considerably later, it would appear, in the life of its author. Born in 1313, Boccaccio fell in love with Maria in 1336 and had enjoyed and lost her by 1339. If his Proemio is to be taken at face value, he wrote his poem while still not possessed of her body. From Chaucer's testimony in the Scrope-Grosvenor trial it seems that he was born in the earlier 1340's; see Oliver F. Emerson, "Chaucer's Testimony as to his Age," reprinted from *MPh.* XI (1913), 117-25, in his *Chaucer Essays and Studies* (Cleveland:

Western Reserve Univ. Press, 1929), pp. 247-62. The consensus of Chaucerians is that the *Troilus* was in process in the earlier 1380's although Professor Tatlock held to the end of his life, it seems to me too hard, that Gower may have been referring to it in *Mirour de l'Omme* of 1377—*The Mind and Art of Chaucer* (Syracuse: Syracuse Univ. Press, ᶜ1950), p. 51. Usk shows knowledge of all five books of the *Troilus* (including IV. 953-1085 added by Chaucer in revision) in his *Testament,* composed very likely in the period, Dec., 1384-June, 1385, and certainly, as his executioners determined, before 1388. See Ramona Bressie, "The Date of Thomas Usk's *Testament of Love,*" *MPh.,* XXVI (1928), 16-29. The reader interested in the dating of the *Filostrato* may begin with the Introduction, pp. 2-24, to Griffin and Myrick's edition and with p. 372 of the notes in Pernicone's; nothing will be said in this book about the evidence for it.

5. The ascending action fills 2344 lines in the *Filostrato* (I. 1-III.93) or 41 per cent of its total, and 4669 lines in the *Troilus* (I. 1-III. 1820), 57 per cent of its total; the descending action occupies 3360 and 3570 lines in the old and new works respectively.

6. See Robert A. Pratt, "Chaucer and *Le Roman de Troyle et de Criseida,*" *StPh.,* LIII (1956), 509-39, for our poet's use of Beauvau's translation, printed by L. Moland and C. d'Héricault in their *Nouvelles Françoises en prose du XIVᵉ Siècle* (Paris: Jannet, 1858), pp. 115-304. Of the some three hundred verbal parallels between the translation and Chaucer's poem noted by Pratt, I have recorded those most pertinent to my study in the following notes: Ch. I. 6. notes 39, 63; 8. notes 19, 24; 9. note 6; 10. notes 4, 5; 11. notes 5, 9; Ch. II. 2. notes 49, 64, 65, 92; 3. note 61; 4. notes 71, 72, 74, 91, 100, and 106; 5. notes 48, 54; 6. notes 108, 130, 201; Ch. III. 2. note 50; 3. notes 53, 108, 116, 160; 5. notes 102, 163; 6. note 59; 7. note 71; 8. note 87; Ch. IV. 3. notes 63, 139. See Hubertis M. Cummings, *The Indebtedness of Chaucer's Works to the Italian Works of Boccaccio* (Menasha: Banta 1916), Ch. V, for the use made in the *Troilus* of the *Filostrato,* although it is to be noted that he exaggerates Chaucer's dependence upon this work of Boccaccio's no less than in other chapters he under-estimates the poet's use of other works of the Italian. In Ch. I, he goes so far as to deny altogether our poet's recourse to the *Filocolo* established by Professor Young. See the latter's *Origin and Development,* Ch. IV, for influence of that poem upon the *Troilus,* a chapter which I have been able to supplement. In all my citations of passages in the *Filocolo,* it may be noted, I shall give page references both to the edition cited by Professor Young, Ignazio Moutier's *Opere volgari di Giovanni Boccaccio* (Florence: Stamperia Magheri, 1824-37), vols. VII and VIII, designated as I and II, and to Salvatore Battaglia's edition of the poem, No. CLXVII of the series Scrittori d'Italia (Bari: Laterza, 1938). See also the *Origin and Development,* Ch. III, for Chaucer's use of the *Roman de Troie* and Guido's *Historia,* which chapter makes referral un-necessary to James W. Broatch, "The Indebtedness of Chaucer's *Troilus* to Benoit's *Roman,*" *JEGP.,* II (1898), 14-28, and to George L. Hamilton, *The Indebtedness of Chaucer's Troilus and Criseyde to Guido delle Colonne's Historia Trojana* (New York: Columbia Univ. Press, 1903). My references to the *Roman* will be to Leopold Constans' edition, *SATF.,* 1904-12; and to the *Historia,* to Nathaniel E. Griffin's edition, Cambridge (Mass.), Mediaeval Academy, 1936. Other scholarship on sources will be cited, as occasion arises, in following sections of the present chapter and in following chapters.

7. For more delicate quantitative analyses of the *Filostrato* and *Troilus* than those attempted in notes 8-19, see Rudolph Fischer, *Zu den Kunstformen des mittelalterlichen Epos* . . . , Wiener Beiträge, IX (1899), 215-370. These I have not used.

8. Analysis of scenes by length is conditioned by the principles followed for their delimitation. In this work, these are: to consider any scene to begin and to end with any indication there may be of a change of place or a lapse of time, even a little time; and when such indication is lacking to rely, perforce, upon subjective judgment. If another system were followed, as for example, a change of scene with every entrance or exit, different statistics would obviously result. According to the one used, there are 56 scenes in the *Filostrato*—27 of fifty lines or fewer, 28 between a floor of fifty and a ceiling of three-hundred lines, and one above that ceiling; 72 scenes in the *Troilus,* with 39 in the first group, 28 in the second, and five in the third. For another tally

of scenes in the *Troilus*, see Thomas R. Price's "Troilus and Criseyde, A Study in Chaucer's Method of Narrative Construction," *PMLA.*, XI (1896), 312-15.

9. In the *Filostrato*, the meeting of Troiolo and Criseida on the night after the parliament (IV. 127-67) runs to 328 lines. In the *Troilus*, the first conversation of confidant and prince (I. 547-1061) runs to 515, the first of confidant and lady (II. 78-595) to 518, the first scene in the little closet of Pandarus' house (III. 743-1528) to 786, the conversation between Troilus and Pandarus after the parliament (IV. 351-658) to 308, and the meeting of the lovers on the ensuing night (IV. 1247-1701) to 455. These correspond respectively to the following much shorter scenes in the *Filostrato*: II. 1-33, II. 34/4-67, III. 31-52/2, IV. 43/5-77, and the above cited IV. 127-67.

10. In the *Filostrato*, 3445 lines, 60 per cent of its total of 5704, give direct discourse; in the *Troilus*, 4821 lines, 59 per cent of its total of 8239. The 3445 lines of the former include 145 divided between a character and the author but counted as entirely the character's; the 4821 of the latter include 396 of this kind.

11. The percentages of lines in direct discourse in the five books of the *Troilus* and in corresponding ranges of the *Filostrato* are severally as follows: *Fil.* I. 1-II. 34/3 and *TC.* I, 47 per cent and 52 per cent; *Fil.* II. 34/4-143 and *TC.* II, 79 per cent and 66 per cent; *Fil.* III. 1-93 and *TC.* III, 53 per cent and 52 per cent; *Fil.* III. 93-IV. 167 and *TC.* IV, 67 per cent and 70 per cent; *Fil.* V-IX and *TC.* V, 55 per cent and 52 per cent.

12. Only fifteen lines of direct quotation come outside of episodes in the *Filostrato*; only twenty-seven, in the *Troilus*.

13. Of the 3445 lines of direct discourse of the *Filostrato*, Troiolo has 1706; Pandaro, 789; Criseida, 747; Diomede, 98; and Calcas, Cassandra, Deifobo, Ettore, Priamo, and anonymi together, 105. Of the 4821 in the *Troilus and Criseyde*, Troilus has 1462½; Pandarus, 1804½; Criseyde, 1154; Diomede, 153; and Antigone, Calkas, Cassandre, Deiphebus, Eleyne, Ettore, and anonymi together, 247. In this computation, lines divided between a character and the narrator in each poem, as explained in n.10 are counted as the character's. In the *Troilus* alone, some lines are divided between two characters; each of these is counted as a half line for each speaker. In Troilus' total, seven such half lines are included; in Pandarus', eleven; in Criseyde's, four; and in Deiphebus', two. Lines in each poem in which one character quotes another are counted as the quoter's.

14. Contexts of Troiolo's not directed in any part to a hearer or epistolary correspondent, though spoken in some cases in the presence of others, run to 468 lines (*Fil.* I. 38/2-39, 43/3-8, 50/3-56; II. 80/7-8, 107/7-8, 129/3-8, 132/3-8; III. 25/6-8, 74-89; IV. 30/2-40, 121/2-123/7; V. 3/6-5/5, 19/4-21/6, 44/3, 48/7-8, 53/3-8, 54/4-55, 56/2-57, 58/3-7, 59, 60/5-6, 62-66, 69/5-8, 70/8; VII. 77/7-8, 88/8; VIII. 10/7-8). These include monologues; songs; apostrophes to deities, persons absent or oblivious, and inanimates; and silent streams of consciousness. Against this 468, there are 958 spoken by him to others with the intention of being heard (the line references for conversational passages of the hero—as for those of other characters later—being omitted to save space) and 280 written by him in two letters (*Fil.* II. 96-106; VII. 52-75). Self-communicative passages of Troilus run to 558 lines (*TC.* I. 205, 400-20, 422-34, 458-62, 507-39, 936-38; II. 972-73, 1091-92, 1348, 1754-55; III. 52-55, 705-7, 712-35, 1077-78, 1254-74, 1450-63, 1465-70, 1744-71; IV. 165-68, 250-52, 260-336, 958-1082, 1166, 1175-76, 1192-1210; V. 39-49, 205, 218-45, 465-67, 502-4, 540-53, 565-81, 582-602, 606-16, 620-21, 627, 638-44, 650-58, 663-65, 669-79). Against these 558, there are 799½ spoken by him to others and 105 written by him in one letter (V. 1317-1421).

15. Pandaro had only seven lines of self-communication (*Fil.* V. 49/4-8; VII. 10/7-8), and Pandarus, despite the great increase in his line total, only eighteen (*TC.* II. 267-73, 1296-98; IV. 524-25; V. 505, 507-8, 1174-76).

16. With 1015½ lines more than Pandaro all told (1804½ as against 789), Pandarus has only sixty-odd more than he to deliver after the lover has possessed himself of the lady.

17. Criseida had 189 lines of self-communication (*Fil.* II. 69-74, 75/2-78/2, 115/7-117; IV. 79/3, 88-94; V. 6/6-7/8; VI. 4/3-7/8). Against this 189, there are 502

spoken by her to others and 56 written by her in a letter (*Fil.* II. 121-27). Criseyde has 281 lines of self-communication (*TC.* II. 387, 456-62, 651, 653-55, 703-63, 771-805, 807-8, 1582; III. 641-44, 813-40; IV. 743-49, 757-98; V. 58, 689-707, 731-65, 1006-8, 1054-77. 1079-85). Against this 281, there are 831 spoken by her to others and 42 written by her in a letter (*TC.* V. 1590-1631).

18. Criseida had 267 lines of conversation with Troiolo to his 151 with her; 188 with Pandaro to his 252, and 47 with Diomede to his 91. Criseyde has 500½ of conversation with Troilus to his 216½ with her, 275½ with Pandarus to his 702½, and 49 with Diomede to his 128, as well as six with other characters. Pandaro had 530 lines of conversation with Troiolo to the latter's 664 with him; and Pandarus has 1019 with Troilus to the latter's 532, as well as 65 with other characters. Finally Troiolo had 143 lines of conversation with characters beside the heroine and confidant, and Troilus has 51.

19. Boccaccio's Diomede has seven lines of self-communication (*Fil.* VI. 10/2-8) and Chaucer's twenty-five (*TC.* V. 94-98, 100-5, 783-84, 786-94, 796-98). See n. 18 for his lines of conversation.

20. *Dramatic Irony in Chaucer*, Stanford Univ. Publs., Univ. Series, Lang. and Lit., IV, No. 3 (1932), 10-26, 94-98. Comments of mine in the following sections on the ironies of particular scenes have been partly inspired by hers. In his "The Art of Geoffrey Chaucer" (Gollancz Memorial Lecture, 1930), *Proceedings of the British Academy*, XVI, 28-29, Professor Lowes recognizes the fructifying influence of the *Filostrato* upon our poet and includes in it the encouragement of irony.

21. In his *Chaucer in seinen Beziehungen zur italienischen Literatur* (Bonn: Marcus, 1867), Alfons Kissner pronounces the *Troilus* inferior to the *Filostrato*. Summing up, he says, "In Betreff des allgemeinen künstlerischen Wertheshat die englische Nachbildung das italienische Original nicht erreicht: die einheitlich abgerundete Composition ist verlassen und zu einer vieltheiligen, bunten Mosaik geworden," p. 58. Professor ten Brink reverses Kissner's judgment in *Chaucer Studien* (Münster: Russell, 1870), on the ground that Chaucer's aims are loftier than Boccaccio's, but only after conceding that his reach exceeds his grasp: "Es ist dem englischen dichter eben nicht gelungen . . . die verschiedenen gesichtspunkte, welche sich ihm bei der verarbeitung seines stoff geltend machten, bis zu jener höhe zu erheben, wo sie in eine künstlerische gesammtanschauung zusammenflossen," pp. 76. Émile Legouis, though recognizing with ten Brink the ambitiousness of the *Troilus*, is less charitable than he. Likening the poem to a landscape with a Kentish sky "behind the luxurious vegetation of a Neapolitan foreground," he terms the poem a failure, though a glorious one, *Geoffrey Chaucer*, tr. L. Lailavoix (London and New York: Dent, Dutton, 1913), pp. 133-34.

22. For example, Professor Lounsbury observes in his *Studies in Chaucer His Life and Writings* (New York: Harper, 1892), III. 328, "But if the demand were made upon the most censorious critic for a selection of parts to be cut out or compressed, he would with the exception of two passages [Criseyde on worldly felicity and Troilus on predestination] be sorely embarrassed in the task of pointing them out."

23. For scholarship on profane love in the *Troilus*, see Ch. IV. 3.

24. For that stressing religious and moral implications see Ch. IV. 3 and also, as it concerns Troilus' soliloquy and the Epilog, Sections 7 and 11 of the present chapter.

25. *Chaucer and his Poetry*, pp. 110-11.

26. For example, Professor Tatlock, "The People in Chaucer's *Troilus*," *PMLA.*, LVI (1941), 104: "All these, the insight into actual people and the traditional literary usage, the loftiness and the everyday dialog, the unreal ideality in Troilus and the keen even prosaic naturalness of the others, the immersion in unchristian ethics and the abjuring of them in the Epilog, give the poem a clashing discord, which however adds to its appeal."

27. "It is in the *Troilus*, too, that one also feels, again for the first time, that detachment which is also the distinctive note of the greater Canterbury Tales—that wise and urbane detachment with which Chaucer came in the end to view the human comedy. And often when Pandare speaks, one is curiously aware of something in the background—like Meredith's comic spirit with its 'slim feasting smile'—which is playing

the game with Pandare no less urbanely and ironically than he with Troilus and Criseyde," "The Art of Geoffrey Chaucer." p. 29.

Section 2 *Entrances of Hero and Heroine—and of the Narrator*

1. *TC.* I. 1-546 (*Fil.* I. 1-57).
2. Thereafter only in the following passages: *Fil.* III. 1-2, IV. 23-25, IX. 1-8.
3. *TC.* I. 1-56 (*Fil.* I. 1-6). For an *explication de texte* of the opening of each of Hopkins Press, (1951), Ch. VI.
Chaucer's five books, see Professor Malone's *Chapters on Chaucer* (Baltimore: Johns
4. I. 57-147 (*Fil.* I. 7-16). In his "Destiny in Chaucer's *Troilus,*" pp. 135-36, Professor Curry begins his extensive listing of destinal suggestions in the poem with the two additions to the source here noted.
5. I. 148-322 (*Fil.* I. 17-31). For the reflection of Boccaccio's own enamorment in this scene of the *Filostrato* and in similar ones in other of his romances, see Griffin's Introduction, pp. 14-16, 50-56. In his *Origin and Development,* pp. 167-70, Professor Young suggests that Chaucer may have here supplemented the *Filostrato* with the *Filocolo* and with the *Roman de Troie:* that he drew on Boccaccio's description of his own enamorment at the start of the one, p. 6 (ed. Battaglia), I. 5 (ed. Moutier) for Troilus' reaction to love as particularized in *TC.* I. 271-78; and that he drew on Benoit's account of what befell at the commemoration of Hector's death in the other— on ll. 17552-58 for further particulars of Troilus' reaction, *TC.* I. 295-98, 365-67, and on ll. 17495-96, 17500-01, 17515-16, and 17519-20 for picturesque circumstances of the Palladian festival, *TC.* I. 162-68. Since Chaucer used these works later in the *Troilus,* he may have been influenced at this point by one or both, but the similarities adduced do not seem to me to prove conclusively that he was.
6. I. 323-546 (*Fil.* I. 32-57).
7. I. 400-20 (Sonnet No. 132 in Petrarch's *Canzoniere*). See Ernest H. Wilkins, "Cantus Troili," *ELH.*, XVI (1949), 167-73, for a text of the original, an account of it, and an analysis of Chaucer's translation.
8. I. 393-99.
9. *Harvard Studies in Classical Philology,* XXVIII (1917), 47-133. See also Will Héraucourt, *Die Wertwelt Chaucers, Die Wertwelt einer Zeitwende* (Heidelberg: Winter, 1939), p. 161.
10. *TC.* II. 18, 49.
11. II. 12-14.
12. II. 700; III. 502, 575, 1196, 1325, 1817.
13. V. 1653-55.
14. As indicated by Kittredge, pp. 55-72.
15. Horace, *Epistle,* I. ii, begins,
> Troiani belli scriptorem, Maxime Lolli,
> dum tu declamas Rome, Praeneste relegi,

and goes on at some length to praise the work of the "scriptorem" as morally instructive. With "maxime" taken to be, not part of Lollius' name, but an adjective "greatest," and with "scriptorem" misread as "scriptorum," Lollius would be assumed to be the author who is lauded. R. E. Latham, as far back as 1868, suggested that Chaucer had misinterpreted the Epistle, and ten Brink in 1870 that he had been led to do so by a mistranscription. Kittredge endorsed both suppositions, pp. 72-91. Professor Pratt's article, "A Note on Chaucer's Lollius," *MLN.*, LXV (1950), 183-87, by its citation of a manuscript of the *Policraticus* with the reading "scriptorum" and of Foullechat's French translation of 1372 with its misrendering of the line in question makes the conjecture of these scholars a virtual certainty. Other solutions of the Lollius question are in my opinion so implausible as safely to be ignored here. For Chaucer's knowledge of John of Salisbury, see Professor Pratt, "A Note on Chaucer and the *Policraticus . . .*" *MLN.*, LXV (1950), 243-46. For his probable lack of first-hand acquaintance with Horace, see Harriet Seibert, "Chaucer and Horace," MLN., XXXI (1916), 304-07.
16. *HF.* 1464-72. Whether "Gaufride" was Geoffrey of Monmouth—or less probably Geoffrey Chaucer himself—need not concern us here.

17. *TC.* I. 145-47; V. 1770-71. See Sect. 1. n. 1 for Dares and Dictys. There is no evidence that Chaucer knew either at first hand. The first passage may be derived either from Benoit's *Roman de Troie,* 11. 71ff. or from the adaptation of these lines in Guido's *Historia,* p. 4, as pointed out by Young, *Origin and Development,* pp. 129-30. In his "Chaucer's Dares," *MPh.,* XV (1917), 1-22, Professor Root tells us that Joseph of Exeter's twelfth-century adaptation of Dares, used by Chaucer, is itself denominated as the work of Dares in its manuscripts and infers therefrom that our poet may have the adaptation in mind whenever he cites the supposed historian of Troy.

18. III. 91, 1199; V. 1562, 1753, 1854-55. In his note to the last passage, p. 563, Root interprets "forme" as bearing the scholastic sense, "the essential principle of a thing which makes it what it is."

19. E.g.: I. 159, 495; III. 450, 971, 1774 (*Fil.* III. 90); IV. 18, 1415, 1421; V. 19, 799, 816, 834, 1037, 1044, 1050, 1051, 1651, 1758, 1776. In Appendix I to his "Chaucer's Lollius," pp. 92-110, Kittredge lists all passages in the *Troilus,* in the discourse of characters as well as in lines of the narrator, which specify or imply dependence upon authority.

20. Father Denomy sees an extraliterary motive in the pose and hence in the insistence on mere translatorship which contributes to it; namely, a prudential desire to avoid censure from the moral and pious by disclaiming responsibility. See his article cited in Ch. IV. 2. n.23.

21. *Fil.* I. 46; III. 90.

Section 3 *Entrance of the Confidant*

1. Consult the authorities on Boccaccio's sources named in Sect. 1. n.2, for his debt to literature in developing a new role and a personality for Pandarus de Sezile (who in the *Roman de Troie,* 8135, 11315, 11353-56, appears only as a king fighting on the Trojan side and is a minor figure even in that capacity) and in bringing Troilus under the guidance of this transformed character.

2. In his *Origin and Development,* pp. 161-67, Professor Young cites utterances of Feramonte in two conversations with Florio − *Filocolo,* ed. Battaglia, p. 171 (ed. Moutier, I. 219), 188 and 172 (I. 241 and 220), 188 (I. 242), 168 (I. 215-16) − as parallel to the parading of "ensaumples," condemnation of persistence in grief, exculpation of Fortune, and resort to a medical analogy by Pandarus in his first conversation with Troilus − *TC.* I. 652-56 and 696-700, 761-64 and 778-84, 841-54, 855-58. Young also sees in Troilus' disparagement of his friend's "ensaumples," *TC.* I. 755-60, a possible reminiscence of Florio's citation of many in a soliloquy and his conclusion that they do not measure up to his own woe, pp. 199-200 (I. 256-57). And he suggests that the rousing of Florio by Ascalione, Feramonte's companion in the latter's second conversation, p. 186 (I. 238), gave the hint for Pandarus' doing the like with Troilus, *TC.* I. 722-31. As in the enamorment scene (see Sect. 2. n.5), so in this talk of the confidant and hero, indebtedness to the *Filocolo,* while possible because of the use made of it later, does not seem to me to have been positively established.

Dean S. Fansler, *Chaucer and the Roman de la Rose* (New York: Columbia University Press, 1914), pp. 153-56, 187-91, 209-10, points out that Pandarus fulfills all the requirements for a confidant set forth by Love in Guillaume de Lorris' part of the *Roman,* that he derives bits of wisdom from the Amis in Jean de Meun's continuation of it, and that he holds views on Fortune similar to Reason's in the continuation. Yet he says of Pandarus, p. 156, "Altogether there is no one character in the *Roman de la Rose* that approaches him." Noting further that Troilus conforms to Love's prescriptions for a lover, pp. 149-53, he does not claim that Troilus duplicates the Amant in any of his actions or utterances.

Bernard L. Jefferson, *Chaucer and the Consolation of Philosophy of Boethius* (Princeton: Princeton Univ. Press, 1917), pp. 123-25, observes that Troilus corresponds ideologically to Boethius as a character in that dialogue, but Pandarus only in a limited way to Philosophy. Remarking the likeness between the confidant's first visit to the prince and Philosophy's first to Boethius, he qualifies it as follows: "Pandarus is able to administer to Troilus only the 'lighter remedies' of Dame Philosophy; he does not administer the 'stronger remedies' of which Troilus on his higher intellectual plane stands in need, but which Chaucer himself reserves to state in the conclusion."

Noting parallels to *Epistles* of Seneca in the confidant's speeches to Troilus in their first conversation, which even in sum are not very impressive, Harry Morgan Ayres claims that it is with the help of that sententious author "that Pandarus is transformed out of the youth Pandaro," "Chaucer and Seneca," *Rom. Rev.*, X (1919), 11-15.

3. *TC.* I. 547-1061 (*Fil.* II. 1-33).

4. I. 624-721 (*Fil.* II. 10-14).

5. The thesis about contrarieties appears to have been suggested by the *Roman de la Rose*, 21545-82. This and subsequent references to the *Roman* are to the edition of Ernest Langlois, *SATF.*, 1914-24.

6. Ovid, *Her.* v.

7. Ovid, *Met.*, VI. 312.

8. *TC.* I. 722-875 (*Fil.* II. 15-20).

9. I. 876-1061 (*Fil.* II. 21-33).

10. This sentiment, *TC.* I. 977-79, may have been derived from an unmetaphorical phrasing of it in Dante, *Purg.*, xvii, 91-93, as claimed by Mario Praz, "Chaucer and the Great Italian Writers of the Trecento," *Monthly Criterion*, VI (1927), 133-34.

11. *TC.* I. 1062-II. 77 (*Fil.* II. 34/1-3). For an *explication de texte* of the ending of each of Chaucer's five books, see Malone, *Chapters on Chaucer*, Ch. VII.

Section 4 *Preliminary Negotiations*

1. *TC.* II. 1-49.

2. The metaphor is adapted from Dante, *Purg.*, i. 1-3, as pointed out by Professor ten Brink, *Chaucer Studien*, pp. 80-81.

3. As suggested by Boyd A. Wise, *The Influence of Statius upon Chaucer* (Baltimore: Furst, 1911), 7-8, the invocation of Cleo may have been suggested by a briefer one in the *Thebaid*, I. 41.

4. That he was here forestalling surprise at fleshliness is assumed by Professor Tatlock, "The Epilog of Chaucer's *Troilus*," *MPh.*, XVIII (1921), 638, n.3. Professor Young conjectures a tacit apology for the brokerage of Pandarus in this for the affair as a whole, "Aspects of the Story of Troilus and Criseyde," *Univ. of Wisconsin Studies in Language and Literature*, No. 2 (1918), 374-75.

5. *TC.* II. 50-77. The opening lines are:

> In May, that moder is of monthes glade,
> That fresshe floures, blew and white and rede,
> Ben quike agayn, that wynter dede made,
> And ful of bawme is fletyng every mede;
> Whan Phebus doth his bryghte bemes sprede,
> Right in the white Bole, it so bitidde.

A passage from the *Teseida* and one from the *Roman de la Rose* have been proposed as joint sources for them, and I would suggest, as alternate or complement to the former, a passage from the *Filocolo*. In that poem, Boccaccio relates that Florio, who had reached Alexandria when the sun was in its house, found himself at a loss as to how to reach Biancofiore, there immured in a tower. He remained in that state, the poet continues, "infino a tanto *che Febo in quell' animale, che la figliuola d'Agenore trasportò da' suoi regni, se ne venne a dimorare*, e quivi quasi nella fine congiunto con Citerea, rinnovellato il tempo, cominciò gli amorosi animi a riscaldare, e a raccendere i fuochi divenuti tiepidi *nel freddo e ispiacevole tempo del verno*: e massimamente quello di Filocolo," p. 388 (ed. Battaglia), II. 149 (ed. Moutier). Even thus enkindled, Florio, or Filocolo, as he now called himself, did nothing effective until the sun had moved from Taurus into Gemini. Then he galloped off boldly to the tower, and gained the friendship of its castellano, Sadoc. He thus initiated the procedures which were eventually to bring him to the couch of Biancofiore—a sequence of which Chaucer was to make extensive use in his account of the consummation of Troilus' affair. If this passage gave Chaucer the initial suggestion for his above dating, he must still have drawn upon the *Roman* but might or might not have upon the *Teseida*. The mention of winter as past in the *Filocolo* could have recalled to him the description of the vernal countryside in the *Roman,* 45-66, since it contains reference to that dead time as happily over. This description would have provided all necessary inspiration for his vegetational details. If, on the contrary, the stanzas in the *Teseida* III. 5-6, proposed as a source, gave him the initial hint, he must still have used the *Roman,* 45-66, but not necessarily the *Filocolo.* The first of the two contexts dates the enamorment of Arcita and Palemone by the presence of Febo in that "umile animale" which bore Eüropa away, and the second describes the burgeoning of vegetation, but without mention of departed winter or of the hues of flowers.

For Proigne's awakening of Pandarus, *TC.* II. 64-70, no one source can be positively distinguished. There is a detailed if short mention of her tragedy in the seventh question of love adjudged by Fiammetta in the *Filocolo,* p. 342 (ed. Battaglia), II. 89 (ed. Moutier), but no suggestion of her singing as a bird. Passages in the *Teseida,* IV. 73, and the *Purgatorio,* ix. 13-15, which have been adduced as sources, do not seem likely as such, since in them it is not the metamorphosed Proigne who sings but her sister Philomela. Chaucer would have had in mind the full account of the tragedy given by his favorite, Ovid—*Metamorphoses,* VI. 424-674—whatever his immediate source.

6. Since Palamon escapes from prison on May third (*CT.* I. 1462-69) and was immediately involved in an altercation with Arcite and since Chauntecleer was seized by the fox on that day (*CT.* VII. 3187-97), it would appear that Chaucer thought it portentous, though we cannot be sure why. Professor Manly provides much scholarly conjecture on the former passage in his partial edition of the *Canterbury Tales* (New York: Holt, ᶜ1929), pp. 549-51, and Professor Robinson also in his note to it, pp. 775-76. In the course of her article, "Joan of Kent and the Order of the Garter," *Univ. of Birmingham Hist. Journal,* I (1947), 13-50, Miss Galway argues that the date was significant to Chaucer, at least partly, because Joan, his supposed inspiration, was released as of May 3, 1348, by papal mandate from the custody of her then husband, Montague, in the sequence of proceedings to restore her to Holland, to whom she had contracted herself in girlhood. On p. 49, Miss Galway finds confirmation for this belief in the *Troilus* from the alleged fact that the flowers mentioned in the stanza bringing up May third are of Joan's heraldic colors, white and red (unfortunately the flowers are "*blew* and white and rede"). See Ch. IV. 2. n.21 for critical reception of Miss Galway's theories about Joan. In his already cited article, "Chaucerian Tragedy," p. 19, Professor Robertson would have it that the poet considered the date to be unlucky for Pandarus—and all other benighted followers of Venus—because it was the day of Saint Helena, who cast down the idol of that goddess and who set up the cross in Jerusalem. This conjecture is indemonstrable, and I see no support for it in the facts earlier pointed out by Roland M. Smith, "Three Notes on the Knight's Tale," *MLN.,* LI (1936), 319-20, that in the *King of Tars,* a defeat of Christians takes place on May third and that, in one manuscript thereof, the day is identified, without comment, as "Of seynt Eline."

7. Willard Farnham, "The Dayes of the Mone," *StPh.,* XX (1920), 70-82, esp. 71. Professor Curry, however, assumes astrological proficiency on the confidant's part at this juncture—"Destiny in Chaucer's *Troilus,*" pp. 137-38.

8. *TC.* II. 78-597 (*Fil.* II. 34/4-67).

9. In his *Chaucer and the Roman Poets,* Harvard Studies in Comparative Literature, VII (1929), 160-68, Professor Edgar Finley Shannon argues that Ovid's Helen was the literary model for Criseyde. He cites general resemblances between their situations and passages in the former's letter to Paris, *Her* xvii (xvi), which he considers parallel to lines spoken by Criseyde, mainly in Book II. Neither general nor particular likenesses are close enough to be convincing. Miss Galway would have it that Criseyde is partially to be identified with Joan of Kent—see Ch. IV. 2. n. 21.

10. *TC.* II. 78-217 (*Fil.* II. 34/4-35/7).

11. Criseyde's designation of the volume as a "romaunce" points to the *Roman de Thèbes* (ed. Léopold Constans, *SATF.,* 1890), and her entitling Amphiorax a "bisshop" echoes the designation of him in that poem as "arcevesque," 2026, 2072, and "evesque," 5053, but the remark made by Pandarus, to show his erudition, that the work was in twelve books identifies it with the *Thebaid.* Chaucer would naturally prefer the lesser anachronism of the reading by Trojans of a Roman author to the greater of the

reading of a medieval. He avoids making even the former an explicit one by not naming Statius as the author of the twelve-book production. For Amphiorax's death, see the *Roman*, 4829-38, and the *Thebaid*, VII. 794-823. For further light on allusion here to the *Roman*, see Wise, *The Influence of Statius upon Chaucer*, pp. 8-9, 127-29, 137.

12. *TC*. II. 218-385 (*Fil*. II. 35/7-46).

13. II. 386-597 (*Fil*. II. 47-67).

14. In his *Origin and Development*, pp. 162-63, Professor Young suggests that Pandarus' account of his rousing Troilus from brown study on the first of the days, *TC*. II. 542-50, was derived from Ascalione's so rousing Florio in the *Filocolo*, p. 186. (ed. Battaglia), I. 238 (ed. Moutier), and perhaps also from Feramonte's doing the like, p. 167 (I. 214). The parallels are not conclusive.

15. *TC*. II. 598-812. (*Fil*. II. 68-78).

16. The mention of the gate of Dardanus as Troilus' point of re-entry indicates use of Benoit's *Roman de Troie*, as remarked by Young, *Origin and Development*, pp. 137-39. Of the six gates enumerated in the *Roman*, 3139-72, only this one figures in accounts of warfare: in that of the second battle, where it is described at length, 7671-86, and in that of the twenty-first, 23511. The account of the second apparently proved useful to Chaucer. Benoit's comment that Fortune was responsible for the Trojans not completing the discomfiture of the Greeks, 10121-86, appears to have suggested our poet's comment on Troilus' destiny, the last two lines of which resemble the last two of Benoit's:

> Si ert la chose a avenir
> Que rien nel poëit destolir.

(Boethius' *Consolation*, V. pr. vi, may also have contributed here—through association.) The public acclamation of Hector, when he returned, honorably scarred, from the battle, 10201-32—to which he had gone through the aforementioned gate, opened at his command, 7671-72—probably suggested to Chaucer the triumph of his hero. The transfer of a popular welcome from the one brother to the other would have been easy enough, since Troilus is extolled for valor by Benoit, *in propria persona*, and through the lips of Hector, before the battle, 7749-72, and is made to take an active part in it. The conclusion of another battle, the sixteenth, may also have contributed to Chaucer's spectacle, although there is no mention in it of the aforesaid gate; Benoit, in there describing triumphant return of Troilus himself, 20597-627, represents him to have borne many marks of combat, as our poet does.

17. As acknowledged by Robinson in a note, p. 931, the influence here of the *Roman d'Eneas* was remarked to him by Professor Lowes. The episode concerned in it, 8025-8398, in Salverda de Grave's edition, Les classiques français du moyen age, XLIV, LXII (1925, 1929), bears a general similarity to Criseyde's viewing of Troilus, with Lavine beholding Eneas from her window when, in time of truce, he rides past the city which he is beleaguering. And, although Lavine's response is much more precipitate than Criseyde's, the question with which she begins a long soliloquy:

> "Lasse," fait ele, "que ai gié?
> Qui m'a sorprise, que est cié?" 8083-84

may have suggested the latter's laconic "Who yaf me drynke?"

18. For astrological interpretations of the passage *TC*. II. 680-86—see Root's note, p. 446, and Curry, "Destiny in Chaucer's *Troilus*," pp. 139-41.

19. *TC*. II. 813-931.

20. *TC*. III. 1744-71, replacing *Fil*. III. 74-89.

21. *Origin and Development*, pp. 173-76.

22. See Kittredge's brief note, "Antigone's Song of Love," *MLN*., XXV (1910), 158. The *Paradis*, a poem of 198 lines in varying stanzas, is to be found in Machaut's *Poésies lyriques* edited by V. Chichmaref (Paris: Champion, 1909), II. 345-51. Parallels to concepts in Antigone's song, as I distinguish them, are as follows. Her thankful devotion to love expressed in feudal terms, *TC*. II. 827-30 and 848-50: *Paradis*. 33-37, 109-22, and 183-93; her happiness in love, *TC*. II. 831-36: *Paradis*. 1-32, 59-76, and 153-62; the manifold excellence of her lover, *TC*. II. 837-47: *Paradis*. 42-58, 95-108; her moral improvement by love, *TC*. II. 851-54: *Paradis*. 77-86, 133-52, 163-82; her condemnation and refutation of disprizers of love, *TC*. II. 855-68: not in *Paradis*,

but instead an assertion that one who is not in love would be if he knew its weal, 123-32; determination to cherish her lover forever, *TC*. II. 869-75: *Paradis*, 38-41.

23. Chaucer and the Great Italian writers of the Trecento," *Monthly Criterion*, VI (1927), 29-31, Praz aptly suggests that the "grifo" (snout) of the boar in Troiolo's dream may have led Chaucer, by association, to Dante's "grifon," the symbol of Christ, which as described in *Purg.* xxix, 106-14, is not only half eagle but also partly white, and thence to the spectacular descents of an eagle upon a tree and upon the chariot left tied to it by the "grifon," *Purg.* xxxii, 109-26, with this eagle perhaps then reminding our poet of that other eagle which descended upon Dante himself in his dream, *Purg.* ix, 1-33. Praz confines himself to sources, not offering interpretation of Chaucer's purposes in either dream.

24. For a notion of the eagle which contravenes my belief that its opposition to the boar is favorable to Troilus, see Charles A. Owen, Jr., "Chaucer's *Troilus and Criseyde*, II. 925-31," *Explicator*, IX (1951), item 26. He supposes that Chaucer would have us take the bird ironically—as a symbol of the masterful male whom Criseyde subliminally wanted but who Troilus could never be.

25. *TC*. II. 932-1327 (*Fil*. II. 79-129).

26. In Pandarus' excursus on letter writing, II. 1023-43, the warning against pretentious style comes from Ovid's *Ars amatoria*, I. 463-66, and the suggestion of blotting with tears perhaps from his *Heroides*, iii. 3; the figures of the harper who sticks to one string, perhaps from Horace's *Ars poetica*, 355-56, and that of the painter who makes monstrous combinations, certainly from the *Ars*, 1-5. See Ch. III. 4. n. 75 on the lines from Horace.

27. *TC*. II. 1328-51 (*Fil*. II. 130-32).

Section 5 *Commitment to a Tryst*

1. *TC*. II. 1352-1757 and III. 1-504 (*Fil*. II. 133-43 and III. 1-20).

2. "The Prologue to the *Legend of Good Women* Considered in its Chronological Relations," *PMLA.*, XX (1905), 840. Professor Lowes also sees, p. 839, another foreshadowing here: of Criseyde's woeful hearing of the misdirected consolation of woman friends for her exchange, IV. 701-7 (*Fil*. IV. 83) in her listening gladly to praises of Troilus uttered by her fellow guests at Deiphebus' house, II. 1590-94. This may be of course, but I am dubious of it.

3. *Fil*. VII. 77-103, as noted in Cummings, *The Indebtedness of Chaucer's Works to the Italian Works of Boccaccio*, pp. 59-60.

4. The suggestion is made with admirable scholarly caution by Charles Muscatine in his article, "The Feigned Illness in Chaucer's *Troilus and Criseyde*," *MLN.*, LXIII (1948), 372-77. The story to which he calls attention is to be found in II Samuel, xiii. 1-20; in Peter Comestor's *Historia scholastica*, with only inconsequential variations from the Vulgate; and in the *Jewish Antiquities* of Josephus, with elaboration of several details beyond what is given in the other two versions. In brief, it runs as follows: Amnon, a son of David, who is enamored of Tamar is advised by Jonadab to feign indisposition and to ask his father to send Tamar to him to supply food. Carrying out these instructions, the lover succeeds in raping the lady.

5. *TC*. II. 1352-1535.

6. For possible sources for the name, "Poliphete"—not the lie about him—see Root's note, p. 455, to II. 1467.

7. II. 1536-54.

8. II. 1555-1624. See n.2 for possible anticipation here of IV. 701-7.

9. II. 1625-1757.

10. III. 1-49.

11. *Fil*. III. 74-79. For discussion of ideological forerunners of these stanzas, see Albert S. Cook's "Chaucer's *Troilus and Criseyde* 3. 1-38," *Archiv*, CXIX (1907), 40-54; and, for an argument for direct use in them of Lucretius, an argument developed from Cook's noting of parallels to the *De rerum natura*, see Morton W. Bloomfield, 'The Source of Boccaccio's *Filostrato* III. 74-79 . . . ," *Classical Philology*, XLVII (1952), 162-65. The latter scholar considers the case for Lucretius' poem as source to be

stronger than the generally accepted one for Boethius' *Consolation*, II. m. viii. And for an exegesis of the astronomy and mythology of Chaucer's rendition of the stanzas, see

12. *Purg* i. 7-12, remarked as a source by ten Brink, *Chaucer Studien*, pp. 80-81.
13. *TC* .III. 50-203.
14. III. 204-26.

Root's notes, pp. 463-65.

15. *TC*. III. 227-420 (*Fil*. III. 3-19). As previously remarked, Chaucer does not use Boccaccio's invocation of Maria (*Fil*. III. 1-2).
16. III. 239-45 (*Fil*. III. 5), 360-64 (*Fil*. III. 13).
17. III. 372-85 (*Fil*. III. 15), anticipating V. 1805-6 (*Fil*. VIII. 27).
18. The latter conference, III. 1583-1666 (*Fil*. III. 56-63).
19. III. 421-504 (*Fil*. III. 20).

Section 6 *Union*

1. The sequence: *TC*. III. 505-1666 (*Fil*. III. 21-63); the following period of happiness, III. 1667-1806 (*Fil*. III. 64-93); and Chaucer's conclusion, III. 1807-20, which replaces Boccaccio's, *Fil*. III. 94. The whole is expanded two and a quarter times.
2. III. 505-1190 (*Fil*. III. 21-30).
3. III. 1191-1528 (*Fil*. III. 31-52/2).
4. III. 1529-1666 (*Fil*. III. 52/3-63).
5. III. 1667-1715 (*Fil*. III. 64-71), 1716-36 (*Fil*. III. 72), 1737-71 (*Fil*. III. 73-89), 1772-1806 (*Fil*. III. 90-93).
6. III. 1807-20, replacing *Fil*. III. 94.
7. Ch. I. 2. n.5; 3. n.2; 4. n.5 and n.14; 7. n.24; 8. n.22; 11. n.22.
8. "Chaucer's Use of Boccaccio's 'Filocolo'," *MPh*., IV (1906), 169-77.
9. "The *Franklin's Tale*; the *Teseide*, and the *Filocolo*," *MPh*., XV (1918), 705-13.
10. *TC*. III. 505-46.
11. *Filocolo*, p. 382 (ed. Battaglia), II. 140-41 (ed. Moutier). As I said in Ch. I. 1. n.6, all my citations of the *Filocolo* are to both editions. The shaking of the laurel may derive from Ovid, *Met*. I. 566-67, as remarked by Skeat, II. 477, in his note to *T.C.* II. 542, although there is nothing in Ovid's account of Daphne's metamorphosis to suggest that Apollo ever spoke out of the laurel which she became.
12. *TC*. III. 547-94.
13. For the "chaungynge of the moone," see Root's note, pp. 472-73.
14. Young, *Origin and Development*, pp. 143-44, 145, suggests that Pandarus' ambivalent declaration, III. 568-74, may have been inspired by very different pretenses of Glorizia, *Filocolo*, pp. 405-6 (II. 171), 408 (I. 174), 409 (I. 175).
15. *TC*. III. 595-603.
16. *Filocolo*, pp. 403-4 (II. 167-69), 406-7 (II. 172), as remarked in *Origin and Development*, pp. 144-45.
17. *TC*. III. 604-93, with *Filocolo* and *Origin and Development* as in note 16.
18. In his note, "Concerning Wade," *MLR*., XXXI (1936), 202-3, J. A. W. Bennett suggests that the story of this hero may have been such as would recommend love to Criseyde.
19. See *Inf*. vii. 61-96, esp. 77-84, and Professor Tatlock's "Chaucer and Dante," *MPh*., III (1906), 370-72.
20. For the conjunction and its implications as to the period of composition of the *Troilus*, see Robert K. Root and Henry N. Russell, "A Planetary Date for Chaucer's *Troilus*," *PMLA*., XXXIX (1924), 48-63. The conclusions drawn in this article as to dating are controverted by Professor Tatlock, "The Date of the *Troilus* and Minor Chauceriana," *MLN*., L (1935), 277-89, especially pp. 279-82, and by John J. O'Connor, "The Astronomical Dating of Chaucer's 'Troilus,'" *JEPG*., LV (1956), 556-62.
21. The feast of the Palladium came in April, *TC*. I. 155-61; Pandarus' teen in love, immediately before his visit to Criseyde, on May third, II. 50-63; and the affair at Deiphebus' house, within the same year as the feast, III. 360-64. Indications of lapses of time between the second and third of these points and between the third and the

conjunction make it impossible that the last could have been in the same May as the teen but do not suggest that it was later than the next.

22. See Root's note, p. 475, to *TC.* III. 659-68, and also his notes pp. 475-76 to III. 671 and 674. In his "Chaucer's Ancient and Biblical World," *Mediaeval Studies,* XV (1953), 134-35, Francis P. Magoun charts accommodations at Pandarus' house very differently than Root, and with fundamental errors. These are: the misassignment of the "closet" of III. 663 to Pandarus, which is obviously the same as that of III. 687 occupied by Criseyde; the misassignment to her of the "chaumbre" of III. 676, which is that occupied by her women, III. 666, after it has served for the evening's festivities.
23. *TC.* III. 694-742.
24. For the astrology and mythology here, see Root's notes, pp. 476-78.
25. *Filocolo,* p. 400 (II. 164).
26. *TC.* III. 743-952.
27. *Origin and Development,* pp. 145, 157-61.
28. *Filocolo,* p. 409 (II. 175).
29. Pp. 190-237 (I. 244-305), 279-84 (II. 8-14), 487-93 (II. 277-84).
30. For discussion of this name, see Root's note, p. 479, to *TC.* III. 797, and Robinson's, p. 937.
31. Professor Young, pp. 160-61, suggests that Criseyde's exclamation "Allas, what *wikked spirit* tolde hym thus," *TC.* III. 808, may echo the injunction, "Caccia dalla tua nave quello *iniquo spirito,*" which in a dream of voyaging, Filocolo fancied he heard from Biancofiore, *Filocolo,* p. 202 (I. 259-60). "Wikked spirit," however, is not applied specifically to jealousy as "iniquo spirito" was. See n.36, for further parallels re jealousy suggested by Young.
32. There can be no question that it is a lie. In his note, "A Defense of Troilus," *PMLA.,* XLIV (1929), 1246-47, Professor J. Milton French conclusively disproved the arguments for the actuality of Troilus' jealousy advanced by Joseph S. Graydon in his "Defense of Criseyde," *PMLA.,* XLIV (1929), 160-63. See also Joseph M. Beatty, Jr., "Mr. Graydon's 'Defense of Criseyde,'" *St Ph.,* XXVI (1929), 471-74, for dismissal of jealousy in the hero as a major factor.
33. *Filocolo,* p. 402 (II. 166).
34. *Consolation,* II. pr. iv.
35. *TC.* III. 953-1190.
36. Merits of the lover, *TC.* III. 995-98: *Filocolo,* pp. 210-11 (I. 270-71); promise of happiness, *TC.* III. 1003-8: *Filocolo,* p. 213 (I. 274); jealousy versus love, *TC.* III. 1023-24: *Filocolo,* pp. 218-19 (I. 280-81); jealousy as an illusion, *TC.* III. 1030-34, 1040-41: *Filocolo,* p. 211 (I. 271); assurance of fidelity, *TC.* III. 1045-54: *Filocolo,* pp. 210-11, 213 (I. 270-71, 273-74)—as remarked in *Origin and Development,* pp. 157-60.
37. *Consolation,* I. m. v. esp. 22-35, as remarked in Root's note, p. 482, to *TC.* III. 1016-19.
38. *Filostrato,* IV. 18-21, as remarked by Praz in his "Chaucer and the Great Italian Writers of the Trecento," *Monthly Criterion,* VI (1927), 26-27.
39. *Filostrato,* IV. 19. "Pous" does not occur elsewhere in Chaucer's writings and "revoken" again only in his Retraction appended to the *CT.* As noted by Pratt, *StPh.,* LIII (1956), 522-23, there are verbal echoes in Chaucer's lines also of the rendering of Boccaccio's in *Le Roman de Troyle et de Criseida,* p. 204: "et lui *frotoient* le pouls . . . et arrousoient *ses temples.*"
40. *Filocolo,* p. 413 (II. 181), as remarked in *Origin and Development,* pp. 145-46.
41. *TC.* III. 1191-1528.
42. III. 1191-1309.
43. *Filocolo,* p. 401 (II. 165-66). In his note to *TC.* III. 1192, Robinson, p. 938, remarks the parallel without comment.
44. P.412 (II. 180).
45. Pp. 411-12 (II. 178-79). Moutier's edition has the reading *mamelle* instead of *menne.*
46. *Origin and Development,* pp. 146-47.
47. *Filocolo,* pp. 413 (II. 181), 414 (II. 182), 415 (II. 183).

48. The two other mentions of Imeneus by Chaucer are both later than this one and both in connection with marriage, *CT.* IV. 1729-31, *LGW.* 2249-50.

49. Dante, *Par.* xxxiii. 13-18, as remarked by Root, p. 484, in his note to *TC.* III. 1262-67.

50. Professor Young, *Origin and Development,* pp. 146-47, is of the opinion that it may have been suggested by these ceremonials.

51. *Filostrato,* III. 31-52/2.

52. *TC.* III. 1310-1528.

53. This profession, it may be noted, occurs at a later point in the β state of the text, not coming after III. 1323 as in the γ state, the basis of Robinson's text (which I follow), but after III. 1414 according to his numeration. Root, who bases his text on the β state, prints it in that position. Professor Tatlock, "The Epilog of Chaucer's *Troilus,*" *MPh.,* XVIII (1921), 639-40, takes the profession as an apology for carnality.

54. *Origin and Development,* p. 146.

55. *Filocolo,* p. 413 (II. 181).

56. *TC.* II. 584-85 (with "ruby" particularized from "gemma," *Filostrato.* II. 43); V. 549. See also Pandarus' figure of "the faire gemme vertulees," II. 344.

57. II. 1086-88 (with the same particularization, *Filostrato.* II. 107).

58. See Margret Schinnagel, *Schmuck als Lebensäusserung in den Werken Chaucers* (Würzburg: Triltsch, 1938), for comment on the brooch, pp. 31-33; the ruby in Troilus's signet, p. 47; Criseyde's "blewe ryng," p. 48; their exchange of rings, p. 50; and the metaphors of ruby and virtueless gem, p. 59. For ruby symbolism in other works of Chaucer, see Howard R. Patch, "Precious Stones in *The House of Fame,*" *MLN.,* L (1935), 314-17, and James J. Lynch, "The Prioress's Gems," *MLN,* LVII (1942), 440-41.

59. *TC.* III. 885-87.

60. Dante, *Purg.* xx, 106-8, 116-17, as remarked by Professor Lowes, "Chaucer and Dante," *MPh.,* XIV (1917), 711-14. And for sources supplementary to the *Purgatorio* here, see Professor Shannon, *Chaucer and the Roman Poets,* p. 133. n.2.

61. The epithet is taken from the *De planctu Naturae* of Alanus de Insulis, *PL.,* CCX, 436, as remarked by Robinson in his note, pp. 938-39, to *TC.* III. 1415-26.

62. Mention of Fortuna Major as a harbinger of dawn probably derives from Dante, *Purg.,* xix. 4-6. For astronomical comment on Lucifer and Fortuna Major, see Root and Russell, "A Planetary Date for Chaucer's *Troilus,*" pp. 56-58. An unconvincing interpretation of the latter, contrary to theirs, is offered by Curry, "Fortuna Major," *MLN.,* XXXVIII (1923), 94-96.

63. "The *Franklin's Tale,* the *Teseide,* and the *Filocolo,*" pp. 708-9. As noted by Pratt, *StPh.,* LIII, 520, "O cruel day," *TC.* III. 1450, in Troilus' longish apostrophe corresponds to "O jour cruel" in *Le Roman de Troyle et de Criseida,* p. 185, which in turn renders "o dispietato giorno" in Troiolo's three-line apostrophe of day in the *Filostrato.* III. 46.

64. *Filocolo,* pp. 134-35 (I. 173). "Hemysperie" appears elsewhere in Chaucer's works only in *CT.* IV. 1799 and in the *Treatise on the Astrolabe.* The confusion of Titan the Sun and Tithonus, of course antedates Boccaccio, as Professor Lowes is careful to state. And it appears, not only here, but later in the *Filocolo,* p. 562 (II. 374), and also in the *Teseida,* IV. 72. See note 72, for a suggestion of further influence of this passage—not Lowes' but my own.

65. In his *Chaucer and the Roman Poets,* pp. 133-38, Professor Shannon argued that the twin apostrophes were suggested by Ovid, *Amores.* I. xiii, a reproach to Aurora for haste. It may well have been a companion source here to the *Filocolo* but hardly, as he presumed, the basic source. Reproach in it of Aurora for bringing toil and sorrow may have inspired Criseyde's of night for not affording proper surcease; and its allusion to Jove's long consummation with Alcmena, Criseyde's to the same marvel. Its allusion to Tithonus, as lover of the goddess could have been misinterpreted as to Titan, if the name was erroneously transcribed or glossed.

66. *TC.* III. 1529-47 (*Filostrato,* III. 52/3-54).

67. III. 1548-54 (*Filostrato,* III. 55).

68. III. 1555-82.

69. *Filocolo,* pp. 416-17 (II. 185-86).
70. *TC.* III. 1583-1666 (*Filostrato,* III. 56-63).
71. III. 1667-1715 (*Fil.* III. 64-71).
72. See the passage quoted, pp. 75-76, from the King's diatribe. In Troilus' stanza, *TC.* III. 1702-08, the fancy that "Pirous and tho swifte steedes thre" have taken a shortcut may have been suggested by the opposite fancy of the King's that the sun had reversed its course, and the threat to the sun, "Ne shal I nevere don him sacrifise," by the King's lengthier remarks on sacrifice. The name of Apollo's horse may have come from Ovid, *Met.* II. 153-55, as noted by Root, p. 493.
73. *TC.* III. 1716-36 (*Fil.* III. 72 supplemented by II. 84).
74. III. 1737-43 (*Fil.* III. 73).
75. III. 1744-71 (*Consolation,* II. m. viii). This song, which replaces *Fil.* III. 74-89, may have been added in revision, since it does not appear in two of the four manuscripts representing the *a* state of the text from III. 399 to IV. 196—see Root, *Textual Tradition,* pp. 155-57. For a contrary opinion, see John V. Hagopian, "Chaucer's *Troilus and Criseyde,* III. 1744-71," *Explicator,* X (1951), item 2.
76. See Ch. I. 5. n.11 for the commonly supposed dependence of Troiolo's opening stanzas upon the very metre to which Chaucer resorted.
77. III. 1772-1806 (*Fil.* III. 90-93).
78. *Fil.* III. 94.
79. *TC.* III. 1807-20.
80. *Tes.* I. 3, XI. 63, and *Par.* viii. 1-3, 7-9. See Lowes, "Chaucer and Dante," pp. 731-32, and Root's note, pp. 495-96.

Section 7 *Separation in Prospect*

1. The increase is 127 per cent from 1344 lines to 1701: *TC.* IV. 1-1701 (*Fil.* IV. 1-167, with *Fil.* III. 94 used at the beginning).
2. See Ch. I. 1. n.6; 2. n.5, n.17; 3. n.1; 4. n.16.
3. See Ch. I. 1. n.6; 2. n.17. As stated in the first note, my citations of the *Roman* are to Constans' edition and of the *Historia* to Griffin's, while my principal authority for Chaucer's use of both works is Young, *Origin and Development,* Ch. III. Root's notes supplement Young.
4. *TC.* IV. 1-28.
5. IV. 1-11, expanded from *Fil.* III. 94 as already remarked.
6. As remarked in Professor Lowes, "Chaucer and Dante," pp. 718-24, 733-34, Chaucer's conception of the Furies derives from *Inf.* ix. 37-51 and that of Mars from *Par.* viii. 130-32 perhaps in combination with Ovid, *Met.* XV. 863.
7. *TC.* IV. 29-140 (*Fil.* IV. 1-13/2).
8. An adaptation of Ovid, *Ars am.* I. 68, as remarked by Root, p. 500, in his note to *TC.* IV. 31-32.
9. "The Date of the *Troilus:* and Minor Chauceriana," *MLN.,* L (1935), 282-84.
10. *Roman de Troie,* 12551-65, as remarked by Root, pp. 501-2, in his note to *TC.* IV. 50-54.
11. *Roman,* 12853-13008, and *Historia destructionis Troiae,* p. 160, as remarked by Root, p. 502, in his note to *TC.* IV. 57-58. In the original or *a* state, the lines agree with the *Filostrato.*
12. The reference to Phebus and Neptunus may be due, in part, but only in part, to the *Roman,* 25918-23. See Root's note, p. 503, to *TC.* IV. 120-26.
13. *Roman,* 13079-120, and *Historia,* pp. 160-61. In both works, Antenor is exchanged for Thoas alone, with Briseïda released to her father without compensation; in the second, however, her release is mentioned in the same sentence as the exchange. See Young, *Origin and Development,* pp. 115-16.
14. *TC.* IV. 141-217 (*Fil.* IV. 13/3-17).
15. I. 106-26 (*Fil.* I. 12-14), II. 1450-56.
16. *Sat.* x. 2-4.
17. Chaucer might have learned of Antenor's and Eneas' treachery from—among various sources—the *Roman,* 24397-25734, or the *Historia,* pp. 217-29, as observed by Root, pp. 504-5, in his note to *TC.* IV. 203-5.

18. Carleton Brown, "Another Contemporary Allusion in Chaucer's *Troilus*," *MLN.*, XXVI (1911), 208-11. For the interpretation, in this article, of a metaphor of a straw-fed fire as an allusion to Jack Straw, see Ch. III. 8. n.109. The article is controverted by Professor Tatlock in his "The Date of the *Troilus*: and Minor Chauceriana," pp. 277-78. See Willy Pieper, "Das *Parlament* in der me. Literatur," *Angl.*, CXLVI (1923), 205-6, for echoes of English in the Trojan parliamentary procedure.
19. *TC.* I. 211 (*Fil.* I. 25), III. 620.
20. John Speirs, *Chaucer the Maker* (London: Faber and Faber, 1951), p. 65, n.2.
21. *TC.* III. 1086-1120, suggested by *Fil.* IV. 18-21.
22. IV. 218-343 (*Fil.* IV. 22-41).
23. *Inf.* iii. 112-17.
24. The appeal for graveyard contemplation may possibly have been suggested by Florio's equally sentimental anticipation of an inscription for his tomb in his reproachful letter to Biancofiore, *Filocolo*, p. 207 (ed. Battaglia), I. 266-67 (ed. Moutier)—Young, *Origin and Development*, p. 176. See also *Tes.* XI. 91, for the inscription on Arcita's funeral urn.
25. *TC.* III. 407-13 (*Fil.* III. 18).
26. IV. 344-658 (*Fil.* IV. 42-77).
27. *Amores*, II. iv. 10-44, as remarked by Skeat, II. 487, in his note to *TC.* IV. 407.
28. *TC.* III. 1625-28.
29. IV. 659-730 (*Fil.* IV. 78-86/3).
30. IV. 731-805 (*Fil.* 86/3-95/4).
31. *TC.* IV. 806-945 (*Fil.* IV. 95/5-108).
32. III. 1555-82.
33. III. 813-36.
34. *Textual Tradition*, pp. 216-20.
35. As numbered in Robinson's edition and Root's, *TC.* IV. 946-52 and 1086-92, corresponding to *Fil.* IV. 109.
36. As numbered in these editions, *TC.* IV. 1079-85.
37. IV. 953-1078, with all but the stanza introducing the soliloquy (IV. 953-59) and the second stanza of it (IV. 967-73) deriving from the first half of prose iii. of Book V of the *Consolation*.
38. *TC.* IV. 946-1123, as against *Fil.* IV. 109-13.
39. *Fil.* III. 4.
40. *Chaucer and his Poetry* (Cambridge: Harvard Univ. Press, ᶜ1915), p. 116.
41. "Destiny in Chaucer's *Troilus*," *PMLA.*, XLV (1930), 150-56, with quotations from pp. 152, 153. For another favorable judgment, see Farnham, *The Medieval Heritage of Elizabethan Tragedy* (Berkeley: Univ. of Cal. Press, 1936), pp. 144-47.
42. "Troilus on Predestination," *JEGP.*, XVII (1918), 399-422, with quotation from p. 410.
43. *The Poetry of Chaucer* (Boston: Houghton Mifflin, ᶜ1922), pp. 117-18.
44. "The People in Chaucer's *Troilus*," *PMLA.*, LVI (1941), 91-92. For a repetition of this view, see Tatlock's *Mind and Art of Chaucer*, pp. 43-44.
45. "Chaucer's *Troilus and Criseyde* as Romance," *PMLA.*, LIII (1938), 49-50.
46. *Chaucer's Troilus A Study in Courtly Love* (University: Louisiana State Univ. Press, 1940), pp. 260-64, with quotation on p. 262.
47. *TC.* IV. 1124-1701 (*Fil.* IV. 114-67).
48. IV. 1124-1246 (*Fil.* IV. 114-26).
49. IV. 1247-1701 (*Fil.* IV. 127-67).
50. *Roman de Troie*, 13768-73, or *Historia destructionis Troiae*, pp. 165-66, as remarked by Young, *Origin and Development*, pp. 119-20.
51. For the sources of "drede fond first goddes," *TC.* IV. 1408, see Robinson's note p. 944.
52. As remarked by Robert P. ap Roberts, "Notes on *Troilus and Criseyde*, IV, 1397-1414," *MLN.*, LVII (1942), 92-97—with special emphasis upon Criseyde's reference to her father's experience at Delphi, *TC.* IV. 1411.
53. This irony is recognized by Professor Kittredge, *Chaucer and his Poetry*, 133-34; Curry, "Destiny in Chaucer's *Troilus*," p. 149; and ap Roberts as cited above.
54. Punishment invoked from Juno, *TC.* IV. 1534-40, suggested by Dante, *Inf.*

xxx. 1-12, as pointed out by Lowes in his articles, "Chaucer and Dante," *MPh.,* XV (1917), 715-17. Swearing by demigods thereafter, suggested by listings of such in Ovid, *Met.* I. 192-93, VI. 392-94; and asseveration by Simois, suggested by protestations by Xanthus in Ovid, *Her.* V. 29-32, and by Simois in his *Amores,* I. xv. 9-10—see Shannon, *Chaucer and the Roman Poets,* pp. 146-49.

55. See Root's note, p. 527, to the quoted stanza, *TC.* IV. 1590-96.

56. "Chaucer's *Troilus and Criseyde* as Romance," pp. 55-56.

Section 8 *Parting of the Ways*

1. *TC.* V. 1-1869 (*Fil.* V. 1-71, VI. 1-34, VII. 1-106, VIII. 1-33, and IX. 1-8), with the line total of the book amounting to 93 per cent of that of the parts.

2. The hypothesis of purposiveness rests on the assumption that Book V is essentially a finished product. The latter has been tentatively questioned: "It is therefore not strange . . . that he made many retouches on the text in the first four books of 'Troilus and Criseyde,' leaving the fifth book, perhaps, a mass of undigested materials, because he had not proceeded so far in the revision," John M. Manly and Edith Rickert, *The Text of the Canterbury Tales* (Chicago: Univ. of Chicago Press, c1940), II. 36. While Chaucer may have scanted Book V in revision, he did not leave it "undigested."

3. *TC.* V. 1-7.

4. See Ch. II. 6. n.240.

5. *TC.* V. 8-14 (*Tes.* II.1, in which stanza, however, the sun and wind are noted to have returned twice, not thrice).

6. V. 15-196 (*Fil.* V. 1-14).

7. Skeat's note, II. 495, to *TC.* V. 67.

8. *Roman,* 13529, with the identity of naming, but not the similarity of action, remarked by Young, *Origin and Development,* pp. 131-32. The suggestion of William M. Rossetti, *Chaucer's Troylus and Cryseyde . . . Compared with Boccaccio's Filostrato,* Chaucer Soc., Ser. I, Vols. XLIV and LXV, p. 235, that "by the reyne hire hente," *TC.* V. 90, resulted from a misunderstanding of "nascosamente sé di colei piglia," *Fil.* V. 13, seems untenable in view of the former's resemblance to the line in the *Roman.*

9. Diomede's visit to Criseida in camp, *Fil.* VI. 9ff., treated in Section 9.

10. *Roman,* 13529ff. The meager condensation of this in Guido's *Historia,* pp. 164-65, seems to have had nothing to give Chaucer for the ride.

11. Closest parallels between the proffer and the *Roman:* promise of alleviation of the lady's evident unhappiness, *TC.* V. 108-16, and *Roman,* 13604-10; assertion that the present declaration of love is the speaker's first, *TC.* V. 155-58, and *Roman,* 13556-58 and 13591-98; possibility of love, as in his case, sight unseen, *TC.* V. 164-65, and *Roman,* 13552-55; and plea for himself as one suitor among many anticipated, *TC.* V. 169-76, and *Roman,* 13573-81—as indicated by Young, *Origin and Development,* pp. 131-32. Closest parallel between the proffer and the *Filostrato:* availability to her of a lover among the Greeks as true as any Trojan, *TC.* V. 124-26, and *Fil.* VI. 22—as indicated, among other parallels, by Young, p. 132. n.1.

12. For this as one of the word plays in Chaucer, see John S. P. Tatlock, "Puns in Chaucer," *Flügel Memorial Volume* (Stanford: Stanford Univ. Press, 1916), pp. 230-31.

13 *TC.* V. 176: *Roman,* 13618; *TC.* V. 177, 180: *Roman,* 13637-39; *TC.* V. 183, 185: *Roman,* 13707-8—as remarked by Young, pp. 121-22.

14. *TC.* V. 190-96 (*Fil.* V. 14 and *Roman,* 13713-17). In the *Roman,* Briseïda, goes on to scold her father at length for treason.

15. *TC.* V. 197-431 (*Fil.* V. 15-39).

16. *TC.* V. 274-79 (*Tes.* VII. 94).

17. *TC.* V. 302-315, as culled from stanzas relating to Arcita's funeral, *Tes.* XI. 13, 14, 35, 50, 52-62, 69, 89-90, and from those relating to matters before the funeral, VII. 4, 27, X. 37, 89, 93-99. See Young, pp. 177-78; Kittredge, "Chaucer's Lollius," *Harvard Studies in Classical Philology,* XXVIII (1917), 110-12; and also Root's note, p. 535, and Robinson's, p. 945, to the passage.

18. The dreams of pursuit, capture, and falling which Chaucer takes from Troiolo's morning speech to Pandaro to report them *in propria persona* in his account of the preceding night, *TC*. V. 246-59 (*Fil*. V. 26-27). In his *Chaucer and the Medieval Sciences* (New York: Oxford Univ. Press, 1926), pp. 208-9, Professor Curry puts these in the category of the *somnium naturale*, that is the physiologically produced and hence non-prophetic dream. Doubtless correct in the categorization, he is wrong in implying that Pandarus knew their content and was influenced by it to minify dreams in general. Since Chaucer, having already given the content of the dreams in his own person, allows Troilus to tell his friend no more than that he has had "dremes now and yore ago," *TC*. V. 317, such is not the case.

In his article "Destiny in Chaucer's *Troilus*," *PMLA.*, XLV (1930), 157, Professor Curry repeats that such dreams of Troilus as are mentioned are not prophetic, but then goes on to say, "Still, he himself is convinced that these dreams and the shrieking of . . . the owl undoubtedly foretell his approaching death (V. 316-20). And Troilus's qualm . . . communicates itself to the sympathetic reader, who is also made to feel that the protagonist has not long to live."

19. The confidant chooses the host in *TC*. V. 430-31 and in *Le Roman de Troyle et de Criseida*, p. 251; the hero, in *Fil*. V. 38, as noted by Pratt, *StPh.*, LIII, 530.

20. *TC*. V. 432-511 (*Fil*. V. 40-49).

21. *TC*. V. 512-686 (*Fil*. V. 50-71).

22. V. 551-52, perhaps, as is proposed by Young, *Origin and Development*, pp. 171-73, adapted from the kissing of the doors of his father's palace by Florio, who had stolen back at night from Montorio to Marmorina to prowl loverlike beside this abode of his Biancofiore, *Filocolo*, p. 97 (ed. Battaglia), I. 124 (ed. Moutier). It may be added that he later kissed the walls of the tower in Alexandria then her place of confinement, p. 389 (II. 149-50).

23. As pointed out by Lowes, "Chaucer and Dante," *MPh.*, XIV (1917), 715-17, Troilus' allusion to Juno, V. 599-602, derives from Dante, *Inf.* xxx. 1-12, like Criseyde's, IV. 1534-40.

24. As noted by Pratt. *StPh.*, LIII, 531, "And after this," V.603, corresponds to the time link. "Puis" in *Le Roman de Troyle et de Criseida*, pp. 256-57, added in its rendering of *Fil*. V. 58.

25. See Root's note, p. 540, to this stanza, *TC*. V. 652-58, for its chronological compatibility with the poet's placing of the sun in Leo, IV. 31-32, and Criseyde's premise, IV. 1590-96, and also his notes, pp. 500, 527, to these passages respectively.

Section 9 *The Heroine's Moral Eclipse*

1. *TC*. V. 687-1099 (*Fil*. VI. 1-34).

2. V. 687-765 (*Fil*. VI. 1-7).

3. V. 743-49, with the notion of three-eyed Prudence from *Purg*. xxix. 130-32, as noted by Professor Tatlock, "Chaucer and Dante," *MPh.*, III (1906), 367-68.

4. V. 766-77 (*Fil*. VI. 8).

5. V. 778-98 (*Fil*. VI. 10-11/7). See notes 8 and 10 for Chaucer's adaptations of *Fil*. VI. 9 and 11. 7/8.

6. V. 799-840. In his *Origin and Development* (1908), pp. 108-13, 133, Young showed that Chaucer's portraits resemble Benoit's of the three parties more closely than they do Guido's. In his "Chaucer's Dares," *MPh.*, XV (1917), 6-18, Root announced his discovery that they are indebted to Joseph's of the parties as well as to Benoit's. In the notes in his edition of the *Troilus*, pp. 541-45, Root gave Joseph's from the MS. in the Chapter Library of Westminster Abbey, and while not overstressing their influence, somewhat neglected that of Benoit's. The following analysis combines the finding of these scholars:

Diomede, V. 799-805: Dares, Ch. xiii; Joseph IV. 124-27; Benoit, 5211-24; Guido (ed. Griffin), p. 84; *Fil*. VI. 33 supplemented by 24. Correspondences to Joseph: "With sterne vois and myghty lymes square" to "Voce ferox" and to "validos quadratur in artus Titides" (closer than to Dares' "quadratum" or Benoit's "quarrez"), and "chivalrous Of dedes, lik his fader Tideus" to "plenisque meretur

447

Tidea factis." Correspondence to Benoit: "Hardy, testif" to "Mout fu hardiz, mout fu noisos." Correspondences to Boccaccio: "of tonge large" to "parlante quant' altro Greco mai" and royal heirship to royal heirship. And as noted by Pratt, *StPh.*, LIII, 533, correspondence of "Hardy" to "hardy" in *Le Roman de Troyle et de Criseida*, p. 268.

Criseyde, V. 806-26: Dares, Ch. xiii; Joseph, IV. 156-62; Benoit, 5275-88; Guido, p. 85. Correspondences to Joseph: "Criseyde mene was of hire stature" to "In medium librata statum Briseis"; mention of Criseyde's disposition of her hair to a mention of Briseis' rather different one; rivalry of beauty and love in her to "Diviciis forme certant insignia morum (*var.* amorum)"; and the lines,

> . . . .
> She sobre was, ek symple, and wys withal,
> . . . .
> And goodly of hire speche in general,
> . . . .
> Ne nevere mo ne lakked hire pite,

to the lines,

> Sobria simplicitas, comis pudor, arida numquam
> Poscenti pietas, et fandi gracia lenis.

Correspondences to Benoit: mention of Criseyde's joined eyebrows expressly as a blemish to the like mention of Briseïda's (such mention also in Guido); "The best ynorisshed ek that myghte be" to "Mout fu de bon afaitement"; and "slydynge of corage" to "Mais sis corages li chanjot." For conflicting interpretations by scholars of "slydynge of corage," see Fred M. Smith, "Chaucer's Prioress and Criseyde," *West Va. Univ. Bulletin: Philological Papers,* VI (1949), 5-6. For the change in taste which made joined eyebrows a blemish instead of a beauty, see George P. Krapp, "Miscellaneous Notes," *MLN.,* XIX (1904), 235, and George L. Hamilton, "Supercilia Juncta," *MLN.,* XX (1905), 80. On the blemish, see also Nathaniel E. Griffin, "Chaucer's Portrait of Criseyde," *JEGP.,* XX (1921), 39-46. The fancy of Paradise in the eyes comes from Dante, *Par.* xviii. 21, as noted by Albert S. Cook, "Chauceriana," *RomRev.,* VIII (1917), 226. For parallels between this portrait and the Prioress', see A. C. Cawley, "A Note on Chaucer's Prioress and Criseyde," *MLR.,* XLIII (1948), 74-77, as well as Smith's just cited article, pp. 1-11.

Troilus, V. 827-40: Dares, Ch. xii; Joseph, IV. 60-63; Benoit, 5393-5446; Guido, p. 86. Correspondence to Benoit: description of Troilus as "wel woxen . . . in highte" and perfectly proportioned to

> Granz ert, mais bien li coveneit
> O la taille, que bone aveit.

Correspondences to Joseph: "Yong" to "etate puer"; claim

> That Troilus was nevere unto no wight,
> As in his tyme, in no degree secounde
> In durring don that longeth to a knyght

to "nullique secundus Audendo virtutis opus"; and "geant" in "Al myghte a geant passen hym of myght" to "gigas" in the very different collocation "Mente gigas."

7. In his note, p. 947, to *TC.* V. 799ff., Robinson touches on the convention of the formal portrait in ancient and medieval writers, without evaluation of Chaucer's employment of it. In "The Portraits in *Troilus and Criseyde,*" *PhQ.,* XVII (1938), 220-23, Louis A. Haselmayer, Jr., treats of the portrait series exemplifying the convention in Dares and his derivatives and expresses the opinion that Chaucer's group of three is an inartistic token representative of that: "The story partially resembles the traditional form in having a fragment of the series of portraits . . . Chaucer's motive is most conservative, and he seems so eager to keep within the stylistic tradition that he produces a dramatic ineptitude. The portraits are useless from an organic point of view." Professor Young in his "Chaucer's *Troilus and Criseyde* as Romance," *PMLA.,* LIII (1938), 56, opines that the group "may be a somewhat mechanical reflection of romantic convention." In *The Mind and Art of Chaucer* (Syracuse: Syracuse Univ. Press, ᶜ1950), pp. 46-47, Professor Tatlock asserts that the portrait of Criseyde is a belated and clumsy attempt to prepare for her defection, "Her susceptibility and

unsteadiness are the explanation, but mentioned late and crudely here"; and that the three portraits are imperfectly managed for contrast. Alberto Castelli, however, pays them strong tribute in his *Geoffrey Chaucer* (Brescia: Morcelliana, 1946), pp. 151-53.
8. *TC.* V. 841-47 (*Fil.* VI. 9).
9. Boccaccio's statement that Criseida had not been in camp "il quarto giorno" ere Diomede found occasion to visit her, whether intended or not to make the call coincide with Troiolo's stay with Sarpidone, appears to have been taken from the *Roman de Troie*—from Benoit's remark, which is not a prelude to any call, that Briseïda,

> Anceis que veie le quart seir,
> N'avra corage ne voleir,
> De retorner en la cité, 13859-61

10. *TC.* V. 848-54 (*Fil.* VI. 11/7-8).
11. V. 855-1015 (*Fil.* VI. 12-32).
12. V. 876-917 (*Fil.* VI. 15-20), with the cogency of the argument to our poet's theme of fate remarked by Professor Curry, "Destiny in Chaucer's *Troilus*," *PMLA.,* XLV (1930), 159.
13. V. 1000-4, with 1000-1 apparently and 1004 possibly suggested by Roman, 13676-80,

> Si poëz bien estre certains,
> S'a ço me voleie aproismier,
> Nul plus de vos n' avreie chier.
> Mais n'en ai pensé ne voleir,
> Ne ja Deus nel me doint aveir,

but with 1002-3 more likely suggested by the *Historia*, p. 164, "Amoris tui oblaciones ad presens nec repudio nec admitto," than by *Roman*, 13673,

> Ne jo nos refus autrement.

See Young, *Origin and Development*, p. 123.
14. V. 1009-15 (replacing *Fil.* V. 32), with the locution "Gan . . . faste hire mercy preye" perhaps echoing Benoit's line, *Roman*, 15056, about Diomede after the eighth battle,

> Sovent li vait merci criër,

and with the circumstance of glove taking, to the delight of the taker, certainly coming from the like recorded at the end of the ride to camp after the seventh, *Roman*, 13709-11,

> Un de ses guanz li a toleit,
> Que nus nel set ne aparceit:
> Mout s'en fait liez.

See Young, p. 124.
15. V. 1016-22. For the astronomy of the passage, see Root's note, p. 547; and for Claudian's *De raptu Proserpinae*, I, 101-2 (quoted and glossed in the schoolbook, the *Liber Catonianus*) as the source of "Signifer his candels sheweth brighte," see Robert A. Pratt, "Chaucer's Claudian," *Spec.* XXII (1947), 420-21. If Chaucer needed a suggestion for the "fadres faire brighte tente," it may have been the elaborate account of Calcas' in the *Roman*, 13818-45, at the end of Briseïda's ride or, less probably, the brief one, 14302-6, in the eighth battle.
16. V. 1023-29 (replacing parts of *Fil.* VI. 33-34). See n.6 for use earlier of part of *Fil.* VI. 33.
17. V. 1030-36 (replacing part of *Fil.* VI. 34).
18. In his Introduction to the *Filostrato*, p. 33, Dr. Griffin remarks that it would have been embarrassing for Boccaccio, the suitor of Maria d'Aquino, to follow Benoit in extenso when the latter told "of the gradual estrangement of the heart of Briseida and of her final surrender to Diomede."
19. V. 1037-50. In the *Roman*, Briseïda approbriously returned to Diomedès, at his request, Troilus' "destrier" of unspecified color, 15079-172—which he had captured in the eighth battle and sent to her from the melee, 14286-352—as a replacement for his own lost later in that battle and passed on to Troilus, 14415-21; and, on the same occasion, she gave him, without being asked, her right sleeve "en lieu de confanon," 15176-78. And when he had been wounded, "Par mi le cors de plain eslais," by Troilus in the fifteenth battle, 20071-102, Briseïda comforted him as much as she could,

betrayed for the first time unmistakably that she'loved him, and thenceforth often visited him so that men might well perceive that she had bestowed upon him "S'amor, son cuer e son pensé, 20202-28. In the *Filostrato,* VIII. 8ff., we read of the hero's brooch discovered on his enemy's garment, and correspondingly in *TC.* V. 1646ff. See Young, *Origin and Development,* pp. 125-26, 134-35.

20. V. 1051-85, with lines in Criseyde's soliloquy corresponding to lines in Briseïda's most closely as follows: 1056-57 to 20242-44, 1058-60 to 20238-39, 1061-66 to 20255-62, 1067-71 to 20275-78, 1072-74 to 20318-20—Young, pp. 135-36; and, less closely: 1075-77 to 20265-66 and 1084 to 20242-44 again. Of Benoit's representation of Briseïda, Marchette Chute remarks, "She is a thoroughly believable woman, in her regrets, in her fear of what people will think of her, in the excuses she makes to herself for her conduct, and in her pathetic resolves to do better in the future," *Geoffrey Chaucer of England* (New York: Dutton, 1946), p. 162.

21. V. 1086-99. In his note, pp. 549-50, to 1086-92, Root observes that, though Chaucer's "authors do not say in so many words how long a time elapses before Criseyde surrenders to Diomede," Benoit so spaces his battles in time from the seventh, after which she was exchanged, through the fifteenth, after which she capitulated, as to indicate that the period "can hardly be less than two full years."

22. "The Character of Criseyde," *PMLA.,* XXII (1907), 531-47, esp. 540-47.

23. "The People in Chaucer's *Troilus,*" *PMLA.,* LVI (1941), 96-102, with the quotations from pp. 99-101. The views about the treatment of Criseyde set forth in the article are reiterated in substance in Tatlock's *Mind and Art of Chaucer,* pp. 45-48. See n.7 above for a quotation from this book.

24. "Character and Action in the Case of Criseyde," *PMLA.,* LIV (1939), 65-81, with quotations from pp. 67, 79.

25. *Courtly Love in Chaucer and Gower* (Boston: Ginn, 1913), pp. 154-78, with quotation from p. 176.

26. *Chaucer and his Poetry* (Cambridge: Harvard Univ. Press, ᶜ1915), pp. 126-36, with quotation from p. 135.

27. *The Allegory of Love* (Oxford: Clarendon Press, 1936), pp. 182-90, with quotations from pp. 185, 189. H. S. Bennett, *Chaucer and the Fifteenth Century* (Oxford: Clarendon Press, 1947), pp. 54-58, agrees in substance with Lewis, saying of Criseyde, "Her timid amorous, dependent nature cannot stand the burden," p. 58. Margaret Galway, "Joan of Kent and the Order of the Garter," *Univ. of Birmingham Historical Journal,* 1 (1947), 49-50, agrees with him also as to Criseyde's flaw and ventures to suppose it a reflection of Joan's: "His heroine separated from Troilus took another lover chiefly through her dread of insecurity, the gravest weakness alike in her and in Joan," p. 49.

28. *Chaucer's Troilus A Study in Courtly Love* (University, La.: Louisiana State Univ. Press, 1940), pp. 192-238, with quotations from pp. 235, 237.

29. For further discussion of the letter, *TC.* V. 1590-1631, see section 11.

Section 10 *Attrition of the Lover's Hopes*

1. *TC.* V. 1100-1540 (*Fil.* VII. 1-106).
2. V. 1100-1232 (*Fil.* VII. 1-22).
3. V. 1107-11 and II. 64-70. The story of Scylla and Nisus is told in Ovid, *Met.* VIII. 6-151. That the bird "ciris," which she is there said to have become, was a lark Chaucer may have learned from a gloss in some MS. of the *Met.* or from the *Ovide Moralisé*—Meech, "Chaucer and the *Ovide Moralisé*—A Further Study," *PMLA.,* XLVI (1931), 188-89. For possible sources of the stanza on Proigne, see Ch. I. 4. n.5.
4. V. 1112-13 (*Fil.* VII. 1), with "on the walles" replacing " 'n verso il campo"; V. 1145 (*Fil.* VII. 6), with the gesture of craning either a misrendering of "sospeso"— in suspense—or, more probably, a deliberate substitution for it; and V. 1194-95 (*Fil.* VII. 14), with pacing on the walls instead of unvisualized tarrying outside. Troilus, posted as he is on the tenth day, must propose at its end to go to the gate to order the porters to keep it open, not, as Troiolo did, to remain outside to prevent the guards from detaining his lady, V. 1138-41 (*Fil.* VII. 5). In its renderings of *Fil.* VII. 1, 5, *Le*

Roman de Troyle et de Criseida, pp. 268, 269, represents the hero and confidant to have stayed inside up to intercession with the porters, though not to have mounted upon the walls—Pratt, *St.Ph.*, LIII (1956), 534.

5. As noted by Pratt, p. 534, the hero in *Le Roman*, p. 269, is made to propose "Desoresmais *allons nous en disgner*"; the confidant in the *Troilus*, V. 1129, "And forthi lat us dyne." Neither of the men explicitly proposed dinner in the *Filostrato*, VII. 3, 4.

6. V. 1134, an adaptation of the less meaningful "ma gl' ingannò 'l pensiero," *Fil.* VII. 4.

7. V. 1184-91 (*Fil.* VII. 12-13). Criseida promised return explicitly on the tenth day, *Fil.* IV. 154, not after ten as Troiolo would have it; and Criseyde "Er dayes ten," *TC.* IV. 1320, and "Or nyghtes ten," IV. 1685, as well as before the moon should pass through the Lion, IV. 1591-92.

8. V. 1222, added in adaptation of *Fil.* VII. 20.

9. V. 1233-1435 (*Fil.* VII. 23-76).

10. II. 925-31. See Ch. I. 4. n.23 for sources, besides the *Filostrato*, of Criseyde's dream.

11. In his "Destiny in Chaucer's Troilus," *PMLA.*, XLV (1930), 157-58, Professor Curry accepts the boar dream, *TC.* V. 1233-41 (*Fil.* VII. 23-24) as an authentic "*somnium coeleste*" because of its substantiation by events. The hero's attribution of it to the gods, V. 1250-51 (*Fil.* VII. 26) and to Jove, V. 1445-49, is therefore justified.

12. "Chaucer and the Great Italian Writers of the Trecento," *Monthly Criterion*, VI (1927), p. 31.

13. *TC.* V. 1275-88 (*Fil.* VII. 40-41). In his note, p. 551, to V. 1275-78, Professor Root observes, "Pandarus, who had previously (5.360-85) denied the significance of dreams, now takes the more orthodox position that dreams deceive us because we wrongly interpret them."

14. IV. 624-28 (expanded from *Fil.* IV. 75/5-7).

15. V. 764-70.

16. Chaucer's digest of this letter of Criseyde's given at the end of his second sequence, V. 1424-30, is evidently expanded from Boccaccio's of Criseida's tardier one given at the end of his third, *Fil.* VII. 105.

17. V. 1436-1540 (*Fil.* VII. 77-106).

18. In his "Defense of Criseyde," *PMLA.*, XLIV (1929), 165, Joseph S. Graydon counts the resort to Cassandre among actions of Troilus which, in his opinion, justify Criseyde's abandoning the hero. J. Milton French demolishes Graydon's reasoning about this incident—as about others—in his "Defense of Troilus," *PMLA.*, XLIV (1929), 1247. See also Joseph M. Beatty, Jr., "Mr. Graydon's 'Defense of Criseyde,' " *StPh.*, XXVI (1929), 474-76.

19. In his note, pp. 552-53 to *TC.* V, 1450, Root observes "The term sibyl is used generically for a female prophet. . . . Chaucer . . . clearly regards the names *Sibille* and *Cassandre* as alternative names of the same person."

20. As remarked by Professor Farnham in *The Medieval Heritage of Elizabethan Tragedy* (Berkeley: Univ. of Cal. Press, 1936), pp. 147-49. He terms the lady's excursus "a brief *De Casibus*."

21. V. 1457-84, with the Calydonian details taken from Ovid, *Met.* VIII. 260-546.

22. V. 1485-1512. For Chaucer's use of the twelve-line Latin argument of the *Thebaid*, which is inserted in MSS. of the *Troilus*, after V. 1498; of twelve-line arguments severally of Books II-XII of that poem; and of the work itself, see Francis P. Magoun, Jr., "Chaucer's Summary of Statius' *Thebaid* II-XII," *Traditio*, XI (1955), 409-20.

23. As suggested by Farnham in his pages cited in n.20.

Section 11 *Finale*

1. *TC.* V. 1541-1869 (*Fil.* VIII. 1-33 and IX. 1-8).

2. V. 1541-1638 (*Fil.* VIII. 1-7/4).

3. With verbal echo of *Inferno*, vii. 77-84, as pointed out by Professor ten Brink, *Chaucer Studien* (Münster: Russell, 1870), p. 74, and also of *Ecclus.*, x.8, as orally communicated by Alfred M. Kellogg at an MLA. meeting, Dec. 27, 1954.

4. *Roman de Troie*, 16215-30, with possible reinforcement by Guido's *Historia destructionis Troiae*, p. 175, as noted by Professor Young, *Origin and Development*, pp. 127-28. As to Ector's "aventaille," one of the particulars, from the *Roman*, see George L. Hamilton, "Ventaille," *MPh.*, III (1905), 541-46.

5. As indicated by Pratt, *StPh.*, LIII, 535, "Hymselven lik a pilgrym to *desgise*," V. 1577, is closer to "en habit *dissimulé*, en *guise* de pelerin," *Le Roman de Troyle et de Criseida*, p. 296, than to "di pellegrino in abito," *Fil.* VIII. 4. On the pilgrim disguise as a medieval literary convention, see Francis P. Magoun, Jr., " 'Hymselven Lik a Pilgrym to Desgise': *Troilus*, V. 1577," *MLN.*, LIX (1944), 176-78, and B. J. Whiting, "Troilus and Pilgrims in Wartime," *MLN.*, LX (1945), 47-49. The latter interprets the renunciation of the project as indicative of weakness: "The remaining lines of the stanza are all to characteristic of Troilus's fatal flaw. . . . As so often before, he could not bring himself to take a chance, and this time there was no one to lead him 'by the lappe'." That Chaucer meant to convey this implication is possible but not demonstrable. He gives the hero the same plausible reasons for abandonment of the venture as Boccaccio did—penetrability of disguise and complete quandary if it should be penetrated.

6. *TC.* V. 1592-96 (*Fil.* II. 96, the opening stanza of Troiolo's letter); V. 1599-1600 and 1625-30 (*Fil.* II. 122/7-8 and 126/1-6 from Criseida's letter). Chaucer, it will be remembered, reduced these early letters to digests in his Book II.

7. V. 1639-66 (*Fil.* VIII. 7/5-10).

8. For Lollius, see Ch. I. 2.

9. *TC.* V. 1667-1743 (*Fil.* VIII. 11-24). As noted by Pratt, *StPh.*, LIII, 536, one finds in *Le Roman de Troyle et de Criseida*, pp. 297-98, "Puis se partit Troïlus . . . pour aller en sa chambre"; in Chaucer's poem, V. 1667, "He goth hym hom"; in the *Filostrato*, VIII. 11, only "Quindi partito Troiolo."

10. As Professor Young has suggested, *Origin and Development*, p. 136, the hope to make Diomede's "sydes blede," V. 1705, may reflect the circumstance, recorded by Benoit, that, in the fifteenth battle, Troïlus pierced the rival with his lance "par mi les costez," *Roman de Troie*, 20071-78. He added verbal insult to this injury, 20079-102.

11. *TC.* V. 1744-71 (*Fil.* VIII. 25-30).

12. Troilus greatly distinguished himself from the thirteenth through the eighteenth battles chronicled in the *Roman de Troie*, 19281-21189.

13. In adapting Boccaccio's account of the encounters of the pair, Chaucer may possibly have had episodes of the *Roman* in mind—that mentioned in n.10, Troïlus' wounding of Diomedès in the fifteenth battle; and one, also singled out by Young, pp. 128-29, the Greek's wounding of Troïlus in the tenth, 15638-56.

14. For Dares, see Ch. I. 1.n.1.

15. *TC.* V. 1772-85.

16. Of Chaucer's procedure here, Professor Malone writes in part as follows: "He preferred to phrase the moral in such a way that it holds for women only: beware of men. In making this the moral of *Troilus and Criseyde* the poet was making fun, of course. He could have found no moral for his tale more completely paradoxical. . . . And his fun-making went on, to the very end of the stanza. . . . There is one man they can believe, and Chaucer is that man." *Chapters on Chaucer* (Baltimore: Johns Hopkins Press, 1951), p. 132.

17. In his "Epilog of Chaucer's *Troilus*," *MPh.*, XVIII (1921), 625. n.1, Professor Tatlock qualifies his distinction of the last twelve stanzas as the Epilog in this manner: "The preceding two stanzas as well, on Criseyde's and others' treason to love, are general in application, and might be called part of the Epilog."

18. *TC.* V. 1786-99.

19. As Root observes, p. 558, in his note to V. 1788, "It is not necessary to assume that Chaucer had any specific work in mind."

20. Says Professor Tatlock in "The Epilog," p. 630. n.8, "As to the nature of the distinction, it is not so much that he uses 'makyng," etc., of vernacular verse, and 'poetrye,' etc., of Latin. The latter refers to the loftier . . . literature which is of course mostly in verse, and which to the Middle Ages is nearly all in Latin, the *Divine Comedy* being the chief exception." In "An Unusual Meaning of 'Make' in Chaucer," *MLN.*, LII (1937), 351-53, Richard C. Boys argues that *make*, V. 1788, signifies

"match" (Oxford Dictionary, Make, v^2) not "compose." Since *makere* and *makyng* in the preceding and following lines unquestionably mean "composer" and "composing," his argument is unconvincing to me.

21. *Filostrato*, IX. 1-8.

22. *Filocolo*, pp. 563-65 (ed. Battaglia), II. 376-78 (ed. Moutier), with the source relationship pointed out by Young, *Origin and Development*, p. 178. Boccaccio addresses the poem as "mio libretto," p. 563. And calling himself "tuo fattore," he gives it counsel in part as follows: "e però agli eccellenti ingegni e alle robuste menti lascia i gran versi di Vergilio. . . . E quelli del valoroso Lucano . . . lasciali agli armigeri cavalieri insieme con quelli del tolosano Stazio. E chi con molta efficacia ama, il sulmontino Ovidio seguiti, delle cui opere tu se' confortatore. Né ti sia cura di volere essere dove i misurati versi del fiorentino Dante si cantino, il quale tu si come piccolo servitore molto devi reverente seguire. Lascia a costoro il debito onore, il qual volere usurpare con vergogna t' acquisterebbe danno," p. 564. Since the apostrophe to the "canzon" in the *Filostrato* resembled this to the "libretto" in being a dedication to the poet's beloved and in employing the metaphor of landing after a voyage, the one would naturally have led Chaucer to the other. The notion of kissing "the steppes" may have come from Statius' envoy to his *Thebaid*, as Young suggests:

> nec tu divinam Aeneida tempta,
> sed longe sequere et vestigia semper adora. XII. 816-17.

See Tatlock, "The Epilog," pp. 627-30, for the history of the "Go little book" formula, which starts with Ovid.

23. Professor Tatlock speaks of Chaucer's concern here as "one of the earliest expressions in English of the self-consciousness of literary art," "The Epilog," pp. 625-26; and adds, "This is the earliest time in his works that Chaucer expresses this solicitude," p. 626. n.1.

24. *TC*. V. 1800-6 (*Fil*. VIII. 27).

25. V. 1807-27.

26. *Tes*. XI. 1-3. See Howard R. Patch, "Chauceriana," *ESt.*, LXV (1931), 357-59, for the *Pharsalia*, IX. 1-14, and the "Somnium" as Boccaccio's sources. In the former, Pompey's soul rose from the funeral pyre in Egypt nearly to the moon's orbit, saw the light there and above and the darkness beneath, and smiled at the mockery performed for his headless body—"risitque sui ludibria trunci." In the latter, the dreaming Scipio saw earth and spheres from the Milky Way in company with his deceased ancestor and was taught by him to prefer the life to come to life on earth. For the *Paradiso* as a source see Clark as cited in n.27.

27. Indebtedness of Chaucer here to either *Pharsalia* or *Paradiso* cannot be conclusively established. However, in his article "Dante and the Epilogue of the *Troilus*," *JEGP.*, L (1951), 1-10, John W. Clark hypothesizes that Chaucer's mind proceeded along the following path of association: from comment of Dante's on the spheres viewed from that of the sun, *Par*. xiv. 25-33 (of which passage 11. 28-30 are used in the concluding stanza of the *Troilus*); to Dante's viewing of the spheres from that of the fixed stars, *Par*. xxii. 100-54; to the three stanzas in the *Teseida*, which have verbal echoes of the latter.

28. Some MSS. have the reading "eighthe," others "seventhe"; the former is established as correct by "ottava" in the *Teseida*. As Root explains, pp. 560-62, in his note to *TC*. V. 1809-13, the context clearly shows that by "cielo ottava" Boccaccio meant the sphere of the moon, counting the spheres from outmost to inmost. If Chaucer understood the context, and as an amateur scientist he should have, he presumably intended to convey the same meaning. Clark, "Dante and the Epilogue," p. 8, argues that, though he understood, he was purposely unclear, leaving it indefinite as to whether the eighth sphere was the moon's, or, counting in the opposite direction, that of the fixed stars. Since the poet does not change his original one iota, such purpose is indemonstrable, though it is possible because the original itself would not be clear to everyone. In "Chaucer, Venus, and the 'Seventhe Spere'," *MLN.*, LXVII (1952), 245-46, Jackson I. Cope argues for the reading "seventhe spere" and its interpretation as the seventh counting outward, on the fanciful ground that the heaven of Saturn would be an appropriate one for Troilus in the light of Dante's account of it. Forrest S. Scott also argues for the reading "seventhe spere" but for its interpretation as Mercury's the

seventh counting inward from Saturn's "The Seventh Sphere. . . ," *MLR.*, LI (1946), 2-5.

29. See Root's note, p. 562, to *TC.* V. 1814-19 for the "Somnium" as ideological source for this expansion and for his comment, "Chaucer's 'pleyn felicite' is his own Boethian addition."

30. In his *Textual Tradition of Chaucer's Troilus*, Chaucer Soc., Ser. I., XCIX (1916), pp. 245-48, Professor Root confesses himself at a loss to explain the absence of the passage in three MSS. only of the poem, one of the *α* variety and two of the *β*, but concludes that "in the absence of certain evidence, the probabilities both external and internal favour the hypothesis that the *Teseide* passage was not present in Chaucer's earliest draft of the poem."

31. The similarity in function of the two passages has been pointed out by Erich Ballerstedt, *Ueber Chaucers Naturschilderungen* (Göttingen: Dieterischen Buchdruckerei, 1891), pp. 63-65, and by Bertrand H. Bronson, "In Appreciation of Chaucer's *Parlement of Foules*," *Univ. of Cal. Publs. in English*, III. v (1935), 199-202.

32. The ambiguity of "Ther as Mercurye sorted hym to dwelle," reproducing Boccaccio's "nel loco che Mercurio li sortio," is obvious and artistically right. Though divine forgiveness and reward are not denied, they are not assured and could not be. To proceed from a fleshly lover in high place in the other world to caution against love as dangerous to salvation would be a non sequitur indeed. Professor Kirby misinterprets, I believe, in saying, "On his death the hero ascends directly to heaven; he lingers in no limbo, no purgatory; there is no period of purgation of any kind. On the contrary, his love has been so noble, so spiritual, that he passes at once to his eternal reward," *Chaucer's Troilus*, p. 282. Troilus, indeed, reaches the "eighthe spere" but does not remain there; is illuminated but not assured of further benefit.

33. Even Professor Tatlock, who deems the renunciatory stanzas in the poem an irreconcilable contradiction of the body of it, recognizes the transitional value of the insertion before them, "In the earlier form of the poem the blow is particularly sudden, and it was probably to lessen the shock that Chaucer inserted the three stanzas from the *Teseide*, and made Troilus himself gently lead us upward," "The Epilog," p. 638.

34. *TC.* V. 1828-34 (*Fil.* VIII. 28). Premising, as recorded in n.32, that Chaucer has brought Troilus to an eternal reward, Kirby, p. 282, concludes that "Swych fyn" signifies, not such a wretched end, but such a fine one: "it clearly refers not to Troilus' death and the end of everything but rather to the event recounted in the immediately preceding lines, the ascent to heaven." If Chaucer had meant this, he would not have added "Swych fyn hath false worldes brotelnesse" to the preceding "Swych fyn's."

35. *TC.* V. 1835-48, replacing *Fil.* VIII. 29-33.

36. See Professor Tatlock's discussion "The Epilog," pp. 635-40, of the two stanzas. Though recognizing that Chaucer has sounded notes of warning, he denies that they prepare at all for this passage: "The . . . stanzas express the natural enough revulsion of a medieval mind to the strong emotion and painful outcome of the love story. . . . A revulsion it is, or, if anyone prefers, a sudden transcending. . . . Though in the opening lines of the poem and all through we are warned of the tragedy to come, . . . there is a sense that nothing is better than happy love, and a pretense that the poet is a wistful outsider to the greatest thing in the world. There is not a hint of detachment or sense of the vanity or unworthiness of love," p. 637. The "sense" and the "pretense" mentioned are certainly present, but opposed, I think, more strongly than he admits by reservations implicit and explicit.

37. As to the implications of the negation, Professor Tatlock suggests that it may center on the fleshly element in the affair. "High and ennobling as the poem is, in no other medieval work is physical passion depicted with such naturalness and sympathy and made so attractive. . . . The senses, being outlawed by medieval theory, could be indulged only in a light mood. None of Chaucer's other love stories is intense enough to call for such a disclaimer," "The Epilog," p. 638. In his "Chaucer's Renunciation of Love in *Troilus*," *MLN.*, XL (1925), 270-76, Professor Young offers a supplementary interpretation. Calling Tatlock's "truly illuminating and convincing," he says that "there is no obstacle to one's surmising that Chaucer's revulsion of feeling arose as much from the false principles of courtly love in the poem as from the intensity and reality of the physical passion. Possibly, indeed, the influence arising from

454

courtly love was the greater," pp. 272, 273. In her essay, "O Yonge, Fresshe Folkes," *A Lost Language and Other Essays on Chaucer* (New York: Sheed and Ward, 1951), pp. 119-30, Sister M. Madaleva stresses the poet's concern for the welfare of the young. She writes: "His thought no doubt moves back to all who will read his book but especially to the 'yonge, fresshe folkes.' . . . He is solicitous for them," p. 129.

38. *TC.* V. 1849-55.

39. In his note, p. 563, to *TC.* V. 1854, Root observes, "The context suggests that *forme* is here used in the sense given to *forma* by scholastic philosophy, i.e., 'the essential principle of a thing which makes it what it is.' "

40. See Tatlock, "The Epilog," pp. 640-59, for a discussion of the passage in the light of the classical coloring of the *Troilus* on the one hand and fourteenth-century uneasiness about such cultivation of paganism on the other, the latter as illustrated particularly in Boccaccio's *De genealogia deorum*. Making the plausible assumption that our poet is here influenced by his own and others' religious scruples, he considers the result to be compromising of art: "Chaucer . . . felt the extraordinary novelty of his complete substitution of paganism for Christianity and its view of the universe. He himself may have felt the chill of this alien and calamitous world in which he had lived so intensely, and comes home to the warmth and glory of his own faith. Even at some sacrifice of art, he wished to effect a makeshift unification of his poem with everything else in his friends' minds and his own, that it should not be encysted, as it were, by itself," pp. 656-57. See Young, *Origin and Development*, pp. 120-21 for possible particular influence of Benoit, *Roman de Troie*, 21713-17, 21732-40, and Guido, *Historia*, *pp.* 93-97.

41. As Malone interprets the passage in his *Chapters on Chaucer*, p. 140, "It was part of the tragedy of Troilus that he lived in a time and place far from the grace of God, the gift of Jesus Christ to mankind. . . . Only after death did he win that insight which the Christian may win in earthly life."

42. I differ here from Professor Kittredge, who writes, "Chaucer cannot say farewell without turning his irony upon himself. . . . Who am I, that I should exhort you to turn aside from the follies of love and the vanities of human endeavor? A mere student, poring over my ancient books and repeating . . . the wonderful and transitory things that they record," *Chaucer and his Poetry*, p. 145.

43. *TC.* V. 1856-59.

44. For the convention and particularly in the works of Boccaccio, see Professor Tatlock, "The Epilog," pp. 631-35.

45. For Strode, see Robinson's note, pp. 951-52, to *TC.* V. 1856ff.

46. *TC.* V. 1860-69.

47. V. 1863-65 (Dante, *Par.* xiv. 28-30).

48. "Destiny in Chaucer's *Troilus*," *PMLA.*, XLV (1930), 165, 168.

49. "The Epilog," p. 636. See other quotations from this article in notes 36 and 40 and Tatlock's *Mind and Art of Chaucer* (Syracuse: Syracuse Univ. Press, ᶜ1950), pp. 48-49. Fritz Krog also finds the Epilog incompatible, *Studien zu Chaucer und Langland*, Anglistische Forschungen, LXV (1928), 86-91.

50. *Chapters on Chaucer*, p. 141. Others in the majority may be cited, as follows, in order of publication. Willard Farnham. *The Medieval Heritage of Elizabethan Tragedy* (Berkeley: Univ. of Cal. Press, 1936), pp. 151-54. Howard R. Patch. *On Rereading Chaucer* (Cambridge: Harvard Univ. Press, 1939), pp. 58-62, 117-21. Will Héraucourt, *Die Wertwelt Chaucers, Die Wertwelt einer Zeitwende* (Heidelberg: Winter, 1939), pp. 321-22. James L. Shanley, "The *Troilus* and Christian Love," *ELH.*, VI (1939), 271-81. Thomas A. Kirby, *Chaucer's Troilus* (La. State Univ. Press, 1940), pp. 283-84. Nevill Coghill, *The Poet Chaucer* (London: Oxford Univ. Press. 1949), pp. 83-85. John Speirs, *Chaucer the Maker* (London: Faber and Faber, 1951), pp. 80-82. William A. Madden, "Chaucer's Retraction and Mediaeval Canons of Seemliness," *Mediaeval Studies*, XVII (1955), 173-84, esp. 182.

CHAPTER II *Physical Particulars and Time and the Supernatural*

Section 2 *Age, Person, and Dress*

1. *Fil.* IV. 84, II. 41; VII. 52, VI. 14; IV. 8.
2. II. 54; 69, 70, 71.
3. III. 71.
4. VIII. 30.
5. I. 27.
6. IV. 87 (two contexts), III. 46, VI. 1, I. 28; V. 19, III. 29, 82, 62, V. 37.
7. I. 13, 19.
8. I. 42; I. 38, III. 58; IV. 50-52, 164; III. 84; V. 62. However, in offering Polissena or Elena to Pandaro as a mistress, Troiolo spoke of the one as "piú di bellezza che altra pregiata" and of the other as "bellissima," III. 18.
9. II. 44.
10. Criseida's beauty in general: II. 81, 84. Beauty of her countenance: I. 33; II. 35; IV. 82; V. 45. Beauty of her eyes: I. 29, 41; III. 36.
11. Her beauty in general: I. 43; II. 57, 59, 88, 98, 99, 104; III. 29, 47, 62, 83, 88; IV. 143; V. 24, 25, 28; VII. 70, 93. Beauty of her countenance: I. 39, 55; V. 19; VII. 69; VIII. 15. Beauty of her eyes: II. 58, 86, 98; III. 88; IV. 51, 123; V. 55.
12. Her beauty in general: II. 21, 36, 42, 43, 54, 137; IV. 98; V. 34. Beauty of her face and eyes: II. 64.
13. II. 69; VI 20.
14. IV. 164.
15. I. 12.
16. I. 19, 26, 30.
17. I. 38.
18. II. 54, 60.
19. IV. 90.
20. Introduction to Griffin and Myrick's edition of the *Filostrato*, pp. 55-56.
21. *Fil.* III. 32.
22. III. 71.
23. II. 110.
24. I. 35, II. 34, 128, III. 63, IV. 41; I. 20; V. 11; VII.33.
25. IV. 109, VII. 45.
26. VIII. 29. That Troiolo was youthful may be hinted also in the narrator's remark that it pleased the prince to see "giovani" honored, III. 92.
27. I. 40, III. 90.
28. II. 42, 71.
29. IV. 128, VII. 29.
30. II. 84, III. 91.
31. II. 107; VIII. 9; IV. 120, 123, 125, and VII. 33, 36.
32. V. 10, VIII. 4.
33. VI. 33.
34. VIII. 8-9.
35. II. 1, V. 11 and VII. 45.
36. IV. 10, 12.
37. IV. 93, 136; IV. 38, V. 4, 25, VII. 3, 28, 56. Avariciousness is mentioned in IV. 136, VII. 56.
38. See Ch. I. 1. n.4 for the ages of Boccaccio and Chaucer at the periods respectively when the *Troilus* and *Filostrato* were composed. In view of Chaucer's de-emphasis of the youthfulness of the main characters, Professor Patch seems to overestimate the poet's consideration of this factor. In *On Rereading Chaucer* (Cambridge: Harvard Univ. Press, 1939), he says of the *Troilus*: "The preoccupation of its story with the concerns of youth meant perhaps a lack of range in the artistic possibilities open to the poet's imagination, but the emotional patterns fell within correspondingly easier compass. Ironies of a youthful misadventure would seem to be more steadily

congenial to Chaucer, or to the people for whom he was writing, than tragic implications of disaster among an older group," pp. 56-57. And he dwells on the youth and youthful attributes of the hero after this introductory statement, 67, 71, 83-88, 92-93.

39. In his "The People in Chaucer's *Troilus,*" *PMLA.,* LVI (1941), Professor Tatlock writes, "the poet would probably not have denied that Troilus was in the early twenties," p. 92; and as for the lover's friend, "he is Criseyde's uncle. . . , but there is not another syllable to suggest that he belongs to a different generation. . . . He is still a youngish man, carrying on a . . . love-affair, going in for athletic sports with Troilus. . . . Nearly twenty times, one of them calls the other 'brother,' " p. 95. Professor Kirby feels sure that the go-between is in his early thirties, *Chaucer's Troilus,* p. 187. Chaucer gives the years of one female and five male characters whom he calls "yong": Queen Anelida is twenty, *AA.* 78, and the Squire in the *General Prologue,* Theseus in the *Legend,* Blanche's relict, Emetrius, and the Monk in the *Shipman's Tale* are respectively twenty, twenty-three, twenty-four, twenty-five, and thirty, *CT.* I. 79 and 82, *LGW.* 2075, *BD.* 454-55, *CT.* I. 2172 and 2598, and *CT.* VII. 26 and 28. Theseus, the relict, and Emetrius are knights like Troilus, and the last compared—as he is—to Mars, *CT.* I. 2159. Januarie will have no bride as old as thirty, *CT.* IV. 1421.

40. On details of person, dress, and character in the *Troilus* and their literary antecedents, see Claes Schaar, *The Golden Mirror Studies in Chaucer's Descriptive Technique and its Literary Background,* Skrifter Utgivna av Kungl. Humanistiska Vetenkapssamfundet i Lund, LIV (1955), 183-92, 278-90.

41. See Sister Mary Ernestine Whitmore, *Medieval English Domestic Life and Amusements in the Works of Chaucer* (Washington, D. C.: Catholic Univ., 1937), Ch. IV; and Stephen J. Herben, Jr., "Arms and Armor in Chaucer," *Spec.,* XII (1937), 475-87, for the poet's unobtrusive accuracy with respect to dress in general and arms in particular.

42. *TC.* I. 981-87 (*Fil.* II. 27).

43. II. 393-406 (*Fil.* II. 54).

44. II. 750-53 (*Fil.* II. 69).

45. *Courtly Love in Chaucer and Gower* (Boston and London: Ginn, 1913), p. 130.

46. *TC.* III. 468-69, V. 826.

47. I. 281-84 (*Fil.* I. 27). In "The 'Troilus' Frontispiece," *MLR.,* XLIV (1949), 168. n.4, Miss Galway would have it that Chaucer chose not to leave Criseyde expressly tall because of his semi-identification of her with Joan of Kent. See Ch. IV. 2. n.21 for this scholar's work on Chaucer and Joan. On Criseyde's person in general, see D. S. Brewer, "The Ideal of Feminine Beauty in Medieval Literature. . . ," *MLR.,* L(1955), 264-65.

48. III. 1247-50. See Ch. I. 6 for Chaucer's use of the *Filocolo* in the consummation sequence and for his indebtedness to it in the particular passage, see pp. 72-73.

49. IV. 736-38 (*Fil.* IV. 87), 816-17 (*Fil.* IV. 96). "Avecques les cheveulx respanduz," *Le Roman de Troyle et de Criseida,* p. 223, renders *"scapigliata,"* *Fil.* IV. 96, as indicated by Pratt, *StPh.,* LIII, 526.

50. V. 806ff. See Ch. I. 9. n.6 for the sources.

51. It may be noted that Diomede invokes the goddess of wisdom as "Pallas with hire heres clere," V. 999.

52. III. 106, 1296, 1740-41, V. 244, 473, 575-80.

53. IV. 752 (*Fil.* IV. 87), V. 708 (*Fil.* VI. 1).

54 V. 815; IV. 663, 740; V. 1573, 516, 1241.

55. V. 219 (*Fil.* V. 19).

56. III. 129, 1353, V. 220, 566, 1338, and IV. 310; III. 1485, V. 465, 1247, 1264, and V. 1712. The "lady bright" of V. 465 replaces an image of light applied to the lady, *Fil.* V. 44.

57. V.162, 922.

58. For our poet's frequent use of "bright," see Ruth Crosby, "Chaucer and the Custom of Oral Delivery," *Spec.,* XIII (1938), 421. In the *Troilus,* he applies it to females beside Criseyde: to the sex in general, "ful many a lady bright of hewe" and "every lady bright of hewe," III. 303, V. 1772; to Venus, "lady bryght," III. 39, 1807; and to Fortune "hire brighte face," IV. 8. Note also "Minerva, the white," II. 1062, and designations of Antigone as "the shene" and "the white," II. 824, 887.

59. *TC.* I. 100-1 (*Fil.* I. 11), 172 (*Fil.* I. 19), 455 (*Fil.* I. 42).
60. IV. 1155, V. 807-8.
61. III.1280-81; IV. 449-51, answering IV. 400-4.
62. II. 744-48 (*Fil.* II. 69).
63. Two by the narrator, III. 515, 1741; one by Troilus, I. 277; five by Pandarus, I. 882 (*Fil.* II. 21), 982, II. 288 (*Fil.* II. 44), 341, 584 (*Fil.* II. 43); two by Diomede, V. 170, 914 (*Fil.* VI. 20). Also described, without superlatives, as fair are: Eleyne, II. 1556; Polixene, III. 409 (*Fil.* III. 18); Antigone, III. 597; and Europe, III. 722.
64. I. 109 (*Fil.* I. 12). The reading in *Le Roman de Troyle et de Criseida*, p. 122, is "en habit de veufvage," as noted by Pratt, *StPh.*, LIII, 513.
65. I. 170 and 177 (*Fil.* I. 19), 309 (I. 30), 175. As noted by Pratt, p. 514, "habit blak," I. 170, corresponds to "habit de noir," *Le Roman*, p. 124, rather than to "bruna vesta," *Fil.* I. 19.
66. II. 110, 222.
67. II. 533-34.
68. IV. 778-81 (*Fil.* IV. 90).
69. III. 885 and 1368-69, 1370-72.
70. For the symbolism, see the authorities cited in Ch. I. 6. n. 58.
71. V. 1037-43, 1012-13. See Ch. I. 9. n.19 and n.14 for passages in Benoit which supplied Chaucer with the details of horse, sleeve, and glove.
72. I. 437-38 (*Fil.* I. 40).
73. II. 175.
74. II. 624, V. 1037-39. The bay is also mentioned in I. 1072-74.
75. II. 631-42. The realistic particularity as to arms and armor of this passage is to be found also in Chaucer's accounts of the battle in which Antenor was captured and of the slaying of Ector by Achilles, IV. 43-46, V. 1558-61.
76. II. 660ff., 676-77. See Ch. I. 4 n.17 for the influence of the *Roman d'Eneas* upon the incident.
77. II. 1010-15.
78. II. 1086-88 (*Fil.* II. 107).
79. II. 1261-63, 1267.
80. III. 738-742, 1098-99.
81. III. 1126.
82. III. 1168.
83. III. 1368-69.
84. III. 1716-29 (*Fil.* III. 72, supplemented by II. 84), with the circumstance of change of costume, III. 1719, probably suggested by *Fil.* II. 84.
85. III. 1772-79 (*Fil.* III. 90).
86. IV. 1184ff. (*Fil.* IV. 120ff.).
87. IV. 1666-1680, converted from Troiolo's tribute to Criseida, *Fil.* IV. 164-65.
88. V. 64-67 (*Fil.* V. 10).
89. V. 799-805, 827-40. See Ch. I. 9. n.6 for the sources of these portraits. Troilus' ejaculation, "by myn hood," during his vigil on the tenth day, V. 1151, does not indicate, of course, that he was then wearing this article of apparel.
90. V. 1254-56 (*Fil.* VII. 29).
91. V. 1576-82 (*Fil.* VIII. 4). See Ch. I. 11. n.5 for the comments of Magoun and Whiting on this passage.
92. V. 1040-41, 1646ff. (*Fil.* VIII. 8ff.). As noted by Pratt, *StPh.*, LIII, 535, "A manere cote-armure" and "The whiche cote," V. 1651, 1653, have as correspondents in *Le Roman de Troyle et de Criseida*, p. 297, "une riche cothe" and "celle cote," which render respectively "uno ornato vestimento" and "lo," *Fil.* VIII. 8, 9.
93. V. 1835ff. (*Fil.* VIII. 29ff.).
94. His phrase, "us yonge," III. 293, does not mean "us who are *now* in our youth."
95. III. 323-25, III. 1572-73.
96. II. 1180-82. Shortly before, Pandarus spoke figuratively of her finding game in his hood, II. 1109-10.
97. IV. 103-5 (*Fil.* IV. 10), 127-33 (*Fil.* IV. 12). Calkas is accompanied by "lordes olde," IV. 66.
98. IV. 1366ff. (*Fil.* IV. 136).

99. IV. 330-36 (*Fil.* IV. 38), V. 1126-27 (*Fil.* VII. 3), 1135-37 (*Fil.* VII. 5, mention of Calcas, but not as old). Pandarus hypothesizes that the dream boar may signify Calkas "which that old is and ek hoor," V. 1282-88. It may be added that Troilus' father is once designated "the olde Priam," IV. 141-42. For the signification of "olde" in terms of years, see George R. Coffman, "Old Age in Chaucer's Day," *MLN.*, LII (1937), 25-26, and Brother C. Philip, F.S.C., "A Further Note on Old Age in Chaucer's Day," *MLN.*, LIII (1938), 181-82.

Section 3 *Ravages of Passion*

1. *Fil.* II. 38, 47, 118; 139; 115-16.
2. IV. 87, 88, 89, 92.
3. IV. 100.
4. IV. 105.
5. IV. 117ff.
6. IV. 125-26, 157, 162.
7. VI. 1, 4.
8. VI. 7.
9. VI. 9-10, 14-20.
10. I. 43, 47.
11. II. 15, 96.
12. III. 20. Having had no time for slumber on the first night of love, he could not sleep, because of delightful reminiscence, after he had returned from it to his palace, III. 53.
13. IV. 18ff.
14. IV. 109.
15. V. 3, 13.
16. V. 19ff., 26-27.
17. V. 32.
18. V. 52; 60 reinforced by 66.
19. V. 67-68.
20. VII. 18ff.
21. VII. 23-24.
22. VII. 36.
23. VII. 46; 60, 75.
24. VII. 77; 81, 90; 103-4.
25. I. 54, 56.
26. II. 2, 7. See also II. 3.
27. II. 19.
28. II. 59, 64.
29. II. 86, 89; 104.
30. II. 109.
31. II. 132, 137.
32. III. 45, 59.
33. IV. 14; 28, 30-32, 34, 36; 40.
34. IV. 45, 50, 60-62, 70, 76 answering 71ff.
35. IV. 102, 105, 107.
36. IV. 120ff., with Criseida learning of his intention, IV. 125.
37. IV. 139-40, 143.
38. V. 3, 12.
39. V. 17; 24, 27.
40. V. 57, 62ff.
41. VII. 19, 25, 32ff.
42. VII. 61, 73.
43. VIII. 11, 15, 20-21.
44. VIII. 25-27.
45. VI. 11.
46. VI. 23.
47. III. 59.

48. VII. 37-38, 43-45.
49. IV. 9.
50. On psychophysical states and expressive actions in the *Troilus* and their literary antecedents, see Claes Schaar, *The Golden Mirror*, Skrifter Utgivna av Kungl. Humanistiska Vetenkapssamfundet i Lund, LIV (1955), 27-49, 132-39.
51. *TC.* II. 302-3.
52. II. 652, 770.
53. II. 1256; 1198 (*Fil.* II. 118).
54. II. 1470.
55. III. 956, 1569-70.
56. III. 1698.
57. IV. 740-41, 843-45; 862-63 and 869-70 (*Fil.* IV. 100).
58. IV. 1150ff. (*Fil.* IV. 117ff.).
59. V. 181-82.
60. V. 243-45.
61. V. 708-12 (*Fil.* VI. 1). As indicated by Pratt, *StPh.*, LIII, 532, "*Ful* pale ywoxen was hire brighte *face*," V. 708, shows verbal correspondence to "son beau *visage* frays et delyé luy estoit devenu *tout* palle et maigre," *Le Roman de Troyle et de Criseida*, p. 260, an adaptation of lines 6-7 in *Filostrato*, VI. 1.
62. V. 914-15 (*Fil.* VI. 20).
63. V. 1590-96. The lines embody a conceit similar to that (*Fil.* II. 96) in the early letter of Troiolo—a missive which Chaucer did not reproduce. See n.110 below.
64. I. 95.
65. II. 124; 409, 427.
66. II. 449-51.
67. III. 805, 1049.
68. III. 1697.
69. IV. 733-34.
70. IV. 738-39 and 753 (*Fil.* IV. 87), 762-63 (*Fil.* IV. 88), 771-77 (*Fil.* IV. 89).
71. IV. 818-19, 839.
72. IV. 904-10 (*Fil.* IV. 105).
73. IV. 1223-42 (*Fil.* IV. 125-26).
74. IV. 1251.
75. IV. 1412-14, 1415-21.
76. IV. 1560.
77. IV. 1605-7 (*Fil.* IV. 157), 1616-17; 1650-51 (*Fil.* IV. 162).
78. V. 689-90, 700; 701-3.
79. *KnT.* I. 1361-76. See Professor Lowes, "The Loveres Maladye of Hereos," *MPh.*, XI (1914), 491-546, and "Hereos Again," *MLN.*, XXXI (1916), 185-87.
80. I. 400-20; 441; 484-87 (*Fil.* I. 47) and 488-91.
81. I. 553, 575-76.
82. I. 722-28, 737ff.
83. I. 867 (*Fil.* II. 15), 871.
84. I. 914-21. See I. 195-96 for Troilus on the sleeplessness of lovers.
85. II. 551-53, 645-46.
86. II. 1506ff., 1527-30. For a suggested source of the feigned illness, see Ch. I. 5. n.4.
87. II. 1541-45, 1571-73.
88. II. 1576-82.
89. II. 1646ff., 1728-31; 1736.
90. III. 61, 69-70.
91. III. 57-58, 82, 92-95.
92. III. 193-99, 370-71.
93. III. 439-41 (*Fil.* III. 20). Like Troiolo, Troilus, wasting no time in slumber during his first night of love, was unable to sleep for happy reminiscence after returning from it to his palace, III. 1534-40 (*Fil.* III. 53).
94. III. 792-98.
95. III. 1086-92. See Root's note, p. 483, to ll. 1088-89.
96. III. 1190.
97. III. 1698.

98. IV. 150, 235.
99. IV. 342-43 (*Fil.* IV. 41, with Troiolo falling, not into a trance, but asleep),
915-17.
100. IV. 1091-92 (*Fil.* IV. 109).
101. V. 34-35, 36-37 (*Fil.* V. 3).
102. V. 85-86 (*Fil.* V. 13).
103. V. 211ff. (*Fil.* V. 19ff.), 246-59 (*Fil.* V. 26-27).
104. V. 358-61 (*Fil.* V. 32).
105. V. 532; 536 (*Fil.* V. 52), 555, 559.
106. V. 617-23 (*Fil.* V. 60).
107. V. 645-65 (*Fil.* V. 67-69).
108. V. 1212ff. (*Fil.* VII. 18ff.).
109. V. 1233-41 (*Fil.* VII. 23-24).
110. V. 1401-4 (*Fil.* VII. 75); 1414-16 (*Fil.* II. 96). See n.63 above for the use of
Fil. II. 96 also in Criseyde's last letter.
111. V. 1439 (*Fil.* VII. 77), 1440.
112. V. 1536-37.
113. V. 646-48.
114. I. 306-7, as interpreted in terms of medieval medicine by Root in his note, pp.
416-17.
115. I. 459-60, 535-36; 526-27 (*Fil.* I. 54).
116. I. 571-74 (*Fil.* II. 2); 577-79 (*Fil.* II. 3), 603-9 (*Fil.* II. 7).
117. I. 616, 758; 778-819.
118. I. 875.
119. I. 1014, 1034-36.
120. II. 316-85.
121. II. 432-45.
122. II. 475-89.
123. II. 536, 565-67; 577-78.
124. II. 653-55, 663-65.
125. II. 1046-50.
126. II. 1125-27 (*Fil.* II. 109).
127. II. 1208-9.
128. II. 1277-81, 1281.
129. II. 1506-12.
130. II. 1592-94.
131. II. 1736.
132. III. 63.
133. III. 106-12.
134. III. 118-19, 122-23, 150-55.
135. III. 347-48, 360-62.
136. III. 796-98.
137. III. 867-68 reinforced by 876-82; 891-93.
138. III. 904-5.
139. III. 1069-71 and 1072-73, 1081 with 1086ff.
140. III. 1171.
141. III. 1267-73, 1289-1302.
142. III. 1475-77 and 1481-83 (*Fil.* III. 45).
143. III. 1611-14 (*Fil.* III. 59).
144. III. 1697.
145. IV. 151 (*Fil.* IV. 14), 162-63.
146. IV. 250 (*Fil.* IV. 28), 251-52, 260-87 (*Fil.* IV. 30-32), 300-1, 302-8 (*Fil.* IV.
34) and 316-22 (*Fil.* IV. 36), 323-29 (see Ch. I. 7. n.24 for possible source), 333-34
(*Fil.* IV. 39).
147. IV. 373 (*Fil.* IV. 45), 428-31.
148. IV. 432-34, 440-41 (*Fil.* IV. 50), 455, 498-518 (*Fil.* IV. 60-62).
149. IV. 524-25.
150. IV. 580, corresponding to Troiolo's wish that he had died at first sight of
Criseida, *Fil.* IV. 70.

461

151. IV. 582ff. (*Fil.* IV. 71ff.)—esp. 622-23 (*Fil.* IV. 72); 634-37 (*Fil.* IV. 76).
152. IV. 883-84; instead of *Fil.* IV. 102; 918-24 (*Fil.* IV. 107).
153. IV. 953-55, 1079-82.
154. IV. 1184ff. (*Fil.* IV. 120ff.), with Criseyde learning of his intention, IV. 1223-34 (*Fil.* IV. 125).
155. IV. 1251.
156. IV. 1440-46 (*Fil.* IV. 139-40), 1471-77.
157. IV. 1497-98 (*Fil.* IV. 143).
158. V. 40-42 (*Fil.* V. 3), 84 (*Fil.* V. 12); 208-10 (*Fil.* V. 17), 225-31 (*Fil.* V. 24).
159. V. 295-322. See Ch. I. 8. n. 17, for contributions of the *Teseida* to this passage.
160. V. 638-44, substituted for *Fil.* V. 62ff.
161. V. 1209-11, 1215-16 (*Fil.* VII. 19); V. 1245-46 (*Fil.* VII. 25), 1269-74 (*Fil.* VII. 32).
162. V. 1368-72, 1387-93, 1399-1400, 1412-13.
163. V. 1672-73 (*Fil.* VIII. 11), 1684-86, 1699 (*Fil.* VIII. 15), 1716-19 (*Fil.* VIII. 20).
164. V. 1751-64 (*Fil.* VIII. 25-26), 1800-6 (*Fil.* VIII. 27).
165. V. 795-97 (*Fil.* VI. 11), 798.
166. V. 925-26 (*Fil.* VI. 23).
167. I. 877ff.—esp. Pandarus' gladness to have been born now that his friend had chosen so well, 904-5; and his asseveration, by his own death, that the latter was no trifler in love, 930-31; 1053.
168. II. 323-25 and 327-28; 432-34 and 439-46. See II. 172-74, for an incidental asseveration of Pandarus by his own death.
169. II. 449ff.
170. II. 572-74, 575-78.
171. II. 1355-56.
172. III. 118-19.
173. III. 262-63, 414-17. Eugene E. Slaughter, "Chaucer's Pandarus: Virtuous Uncle and Friend," *JEGP.,* XLVIII (1949), 188-91.
174. III. 1611-14 (*Fil.* III. 59).
175. IV. 379.
176. IV. 428-31, 524-25.
177. IV. 538-39, 624-28. The latter passage is analogous in spirit to Pandaro's offer after the boar dream to die with Troiolo in battle against the Greeks, *Fil.* VII. 43-45, a passage omitted by Chaucer.
178. IV. 883-84, V. 1275-76.
179. II. 352-54, 1145-48, III. 571-74.
180. III. 1572-73.
181. II. 57-63; 1165-66; III. 342-43, IV. 397-99.
182. IV. 97-99 (*Fil.* IV. 9).

Section 4 *Expressive Actions*

1. *Fil.* I. 12.
2. I. 19, 27-28.
3. V. 9.
4. II. 82.
5. III. 26, 30.
6. III. 31-32.
7. III. 34-35.
8. III. 36-37.
9. III. 40-41.
10. III. 42-44, 50.
11. III. 66.
12. III. 69.
13. IV. 84, 86, 87, 96, 98, 99, 101, 106, 114, 115, 116, 118, 127, 167; V. 12; VI. 1, 2, 3.

14. IV. 87.
15. IV. 96, 106.
16. IV. 114-17.
17. IV. 126.
18. IV. 127.
19. IV. 167.
20. V. 12.
21. V. 54.
22. VI. 26.
23. II. 34.
24. II. 36, 47.
25. II. 108.
26. II. 113. See the passages cited in n.15 for her behavior during Pandaro's last visit.
27. I. 20-21.
28. I. 30.
29. V. 11. Note also his "falso riso" at the start of his sentimental jaunt through Troy and his raising his head at thought of battle when he was visited abed by Deifobo, V. 51, VII. 81.
30. I. 53, 55, 57; II. 1, 16, 20.
31. II. 62, 61.
32. II. 81.
33. II. 100, 107. In her reply, Criseida alluded to tear blots on his letter, II. 122.
34. III. 29; 32; 36; 37; 44, 46, 51.
35. IV. 28, 29, 30, 34, 35, 41, 44, 49, 50, 63, 65, 66, 70, 101, 103, 114, 115, 116, 118, 124, 127, 160, 167; V. 16, 17, 19, 20, 23, 24, 35, 36, 58; VII. 17, 18, 25, 33, 46, 60, 61, 74; VIII. 12, 25.
36. IV. 21-22.
37. IV. 27.
38. IV. 29.
39. IV. 114ff., 124.
40. V 19-20.
41. VII. 33-36.
42. II. 16, 18, 20.
43. II. 31.
44. II. 33, 81.
45. III. 13.
46. III. 56-57, 73.
47. IV. 44, V. 51.
48. VI. 11, 23.
49. II. 34, 35, 56. Pandaro implied to Criseida that his own love gave him cause to weep, II. 44.
50. II. 108, 118.
51. IV. 101.
52. IV. 44, 46, 101, 103, VII. 37, and VIII. 23; II. 21 and 32; VII. 33-36.
53. IV. 12. See also IV. 4.
54. *TC.* I. 110-12 (*Fil.* I. 12). On emotional behavior of Criseyde and her fellow characters, see Schaar as cited in Ch. II. 3. n.50.
55. I. 178-82 (*Fil.* I. 19), 288-94 (*Fil.* I. 28).
56 III. 211-17. During the party, Eleyne condescended to hold Criseyde's hand and to favor her with an approving look, II. 1604-6.
57. See the stanza of the *Filostrato* cited in n.3.
58. II. 656-58, 689.
59. II. 1254.
60. III. 71-72, 155-58, 182. Eleyne had laid her arm comfortingly over Troilus' shoulder, and she and Deiphebus were to kiss him on leave-taking, II. 1671-72, III. 225-26.
61. III. 885.
62. III. 939-40, 948.
63. III. 967-73.

64. III. 1051-57.
65. III. 1109-11, 1114-15, 1116-17, 1128-29.
66. III. 1198-1201.
67. III. 1350, 1370-72, 1519 (*Fil.* III. 50).
68. III. 1230-32, 1315-16 (*Fil.* III. 32), 1338-44 (*Fil.* III. 34), 1368-69, 1401-4 (*Fil.* III. 40), III. 1408-9 (*Fil.* III. 41).
69. IV. 708-9 (*Fil.* IV. 84), 742, 750-51 (*Fil.* IV. 87), 814-15 (*Fil.* IV. 96), 911-12 (*Fil.* IV. 106), 1135-39 (*Fil.* IV. 115); V. 82 (*Fil.* V. 12), 712 (*Fil.* VI. 1), 725-26 (*Fil.* VI. 3).
70. IV. 730-38 and 752 (*Fil.* IV. 87), with the detail of the fingers an addition to the source.
71. IV. 820-21 (*Fil.* IV. 96), 911-12 (*Fil.* IV. 106). As indicated by Pratt, *StPh.*, LIII, 527, "Fil gruf," IV. 912, corresponds to "se remist *adens* sur son lit," *Le Roman de Troyle et de Criseida*," p. 226, not to "ricadde supina," *Fil.* IV. 106.
72. IV. 1128-55 (*Fil.* IV. 114-17). As indicated by Pratt, p. 527, "*and* therwithal *hire* face Upon *his* brest she *leyde*," IV. 1150-51, is closer to "*Et* puis luy *laissa cheoir son* visaige sur *sa* poitrine," *Le Roman de Troyle*, p. 228, than to "Poi gli ricadde col viso in sul petto," *Fil.* IV. 117.
73. IV. 1229-30, 1243-46 (*Fil.* IV. 126).
74. IV. 1247-51 (*Fil.* IV. 127), 1688-90 (*Fil.* IV. 167). As indicated by Pratt, p. 529, "And ofte *ykist*, and streite in armes folde," IV. 1689, echoes "se sont recommencez à baiser et à acoler," *Le Roman de Troyle*, p. 242, rather than "l'un l'altro abbracciava," *Fil.* IV. 167.
75. V. 568-69 (*Fil.* V. 54).
76. V. 778-81.
77. V. 848-49 (*Fil.* V. 11), 851-52.
78. V. 1005 as against *Fil.* VI. 26.
79. V. 1044-47. See Ch. I. 9. n.19 for Chaucer's indebtedness to the *Roman de Troie* for this circumstance.
80. II. 88-91 (*Fil.* II. 34).
81. II. 98-99.
82. II. 141-42, 253; 408 (*Fil.* II. 47).
83. II. 447-48.
84. II. 1107-8.
85. II. 1114-17; 1159 after 1154-55.
86. II. 1162-69.
87. II. 1180-82.
88. II. 1723-26.
89. III. 561-62.
90. III. 1569-70. See the passages cited in n.71 for her behavior during Pandarus' visit after the parliament.
91. I. 183-96 (*Fil.* I. 20-21), 204-5. As indicated by Pratt, p. 514, "He wolde *smyle*," I. 194, corresponds to "il *sourrioit*," *Le Roman de Troyle*, p. 125, instead of to "ridendo," *Fil.* I. 21.
92. I. 309-15 (*Fil.* I. 30).
93. II. 645-48.
94. V. 77 (*Fil.* V. 11).
95. I. 543 (*Fil.* I. 57); 701 (*Fil.* II. 13, reproved for sighs), 806.
96. II. 540-41 (*Fil.* II. 61), 1086-88 (*Fil.* II. 107).
97. II. 1257-58.
98. III. 69-70, 71-72, 96.
99. III. 953ff., 1079ff.
100. III. 1186-87 reinforced by 1205; 1247-53 (*Filocolo*, as cited in Ch. I. 6. n.45); 1275; 1345-46 (*Filostrato*, III. 35, with Troiolo and Criseida both in gaze); 1352-53 (*Fil.* III. 36); 1359, 1448-49 (*Fil.* III. 44), 1522-23 (*Fil.* III. 51). As indicated by Pratt, p. 520, "in his armes took his lady," III. 1522, corresponds to "l'eut . . . acollée," *Le Roman de Troyle*, p. 186, instead of to "ribasciata l'ebbe," *Fil.* III. 51.
101. Cited in n.68.
102. IV. 246-59 (*Fil.* IV. 28-29), 309-12 (*Fil.* IV. 35), 340 (*Fil.* IV. 41), 365-67

(*Fil.* IV. 44), 510-11, 519-20 (*Fil.* IV. 63), 575 (*Fil.* IV. 70), 1132-48 (*Fil.* IV. 114-16), 1172-73 (*Fil.* IV. 119); V. 214-15 (*Fil.* V. 19), 408-9 (*Fil.* V. 35), 1181-82, 1335-37 (*Fil.* VII. 74), 1747 (*Fil.* VIII. 25).
103. IV. 218-24 (*Fil.* IV. 22), 239-45 (*Fil.* IV. 27), 255-56 (*Fil.* IV. 29).
104. IV. 1128ff. (*Fil.* IV. 114ff.), 1219 (*Fil.* IV. 124).
105. See passages cited in n.74.
106. V. 78-81 (*Fil.* V. 12), 211-12 and 222-24 (*Fil.* V. 19 and 20). As indicated by Pratt, p. 530, "*caste* his eye upon hire" and "*Save* a pilowe, I *fynde naught* t'enbrace," V. 79 and 224, are closer respectively to "les yeulx s'entre *gittèrent* l'un à l'autre" and "or, maintenant *n'ay* je à embracer *que* mon oreiller," *Le Roman de Troyle*, pp. 245, 247, than to "dentro agli occhi l'un l'altro guatârsi" and "ora abbracciando vado il piumaccio," *Fil.* V. 12, 20.
107. I. 1044-45 (*Fil.* II. 33), II. 974 (*Fil.* II. 81).
108. II. 1259-60, 1637-39.
109. III. 358-59 (*Fil.* III. 13).
110. III. 1590-96 (*Fil.* III. 56).
111. III. 1737-38 (*Fil.* III. 73).
112. V. 554-55.
113. V. 90—see Ch. I. 8. n.8 for the line in the *Roman de Troie*, which, rather than *Fil.* V. 13, appears to have suggested this circumstance; V. 1012-13—see Ch. I. 9. n.14, for the lines in the *Roman* which suggested this one; V. 927 (*Fil.* V. 23).
114. II. 96-99.
115. II. 250, 254, 264-65 (*Fil.* II. 35) and 274 (*Fil.* II. 36), 293.
116. II. 323-26.
117. II. 407, 447.
118. II. 505 (*Fil.* II. 56).
119. II. 1114-17.
120. II. 1142, 1154-55 (*Fil.* II. 113).
121. II. 1202-4.
122. II. 1464-65.
123. II. 1725.
124. III. 59-64.
125. III. 115-16.
126. III. 183-84.
127. III. 199.
128. III. 566-67.
129. III. 606, 629.
130. III. 680-83.
131. III. 754-56.
132. III. 1571-75.
133. IV. 872-73 (*Fil.* IV. 101).
134. I. 868-70.
135. I. 1037 (*Fil.* II. 32).
136. II. 507ff. This corresponds to Pandaro's account of time spent in "selve ombrose," *Fil.* II. 56, but with the addition of both exercise and spying.
137. II. 939-43, 953-54.
138. II. 1320.
139. II. 1637-38.
140. Passages cited in notes 124, 125.
141. III. 229-38.
142. III. 698-700, 738-42.
143. III. 953ff., esp. 964-65.
144. III. 974-77.
145. III. 978-80.
146. III. 1093ff.
147. III. 1588-89.
148. IV. 353-61, 365-69 (*Fil.* IV. 44).
149. IV. 521-22.
150. V. 293-94.

151. V. 512-18.
152. IV. 129-30 (*Fil.* IV. 12), V. 190-91.

Section 5 *Place*

1. *Fil.* I. 17, 18.
2. The edifice is referred to as the "tempio," I. 19, 30, the "gran tempio," I. 20, and the "nobil tempio," I. 32. See Ch. I. 2. n.5, for the reminiscence.
3. III. 4ff. In his letter to Criseida in camp, it may be noted, Troiolo wrote that he had come to shun "i templi e le gran feste," which once he sought, VII. 62.
4. The Greeks to whom the decision reached in the "parlamento" was communicated are termed "ambasciatori," IV. 13, and thus implied to have come for it to the city— Troiolo was seated during the proceedings, IV. 14, and therefore, more likely than not, indoors.
5. I. 32; III. 29, 52, 53, 64; IV. 22; V. 15, 51. That the establishment stood apart from the King's is indicated by Pandaro's suggestion, given in it to Troiolo, that they return to court, IV. 77.
6. Pandaro, of course, *passim;* also, "compagni," I. 20, 32, V. 10; "amico e servitor quantunque caro," IV. 22, and "un suo privato valletto," IV. 42.
7. "In camera," I. 33; "nella camera sua," II. 1, and, with backward reference, "nella sua camera," II. 62; "alla camera sua," II. 95; chamber implied by Troiolo's going to bed in his palace, III. 53; "nella camera," "nella camera sua," and "nella camera," IV. 22, 26, 43; "in camera," V. 15; "in camera," V. 50; "nella camera," VII. 33; and "la sua camera," VII .84.
8. I. 32 (outside the chamber, since Troiolo later proceeded to it, I. 33); II. 86-95 (outside, for the same reason, II. 95). Conversations with Pandaro, not expressly, but probably within the chamber, II. 79-81, IV. 109-13.
9. Sitting "a piè del letto," I. 33; lying "sopra il suo letto," and while on it twice hiding his face, then rising from it to embrace Pandaro, II. 1, 16 and 20, 33, with backward reference to II. 1 in II. 62; lying down "nel letto" and, risen therefrom, embracing Pandaro again, III. 53, 56; throwing himself "sopra il suo letto," rising to go to the door, again embracing the friend, IV. 29, 42, 44; tossing abed with business with a pillow and, after summoning Pandaro, exhorted by the latter to rise, V. 19 and 20, 35; sitting a while with him, V. 50; dreaming of the boar presumably in bed and, after again summoning the friend, running for a knife which hung in the chamber, but deprived of it by Pandaro and made to sit beside him, VII. 23-25, 33-36; taking to his bed, there to remain until after the visit of Deifobo and repeated ones of the ladies, VII. 77, 103-4.
10. It is recorded on only three occasions that Pandaro was seated in his friend's presence, II. 79, V. 50, VII. 36, and then not on what. There is no indication whether he sat or stood for long stretches of talk with the bedded lover.
11. IV. 22, 26, 42, 43.
12. II. 56, III. 73.
13. Returning "a casa sua" from her interview with Ettore, Criseida remained in it while in Troy "con quella famiglia ch' al suo onor convenia di tenere," I. 14, 15; "in questa casa," she reminded Pandaro, "son donne ed altre genti meco," II. 143; if some of these were away on the night of consummation as she had anticipated, some were still with her, for, with Troiolo "nella casa" downstairs, she, above, had to speed everyone to bed and wait until "la casa" was all quiet, before descending to him, III. 24, 26-27; passing by the "magione" after her departure, Troiolo thought his heart would break at sight of its closed door and windows, V. 51, 52. In an episode in her dwelling in which no name for it occurs, she is said to quit "la compagnia con la quale era," and, a little later, to quit the same group again, designated this time as "le compagne," II. 108, 114.
14. "Nella camera sua," II. 68; "nella sua camera," II. 114; "dall' un canto della camera sua," II. 120; " 'n camera," III. 30; "nella camera," III. 65; "nella camera sua," IV. 86, and " 'n camera," IV. 95; chamber implied by Criseida's proposal of bed, IV. 126, as well as explicitly indicated before the event by Pandaro, IV. 107.

15. Criseida and Troiolo lying down "nel letto," III. 31, and his rising therefrom, III. 51; bed implied by their lying down together, III. 65, and their rising, III. 70; Criseida alone "in sul suo letto," IV. 87, and still there when visited by Pandaro, IV. 95ff., but promising him to rise, IV. 108; her proposing to Troiolo that they should go "a letto," IV. 126, and their rising, IV. 167.

16. II. 34.

17. II. 82.

18. II. 108, 114, as cited in note 13.

19. II. 118-20; 128; 133-43, with Criseida wishing that she had died on the day that Pandaro had inclined her to love "qui nella loggia," II. 139.

20. III. 26.

21. III. 25, 27-29.

22. III. 30.

23. III. 64-65.

24. IV. 114.

25. IV. 115-26.

26. IV. 80-86 (outside the chamber, since Criseida finally went to it, IV. 86).

27. V. 54-55.

28. V. 40, 41.

29. V. 42-43, according with III. 88 and contrasting with III. 91-93.

30. V. 40.

31. V. 6, 9, 10, 11, and 13; 54.

32. "Fossi," I. 16—and again in incidental fashion, VII. 79.

33. V. 1-15, esp. V. 10.

34. V. 58.

35. V. 70.

36. VII. 1-14.

37. VII. 14.

38. IV. 1 (in Griffin and Myrick's text, "negli ampi piani").

39. V. 70, VI. 4.

40. VII. 63-66. As Griffin points out in his Introduction, p. 57, the contemplation of the natural scene mentioned in Troiolo's letter parallels the forlorn narrator's reported to Maria in the Proemio, "e questa è riguardare quella contrada, quelle montagne, quella parte del cielo, fra le quali e sotto la quale io porto ferma opinione che voi siate," p. 5. The Italian mountains of the Proemio have been transferred to the Trojan littoral in the hero's letter.

41. V. 70, VII. 68.

42. VII. 68. What Troiolo made explicit in this stanza, the narrator implied in VI. 1. Incidental reference to the seaside location of the camp is made in another stanza, VII. 6.

43. *Mediaeval Studies*, XV (1953), 107ff., esp. "Troie," pp. 132-36, also "Est-see," p. 117, and "Symois," p. 129.

44. "The Trojan Background of the *Troilus*," *ELH.*, IX (1942), 252-56. In these pages, Dr. Mayo differs from Professor Lowes, who, in his *Geoffrey Chaucer and the Development of his Genius* (Boston and New York: Houghton Mifflin, c1934), pp. 180-85, stressed the effectiveness of settings in the *Troilus*.

45. "The yate . . . Of Dardanus" and "Symois," II. 617-18, IV. 1548-53; "Delphos" (visited by Calkas), IV. 1411; "Elicone In hil Pernaso" (haunted by the Muses, with erroneous placing of spring on mountain), III. 1809-10—all without parallel in the source. As there is mention in the *Filostrato* of "Argo," VI. 24, "Calidonia," VI. 24, VII. 27, and "Tebe," VI. 24, so is there in the *Troilus* of "Arge" and "Calydoigne," V. 805, 934, and of "Thebes," II. 84, 100, 107, V. 602, 937, 1486, 1490. That the opposing forces are Trojan and Greek is, of course, abundantly emphasized in both works. See Ch. I. 4. n.16 for Benoit's *Roman de Troie* as source for the gate.

46. For the residences of Chaucer's Trojans, see Magoun's just cited article, pp. 134-35, H. M. Smyser's "The Domestic Background of Troilus and Criseyde," *Spec.*, XXXI (1956), 297-315, esp. 300-10; and for realistically fourteenth-century interiors throughout the poet's writings, see Sister Mary Ernestine Whitmore, *Medieval English Domestic Life and Amusements in the Works of Chaucer* (Washington: Catholic University, 1937), Chs. I and II. For the glamorization in the *Troilus* of aristocratic

life after the fashion of the romance genre, see Professor Young's "Chaucer's *Troilus and Criseyde* as Romance," *PMLA.*, LIII (1938), 42-44, 57-58.
47. *TC.* I. 148-61 (*Fil.* I. 17-18).
48. "Temple": I. 162, 267, 317 (*Fil.* I. 30, "tempio"), 323 (*Fil.* I. 32, "nobil tempio"), 363, and "thilke large temple," I. 185 (*Fil.* I. 20, "lo gran tempio"); the heroine at the door, 178-80 (*Fil.* I. 19). Late in the story, Troilus is made to recall his enamorment in this "temple," V. 566-67. As noted by Pratt, *StPh.*, LIII, 514, "temple," I. 162, matches "temple" in *Le Roman de Troyle et de Criseida*, p. 124.
49. III. 383-85.
50. III. 539-46. See Ch. I. 6. n.11 for possible sources.
51. IV. 946ff. (*Fil.* IV. 109ff.).
52. IV. 141ff. (*Fil.* IV. 13ff.).
53. "Paleys" or "paleis": I. 324 (*Fil.* I. 32, "palagio"); II. 616, 933, 1252, 1537; III. 1529 (*Fil.* III. 52, "palagio"), 1534 (*Fil.* III. 53, "palagio"); V. 201 (*Fil.* V. 15, "palagio"), 512. Pandarus' suggestion made to the lover in this palace that he go "to the kyng," like Pandaro's that they both return "a corte," indicates that it stood apart from Priam's establishment, IV. 645-47 (*Fil.* IV. 77).
54. At the Palladian festival: "His yonge knyghtes," whom "as he was wont to gide," Troilus there led up and down, I. 183-87 (*Fil.* I. 20, "compagni," neither guided nor led), and "knyght or squyer of his compaignie," 191 (*Fil.* I. 21, "alcun" pointed out to "suoi compagni"); in the palace after the festival: "his folk" dismissed, I. 357 (*Fil.* I. 32, "ciascun"—of "suoi compagni"—dismissed). With Troilus on his triumphant return from battle: "al his folk . . . in routes tweyne," II. 619-20; with him on his next ride by Criseyde's palace: "his tenthe som," II. 1249. In his chamber after the parliament: "a man of his or two" there with him bidden to leave, IV. 221-23 (*Fil.* IV. 22, "ognuno, amico e servitor" leaving at a hint), and "A certeyn knyght, that for the tyme kepte The chambre door" opening it to admit Pandarus, IV. 351-52 (*Fil.* IV. 42, "un suo privato valletto," outside the door, dispatched to summon Pandaro). At Criseyde's exit from Troy: awaiting her with Troilus, "certeyn folk," V. 32-33, and with him accompanying her out of town "an huge route Of knyghtes," V. 64-67 (*Fil.* V. 10, "piú compagni" with Troiolo)—neither folk nor knights, however, expressly his retainers. Pandarus, of course, like Pandaro, was much in and out of the palace. He is called a knight on one occasion, II. 452, and a lord on another, V. 1311, while Pandaro, on one, was said to have been "d'alto legnaggio," II. 1. As noted by Pratt, *StPh.*, LIII, 514, "His yonge knyghtes," I. 184, corresponds to "ses jeunes seigneurs," *Le Roman de Troyle et de Criseida*, p. 124.
55. I. 323-57 (*Fil.* I. 32).
56. "In chambre," I. 358 (*Fil.* I. 33, "in camera"); "in his chambre," I. 547 (*Fil.* II. 1, "nella camera sua"), and, with backward reference, "Into his chaumbre," II. 556 (*Fil.* II. 62, "nella sua camera"); "in his chaumbre," II. 935, introducing long scene (corresponding to scenes in the original respectively perhaps in the chamber, by implication, not in it, and expressly in it, *Fil.* II. 79ff., 86ff., 95ff.); chamber implied by lover's being abed, II. 1305 (as not in corresponding episode, *Fil.* II. 128ff.); chamber implied by lover's going to bed in his palace, III. 1534-36 (*Fil.* III. 53, likewise); "unto his chambre," IV. 220 (*Fil.* IV. 22, "nella camera"), "aboute the chaumbre," IV. 242, and "Into the derke chaumbre," IV. 354 (*Fil.* IV. 43, "nella camera"); "To chaumbre," V. 202 (*Fil.* V. 15, "in camera"), and "to chaumbre," V. 292; "to the chambre," V. 514 (*Fil.* V. 50, "in camera"); chamber implied by lover's lying down to sleep, though not expressly in palace, V. 1233 (*Fil.* VII. 23, likewise, but confirmed by "nella camera," VII. 33); and again by his taking to his bed, V. 1439 (*Fil.* VII. 77, likewise, but confirmed by "la sua camera," VII. 84); with subsequent invited visit of Cassandre as replacement for the uninvited ones of Deifobo and the ladies.
57. Troilus: sitting "upon his beddes feet," I. 359 (*Fil.* I. 33, likewise); lying as if he were dead, I. 723 (*Fil.* II. 16, supine), going down on his knees to embrace the confidant, I. 1044-45 (*Fil.* II. 33, embracing Pandaro), and backward reference to his lying "Upon his bed," II. 555-57 (*Fil.* II. 62, likewise); sitting in his chamber, II. 935, going to bed for the night, II. 947, but rising to write a letter, II. 1059, and sitting down for composition, II. 1064; abed again, II. 1305, asked by confidant to rise to read answering letter from Criseyde, II. 1313-16; stealing "into his bed," III. 1535 (*Fil.* III. 53,

likewise), restlessly lying there for a long time, III. 1584, and, upon the confidant's arrival, falling on knees to him, III. 1592 (*Fil*. III. 56, embracing Pandaro); lying down, "upon his bed," IV. 224, rising from it; IV. 232, again lying down "Upon his bed," IV. 256 (*Fil*. IV. 29, likewise), still there upon confidant's arrival, IV. 353-55, and bidden by him to rise, IV. 645; tossing abed, with business of a pillow, V. 211-13 and 223-24 (*Fil*. V. 19, 20, likewise), still in bed when confidant came, V. 294, and exhorted by him to rise, V. 407 (*Fil*. V. 35, likewise), and doing so, V. 433-34; going to rest in the chamber, V. 518; dreaming of the boar, presumably in bed, V. 1233-43 (*Fil*. VII. 23-24, likewise), and sitting down to write letter, V. 1312; taking to his bed, V. 1439 (*Fil*. VII. 77), summoning Cassandre, V. 1450-51, and starting "from his bed" directly after the interview, V. 1536-37.

58. Pandarus: shaking the bedded lover, I. 869; sitting down on his "beddes syde," III. 1589; going softly "Toward the bed," IV. 353-55, and standing with folded arms to behold its occupant, IV. 359-61; sitting down "on the bed," V. 294.

59. II. 947, V. 518; III. 229-30.

60. IV. 232-33, 351-55. See n.11 for like circumstances in the *Filostrato*.

63. "Palays," "palais," "paleys," or "paleis": II. 76, 1094; V. 523, 525 (*Fil*. V. 50, 61. II. 507ff. (*Fil*. II. 56ff.).

62. III. 1737-38 (*Fil*. III. 73).

"casa"), 540, 542, 544, 547. "Hous": I. 127 (*Fil*. I. 14-15, "casa"); II. 437, 1461; III. 1581; IV. 823; V. 528 (*Fil*. V. 51, "magione"), 541.

64. Following Boccaccio, Chaucer tells us that the heroine lived "with swich meyne As til hire honour nede was to holde," I. 127-28 (*Fil*. I. 15). And he particularizes on his own account. Pandarus, coming to her for his first visit, asked "hire folk" where she was, found her with two other ladies listening to "a mayden" read, and had private conversation with her after the withdrawal of "everi wight that was aboute hem tho," II. 79, 81-84, 215-17. "Al hire meyne" shouted upon Troilus' return from combat, II. 614-15. Three nieces "And other of hire wommen, a gret route" were with her in her garden, and, when night came, "Hire wommen" attended her to rest, II. 815-19, 914. Next day, Pandarus warned her, in the garden, that "folk" might wonder if she cast away the letter he had brought, and, in hall, quizzed her about it when he saw "hire folk were alle aweye"; before the quizzing, she had left the hall momentarily with "some of hire wommen," II. 1156-57, 1194, 1172-73. She went to Deiphebus' house with two of her nieces, and to Pandarus',

> With a certein of hire owen men,
> And with hire faire nece Antigone,
> And other of hire wommen nyne or ten. II. 1562-63, III. 596-98.

65. Criseyde would surrender what Poliphete was allegedly suing for, saying to Pandarus, "Withouten that I have ynough for us," II. 1478. She schemes to palm off on her father, as property sent to him in trust by others, "The moeble which that I have in this town," IV. 1380-87. Troilus argues to her that they have "tresour" enough between them to live well in exile, IV. 1513-16.

66. "Withinne a paved parlour," II. 82 (*Fil*. II. 34, "in una loggia"). "Into hire closet," II. 599 (*Fil*. II. 68, "nella camera sua"), said closet commanding a view of the street, II. 610ff.; "into a closet," II. 1215 (*Fil*. II. 120, "dall' un canto della camera sua"). "Under the chambre wal ther as she ley," II. 919; "from the chaumbre down," II. 1117; "into hire chambre," II. 1173 (*Fil*. II. 114, "nella sua camera"); "Into hire chambre," IV. 732 (*Fil*. IV. 86, "nella camera sua"); lover's coming to chamber implied, IV. 919-21 (*Fil*. IV. 107, likewise), and explicitly stated his going "out of the chaumbre," IV. 1701. "Into halle," II. 1170, with a window commanding a view of the street, II. 1186, 1192, 1015, presumably, it seems to me, in the hall; "out of the halle," IV. 732. "Into the garden," II. 814, and "in the garden," II. 819; "Into the gardyn from the chaumbre down, II. 1117. The garden is described as follows:

> This yerd was large, and rayled alle th' aleyes,
> And shadewed wel with blosmy bowes grene,
> And benched newe, and sonded alle the weyes, II. 820-22.

A *large* portal seems indicated by the shout of Criseyde's household, "A go we se! cast up the *yates* wyde!" II. 615—on which passage see Professor Kittredge, "Chauceriana,"

MPh., VII (1910), 479-80. Troilus, passing the house after her departure, saw "every wyndow" closed as Troiolo saw "la porta serrata e le finestre," V. 533-34 (*Fil.* V. 52). The reader had best assume that the two mentions of a closet refer to one room and the several of a chamber all to another, even if he doubts that Chaucer kept them sharply defined in his own consciousness. The reader must further assume, I would suggest, that both rooms were on the second floor—the former because Criseyde descended from it to the garden "Adoun the steyre," II. 813-14, and the latter because she and Pandarus went down from it, though not expressly by a staircase, into the garden. See Magoun's "Chaucer's Ancient and Biblical World," p. 134, for an interpretation of the scattered data more positive than mine and somewhat at odds with it. He believes that the closet was on the second floor, indeed, but that the stair mentioned in connection with it reached only to the first; that it was by this short stair, presumably, that Criseyde and Pandarus went from the chamber of II. 1117 into the garden, and that this chamber was therefore on the ground floor, and thus not the same as the chamber mentioned in other contexts allowed by him to be on the second; and that the window which I vision as in the hall, was in another, unnamed apartment—a "living room."

67. II. 78ff. (*Fil.* II. 34ff.), 598ff. (*Fil.* II. 68ff.), 813ff., 904ff.

68. II. 1093ff. (*Fil.* II. 108ff., without localization).

69. II. 1170ff. (*Fil.* II. 114ff., Criseida leaving companions that she may read letter in her chamber), 1185ff. (*Fil.* II. 118ff., Pandaro's pressing at an unspecified place for an answer and Criseida's writing it in chamber), 1226ff. (*Fil.* II. 128, her giving letter to him at place unspecified). For the "quysshyn," see O. F. Emerson, "Some Notes on Chaucer and Some Conjectures," *PhQ.,* II (1923), 85-89, reprinted in his *Chaucer Essays and Studies* (Cleveland: Western Reserve Univ. Press, 1929), pp. 384-92.

70. II. 1460ff., III. 547ff.

71. IV. 680ff. (*Fil.* IV. 80ff., without localization), 731ff. (*Fil.* IV. 86ff., in chamber).

72. IV. 918-21 (*Fil.* IV. 107).

73. IV. 1124ff. (*Fil.* IV. 113ff.).

74. "Morter," IV. 1245 (*Fil.* IV. 126, "torchio"), "swerd," IV. 1215.

75. Deiphebus referred to Criseyde as "my frend" and, "of his owen curteisie," came in person to her house to invite her to his, II. 1424, 1486-89; Eleyne showed affection toward her by word and gesture, II. 1604-10; and both spoke so well of her that it was a joy to hear them, III. 214-17. As for Ector, who was not at the party, Deiphebus said that he had heard him speak in superlatives of Criseyde, II. 1452-54. It may be added that Troilus' reminiscences about his lady after the exchange, like Troiolo's, imply that she circulated socially, V. 565-81 (*Fil.* V. 54-55).

76. II. 1514, 1540.

77. Troilus put to bed on the first night, II. 1541-45, and dormant until the morning of the next, III. 423-24. Of his resting place, Pandarus said, "the chaumbre is but lite," II. 1646.

78. "Grete chaumbre," II. 1712; "steire," II. 1705, III. 205; "herber," II. 1705, also called "gardyn," III. 221.

79. II. 1692-1701. While at the bedside, Eleyne laid a friendly arm over Troilus' shoulder, II. 1671.

80. III. 59-60.

81. III. 71-72, 182.

82. III. 183-84.

83. III. 193-200 (bringing the affair to the same point as *Fil.* II. 143).

84. III. 227-38.

85. III. 239-420 (*Fil.* III. 5-19).

86. II. 61-70.

87. "Hous": III. 195, 514, 560, 635, 767.

88. As stated in Ch. I. 6. n.22, I follow Professor Root's interpretation of the disposition of apartments, not Professor Magoun's. And not, I may add, that of Sister Mary Ernestine Whitmore, *op. cit.* p. 32.

89. III. 595-603.

90. III. 659-62.

91. III. 673-75, 680-86.

92. III. 687-700, 741-42. Pandarus told Criseyde that he had entered by "this *secre* trappe-dore," III. 759.

93. III. 747-49, 785-91. See Ch. I. 6. n.33 for influence of the *Filocolo* upon the second context.

94. III. 953ff., esp. 953-56, 964-66, 974-80, 1079-99, 1141, 1188-90.

95. III. 1191ff., 1555ff.

96. III. 1667ff. (*Fil.* III. 64ff.).

97. "And many a nyght they wroughte in this manere," III. 1713, that is in the manner of the second night.

98. V. 428ff. (*Fil.* V. 38ff.).

99. V. 449ff. (*Fil.* V. 42ff.), III. 1786-1806 (*Fil.* III. 92-93).

100. II. 610-18.

101. II. 1247-52.

102. II. 1185-90, 1145-48.

103. III. 1782-85. It cannot be determined from this context whether Troilus was coming "into town" from his palace or from somewhere outside the walls.

104. V. 522ff. Troilus' finding a pretext "in towne for to go" to cover his pilgrimage from his abode to hers, V. 526-28, suggests that the former was further away from the center than hers. The corresponding pilgrimage of Troiolo with Pandaro, *Fil.* V. 50ff., cannot be assigned to a street since none is mentioned in preceding episodes.

105. Pandarus, having spent a wakeful night, presumably in his own house, got up in the morning to repair to "his neces palays ther beside," II. 62-76. If his claim that he had run (not ridden) from Deiphebus' house to hers, II. 1464, can be taken at face value, it would appear that the distance between the two was not great. "But a myle" to Sarpedoun's abode from the hero's, V. 403 (*Fil.* V. 40, "quattromila passi").

106. V. 431, 513.

107. V. 32-35, 64-70, 197-202. Troilo, setting out, not expressly from the city gate, but from some point unspecified, accompanied Criseida "infin di fuori a tutto il vallo," *Fil.* V 1ff., esp. 10. As remarked in Ch. I. 8. p. 101, "valeye" is likely, not a mistranslation of "vallo," but a deliberate substitution made because Chaucer had fixed the start of the ride at the gate.

108. V. 603-16. Troiolo, in his corresponding visit to the gate, *Fil.* V. 58-59, spoke vaguely of conducting Criseida "a quel loco." As remarked in the preceding note, he had quitted her outside the wall.

109. V. 666-70. Troiolo is left unplaced for viewing the camp, *Fil.* V. 70.

110. V. 1107ff. (*Fil.* VII. 1ff.). Chaucer's principal change is moving the pair from outside the gate to the walls, an obviously better point of vantage: "And on the walles of the town they pleyde," V. 1112; "And fer his hed over the wall he leyde," V. 1145. As remarked in Ch. I. 10. n.4, the second of these lines may be purposive reworking, rather than a mistranslation, of "il quale in vêr lo campo sospeso era," *Fil.* VII. 6.

111. V. 1192-97. Again Chaucer departs from Boccaccio (*Fil.* VII. 14) in placing the hero "Upon the walles," V. 1194. He has already made Calkas assure the Greeks that Phebus and Neptunus would destroy Troy because Lameadoun did not compensate them for building its walls, IV. 120-26, and made Troilus anticipate that the priest would confront his daughter with the Greeks' oath to raze them, IV. 1478-82.

112. I. 1072-75; possibly, II. 190-204; II. 610ff.; IV. 38-49 (*Fil.* IV. 1-2, with fighting specified to be "ne' campi piani").

113. V. 729-33 (*Fil.* VI. 4). The part of Troiolo's letter, in which "monti" surrounding the camp are mentioned, *Fil.* VII. 63-66, Chaucer rejects for his hero.

114. IV. 1307-9.

115. Troilus could see "the tentes," V. 670 (*Fil.* V. 70, Troiolo, "li Greci attendati").

116. V. 148-50, 841-52, 1016-27.

117. Criseyde is made to swear by Simois running "ay downward to the se," IV. 1548-53. The narrator speaks of the sun as rising out of "the est se," V. 1107-9. See Robert A. Pratt, "A Geographical Problem in *Troilus and Criseyde*," *MLN.*, LXI (1946), 541-43, for an hypothesis that Chaucer visioned "a sea stretching to the east, beyond Troy" and did so on the basis of a passage in Guido's *Historia*, ed. Griffin, pp. 6-7. This article is questioned by Professor Magoun, *op. cit.*, p. 117.

118. V. 1807-27 (*Tes.* XI. 1-3). See Ch. I. 11. n.27, for other sources.

Section 6 *Time and the Supernatural*

1. See Ch. I. 1. pp. 5-6.
2. *Fil.* I. 16, 46; III. 90.
3. I. 1.
4. I. 24; III. 74, 76, 88; IV. 121-22; VIII. 17-18.
5. V. 6-7, IV. 97.
6. A wish of the narrator's addressed to "Iddio," III. 39, and an exhortation of his "per Dio," VIII. 29.
7. III. 15, 85. The prince's mentions of "Iddio" or "Dio," without specification of attributes are: appeals to "Iddio," I. 43, III. 14, V. 37, and to "Dio," III. 51, IV. 53, VII. 75, 100, VIII. 21; thanks to "Dio," III. 35; assumption that his life is no longer pleasing to "Dio," VII. 25; exhortations "per Dio," II. 8, 59(2), IV. 55, 62(2), 144, 156, V. 46, 65, VII. 8, 34, 48; and the exclamation "Oh Dio," V. 48.
8. Appeals to or asseverations by "Iddio," II. 65, 113, 118, 120, 127, IV. 105, 130, and the like to or by "Dio," II. 48, IV. 93, 128, VIII. 12; thanks to "Dio," III. 35, IV. 126; and exhortations "per Dio," II. 51, III. 28, and "per amor di Dio," II. 111.
9. II. 44; and II. 11, VIII. 24, V. 32, III. 7. Without specification of attributes: appeal to "Iddio," II. 67; thanks to "Iddio," II. 36; exhortations "per Dio," III. 10, V. 33, and a suggestion to Troiolo that he make one "per Dio," II. 91.
10. II. 41.
11. Diomede, thanks to "Dio," VIII. 25, as reported by the narrator; and Calcas, asseveration "per Iddio," IV. 11, and exhortation "per Dio," IV. 10.
12. III. 74-89. Though never named in the hymn, Venere is plainly identified. She is called friend of the sun and daughter of Giove in 74; "bella dea" or simply "dea" in 76, 77, 78, 79, 82, 87(2); linked amorously with Marte in 77, and given a son—obviously the love god—in 79 and 83. In 74 again, she is referred to as the eternal light whose splendor makes the third heaven fair; and, in 82 and 89, characterized as luminous.
13. "Lodato sia il tuo summo valore, Venere bella, e del tuo figlio Amore," II. 80; "ch'a Vener non sono util né a Marte," VII. 59; "per Venere dea," VIII. 16.
14. Whether the word "amor(e)" is used with personification or not is sometimes hard to determine. In Pernicone's edition, it is capitalized in most but not quite all of the instances in which it is apparently so employed. The narrator refers plainly to Love the person in the following stanzas: I. 1, 4, 6, 25, 29, 38, 50; II. 115, 132; III. 1, 33, 55, 93; VI. 11, 13; VII. 12, 15; VIII. 33; IX. 8; and perhaps also in IV. 120, despite Pernicone's failure to capitalize. The hero as plainly in the following: I. 50, 51, 52, 55; II. 7, 19, 20, 80, 95, 97, 105, 106, 129; III. 58; IV. 33(2), 53; V. 27, 56, 63(2), 66; VII. 52, 60; and probably also in III. 61, despite Pernicone's failure to capitalize. Criseida as plainly in: II. 110, 121; IV. 150, and presumably—despite such failure—in III. 48. And Pandaro as plainly in: II. 21, 24, 57, 94, 119.
15. II. 80 and III. 79, 83 as cited in notes 13 and 12.
16. The hero's prayer, "Amore e Dio e 'l mondo questo cessi," IV. 53, does not imply that he expects joint response.
17. "Signor(e)": I. 38, 39; II. 57, 58, 59, 60(2), 98; IV. 33(2); V. 57.
18. I. 1 and IX. 8; VII. 90 with 88.
19. III. 74, V. 68. Troiolo also personifies the sun in III. 58 and VII. 66, but without mythological reminiscence.
20. I. 1.
21. IV. 78.
22. I. 17-18, III. 88. See also V. 30, in which Troiolo swore by Pallade without indicating her function.
23. III. 20, 88, VII. 59; and III. 77.
24. III. 80.
25. Troiolo put the blame for anticipated death upon "dispietati iddii," IV. 36; told Fortuna that he had cherished her above "altro iddio," IV. 30; cursed "gli dii e le dee e la natura," V. 17; attributed the boar dream to "gli dii," VII. 26, VIII. 19; and, in a letter to Criseida, reminded her that she had sworn return by "ciascheduno iddio," VII. 54. Pandaro anticipated the help of "gl' iddii" for her abduction, IV. 75. And Ettore

invoked punishment from "gli dii" upon Calcas, I. 14. Diomede mentioned, if somewhat sceptically, his reputed descent "di dio," VI. 24.

26. Before Calcas' flight, the Greeks were stepping up their efforts "di giorno in giorno," I. 7; between the Ettore episode and the festival, the Trojans sallied forth "tal volta" and the enemy countered "spesse volte," I. 16. The festival occurred in the springtime, according to the stanza introducing it, I. 18; the flight, after dark, as Calcas recalled long after it, IV. 7.

27. Having gone to palace—and into chamber—from the temple, Troiolo reviewed what he had experienced in the latter during "la mattina," I. 33.

28. Between the festival time and Pandaro's first visit, the lover fed his flame "di giorno in giorno," I. 41; was in the thick of battle "spesso," I. 45; and experienced a hundredfold increase of torment "ciascun giorno," I. 57. After his visit to Troiolo, "un dí," II. 1, Pandaro proceeded to Criseida on the same, II. 34, and mentioned the woodland interlude to her as having taken place "L' altrieri," II. 56, and the conference in chamber as having done so today, "oggi," II. 62. Leaving her, he went to her lover "diritto," II. 79.

29. Troiolo, *inter alia*, attended to his toilet "spesso" and Criseida favored him with sight of herself, "a tempi," II. 84. Appealed to by the prince "talvolta," II. 86, Pandaro suggested a missive to the lady, which the former wrote "presto," II. 95. Taking it to the lady, perhaps as soon as written, II. 108, he did not press for an answer until solicited by Troiolo, "sovente," II. 118. She promptly composed a letter, II. 120, and gave it, apparently as soon as written, to her cousin, II. 128, who went in search of the prince "tosto," II. 128.

30. Hopeful from the reply, Troiolo longed for fruition "dí e notte," II. 130; with ardor waxing "di giorno in giorno," he wrote "piú volte" and had from Criseida "riposta . . . e spessa e rara," II. 131. Pandaro appealed to her "spesso," II. 133 before extorting the commitment for the festival, II. 143. Informing the prince of it instanter, he remarked that delight was not far away, III. 6.

31. After some days, III. 20, there came "il tempo disïato da' due amanti," and with it Pandaro's instruction of the pair, III. 21-23. Supposing as one must that it was the time set by the lady, one wonders why the ardent lover had wandered off " 'l dí davanti."

32. III. 24 and 42ff.; 56.

33. III. 64ff.

34. III. 71ff. On the one hand, we have the author's lament, "Ma poco tempo durò cotal bene," III. 94; on the other, his statements that Troiolo resorted to a garden "talvolta," III. 73, that in warfare he excelled "sempre," III. 90, and that he went hawking "Ne' tempi delle triegue" and hunting "tal fiata," III. 91, as well as Criseida's reminder to her lover in their last tryst that, "talor," they had passed "piú dí" without seeing each other, IV. 133.

35. IV. 1ff. The only specific note of time is that the battle resulting in the capture consumed all of one day.

36. 2192 lines (IV. 13-167, V. 1-71, VI. 1-34, VII. 1-14), 38 per cent of the total of 5704. As remarked in Ch. I. 1. n.5, the ascending action comprises 41 per cent of the line total, leaving 59 per cent to the entire descending action.

37. Betaking himself to his palace from the parliament, IV. 22, Troiolo, after lengthy indulgence in grief and a bit of napping, summoned Pandaro to his chamber, IV. 42, and was promised an assignation "stasera," IV. 77. Criseida, informed of her fate by "La fama velocissima," IV. 78-79, was kept from her chamber by visitors similarly informed but went to it as soon as they had departed, IV. 86. Coming to her, Pandaro referred to sorrows of earlier in the day, IV. 97, 103, to her exchange as set for the present week, IV. 102, and to the hour of Troiolo's coming as near at hand, IV. 106. Returning to the prince, the go-between confirmed the promise for "stasera," IV. 112, and the former availed himself of it, IV. 114ff.

38. IV. 154.

39. IV. 155-56, 157.

40. IV. 167, V. 1ff., 15ff.

41. V. 22, 31ff., 37-38.

42. V. 40, 46; 47-48.

43. V. 49.

44. V. 50-57.
45. V. 58ff. See n.247 for full analysis of these stanzas.
46. VI. 8, 9ff.
47. VII. 1ff., esp. 12-13.
48. VII. 14.
49. VII. 15ff.; 23ff.; 51ff., esp. 54, 63.
50. VII. 76-77; 77ff., esp. 78; 84ff.
51. VII. 103, 104-5, 106.
52. VIII. 1, 3, 4, 5.
53. VIII. 8ff., 25-27.
54. III. 74ff., 86.
55. II. 44. In Pernicone's edition, " fortuna," unlike "amore," is not capitalized even when used with personification.
56. II. 51, 77.
57. III. 7. In this context the word "fortuna" may not be used with personification, as it clearly is in the others cited.
58. III. 45.
59. III. 94. See also IV. 113, 120.
60. IV. 30-32 and 45, 121-22. See also IV. 56, 166, V. 66, VII. 32.
61. IV. 73.
62. IV. 88, 104, 154.
63. V. 6-7.
64. VIII. 15.
65. VIII. 25-26, 28.
66. V. 26-27, 32.
67. VII. 25-28, 39-41, 48, 76; VIII. 6-10, 19-20.
68. I. 8, IV. 11.
69. VI. 17-18; 27, 31.
70. III. 74ff., esp. 75.
71. I. 18; VII. 63, 78.
72. IV. 7.
73. III. 24, 64.
74. III. 42-43, IV. 167.
75. V. 69.
76. VII. 9, 11.
77. In his invaluable study, "Chaucer's Lollius," *Harvard Studies in Classical Philology,* XXVIII (1917), 50-54, Professor Kittredge calls attention to "touches of antiquity" in the *Troilus,* some hundred in number. Asserting that they "are present as parts of an artistic design," he continues: "They are meant to produce or to intensify an atmosphere of high antiquity—a Trojan or Lollian atmosphere. Chaucer pretends—in an artistic fiction—to be translating from an ancient author, and he tries to make his characters talk and think like persons of the heroic age in such matters of detail as do not interfere with their truth to eternal and unchanging humanity. He could not dig up Troy. It was out of his power to archaeologize in dress and manners and topography. But he could make Pandarus swear like a heathen of the heroic age, and speak familiarly of the letter he had seen that Oenone wrote to Paris, and refer to Niobe and her tears as still visible in stone. . . . And all this he did, and much more, with the same artistic purpose that had prompted him to describe his whole poem as translated from an ancient Latin author—one Lollius," p. 54. Accepting this most gratefully, I would remark, however, that there is little evidence that Chaucer tried to make his characters really "*think* like persons of the heroic age" and that, while Pandarus sometimes swore "like a heathen," he often asseverated by God, and otherwise named Him, very much like a Christian.

Professor Tatlock, when discussing the condemnation of paganism, V. 1848-53, in his "Epilog of Chaucer's *Troilus,*" *MPh.,* XVIII (1921), 640-59, approves Kittredge's point about deliberate ancient coloring, noting incidentally the poet's care to gloss recherché touches; and makes this complementary point: "It is certain that Chaucer took pains to avoid such an excess of contemporary medieval color as would have marred the remote romantic background which gave dignity to the emotional romance. The penetrating modern is surprised at the small number of anachronisms," pp. 641-42. These sentences, as interpreted by footnotes which I have not quoted, are sound enough. It is to be remarked, however, as Tatlock does not, that the *Troilus* is no less medievally colored than the *Filostrato*. And whether this scholar is right or wrong in inferring from the condemnation a serious concern for audience reaction, he goes too far in thus phrasing the reason for it, "Chaucer, once more, felt the extraordinary novelty of his complete substitution of paganism for Christianity and its view of the universe," p. 656; and, recognizing that he has been extreme, qualifies by footnote: "When all is said and done, there is not much in the poem about pagan rites or about the gods as moving forces. The moving force behind it all is destiny, an idea familiar to the medieval. But on the surface paganism is everywhere and Christianity is gone. He disavows more than there is to disavow, because he is heading off not an indictment but a feeling." Needless to say, even on the surface paganism is not "everywhere."

Harry Morgan Ayres, in his article, "Chaucer and Seneca," *Romanic Review*, X (1919), 9-11, notes as evidential of the poet's avoidance of anachronism the fact that his characters in the *Troilus* do not cite authors postdating them.

Root provides a significant corrective to overestimation of Chaucer's care for antique semblance. In his *Textual Tradition of Chaucer's Troilus*, Chaucer Soc., Ser. I, No. XCIX (1916 for 1912), 261-62, he notes that our author in revision, if sacrificing but one pagan touch at most, II. 115, added only four, I. 9, 164, IV. 300, 644.

C. S. Lewis, who concentrates upon courtly love in the *Troilus*, takes a position antipodal to Tatlock's with respect to period flavor, and consequently is as extreme. In "What Chaucer Really Did to *Il Filostrato*," *Essays and Studies*, XVII (1932), 56-75, he writes "I shall endeavour to show that the process which *Il Filostrato* underwent at Chaucer's hands was first and foremost a process of *medievalization*," p. 56; and, "The majority of his modifications are corrections of errors which Boccaccio had committed against the code of courtly love . . . these are only part and parcel of a general process of medievalization," p. 59. And he continues of the same mind when discussing the *Troilus* in *The Allegory of Love A Study in Medieval Tradition* (Oxford: Clarendon Press, 1936), pp. 176-97, writing of Chaucer's adaptation of the Italian poem, "The effect of all his alterations is to turn a Renaissance story into a medieval story," p. 177.

In the article "Chaucer's *Troilus and Criseyde* as Romance," *PMLA.*, LIII (1938), 38-63, which maintains that courtly love and other elements in the work accommodate it to that medieval genre of fiction, Professor Young has this to say about the poet's development of atmosphere: "The fact seems to be that in his medievalizing, as in his archaizing, he was ambitious mainly to convey, not an impression of contemporary actuality, but an effect of glamor and strangeness," p. 43. Agreeing that he was ambitious in this direction, I am dubious that he was "mainly" so.

For the temporal flavor of oaths and prayers in works of our poet, see Ruth Crosby, "Chaucer and the Custom of Oral Delivery," *Spec.*, XIII (1938), 425-26, and the authorities cited by her, p. 425, n.5; and see Herbert W. Starr, "Oaths in Chaucer's Poems," *W. Va. Univ. Bull., Philol. Studies*, IV (1943), 44-63.

Also to be cited is Morton W. Bloomfield's "Chaucer's Sense of History," *JEGP.*, LI (1952), 301-13. In this, he observes, "What is remarkable is that Chaucer is historically minded as compared with his English contemporaries and that on the whole, in his later works, he has a considerable sense of historic succession and cultural relativity," p. 305.

78. First to be mentioned are the articles already cited in Ch. I. 6. n.20: Robert K. Root and Henry N. Russell, "A Planetary Date for Chaucer's *Troilus*," *PMLA.*, XXXIX (1924), 48-63; and John S. P. Tatlock, "The Date of the *Troilus*; and Minor Chauceriana," *MLN.*, L (1935), 277-89. The former is an argument that Chaucer meant to refer to a conjunction of 1385, which had not occurred since 769, and that he did so near the time of the event; the latter, pp. 279-84, admits the possibility of reference to it but reasons that Chaucer could have anticipated the event, and hence have made allusion to it long before it occurred. The contexts involved are III. 624-25 (with 549-50) and III. 1417-18. In the one, which comes in the account of Pandarus' supper party, the crescent moon, Saturn, and Jupiter are located together in Cancer. The presence of the crescent in the sign establishes that the time was May or perhaps early June, and it was in that period of 1385 that the rare conjunction occurred. In the

other, which comes in the account of dawn, Venus—"Lucyfer"—is mentioned as rising, as she would not have done in 1385, being then conjoined in the evening sky with the other three planets. Root and Russell accept the discrepancy, reasonably enough it seems to me, as poetic license. In the course of argument about the conjunction in Book III, Tatlock offers valuable comment, pp. 282-84, on astronomical datings beginning with IV. 31-32—for which see n.236.

Root, in the Introduction to his edition of the *Troilus*, pp. xxxiii-xxxiv, gives an outline of the chronology of the poem, observing apropos of the "compelling sense of actuality" in the work that "One of the elements which contributes to this sense of the actual is the care with which Chaucer has marked the passing of his dramatic time." The notes of this editor to contexts indicative of date are invariably helpful.

In the "Defense of Criseyde," *PMLA.*, XLIV (1929), 141-77, Joseph S. Graydon, puts such construction upon the remarks about time in Book V as to support his thesis that Chaucer would have us believe that Troilus' suspicions of the lady were premature —construction, in my view, as strained as the thesis is palpably wrong. Professor Mizener, though speaking more charitably than I of Mr. Graydon, disagrees with him, opining that the chronology of the Book is deliberately obscured to leave the impression, erroneous but necessary for tragic effect, that her fall was very sudden, "Character and Action in the Case of Criseyde," *PMLA.*, LIV (1939), 76-81. Acquainted with Benoit, Chaucer is perhaps a little disingenuous in saying, V. 1086-88, that "non auctour" tells how long it was before Criseyde surrendered to Diomede—see n.256. Yet his failure to avail himself of chronological data in this secondary source is hardly proof of an intention to be above. And it is to be noted that he gives more information about time in Book V than Boccaccio in the corresponding parts of the primary source.

In "The Dual Time-Scheme in Chaucer's *Troilus*," *MLN.*, LVI (1941), 94-100, H. W. Sams argues that beside a literal time-scheme of three years, there is in Chaucer's poem a figuratively suggested scheme of "one year, or the coming and departure of one summer," p. 100. The images which he cites as creating this illusion are not, I feel, sufficiently numerous to do so for any listener or for any but the most ingenious reader and hence not meant by Chaucer to achieve it.

79. In *Chaucer and his Poetry* (Cambridge: Harvard Univ. Press, ᶜ1915), Professor Kittredge provides a matchless summary impression of the destinal atmosphere of the *Troilus*, beginning: "Fate dominates in the Troilus. The suspense consists not in waiting for the unexpected, but in looking forward with a kind of terror for the moment of predicted doom. The catastrophe is announced at the outset," p. 112; and ending, "Thus, from first to last, the loves of Troilus and Cressida are bound up with the inexorable doom that hangs over the city. The fate of Troy is their fate. Their story begins in the temple of the Palladium; it is Calchas' foreknowledge and the people's infatuation that tear them asunder; it is the peril of the town that thwarts woman's wit, until Diomede subdues the inconstant heart. The tragedy of character grows out of the tragedy of situation," pp. 120-21.

Professor Curry, holding views very much like Kittredge's, documents them thoroughly in his "Destiny in Chaucer's *Troilus*," *PMLA.*, XLV (1930), 129-68. The following excerpts are representative of his—to me—extreme but illuminating interpretation. "In this tragedy the poet has not been able, or perhaps has been unwilling, to define the limits of the destiny back of the story's action with such precision and accuracy as he has employed elsewhere. . . . Still one is made to feel . . . that the days of Troy are numbered and that the cloud of fate hovering over Troilus and Criseyde will presently overwhelm them in the general disaster," p. 135. "He was probably orthodox in his own beliefs; but in the drama proper I can find no indication of his personal views. But he was, for his time, undoubtedly an extremely intrepid artist who conceived that the action of a great tragedy should be under the direction of a stern necessity and that the doom of a struggling protagonist should be inevitable," p. 156. Summing up that the hero's "common and individual fortunes have been, in the Providence of God, directed in part by Nature-as-destiny and partly by that destiny inherent in the movements of erratic stars," Curry adds: "We must observe in passing, however, that there is a third destinal force, postulated by Boethius, which Chaucer has not forgotten in presenting the spectacle of Troilus caught in a web of fate. . . . For a character, with the stamp of Nature and of the stars upon it at birth, is itself responsible in large measure for whatever fortune it suffers," p. 160.

See also Claes Schaar, *Some types of Narrative in Chaucer's Poetry*, Lund Studies in English, XXV (1954), 34-37, 119-26, 203-15.

Germaine Dempster notes the advantage to dramatic irony of the destinal atmosphere of the poem, *Dramatic Irony in Chaucer* (Stanford Univ. Press, 1932), pp. 10-13.

In "The Trojan Background of the Troilus," *ELH.*, IX (1942), 245-52, Robert D. Mayo minimizes the fate of Troy—unduly, I believe—as a theme designedly complementary to that of the fate of the hero.

In *The Medieval Heritage of Elizabethan Tragedy* (Berkeley: Univ. of Cal. Press, 1936), pp. 155-58, Professor Farnham asserts a contradiction between the deterministic implications of the poem, which he has argued make it a tragedy in the *De Casibus* tradition, and its lively characterizations of hero and heroine, which he says are convincing of their partial freedom. The *Troilus*, he feels, would have been more vitally dramatic than it is, "if Chaucer had permitted his keen observation of human character and its effects to alter his deterministic philosophy of tragic causes and his deterministic tragic paraphernalia," p. 157.

In "Troilus on Determinism," *Spec.*, VI (1931), 225-43, reprinted in *On Rereading Chaucer* (Cambridge: Harvard Univ. Press, 1939), pp. 104-22, Professor Patch argues that the poet clearly manifests a Boethian—an orthodox—belief in free will and that his tragedy should and can be interpreted as coherently developed according to this belief. A salutary corrective to disproportionate attention to the destinal element in the *Troilus*, the essay is perhaps too absolute, assuming from the many unquestionable suggestions of free will in the work that the whole is sytematically worked out on that basis. See also Professor Patch's article about the hero's soliloquy in the temple, "Troilus on Predestination," *JEGP.*, XVII (1918), 399-422, along with his "Chaucer and Lady Fortune," *MLR.*, XXII (1927), 377-88, esp. 383-85; *The Goddess Fortuna in Medieval Literature* (Cambridge: Harvard Univ. Press, 1927), 31-32; and *The Tradition of Boethius* (New York: Oxford Univ. Press, 1935), 61-72.

James Lyndon Shanley also dwells on free will in "The *Troilus* and Christian Love," *ELH.*, VI (1939), 271-81. Giving due recognition to the importance of destiny in the lives of hero and heroine he writes, "But the story does not depend on destined events alone, nor is the final unhappiness of either owing only to fate. They are free to choose what they wish, and as they choose they determine their lot. (Chaucer's philosophical reconciliation of these elements we do not know; the *Troilus* is not . . . a philosophical poem; but it is controlled by Chaucer's philosophy)," p. 275.

So too D. W. Robertson, Jr., in his "Chaucerian Tragedy," *ELH.*, XIX (1952), 1-37, which I have discussed somewhat sceptically in n.1 of the Preface.

In "Boethius' Influence on Chaucer's *Troilus*," *MPh.*, XLIX (1951), 1-9, Theodore A. Stroud approaches the poem as "a philosophical 'quest' in certain respects parallel to the *Consolation*," p. 3.

For the astral component of deterministic suggestion in Chaucer's works, see Theodore O. Wedel, *The Mediaeval Attitude toward Astrology Particularly in England*, Yale Studies in English, LX (1920), 142-53.

80. See Preface, n.2. See also Claes Schaar, *The Golden Mirror*, Skrifter Utgivna av Kungl. Humanistiska Vetenskapssamfundet i Lund, LIV (1955), 398-403, 448-50.

81. *TC.* III. 15-21 (*Fil.* III. 76, "Giove") with III. 3 (*Fil.* III. 74, "figliuola di Giove"). The narrator's mention of Jove, Saturne, and the moon in III. 624-25 is purely astronomical.

82. V. 1-7, 1541-47, 1849-53.

83. III. 715-21, 722-23.

84. IV. 335-36, 1079-82; 1192-1204 (*Fil.* IV. 121-22, "Giove"), 1683-86. See note 105 below for comment on IV. 1079-82.

85. V. 207-10, 1445-49.

86. V. 1525.

87. III. 1015, 1016-22; 1427-28. See Robinson's textual note, p. 1025, to II. 115 for the reading "by Joves" found in some MSS. instead of "By God" in this line of the heroine's.

88. IV. 666-70.
89. IV. 1149, 1337.
90. V. 957-58.
91. I. 878.
92. II. 233, III. 150-51. See Robinson's note, p. 935, to the latter context.
93. IV. 644. As remarked in Robinson's textual note to the line, p. 1028, "Jove" has been substituted for the anachronistic "aungel" of the α version.
94. II. 1607-10.
95. III. 617-20; V. 1835-48, 1863-69; III. 12. Compare with the exalted reference to the crucifixion in V. 1842-44, the narrator's impious one in III. 1577-78 and another irreverent locution of his in III. 1184-86.
96. I. 32-34, 40-42, 43-46.
97. I. 436; II. 1272-73, 1274; III. 49, 56, 1058-59, 1246, 1384-86 (*Fil.* III. 39, "Iddio"), 1387-93; V. 157-58; V. 1212-14, 1781. See also III. 545.
98. V. 1748-50; 1786-88, 1793-96 and 1797-98. See also V. 1434-35.
99. III. 1399-1400; IV. 1212-13; V. 538-39, 1805.
100. I. 826; II. 686, 1261-62, 1263, 1551-52; III. 609, 1410; IV. 696, 722-23; V. 766 67, 1105-6, 1761-62. Also II. 1561, IV. 1162.
101. II. 1757; III. 1326-27, 1378-79.
102. II. 1564-65; III. 1224-25.
103. II. 667-69.
104. I. 877; II. 597, 694; III. 57, 82, 206, 956, 1345, 1373, 1380; IV. 362; V. 82, 529. See also V. 1862.
105. IV. 958ff., with the word "God" occurring in 963, 974, 975, 986, 991, 993, 1011, 1046, 1062, 1066. He concluded with the already cited prayer to "Almyghty Jove in trone," IV. 1079-82, obviously God under another name since credited by Troilus with knowledge of the point which he had been debating. The hero's phrase is echoed in the confidant's "O myghty God . . . in trone."
106. III. 1765-68.
107. III. 1456, 1470.
108. I. 276, 459-60 (*Fil.* I. 43, "Iddio"), 519-22, 526-27, 533, 597-98, 1055; II. 1060-62, 1690-91; III. 1124, 1277-78, 1526 (*Fil.* III. 51, "Dio"); IV. 325-26, 439-41 (*Fil.* IV. 50, "Dio"), 566-67; V. 227, 423-24 (*Fil.* V. 37, "Iddio"), 608-9, 1127, 1359, 1362-63, 1411 (*Fil.* VII. 75, "Dio"), 1702-3 (*Fil.* VIII. 21, "Dio"), 1705-7 (*Fil.* VIII. 17, "Giove"). The last is a wish implied by a question. See also Troilus' nonwishful question addressed to God, I. 400. As indicated by Pratt, *StPh.*, LIII, 535, 536, the phrasings of V. 1411 and 1702-3 are partly echoic of *Le Roman de Troyle et de Criseida*, pp. 287 and 300.
109. I. 517-18.
110. I. 1047.
111. III. 376-78, 1290.
112. I. 195, 334, 835; III. 100, 1084-85, 1357, 1481, 1644-45; IV. 498; V. 1264-65, 1713-15. The last context is a curious combination of contemporary phrase and the old polytheism. Also III. 66.
113. Omniscience, IV. 1654-57; sway, III. 372-73 (*Fil.* III. 15, "Iddio"); redemption, II. 977-79, III. 100-3, and perhaps IV. 1444-45. Also "by God and by my trouthe," I. 770; "Have God my trouthe," II. 1684-86; "And by that feyth I shal to God and yow," III. 1648-50; "thorugh the myght of God," II. 1317; "And God toforn," I. 1049, III. 1639-42; "By God," V. 1147.
114. I. 571-72, 612-13 (*Fil.* II. 8, "per Dio"); III. 416-17, 1289-95, 1300-2; IV. 1600-1 (*Fil.* IV. 156, "per Dio"); V. 522-23, 655-56, 1390-93. And V. 481-82 (*Fil.* V. 46, "per Dio").
115. "Parde(e)": I. 1047; III. 399; IV. 541, 975, 1013. "Pardieux," I. 197. "Depardieux," II. 1058.
116. I. 330, 350, 528; II. 975, 981, 1754. Besides IV. 1175-76, V. 502-4.
117. III. 1429-31, 1436-40.
118. II. 113, 163, 1212 (*Fil.* II. 120, "Iddio"); III. 1565; IV. 1231, 1555-57, 1561, 1604, 1647; V. 707, 959 (continuing a prayer to the Almighty under the appellation

Jove), 1006-8, 1074-77, 1631. And we learn from lines of the narrator, IV. 738-39, of still another prayer of Criseyde's to God. Note also her "benedicite" in III. 757.

119. II. 243-44, 467-69; III. 930-31; IV. 1664-65. Criseyde once averred, however, that if Troilus' affection were unquestionable "God myghte nought a poynt my joies eche," III. 1508-9.

120. II. 750-51; III. 1039-40, 1349 (*Fil*. III. 35, "Dio"). Another instance of her thanking God is mentioned by the narrator, III. 474. She apostrophized God, without prayer or thanksgiving, in II. 127, III. 813-15.

121. "God woot": III. 816-17; IV. 904; V. 983, 1604-5. "But that woot heighe God that sit above," III. 1027-28. "God, thow woost," III. 1053-54, IV. 1619-22.

122. III. 1165-66. Also suggestive of redemption are her "As wisly verray God my soule save," III. 1499-1502, and "As wisly God at reste My soule brynge," III. 925-26, with the oath which she challenged Pandarus to take, "so God yow save," II. 114. Her other asseverations are as follows. "As help(e) me God," II. 133, 590. "God help(e) me so," II. 1213-14; III. 807, 1566. "And helpe me God so at my mooste nede," IV. 1532-33. "As wisly help me God the grete," II. 1230-32. "So God me spede," II. 744-47. "As wisly God myn herte brynge at reste," II. 1515-18. "As wisly God my soule rede," IV. 1364-65. "By God," II. 115, 183, 213-14; III. 869-70; IV. 1319-20. "By God and by my trouthe," III. 120-21, 1512; with "by God and by youre trouthe," II. 1137-40. "By God that sit above," V. 1004. "And God toforn," III. 848-49, V. 962-63.

123. "For (the) love of God": II. 225-26, 246-49, 1130-32, 1476-77; III. 73-74, 941-44, 1045-48, 1503-5; IV. 1286-87. "For Goddes love": II. 122-23, 309-10; III. 162-66; IV. 1651-52. "For his love . . . ," II. 500.

124. "Parde": II. 497, 732; IV. 1368, 1584, 1613. "Par dieux," II. 759. "Depardieux," II. 1212.

125. IV. 1236-39. "Lord": II. 276, 464, 885; IV. 1564; V. 735.

126. I. 552, 558-60, 1041; II. 85-86, 582-83, 588, 1019, 1638, 1713, 1731; III. 61, 761, 966; IV. 383, 407-8; V. 1742-43 (*Fil*. VIII. 24, "Dio"). On one occasion, he asked Troilus to pray to God for him, III. 342-43. Note also his "bendiste" in I. 780 and "benedicite" in III. 860.

127. I. 715-16; II. 92-93, III. 794-95. And II. 155, 1319-20.

128. I. 1002-8, with God mentioned in 1005, 1006. Note also the metaphor for lovers, "verray Goddes apes," which Pandarus quoted from Troilus, I. 911-13.

129. IV. 1086 echoing 1079. His ejaculation to his niece, "Allas, that God yow swich a beaute sente," II. 336, implied that the Deity was her Creator. Note also his ejaculation "O verray God," II. 1464.

130. "God woot": II. 568-71, 995-96, 1234-35, 1360; III. 239-45, 1618-19; V. 333, 347, 507-8, 1733, 1738-39. "But God, that al woot, take I to witnesse . . . ," III. 260-63 (*Fil*. III. 7, "Ma come Dio, che tutto quanto vede, e tu che 'l sai . . ."). As noted by Pratt, *StPh.*, LIII, p.519, the preceding Italian context is translated as "Mais Dieu qui tout voit, et *scet* bien, et aussi faittes vous," in *Le Roman de Troyle et de Criseida*, p. 175.

131. II. 381-82, 563-64.

132. "God help(e) me so": II. 182, 364, 1003-7, 1282; III. 862-64, 1620-21; IV. 610-14; V. 363 (followed by a pagan-colored statement that "prestes of the temple" claim dreams to be the revelations "Of goddes"), 392, 486-89; and "helpe me God," II. 1126-27. "So God me sende hele," III. 321-22. "I bidde God I nevere mote have joie," III. 872-75. "By God": II. 137, 430, 1107; III. 663; V. 430-31, 1161. "By God and by my trouthe," II. 957-59. "By God and yonder sonne," III. 1235-37. "By that God above," III. 878-80. "And God toforn": II. 431, 991-92, 1363-65; III. 334-35.

133. "For the love of God, that us hath wrought," II. 577-78. "For (the) love of God": II. 290-91; III. 118-19, 755, 950-51 (followed by praise of Venus), 1138-40; IV. 895-96. "For Goddes love": I.1027; IV. 96, 1200, 1728-29; III. 122-23, 264-66.

134. II. 366, 995, 1319, 1523; III. 337, 635, 913; IV. 524, 1090.

135. II. 1053-55. "Lord": I. 803, 1025; II. 943; III. 656.

136. Deiphebus: "parde . . . and God tofore," II. 1408-11. Eleyne: "For love of God," II. 1674-78. Calkas: "for the love of God," IV. 109-10, and, as indirectly reported by the narrator, "For love of God," IV. 68-70. One of Criseyde's gossips: "almyghty God hire gide," IV. 693. Diomede: "But wolde nevere God," V. 124-26; "parde," V. 142;

479

"for the love of God," V. 144-45, 159; "God helpe me so," V. 152-54; "God myn herte as wisly glade so," V. 156-58.

137. I. 623; and I. 805, II. 1737, IV. 630; I. 153; and II. 117-18 and 758-59. In her "Pandarus a Devil?" *PMLA.*, LXXI (1956), 275-79, Charlotte D'Evelyn argues, convincingly that "devel" in Troilus' line, I. 623, seems to be an expletive, rather than a vocative for Pandarus as assumed by D. W. Roberston, Jr., in his "Chaucerian Tragedy," *ELH.*, XIX (1952), 17. Note also Criseyde's reference to Amphiorax as "the bisshop," II. 104-5, which I agree with Tatlock, "Epilog," p. 642. n.1, is as minor an anachronism as a modern's reference to an ancient holy man as a 'priest." And recall the circumstance, taken over from the *Filostrato*, of the hero's planning to visit the camp in pilgrim's disguise, V. 1576-77 (*Fil.* VIII. 4), on which see Ch. I. 11. n.5.

138. II. 680-86.

139. III. 1-38 (*Fil.* III. 74-79), 39-48. Chaucer did not call her a goddess as Troiolo had done (n.12) but gave her name, III. 48, as the latter had not.

140. III. 1807-13. The narrator also included Venus in his kinetic picture of the Zodiac, V. 1016-20.

141. I. 1014, II. 972-73 (*Fil.* II. 80, exalting Amore as well as Venere).

142. III. 712-21. See Root's note, p. 477, to 715-17 for the astrology therein.

143. III. 1202-3.

144. III. 1255-58 in III. 1254-74.

145. V. 206-210.

146. IV. 1216, 1661-63.

147. II. 232-37, 1524-26; III. 185-89, 951.

148. So identified in the just cited contexts, III. 1254-57, 1808.

149. In the narrator's lines: "Cupide": III. 461, 1808; V. 207. "God of Love": I. 15, 206 (*Fil.* I. 25, "Amor"), 421 (*Fil.* I. 38, "Amore"). "Love": I. 16, 27, 31, 42, 46, 48, 237, 255, 303, 304 (*Fil.* I. 29, "Amor"), 308, 319, 328; III. 1328, 1552 (*Fil.* III. 55, "Amore"), 1794; IV. 1189 (*Fil.* IV. 120, "amore").

In Troilus': "Cupide," V. 582 (*Fil.* V. 56, "Amor"). "God": II. 526 (as quoted by Pandarus), IV. 288; V. 590. "Charite," III. 1254. "Love": I. 518, 603 (*Fil.* II. 7, "Amore"); III. 1254, 1261, 1610 (*Fil.* III. 58, "Amor"), 1744, 1745, 1746, 1748, 1757, 1762, 1764, 1766; IV. 288 (*Fil.* IV. 33, "Amor").

In Criseyde's: "Love," IV. 1306. She addressed Troilus as "Cupides sone," V. 1590.

In Pandarus': "Cupid," III. 186. "God of Love": I. 932, 967 (*Fil.* II. 24, "Amor"). "God": I. 940, 942; III. 185. "Love": I. 879 (*Fil.* II. 21, "Amore"), 909, 912, 998; II. 522 (*Fil.* II. 57, "Amor").

In Diomede's: "God of Love," V. 143, 167.

In Antigone's: "God of Love," II. 848. "God," II. 834. "Love," II. 827, 860.

150. In Troilus' lines: I. 422 (*Fil.* I. 38, "Signor"), 424, 430 (*Fil.* I. 39, "signor"), 936; II. 523, 525 (*Fil.* II. 57, "Signor"), 533 (*Fil.* II. 60, "signor"); IV. 288 (*Fil.* IV. 33, "signor"); V. 582, 589 (*Fil.* V. 57, "signor"), 591, 599. Pandarus quoted him as having called Love, "Seynt Idyot, lord of thise foles alle," I. 910.

In Antigone's: II. 829, 837, 850.

151. I. 1-56, replacing *Fil.* I. 1-6; 204-59, of which 204-17 owe something to *Fil.* I. 25.

152. I. 422-34 (*Fil.* I. 38-39).

153. I. 904-1008. If Pandarus' statement to his niece can be trusted, the prince had professed repentance to Love, earlier and on his own initiative, in the palace garden, II. 523-32.

154. III. 1254-74.

155. III. 1744-71 (*De cons. Phil.* II. m. viii).

156. V. 582-95 (*Fil.* V. 56-57).

157. II. 827-75. For source, see Ch. I. 4.n. 22.

158. Narrator's references to the sun as "Phebus": II. 54-55; IV. 31-32; V. 8-10 (*Teseida*, II. 1), 278-79, 1016-17, 1107-9. He personified the sun, without naming it, in II. 904-5. Troilus' reproach to the sun under the name of "Titan," III. 1464-70. (For his confusion of Titan with Tithonus, see Root's note, p. 490, to the passage, and Robinson's p. 939.) His reference to the sun, under name of "Phebus" in the song to

Love, III. 1755. He spoke of the horses of the solar chariot, III. 1702-5; alluded to the myth of "Pheton" in a statement about the sun, V. 663-65 (*Fil.* V. 68); personified it in III. 1604-7 (*Fil.* III. 58); and implied its divinity in III. 1707-8, all without naming it. Criseyde referred to the sun as "Phebus" in an asseveration, III. 1493-98, and in her promise of return, IV. 1591-93.

159. Pandarus' comparison of himself to "Phebus," I. 659-66; a metaphor of "Apollo" in Antigone's song, II. 843.

160. I. 64-77 (*Fil.* I. 8, "grande Apollo"). See Tatlock, "Puns in Chaucer," *Flügel Memorial Volume* (Stanford Univ. Press, 1916), pp. 230-31.

161. IV. 113-26, of which 113-19 is adapted from *Fil* IV. 11. For Calkas' modes of foreknowing, see Root's note, p. 503, to 11. 114-17; and, for sources of the walling incident, his note to 11. 120-26 and Robinson's, p. 940, to the same.

162. IV. 1394-1414. See Ch. I. 7. notes 51, 52, 53 for scholarship on this passage.
163. III. 533-46, 726-28.
164. V. 207.
165. V. 1852-53.
166. III. 715-19, 724-25.
167. III. 731-32, 729-31.
168. III. 624-25, IV. 1534-40.
169. V. 1852-53.
170. III. 22 (*Fil.* III. 77), IV. 22-28.
171. II. 628-30, III. 436-37 (*Fil.* III. 20).
172. V. 306-8.
173. II. 435-38, 592-93, 988.
174. IV. 1608-9; V. 1464-70; IV. 1591-93, V. 655-56, 1018-19. See Root's note, p. 540, and Robinson's, p. 946, to the next to the last passage for the reading "Latona" completely supported by the MSS.

175. V. 321-22, 1826-27. See Root's note, p. 535, to the former passage, for possible sources.

176. I. 152-64 (*Fil.* I. 17-18, "Pallade" and "Palladio").
177. III. 729-30, V. 308. See Root's note, p. 478, to the former context.
178. II. 425-27, 1062-63; V. 977-78, 999-1001.
179. II. 232-38.
180. V. 601-2; IV. 1534-40, 1594-96; IV. 1116-17. The first context, as noted by Root, p. 539, is apparently from *Inf.* xxx. 1-2, and the second, as noted by him, p. 525, apparently from 11. 1-12 of that canto.

181. II. 442-45, IV. 120-26.
182. II. 8-10; III. 45-48, 1807-13. See Root's note, pp. 495-96, on the last context for its geographical error and sources thereof.

183. I. 6-11, IV. 22-28. On sources and analogues for Chaucer's conception of the Furies, see Root's notes, pp. 409, 499-500, to the passages and Robinson's, pp. 924-25, 939.

184. II. 435-36, V. 1498. See Root's note, p. 442 to the first context, and Robinson's, p. 949, to the second.

185. II. 64-70; 77; III. 1389; 1807, IV. 22, 25; 31-32; 659-65 (*Fil.* IV. 78); 1138-39; 1188; V. 10-11; 208; 211-12; 1110; 1777-78. Blanket reference may be made to the notes of Root and Robinson to contexts cited in my notes 185-191. Apropos of the Germanic "tale of Wade," which, according to the narrator, was recounted at Pandarus' house, III. 614, see Ch. I. 6. n.18.

186. I. 759; III. 720-21, 722-23, 726-28, 729-31; 1258, 1469; IV. 299-301; 473-74; 1459; V. 319-20; 601-2; 642-44; 663-65; 1527-33. Troilus also referred to Flegetoun, "the fery flood of helle," III. 1600.

187. II.100-5; III. 1427-28; IV. 788-91, 1538-40; 1541-45.
188. I. 652-65; 697-700, 785-88; 859-61; III. 589-93.
189. V. 890-93, 932-38.
190. V. 1485-1510, after 1464-84.
191. IV. 120-26.
192. Narrator: I. 150-51 (*Fil.* I. 17, "li divin sacrificii"), III. 622-23, 1671-72, IV. 949-51, V. 1850. Troilus: III. 383-85, IV. 268-69 (*Fil.* IV. 30, "altro iddio"), V. 1250-

51 (*Fil.* VII. 26, "gli dii"), 1713-15 (*Fil.* VIII. 19, "gli dèi"). Criseyde: IV. 1401-11 (4), V. 1604-6. Pandarus: V. 365-67.
193. 4669 lines against 2344 in the *Filostrato.*
194. 2898 lines, IV. I-V. 1197, against 2296, *Fil.* III. 94-VII. 14.
195. 672 lines, against 1064.
196. I. 57-60.
197. "Som day" the Trojans suffered in warfare and "eft" the Greeks, I. 136-37 (*Fil.* I. 16). Dating of the festival, I. 155-61 (*Fil.* I. 18).
198. After return home from the temple, I. 323-24 (*Fil.* I. 32), the hero experienced increase of love "day by day," I. 442-44 (*Fil.* I. 41), and, because of it, distinguished himself in arms "Fro day to day," I. 482-83, all before Pandarus "Com oones in unwar," I. 547-49 (*Fil.* II. 1). That this coming was in April is established in III. 360-64.
199. I. 1062-71.
200. II. 50-77. Lines 50-62 seem clearly to indicate that it was Pandarus' reverse which fell on May 3, not his visit to his niece. In Root and Russell's article, however, p. 50. n.6, it is said that the latter occurred "on May 3, or perhaps May 4"; and in Root's edition, p. xxxiii, categorically that it occurred on the third.
201. II. 554-57 (*Fil.* II. 62), 507-11 (*Fil.* II. 56). As noted by Pratt, *St.Ph.*, LIII, 517, "L'altrieri," *Fil.* II. 56, is rendered as "L'autre jour" in *Le Roman de Troyle et de Criseida*, p. 150. In "Troilus' Confession," *MLN.*, LXIX (1954), 468-70, Arthur E. Hutson too confidently assumes that Pandarus' account of discovery of his friend's love, II. 506-74, involved a "little fib." Though he was certainly capable of such, there is no evidence that he misrepresented the discovery—as there is none that the uninventive Pandaro did.
202. Nightfall and night, II. 904-24.
203. II. 932-49. See II. 960-62, 990-92 for backward and forward time links.
204. II. 1093-94; 1163, 1171, 1179, 1184; 1185-88; 1301-2. Pandarus thought that Criseyde's resolve, announced during this second visit of his, to go only part way in love would not be kept "fully yeres two." II. 1296-98. On this estimate, which does not contribute to the timetable of events, see Thomas A. Kirby, "A Note on 'Troilus,'" II. 1298," *MLR.*, XXIX (1934), 67-68; and " 'Troilus,' II. 1298, Again," *MLR.*, XXXIII (1938), 402, as well as Ellsworth G. Mason, " 'Troilus,' II. 1298," *MLR.*, XLII (1947), 358-59.
205. II. 1303-7, with 1312, 1320.
206. Troilus wrote to his lady "Fro day to day," II. 1343-44 (*Fil.* II. 131);
        And after swiche answers as he hadde,
        So were his days sory outher gladde, II. 1350-51 (*Fil.* II. 131).
207. II. 1362-65, 1399-1400, 1402, 1431-35, 1460-63 (including reference to dining), 1485-90, 1492-98, 1513-23.
208. II. 1540, 1544-45, 1548-50.
209. II. 1555-60, 1562-63.
210. II. 1569-70, 1597ff.
211. II. 1702-8.
212. III. 204-10, 222-26.
213. III. 227-31, with 420, 423-24.
214. III. 360-64.
215. III. 202-3.
216. Troilus devoted days and nights respectively to warfare and amorous contempla tion, III. 435-41 (*Fil.* III. 20), and had occasional contact with his lady, III. 451-52, and voluminous correspondence, III. 501-4, with 488. See the variant in 503, given by Robinson, p. 1026.
217. III. 547-67, esp. 549-51, 559-60, 562. Whether the host timed his supper party in anticipation of a storm Chaucer leaves to our conjecture—see III. 531-32.
218. III. 595-603.
219. III. 624-48, esp. 624-25.
220. In the article of Root and Russell cited in n.78, after correlation of III. 624-25 with 549-50, it is stated: "Now if the thin crescent moon is in the sign of Cancer, the Sun must be in, or approaching, the next preceding sign of Gemini; and the time of year when Pandarus gave his supper party is clearly designated as May or early June.

By Chaucer's calendar the Sun entered Gemini on or about May 12," p. 50. In his article cited in my same note, Tatlock observes incidentally, "the new moon would be in Cancer only in late spring," p. 279. n.8. Root and Russell opine that the astronomically dated consummation took place "presumably one year after the first wooing," p. 50, n.6.

221. "A slight knowledge of astrology is sufficient to show that it should produce this effect [i.e. a rainstorm]," Root and Russell, p. 58. They raise the interesting question, "Is it possible that Chaucer's thunderstorm may have been suggested by the storm of hail and thunder which drove Dido and Aeneas to take shelter together in the fateful cave (*Aen.* 4. 160-172)?" p. 49. n.5.

222. See note 78.

223. III. 656-63, 677-79, 743-46. See also Pandarus' humorous backward reference to the storm, 1557-61.

224. III. 673-76. See Root's note, p. 475, to l. 671.

225. III. 1415-20. The detail of cockcrow is elaborated from *Fil.* III. 42. For Venus, see my note 78 and, for *Fortuna Major*, Root's note, pp. 488-89, to 1419-20, and Robinson's, pp. 938-39, to 1415-26.

226. III. 1520-30; 1555-56 with 1569-70 and 1581; and 1583-89, 1665-66.

227. III. 1667-70 (*Fil.* III. 64), with dawn terminating the rendezvous, III. 1695-1711, as in *Fil.* III. 70-71.

228. Adapting the account in *Fil.* III. 71 of the lovers planning future meetings at the end of their second, Chaucer adds the specification, "And many a nyght they wroughte in this manere," III. 1713.

229. IV. 1324-30 (*Fil.* IV. 133).

230. III. 1737-43 (*Fil.* III. 73), 1772-85 (*Fil.* III. 90-91), 1786-1806 (*Fil.* III. 92-93). It may be noted that Chaucer, like Boccaccio, speaks of the undue brevity of the lover's joy, IV. 1-2 (*Fil.* III. 94).

231. Of the total of 4669 lines in Books I-III, 3977 lines are allotted to the ten days as follows. The day in April of Troilus' enamorment and subsequent meditation in chamber, I. 155-434 (whether the meditation ends with or before 434 is not clear); the day in that month of Pandarus' first talk with him, I. 547-1061; the three days in the next month in which the confidant suffered from love and paid his first and second visits to Criseyde, repairing to Troilus after each visit, II. 50-1330; the two, of month unspecified, in which he arranged for and managed a gathering at the house of Deiphebus and conferred with the hero afterward, II. 1352-1757 and III. 50-424; and the three in May, presumably a year after the enamorment, in which

232. I. 106-26, III. 1667-1712, 1737-71, totalling 102 lines.

233. IV. 31-34. See n.236.

234. IV. 36-37. Greeks and Trojans fought "The longe day," IV. 43-46 (*Fil.* IV. 2).

235. Calkas, among the first to learn of the truce for exchange, repaired promptly to the Grecian assembly and as promptly instructed the ambassadors when he had won his petition for Criseyde, IV. 61-67, 135-38. They went to Troy as soon as they had Priam's safe-conduct, and the King held his parliament directly upon their arrival, IV. 139-43.

236. "The Date of the *Troilus* . . . ," *MLN.*, L (1935), 282-84. The date of Ector's resolve as indicated by the sun's presence in Leo may, Tatlock says, be "at any time between about 12 July and 12 August," p. 282. As he notes, Criseyde promised on the night after the parliament that she would return before the moon was beyond Leo, IV. 1590-93, and Troilus remembered seeing its "hornes olde" at that time and hoped that she would be back when its "hornes newe" began to sprout, V. 652-58 (*Fil.* V. 69). The narrator thus described the celestial pageant on the night after Diomede's call (the tenth after that in which she had made promise):

> The brighte Venus folwede and ay taughte
> The wey ther brode Phebus down alighte;
> And Cynthea hire char-hors overraughte
> To whirle out of the Leoun, if she myghte;
> And Signifer his candels sheweth brighte, V. 1016-20.

Tatlock writes of these lines: "Venus therefore is visible and is evening-star, the moon is about to leave Leo, it is fully night, and therefore Venus' distance from the sun is consummation was effected and reviewed, III. 547-1666.

considerable. The sun is still in Leo and west of the moon, for the moon in Leo is new [as established in V. 650-58]; this harmonizes fully with the estimate . . . that this night is not much more than ten days after the day we started with, when the sun was in Leo," p. 283. Criseyde's promise by the moon, it may be added, was recalled by Troilus on this tenth night, V. 1187-90. See also Root's notes, pp. 527, 540, 547, and 551 to IV. 1590-96, V. 652-58, 1016-20, and 1185 respectively.

237. See n.240.

238. Troilus sped "faste" from parliament to chamber, IV. 218-20 (*Fil.* IV. 22). The friend came there "in a rees," IV. 344-50, without being summoned as in *Fil.* IV. 43; and promised Troilus an assignation "this nyght som tyme," IV. 652-54 (*Fil.* IV. 77). Criseyde, apprised of misfortune by "swifte Fame," IV. 659-70 (*Fil.* IV. 78-79), sought her chamber after female visitation, IV. 729-32 (*Fil.* IV. 86). Joining her, Pandarus spoke of his contact with the lover, "this day," IV. 885-86. (*Fil.* IV. 103) and of hers presently to come, IV. 913-15 (*Fil.* IV. 106). Back with the prince, he confirmed the assignation, IV. 1114-15 (*Fil.* IV. 112). Troilus sought his mistress at the appropriate hour and remained with her till daybreak, IV. 1124-26 (*Fil.* IV. 113), 1688-1701 (*Fil.* IV. 167).

239. In his adaptation of Criseida's first long speech, Chaucer makes his heroine give assurance to Troilus that she would be back "Er dayes ten" and to ask if he could not contain himself for "ten dayes" for the sake of her reputation, IV. 1317-20, 1328-30. The question is similar to one, *Fil.* IV. 157, in a later speech of Criseida's. In his adaptation of a speech of hers between these two, he complements the promise to return on the tenth with its astronomical equivalent, IV. 1590-96 (*Fil.* IV. 154), and he preserves the reference to the promised tenth in the hero's unhappy rejoinder, IV. 1597-99 (*Fil.* IV. 155). In Criseyde's final speech substituted for one of Troiolo's, he makes her pray Jupiter for reunion "Or nyghtes ten," IV. 1683-86.

240. V. 8-14. The conjunctive "Syn that" indicates to me that the spring of the enamorment is not to be counted as one of the three mentioned as brought by Phebus and Zepherus and hence that three years, not two, have elapsed. Doubt is expressed, unnecessarily, I think, as to whether it should be so counted or not in Root and Russell's article, p. 50, n.6; and in Root's edition, p. xxxiv, there seems to be implication that it should be.

241. V. 15-16. In accord with the mention of "prime" here is Diomede's recollection that Criseyde left Troy "by the morwe," V. 874, if not Troilus' that he came home at "eve" after escorting her part way, V. 610-16.

242. V. 92ff. See Chapter I. 8. pp. 101-3, for Chaucer's employment here of the *Roman de Troie* in conjunction with the *Filostrato*.

243. Troilus, returning to chamber, V. 197-202 (*Fil.* V. 15), abandoned himself to furious grief, "neigh til day," V. 213, and then asked in the course of a lament how he might endure the ten days, V. 239-40. The indication of time in 213 is similar to that in *Fil.* V. 26.

244. V. 274-94, expanding *Fil.* V. 22.

245. Before they left the chamber for Sarpedoun's establishment, V. 432-34 (*Fil.* V. 40), both men showed their preoccupation with time, Pandarus twice referring to the ten-day span, V. 353 (*Fil.* V. 31), 397-99, and Troilus once, V. 423-24 (*Fil.* V. 37). At the end of the fourth day with Sarpedoun, Troilus proposed departure as Troiolo before three were over, V. 475-83 (*Fil.* V. 46); Pandarus successfully argued for rounding out a week as Pandaro for staying two days longer, V. 484-501 (*Fil.* V. 47-48).

246. V. 512-25 (*Fil.* V. 50).

247. Boccaccio who begins the pilgrimage with a visit to the lady's vacant palace seems to end it with the lover's address to Amore, *Fil.* V. 51-57. He goes on to record that Troiolo sometimes, "talvolta," visited the gate, V. 58-59, conceived the fancy that he was sometimes pointed at because of change in appearance and for that reason composed a song, V. 60-66; kept impatient track of time, with reproach for slowness to the sun and wish to the moon that she might become newly horned, V. 67-69; directed his gaze campward, V. 70; and in such and other ways passed the hours away, V. 71. The visits to the gate could only have come after that to Sarpedoun; some of the other activities would have been possible during it as well as after. Chaucer includes as much

certainly as Boccaccio in the pilgrimage, V. 526-602; and perhaps also in it the visitation of the gate, V. 603-16. In adapting the circumstances recorded by his authority after the business at the gate, he replaces the song with an altogether different one which makes mention of the tenth night, V. 638-44; effects rhetorical improvement in the wish to the moon, V. 652-58; and, as remarked in my text, indicates that he has brought the hero through the ninth night, V. 680-81.

248. Ch. I. 9. pp. 120-21.

249. V. 701-6, 750-54 (*Fil.* VI. 7). Criseida phrased her resolution without saving when it would be carried out; Criseyde said that it would be "to-morwe at nyght." That the morrow was the tenth day on which she had promised to return might be guessed, but since her resolve, like Criseida's, is undated, there is no certainty of this.

250. V. 766-67 (*Fil.* VI. 8).

251. V. 841-46 (*Fil.* VI. 9).

252. V. 943-51, with 995-96; 1014-15.

253. V. 1016-22. See n.236.

254. V. 1023-29, instead of *Fil.* VI. 33-34.

255. V. 1030-36. Boccaccio noted abatement of her sorrow without attributing it to a visit of Diomede on the morrow or otherwise dating it precisely, *Fil.* VI. 34.

256. V. 1086-92. In his note, pp. 549-50, to this passage, Root writes: "It is true, as Chaucer says, that his authors do not say in so many words how long a time elapses before Criseyde surrenders to Diomede; but if one takes careful heed of the time indications in the book of Benoit, one finds that between the arrival of Briseida at the Grecian camp and her final acceptance of Diomede there is an interval of *at least* twenty-one months."

257. V. 1100-13, corresponding to *Fil.* VII. 1, in which neither of the chronological particulars is noted.

258. The friends allowed themselves a break at noon as in the source—and expressly for dinner as not in the source—V. 1114-32 (*Fil.* VII. 2-4). See Root's note, p. 550, to 1.1126. The coming of evening and then of night is registered much as in the original: V. 1135-1176 (*Fil.* VII. 5-10), 1177-1183 (*Fil.* VII. 11).

259. V. 1184-1191 (*Fil.* VII. 12-13). See Root's note, p. 551, to 1.1185.

260. V. 1192-97 (*Fil.* VII. 14).

261. V. 1198-1316 (*Fil.* VII. 15-51).

262. "But in two monthes yet ye nat retounre," V. 1351 (*Fil.* VII. 54, "né fra quaranta ancor fatt' hai ritorno"). The omitted notice of springtime, *Fil.* VII. 63.

263. V.766-67, IV. 31-34.

264. In the transition from letter writing to conference, V. 1422-1449, Chaucer implies that Criseyde replied promptly but states that Troilus' woe increased nonetheless "fro day to nyght"; in that from the writing to the visits, *Fil.* VII. 76-77, Boccaccio stated that Troiolo waited many days in vain for reply and that his woe increased from day to day. The conference itself, V. 1450-1533 replacing the visits, *Fil.* VII. 77-103.

265. Troilus started from bed immediately after Cassandre's interpretation of his dream and "day by day" sought to check it, V. 1534-40, whereas, soon recovering his strength after the visits, Troiolo took part in many battles, *Fil.* VII. 104-6. Fortune plucked Troy "Fro day to day," and fate deprived the city of Ector to the great sorrow of Troilus and others, V. 1541-1568, while in the source it is recorded that the death of Ettore kept Troiolo in grief for a long time, *Fil.* VIII. 1. Like Troiolo, Chaucer's prince kept enough hope to be often of a mind to visit the camp and often to appeal to the lady in writing, V. 1569-1638 (*Fil.* VIII. 2-7), until discovery of the brooch left him no resort but complaint to the friend, V. 1639-1743 (*Fil.* VIII. 8-24). Like Troiolo, he was much in combat, and often against Diomede, from the discovery until his death at the hand of Achilles, V. 1744-1764 and 1800-6 (*Fil.* VIII. 25-27).

266. V. 1807-27 (*Teseida*, XI. 1-3).

267. Of the 3570 lines of Books IV-V, 1981 are devoted to the three days beginning with the parliament, IV. 141-1701 and V. 15-434; 391 to days later in the sequence, V. 499-602, 841-1036, and 1107-97; 371 to the three days after it, V. 1233-1421, 1450-1533, 1646-1743.

268. See note 79.

269. I. 64-77 (*Fil.* I. 8).

270. I. 93.
271. I. 138-40.
272. I. 211-59, of which 211-17 corresponds in part to *Fil.* I. 25.
273. II. 50 63. For scholarship on May 3, see Ch. I. 4.n.6.
274. II. 619-23.
275. II. 680-86. See Ch. I. 4. n.18 for scholarship on the passage.
276. III. 1-38 (*Fil.* III. 74-79).
277. III. 617-23.
278. III. 1667-70; in the corresponding stanza of the source, *Fil.* III. 64, the word fortuna" is employed but without personification. III. 1714-15.
279. IV. 1-11 (*Fil.* III. 94).
280. V. 469, 1134.
281. V. 1541-47.
282. V. 1745-47 (*Fil.* VIII. 25), 1763-64 (*Fil.* VIII. 26).
283. V. 1097-99.
284. I. 837-40.
285. III. 712-35.
286. III. 1202-3, 1254-74.
287. III. 1744-71 (Boethius, *Cons.* II. m. viii.)
288. IV. 260-87 (*Fil.* IV. 30-32), 323-26.
289. IV. 958-1078.
290. IV. 1184-1204 (*Fil.* IV. 120-22).
291. IV. 1208.
292. V. 204-10 (*Fil.* V. 17); 1250-51 (*Fil.* VII. 26), 1713-15 (*Fil.* VIII. 19).
293. V. 1699-1701 (*Fil.* VIII. 15, " 'n malora").
294. III. 813-40 (*Cons.* II. pr. iv.). See also IV. 834-40.
295. IV. 745 (*Fil.* IV. 88, " 'n mal punto").
296. IV. 1394-1414.
297. Criseyde spoke more or less piously of Jove or Jupiter, III. 1015-23, 1427-28, IV. 666-70, 1149, 1337, V. 957-58, and always very piously and much more frequently of God, as cited in notes 117ff.; of Venus, IV. 1216, 1661-63; of Cinthia, IV. 1608-9; of Pallas, II. 425-27, 1062-63, V. 977-78, 999-1001; of Saturne's daughter Juno, Attropos, celestial and infernal deities collectively, nymphs, satyrs and fauns in one long protestation, IV. 1534-47; and of "goddes" collectively in a letter, V. 1604-6.
298. IV. 1583-89 (*Fil.* IV. 154), 1681-82. The second passage corresponds to *Fil.* IV. 166 in a speech not of the heroine's but of the hero's. Criseida's defiance of Giove and Fortuna, *Fil.* V. 6, Chaucer omits.
299. V. 1054-77, esp. 1067-68.
300. II. 74-75. For scholarship on these lines, see Ch. I. 4 n.7.
301. I: 841-54, IV. 384-92, 600-2 (*Fil.* IV. 73). See also II. 281-87 (*Fil.* II. 44).
302. V. 358-85, of which 358-64 corresponds to *Fil.* V. 32. See Ch. I. 8. n.18.
303. IV. 113-26, instead of *Fil.* IV. 11.
304. V. 897-910 (*Fil.* VI. 17-18).
305. V. 1457-63.
306. I. 155-58 (*Fil.* I. 18).
307. II. 50-56.
308. II. 64-70. See Ch. I. 4. n.5 for sources of this stanza and that cited in n.307. In his article "Chaucer's Use of the *Teseida*," *PMLA.*, LXII (1947), 608-11, Professor Pratt remarks the indebtedness of these two "heightened time descriptions" and two later ones, V. 8-11, 274-279, respectively to *Teseida*, III. 5-6, IV. 73, II. 1, VII. 94; and of three more, III. 1415-20, V. 1016-20, 1107-10, not to any particular passage in that romance, but to its general example of employment of such descriptions.
309. II. 112. Note also Pandarus' later reference to Maytime, II. 1096-99.
310. II. 820-22. The garden in which Pandarus discovered his friend's love—though more explicitly described by him, II. 506ff., than the woods in which Pandaro made such discovery are by him, *Fil.* II. 56—is not made definitely springlike.
311. II. 904-10, 918-22. There is indication in lines of Pandarus that the sun was shining on his second day with his niece and the moon on the night which followed it, II. 1237, 1312.

312. III. 1-2 (*Fil.* III. 74), 8-11 (*Fil.* III. 75). Note also the mention of Deiphebus' "herber grene," II. 1705.
313. III. 548-52, 562, 624-28, 656, 677-79, 743-44, 786-88, 1560-61.
314. III. 1415-20. See Ch. I. 6. notes 61, 62 for sources. In the *Filostrato,* IV. 42-43, there is notice of cocks, though without visualization; there is none of celestial bodies.
315. III. 1427-42, 1450-70. For sources, see Ch. I. 6. pp. 75-76, and notes 63-65. Boccaccio did no more than state in the briefest possible fashion that Troiolo cursed the approaching day, *Fil.* III. 44.
316. III. 1702-8. Like Boccaccio, Chaucer briefly states that, in this second meeting, both lovers cursed the day, III. 1699-1701 (*Fil.* III. 70).
317. III. 1751-61. The song is derived from the *Consolation,* II. m. viii.
318. IV. 31-34, 1590-93. See n.236 for the interrelationship of these passages and V. 652-58, 1016-20, 1187-90.
319. V. 8-14.
320. V. 645-79 (*Fil.* VII. 67-70).
321. V. 1016-22.
322. V. 1107-11.
323. V. 1186-91. In *Fil.* VII. 12-13, Troiolo misinterpreted his mistress' promise as phrased in terms of days.
324. V. 1807-19. See Ch. I. 11. pp. 135-36, and notes 26-33 for sources and interpretation.

CHAPTER III *Figurative Associations in Seven Areas*

Section 1 *Preview*

1. "Figurative Contrasts in Chaucer's *Troilus and Criseyde,*" *English Institute Essays, 1950* (New York: Columbia Univ. Press, 1951), 57-88. Friedrich Klaeber surveyed the Chaucerian canon for imagery in his large volume, *Das Bild bei Chaucer* (Berlin: Heinrich, 1893), analyzing this element successively, in the four parts of his book, by the context of the vehicle, by rhetorical and syntactical form, by mode of treatment of sources, and by tonal characteristics. Finding it easier to devise my own approaches than to adapt his, scholarly though they were, I did not make use of his work either in my article or in the present book. In the article, "Chaucer's Imagery," *Transactions of the Royal Society of Canada,* Ser. III., Vol. XXXIII (1939), Sect. II, 81-90, R. K. Gordon gave a selection of images from Chaucer's poems as evidence of the poet's experiences and interests. Not believing that the latter can be deduced from the former, I passed over this article too. I have also passed over the collections of associative figures from Chaucer made by Claes Schaar, *The Golden Mirror,* Skrifter Utgivna av Kungl. Humanistiska Vetenskapssamfundet i Lund, LIV (1955), 110-19, 259-64, 428-30. Other scholarly efforts relating in one way or another to associative figures I have drawn on with profit, as will be acknowledged in notes in later sections of the chapter.
2. *TC.* I. 353, III. 1309. For further instances of metaphor in the *Troilus,* see the long ones cited in n.16; and for instances thereof in the *Filostrato,* the long ones cited in n.4. Metonymies may be found listed in Section 5: of the adaptation, in notes 103, 164, 165; of the source, in notes 3, 27, 54.
3. I. 525 (*Fil.* I. 53), IV. 337 (*Fil.* IV. 41), V. 838; II. 47, III. 1062, V. 741-42. All similes and illustrations of the *Troilus* are listed in n.18; and of the *Filostrato* in n.6.
4. There are twenty-five figurative utterances in Boccaccio's poem which run to four lines or more. Of these, the narrator has four metaphors: *Fil.* I. 2, 40-41, III. 1, IX. 3-8; and the eight similes designated as long in n.6. Troiolo has nine metaphors: I. 38-39, II. 86-89, III. 61-62, 67-68, IV. 51-52, 61, V. 53, 56-57, VII. 97; and the long simile cited in n.6. Pandaro quotes a long metaphor from his friend, II. 57-60. Criseida has a long metaphor, II. 115-16; and the long illustration cited in n.6.
5. These three of the twenty-five longest are I. 38-39 and V. 56-57 in Troiolo's lines and II. 57-60 quoted from him in Pandaro's.

6. Narrator: long similes, II. 80, 85*, III. 12, IV. 18, 26-27*, 85*, 138*, VII. 80*; short similes, I. 3, 19, 40 (within a long metaphor), 46, II. 38, 47, 108*, III. 91*, IV. 28, 41*, V. 42, VI. 23*, VII. 20, 84, VIII. 30. Troiolo: long simile, V. 37*; short similes. I. 22*, 53 (three in this stanza)*, 56*, IV. 139, 140*, VII. 31*; short illustration, VII. 93*. Pandaro: short similes, II. 22, 135; short illustrations, II. 10 (two in this stanza)** Criseida: short simile, II. 71; long illustration, II. 74*. Stars in notes 6 and 18 indicate contexts classified as proverbial by Professor B. J. Whiting, *Chaucer's Use of Proverbs*, Harvard Studies in Comparative Lit., XI (1934), Ch. III. This book supersedes Willi Haeckel, *Das Sprichwort bei Chaucer* . . . , Erlanger Beiträge, VIII (1890).

7. See note 6. As recorded in n.4, the narrator has four long metaphors against his eight long similes; Troiolo nine against his one; Pandaro, a long metaphor quoted from the prince; Criseida, a long one beside her long illustration.

8. Narrator: his nine starred similes in n.6 and two metaphors, I. 25, IV. 78. Troiolo: his six similes and one illustration starred in n.6. Pandaro: his two starred illustrations and two metaphors, V. 32, VII. 10. Criseida: her starred illustration and three metaphors, III. 48, IV. 152, VI. 7. See n.25 for Professor Whiting's classification of the material.

9. IV. 85.

10. I. 1-2, III. 68. A conceit, which does not fall within the scope of this chapter, is the hero's assumption that the wind from camp was his lady's sighs, V. 70.

11. *TC.* IV. 305-6, V. 423-24, 1418.

12. II. 1380-90.

13. III. 710-11.

14. II. 1501-3, 964.

15. See Ch. I. 1. notes 10, 13, for my system of counting the lines of narrator and characters in the two poems.

16. There are sixty-three figurative utterances in the *Troilus* which run to four lines or more as against the twenty-five in the source which have been listed in n.4. Of the sixty-three, the narrator has eight metaphors, I. 21-46, 435-50 (*Fil.* I. 40-41), II. 1-7, 659-62 (*Fil.* II. 68, less than four lines), III. 526-29, 617-20, 1730-36, V. 771-77; and the thirteen similes and three illustrations designated as long in n.18. Troilus has eleven long metaphors, I. 330-35, 336-40, 415-18, 422-34 (*Fil.* I. 38-39), III. 131-46, 1744-50, IV. 302-8, 442-48, V. 582-90 (*Fil.* V. 56-57), 638-44, 1688-91, and the two long similes and one long illustration cited in n.18. Pandarus has two long metaphors quoted from the prince, II. 523-32 (*Fil.* II. 57-60), 533-36, and the five long similes and six long illustrations cited in n.18. Criseyde has four long metaphors. II. 778-81, III. 169-77, 1009-15, 1429-35, and the three long illustrations cited in n.18. Diomede has three long metaphors, V. 172-75, 918-24, 939-45 (*Fil.* VI. 25, less than four lines). Antigone has the two long illustrations cited in n.18.

17. Thirteen of the sixty-three figures listed in n.16. belong to the pattern of subjugation and feudal relationship. Of these, seven are in Troilus' lines: I. 330-35, 422-34 (*Fil.* I. 38-39), III. 131-46, 1744-50, IV. 442-48, V. 582-90 (*Fil.* V. 56-57), 1688-91; and two more, quoted from him, in Pandarus': II. 523-32 (*Fil.* II. 57-60), 533-36. One is in Criseyde's: III. 169-77. And three are in Diomede's: V. 172-75, 918-24, 939-45 (*Fil.* VI. 25).

18. Narrator. Long similes: I. 101-5 (*Fil.* I. 11), 218-24*, 1086-91, II. 764-70 (including a metaphor), 967-72 (*Fil.* II. 80), 1331-34 (*Fil.* II. 85)*, III. 351-57 (*Fil.* III. 12), 1233-39, 1240-45, IV. 225-29, 239-45 (*Fil.* IV. 27), 1135-39*, 1432-35 (*Fil.* IV. 138); short similes: I. 482-83 (*Fil.* I. 46), 871-72, II. 600*, 628-30, 926*, 1256*, 1335*, 1461-62*, 1493-94*, 1553-54, 1615-16*, III. 228, 425-26*, 433-34*, 699-700*, 1200-1*, 1230-32, 1371, 1783-85 (*Fil.* III. 91)*, IV. 183-84*, 233-35, 246-47 (*Fil.* IV. 28), 337-38 (*Fil.* IV. 41)*, 353-55*, 366-67, 519-20, 726-28 (*Fil.* IV. 85)*, 750-51, 864-65, 1697-98, V. 211-12, 533-35*, 830*, 831*, 836-38, 844-45*, 1536-37, 1728-29*, 1841. Long illustrations: I. 738-42*, 1065-71, III. 1212-18*; short illustrations: I. 257-59*, 448-50*, II. 19-21*, 36-37*, 42, 47-48, III. 1060-61*, 1062*, 1063-64*, 1191-92, 1577-78*.

Troilus. Long similes: IV. 463-66,* V. 1527-33; short similes: I. 523-24 (*Fil.* I. 53)*,

525 (*Fil.* I. 53)*, IV. 300-1, 1459*, V. 425-27*. Long illustration: V. 415-20; short illustrations: 985-87*, IV. 1453-54*, 1455-56*, 1457-58*.

Pandarus. Long similes: I. 659-69, 697-700, 731-35*, 785-88, 963-66; short similes: I. 670-71, 889 (*Fil.* II. 22), II. 193-94*, 1383-84 (within a long illustration), IV. 594-95*, 625-27, 1097-99. Long illustrations: I. 946-49*, 1002-8*, II. 1028-36*, 1037-43, 1380-89*, III. 855-61*; short illustrations: I. 628-30 (*Fil.* II. 10)*, 631-32*, 638-39*, 642-44, 694-96*, 856-58*, 950*, 951*, II. 344, 345, 347, 372-73, 537-39 (quoting Troilus)*, 1531-33*, III. 764-66*, IV. 411-13, 931*, 1104-6.

Criseyde. Short similes: IV. 789-91, 1354-56*, 1548-49*. Long illustrations: II. 715-18*, IV. 767-70*, 1373-76*; short illustrations: II. 481-83*, 804-5*, IV. 765-66*, V. 741-43*.

Antigone. Long illustrations: II. 862-65, 893-96.

See note 6 for the significance of the stars.

19. See n.18. As recorded in n.16, the narrator has only eight long metaphors; the hero, eleven; the confidant, only the two quoted from Troilus; the heroine, four; and Diomede, three.

20. Proverbial similes and illustrations of the several speakers as distinguished by stars in note 18. Metaphors as follows. Narrator: I. 210, 215-16, 236-38, 300, 353, 384-85, 1074, II. 1275-76, III. 87-88, 113-14, 694-95, 1162, IV. 6-7, 1166, V. 469, 1432-33. Troilus: I. 202-3, 406, 509, 836-40, IV. 460, 461, V. 1264-65. Pandarus: I. 912-13 (quoting Troilus), 976-79, 1023-24, II. 327-28, 402-3, 1021-22, III. 198-99, 710-11, 736-37, 775-76, 890, 1137, 1630, IV. 622, V. 349-50, 484-85, 505, 1174-75, 1176. Criseyde: II. 754, 784, 791, 1104, III. 813-15, 930-31, 1034-35, IV. 1261-63, 1370-71, 1567-68, V. 1062. Diomede: V. 897-99. Antigone: II. 859-61, 867-68. See n.25 for Professor Whiting's classification of the material.

21. Metaphors: III. 87-88, V. 469, V. 1432-33, II. 1275-76, I. 210, I. 300, III. 1162; similes: I. 218-24, IV. 726-28 (*Fil.* IV. 85).

22. II. 985-87, IV. 1453-59.

23. Metaphors: III. 775-76, II. 327-28, III. 736-37, III. 710-11. III. 1630, V. 484-85; similes: III. 319-20, I. 731-35, IV. 594-95; illustrations, I. 631-32, II. 1531-33, III. 764-65.

24. Metaphor: IV. 1261-63; illustrations: II. 715-18, IV. 765-66, IV. 1373-74.

25. In Chapter III of his *Chaucer's Use of Proverbs*, Professor Whiting has collected from the *Troilus* as from the *Filostrato* all instances of the following three kinds of proverbial material: proverbs—monitory sayings popular either in origin or through long use; sententious remarks—also monitory but not popular; and proverbial phrases—current expressions which are ordinarily not monitory. In the last group, he distinguishes comparative from other phrases. All of the comparative phrases are associative figures. needless to say; and so are not a few of the other expressions—in the English poem, nearly half of the remaining phrases, and more than a third of the proverbs and sententious remarks. Generalizing, it appears, mainly on the first kind, he says:

> Chaucer uses proverbs in *Troilus and Criseyde* largely for purposes of characterization. There are some in the narrative, but less than half as many as occur in the dialogue. The greatest number of proverbs are put in the mouths of the most sophisticated and self-possessed characters, Pandarus and Cressida. Troilus uses few, and three of his few seem to have been evoked in desperate parody. Even Antigone and Diomede, who say relatively little, quote two proverbs each to Troilus's four. Neither here nor elsewhere does Chaucer regard proverbs as fitting wisdom for peasants and rustics. He feels that they add *ton* and a touch of sophistication to the characters who use them, pp. 74-75.

In his article, "The Function of the Proverbial Monitory Elements in Chaucer's *Troilus and Criseyde*," *Tulane Studies in English*, II (1950), 5-48, Dr. R. M. Lumiansky examines the proverbs and sententious remarks in the poem for their function in characterization and, along with them, "ancient moral stories, exampla, and 'ensaumples,' " but not proverbial phrases. He summarizes as follows—rather too disparagingly, it seems to me as far as the hero is concerned:

> First, one aspect of Troilus' naivete is his view of a proverb, a maxim, or an example as a complete piece of wisdom upon which he can depend for

guidance in his thinking and acting. The reader is made aware in Book I of Troilus' attitude toward proverbial monitory material, and is reminded of it throughout the poem. Second, Pandarus, as a more sophisticated person, realizes the half-truth inherent in proverbial wisdom; he also recognizes Troilus' dependence upon it, and uses maxims and the like as a method of influencing Troilus. . . . Third, Criseyde also makes use of a large stock of proverbs. In her own private thinking, she often uses maxims to state her conclusions pithily, but she does not lean upon them for guidance as does Troilus. . . . In the last scene of Book IV, . . . she finds it necessary to adopt strategy similar to that which Pandarus employs in Book I and elsewhere: she looses a flood of proverbs at Troilus in order to win his agreement to her proposal. . . . Fourth, proverbial monitory matter plays an important part in the battles of wits which take place between Criseyde and Pandarus in Books II and III. The latter tries to influence his niece by means of proverbial monitory remarks, but she recognizes what he is doing and even employs similar material as a part of her strategy with him. pp. 47-48.

26. I. 752-60. The proverbial utterances of Pandarus, as identified by Whiting, were I. 628ff. and 731-35; and his example of Nyobe came in lines 697-700. The narrator's interpretation of the hero's silence is in 737-49.

27. IV. 463-66. Pandarus had advised taking a new mistress on the proverbial ground that "The newe love out chaceth ofte the olde," IV. 415.

28. Criseyde's proverbialism, IV. 1373-76; and Troilus', IV. 1453-58. When in camp, the lady recognized her error with another proverbialism, V. 741-42.

29. *Op. cit.*, p. 66.

30. I. 465-68, IV. 519-20, V. 767-69.

31. III. 1356-57, 1461-62, IV. 292-94, 305-6, 776. A conceit of Troilus, not within the scope of this chapter, is his fancy that the wind from camp was his lady's sighing, V. 673-79 (*Fil.* V. 70).

32. II. 964, 1534-35, 1310-11, 1638, III. 185-89, 340.

33. Diomede has, however, an ingenious play on words, V. 143-45.

Section 2 *Religion and Mythology*

1. Narrator: *Fil.* IV. 84, 96, 100, 124; and III. 42, 71, IV. 116. Diomede: VI. 14.
2. I. 2.
3. "Dea," I. 38, IV. 139; "Iddio," V. 42.
4. "Angelica," I. 11; "angelico," I. 28, VI. 14 and 22.
5. "Angiola," VII. 84; "angelico," IX. 7.
6. "Celestïale," I. 27; "fatta in paradiso," IV. 100.
7. "Divina," VII. 65.
8. "Santa," III. 8, VII. 31. Pandaro speaks contemptuously of the pretended sainthood of priests who recommend chastity to such as Criseida, II. 135.
9. III. 16 and 56, VII. 69. Complementary to these metaphors, though not themselves associative figures, are Troiolo's declaration that for one winter's night with Criseida he would endure a hundred and fifty in Inferno and Pandaro's that an assignation would be a greater boon to the prince than Heaven had to offer, II. 88, 137. In his address to lovers at the end of the action, Boccaccio credits Amore with some sort of heaven of his own, asking lovers to pray to the god to put Troiolo in that region where the former dwells, VIII. 33.
10. "Martira," II. 100.
11. Narrator: I. 35, II. 85, 130, VII. 17. Troiolo: I. 23, II. 6, III. 84, IV. 54. Pandaro: II. 13, III. 5, IV. 49, 72. The first and last of the hero's applications of the term are respectively to the torment of previous love affairs and to that anticipated in the after life. Applications of it in all other contexts are to current sorrow.
12. III. 80.
13. In his book, *Courtly Love in Chaucer and Gower* (Boston and London: Ginn, 1913), pp. 189-208, William G. Dodd notes the ecclesiastical, along with the feudal, concepts of love involved in Chaucer's presonification of love in the *Troilus*.

14. Eugene E. Slaughter, "Love and Grace in Chaucer's *Troilus*," *Essays in Honor of Walter Clyde Curry* (Nashville: Vanderbilt Univ. Press, 1954), 61-76. He summarizes, in part, as follows: "The imitation of Christian grace and its associated notions contributes much to the extenuation of earthly love in *Troilus*. Love is god, who causes good but cannot cause sin. Since he is irresistible in moving Troilus's will by grace, Troilus's love appears to be good, and the results of it are increased virtue. The effect is a tone of religious love and devotion that infuses Troilus's endeavor and excites in the reader a serious concern for the hero's high purpose in love. Now, of course, this is specious. And irony, which varies in intensity from one passage to another, attaches to the god of Love and his power," p. 75. See D. W. Roberston, Jr., "Chaucerian Tragedy," *ELH.*, XIX (1952), esp. 23-28. As the following excerpt will show, this article concentrates upon censorious implications of the religious linkage, which in Dr. Slaughter's are subordinated to the extenuative. "In fact, the religious imagery is intended to suggest the values from which the hero departs, and, at the same time, to furnish opportunity for ironic humor. . . . Specifically, the religious imagery of Book III is used to show the corruption of Troilus' higher reason as he substitutes the 'grace' of Criseyde for providence. Once this substitution is made, the fall is complete," p. 24.

15. *TC.* I. 1-56, replacing *Fil.* I. 1-5, in which Boccaccio addressed his lady, and I. 6, in which he addressed lovers, beseeching them to pray for him to Amore. See Dodd, pp. 191-96, for a fuller treatment of ecclesiastical echoes in these lines of Chaucer's than I have attempted. He does not venture comment on the intention or spirit of the passage. Dealing with it in "What Chaucer Really Did to *Il Filostrato*," *Essays and Studies*, XVII (1932) 66-68, C.S. Lewis writes, "Chaucer is emphasizing that parody, or imitation, or rivalry—I know not what to call it—of the Christian religion which was inherent in traditional *Frauendienst*." In his "Chaucerian Tragedy," p. 12, D.W. Robertson has this to say, with special reference to 11. 47-51: "The servants of love, already mentioned in line 15, are servants of Cupid, or Satan. Chaucer proposes to describe their 'wo' and live in 'charite.' That is, he will take pity on the followers of the wrong love and seek to maintain the right love in himself. He will 'advance' his own soul best in this way, for, as Boethius explained, one should 'have pite on shrewes.' " With this interpretation, as is obvious from my text, I do not agree.

16. *TC.* I. 245, 308.

17. I. 336-40. See also I. 422-24, cited by Dodd, p. 196, as an instance of ecclesiastical ideology.

18. I. 906-10. See also I. 896, cited by Dodd, p. 199.

19. I. 932-38.

20. I. 995-1008. On these lines and on 906-10, 932-38, see Dodd, pp. 202-3.

21. II.519-25. See Dodd, pp. 197-98; and Arthur E. Hutson, "Troilus' Confession," *MLN.*, LXIX (1954), 468-70—with my caveat of Ch. II. 6. n.201.

22. II. 1501-3.

23. III. 183-89. As recorded in Robinson's textual note, p. 1026, to 189, "merveille" is the reading in five MSS.; *"miracle,"* in the others. For instances in medieval literature of bells ringing without hands, see John S. P. Tatlock, "Notes on Chaucer: Earlier or Minor Poems," *MLN.*, XXIX (1914), 98; Phillips Barry, "Bells Ringing Without Hands,"*MLN.*, XXX (1915), 28-29; and Henry B. Hinckley, "Chauceriana," *MPh.*, XVI (1918), 40. For another hint of Venus' connection with the religion of love, see Troilus' line, III. 712, with the reading "blisful Venus" of the β and γ MSS. replacing the more suggestive "seynt Venus" of the α MSS.—Robinson's textual note, p. 1027. The hero's appeal to Venus for intercession with her father, III. 715-19, is connected by Dodd, p. 200, with the concept of the mediating function of the Virgin.

24. III. 1261-67, V. 593. See Root's note, pp. 484-85, to the former context, for adaptation therein of Dante, *Par.* xxxiii, 13-18, and Robertson, p. 27.

25. III. 1204. In the bidding prayer, Chaucer asks lovers to pray that Love may bring those in Troilus' case "in hevene to solas," I. 31. This "hevene" is, however, literally the other world, not a figurative paradise on earth.

26. III. 1656-59.

27. II. 894-96. Apropos of this and other associations with the infernal region, see Theodore Spencer, "Chaucer's Hell: a Study in Mediaeval Convention," *Spec.*, II (1927), 177-200, esp. 180-87.

28. III. 1577-78.
29. IV. 712-13, 816-19 (*Fil*. IV. 96). Criseyde considers the possibility of residence in a literal hell—with Athamante, IV. 1534-40.
30. IV. 782-84. This ascetic conceit is reminiscent of her literal statement before falling in love that it would better become her, as a widow, to pray and read saints' lives in a cave than to do observance to May, II. 113-18. Pandarus, taking a more earthly view of her youthfulness, said that it did not become her to be "celestial," I. 983.
31. IV. 1138-39. See Root's note, p. 521, for the reference here to Ovid, *Met*. X. 298-502.
32. I. 425-26 (*Fil*. I. 38).
33. I. 102-5 (*Fil*. 1. 11), IV. 864 (*Fil*. IV. 100).
34. V. 816-17. Probably suggested by a similar conception entertained by Dante of Beatrice, *Par*. xviii. 21, as noted by Albert S. Cook, "Chauceriana," *Rom Rev*., VIII (1917), 226.
35. V. 553.
36. III. 267-68 (*Fil*. III. 8).
37. V. 1264-65 (*Fil*. VII. 31).
38. V. 1527-33. There is an echo of this comparison in Chaucer's statement, anticipatory of the *Legend of Good Women*, that he would gladlier write of Penelope and Alceste than of guilty Criseyde, V. 1777-78.
39. III. 1599-1600 (*Fil*. III. 56).
40. III. 704; 1251, 1322. The poet implies that amatory bliss may be spiritually costly, III. 1319-20. It is to be added that Criseyde anticipates that she will be able so to wheedle Calkas that he will dream his soul to be in "hevene," IV. 1394-96.
41. I. 785-88, 871-72, IV. 1697-98, V. 211-12; and V. 1376, 1396. For the first context, Chaucer appears to have drawn on his own translation of the *Consolation*, III. m.xii, as pointed out in Root's note, p. 425.
42. I. 697-700; IV. 300-1, V. 599-602. For the sources of the three contexts, see Root's notes, pp. 423, 506-7, and 539, and Robinson's, pp. 928, 941, 946. As pointed out in Root's note to the second, the reference to Edippe is not present in the *a* text.
43. V. 642-44.
44. II. 628-30.
45. II. 637; III. 1742, II. 826.
46. V. 838. This is a transformation of Joseph of Exeter's characterization "Mente gigas," which exalts Troilus' spirit rather than his brawn.
47. II. 372-73.
48. III. 86-88.
49. IV. 436-88.
50. IV. 622-23. "Presumi pur di fare, gl' iddii ci avranno poscia ad aiutare," *Fil*. IV. 75; "et les Dieux qui veoient voustre *martire* seront à voustre aide," *Le Roman de Troyle et de Criseida*, p. 218. Chaucer's indebtedness here to the *Roman* is noted by Pratt, *St.Ph*., LIII, 525.
51. V. 423-24.
52. V. 1590. To be compared with the likenings of Troilus to Mars and Cupide is that of the lover in Antigone's song to Apollo, with respect to wit, II. 843.
53. I. 652-65.
54. II. 59-60; 495-96, 568-69.
55. IV. 1459, 1471-74.
56. II. 579. See also II. 439-41.
57. III. 151. Later, he swears like a mere mortal that he would rather be in "helle" with Pluto than fail his niece, III. 589-93.
58. V. 88-90.

Section 3 *Subjugation and Feudal Relationship*

1. "Donna," *Fil*. III. 74, "legge," III. 79; "governa," III. 89.
2. "Nemica," II. 132 and V. 23, IV. 104; "vinci" and "soggiacette," IV. 154.
3. "Governa," III. 15.

4. "Trafisse," I. 25; "dardi" and "servi," I. 29.
5. "Signor" (2), "servir" (2), and "acute saette," I. 38-39.
6. "Signor(e)" (5), II. 57-60, with the soul "vinta" and "cinta" in 58; "suggetti," 59.
7. "Ferventi dardi," IV. 150.
8. V. 56-57.
9. "Servir," V. 57.
10. Troiolo's exact words are:
> Amore, incontro al qual chi si difende
> piú tosto pere ed adopera invano, II. 7.

Also to be noted is his statement:
> Amor non ha qual uom ami per legge,
> fuor che colei cui l'appetito elegge, II. 19.
11. "Feristi," V. 63; "amorose ferute," V. 64.
12. "L'amorosa ferita," I. 32, and "l'amorose ferute," I. 44; "il colpo amoroso," V. 29.
13. "Sire," II. 106; "signor(e)," II. 98, IV. 33(2).
14. "Regno d'Amor," III. 1; "fedel servidore," III. 90. Criseida speaks of "amorosi regni," II. 48.
15. The narrator speaks of Troiolo as "d'alto duol ferito," IV. 18; as "vinto" by the exchange and subsequent lamentation, IV. 20, 41; as in "gran battaglia" with his own sighs and plaint, V. 2; as diverting his "anima conquisa," V. 61; as plagued by the "nemico spirto di gelosia," VII. 18; and as "vinto" by sighs, VII. 19. Troiolo speaks of himself as one of "virtú vinta," II. 2; as one left alone to combat—"combatter"—his own distress, II. 8; as one with strength of sight "vinto e conquiso" by weeping, IV. 35; as one borne down by sorrow's "gran percossa," IV. 66; as one alluded to by others as "conquiso," V. 60; as one whom fear robs—"fura"—of delight and hope and conquers—"conquide," VII. 58, 59; and as one whose soul is "legata dal piacere," VII. 67. And Pandaro speaks of him as "vinto" by the times, II. 1; and as his own enemy, "nemico," IV. 49.
16. "In la sua pace," II. 94.
17. "Offese," VI. 11.
18. "Gloria," II. 60.
19. "Trafitta," II. 66, 115.
20. "Sotto lo scudo . . . chiudendo," II. 129.
21. "Amorose saette," IV. 146; "suo signore Amore," VI. 13. On an earlier occasion, Criseida conceives of Amore, not as an archer, but as a spirit which holds tenaciously in its claws anything which it seizes, III. 48. In two contexts, she is represented as beset by psychic forces other than love personified, the narrator speaking of her as "vinta" by grief, IV. 86, and she referring to her own thought process as "nemico," VI. 6.
tion that she is a feudal superior in love.
23. IX. 1, 5.
22. "Fedele e suggetto," I. 4. Maria is called "donna" in I. 2, 4, but without implica-
24. "Sua libertá" put "tra le mani," I. 21; "libero," I. 31.
25. Troiolo: "piagato," II. 103, III. 15. Pandaro: "feruto," II. 40, and "piagato," V. 34.
26. "I focosi dardi d'amor," III. 36.
27. "Libertate," II. 73.
28. III. 28, IV. 158. The "dolce mio signore" of the second stanza may mean either "lord in love" or "lord in rank" or both. "Signor" in III. 28 clearly means only the latter. She once refers to her deceased husband as her "lord," VI. 29.
29. Troiolo: II. 98, 101, 102; III. 47, 88; IV. 165; V. 55, 64, 69; VII. 35, 68, 70. Narrator: I. 44, V. 58, VII. 51.
30. "Corona," II. 134, 135; "re," II. 22.
31. "Suggetto," VII. 73.
32. VIII. 11, 18.
33. VIII. 28. The only other application of the adjective in question is to the reproaches exchanged by Troiolo and Diomede—"rimproveri cattivi e villani," VIII. 26. Troiolo assures Pandaro that he does not desire any "villania" of Criseida, that is, any breach of decorum, II. 31.

34. "Per servente," I. 34; "a servidore," I. 49.
35. "A servir," I. 38.
36. "Ancella," II. 99; "di ben servire," II. 102; "per mio servir," II. 103.
37. "Servo verace," III. 83.
38. "Servidore" and "su maggior," VII. 54; "suggetto," VII. 73.
39. "Furtivamente" and "convien sempre si furi," IV. 153. In quite another vein, Criseida speaks of herself as in the future a "vedova," IV. 90, while comparing herself by implication to "Le nuove spose" on her first night with him, III. 31.
40. Troiolo's esteeming love above power and glory is signalized in several contexts, none of which qualifies, however, as an associative figure. He is made happier by encouragement from Pandaro, the narrator tells us, than if he had been given "mille Troie," II. 81. Awaiting Criseida in her house, he expects to be more joyous than if he were "sol signor . . . del mondo," III. 25; and, when departing from it, he tells her that he would rather be sure of her love than of " 'l troian regno," III. 47. And in his song to Venere, he proposes to spend all his time in contemplation of her beauties, letting him who will pursue

> i regni e le ricchezze,
> l' arme, i cavai, le selve, i can, gli uccelli,
> di Pallade gli studi, e le prodezze
> di Marte, III. 88

She, it may be noted, once assures him that she cares not for "oro . . . cittá né palagio," but only to be with him, IV. 128.
41. "Di sollazzo mendica," II. 132; "a gran divizia," III. 11; "di posa mendico," VII. 18.
42. "Vendea," VII. 106; "vendendosi," VIII. 26.
43. V. 13, VI. 11.
44. "In prigione," VI. 15.
45. "In servidor" and "signoria," VI. 25. Diomede tells Criseida that he would rather be her lover than "re de' Greci," VI. 22, thus—unconsciously—echoing Troiolo as quoted in n.40.
46. *TC.* II. 425; I. 164, 315. See also III. 538.
47. III. 437.
48. II. 8, III. 592, IV. 1594. As Root observes in his note, p. 527, to the last line, Juno's title is the Virgin's, "Regina caeli."
49. V. 1604-6.
50. Fourteen in lines of the narrator, as listed in Ch. II. 6. n.104; eight in Troilus', as listed in Ch. II. 6. n.116; six in Criseyde's, as listed in Ch. II. 6. n.125; and five in Pandarus' as listed in Ch. II. 6. n.135.
51. Narrator: V. 1862, 1864 (*Par.* xiv. 29) with defense asked against "foon" visible and invisible, 1866-67. Troilus: IV. 1175.
52. IV. 1079, 1086.
53. III. 372-73 (*Fil.* III. 15). "*Al* this world," III. 373, "*tout* le monde," *Le Roman de Troyle et de Criseida*, p. 177, " 'l mondo," *Fil.* III. 15, as noted by Pratt, *StPh.*, LIII, 519.
54. III. 1436-40. According to the narrator, both Troilus and Criseyde think of the day which ends their second meeting as a "traitour," III. 1699-1700, but apparently to themselves rather than to God. That which ends their first Troilus figures as a merchant of light to the engravers of small seals, III. 1461-62. Other personifications of agents of time, all given us by Chaucer in his own narrative are of May as "moder" of the glad months, II. 50, of the sun as "The nyghtes foo," II. 904-5, and of Lucifer as "the dayes messager," III. 1417.
55. As remarked in Ch. II. 6, Jove is sometimes thought of as the outmoded pagan, rather than as the equivalent of the Christian Supreme Being. In the former aspect, he may be reprehended, as, for example, in the narrator's lines,

> Lo here, the fyn and guerdoun for travaille
> Of Jove, Appollo, of Mars, of swich rascaille, V. 1852-53.

56. II. 1019, IV. 1561, V. 1434.
57. III. 1165.
58. V. 1835-48.

59. III. 617, IV. 1-5. See also V. 1541-47, in which the narrator asserts that per-
mutation is "comitted" to Fortune by Jove, and V. 1-7, in which he represents that
Jove "Committeth" the destiny of the lovers to the Parcae.

60. I. 837.

61. IV. 1587-89, corresponding to *Fil*. IV. 154.

62. II. 684-85.

63. III. 36 (*Fil*. III. 79), 39-42.

64. III. 1807.

65. I. 15, 34, 48.

66. I. 206-10. See Robinson's textual note, p. 1025, for the α reading of 206-9.

67. I. 225-31.

68. I. 232-38.

69. I. 239-56.

70. I. 302-08.

71. I. 316-29.

72. I. 330-34.

73. I. 422-34 (*Fil*. I. 38-39). "Lord" occurs three times in the English stanzas;
"signor" twice, in the Italian.

74. I. 603-4 (*Fil*. II. 7).

75. I. 910-13, 933, 936.

76. I. 1000-1.

77. "Lord," II. 523, 525, 533; "rebell," 524; "sheld," 532. There are five occurrences
of "signor(e)" in Troiolo's supplication, *Fil*. II. 57-60, to which Troilus' roughly
corresponds.

78. III. 1261-67.

79. III. 1744-71 (*Cons*. II. m. viii). See Ch. I. 6. n.75 and Robinson's textual note,
p. 1027, to III. 1748.

80. III. 1793-95.

81. IV. 288-94. The designation "lord," but not the legal phrasing, comes from
Troiolo's corresponding stanza, *Fil*. IV. 33.

82. IV. 1305-6.

83. V. 582-90 (*Fil*. V. 56-57). Continuing the apostrophe, Troilus addresses Love
as "lord" in 591 and 599.

84. According to the narrator, love made Troilus' food his "foo," I. 484-85. Troilus
anticipates that sorrow may "myne" so long in him as to bring death, IV. 470-71; recalls
that he would once have given "hire" to escape death, IV. 505-6; but eventually thinks
of it as ending all his "werre," V. 1393. And he believes himself to be "defet" in
appearance, V. 617-19 (*Fil*. V. 60, "conquiso"). Pandaro asks him why he would be
his own "fo," IV. 1089.

85. II. 57-58.

86. V. 141-45.

87. V. 166-68.

88. V. 795-98 (*Fil*. VI. 11).

89. The narrator says that Troilus' manliness and suffering made love "myne" in
Criseyde's heart, II. 676-77. Pandarus attributes to the lover the fear that "Daunger"
opposes "Kynde" in the lady's thinking and that "So reulith hire hir hertes gost
withinne" that she will not fall, II. 1373-79. She contemplates abstaining from meat
or drink till she "unshethe" her soul from her breast, IV. 775-76 (perhaps reminiscent
of Dante, *Par*. i. 20-21, as observed in Root's note, p. 514). Troilus asks rhetorically who
can comfort her "hertes werre," V. 234. See also V. 818-19.

90. II. 1324-27 (*Fil*. II. 129).

91. IV. 832-33.

92. The song, II. 827-75, attributed in the "mayde," 880-82. See Ch. I. 4. n.22 on the
real source of the song.

93. I. 323-25; II. 533-36, IV. 472-73. "Criseydes darte" is the only amorous missile
to be named in the *Troilus*. There is, however, the lovely figure of the river Simois
running seaward like "an arwe clere," IV. 1548-49. Pandarus is once imagined to have
scored a touch on the prince—"Tho gan the veyne of Troilus to blede, For he was hit,"
I. 866-67.

94. III. 1358. Troilus exclaims "al brosten ben my bondes," II. 976, upon assurance of his lady's receptivity; and the narrator interprets that she kissed the swooning prince "to deliveren hym fro bittre bondes," III. 1116-17.

95. I. 874, V. 228. Troilus fears to obstruct Criseyde's exchange lest she become his "fo" in earnest, IV. 166.

96. II. 358-59.

97. II. 726-28.

98. II. 754-56 (*Fil.* II. 73). Like Criseida, Chaucer's heroine calls her husband "lord" when mentioning him to Diomede, V. 974-76 (*Fil.* VI. 29).

99. II. 771-73.

100. II. 1215-17, 1221-25.

101. IV. 673-75.

102. IV. 785-87.

103. III. 75-77.

104. III. 169-72.

105. III. 477-83.

106. III. 1063-64.

107. III. 1206-8, 1210-11. Except for Troilus' early reference to ladies as the desired "prey" of lovers, I. 201, his command here is the only passage in which he imagines woman to be the dominated and not the dominator. Confessing surrender at this point, the heroine has given hyperbolical expression to concern for her lover's life by declaring that his recovery from swoon would be dearer to her "Than al the good the sonne aboute gooth," III. 1107-8, and will give it by assuring him that, had he committed suicide, she would not have survived him "to han ben crowned queene Of al the lond the sonne on shyneth sheene," IV. 1236-39. Rhetorically in contrast with these evaluatory expressions are her homely ones: "avayleth nought thre hawes," IV. 1397-98; "naught worth a beene," III. 1167; "if . . . he sette a myte," III. 832; and "As good chep," III. 641-44, on which last, see Thomas A. Kirby, *MLN.*, XLVIII (1933), 527-28. Evaluations by Troilus, Pandarus, and Diomede are cited respectively in notes 143, 164, and 159; cp. the narrator's "al deere ynough a rysshe," III. 1161. Evaluations are not, of course, associative figures.

108. Narrator: I. 493, 825; II. 32, 1065 (*Fil.* II. 98, Troiolo quoted); III. 78, 95, 441, 451, 472, 494, 955, 981, 1157, 1448, 1522, 1663, 1670, 1777, 1783; IV. 10, 172, 1691; V. 24, 210, 452, 457, 636, 1241, 1315 (*Fil.* VII. 51), 1445, 1570, 1666. Troilus: I. 434, 524, 1032; II. 1092; III. 53, 134, 1289, 1355, 1472, 1485 (*Fil.* III. 47); IV. 307, 316 ("lady sovereigne"), 1197, 1201, 1214 ("herte" in *a* MSS.), 1450; V. 218, 229, 312, 467, 565, 567, 576, 581 (*Fil.* V. 55), 653 (*Fil.* V. 69), 669, 675, 1340, 1346, 1362, 1390, 1405, 1674. Pandarus: I. 716, 780, 898; III. 339; IV. 603, 654; V. 1279. Criseyde: V. 1077. Cassandre: V. 1516. As will appear, Diomede also calls Criseyde his "lady," V. 144, 160, 162, 872, 922. And there is generic reference to lovers' ladies by the narrator, I. 45; by Troilus, I. 346; and by Pandarus, I. 811, 812, 815. Like "donna" in the *Filostrato*, "lady" is sometimes used of course, not in the special sense of man's liege in love, but in the general one of female or female of some social consequence. As indicated by Pratt, *StPh.*, LIII, 530, 535, "O lady *myn*" and "Upon his *lady*," V. 229, 1346, correspond to "o *ma* belle dame" and "de sa *dame*," *Le Roman de Troyle et de Criseida*, pp. 248, 281, rather than to "o bella donna" and "del suo maggior," *Fil.* V. 24, VII. 54.

109. Listed in n.29.

110. II. 1735. See Root's note, pp. 456-57, to this cryptic phrase and Robinson's, pp. 933-34, as well as Howard R. Patch, "Two Notes on Chaucer's *Troilus*," *MLN.*, LXX (1955), 8-11.

111. III. 131-46.

112. III. 173-75.

113. III. 259, 339-40.

114. III. 1291-92, 1300-2.

115. V. 1387-93, 1412-13.

116. I. 888-89 (*Fil.* II. 22), II. 1240. As indicated by Pratt, *StPh.*, LIII, 516, "honour," I. 888, seems suggested by "honneur," in *Le Roman de Troyle et de Criseida*, p. 141.

117. V. 1247. The suspicion aroused by the dream was not allayed by Criseyde's letter in answer to his, Troilus deeming it "a kalendes of chaunge," V. 1634.

118. *Fil.* VIII. 11, 28, as already cited in notes 32, 33.

119. *TC.* IV. 19-21.

120. V. 1095-96.

121. In the English poem, concepts of stealth are employed with neutral or with mildly pejorative implications. Troilus or Criseyde speak of "stealing" away together five times, IV. 1503, 1506-7, 1529-30, 1601, V. 739-40, and Criseyde twice speaks of "stealing" out of the Greek camp, V. 701-2, 751-52. Troilus once asks himself why he does not "steal" her away, V. 47-48. Pandarus twice calls the hero "thef," in affectionate jest, I. 870, III. 1098. Cp. *Fil.* IV. 153, as cited in n.39, with its glorification of clandestinity.

122. Troilus: III. 1487, V. 1345-47 (*Fil.* VII. 54, "servidore"). Narrator: III. 983.

123. As cited in notes 128-30.

124. Troilus: III. 1487, IV. 569. Narrator: III. 920, 983; V. 865. Pandarus: III. 915. Criseyde, as cited in note 134. There are other applications of the word "knyght" to the hero, but these are merely in reference to his social rank or military prowess, not to his service to Criseyde.

125. Troilus: III. 1288, V. 1318. Pandarus: I. 958, 963. Criseyde: III. 161, 992. Narrator: II. 678; III. 475, 1815.

126. Troilus: I. 426 (*Fil.* I. 38), 458; III. 144, 1290; IV. 321, 442, 447-48; V. 312, 1389, 1721. Narrator: I. 370, III. 440-41. Pandarus: III. 154. Criseyde: V. 1074-77.

127. Troiolo as cited in notes 35-38; narrator as cited in note 34.

128. I. 426, 432-34.

129. I. 465-68.

130. IV. 447. To "traysen" Criseyde, the prince tells his friend, would be fiendish, IV. 435-38.

131. V. 230.

132. Troilus' early assurance to Pandarus that he intended no "vilenye" to the lady, I. 1030-33 (*Fil.* II. 31), is borne out in conduct, as was Troiolo's. Chaucer's apology for anything exotic in his hero's courtship—on the principle that "ecch contree hath his lawes," II. 42—appears supererogatory in the frame of courtly love. The sole "vilanye"—attributed to him by Pandarus—is his proposed abbreviation of the visit at Sarpedoun's, V. 489-90, and this is motivated by a commendable anxiety about his beloved.

133. V. 1074-77.

134. Criseyde: III. 176, 996, 1309; IV. 746, 1537. In Antigone's song, its authoress calls her lover, who is nonpareil in intent "To serven wel," II. 838-40, "al myn owen knyght," II. 871.

135. III. 479-80. In his formal portrait of Troilus, the narrator characterizes him as "Trewe as stiel in ech condicioun," V. 831. After the parliament, the hero wishes "ay love of stiel" for lovers more fortunate than himself, IV. 325.

136. V. 1591.

137. II. 201.

138. II. 153-54, IV. 187-89. Ector, like Troilus, is an idealist where females are concerned. In protesting, "We usen here no wommen for to selle," IV. 182, he stigmatizes the exchange as a commercial transaction. Criseyde modestly opines that her father "bought" her dear, V. 965-66.

139. I. 334-35.

140. I. 740-42.

141. I. 810-19. Reminiscent of Machaut's *Remede de Fortune* (ed. Hoepffner, *SATF.*), 1636-51, 1662, as pointed out by Professor Kittredge, "Chaucer's *Troilus* and Guillaume de Machaut," *MLN.*, XXX (1915), 69.

142. II. 390-92.

143. Pandarus' report of the first visit made him gladder, the prince declares than would a gift of "A thousand Troyes," II. 977-79 (*Fil.* II. 81, "mille Troie"). At the end of their first night he is to tell Criseyde that assurance of her love would be dearer to him than "thise worldes tweyne," III. 1486-90 (*Fil.* III. 47, " 'l troian regno"). He

497

would not expose her to scandal, he promises his friend, "For al the good that God made under sonne," III. 376-78.

144. II. 985-87.

145. II. 1293-95.

146. III. 349-50 (*Fil.* III. 11), 442-45. At Deiphebus', the hero was so abashed by Criseyde that he could not speak even had decapitation been the alternative, III. 80-81, and so eager to assure Pandarus about the future as to aver that he would prefer dying Agamenoun's captive, "stokked in prisoun," to exposing the affair, III. 379-82. These literal alternatives and others cited in n.150 complement the figurative associations with punishments recorded in my text.

147. III. 850.

148. III. 899-902.

149. III. 1067-68. Criseyde opines that he deserves literally to be flogged:
Wol ye the childissh jalous contrefete?
Now were it worthi that ye were ybete, III. 1168-69.

150. III. 1240-45. Confronted with Troilus on this first night, the heroine could not find words even had decapitation threatened, III. 957-59. And on the next, he declared that he could not banish her from his heart, were he to "dyen in the peyne," III. 1499-1502.

151. IV. 1105-6.

152. V. 1387-1400.

153. V. 1688-91. Troilus' question is substantially Troiolo's, *Fil.* VIII. 14, but the fiefing concept is new, an addition typical of Chaucer's feudalizing of love.

154. V. 1755-56, 1800-1. At the beginning of the poem, the poet records that the enemy sometimes "boughten" war dearly, I. 136.

155. For Chaucer's recourse to Benoit's *Roman de Troie* in replacing Boccaccio's statement about Diomede, "nascosamente sé di colei piglia," with "and by the reyne hire hente," V. 90 (*Fil.* V. 13) and in supplying a declaration for the rival on the way to camp, V. 118 ff., see Ch. I. 8, notes 8, 11.

156. V. 131-33, followed by plea for treatment as a "brother," 134.

157. V. 144-47, 159-61, 162-65, 169-75. "Enseled" is used metaphorically in V. 151.

158. V. 792-98, in lieu of the observation about being a "sovrano artista," *Fil.* VI. 10.

159. The Trojans "In prisoun," V. 883- 84 (*Fil.* VI. 15, "in prigione"), with not one to escape "For al the gold atwixen sonne and se," V. 885-86. Among the Greeks, a lover better able to "serven" the heroine, V. 918-21 (*Fil.* VI. 22, a better lover without specification of service).

160. V. 922-23 (*Fil.* VI. 22), 930-38 (*Fil.* VI. 23-24). As indicated by Pratt, *StPh.*, LIII, 533, "to *serven* yow," V. 923, was suggested by "*digne serviteur*," *Le Roman de Troyle et de Criseida*, p. 265, rather than by "*degno amadore*," *Fil.* VI. 22.

161. V. 939-45. In the corresponding stanza, *Fil.* VI. 25, Diomede, asked to be accepted as "servidor," if he were befitting the heroine's "signoria."

162. V. 972-73.

163. II. 98, IV. 397-99.

164. III. 390-92, 1601-3. Pandarus, of course, is represented quite literally to have served Troilus. He would not keep him dangling, he tells Criseyde, "For al the tresour in the town of Troie," III. 872-75. Rhetorically contrasting with this hyperbolic valuation are denigratory valuations of this and that, in his lines, as not worth "an hawe," III. 854, "a myte," III. 899-900, "two fecches," III. 936, "a grote," IV. 585-86, "A straw" or "a bene," V. 362-63 (*Fil.* V. 32, "un moco").

165. III. 271-73 (*Fil.* III. 8, "trattator," that is, not traitor, but broker).

Section 4 *Acquired Skills and their Products*

1. "Circoscrisse," *Fil.* II. 41; "riveste," I. 18, III. 12.

2. "Ben è la gemma posta nell' anello," II. 43.

3. "Insegnare," II. 119.

4. "Traiamo omai a capo questa tela," II. 142.

5. "Serrato," IV. 108. Later on, the heroine conceives that fate may lock her out of

Troy—"fuor me ne serra," VI. 27; and, earlier, the narrator conceives of the defenders as locked in—"serrati," I. 17.
    6. "Velati," IV. 117; "e gli atti tutti andava disegnando stati tra loro," VI. 2. The narrator admits that the night of consummation could not be "disegnata" by any poetic skill, III. 33.
    7. "L'amorosa danza," IV. 138, as printed in Griffin and Myrick's edition, instead of "l'amorosa usanza," given in Pernicone's.
    8. "Perla orïentale," II. 108; "la chiave," V. 43.
    9. "L'acqua del fabbro," III. 68; "dipinta," III. 82; "la chiave," IV. 143; "non mattasse in mezzo lo scacchiere," VII. 97.
    10. "Immagine," II. 58, 99, III. 67, with the noun modified by "dipinta," in the first context.
    11. "Insegna," IV. 55.
    12. "Figurava," V. 45.
    13. "Effigïato," VIII. 15; "effigïata," I. 5.
    14. "Serra," IV. 123.
    15. "Dipinto," IV. 20; "segnato," V. 66. The narrator also remarks of Troiolo, "e 'l viso alquanto si dipinse con falso riso," V. 51.
    16. "Suona tanto chiara," IV. 150.
    17. "E nell' amor di Troiol vi specchiate," VIII. 29.
    18. "Succinto," II. 90.
    19. "Sovrano artista," VI. 10.
    20. *TC.* I. 138-40, IV. 6-7 and 11, V. 468-69. The second of these contexts derives from Machaut's *Remede de Fortune* (ed. Hoepffner, *SATF.*), 1049-62, as pointed out by Professor Kittredge, "Chaucer's *Troilus* and Guillaume de Machaut," *MLN.*, XXX (1915), 69. In the last context, " 'to glaze his hood' means to deceive or delude or befool him," and "medieval lexicographers specifically associated with the word for 'glass' (*vitrum*) the notion of falsification or delusion," Karl Young, "Chaucer's 'Vitremyte'," *StPh.*, XL (1943), 495-97. Cp. the proverb in Antigone's song,
        And forthi, who that hath an hed of verre,
        Fro cast of stones war hym in the werre, II. 867-68,
in which, as Professor Young points out, pp. 494-95, the head of glass "obviously signifies insecurity or vulnerability."
    21. I. 838-39, IV. 323-29.
    22. I. 848-54. From the *Remede de Fortune*, 2531-38, according to Kittredge as cited in n.20.
    23. V. 1-7, III. 733-35, IV. 1546-47. In the first passage, the mention of Lachesis may derive from *Purg.*, xxv. 79, as suggested by Professor Tatlock, "Dante and Guinizelli in Chaucer's *Troilus*," *MLN.*, XXXV (1920), 43. For an interpretation of the second, see Laura A. Hibbard, "Chaucer's 'Shapen was my sherte'," *PhQ.*, I (1922), 222-25.
    24. III. 1635-37.
    25. II. 1347-48, IV. 1097-99. Pandarus earlier employs a dicing metaphor to counsel Troilus to seize Criseyde before she is exchanged—"manly sette the world on six and sevene," IV. 622, for an interpretation of which see Robinson's note, p. 942.
    26. V. 1863-65 (*Par.*, xiv. 28-30).
    27. V. 1811-13 (*Tes.* XI. 1).
    28. I. 156-57 (*Fil.* I. 18), III. 351-53 (*Fil.* III. 12). The second figure, as in the source, is a metaphor within a metaphor.
    29. III. 1415 (*De planctu Naturae*, PL. CCX. 436; "vulgaris astrologus").
    30. III. 1429-35.
    31. II. 804-5, V. 1062. The figure "bere the belle" applied by Pandarus to both lovers, III. 198, whatever its allusion, has no reference to musical effect and hence will not be considered here. His conception of bells ringing without hands for the "merveille" of Criseyde's acceptance of Troilus, III. 188-89, has already been cited in Section 2. For a list of musical figures in all Chaucer's writings, see Clair C. Olson, "Chaucer and the Music of the Fourteenth Century," *Spec.*, XVI (1941), 86-89.
    32. III. 930-33. See Root's note, pp. 481-82.
    33. IV. 1560-61.
    34. II. 464-66.

35. II. 754.
36. II. 584-85 (*Fil.* II. 43).
37. II. 379-80.
38. III. 775-76.
39. II. 676-77. For a literal use of "myne," see III. 767.
40. II. 899-900.
41. II. 1238-39. For the psychological theory behind this and the other figures of impression, see Marshall W. Stearns, "A Note on Chaucer's Use of Aristotelian Psychology," *StPh.*, XLIII (1946), 15-21.
42. II. 1241.
43. II. 1371-72. Criseyde uses a "graving" figure to describe the appeal which she intends to make to her father's cupidity, IV. 1377-78.
44. V. 716-17 (*Fil.* VI. 2, "disegnando"). Criseyde refers to a letter of Troilus' as "with teris al depeynted," V. 1599-1600.
45. V. 768-69.
46. V. 825, on which, see Ch. I. 9. n.6. Troilus' fear is well founded that Calkas may "glose" his daughter so yielding of disposition, IV. 1471-72, although, as it happens, the father was not to be the principal agent of her alienation from the prince.
47. III. 468-69.
48. III. 1405-7, IV. 1430-31 (*Fil.* IV. 138, for which see n.7).
49. I. 171-72. In "The Date of Chaucer's *Troilus and Criseyde*," *PMLA.*, XXIII (1908), 285-300, Professor Lowes argued that the alphabetical metaphor was an allusion to Anne of Bohemia, whose initial was conspicuously displayed, like Richard's, after their marriage in 1382. This hypothesis has been controverted by Professor Tatlock, "The Date of the *Troilus*: and Minor Chauceriana," *MLN.*, L (1935), 278-79.
50. II. 266.
51. III. 1356-57.
52. V. 540-53.
53. Troilus, it may be noted, has a ruby in the signet ring with which he seals his first letter to Criseyde, II. 1086-88, and another shaped like a heart in the brooch which he gives to her and later sees on Diomede's captured vestment, III. 1370-72.
54. V. 460-62 (*Fil.* V. 43).
55. I. 295-98, III. 1541-44. It may be noted that Pandarus uses the word "impressiouns" for thoughts antecedent to dreams which may produce the latter, V. 372-74.
56. III. 1499-1502.
57. I. 365-66, V. 473-75 (*Fil.* V. 45). The exemplary lover in Antigone's song is called "mirour of goodlihed," II. 842.
58. IV. 470-71.
59. I. 517-18.
60. II. 551-53.
61. I. 384-85, 530-31, IV. 166-68.
62. IV. 1166. Diomede's "refreyn" about Troilus' sickness was "Allas," II. 1571.
63. V. 1432-33.
64. V. 1368.
65. I. 558-59.
66. IV. 233-35, 519-20. The second figure may derive from the *Roman de la Rose*, 6382-83, as suggested in Root's note, p. 510. The word "mat" also is applied to Troilus' physical condition, but with little suggestion left in it of its origin in the game of chess, IV. 342.
67. V. 1417-18.
68. III. 1304, IV. 1672-73.
69. III. 981-82.
70. I. 1000-1.
71. "Loves craft," I. 379; "loves art," III. 1333. The word "craft" is variously employed in I. 747, III. 1634, and V. 90; and the word "art," variously in II. 11, **257**, and IV. 1266.
72. I. 327, 488-89.
73. II. 47.

74. III. 50-52, 83-84.

75. II. 1030-36, 1041-43. The possible indebtedness of the first figure to the *Ars poetica,* 355-56, and the likely indebtedness of the second to it, 11. 1-5, have been discussed by Harriet Seibert, "Chaucer and Horace," *MLN., XXXI* (1916), 306-7. The occurrence of 11. 1-5, in the *Documentum de arte versificandi* of Geoffrey of Vinsauf has been pointed out by Marie P. Hamilton, "Notes on Chaucer and the Rhetoricians," *PMLA., XLII* (1932), 405; and in the *Policraticus* of John of Salisbury, by Robinson in his note, p. 932, to II. 1041-43.

76. I. 1065-69, from the *Nova poetria,* 43-45, as noted by Professor Kittredge, "Chauceriana," *MPh., VII* (1910), 481. Cp. II. 1461-62 and III. 227-28 for other uses of the word "lyne."

77. III. 530-32.

78. I. 631-34. The proverbial comparison to the whetstone occurs in Horace, *Ars poetica,* 304-5, where Chaucer may have encountered it.

79. II. 1106-7. At her laughter at this sally, Pandarus exclaims "Loke alwey that ye fynde Game in myn hood," II. 1109-10, that is to say, always cause for mirth. Cp. II. 954.

80. II. 1304.

81. III. 694-95.

82. II. 262-63, 424.

83. II. 1275-76.

84. II. 1615-16, 1681-82.

85. IV. 460-62.

Section 5 *Corporeal Existence*

1. To avoid repetition in footnotes, it may be stated once and for all in this one that the concept of bitterness is regularly expressed by one word, an adjective in its various forms, "amaro," "amara," "amari," or "amare"; and that the concept of sweetness is predominantly expressed by an adjective, "dolce," "dolci," "piú dolce," or its derivatives, the adverb, "dolcemente," the noun, "dolcezza," "dolcezze," or the noun, "dolzore." The latter concept is alternatively sometimes expressed by the adjective, "soave," or the adverb, "soavemente," as is indicated in every case—see notes 9, 27, 29, 36-39.

2. *Fil.* I. 25.

3. "'L mio bene e 'l mio conforto," I. 2; "isperanza," I. 4; "piú dolce piacere," I. 6.

4. IV. 23.

5. "Lagrimoso," I. 6, IX. 6.

6. IX. 1, 2; "nasca," IX. 2.

7. IX. 6.

8. III. 1, VIII. 33.

9. "Dolce," II. 106; both "soave" and "dolce," IV. 33.

10. II. 60; "L'acqua furtiva assai piu dolce cosa è che il vin con abbondanza avuto," II. 74.

11. III. 30, 33, 35.

12. VI. 4.

13. VII. 70-72.

14. VIII. 3.

15. IV. 86.

16. IV. 97.

17. IV. 127.

18. VI. 1-2. The infinitive, "rammaricar," is used of the heroine's complaining in VI. 3, without suggestion, however, it may be guessed, of its root meaning of bitterness.

19. VI. 20, 9.

20. VII. 56.

21. "Rivolvendo," II. 68.

22. IV. 85.

23. II. 27.

24. V. 23.

25. "Cuor del corpo," III. 35; "cuor del corpo mio," IV. 145, V. 25, 59.
26. "Anima," III. 32, V. 69, VII. 61, 75, and modified by "dolce," V. 24, 25.
27. "Soave vita," V. 58; "ben(e)," III. 29, V. 59, VII. 66, and with "dolce," III. 57, IV. 36, V. 24, VII. 62, 72; "speme," VII. 62. "speranza," III. 29, and the latter with "dolce," II. 97; "conforto," V. 24, and with "dolce," IV. 45; "amor," III. 67, IV. 166, "disiro," IV. 124, "disio," V. 59, all with "dolce"; "diporto," V. 24. The narrator also once refers to Criseida as the lover's "conforto," IV. 113.
28. II. 32.
29. II. 58, 101, 104. Coying with Pandaro, Criseida avers that his friend can discover another lady who will be obliging and "soave," II. 51.
30. III. 3, 6.
31. As cited in n.11.
32. III. 54, 64.
33. III. 67.
34. III. 73, 74.
35. III. 94, IV. 46.
36. "Soave," IV. 37.
37. "Soavemente," IV. 51; "soave," IV. 143.
38. "Soave," IV. 61.
39. Troiolo laments the deprivation thus:

> La dolce vista e 'l bel guardo soave
> de' piú begli occhi che si vider mai,
> ch' i' ho perduti, fan parer sí grave
> la vita mia, ch'io vo traendo guai, V. 62.

He speaks of delusively sweet hope—"pensier dolce," VII. 9. Every sweet song—"ogni canto soave"—that he heard at the house of Sarpidone was an annoyance to him, according to the narrator, V. 43.
40. VII. 70, 71, VIII. 3. In the letter, Troiolo speaks of avoiding "sweet" songs, VII. 62, but, according to the narrator, he felt some "sweetness" on hearing those of female visitors, VII. 85. See also VIII. 2, for his "sweet" preoccupation.
41. II. 15, 64, 131. Pandaro misconjectures at first that it is the "bitter" time for the besieged city which has depressed the prince, II. 1.
42. III. 13, 17.
43. IV. 111, 140.
44. VII. 14.
45. VII. 27, VIII. 17; VII. 106. Forms of the verb "rammaricare" are used for Troiolo's complaining five times—four by the narrator, IV. 63, V. 2, VII. 15, VIII. 11, and once by the prince, VII. 55; and the noun "rammarchio" is once so employed by the narrator, VIII. 25. See n.18.
46. "Nasce," II. 100; "nata," V. 52.
47. "Con gli occhi della mente," V. 42.
48. "Rivolgendo," III. 54; "seco volvendo," IV. 15. There are various dead metaphors of hand or hands applied to Troiolo, III. 8, 21, V. 58, to Ettore, IV. 1, and to the Greeks, IV. 11.
49. "Mole," IV. 18; "quantunque fosse grave questo peso," IV. 71.
50. "Col dare il dosso," IV. 154.
51. "Acutamente," IV. 14; "agre," VII. 104.
52. IV. 158; VI. 6, IV. 98, VI. 13.
53. "Cuor del mio corpo," III. 50, IV. 90; "anima," III. 48, IV. 99.
54. Criseida: "la mia vita," IV. 89, and "dolce mia vita," III. 43; "mio bene," IV. 146, and "ben mio dolce," IV. 157; "dolce mio riposo," IV. 161; "del mio cor diletto," IV. 146; "amor mio," III. 43; "dolce l'amor mio," IV. 88, and "dolce mio amore," IV. 92; "dolce mio disio," III. 28, IV. 88. Narrator: "sua dolce salute," VI. 1; " 'l suo diletto," IV. 87.
55. II. 117, IV. 158.
56. "La morte," I. 46.
57. II. 140, III. 60.
58. II. 35; "per te gittato ho 'n terra il mio onore," III. 6.
59. VII. 37.

60. II. 10.
61. *TC* I. 211-13 (*Fil.* I. 25).
62. IV. 4-7.
63. V. 1823-24. Writing in lighter vein, Chaucer says of Troilus that, when in bed with Criseyde, he "Putte al in Goddes hand," III. 1184-86. The hero, thus situated, termed Venus "Citherea the swete," III. 1255.
64. II. 791, 796-97.
65. III. 813-15.
66. III. 1625-28.
67. II. 904-5, III. 1453.
68. III. 724.
69. II. 765.
70. III. 1758 (Boethius, *De cons, Phil.* II. m. viii. 9, "fluctus auidum mare"), V. 1815-16.
71. II. 539, IV. 119.
72. I. 7 (*Fil.* I. 6).
73. II. 17-21.
74. III. 1193-97.
75. V. 1789-92.
76. III. 508, 1219-20.
77. III. 1701.
78. IV. 708-11, 1135-37.
79. IV. 844. At the same juncture in the source, *Fil.* IV. 97, Pandaro spoke of the prevalence of "amaro languire."
80. V. 731-33. In the corresponding stanza in the source, *Fil.* VI. 4, Criseida spoke of "dolcezze" enjoyed in Troy.
81. V. 913 (*Fil.* VI. 20).
82. II. 267-69.
83. II. 716-18, 782-84.
84. III. 1221, IV. 207-8. The authoress of Antigone's song conceives of herself as bathing in bliss, II. 849.
85. IV. 898, V. 62. With a reversal of the concept of sharpness, Troilus fears that when Criseyde is with the sophisticated Greeks, she will "dullen" of Trojan rudeness, IV. 1489-90.
86. IV. 1618-19.
87. II. 131-32.
88. V. 744-45. For the three eyes of Prudence, Chaucer appears to be indebted to Dante, *Purg.* xxix. 130-32, as pointed out by Professor Tatlock, "Chaucer and Dante," *MPh.*, III (1906), 367-68.
89. II. 387. Of the many occurrences of the word "felen" in the Troilus, this is the only one to suggest ascertainment by exploratory touch.
90. II. 601-2 (*Fil.* II. 68).
91. II. 659-64.
92. II. 696-97. See also V. 1023-27. The expressions, "to have in or on hand," II. 217, III. 937-38, "to hold in hand," II. 477, 1222-23, V. 1678-80, and "to bear on hand," III. 1154-55, IV. 1404-5, which are applied in various forms to Criseyde, are petrified metaphors eliciting little if any reminiscence of manual action.
93. II. 150-51.
94. II. 347.
95. II. 1592-94, IV. 1620.
96. II. 810.
97. II. 924.
98. II. 481-83. It may be added that, when she feels herself succumbing to Troilus' attractions, she asks rhetorically who gave her a love potion, "Who yaf me drynke?" II. 651.
99. III. 1212-18.
100. IV. 726-28 (*Fil.* IV. 85).
101. V. 741-42. The narrator's remarks at other points about "remedie" or "cure" for Criseyde, V. 61, 713, may or may not have been intended to carry medical suggestion.

102. Troilus: "herte," I. 461, 535, II. 982, III. 1181, 1285, 1347 (*Fil.* III. 35, Troiolo and Criseida to one another, "Amor mio"), V. 228 (*Fil.* V. 24, "dolce anima mia," etc.), 569, 1401 (*Fil.* VII. 75, "anima mia"); "swete herte" or "herte swete," III. 69, 98, 127, 147, 1173, 1278, 1525, IV. 1209, 1449, V. 1324, 1344, 1421. The narrator: "herte swete," III. 1820. In the *a* version, Troilus called Criseyde his "herte" also in IV. 1214, but this "herte" was changed to "lady" in later versions—as stated in Robinson's textual note, p. 1029. The paragon of Antigone's song is its authoress' "herte," II. 871, and Pandarus observes that it is wrong for a woman to deceive one whom she calls her "herte," III. 771-77. As indicated by Pratt, *StPh.*, LIII, 527, "*swete* herte," IV. 1209, has no correspondent in *Fil.* IV. 123, but "ma *doulce amour*" in *Le Roman de Troyle et de Criseida*, p. 230.

103. II. 1065-68; V. 607 (*Fil.* V. 58, "la mia soave vita").

104. Troilus: "swete," I. 533, 538, III. 1206, 1343 (Troilus and Criseyde to each other); V. 1399 (*Fil.* VII. 72, "dolce mio bene"); "swete fo," I. 874, V. 228 (*Fil.* V. 24, "dolce bene," etc.); "so swete a wight," III. 1284; "swete may," V. 1720. The narrator: "lady swete," III. 1245.

105. II. 384.

106. I. 469.

107. II. 344-45.

108. II. 570-71.

109. II. 736-41.

110. II. 1066.

111. II. 1313-16.

112. II. 1578-82.

113. IV. 927, 931. For analogues to the first line, see Root's note, p. 516.

114. IV. 944-45. Criseyde's assurances to Troilus that there may be a "remede" or "remedie" for their sorrow, IV. 1272-73, 1623-24, do not seem to carry any medical connotation.

115. III. 1006-8.

116. IV. 760, 1266-67.

117. II. 1638. A pun on "bier" and "bear" (pillow bere) is probably not intended —see Helge Kökeritz, "Rhetorical Word-Play in Chaucer," *PMLA.*, LXIX (1954), 951.

118. III. 508, 1219-20, 1701, IV. 1135-37, as already cited in notes 76-78.

119. I. 384-85.

120. I. 411.

121. I. 1042-43 (*Fil.* II. 32, " 'l dolce fine").

122. III. 178-79.

123. III. 1667-68. In the stanza correspondent in the source, *Fil.* III. 64, Boccaccio refers to the pleasures which Troiolo is to enjoy on his second night as "suoi dolzori."

124. IV. 426.

125. IV. 507-8 (*Fil.* IV. 61, "soave").

126. I. 403-6.

127. III. 1030-35. In III. 1024-26, Criseyde likens jealousy to "venym."

128. V. 1406-7.

129. IV. 337-39. See I. 190-94 for a metaphor of male eyes feeding on womankind.

130. V. 1132-33.

131. III. 1221, 1671. Chaucer once apostrophizes lovers who "bathen in gladnesse," I. 22.

132. III. 906-7, 1182-83.

133. IV. 373, 426, 466, 1501.

134. V. 197-98, 416-18, 1419-20.

135. III. 425-26; V. 1201, 1269. On one occasion, Troilus's heart was now "dul" and now "light," V. 1118.

136. I. 202.

137. I. 211-13 (*Fil.* I. 25), as already cited in n.61.

138. V. 1195.

139. I. 452-54. In his Epilog, Chaucer bids the young, "of youre herte up casteth the visage," V. 1838.

140. III. 1541-42 (*Fil.* III. 54, "ciascuno atto rivolgendo").

141. V. 1313-14. The expression "hold in hand," V. 1371-72, in the letter which he writes is quite dead as a metaphor, as is the same in Criseyde's reply, V. 1614-15.

142. I. 215-16.

143. I. 649-51. Occurrences of "hevy" or "hevynesse" in other contexts about Troilus are uniformly weak in physical suggestion.

144. I. 694-95.

145. II. 1349. See Robinson's note, p. 933, to this line.

146. II. 1553-54.

147. III. 1090-91.

148. V. 1198.

149. III. 1443-45.

150. I. 362-63, 561-64.

151. I. 295-96, 442-43, IV. 631.

152. III. 1546-47. A metaphor of desire breeding fawns in Troilus, I. 465-68, will be considered with the other animal imagery in the next section.

153. I. 411.

154. I. 1083. The authoress of Antigone's song claims that all sorrow is "fro me ded," II. 845.

155. II. 1310-11.

156. II. 1638, as cited in n.117.

157. III. 347, 1171.

158. IV. 1583.

159. V. 1342-43.

160. As cited in notes 106-114.

161. As cited in n.99.

162. V. 49. Three mentions of "remedie" apropos of difficulties of the prince, V. 327-29, 1210-11, 1270, do not seem to be medical in association. Pandarus' jesting characterization of Troilus as he "that hath caught hym an hete," II. 942, if an allusion to his enamorment, is an ambivalent one.

163. Criseyde: "herte," III. 176, 803, 843, 888, 988, 996, 1003, 1039, 1110, 1304, 1349 (Fil. III. 35, Troiolo and Criseida to one another, "cuor del corpo"), 1493, 1510, IV. 759, 792 (Fil. IV. 92, "dolce mio amore"), 796, 858, 1216, 1254, 1311, 1334, 1352, 1528, 1552, 1574; "swete herte" or "herte swete," III. 1183, 1210, IV. 779 (Fil. IV. 90, "cuor del mio corpo"), 1274, 1590, V. 1189 (Troilus quoting Criseyde). The narrator: "herte," III. 1553; "swete herte," V. 63. The beloved of Antigone's song is "of lust fynder and hed," II. 844. As indicated by Pratt, StPh., LIII, 526, "herte" applied to the hero in IV. 858 has as its correspondent "cueur" in Le Roman de Troyle et de Criseida, p. 224, instead of "anima" in Fil. IV. 99.

164. III. 1303, 1422 (Fil. III. 43, "O amor mio"). Life to his mistress, Troilus seems death to the enemy, as the narrator testified:

> Fro day to day in armes so he spedde
> That the Grekes as the deth him dredde, I. 482-83 (Fil. I. 46).

Celebrating his friend's prowess against them on a particular day, Pandarus tells Criseyde,

> He was hir deth, and sheld and lif for us, II. 201.

165. III. 1309, IV. 1640.

166. III. 1163, IV. 1394, V. 572 (as remembered by Troilus).

167. V. 132-33.

168. V. 939.

169. V. 1023-29, to be compared with already cited II. 659-64.

170. V. 1044-50. See Ch. I. 9. n.19 for the passages in Benoit's Roman de Troie correspondent to this stanza.

171. I. 628-29, 638-39. Correspondent to the first lines are Pandaro's:

> e giá veduto s' è andare il losco
> dove l' alluminato non va bene, Fil. II. 10.

172. II. 565-67.

173. II. 1355-58.

174. IV. 363-64.

175. I. 659-69. As shown in my article, "Chaucer and an Italian Translation of the

Heroides," PMLA., XLV (1930), 112-13, our poet had recourse here to Filippo Ceffi's expanded rendering of *Heroides,* V. 151-52, a distich, incidentally, now considered spurious.
176. I. 704-7.
177. I. 757-58.
178. I. 783-84, 789-91.
179. I. 857-58. The observation is taken from Boethius, *De cons. Phil.,* I. pr. iv. In his *Origin and Development,* pp. 164-65, Professor Young suggests that it owes something also to the *Filocolo,* p. 168 (ed. Battaglia), I. 215-16 (ed. Moutier).
180. I. 1086-91.
181. IV. 436-37. Troilus uses a phrase of a medical charm—"Nettle in, dok out"—to characterize the inconstancy in Pandarus' own love life which he ironically infers from the latter's advice to him, IV. 461. See Robinson's note, p. 941, on the phrase. On the day after the parliament, the friend recommends to Troilus the example of lovers who continue hopeful though parted, observing,
> And, for they kan a tyme of sorwe endure,
> As tyme hem hurt, a tyme doth hem cure, V. 349-50.
182. II. 1289. Trading on consanguinity, Pandarus has called his niece "my blood," II. 594. For occurrence of this noun in slightly different sense, see V. 599-601.
183. III. 556-58, V. 1132-33.
184. IV. 131-33. Chaucer refers to Criseyde as the "doughter sweete" of Calkas, V. 191.
185. IV. 1394-1400. See III. 1375 for a metaphorical phrasing of avaricious endeavor.
186. IV. 1456-58, 1462.
187. V. 897-900.
188. II. 1495-96.
189. II. 1742-43.
190. III. 206-7.
191. III. 528.
192. IV. 648.
193. V. 526-27.
194. II. 799-800, III. 582-85 (reported in indirect discourse).
195. V. 1061.

Section 6 *The Brute Creation*

1. "Artigli," *Fil.* III. 48; "ale," IV. 78. The moon, when old and new, is represented as horned, V. 69.
2. "Affrena," II. 27.
3. IV. 138.
4. "Rodendo," V. 14.
5. "Nel laccio preso," I. 50; " 'nretito," I. 52.
6. "Reti," II. 89.
7. "Amorosa rete," III. 36; "reti," III. 61.
8. "Irretire," IV. 164.
9. Troiolo va ora mordendo i difetti
   e' solliciti amor dell' altre genti, I. 25.
                ecco il provveduto
   ch' e' sospir nostri ed amorosi pianti
   morder soleva giá, I. 51.
10.   tu puoi ben vedere
   che pur di ciò pensar tutto mi rodo, IV. 156
   seco rodiesi, V. 3.
11. "Spronar," II. 85. The narrator speaks of Pandaro as goading his friend— "stimolandol," II. 18.
12. "Raffrenando," II. 23.
13. III. 60.
14. "Raffrena," VII. 74.

15. VIII. 29.
16. III. 91. The three lines of the simile are the last of the stanza. The first five record that the protagonist was wont to hawk with falcons, gerfalcons, and eagles and to hunt—with dogs—only the most dangerous of beasts.
17. IV. 26-27.
18. VII. 19-20.
19. VII. 78-80.
20. "Scapestratamente," VII. 89; "la lingua tua pronta raffrena," VII. 92.
21. "Che dài di morso a ciascuna persona," VII. 100.
22. "Bestialitá," VII. 90; "bruttura," VII. 101. Diomede called the Trojans "bruti insensati," VI. 21, and the narrator stigmatized snobbish women as "bestie," VIII. 31.
23. "Cinguettare invano," IV. 86.
24. "Abbaiare," VI. 7.
25. *TC*. III. 617-20.
26. V. 1541-47.
27. I. 209-10.
28. III. 1762-64, from *De cons. Phil.* II. m. viii. 16ff.,

   Hic si frena remiserit,
   Quidquid nunc amat inuicem
   Bellum continuo geret. . . .

In his Prohemium to Book III, the narrator credits Venus with arcane knowledge—*inter alia*,
   As whi this fissh, and naught that, comth to were, III. 35.
29. V. 1852-53. "Raschaille" applied to pagan gods appears in a variant reading of the *Roman de Thèbes*, 4342 (ed. Constans, Appendix I), as pointed out by George L. Hamilton, *The Indebtedness of Chaucer's Troilus and Criseyde to Guido delle Colonne's Historia Trojana* (New York: Columbia University Press, 1903), p. 92. n.2.
30. I. 663. As for the moon, Apollo's sister in myth, the narrator once speaks of her "hornes", III. 624, and the hero of them also and of her as "horned," V. 650-57 (expanded from *Fil.* V. 69).
31. II. 395-96. Pandarus goes on to quote an observation of the king's fool about "crowes feet" in prospect under female eyes, II. 400-5. "Com of," the uncle's adjuration to Criseyde in a later scene, II. 1738, 1742, 1750, is a "figure from falconry or hunting" Robinson tells us in his note, p. 934, to the first of these lines. Likening her postponement of reception of Troilus to delay in putting out a fire, Pandarus observes of the latter:
   The harm is don, and fare-wel feldefare, III. 861.
32. IV. 1490-91.
33. III. 1191-92.
34. III. 1233-39. At the night's end, Criseyde assures Troilus that, ere he can be displaced from her heart, shall "everich egle ben the dowves feere," III. 1496. See Robinson's textual note, p. 1027, to the line for a variant reading.
35. III. 1782-85 (*Fil.* III. 91).
36. IV. 412-13. See n.31 for earlier associations made by Pandarus with birds.
37. IV. 909-10.
38. IV. 1219-22.
39. IV. 1310-13.
40. IV. 1432-35 (*Fil.* IV. 138).
41. II. 750-52.
42. II. 1534-35. For a technical interpretation of this metaphor and the related one in II. 964, see Oliver F. Emerson, "Chaucer and Medieval Hunting," reprinted from *Romanic Review*, XIII (1922), 147-48, in his memorial volume, *Chaucer Essays and Studies* (Cleveland: Western Reserve Univ. Press, 1929), pp. 372-74. And for possibility of a pun on "deer" and "dear," see Helge Kökeritz, "Rhetorical Word-Play in Chaucer," *PMLA.,* LXIX (1951), 951. Inviting Criseyde and Troilus at the house of Deiphebus to come to his own, the uncle anticipates a contest there as to which of them shall "bere the belle" in talk of love, III. 198-99. In his note to the phrase, pp. 935-36, Robinson states that the usual interpretation of it is "lead the flock."
43. IV. 1373-76.

44. IV. 1453-54.
45. IV. 765-66.
46. II. 327-28.
47. IV. 1370-71.
48. V. 748-49.
49. I. 353, 507-9.
50. II. 582-83.
51. III. 1355 (*Fil*. III. 36).
52. III. 1730-36.
53. III. 1481-83.
54. III. 1651-52.
55. IV. 621.
56. V. 36-37 (*Fil*. V. 3, "seco rodiesi").
57. I. 379-83.
58. V. 425-26 (*Fil*. V. 37).
59. IV. 302-8. The concept of birdlike flight does not appear in the corresponding passages, *Fil*. IV. 34 and *Le Roman de Troyle et de Criseida*, p. 208. "Wofulleste" and "evere" are suggested by "plus maleureux" and "oncques" in the latter, as noted by Pratt, *StPh.*, LIII, 524. In an address to Love, Troilus says,

> Whoso wol grace, and list the nought honouren,
> Lo, his desir wol fle withouten wynges, III. 1262-63.

60. I. 218-25.
61. I. 953, III. 1635 (*Fil*. III. 60, "ponghi freno alla mente amorosa").
62. III. 428-29.
63. IV. 1678.
64. I. 730-35. See Robinson's note, p. 928, to I. 731, for the derivation of the simile.
65. I. 747-48, comparable to the *Roman de la Rose* (ed. Langlois), 7557-58, as indicated in Robinson's note to the lines, p. 928.
66. I. 465-68.
67. II. 964. See Robinson's note, p. 932, to the line and Emerson, as cited in n.42. As an alternative to the interpretation of Skeat that "thi sorwe" is Troilus' emotion and therefore a dog to be inhibited from pursuit by maiming, Professor Emerson suggests that it is Criseyde, the cause of his emotion, and therefore a deer to be made more easily pursued by maiming. Though this distinguished authority inclines to the alternative, I still prefer the earlier explanation, as does Robinson.
68. IV. 239-42 (*Fil*. IV. 27).
69. I. 1074, V. 830.
70. II. 193-94. Criseyde anticipates that Troilus will have word of her in exile, since people will probably be travelling between town and camp,

> Alday as thikke as been fleen from an hyve, IV. 1356.

71. I. 300.
72. III. 736-37.
73. IV. 594-95.
74. III. 837, 1010.
75. III. 1162.
76. V. 771-77.
77. III. 526-27.
78. III. 1565.
79. IV. 625-26.
80. IV. 496-97.
81. I. 670-72.
82. III. 582-85.
83. III. 764. The phrase "here and howne," IV. 210, which seemingly means "people of all sorts," may be an animal metaphor. See Robinson's note to it, pp. 940-41, and—for a conjectural emendation—R. C. Goffin, " 'Here and howne' in 'Troilus and Criseyde,' " *MLR.*, XL (1945), 207-10.

Section 7 *Insentient Nature*

1. "Folgore," *Fil.* II. 58.
2. "Fruttevol," II. 95. Criseida's answer to the letter, according to the narrator, made Troiolo hope that the hour to yield fruit—"frutto"—was near, II. 130.
3. "Piove," III. 74; "frutto," III. 78; 'lume," III. 85.
4. III. 94; 'l' alto tuon," IV. 20.
5. "Come al vento si volge la foglia," I. 22; "volubil sempre come foglia al vento," VIII. 30.
6. "La luce chiara e bella," "tenebroso," "la tramontana stella," "porto," and "àncora di salute," I. 2.
7. "Fulvida luce," "raggio," and "lume," III. 1.
8. IX. 3-4.
9. "L' ortica d' amor," II. 132.
10. "Quanto la rosa la vïola," I. 19; "mattutina rosa," II. 38; "rosa di spina," V. 44.
11. "Per ciò che fior caduto è tosto bruno," VII. 93. Pandaro, it may be noted, called Elena "il fior di tutte l' altre donne," IV. 64.
12. I. 53. Apprised of Troiolo's love, Criseida did not show herself hostile in either forest or mountain wise—"né si mostrò selvaggia né alpestra," II. 82.
13. "Fe' de' suoi occhi un' amara fontana," VI. 2.
14. "Qual da mattina l' aër si colora," II. 47. Griffin and Myrick give "scolora" instead of "colora."
15. "Luce," I. 43, II. 88, VII. 65; "luminoso" and "oscuro," V. 53.
16. "La stella giunta col sole," II. 43; "splendor," II. 46.
17. "La stella" and "viso splendido e lucente," III. 29; "chiara stella" and "porto," IV. 143; "luce bella" and "stella mattutina," V. 44.
18. "La luce del sole," VII. 31.
19. "Fresco piú che giglio d' orto," II. 71.
20. "Qual fiore in vivo prato in primavera," I. 56.
21. II. 80, III. 12.
22. IV. 18.
23. "Non fu mai rosa in dolce primavera bella," V. 37.
24. "Due fontane ch' acqua gittassero abbondevol fore," IV. 28; "fiumi," V. 24.
25. "Splendor reale," III. 28; "il lucido splendore," VIII. 28.
26. "Porto," I. 54, II. 132.
27. VII. 10. Fancies involving the wind which do not qualify as associative figures are: the narrator's remark that lamentations of Troiolo were lost in the winds—"venti"— I. 57; the confidant's advice to him to let his dreams and consequent fears go to the winds of which they were composed, V. 32; and Troiolo's conceit reported by the narrator, that a breeze from camp was stirred up by Criseida's sighs, V. 70.
28. Troiolo spoke of his friend's own course in love as a path— "sentiero," IV. 57. Criseida, it may be added, uses this word for the life span of human beings in general, II. 55.
29. *TC.* IV. 846-47. Troilus' terming the day "rosy" when it is ushered in by Phebus, III. 1755 (Boethius, *Cons.*, II. m. viii. 5), the narrator's so terming the god's chariot, V. 278, and the poet's designation of stars as the "candels" of Signifer, V. 1020, do not strengthen the idea, present in their contexts, of an ultimately divine pattern of causation.
30. I. 257-58.
31. I. 384-85.
32. I. 642.
33. I. 816.
34. I. 946-52. The first four lines are from Ovid, *Remedia amoris*, 45-46, as stated by Robinson in his note, p. 928. In the α text, "lilie" appears, instead of "rose," in 949.
35. I. 963-66.
36. II. 36-37.
37. II. 778-81. Defending love, Criseyde's niece Antigone argued that it is no worse for being criticized by wretches than the sun for being unendurable to sight because of its brightness, II. 862-65.

38. II. 1380-89.
39. II. 1744-45.
40. III. 821-26.
41. III. 1058-64. Passages at arms are called "shoures" in two other contexts—in the first with echo of the *Filostrato,* I. 470 (*Fil.* I. 45, "stormi"), IV. 47.
42. IV. 197-201 (Juvenal, *Sat.* x. 1-4).
43. IV. 421-24.
44. IV. 767-70.
45. V. 1840-41.
46. I. 18.
47. II. 1-7 (Dante, *Purg.* i. 1-3). See Swen A. Larsen, "The Boat of Chaucer's 'Connyng.'" *NQ.,* CXCIV (1949), 332, for a nautical interpretation of the gerund in 1.4. In his essay, "Chaucer's Nautical Metaphors," *South Atlantic Quarterly,* XLIX (1950), 67-73, Professor Paull F. Baum makes the point that the maritime figures in the *Troilus* derive from literature rather than experience. Compare "of hope the kalendes" in 1.7 with "kalendes of chaunge," V. 1634, consulting Robinson's note, p. 950, on the latter.
48. II. 1198, 1256.
49. V. 792, 1317.
50. II. 348, III. 1472-73, V. 25-26. The lover celebrated in Antigone's song is called "roote" of virtue, II. 844. See also V. 1245.
51. II. 1272-74.
52. II. 1377-79.
53. III. 890. See Robinson's note to the line, p. 937.
54. III. 1200-1, 1230-32.
55. IV. 1576-77. For evaluations in botanical terms by Criseyde and other speakers, see Ch. III. 3. n.107. These are not associative figures.
56. V. 953-54. Analogous to this metaphor in implication, but not to be considered an associative figure, is Criseyde's declaration to Troilus after union that sooner shall Phebus fall from his sphere and every rock start from its place than he be displaced from her heart, III. 1495-98.
57. I. 523-25 (*Fil.* I. 53).
58. II. 600.
59. I. 873, V. 1330.
60. IV. 1145-46.
61. II. 764-70. Cp. Boethius, *Cons.,* I. m. iii. 3-10.
62. II. 806.
63. IV. 750-51. As Troiolo is reported to have done, Troilus imagines that the wind fanning him from the camp is raised by the heroine's sighs there, V. 673-79 (*Fil.* V. 70). As in the source, this conceit is not an associative figure.
64. IV. 1434-35.
65. III. 1250; IV. 736, 816.
66. I. 174-75 (*Fil.* I. 19).
67. V. 232, 1392, 1405.
68. V. 638-44. The nautical metaphor was suggested to Chaucer by the word "porto" in the corresponding part of his original. There, it means, however, not "harbor" but "I bear," for Troiolo is made to say "disii porto di morte per la partenza," *Fil.* V. 62. Whether Chaucer misunderstood this "porto" or not is of small consequence, for the word set his imagination going in either case—probably, as suggested by Professor Patch, "Two Notes on Chaucer's *Troilus,*" *MLN.,* LXX (1955), 11-12, through association with the noun "porto"—harbor—occurring in *Fil.* I. 54, II. 132, IV. 143.
   Signifying Criseyde's guidance—and, faintly at least, guidance on sea—are Troilus' assumption that she is to be his "steere," i.e., steerer, III. 1291, and the like of the narrator and Pandarus that she can "stere"—steer—his heart, I. 227-28, III. 910. See William A. Read, "On Chaucer's *Troilus and Criseyde,* I. 228," *JEGP.,* XX (1921), 397-98. In IV. 282, Troilus uses the verb of Fortune.
69. V. 543-44, 547-48 (*Fil.* V. 53).
70. II. 967-70 (*Fil.* II. 80).
71. III. 351-54 (*Fil.* III. 12), combined with a literal description of spring in the

Roman de la Rose (ed. Langlois), 45-83, esp. 47-54, 78-80. As indicated by Pratt, *St.Ph.*, LIII, 519, "grene," III. 353, seems suggested by "vertes" in *Le Roman de Troyle et de Criseida*, p. 176.

72. V. 425-26 (*Fil.* V. 37), as recorded in the preceding section.

73. II. 1335-37.

74. III. 1015, 1104-5.

75. IV. 225-29 (*Inf.* iii. 112ff.). On the borrowing from Dante, see ten Brink, *Chaucer Studien*, pp. 82-83, and Praz, "Chaucer and the Great Italian Writers of the Trecento," *Monthly Criterion*, VI (1927), 32-33.

76. V. 505, 1174-76. The second context is a substitution for Pandaro's "Di Mongibello aspetta il vento questo tapinello," *Fil.* VII. 10.

77. V. 1432-33.

78. IV. 467-69.

79. IV. 365-67.

80. IV. 246-47 (*Fil.* IV. 28).

81. IV. 1172.

82. V. 1336, 1373-74.

83. V. 535.

84. IV. 1443-46.

85. III. 433-34. Troilus' trepidation about his lady's shamefastness Pandarus ridicules as care "Lest that the cherl may falle out of the moone," I. 1023-24. "Kankedort" applied to the lover's anxiety at her approach, II. 1752, is interpreted as an astronomical metaphor by Professor Spargo, *MLN.*, LXIV (1949), 264-66, but his view is challenged by Professor Spitzer, *MLN.*, LXIV, 502-4.

86. V. 1565, 1591. Pandarus speaks of Ector as "of worthynesse welle," II. 178, and the lover in Antigone's song is "the welle of worthynesse," too, II. 841.

87. II. 1583-86.

88. IV. 1574-75 (*Fil.* IV. 150, "che del valor tuo suona tanto chiara").

89. I. 415-18. See Ch. I. 2. n.7 for reference to Wilkins' text of the source and his comment on it and the adaptation. For a metaphor of travel not by sea applied to Troilus, see II. 1349, and Robinson's note on the line, p. 933.

90. I. 526-27 (*Fil.* I. 54), 606.

91. I. 969. Cf. *Roman de la Rose* (ed. Langlois), 12760, "A bon port estes arivez."

92. II. 1305-7. Having told of the swoon in Pandarus' house, Chaucer says that the lover began to draw breath "And of his swough sone after that adawe," III. 1119-20.

93. V. 844-45. Troilus vows service to Criseyde "Withouten braunche of vice," III. 132.

94. II. 1104, III. 1566-67. In III. 901, Pandarus spoke of enfeoffing a jealous fool "with a fewe wordes white." Robinson in his note, p. 937, to this line, interprets "white" in it and, by implication in III. 1567 also, to mean "specious, plausible." Haldeen Braddy, however, argues for the sense of "joyful," "Three Chaucer Notes," *Essays and Studies in Honor of Carleton Brown* (New York: New York Univ. Press, 1940), 94-95.

95. IV. 872-73.

96. II. 1492-94, III. 699-700, IV. 353-55, V. 1728-29.

Section 8 *Fire and Heat and Cold*

1. " 'L sentiero . . . dato dal celeste foco," *Fil.* II. 55.

2. "Ferventi dardi," IV. 150.

3. "Folgore," II. 58.

4. "Accende," II. 7; "benedico figliuolto che m' accese," III. 83.

5. II. 60.

6. III. 77; "ardore," III. 89.

7. "E poco parmi le cuoca la pena," II. 27.

8. II. 115-16.

9. "Se crudel foco non m' arda," II. 127.

10. "Ardente" and "ch' ardevan d' egual foco," III. 30.

11. "Fervore," III. 32; "fervente," III. 40; "si raffocò" and "infiammati," III. 42.

12. "Foco," III. 47.
13. IV. 153.
14. "Troppo focoso," IV. 161.
15. "Accese," VII. 70.
16. "Cocenti," IV. 111; "di maggior fuoco," V. 55.
17. "Fredda com' al sereno intero ghiaccio," I. 53. Griffin and Myrick give "interza il" instead of "intero."
18. "S' agghiaccia," II. 138.
19. VI. 34.
20. "Tiepidezza," VII. 50.
21. "Focosi dardi d' amor del qual io tutto incendo," III. 36.
22. "L' ardenti fiamme amorose," I. 40; I. 40-41.
23. "Lo disio fervente . . . nel quale io ardo e 'ncendo," II. 86; " 'nfiammati," "ardor," and "fiamma," II. 87.
24. II. 88.
25. "Arder in sí fatto fuoco," II. 89. Also in this stanza, "Deh, ve' com' io mi cuoco?"
26. "Foco" and "ardor," II. 100.
27. III. 61; "Io ardo piú che mai" and "foco," III. 62.
28. "Focoso," III. 67; "foco," III. 68; "l' acqua del fabbro" and "arde," III. 68.
29. "Ferventi" and "focosi," III. 84; "io accendessi," III. 85.
30. IV. 51-52.
31. "Accese" and "di maggior fuoco," V. 55; "raccende il foco," VII. 67.
32. II. 80. III. 12.
33. "Foco," I. 23; "caldo," I. 49.
34. "Neve al foco," I. 53.
35. "Foco," II. 9; "caldo," II. 23.
36. "Si raccendea," II. 29.
37. "Caldo," II. 74.
38. "Le fiamme accese," II. 133.
39. "Ch' amor vie piú il coce ch' el non facea prima," III. 52; "piú s' accendea," III. 54.
40. "Il giorno ch' io prima m' accesi," IV. 70.
41. "S' io acceso fossi," IV. 71; "quando cuoce . . . la 'nnamorata mente," IV. 72.
42. "S' elle fosser mille volte accese le fiamme mie," IV. 76.
43. "La fiamma amorosa," V. 20; "l' amoroso foco," V. 23.
44. "Focosa," "raffredar," V. 49. Troiolo's suggestion of abbreviating their visit to Sarpidone had moved Pandaro to ask, "Or siam noi per lo foco venuti qui?" V. 47.
45. "Focosi," "cocenti," VII. 17.
46. "Focoso," "caldo," VII. 55.
47. The heat of Troiolo's desires is also suggested, if but weakly, as follows. By "ardor(e)" as employed: by the narrator in I. 31, 36, II. 131; by Troiolo in II. 30, VII. 63; and by Pandaro in II. 13, 53. By the verb "ardere" as used, in some form: by the narrator in II. 114, III. 3; and by Criseida in IV. 152. By "fervore" as used: by the narrator in II. 131; by Criseida in III. 50; and by Troiolo in VII. 58. By "ferventemente" as used by the narrator in II. 84.
48. "Acceso nel dolente foco," IV. 29; "piú che fuoco ardenti," IV. 41.
49. IV. 61.
50. "Acceso," IV. 121.
51. "Infiammati," V. 50.
52. "Fuoco," VII. 19.
53. "Foco di nuovo acceso," VII. 32; "acceso," VII. 46.
54. " 'Nfiammato," VII. 80; "ardente," VII. 104.
55. "Acceso," II. 15.
56. V. 13.
57. "E sí come s' accese prima di lei," VI. 11.
58. "Vermiglio come fuoco nel viso," VI. 23.
59. II. 32.
60. VI. 7.

61. *TC.* I. 976-79 (*Fil.* II. 27).
62. III. 1058.
63. III. 24 (*Fil.* III. 77).
64. III. 1769.
65. II. 890-92.
66. II. 698, 810-11.
67. III. 1060-62.
68. IV. 678, 703-5.
69. V. 720-21.
70. IV. 1261-63.
71. III. 799-800.
72. I. 523-25 (*Fil.* I. 53).
73. I. 226-29.
74. I. 435ff. (*Fil.* I. 40-41).
75. III. 846.
76. III. 855-59.
77. II. 967-72 (*Fil.* II. 80); III. 351-56 (*Fil.* III. 12), 1060-62.
78. II. 1313-16, to which II. 940-42 may be analogous. According to the confidant, Troilus himself jested of lovers' heats and chills, saying that some had a "blaunche fevere" and others "tooke on hem, for the cold, More than ynough," I. 916-19. Chaucer's analogy of recovery from a fever, which he applies to hero and heroine's recovery from sorrow, III. 1212-16, is also evocative of thermal sensation, though very weakly.
79. I. 525 (*Fil.* I. 53).
80. I. 407-8, 419-20.
81. I. 488-90.
82. I. 607 (*Fil.* II. 7), I. 1012 (*Fil.* II. 29).
83. II. 537-39 (*Fil.* II. 58).
84. II. 1331-37 (*Fil.* II. 131 and 85).
85. II. 1343-44.
86. III. 347-48.
87. III. 425-32. As noted by Pratt, *St.Ph.*, LIII, 520. "l' amorose offese," *Fil.* III. 20, is changed to "l' amoureuse flamme" in *Le Roman de Troyle et de Criseida*, p. 179.
88. III. 1539-40, 1546 (*Fil.* III. 54).
89. III. 1630.
90. III. 1650 (*Fil.* III. 61-62).
91. IV. 418.
92. IV. 583-84 (*Fil.* IV. 71).
93. V. 507-8 (*Fil.* V. 49). Pandarus reproved the lovers haste to leave Sarpedoun's abode with a fanciful question expanded from that of Pandaro,
> Be we comen hider
> To fecchen fir, and rennen hom ayein? V. 484-85 (*Fil.* V. 47).
94. V. 1102-3.
95. III. 1443-45.
96. IV. 225-29 (*Inf.* iii. 112-17).
97. IV. 337-38 (*Fil.* IV. 41), 365-67.
98. IV. 509-11 (*Fil.* IV. 61).
99. V. 533-35, 1658-59.
100. "Cares colde": the narrator, I. 264, III. 1202, IV. 1692, V. 1747; Troilus, III. 1260, V. 1342. "Colde care," I. 612.
101. IV. 1429-30.
102. IV. 1567-68, 1583.
103. V. 1761-62.
104. *Fil.* II. 32.
105. *TC.* III. 694-95.
106. III. 484-85.
107. III. 710-11.
108. I. 582, IV. 362-63.
109. III. 628, IV. 183-84, III. 1633-34. That the second context is an allusion to the Peasants Revolt was suggested by Professor Carleton Brown, "Another Contemporary

Allusion in Chaucer's *Troilus, MLN.,* XXVI (1911), 208-11; controverted by Professor Tatlock, "The Date of the *Troilus.* . . ,"*MLN.,* L (1935), 277-78. Criseyde's "ferventliche," IV. 1384-85, is a weak, if not a completely dead, metaphor for sentiments attributed to friends of Calkas.

CHAPTER IV *Composites*

Section 2 *Postures of the Narrator*

1. "Se 'l ver dice la storia," *Fil.* I. 46; "se non erra la storia," III. 90.
2. I. 48.
3. I. 25; II. 85; III. 93, 94; VII. 106; VIII. 28, 30-32.
4. I. 1-5, III. 1-2.
5. IV. 23-25.
6. IX. 5-7.
7. I. 6.
8. III. 33.
9. III. 38-39.
10. VIII. 29, 33.
11. III. 11.
12. III. 31, 33.
13. IV. 44, 87.
14. IV. 95, 99.
15. VI. 3. The narrator said also that sorrow of relatives for Ettore's death could not be told, VIII. 1. No character in the *Filostrato* is made to profess an emotion indescribable. Troiolo, however, confessed inability to do justice to the merits of his lady, and Pandaro paid a similar tribute to the prince, III. 86, II. 42.
16. *Die Funktionen des Erzählers in Chaucers Epischer Dichtung,* Studien zur englischen Philologie, LXXII (1927), 133.
17. "Chaucer and the Custom of Oral Delivery," *Spec.,* XIII (1938), 413-32. See also Charles M. Hathaway, Jr., "Chaucer's Verse-Tags as a Part of his Narrative Machinery,"*JEGP.,* V (1905), 476-84.
18. "Chaucer's Art in Relation to his Audience," *Univ. of California Publs. in English,* VIII, No. 1 (1940), 1-53, esp. 20ff., 31ff. See also George P. Wilson, "Chaucer and Oral Reading," *S. Atlantic Quart.,* XXV (1926), 283-99.
19. Bronson, "*The Book of the Duchess* Re-opened," *PMLA.,* LXVII (1952), 863-81; Charles A. Owen, Jr., "The Role of the Narrator in the *Parlement of Foules,*" *College English,* XIV (1953), 264-69; Ben Kimpel, "The Narrator of the *Canterbury Tales,*" *ELH.,* XX (1953), 77-86; E. Talbot Donaldson, "Chaucer the Pilgrim," *PMLA.,* LXIX (1954), 928-36; and Mary Giffin, *Studies on Chaucer and his Audience* (Quebec: L' Éclair, 1956).
20. *The Art of Satire* (Cambridge: Harvard Univ. Press, 1940), Ch. IV, iv. In Section i of the chapter, Worcester sets up four categories of irony, verbal, of manner, dramatic, and cosmic; defines them—the second as "a deliberate pose on our author's part, a manipulation of the literary personality"; and, though to concentrate in iv upon Chaucer's irony of manner, says here that in the *Troilus,* the poet rides "all four horses abreast." On his irony, see also Miss Dempster and Professor Lowes as cited in my Ch. I. 1. n.20; Howard Patch, *On Rereading Chaucer* (Cambridge: Harvard Univ. Press, 1939), pp. 63-69; Earle Birney, "The Beginnings of Chaucer's Irony," *PMLA.,* LIV (1939), 637-55, and "Is Chaucer's Irony a Modern Discovery," *JEGP.,* XLI (1942), 303-19; and Charles A. Owen, Jr., "The Crucial Passages in Five of the *Canterbury Tales*: A Study in Irony and Symbol," *JEGP.,* LII (1953), 294-311.
21. Miss Galway's three principal publications on Joan are: "Chaucer's Sovereign Lady A Study of the Prologue to the *Legend* and Related Poems, *MLR.,* XXXIII (1938), 145-99; "Joan of Kent and the Order of the Garter," *Univ. of Birmingham Hist. Journal,* I (1947), 13-50; and "The 'Troilus' Frontispiece," *MLR.,* XLIV (1949), 161-77. Her linkings of Chaucer with Joan drew favorable comment from Carleton

Brown, *MLN.*, LVIII (1943), 277-78; unfavorable, from Marshall W. Stearns, *Spec.*, XVII (1942), 570-74; Roger S. Loomis, *MLN.*, LIX (1944), 178-80; Bernard F. Huppé, *MLR.*, XLIII (1948), 393-99; Walter E. Weese, *MLN.*, XLIII (1948), 474-77. She replied to Loomis in *MLN.*, LX (1945), 431-39, and to Huppé in *MLR.*, XLIII (1948), 399-400. See also her brief communications in *LTLS.*, Oct. 10, 1942, p. 499, and 29 Sept., 1945, p. 468, and in *NQ.*, CXCIII (1948), 2-3. Her comments most directly applicable to the *Troilus* are in the second long article, pp. 49-50, and the third, *passim*. In the second, she connected the date May 3, given for Pandarus' teen in love, with an event in Joan's life, as I have recorded in Ch. I. 4. n.6; asserted that Chaucer's reference to himself in *TC*. III. 41 means "the poet of Joan"; and reasoned that his characterization of Criseyde as a charming but weak, because security-craving, woman makes hers a partial portrait of that princess. In the third, she identified as Joan one of a number of figures in a picture in Corpus Christi Cambridge MS. 61 of the *Troilus*, to whom Chaucer is reading, and, on the basis of this and further interpretation of the picture, proposed the theory of a commissioning of the poem by the lady. For the article, see also n.42 below.

22. "The People in Chaucer's *Troilus*," *PMLA.*, LVI (1941), 88, n.6. See also his *Mind and Art of Chaucer* (Syracuse: Syracuse Univ. Press, ᶜ1950), pp. 16-17. Professor Tatlock's point made in the above article is approved and expanded by Marshall W. Stearns, "A Note on Chaucer's Attitude toward Love," *Spec.*, XVII (1942), 571-72. The idea had been partly anticipated by Earle Birney, "The Beginnings of Chaucer's Irony," p. 654.

23. "The Two Moralities of Chaucer's *Troilus and Criseyde*," *Trans. Royal Soc. of Canada*, Ser. III. Vol. XLIV (1950), Sect. 2, p. 45. Compare Bronson, "In Appreciation of Chaucer's *Parlement of Foules*," *Univ. of California Publs. In English*, Vol. III, No. 5 (1935), p. 197.

24. *The Hystorye, Sege and Dystruccyon of Troye* quoted in Caroline F. E. Spurgeon, *Five Hundred Years of Chaucer Criticism and Allusion* (Cambridge: Univ. Press, 1925), Pt. I, p. 25.

25. In his *Europäische Literatur und lateinisches Mittelalter* (Bern: A. Francke, 1948), pp. 91-93, Ernst Robert Curtius shows that modesty in writing as in speaking was an ingratiatory and propitiatory device ancient even in the Middle Ages and extensively practiced in them. There was, for example, much precedent for Chaucer's counsel of meekness to his "litel bok," beside its immediate source the *Filocolo*, and a good deal also for his appeal to Gower and Strode for correction, as appears from Robinson's notes, pp. 950, 951-52, to V. 1786ff. and 1856ff.

26. *TC*. I. 1-5, 52.

27. I. 450; II. 29-35 with reinforcement in 43-44, and 1751-52.

28. III. 495, V. 1032.

29. V. 1785.

30. I. 30, 54, 398; II. 966, 1547; III. 553; IV. 807, 1085; V. 629, 637, 854, 952, 1316, 1589.

31. V. 1797.

32. V. 270-71.

33. Ch. I. 2. pp. 25ff.; Ch. II. 6. pp. 214-15.

34. *TC*. I. 393-99, II. 12-18.

35. III. 1324-36. The apologetic stanzas come later in the consummation scene in the β group of MSS. than in the α and γ. Root, who follows the former's order in his edition, numbers them III. 1401-14.

36. Pandarus, though recognizing the irony of being a counsellor while a failure in love, is self-depreciative but once and then *pro forma*, II. 1002-3 (*Fil*. II. 91); Criseyde, likewise, but once and *pro forma*, IV. 1261-63; and Diomede, though as humble with the lady as Chaucer with his audience, is a patent hypocrite, not the subtly simple wise man. Troilus' undervaluation of himself is ironized, not in his own lines, but in the narrator's:

> And after that he seyde, and leigh ful loude,
> Hymself was litel worth, and lasse he koude, II. 1077-78.

37. III. 1368-69.

38. III. 442-48.

39. I. 492-97 (*Fil.* I. 48); III. 575-81, 967-70.

40. III. 974-77, 1135-37. See also III. 1188-90, 1557-61.

41. Pandarus: I. 803; II. 327-28; III. 148-49, 630, 850; V. 379-82. Troilus: I. 330-36 (*Fil.* I. 21, without irony), 514-16 (*Fil.* I. 51); IV. 496-97. Criseyde: II. 421-23.

42. I. 132-33 (misrepresenting *Fil.* I. 15). In her article, "The 'Troilus' Frontispiece," p. 168. n.4, Miss Galway opines that Chaucer rejected Boccaccio's flat statement that the heroine was childless because he had identified her partially with the fruitful Fair Maid of Kent.

43. III. 502-3. Instead of "Neigh half this book," the β group of MSS. has the more modest reading "An hondred vers"—see Robinson's textual note, p. 1026, to 503.

44. III. 1774 (*Fil.* III. 90, "se non erra la storia").

45. IV. 19-21. In the Prohemium, Chaucer expresses himself as composer, it is to be noted, rather than as reciter:

> And now my penne, allas! with which I write,
> Quaketh for drede of that I moste endite, IV. 13-14.

46. IV. 1415-21, V. 19-21.

47. V. 1049-53.

48. V. 1086-90. In his note, pp. 549-50, to the passage, Root observes that, though Chaucer's sources do not define the period, Benoit gives time indications for it which add up to at least twenty-one months.

49. V. 1093-99. The narrator ventures to suggest the motive—pity—for Criseyde's last letter to Troilus, without authority, and without convincingness in the light of its pain-giving content, V. 1587-89.

50. V. 1772-78.

51. Pp. 215-26.

52. *TC.* I. 232-59.

53. II. 22-48, 666-86.

54. II. 1331-35 (*Fil.* II. 85).

55. III. 1-38 (*Fil.* III. 74-79).

56. III. 1146-48.

57. III. 1204.

58. III. 1223-25.

59. III. 1319-20.

60. III. 1804 (*Fil.* III. 93).

61. Pp. 233-36.

62. *TC.* V. 1434, 1748-49.

63. V. 1832.

64. I. 8-11, 47-51.

65. I. 436.

66. II. 8-11, III. 39-48.

67. III. 49.

68. III. 1246.

69. III. 1373-93 (*Fil.* III. 38-39).

70. IV. 22-28.

71. V. 1212, 1434-35.

72. V. 1781, 1785.

73. V. 1786-88, 1793-96.

74. I. 1863-69.

75. I. 308. Troilus' increase in virtue after consummation moves the narrator again to pagan piety:

> Thus wolde Love, yheried be his grace, III. 1804.

76. II. 77.

77. II. 1272-74.

78. III. 56.

79. III. 1058-59, 1399-1400.

80. Of Troilus: II. 636-37, III. 1742, 113-14; of Criseyde: IV. 855-56 (replacing an aporia, *Fil.* IV. 99), 869-71, V. 722-24 (*Fil.* VI. 3); of Troilus and Criseyde: IV. 1140-41; of Ector: V. 1555-57. Cp. II. 826, of Antigone.

81. III. 344-46 (*Fil.* III. 11), 1310-13 (*Fil.* III. 31, 33).

82. III. 1688-94 (with the second statement perhaps suggested by Dante, *Par.* xix. 8, "Non portò voce mai, nè scrisse inchiostro").
83. IV. 799-805 (*Fil.* IV. 95).
84. IV. 1695-98, V. 267-73.
85. III. 531-32, V. 1432-33. The "us" and "we" are similar in tone to what Professor Tatlock has called "the domestic 'our,' " "The Source of the *Legend,* and Other Chauceriana," *St.Ph.,* XVIII (1921), 425-28. Generalizing on many instances of the latter in the works of Chaucer and other early writers, Mr. Tatlock speaks of it as "Suggesting the intimacy of the household or parish."
86. III. 89-91, 237-38, 435-36, 505-11, 553, 688-89, 1193-97, 1394, 1818-20; IV. 236-38, 258-59, 735, 806-9, 1085, 1127, 1132-34; V. 50-51, 55-56, 195-96, 628-29, 635-37, 771, 847, 853-54, 952, 1100-1, 1316, 1443, 1800-1, 1833-34.
87. II. 687-89, 932-34, 1709-11; III. 218-20, 1583-84; V. 1037.
88. For a complete list of abbreviatory statements in the *Troilus,* see W. Nelson Francis, "Chaucer Shortens a Tale," *PMLA.,* LXVIII (1953), 1127. n.5.
89. II. 965, 1299, 1622; III. 593; V. 946.
90. I. 141-44; II. 1564-66 (with 1564 from the *Roman de la Rose,* ed. Langlois, 18298), 1595-96. See also II. 1219-20, 1405-6; V. 1765-71.
91. III. 1408-9 (a misrendering, very probably intentional, of *Fil.* III. 41, "Ragion non vi si fece di dormire"—"There was no talk there of sleeping"), 1576-78. For a possible gibe at rhetorical embellishment, see II. 904-5.

Section 3 *Gestalten of Heroine, Hero, Rival, and Confidant*

1. See Ch. I. 1. n.13 for distribution of lines among speakers.
2. *Fil.* I. 3, 11.
3. I. 15.
4. I. 19, 27.
5. I. 12, IV. 79, V. 14.
6. II. 21-22, 23, 27-28.
7. III. 8.
8. VIII. 23.
9. II. 98.
10. IV. 164-65.
11. IV. 69.
12. VII. 93-100.
13. VIII. 17-18.
14. II. 38, 49.
15. II. 69.
16. II. 70, 76, 77.
17. II. 139, IV. 151. Criseida came momentarily to regret that she had preferred reputation to certainty of continuance with Troiolo, VI. 6.
18. IV. 93.
19. VI. 29, 30. Cp. her humble apology to Troiolo for a hiding place unworthy of his royal splendor, III. 28.
20. I. 45-46.
21. II. 84.
22. III. 20.
23. III. 90-93. See also III. 72.
24. II. 41-42.
25. II. 54, 67.
26. IV. 109-10, V. 29-30, VII. 41.
27. II. 49, 71, 72.
28. IV. 147-51, 157.
29. IV. 38-40, 31-32.
30. IV. 67-68.
31. V. 4-5.
32. V. 13, VI. 11.

33. VI. 24, 33.
34. II. 1.
35. II. 9, 10-14.
36. II. 25-28, 33.
37. II. 48, 49 ff.; 122, 123 ff.
38. II. 52-54.
39. III. 5-10.
40. III. 13-19, 20.
41. III. 59, 60.
42. IV. 47-49; 64-65, 71-75.
43. IV. 50-62; 66-70, 76.
44. VIII. 23-24.
45. See Ch. I. 1. n.13 for distribution of lines among speakers.
46. "The Prologue to the *Legend of Good Women* Considered in its Chronological Relations," *PMLA.,* XX (1905), 834, 835.
47. Some critics do not touch on Chaucer's display of affection for Criseyde, but none, I believe, expressly minifies it. Joseph S. Graydon's "Defense of Criseyde," *PMLA.,* XLIV (1929), 141-77, has been the only attempt to prove that the poet meant her to be blameless in forsaking Troilus, and it was promptly refuted by J. Milton French, *PMLA.,* XLIV (1929), 1246-51, and Joseph M. Beatty, Jr., *StPh.,* XXVI (1929), 470-81.
48. Pp. 118-20.
49. *Courtly Love in Chaucer and Gower* (Boston and London: Ginn, 1913), pp. 154-78.
50. *Chaucer and His Poetry* (Cambridge: Harvard Univ. Press, ᶜ1915), pp. 126-36.
51. "Aspects of the Story of Troilus and Criseyde," *Univ. of Wisconsin Studies in Lang. and Lit.,* No. 2 (1918), 379-94.
52. "Chaucer's *Troilus and Criseyde* as Romance," *PMLA.,* LIII (1938), 49, 51-56.
53. "Destiny in Chaucer's *Troilus,*" *PMLA.,* XLV (1930), 137-47, with quotation from p. 147. See also. p. 149.
54. *The Allegory of Love* (Oxford: Clarendon Press, 1936), 182-90, with quotations on pp. 183, 185.
55. "Character and Action in the Case of Criseyde," *PMLA.,* LIV (1939), 65-81.
56. *On Rereading Chaucer* (Cambridge: Harvard Univ. Press, 1939), 74-83.
57. *Chaucer's Troilus a Study in Courtly Love* (Louisiana State Univ. Press, 1940), pp. 192-238, with quotations from pp. 234, 237.
58. "The People in Chaucer's *Troilus,*" *PMLA.,* LVI (1941), 96-102, with quotations from pp. 97, 101.
59. "Chaucer (I) Troilus and Criseyde," *Scrutiny,* XI (1942), 84-108, with quotations from pp. 92, 104. On contrast between heroine and hero, see also Claes Schaar, "Troilus' Elegy and Criseyde's," *Studia Neophilologica,* XXIV (1952), 185-91.
60. "Chaucerian Tragedy," *ELH.,* XIX (1952), 23.
61. "In Defense of Criseyde," *MLQ.,* XV (1954), 312-20.
62. "Calchas in the Early Versions of the Troilus Story," *Tulane Studies in English,* IV (1954), 18-19.
63. TC. I. 53-56, 127-31 (*Fil.* I. 15). As indicated by Pratt, *StPh.,* LIII, 513, "Ful wel biloved," I. 131, corresponds to "moult fort amée," *Le Roman de Troyle et de Criseida,* p. 123, rather than to "amata," *Fil.* I. 15.
64. I. 285-87 (*Fil.* I. 27).
65. II. 450-51.
66. II. 673-75.
67. IV. 667-68 (*Fil.* IV. 79).
68. V. 820-25.
69. I. 880-887 (*Fil.* II. 21-22).
70. I. 974-87 (*Fil.* II. 27).
71. III. 267-70 (*Fil.* III. 8).
72. IV. 615-16.
73. V. 1732-33 (*Fil.* VIII. 23).
74. V. 1706-8 (*Fil.* VIII. 17).

75. III. 212-17. See also II. 1452-54.
76. II. 124.
77. II. 758 (*Fil.* II. 69).
78. II. 799-805 (*Fil.* II. 77).
79. III. 1210-11.
80. IV. 1576-82 (*Fil.* IV. 151).
81. V. 974-78 (*Fil.* VI. 29).
82. V. 1054-77.
83. While some of the critics have not vouched explicitly for either point, none, I believe, has denied either one.
84. Pp. 90-91.
85. *Courtly Love in Chaucer and Gower*, pp. 137-54, with quotation from p. 153.
86. *Chaucer and his Poetry*, pp. 122-26.
87. "Destiny in Chaucer's *Troilus*," *passim*, with quotation from p. 164.
88. *The Allegory of Love*, pp. 194-96, with quotations from p. 195.
89. *On Rereading Chaucer*, pp. 83-93.
90. *Chaucer's Troilus*, pp. 246-84, with quotation from pp. 279-80.
91. "The People in Chaucer's *Troilus*," pp. 91-94, with quotations from pp. 93, 94.
92. "Chaucer (I) Troilus and Criseyde," pp. 104-6, with quotation from p. 104.
93. "Boethius' Influence on Chaucer's *Troilus*," *MPh.*, XLIX (1951), 1-9, with quotation from p. 2.
94. "Chaucerian Tragedy," pp. 11 ff., with quotation from p. 13.
95. *TC.* I. 470-83 (*Fil.* I. 45-46), 1072-85. See also I. 565-67.
96. III. 435-41 (*Fil.* III. 20), 1716-25 (*Fil.* II. 84, III. 72), 1772-1806 (*Fil.* III. 90-93).
97. V. 832-37. See Ch. I. 9. n.6 for sources.
98. I. 778-819; III. 1098; IV. 1086-99 (*Fil.* IV. 109-10); V. 330-50 (*Fil.* V. 29-30), 1279-80 (instead of *Fil.* VII. 41).
99. II. 158-61, 169-82, 190-203, 204-7.
100. II. 316-20.
101. III. 781-82.
102. II. 162-68, 183-89.
103. II. 705-14, 722-25, 736-40 (with germinal idea from *Fil.* II. 71). See also III. 169-72.
104. III. 1126.
105. IV. 1555-82 (*Fil.* IV. 147-51).
106. IV. 1667-80 (instead of *Fil.* IV. 164-65).
107. V. 1056-57 and 1074-77, 1611-17.
108. II. 643-44, 1583-94.
109. IV. 330-36 (*Fil.* IV. 38-40), 274-87 (*Fil.* IV. 31-32).
110. IV. 547-53 (*Fil.* IV. 67) and 561-67 (*Fil.* IV. 68); V. 43-56 (*Fil.* V. 4-5).
111. V. 1821-27 (*Tes.* XI. 3).
112. *Chaucer's Troilus*, pp. 239-45, with quotation from pp. 244-45. For our poet's handling of Diomede, see also Tatlock, "The People in Chaucer's *Troilus*," pp. 94-95; and for earlier treatment of him, see Archibald A. Hill, "Diomede: The Traditional Development of a Character," *Univ. of Michigan Publications, Language and Literature*, VIII (1932), 1-25.
113. *TC.* V. 94-96.
114. V. 783-84, 795-98 (first three lines, from *Fil.* VI. 11; fourth line, new).
115. V. 804 (*Fil.* VI. 33).
116. V. 932-38 (*Fil.* VI. 24).
117. *Courtly Love in Chaucer and Gower*, pp. 178-89, with quotation from p. 189.
118. *Chaucer and his Poetry*, pp. 136-42, with quotation from p. 139.
119. "Aspects of the Story of Troilus and Criseyde," pp. 369-79, with quotation from p. 372.
120. "Chaucer's *Troilus and Criseyde* as Romance," pp. 60-61.
121. *The Allegory of Love*, pp. 190-94, with quotation on p. 194.
122. *One Soul in Bodies Twain* (Bloomington, Indiana: Principia Press, 1937), pp. 60-63.

123. *On Rereading Chaucer,* pp. 93-103.
124. *Chaucer's Troilus,* pp. 121-91. Troilus' response, quoted by Kirby, p. 190, is *TC.* III. 393-406.
125. "The People in Chaucer's *Troilus,*" pp. 95-96.
126. "Chaucer (I) Troilus and Criseyde," pp. 92-99.
127. "Chaucerian Tragedy," pp. 16-17.
128. "Chaucer's Pandarus: Virtuous Uncle and Friend," *JEGP.,* XLVIII (1949), 186-95, with quotation from p. 186.
129. *TC.* II. 452 and V. 1311; IV. 344-47 (changed from *Fil.* IV. 43) and V. 284-85.
130. I. 621-23 (*Fil.* II. 9), 624-721 (*Fil.* II. 10-14).
131. I. 901-3 (*Fil.* II. 25) and 990-94 (*Fil.* II. 28); 1051-54 (*Fil.* II. 33).
132. I. 1070-71.
133. II. 50-63, 98.
134. II. 232-38, 239-42.
135. II. 351-64.
136. II. 409-25 (*Fil.* II. 48).
137. II. 1096-99 and 1105-6; 1165-66 and 1167-69.
138. III. 239-343 (*Fil.* III. 5-10).
139. III. 360-420 (*Fil.* III. 13-19). As indicated by Pratt, *StPh.,* LIII, 520, "But sith thow hast idon me this servyse, My lif to save, and *for non hope of mede,*" III. 414-15, corresponds to "Mais je vous pry . . . que vous *ne* cuidez *point* que je pense que vous avez secouru voustre amy 'au besoin *en esperance de guerdon,*" *Le Roman de Troyle et de Criseida,* p. 177, rather than anything in *Fil.* III. 16.
140. III. 487-90, 519-25, 960-61.
141. III. 1077-78, 1611-14 (*Fil.* III. 59).
142. III. 1618-38 (*Fil.* III. 60).
143. III. 1564-68, 1577-79.
144. IV. 393-427 (*Fil.* IV. 47-49 and, transferred from Troiolo, 59), 526-39 (*Fil.* IV. 64-65), and 582-630 (*Fil.* IV. 71-75).
145. IV. 435-518 (*Fil.* IV. 50-62), 540-81 (*Fil.* IV. 66-70) and 631-37 (*Fil.* IV. 76).
146. IV. 428-31.
147. V. 1731-39 (*Fil.* VIII. 23-24).

Section 4 *Conclusion: The Totality*

1. For scholarly opinion on the reflection of courtly love in Chaucer's several characterizations of heroine, hero, rival, and confidant, see the preceding section. For accounts of courtly love literature before Chaucer and Boccaccio, see Dodd, *Courtly Love in Chaucer and Gower,* Chs. I and II; Lewis, *The Allegory of Love,* Chs. I, II, and III; and Kirby, *Chaucer's Troilus,* Pt. I. For distinguishing characteristics of courtly love, see John Wilcox, "Defining Courtly Love," *Papers of the Michigan Academy of Science, Arts and Letters,* XII (1930), 313-25; Alexander J. Denomy, C.S.B., *The Heresy of Courtly Love* (New York: Declan X. McMullen, ᶜ1947), *passim,* and "The Two Moralities of Chaucer's *Troilus and Criseyde,*" *Trans. Royal Soc. of Canada,* Ser. III. Vol. XLIV (1950), Sect. 2, 36-37. Wilcox finds in courtly love "three essential elements, the worship of woman, doctrinaire free love, and the partial sublimation of sexual impulses through chivalric action," pp. 313-14. In *The Heresy of Courtly Love,* pp. 20-21, Father Denomy selects as the basic elements "the ennobling force of human love," "the elevation of the beloved to a place of superiority above the lover," and "the conception of love as ever unsatiated, ever increasing desire"; and in his "Two Moralities," p. 36, the first and third of these. Both authorities mention peripheral characteristics as well as those which they believe central. My own view is that it is not the presence of several concepts in a piece of medieval literature which identifies it as in the tradition of courtly love, since any two or three may be found in nonmedieval works, but the presence of a number along with period-limiting emphases upon some over others and dated modes of projecting all of them. A complex of this kind is to be found in the *Troilus* as evidenced in the preceding section and justifies, I believe, the opinion prevailing among scholars that the work is an instance of a definable category of romantic

love, the courtly. For contrary opinion, see Professor Tatlock, "The People in Chaucer's *Troilus*," *PMLA.*, LVI (1941), 86-89, and *The Mind and Art of Chaucer* (Syracuse: Syracuse Univ. Press, ᶜ1950), pp. 38-40. Even he concedes that "Troilus is in some measure a 'courtly love' hero," "The People," p. 88, though holding that his story is not essentially a courtly love poem but one of dateless romantic feeling.

2. *The Allegory of Love,* p. 197. Also questionable, I believe, is Lewis' assertion later on this page, "Chaucer has brought the old romance of adultery to the very frontiers of the modern (or should I say the late?) romance of marriage." In "Love and Marriage in Chaucer's Poetry," *MLR.*, XLIX (1954), 461-64, D. S. Brewer offers the even more dubious proposition that Chaucer deliberately obscures the illicitness of the hero and heroine's affair in an effort to make it seem an unexceptionable love. The poet actually advertises its furtiveness, it seems to me, by devising elaborate machinations for Pandarus at his own house and at Deiphebus'.

3. "The Two Moralities of Chaucer's *Troilus and Criseyde,*" p. 43.

4. See Ch. II. 6. n.79.

5. *The Indebtedness of Chaucer's Works to the Italian Works of Boccaccio* (Menasha: Banta, 1916), pp. 83-91, esp. 83.

6. *On Rereading Chaucer,* pp. 69-71. Also see Professor Lowes as cited in Ch. I. 5. n.2.

Index

The Notes are not indexed. Literary works, other than the anonymous *Roman d'Eneas*, are entered under the names of their authors. The abbreviations, *Fil.* and *TC.*, stand for the *Filostrato* and *Troilus and Criseyde*.

A

Achille in *Fil.*, 133, 135.

Achille, Achilles in *TC.*, 56-57, 131, 135.

Alain de Lille, *De planctu Naturae*, 293.

Alete. *See* Furies in *TC.*

Almighty. *See* Supreme Being in *Fil.* and *TC.*

Amore. *See* Love, God of, in *Fil.*

Amour courtois. *See* Courtly love in *Fil.* and *TC.*

Andreas Capellanus, *De amore*, 413.

Andromaca in *Fil.*, 50.

Antenor in *TC.*, 51, 81-83, 101, 108, 425.

Antenore in *Fil.*, 81, 101.

Antigone in *TC.*, 10, 42-43, 52, 252, 424.

Antique atmosphere. *See* Time in *Fil.* and *TC.*

Apollo in *Fil.*, 206-7.

Apollo, Appollo, Phebus in *TC.*, 30, 34, 64-65, 77, 81, 95-96, 100, 108, 115, 123, 222-23, 234, 238, 324.

Associative figures in *Fil.* and *T.C.*: summarily viewed in various aspects, 245-61; analyzed in seven content patterns, primarily for application to persons or divinities, 262-363.

Astrology: in *Fil.*, 53-54, 211; in *TC.*, 34, 41, 53-54, 66-68, 72, 91, 143, 215, 217, 220-24, 234-36, 237-38, 255-56, 323.

Atropos, Attropos. *See* Parcae in *TC.*

Augury: in *Fil.*, 103-4; in *TC.*, 104-5, 238.

B

Beauvau, Seneschal of Anjou, *Roman de Troyle et de Criseida* (French prose translation of *Fil.*), 7, 105, 107, 124, 132, 151-52, 153, 268-69, 360.

Benoit de Sainte-Maure, *Roman de Troie*, 4-7, 37, 40-41, 80-81, 95, 100, 102-3, 109-10, 112, 113, 115-17, 131, 152, 230, 423.

Boccaccio: life ignored except for affair with Maria d'Aquino (whom *see*), viii; projection of himself as narrator (*see* Narrator in *Fil.*); *De casibus virorum illustrium*, 211; *Filocolo*, 5-7, 52-53, 56, 60-66, 68, 69, 71-78, 107, 134, 151, 200; *Filostrato, passim;* French prose translation of *Filostrato* (*see* Beauvau, Seneschal of Anjou); *Teseida*, 7, 78, 100, 104, 135.

Bodily existence. *See* Corporeal existence in *Fil.* and *TC.*

Boethius, *Consolation of Philosophy*, vi, 6, 8, 60, 70, 71, 77, 80, 89, 90-92, 135, 222, 278, 323, 403, 404, 408.

Bronson, Bertrand H., 373.

Brown, Carleton, 82.

Brute creation in *Fil.*: birds and animals, amorous in springtime, 211-12; the dream boar (*see* Dreams in *Fil.*); figurative associations with this creation, 320-23.

Brute creation in *TC.*: metamorphosed swallow, nightingale, owl, and "ciris,"

523

Guillaume de Lorris and Jean de Meun, *Roman de la Rose,* 8, 413-14.
Guillaume de Machaut, *Paradis d'Amour,* 7, 43.

H

Herynes. *See* Furies in *TC.*
Homer, 26, 134.
Horace: *Ars poetica,* 8, 299; *Epistles,* 8, 26.
Horaste in *TC.,* 51, 69, 425.

I

Imeneus, Hymen in *TC.,* 41, 73, 220, 236.
Irony in *Fil.*: cosmic, 16, 130; dramatic, 15-18, 24, 43-44, 86, 94, 98, 105, 113, 120, 122-25, 126, 127, 158, 208, 231-32, 256, 259, 271-72, 275, 351, 370, 386-87, 388, 414-16, 417-19, 420-21, 423; of manner, 370-71.
Irony in *TC.*: cosmic, 16, 124, 128, 131, 132, 135-37, 367; dramatic, 15-18, 24-25, 43-44, 49-56, 69-70, 86, 88, 94, 98, 100, 105-6, 113, 120, 122-24, 128, 231-33, 254, 256, 259, 266, 267, 269, 277-78, 285, 286, 287-88, 329, 331-32, 357, 358, 367-69, 397-98, 404, 406-7, 410-11, 412, 414-16, 417-19, 420-21, 423-27; of manner, 15, 265, 367, 372-77, 385; verbal, 377.

J

Joan, the Fair Maid of Kent, 373.
John of Salisbury, *Policraticus,* 26.
Joseph of Exeter, *Frigii Daretis Ylias,* 7, 109, 112, 152.
Jove, Jupiter. *See* Supreme Being in *TC.*
Juno in *TC.,* 37, 97, 98, 107, 224, 276.
Juvenal, *Satires,* 82.

K

Kirby, Thomas A., 91, 120, 396, 403, 410, 413.
Kittredge, George Lyman, 21, 25, 43, 90, 119-20, 396, 403, 413.

L

Lachesis. *See* Parcae in *TC.*
Latona. *See* Diane in *TC.*
Legouis, Émile, 20-21.
Letters between hero and heroine in *Fil.* and *TC.,* 44-46, 124-27, 131, 426.
Lewis, C. S., 119-20, 396, 403, 404, 413, 421.
Locales and movement in them in *Fil.*: in general, 13, 142, 421-22; temples, 191; dwellings, 191-94; fortifications, 194; extramural territory, 194-95.
Locales and movement in them in *TC.*: in general, 13, 142-43, 421-22; temples, 195-96; dwellings, 196-202; street, 201-2; fortifications, 202; extramural territory, 202-3; the celestial spheres, 203.
Lollius, 8, 14, 25-26, 131-32, 375, 376.
Love. *See* Courtly love in *Fil.* and *TC.*
Love, God of: in *Fil.,* called Amore, 4, 16, 23, 83, 106, 111, 133, 143, 209-11, 255, 271-73, 302, 320, 333, 347; in *TC.,* usually called Love, also God of Love, Cupide, Charite, 16, 23-24, 31-32, 41, 42-43, 53, 57, 77-78, 82, 103, 107, 143, 220-22, 234, 236, 255-56, 264-66, 277-81, 323.
Love, Goddess of. *See* Venere in *Fil.* and Venus in *TC.*
Lowes, John Livingston, 21, 49, 60, 75, 395.
Lucan, *Pharsalia,* 135. *See also* 134.
Lucina. *See* Diane in *TC.*
Lüdeke, H., 372-73.
Lumiansky, R. M., 397.
Lydgate, John, 373-74.

M

Macrobius, *Somnium Scipionis,* 135-36.
Magoun, Francis P., Jr., 195.
Malone, Kemp, 138.
Maria d'Aquino, viii, 5, 14, 23, 47-48, 133, 147, 207, 249, 254-55, 262, 273, 301, 333-34, 339, 370.
Mars, Marte in *TC.,* 13, 67, 78, 104, 223, 276, 324.

529